ANY EMPIRE

ISBN 978-1-60309-077-3

1. Fantasy/Imagination
2. Southern American fiction
3. Graphic Novels

Edited by Chris Staros
Design by Tony Ong

First Printing, July 2011. Printed in China.

" hanging from the ceiling, eating off the floor
   retreat without fear, conquer without force
the lion begins to bleat when the lamb begins to roar
disintegration by the dozens, evaporation by the score:

oppress yourself. "

— lungfish

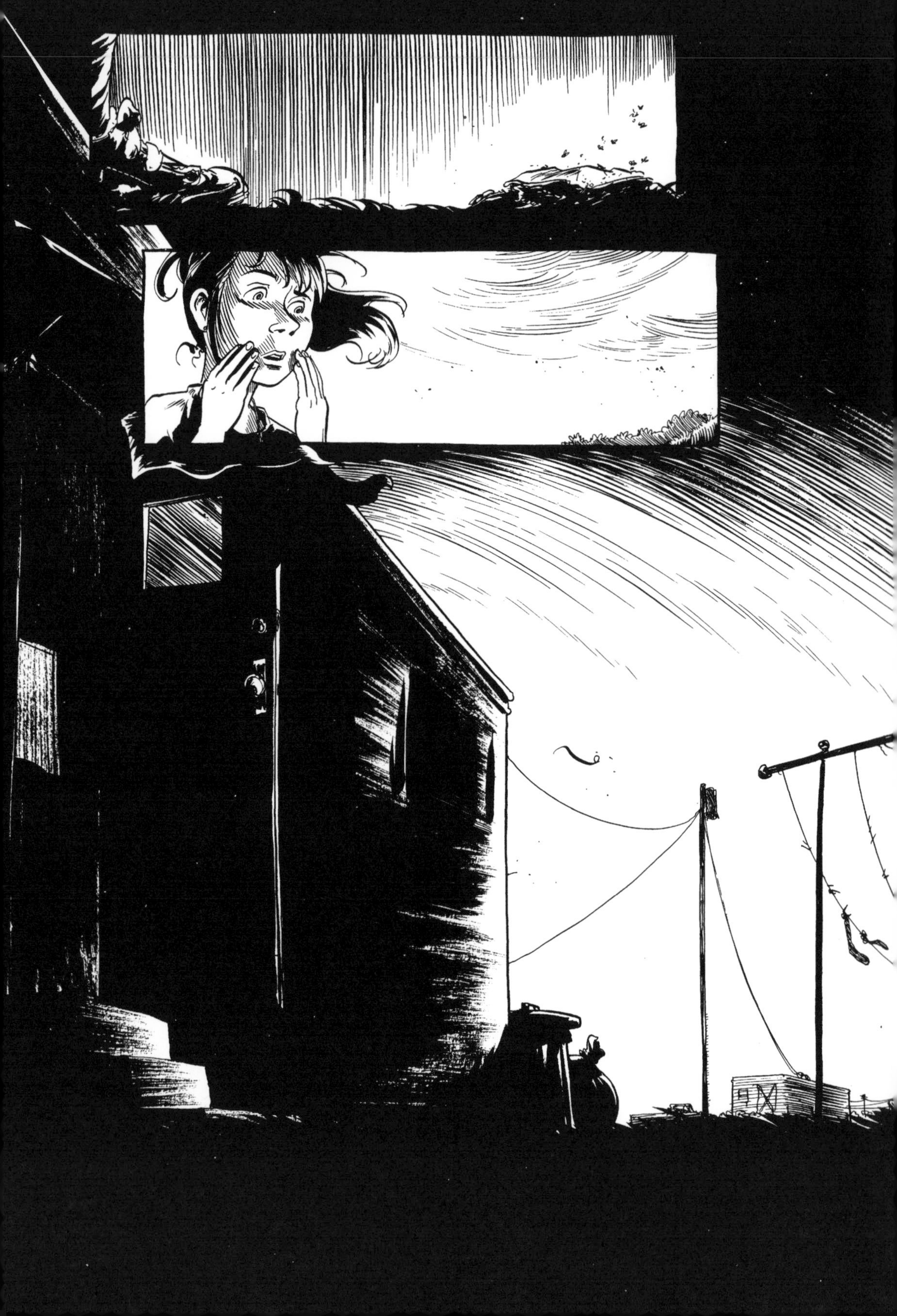

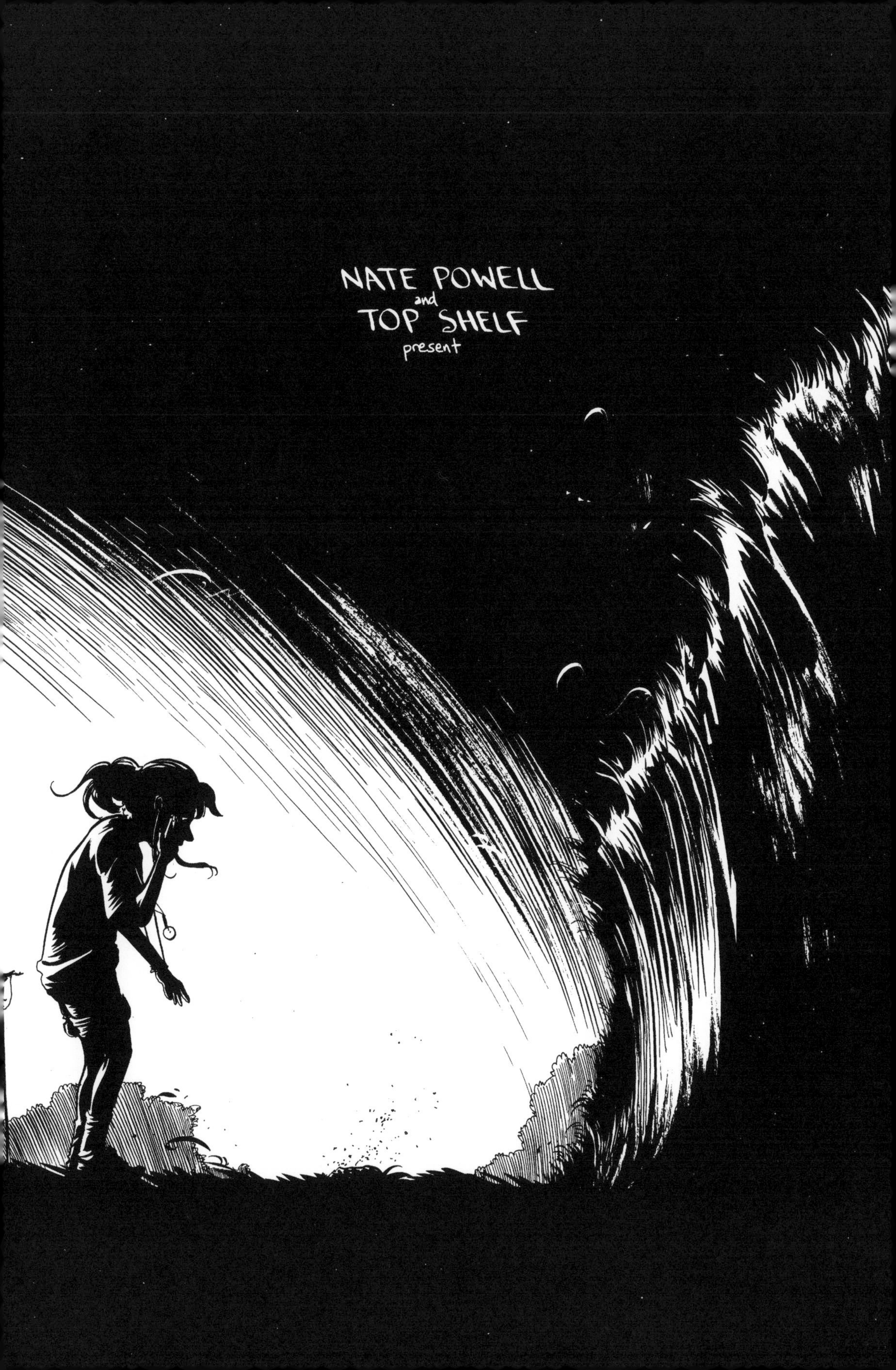
NATE POWELL
and
TOP SHELF
present

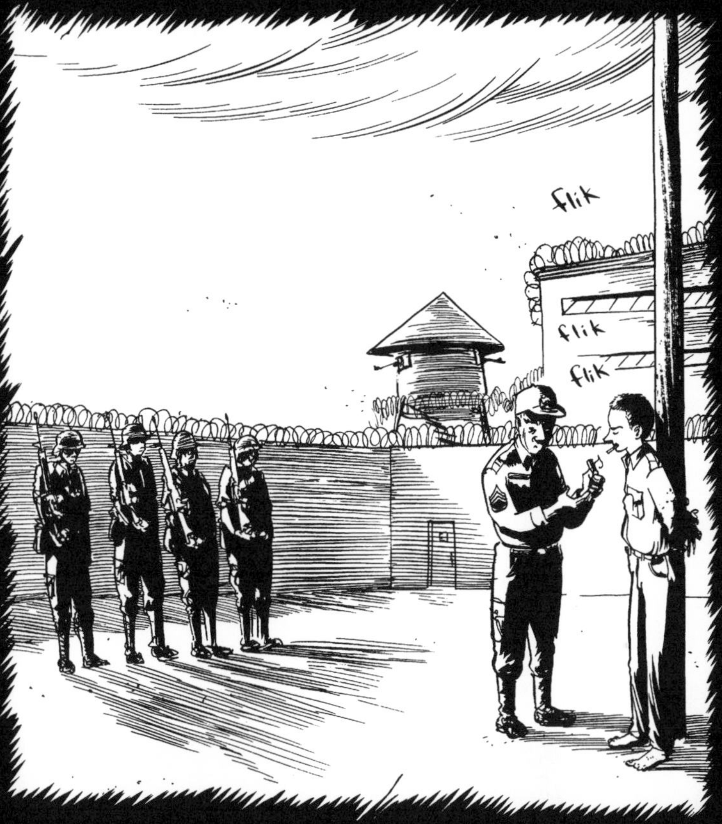
flik
flik
flik

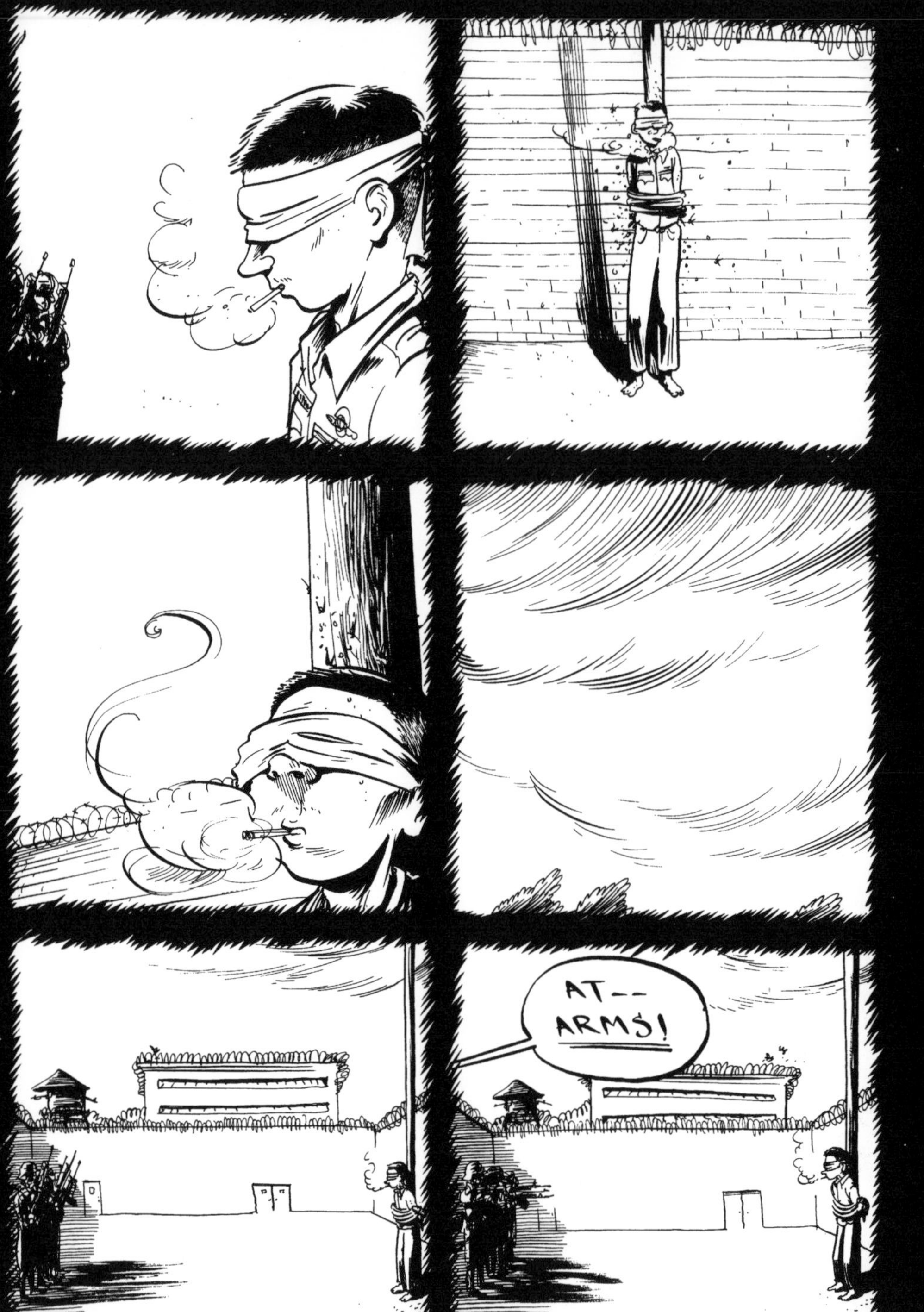
AT--
ARMS!

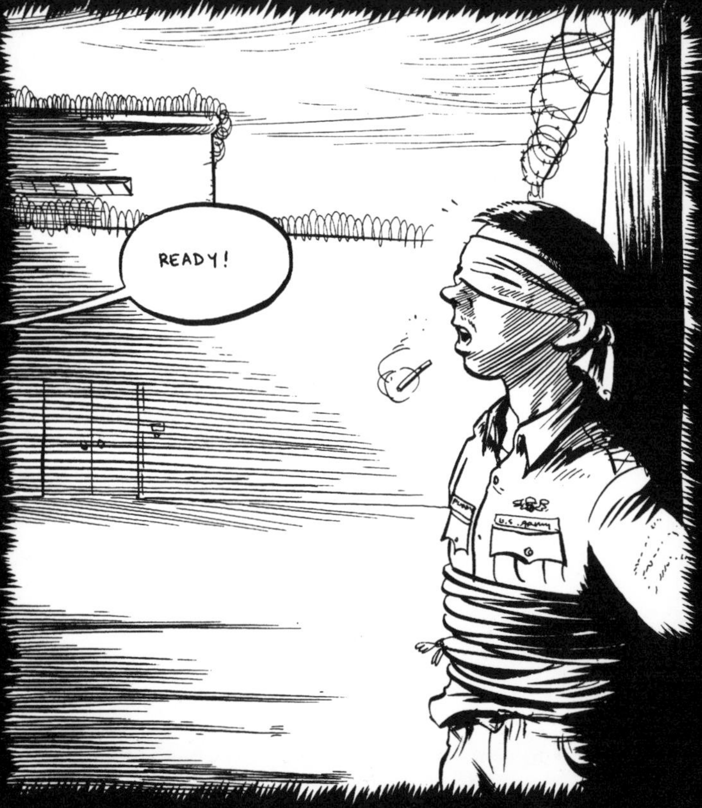
READY!
U.S. ARMY

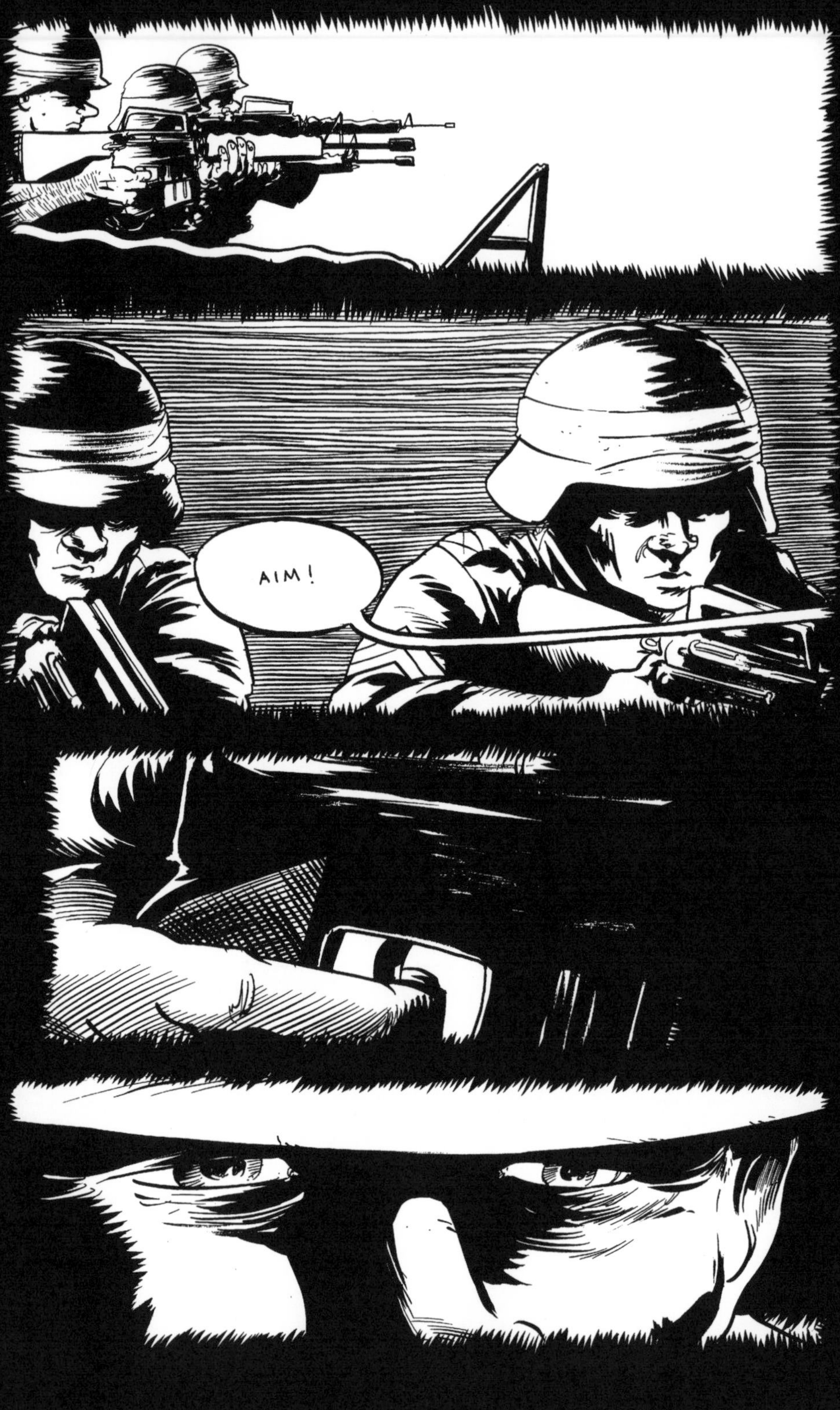
AIM!

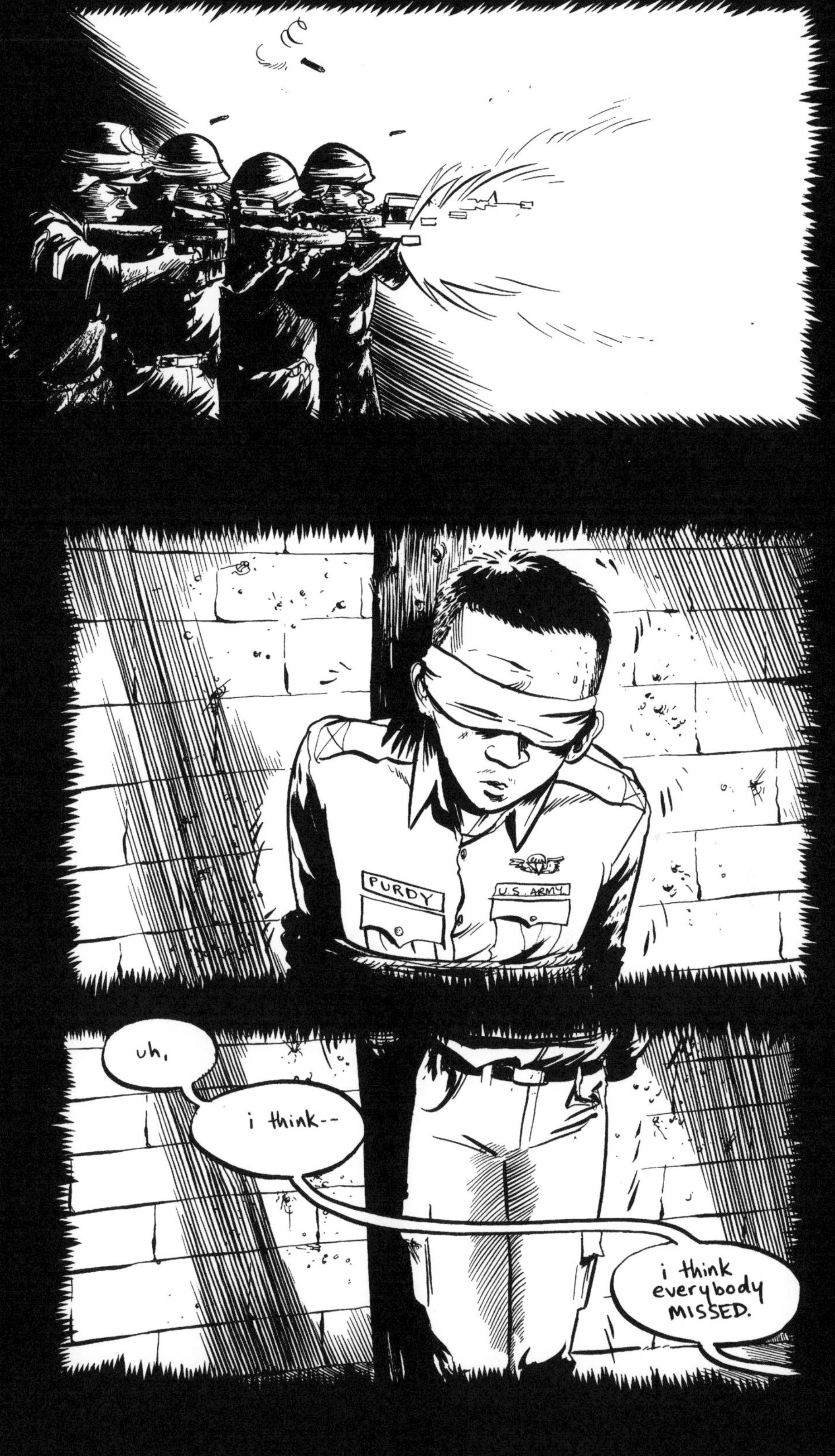
PURDY
U.S. ARMY
uh,
i think--
i think everybody MISSED.

ANY E

well,
now what?

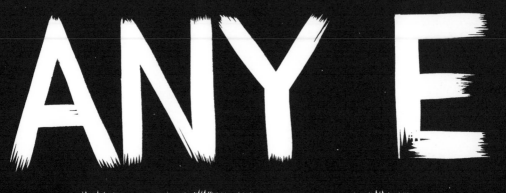

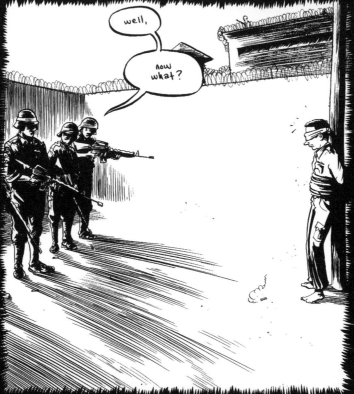

MPIRE

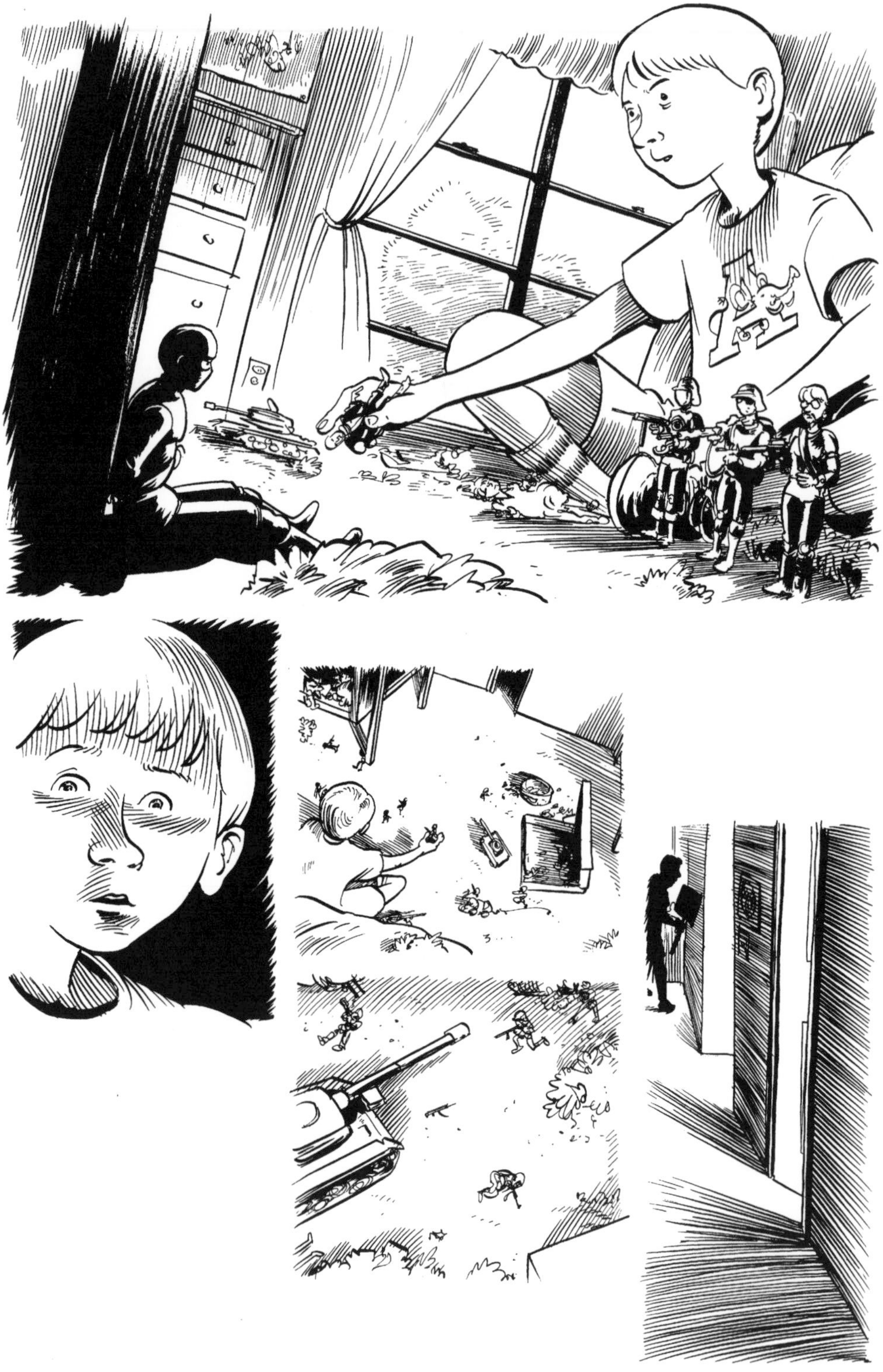

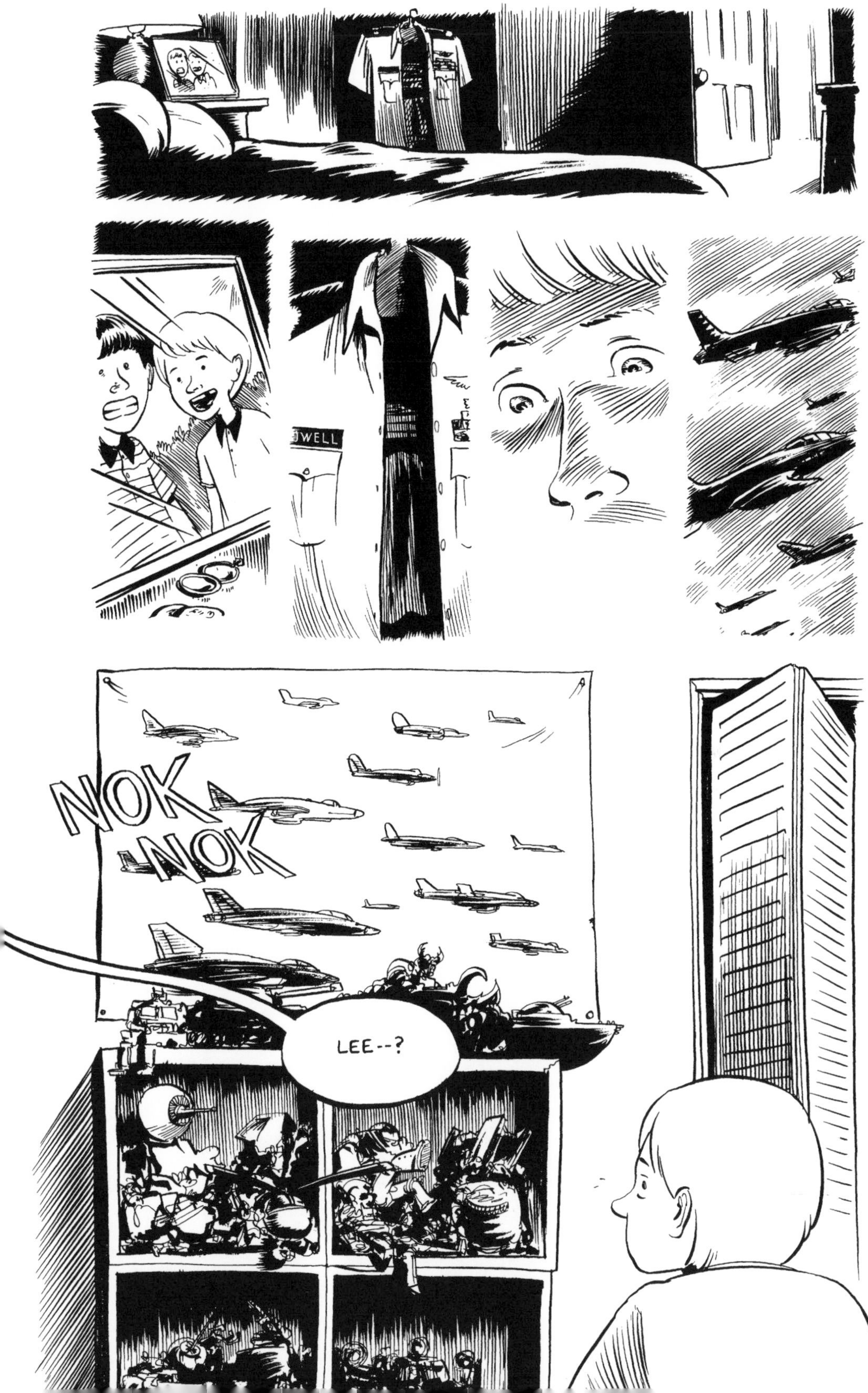
WELL
NOK NOK
LEE--?

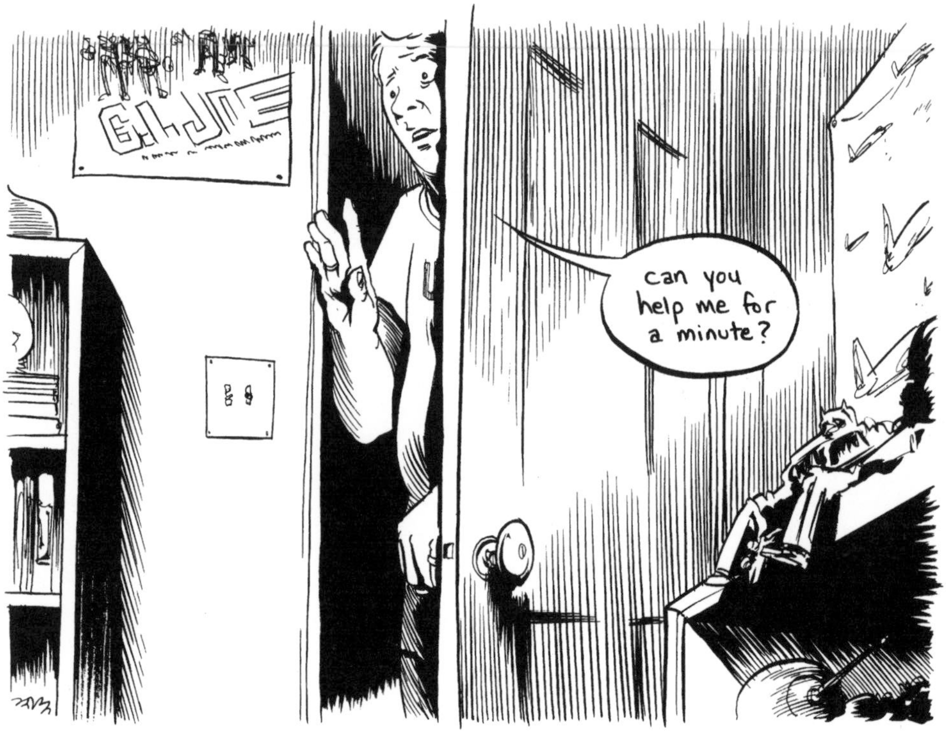
G.I. JOE
can you help me for a minute?

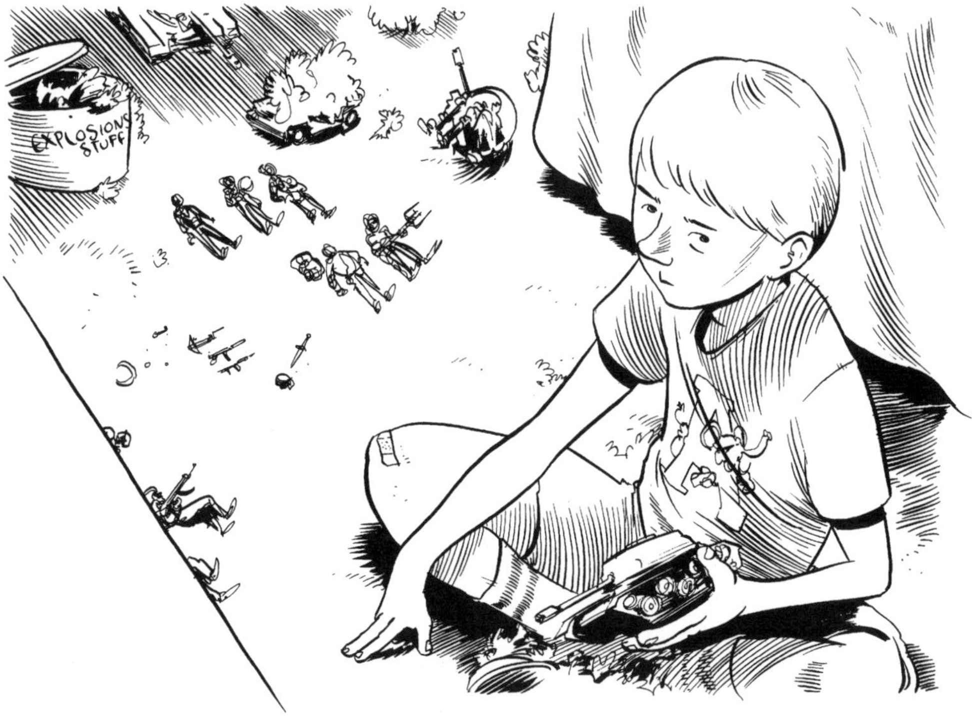
EXPLOSIONS STUFF

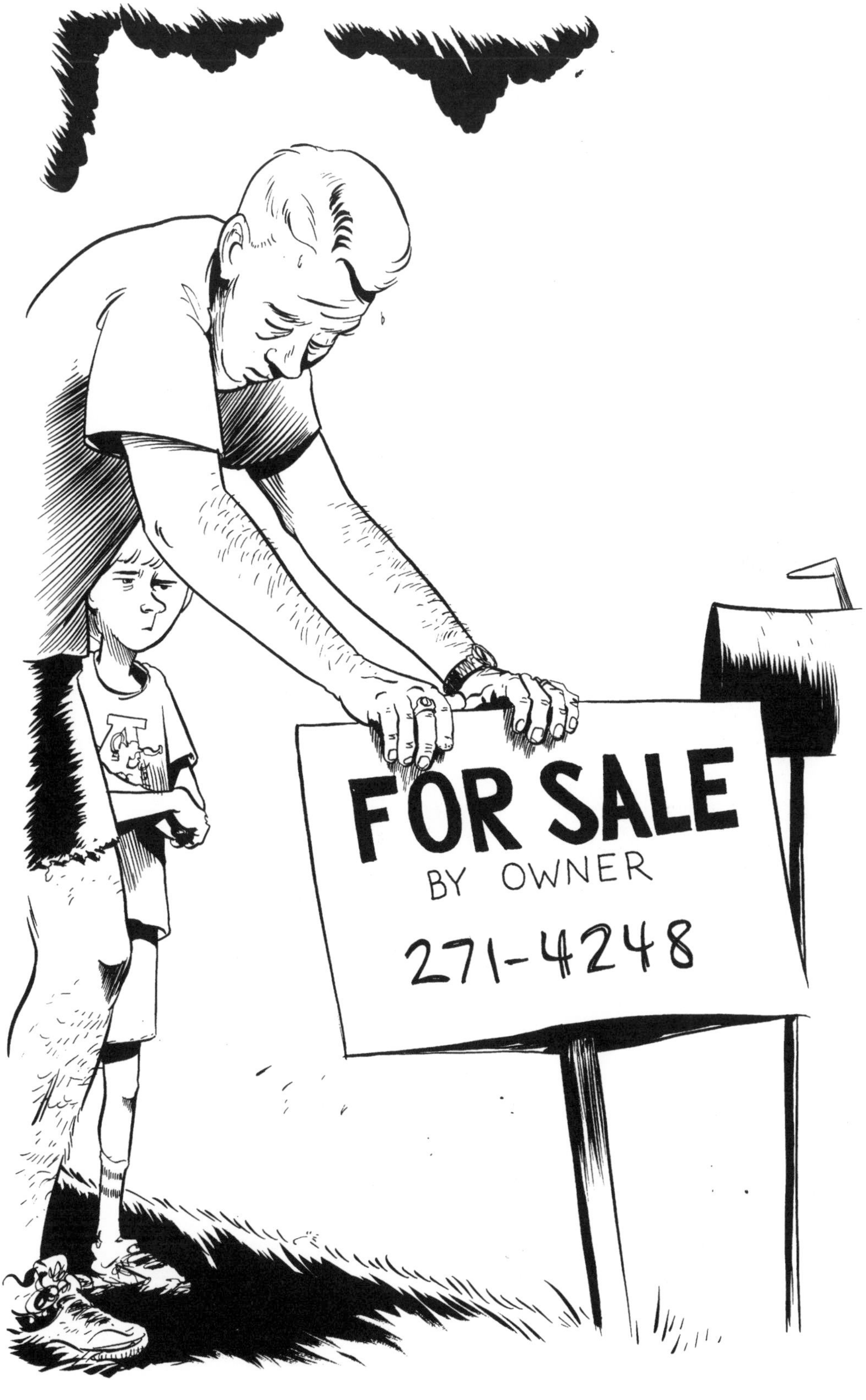
FOR SALE
BY OWNER
271-4248

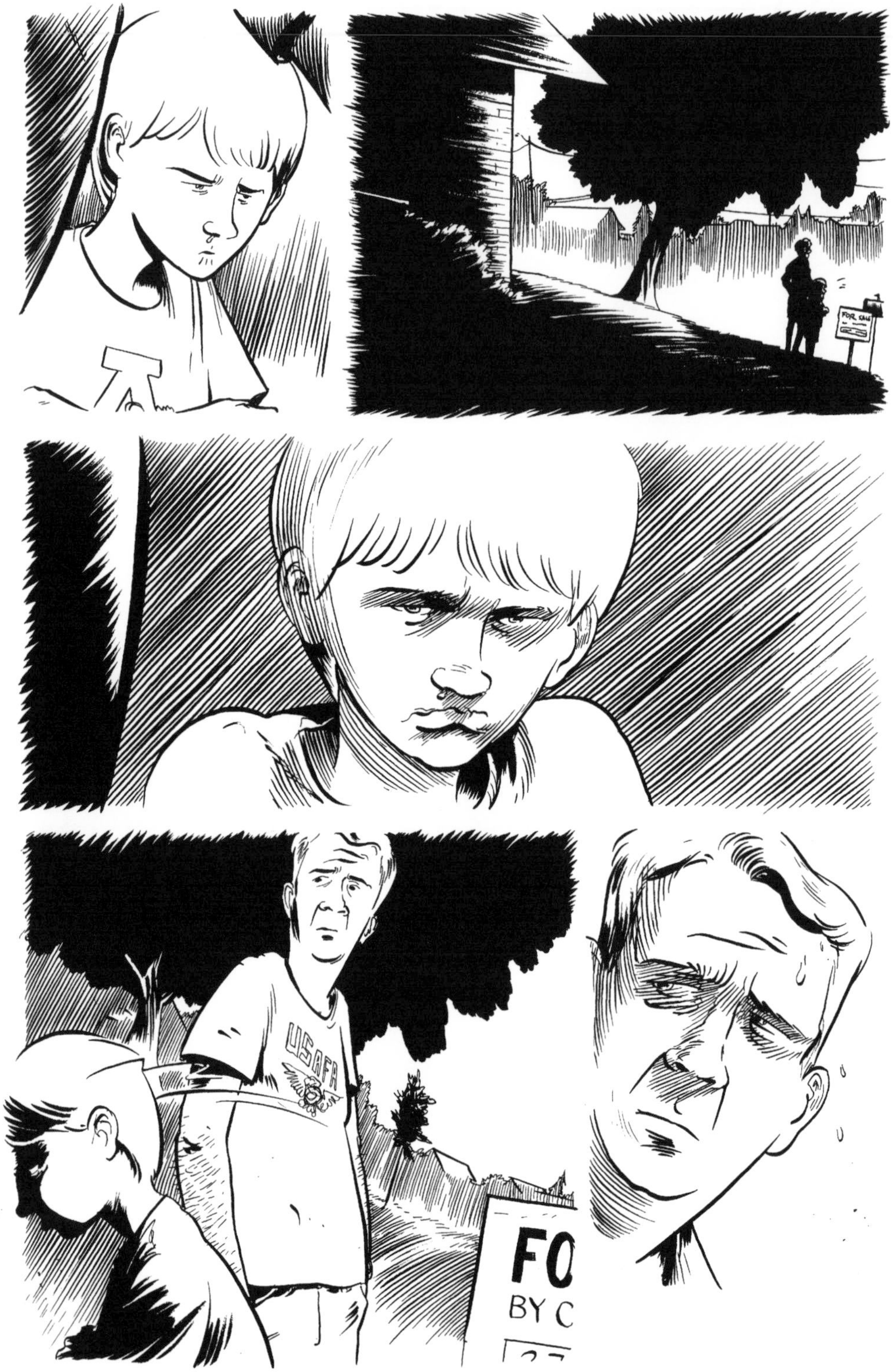
USAFA
FO
BY C

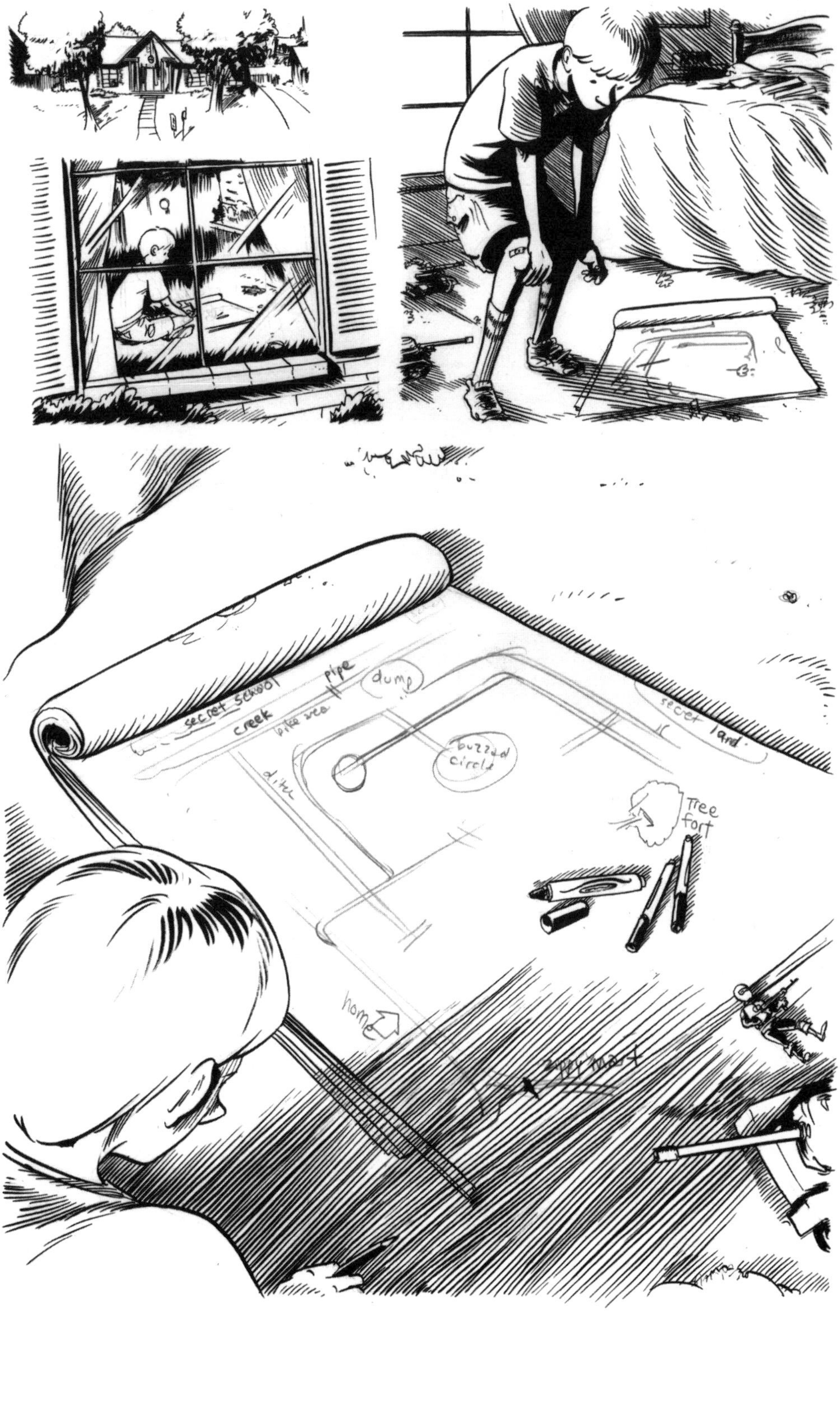
secret school
creek
pipe
dump
bike area
buzzard circle
ditch
secret land
Tree fort
home

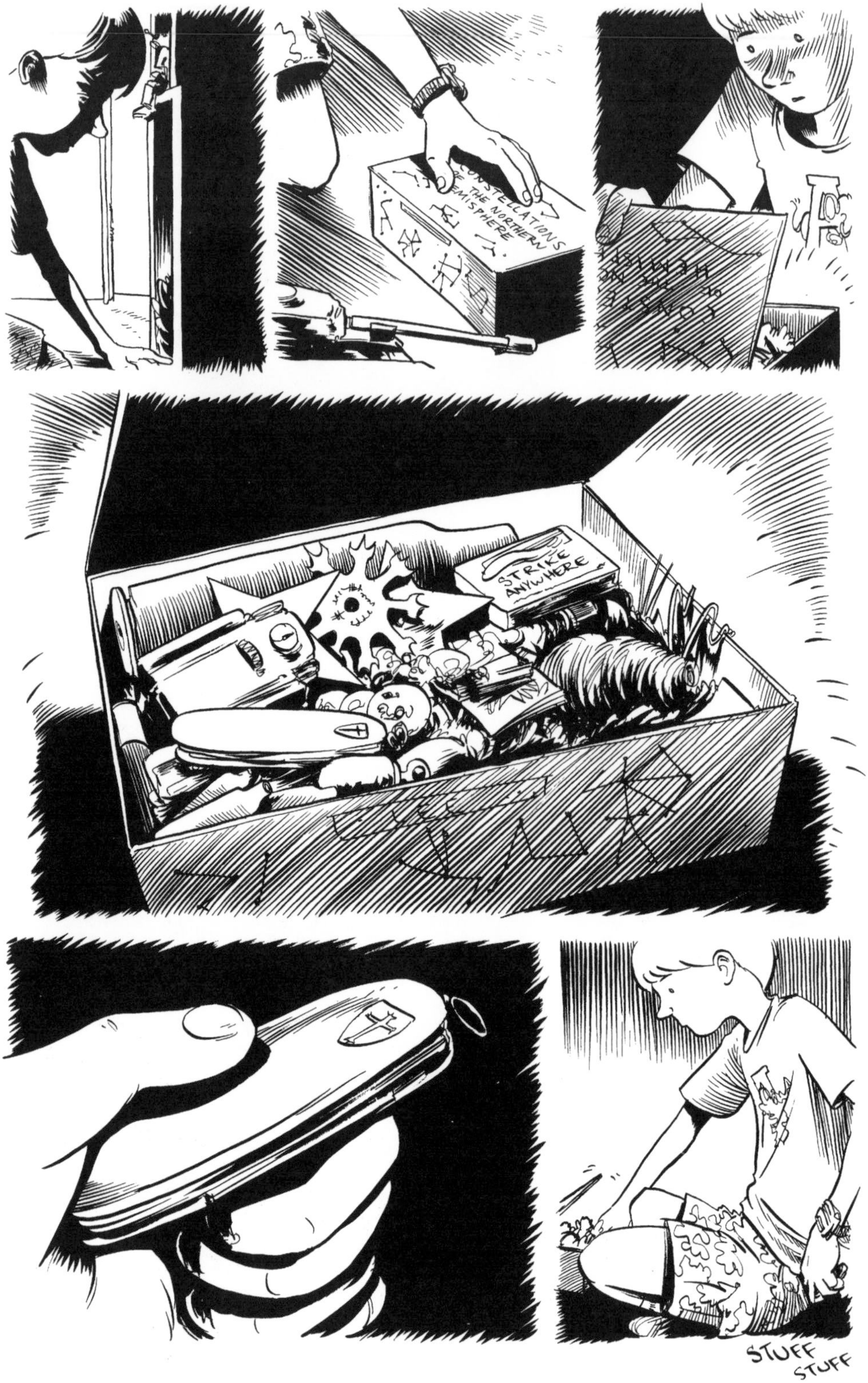
CONSTELLATIONS OF THE NORTHERN HEMISPHERE
STRIKE ANYWHERE
STUFF
STUFF

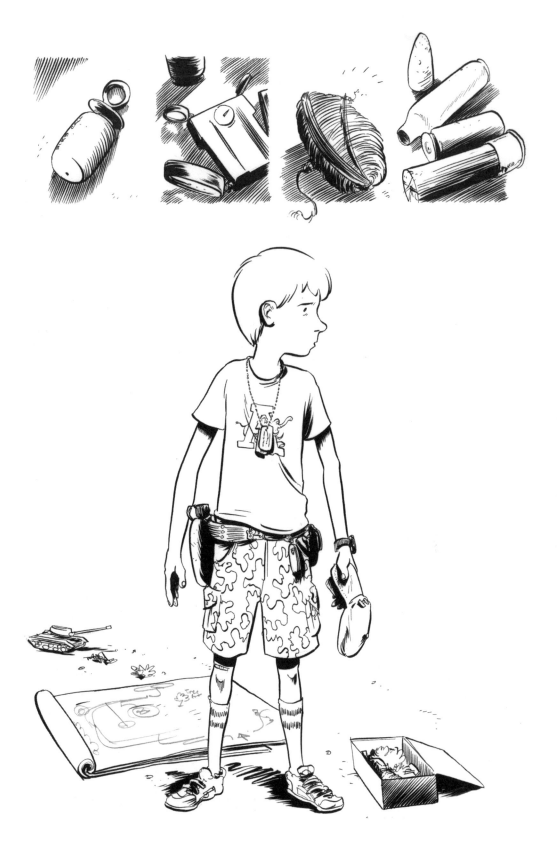

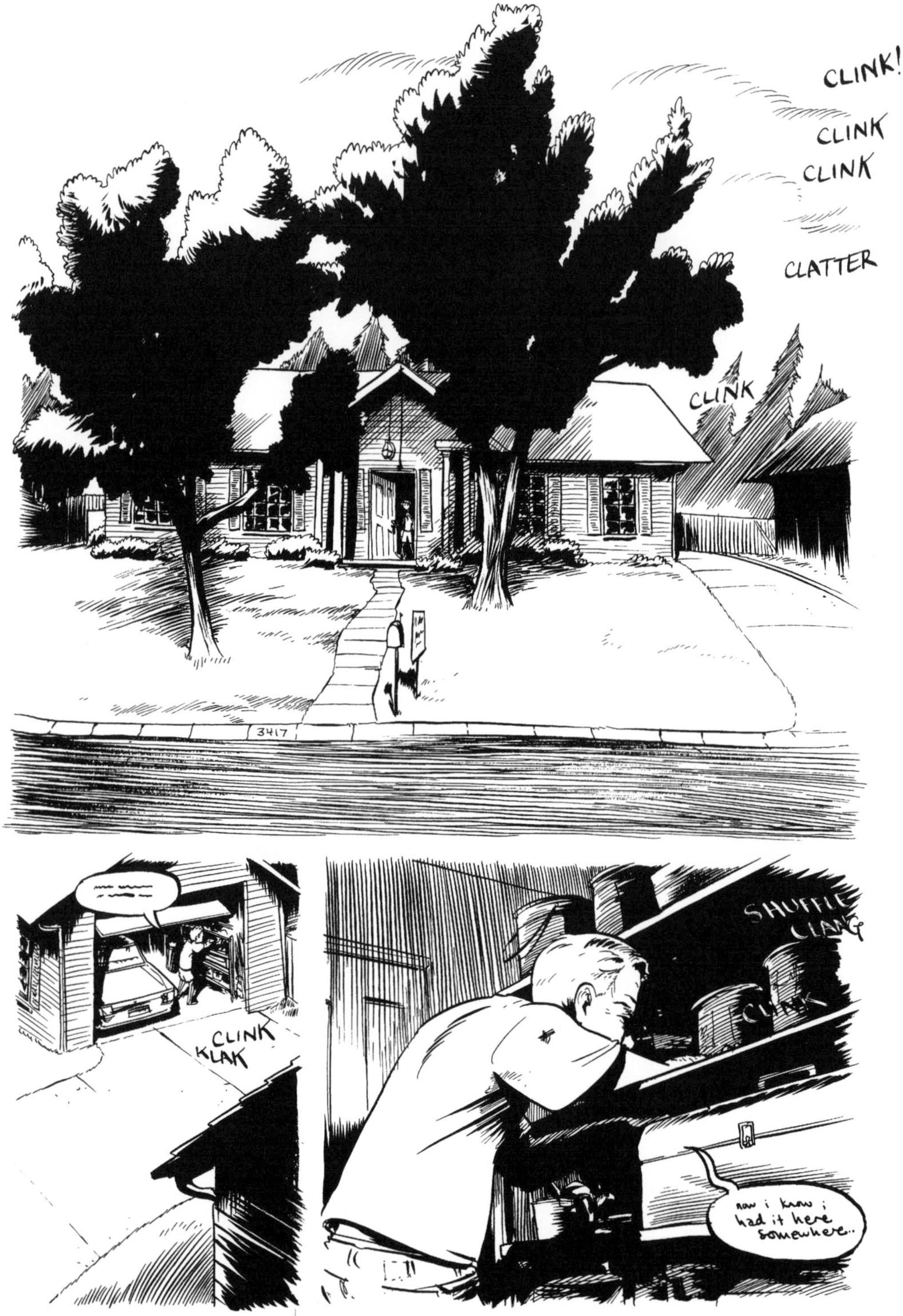
CLINK!
CLINK
CLINK
CLATTER
CLINK
CLINK
KLAK
SHUFFLE
CLANG
CLINK
now i know i had it here somewhere...

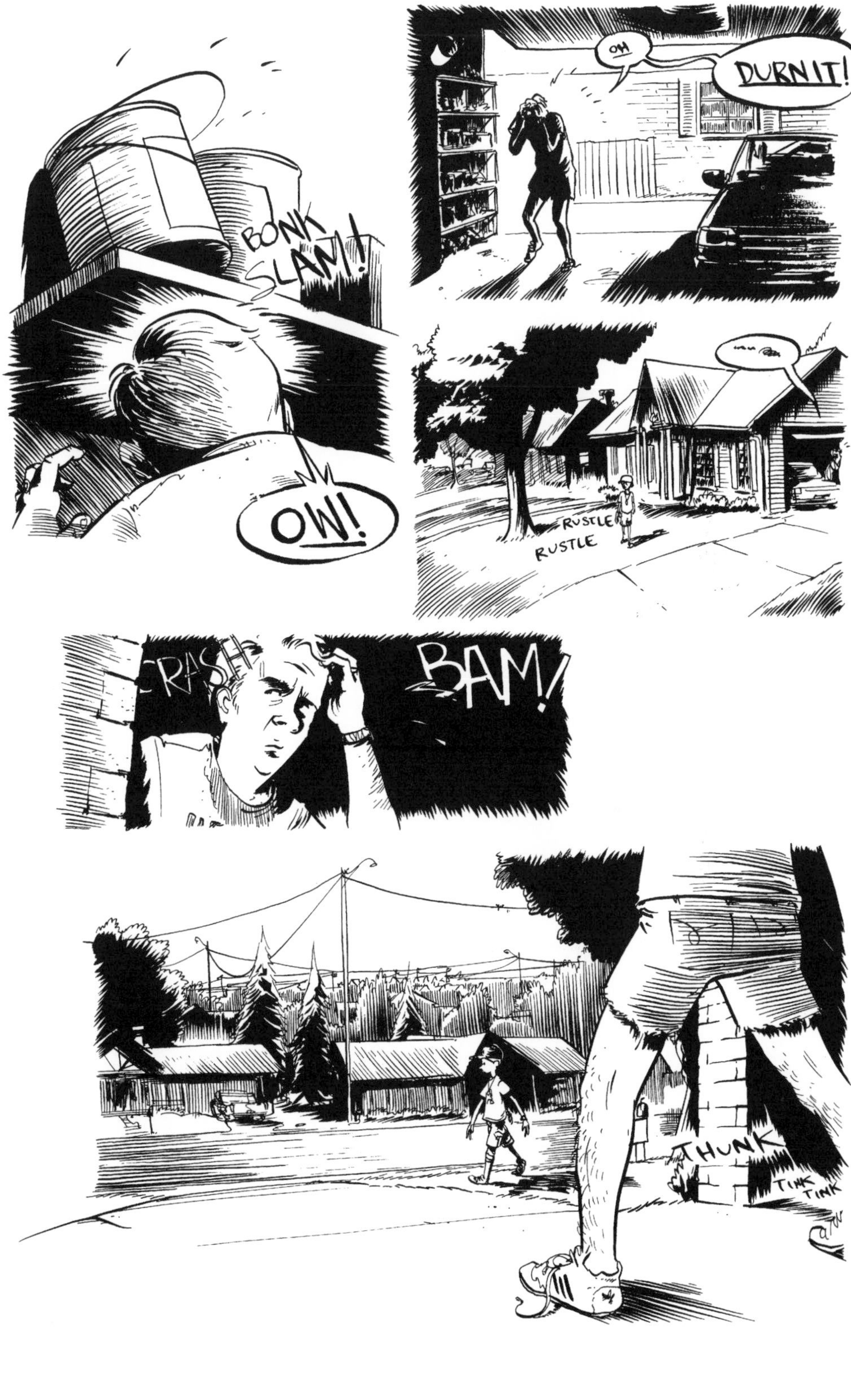
BONK
SLAM!
OW!
OH
DURN IT!
RUSTLE
RUSTLE
CRAS
BAM!
THUNK
TINK
TINK

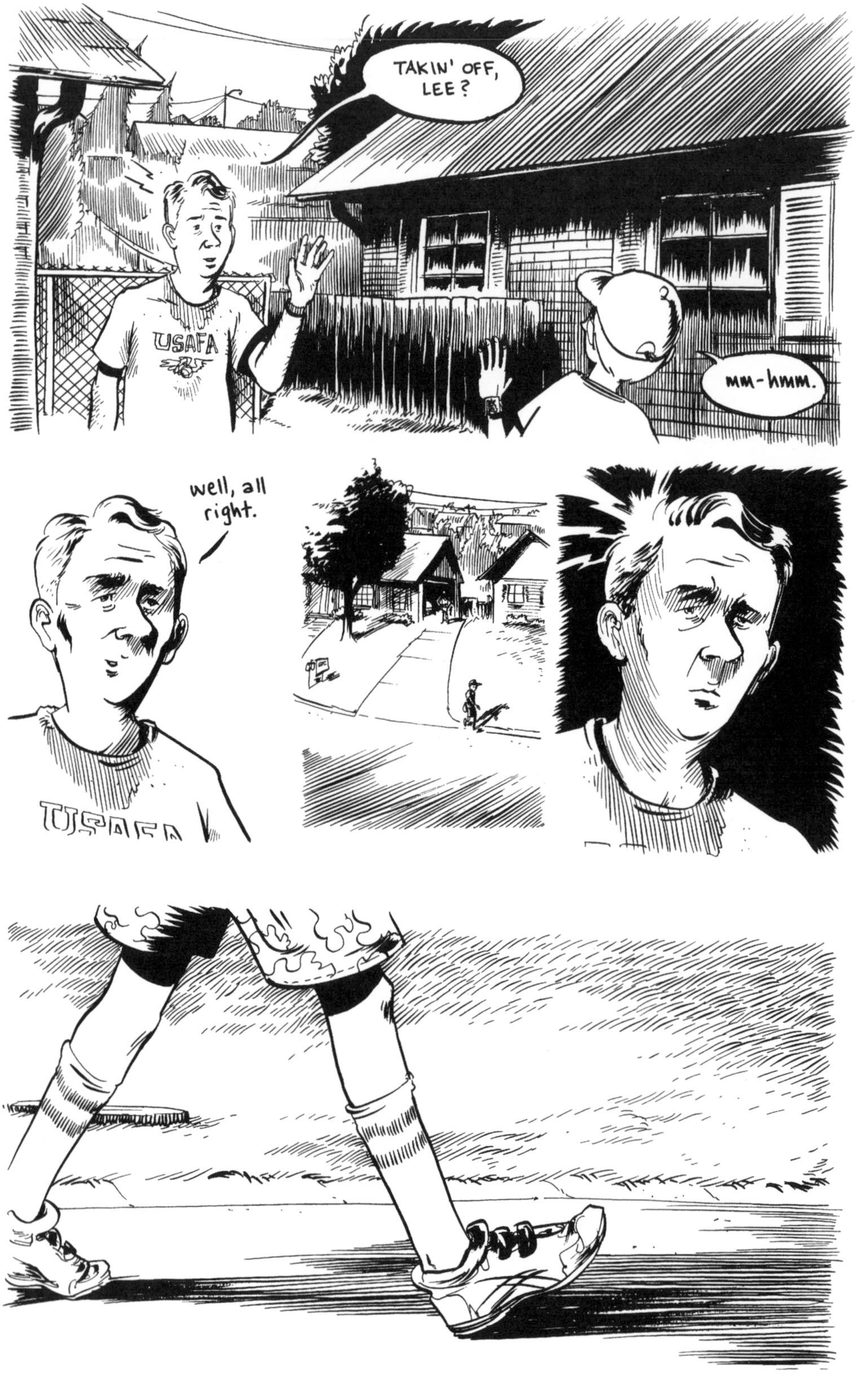
TAKIN' OFF, LEE?
mm-hmm.
USAFA
well, all right.
USAFA

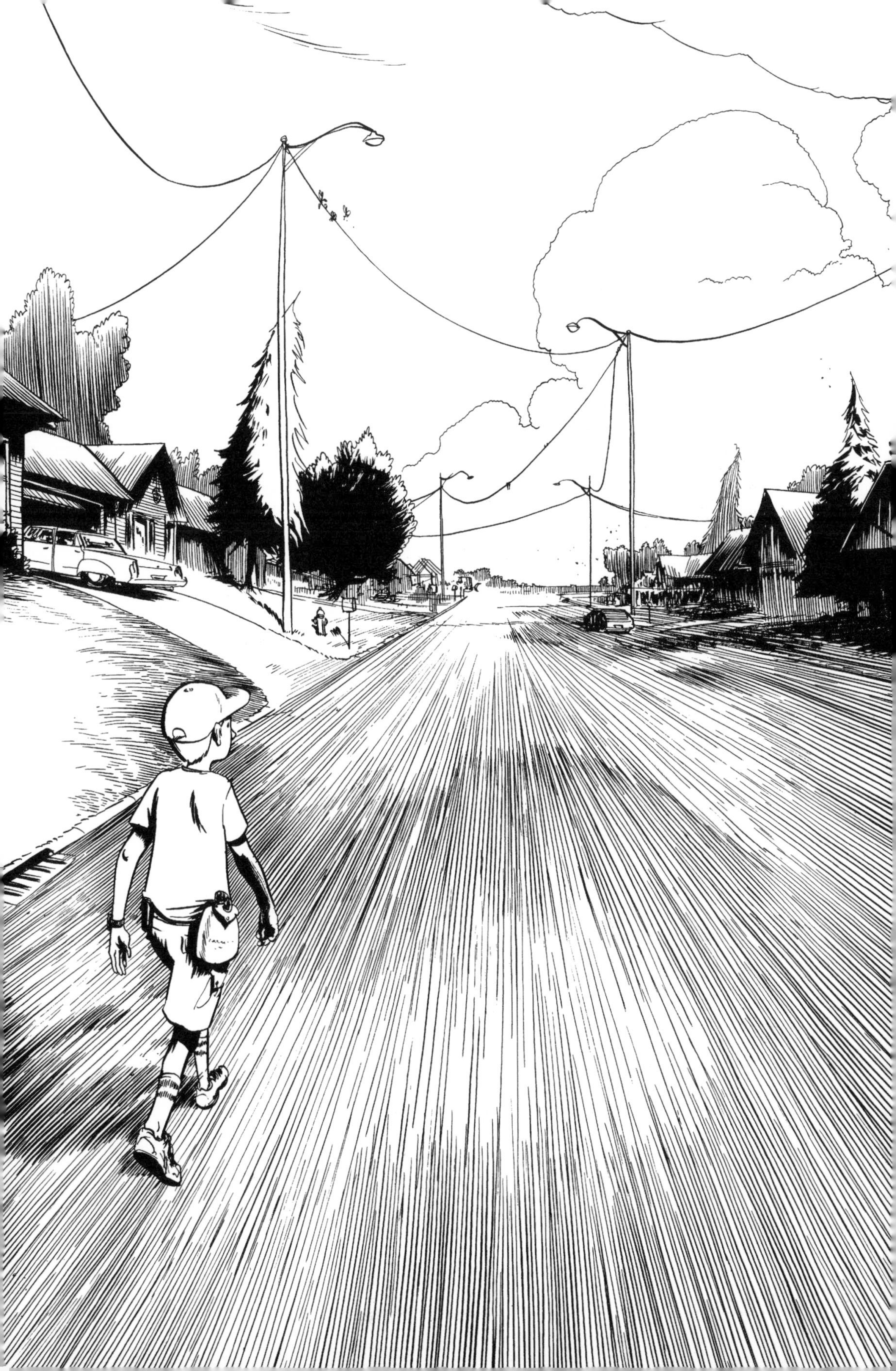

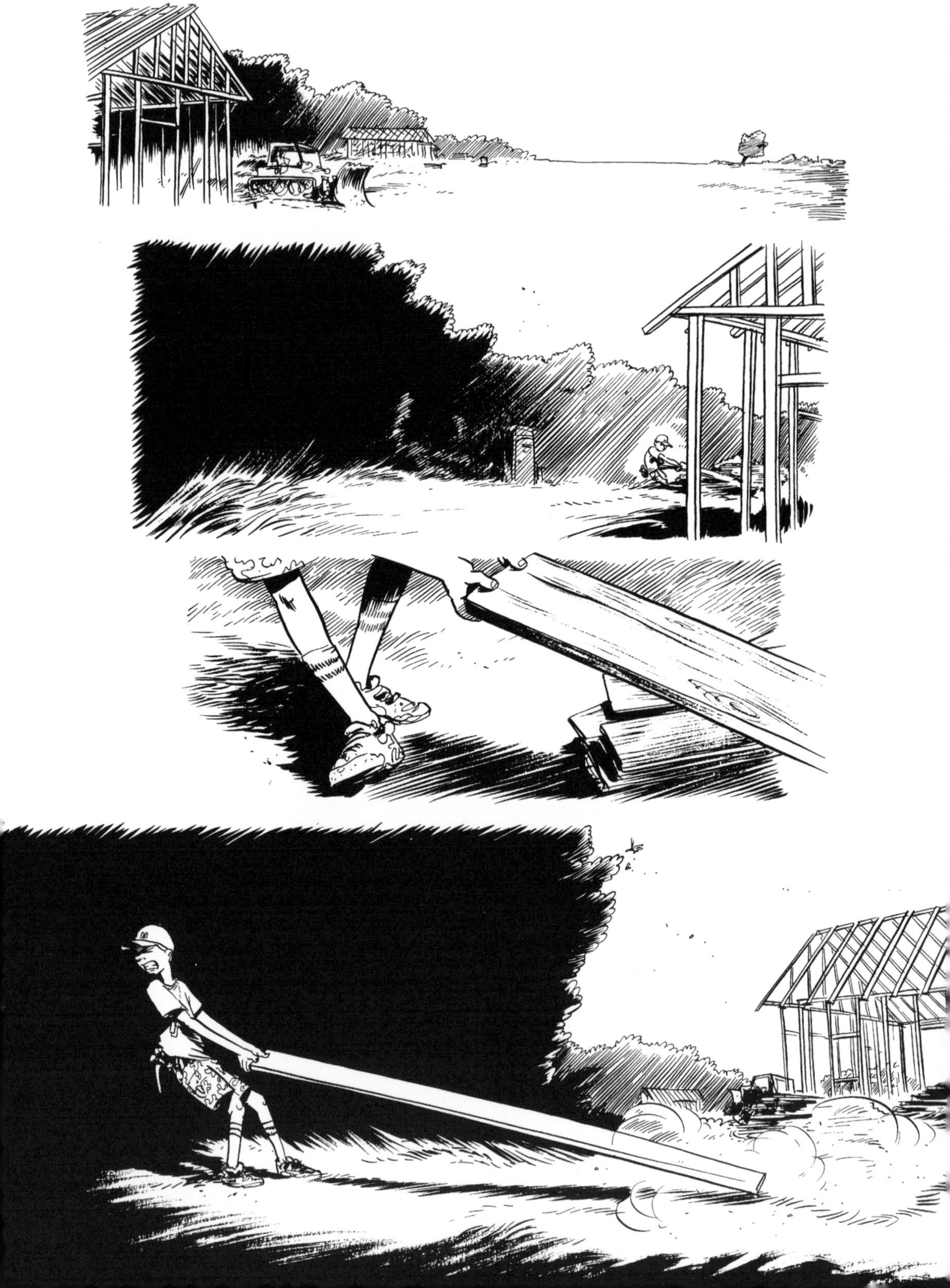

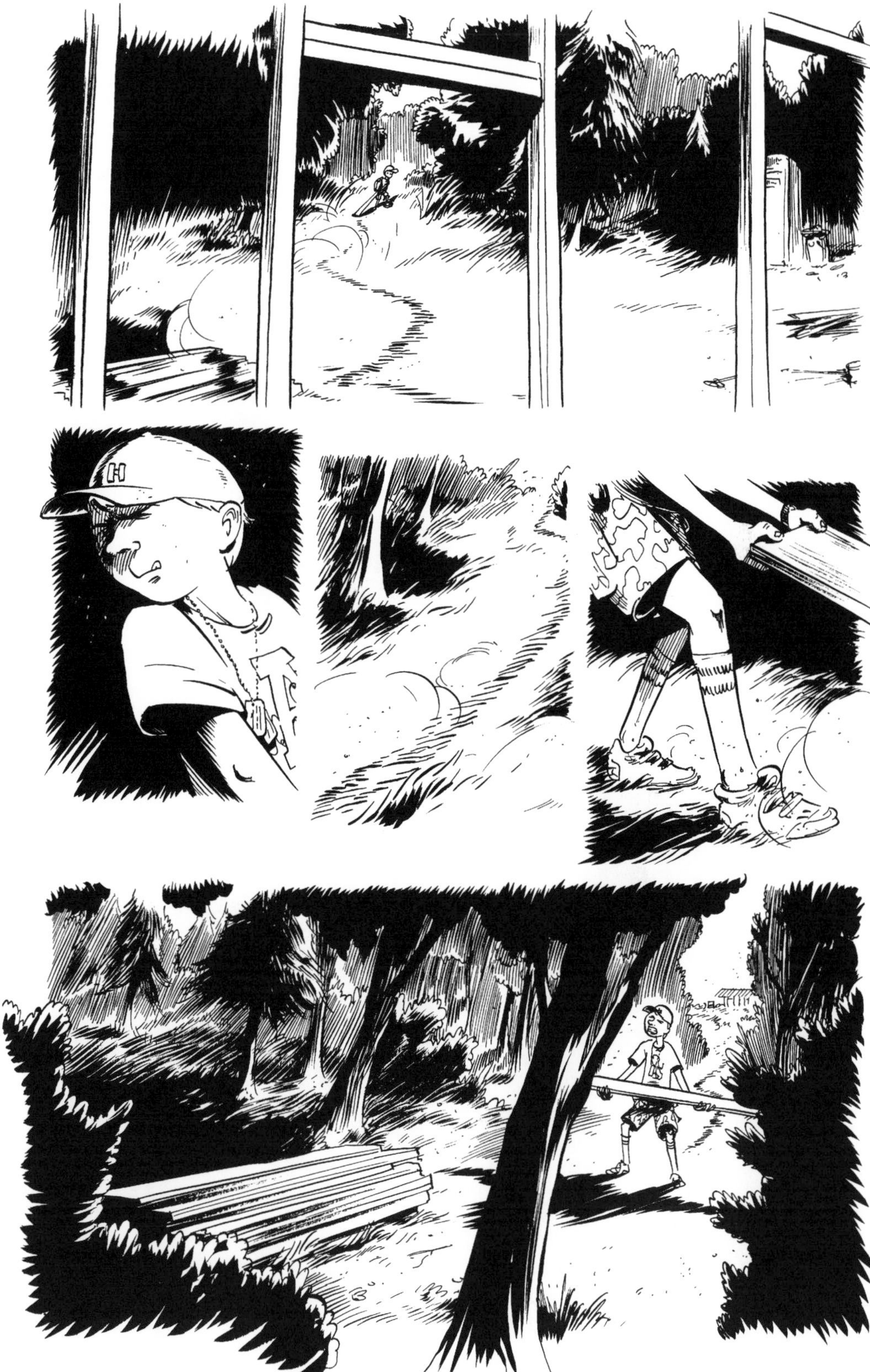

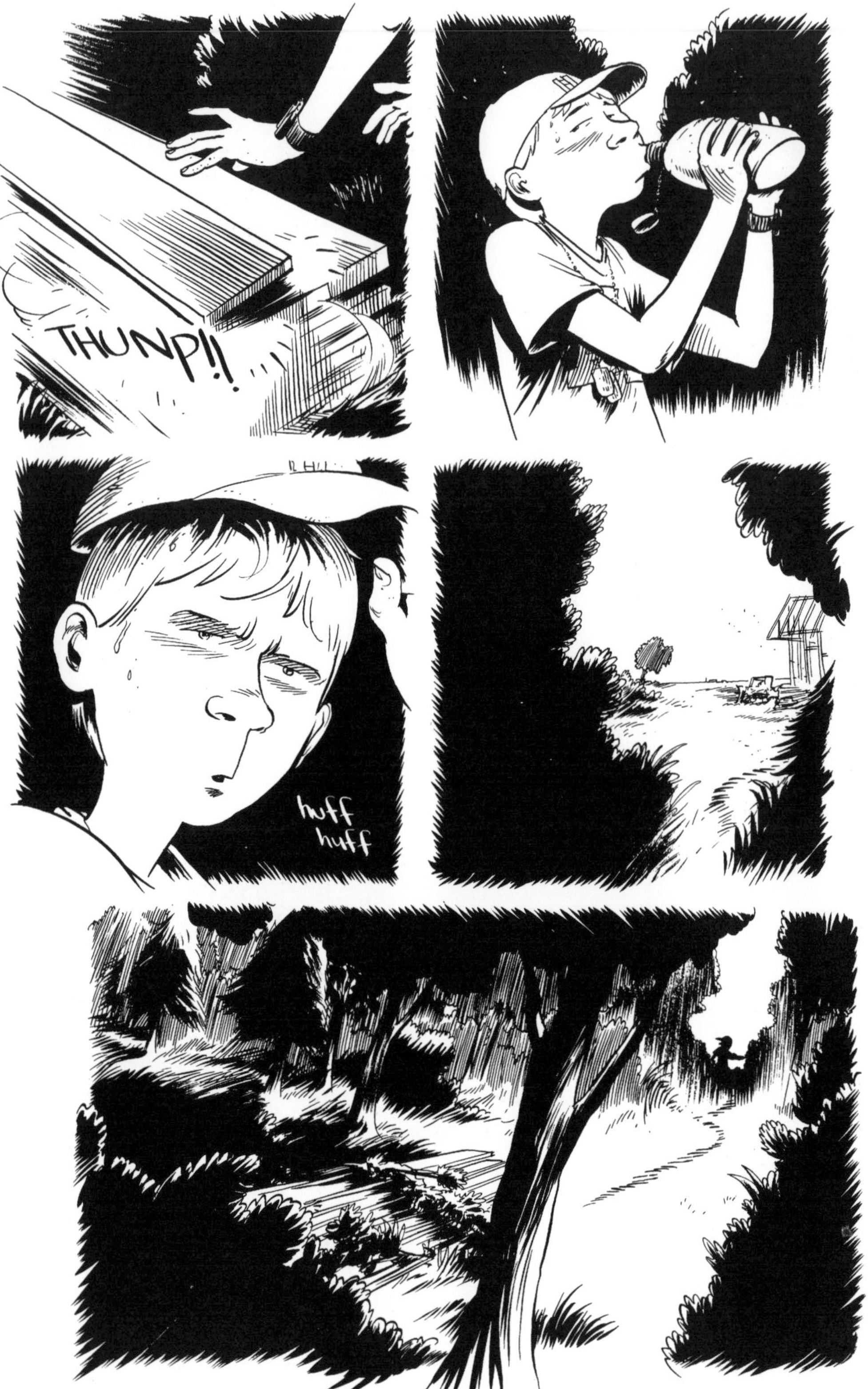
THUNP!!
huff
huff

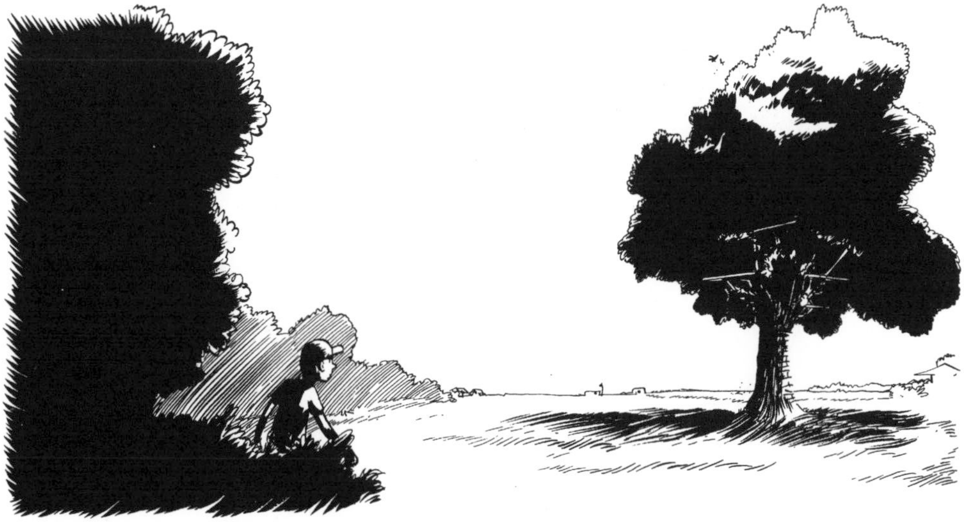
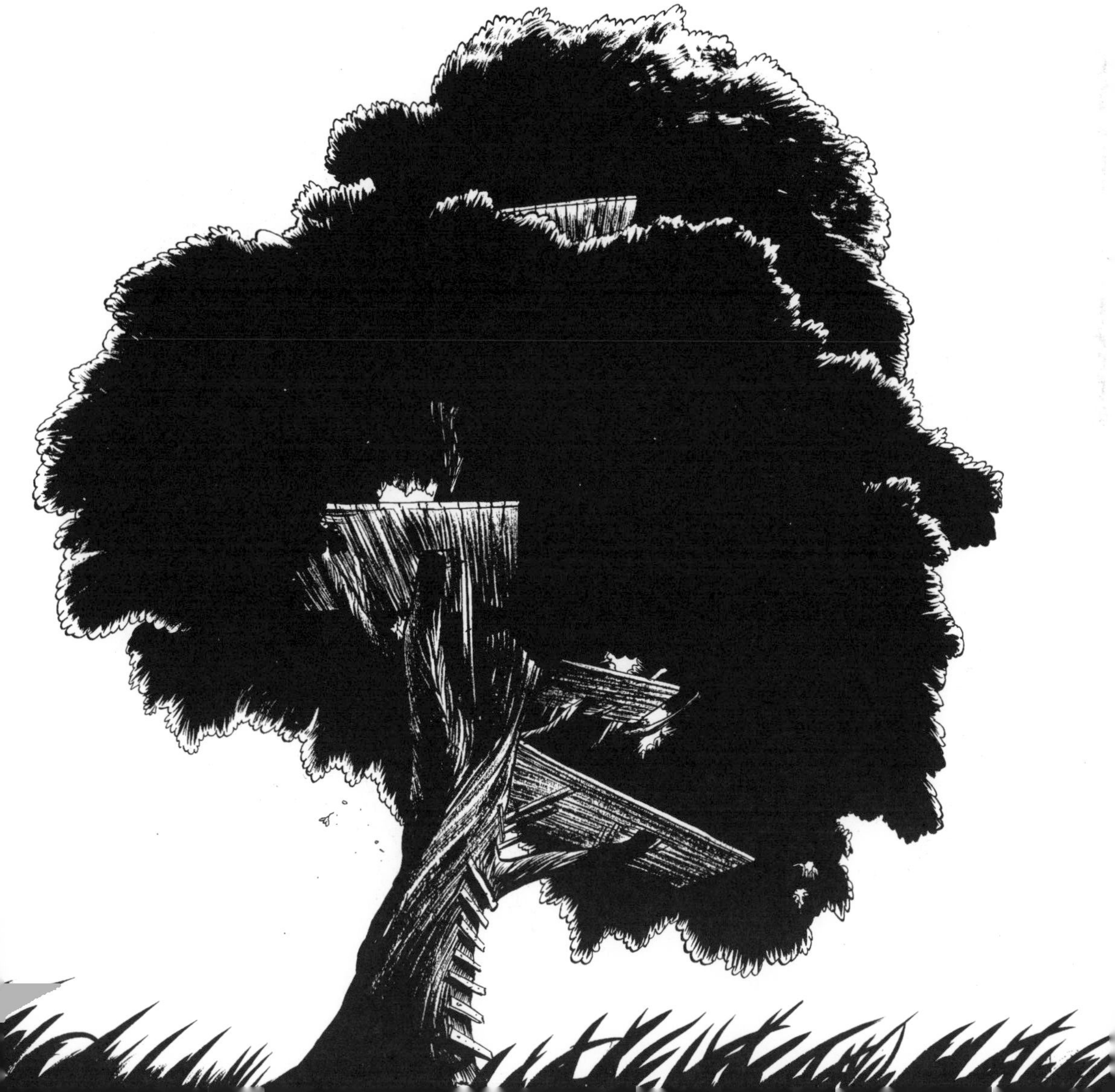

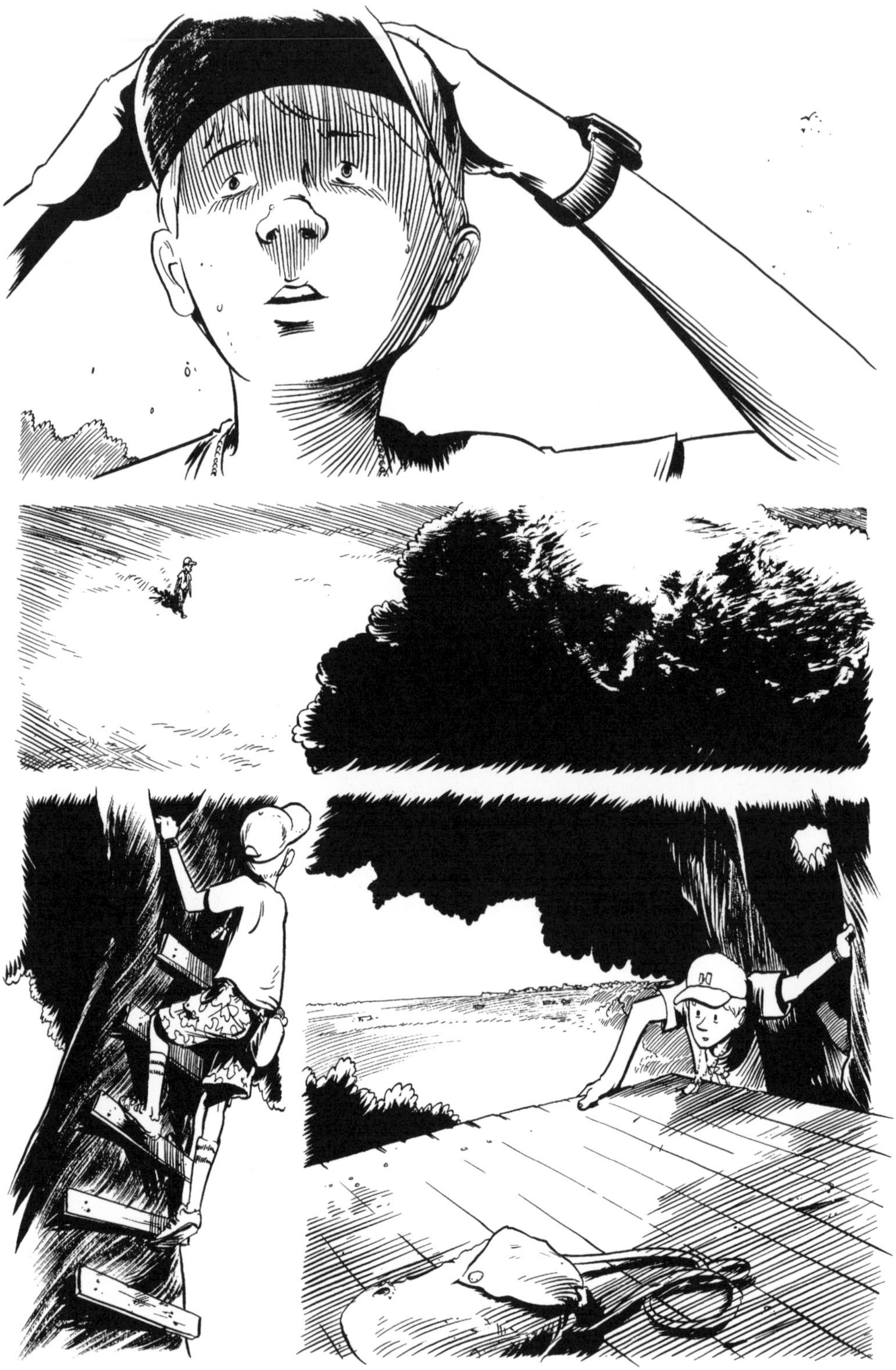

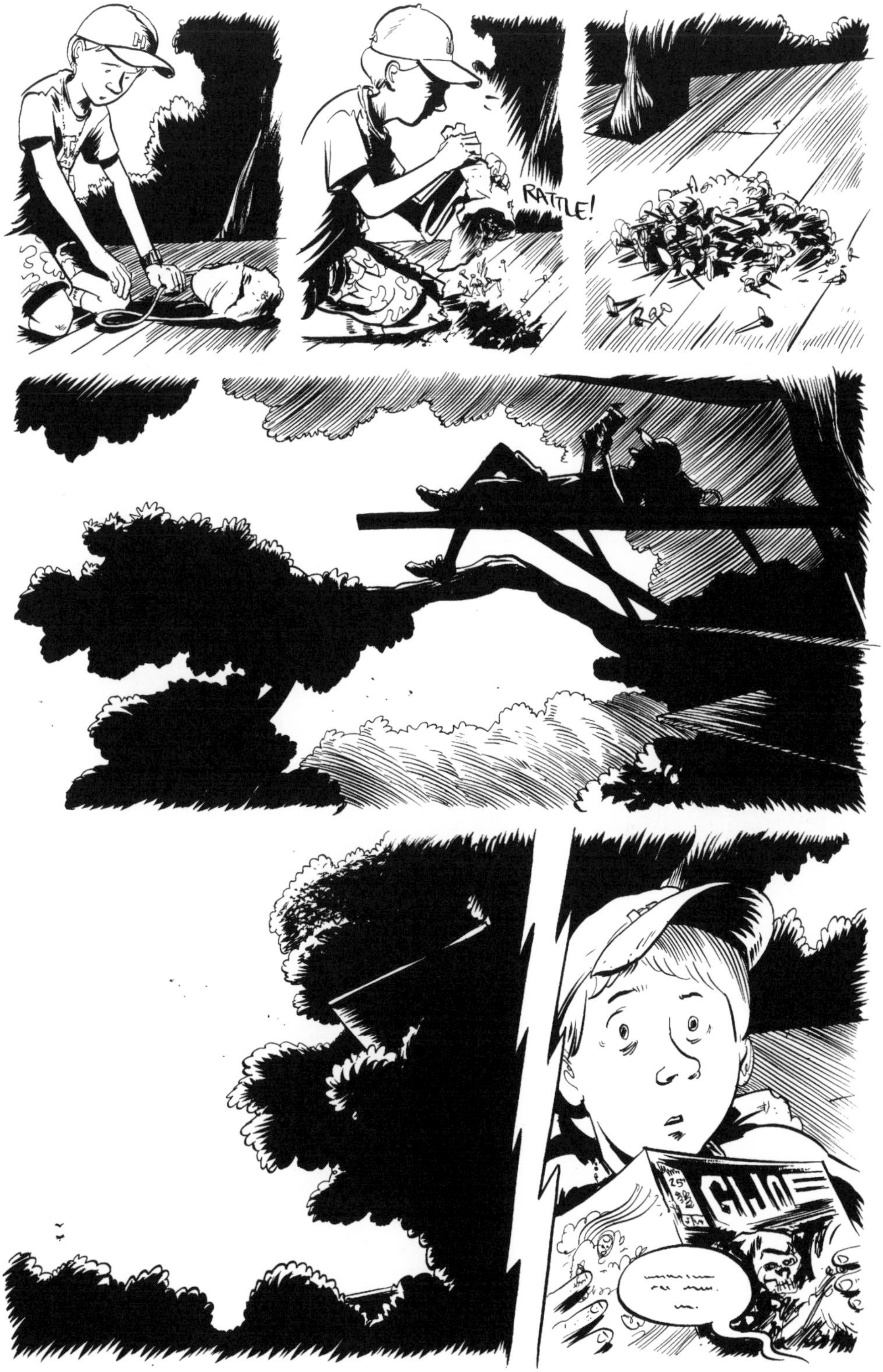
RATTLE!

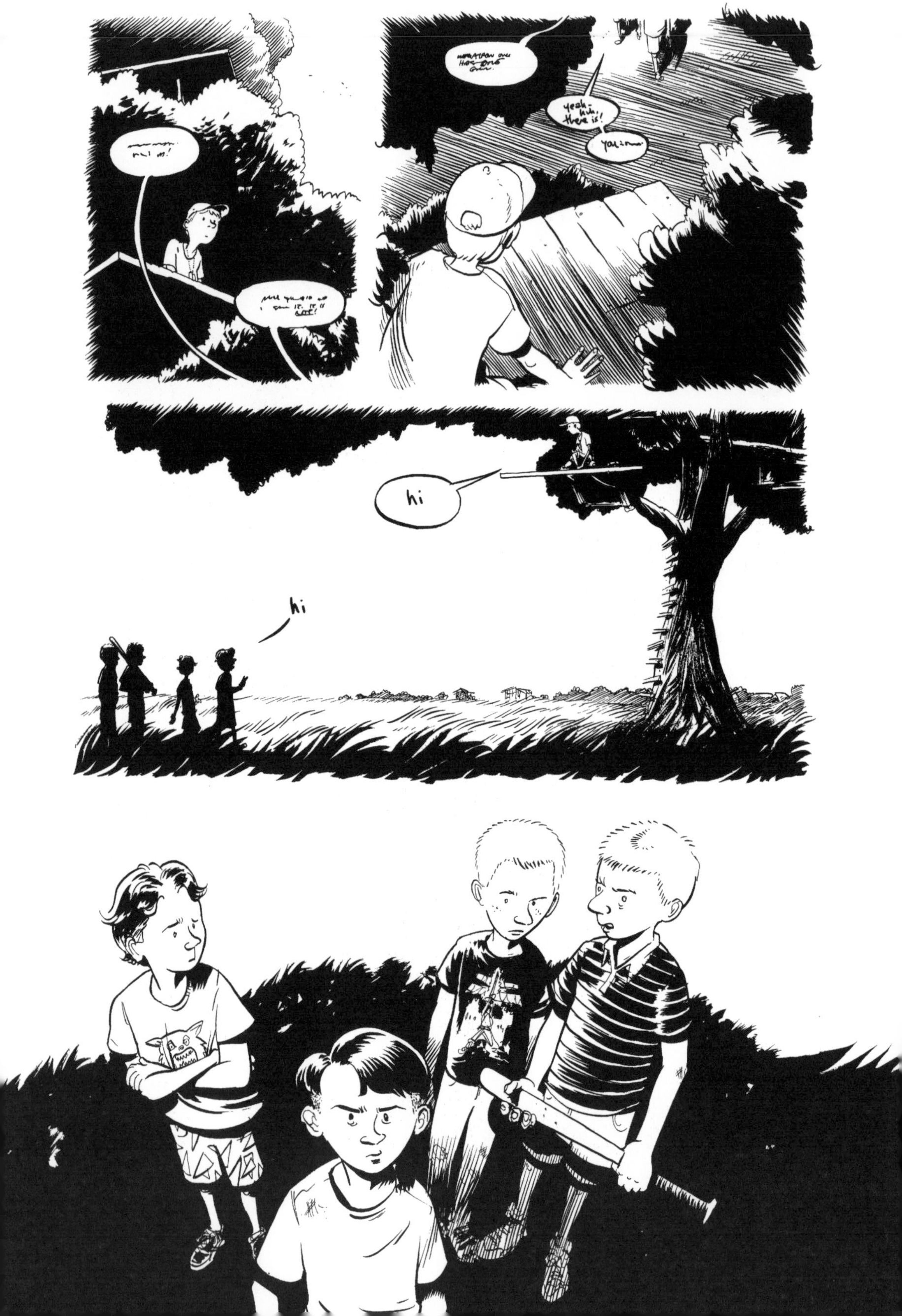

yeah-huh, there is!
hi
hi

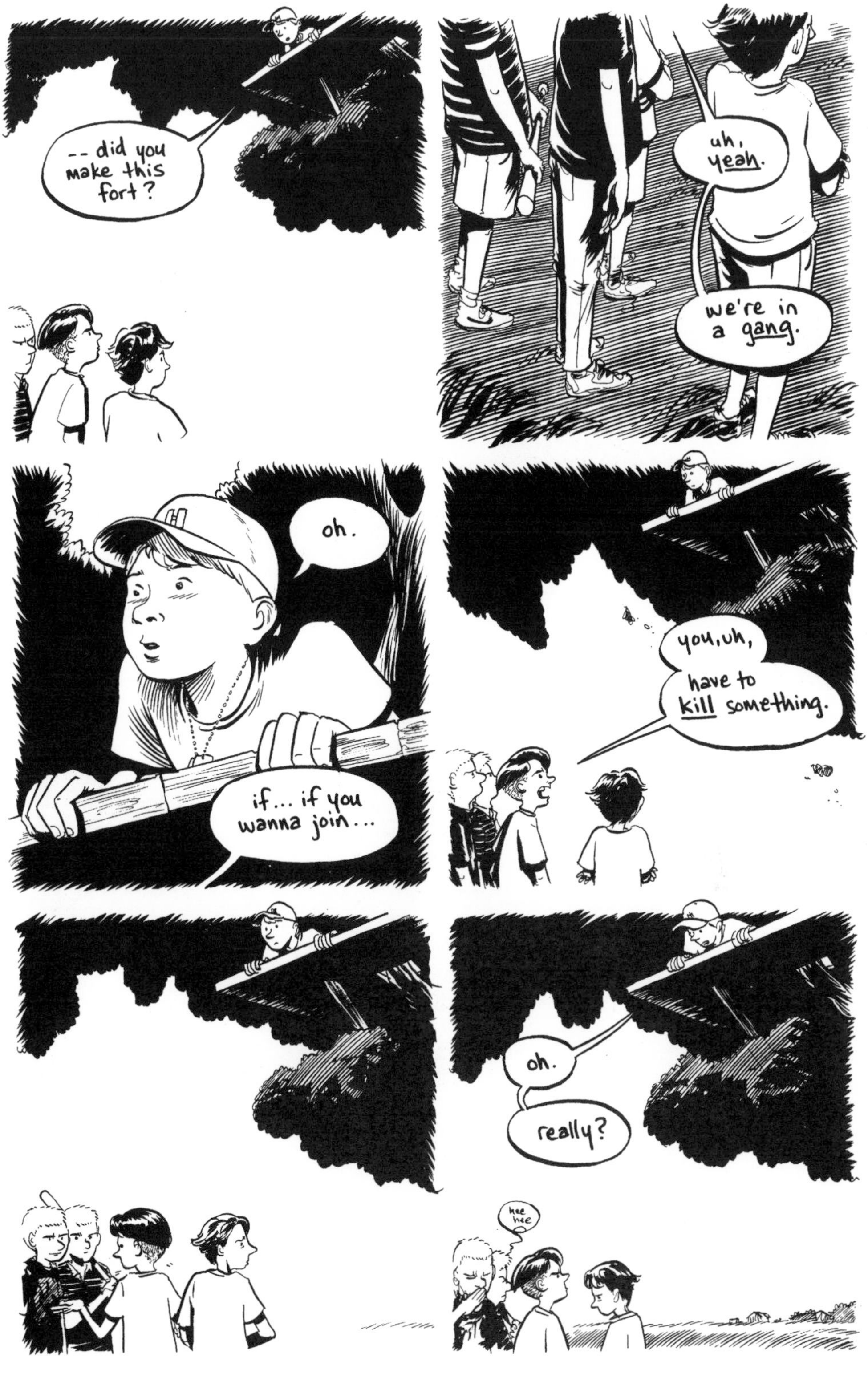
-- did you make this fort?
uh, yeah.
we're in a gang.
oh.
if... if you wanna join...
you, uh,
have to kill something.
oh.
really?
hee hee

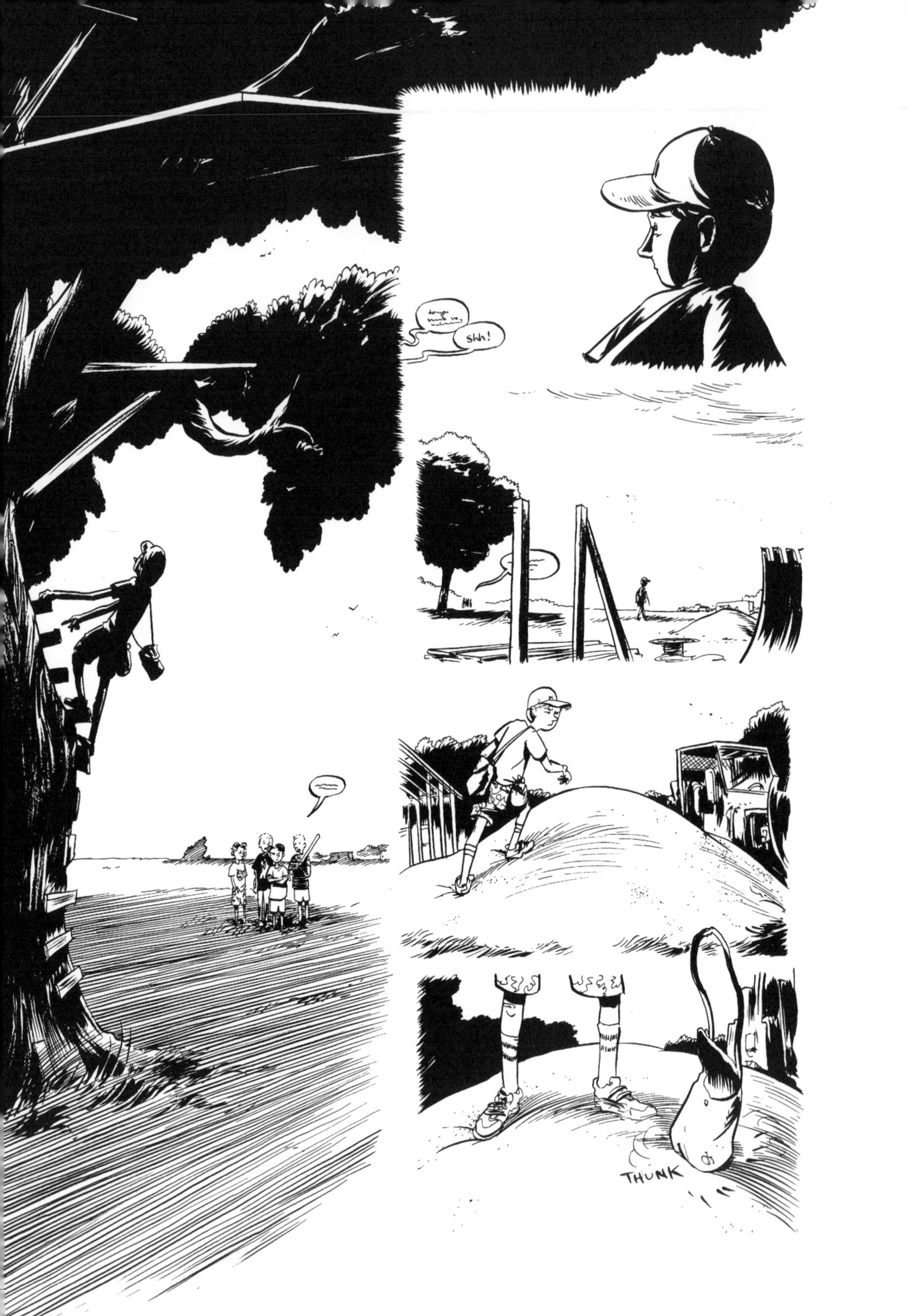
shh!
THUNK

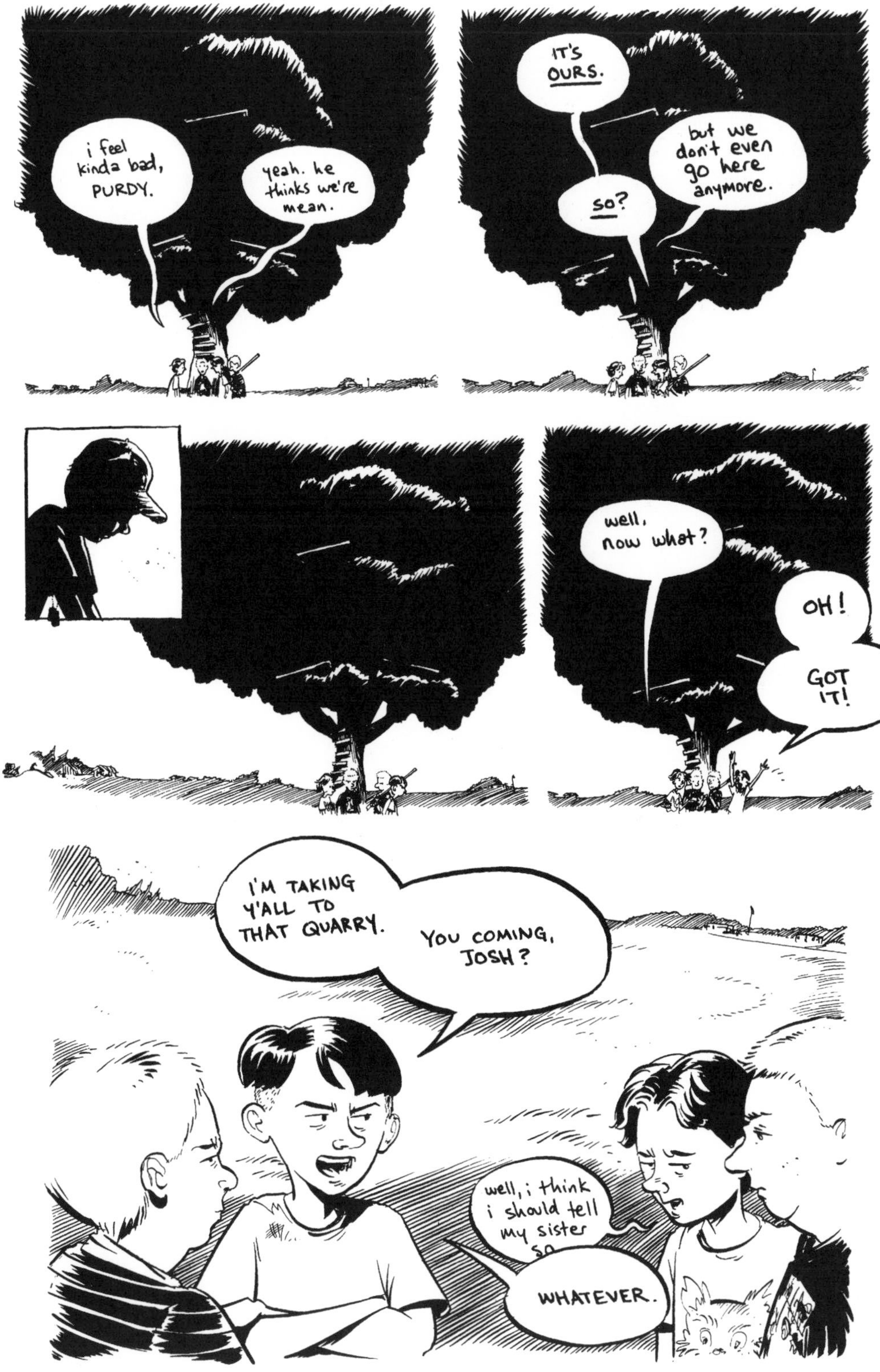
i feel kinda bad, PURDY.
yeah. he thinks we're mean.
IT'S OURS.
SO?
but we don't even go here anymore.
well, now what?
OH!
GOT IT!
I'M TAKING Y'ALL TO THAT QUARRY.
YOU COMING, JOSH?
well, i think i should tell my sister so
WHATEVER.

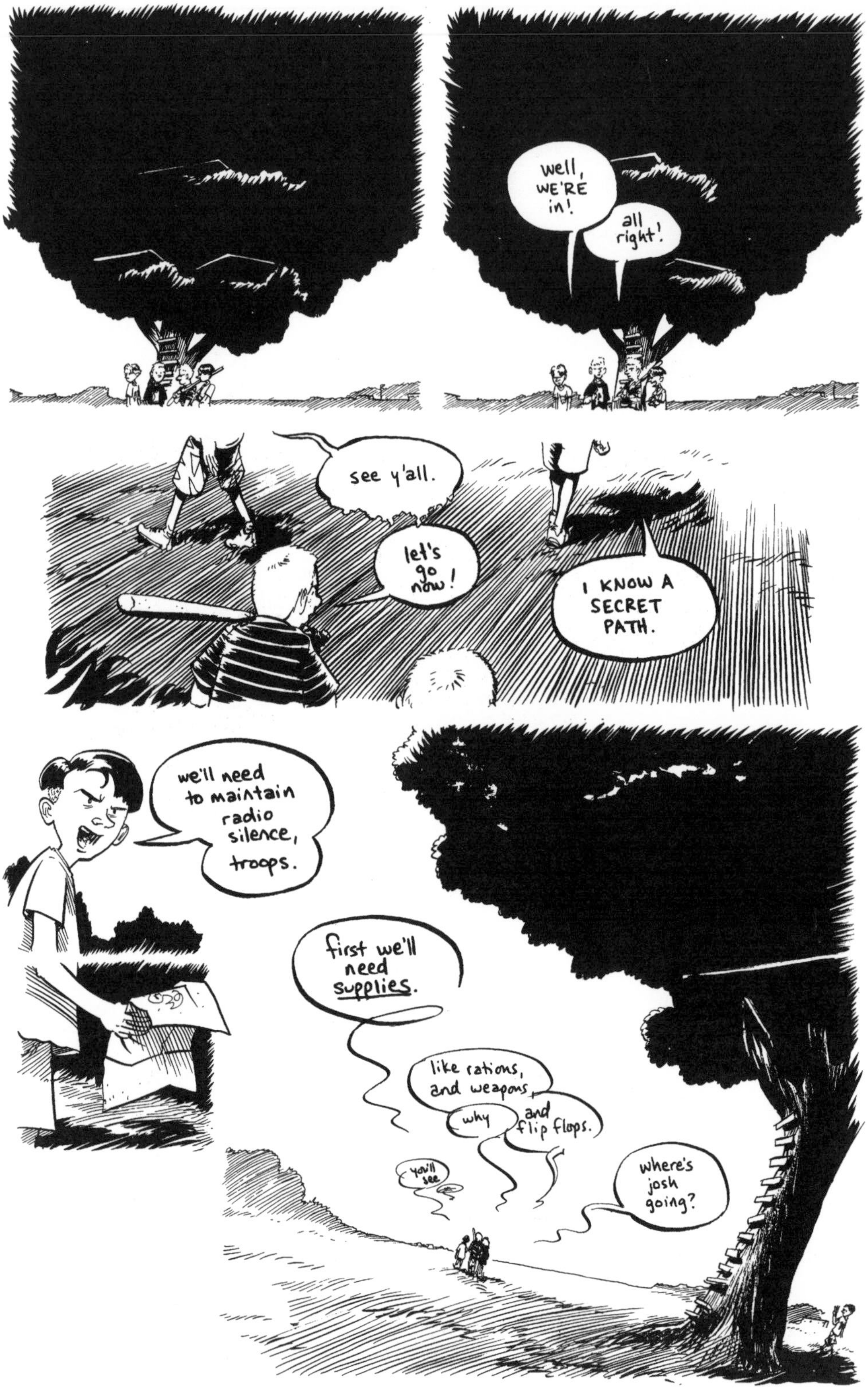
well, WE'RE in!
all right!
see y'all.
let's go now!
I KNOW A SECRET PATH.
we'll need to maintain radio silence, troops.
first we'll need supplies.
like rations, and weapons,
why
and flip flops.
you'll see
where's josh going?

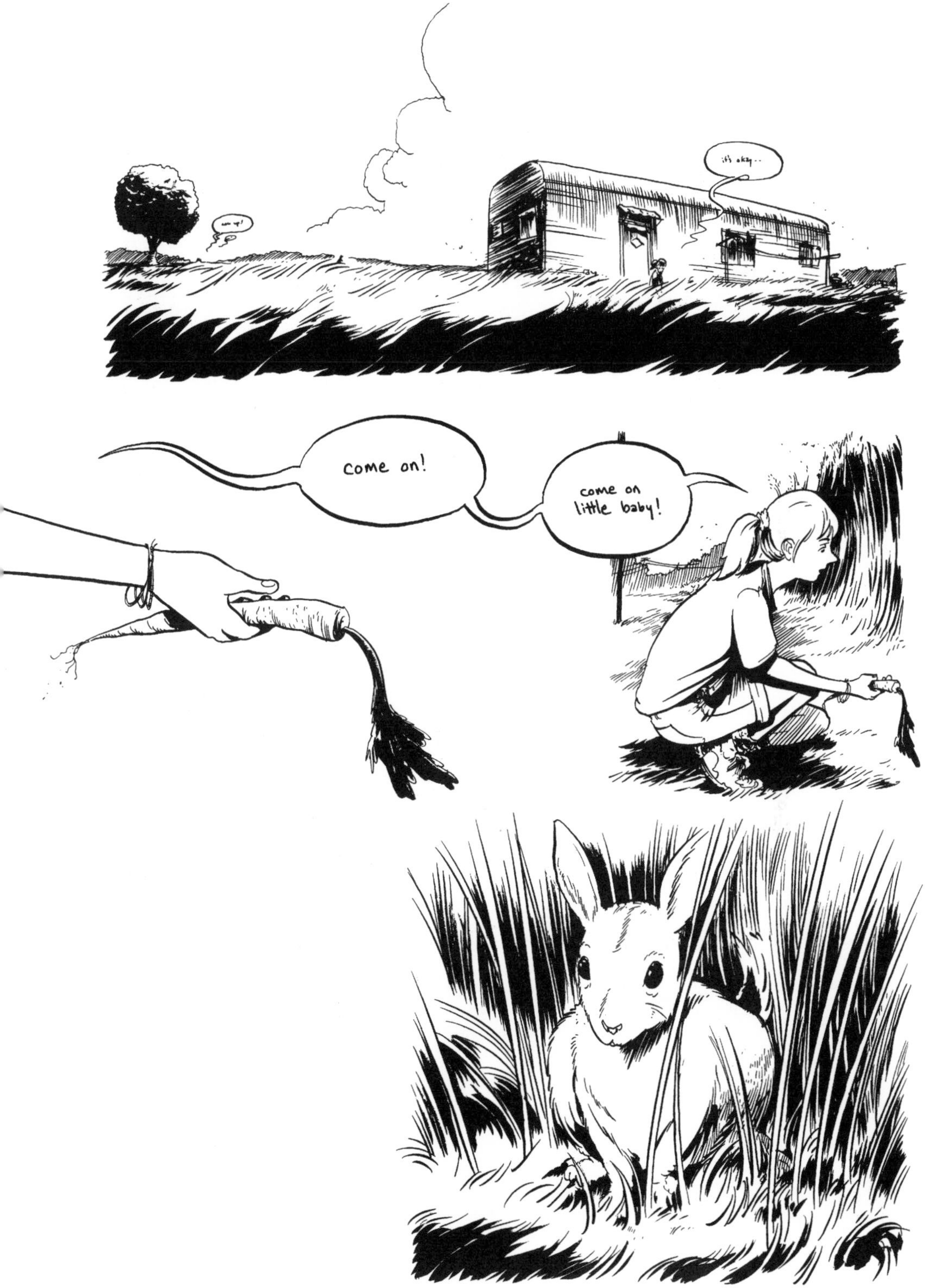
it's okay..
come on!
come on
little baby!

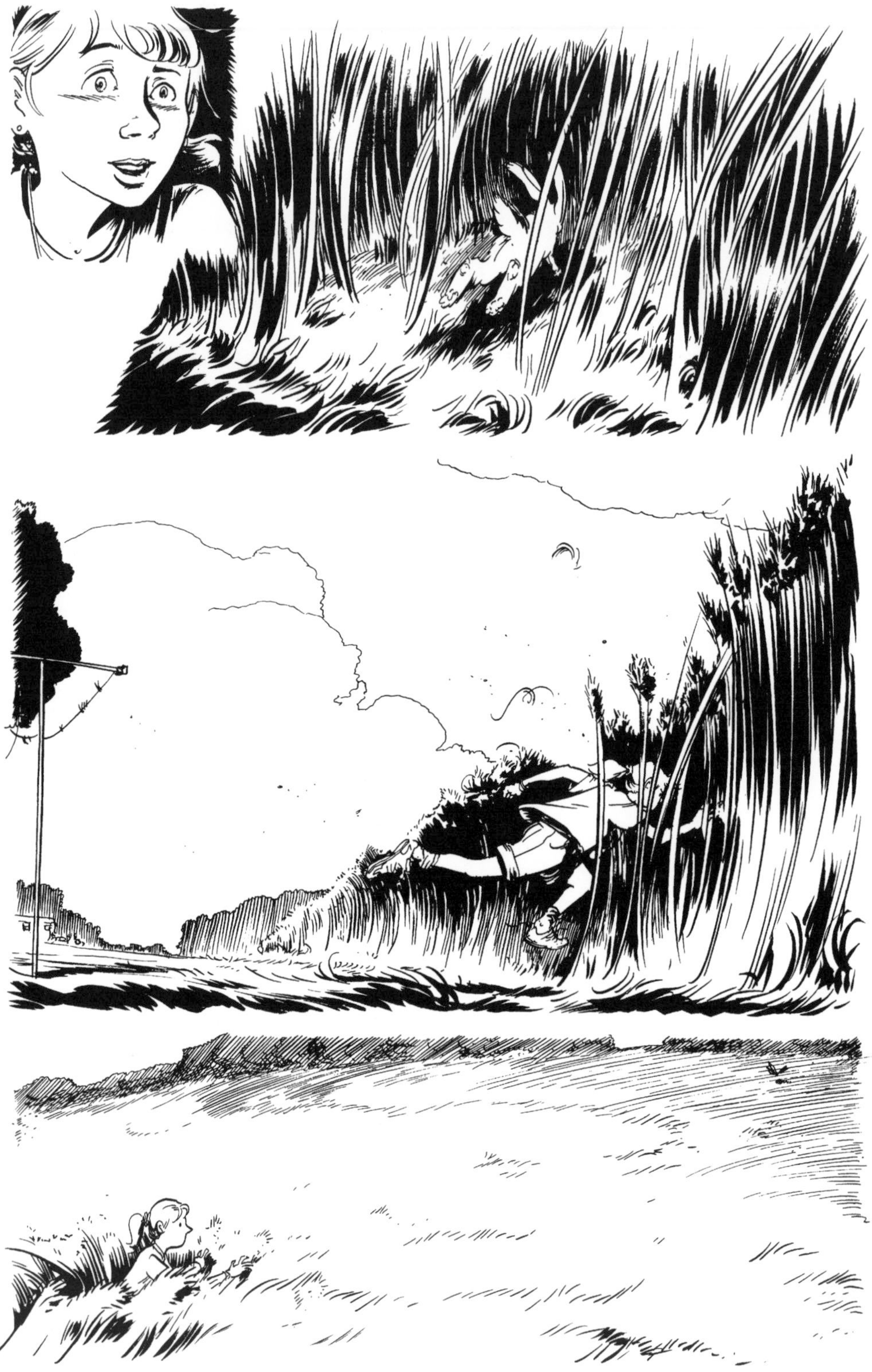

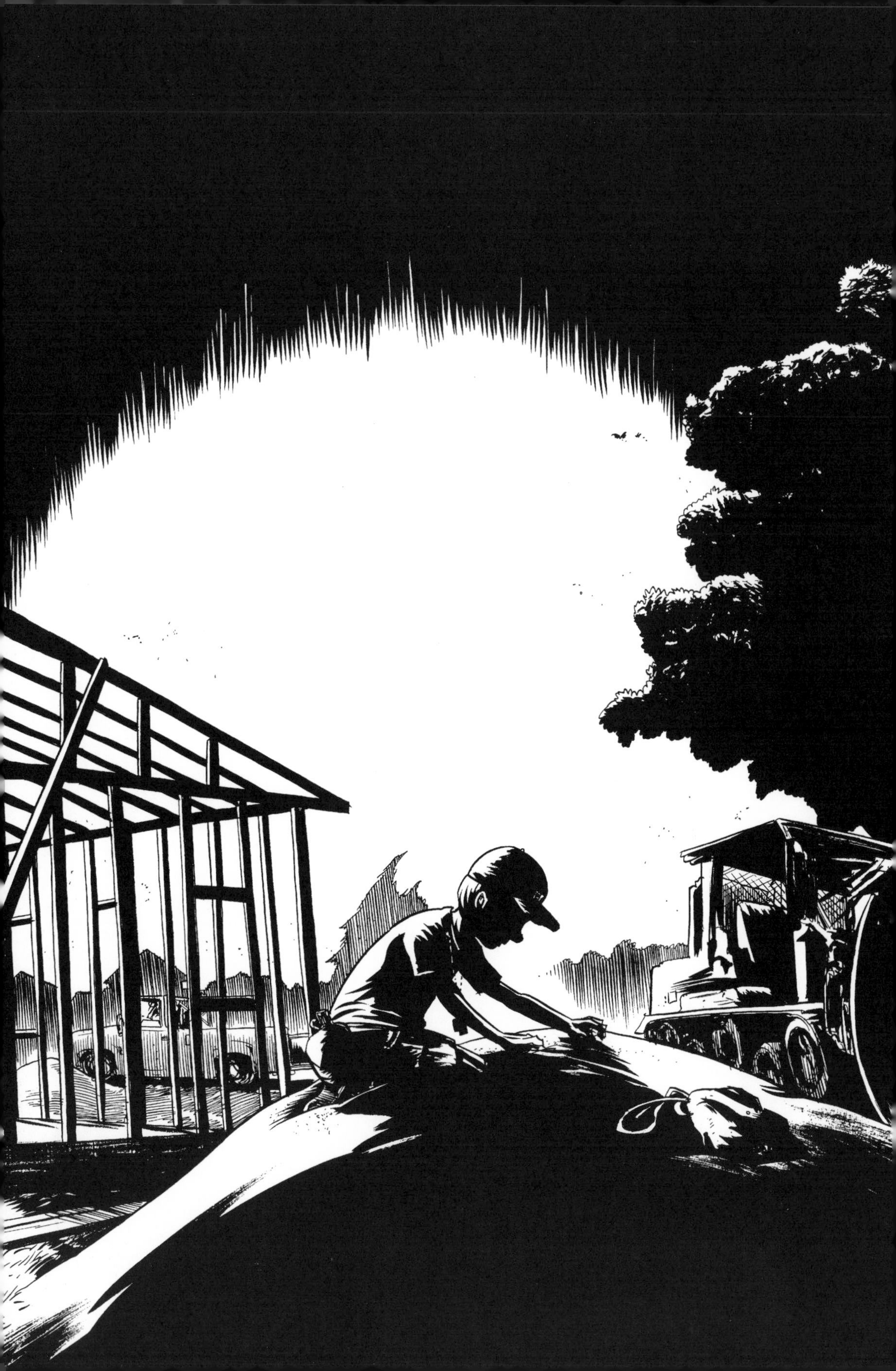

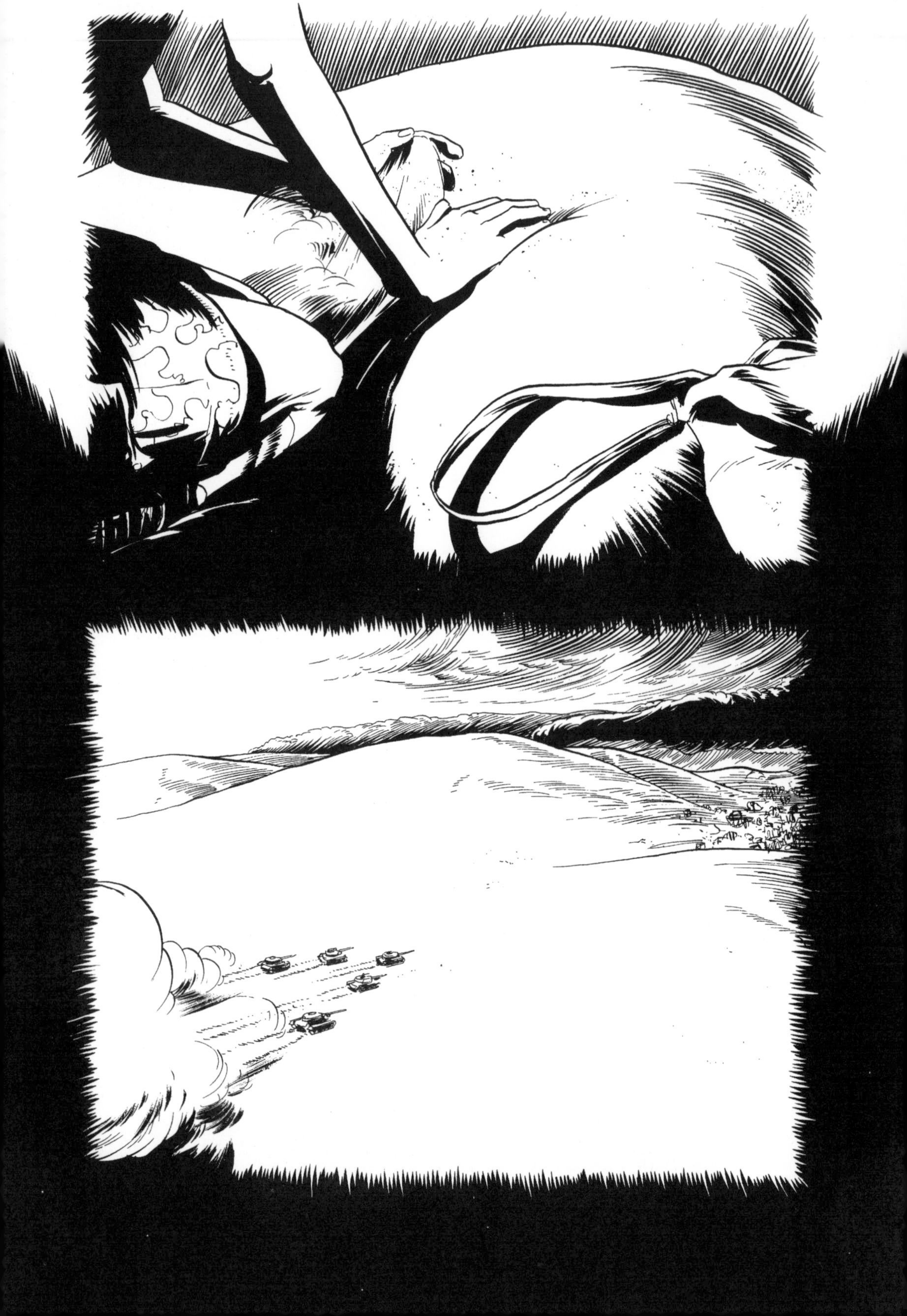

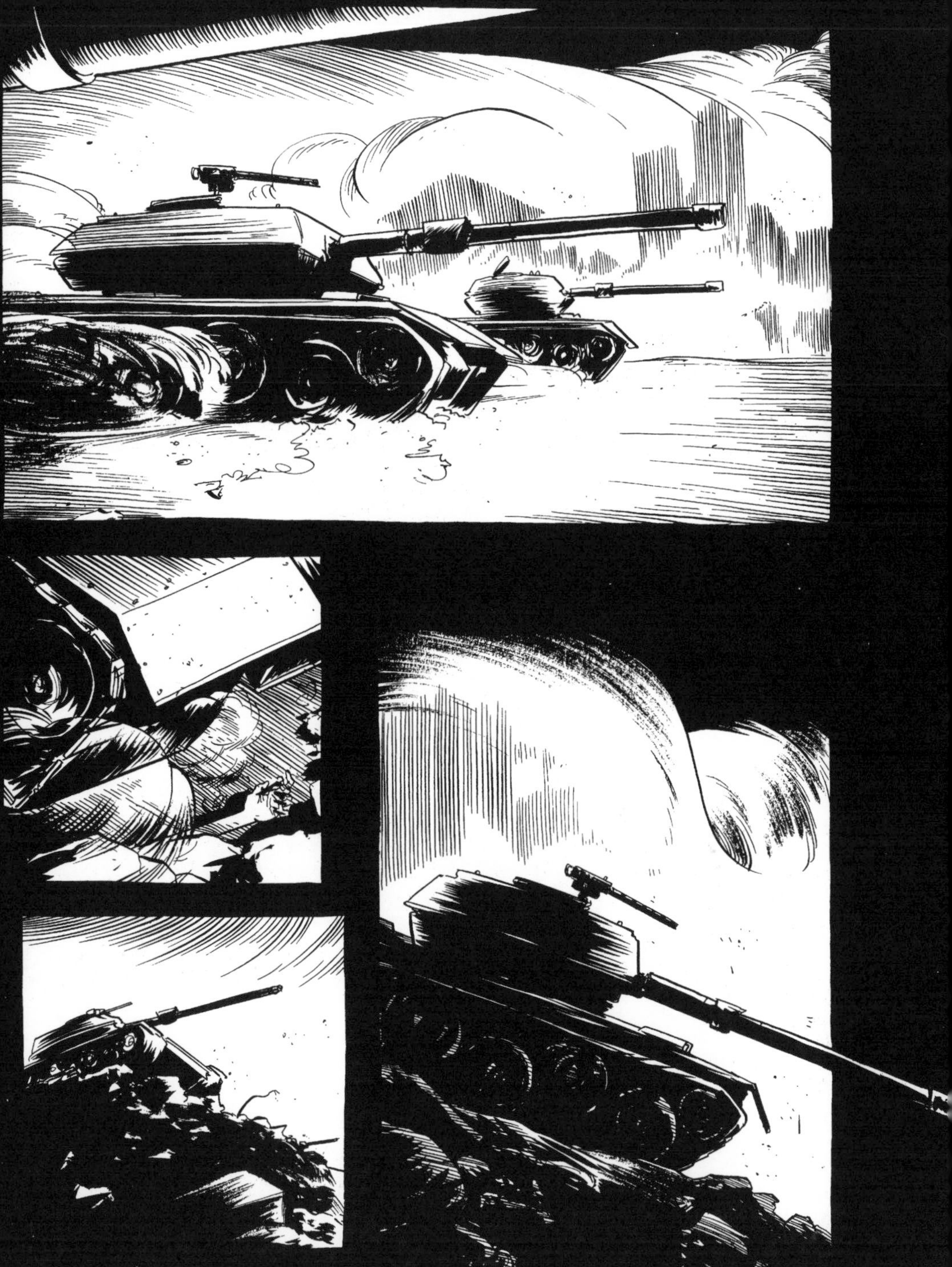

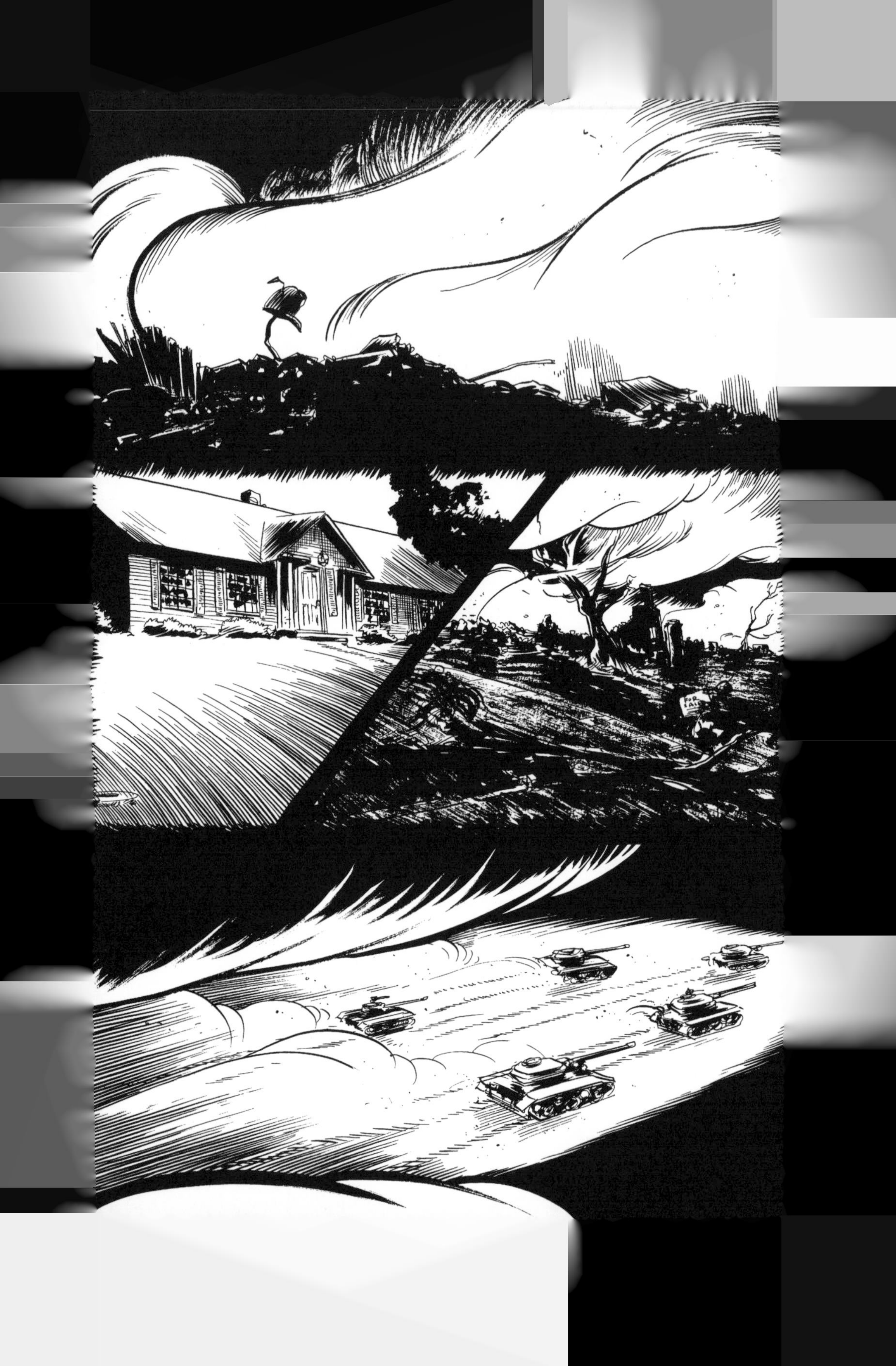

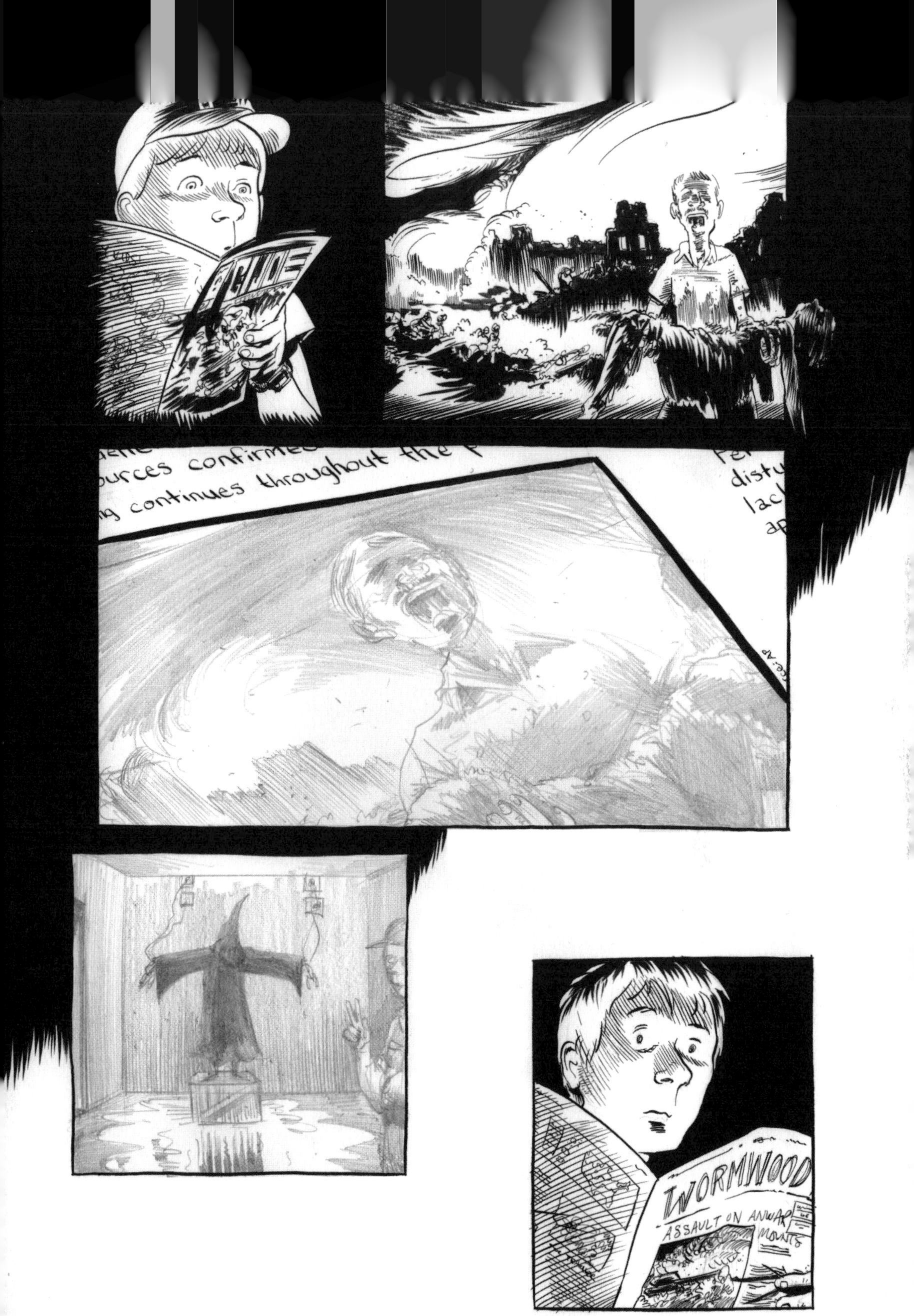

ources confirmed
continues throughout the
WORMWOOD
ASSAULT ON ANWAR
MOUNTS

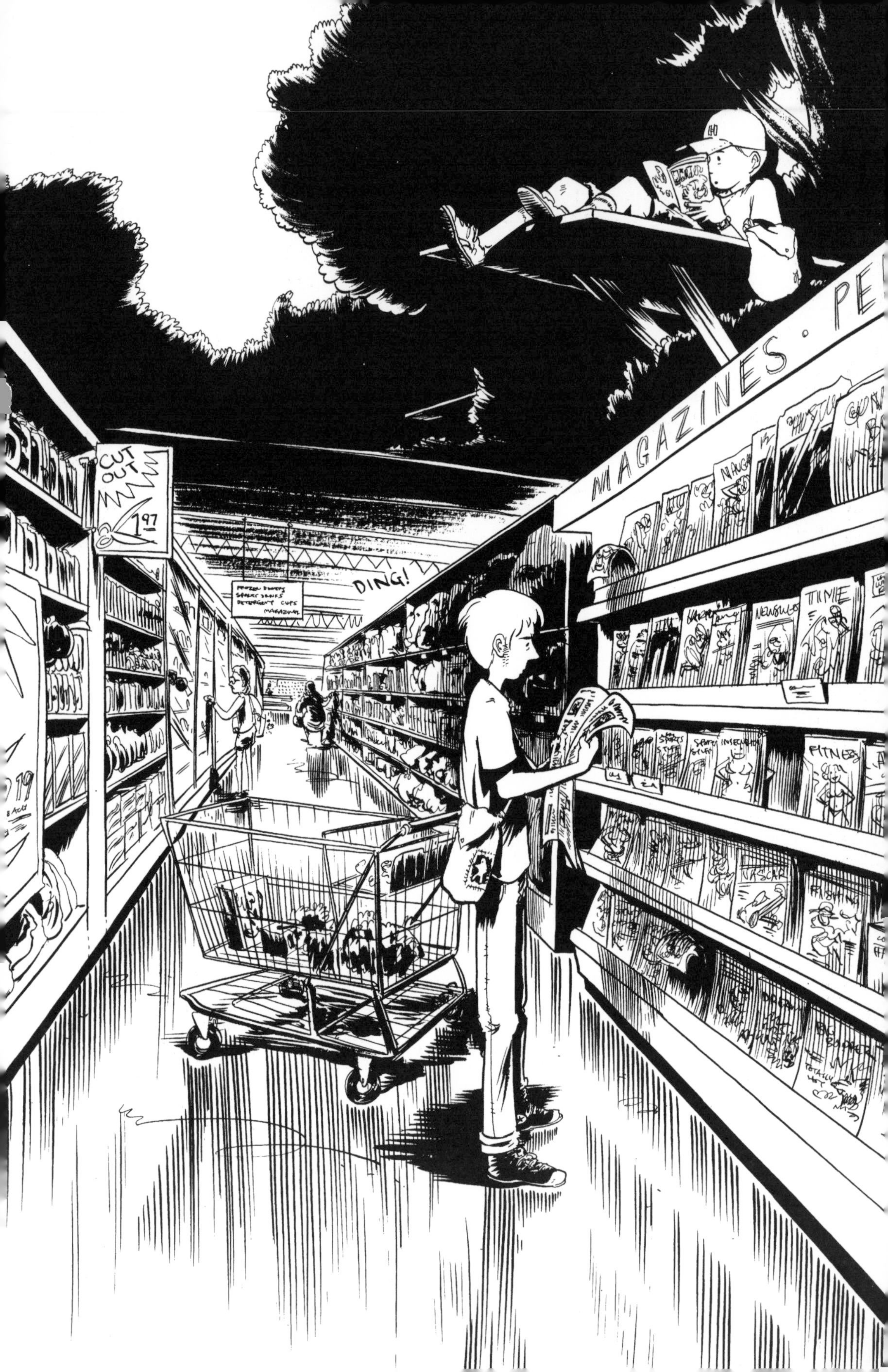
CUT OUT
1.97
DING!
MAGAZINES · PE
TIME
FITNESS
NASCAR

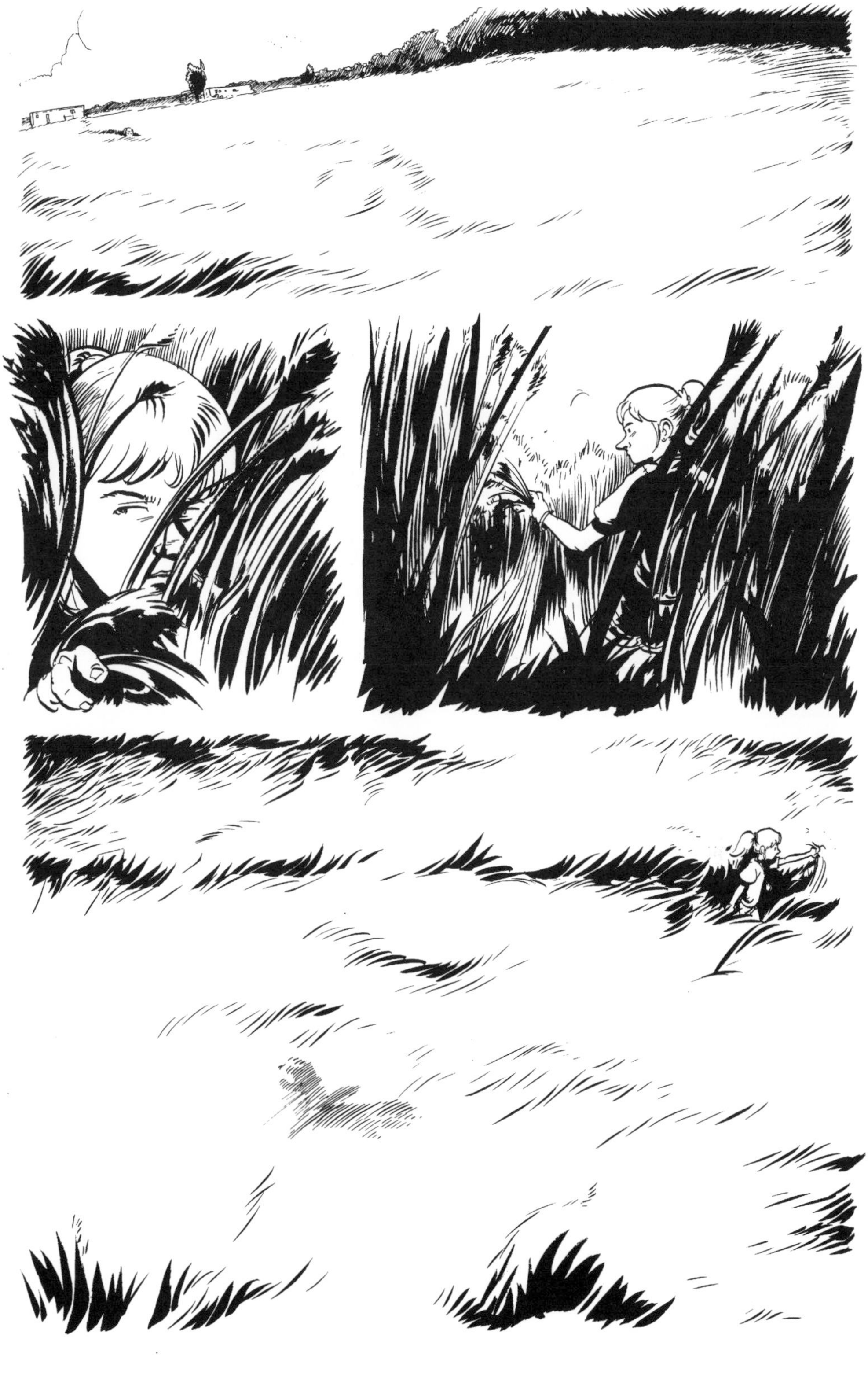

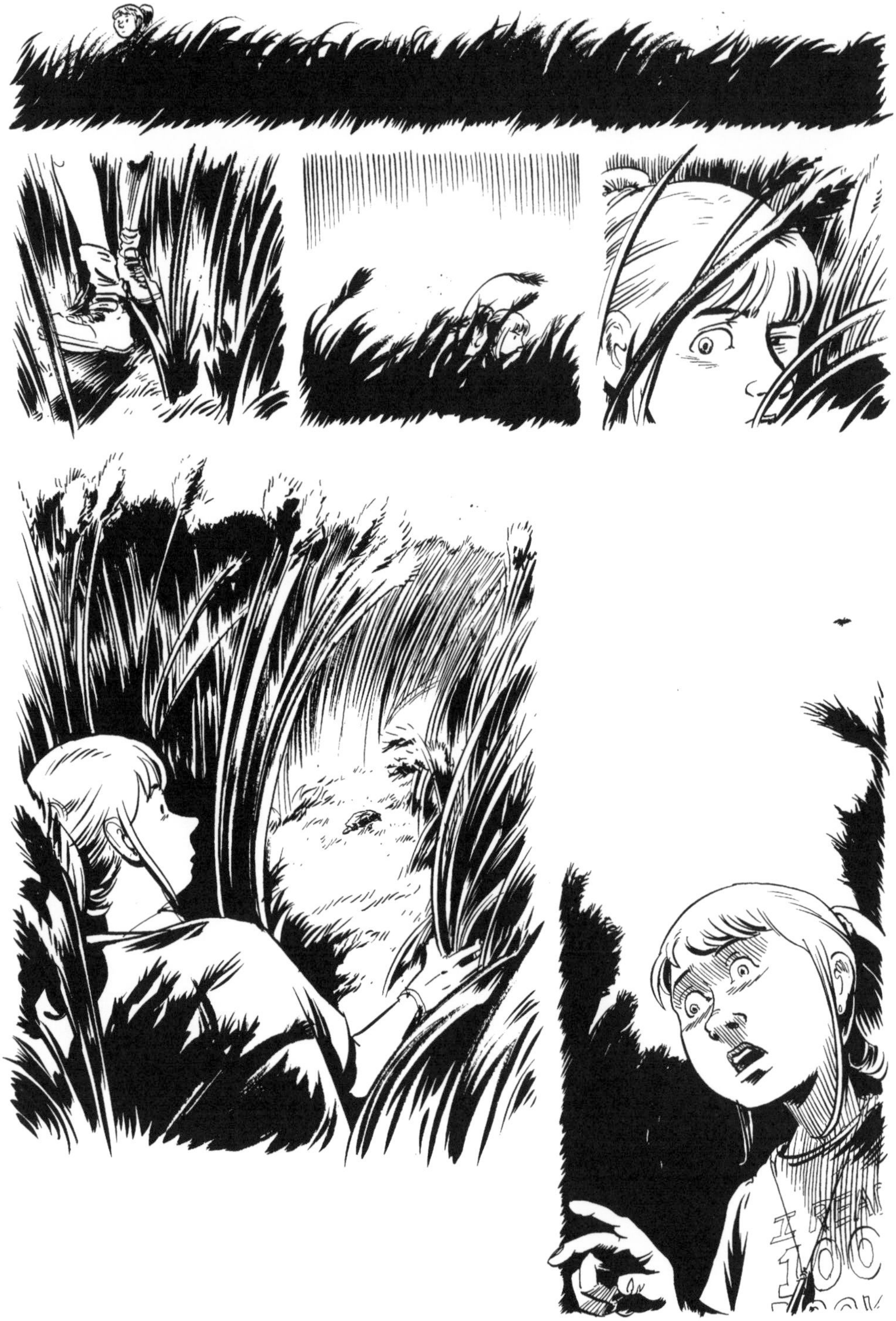

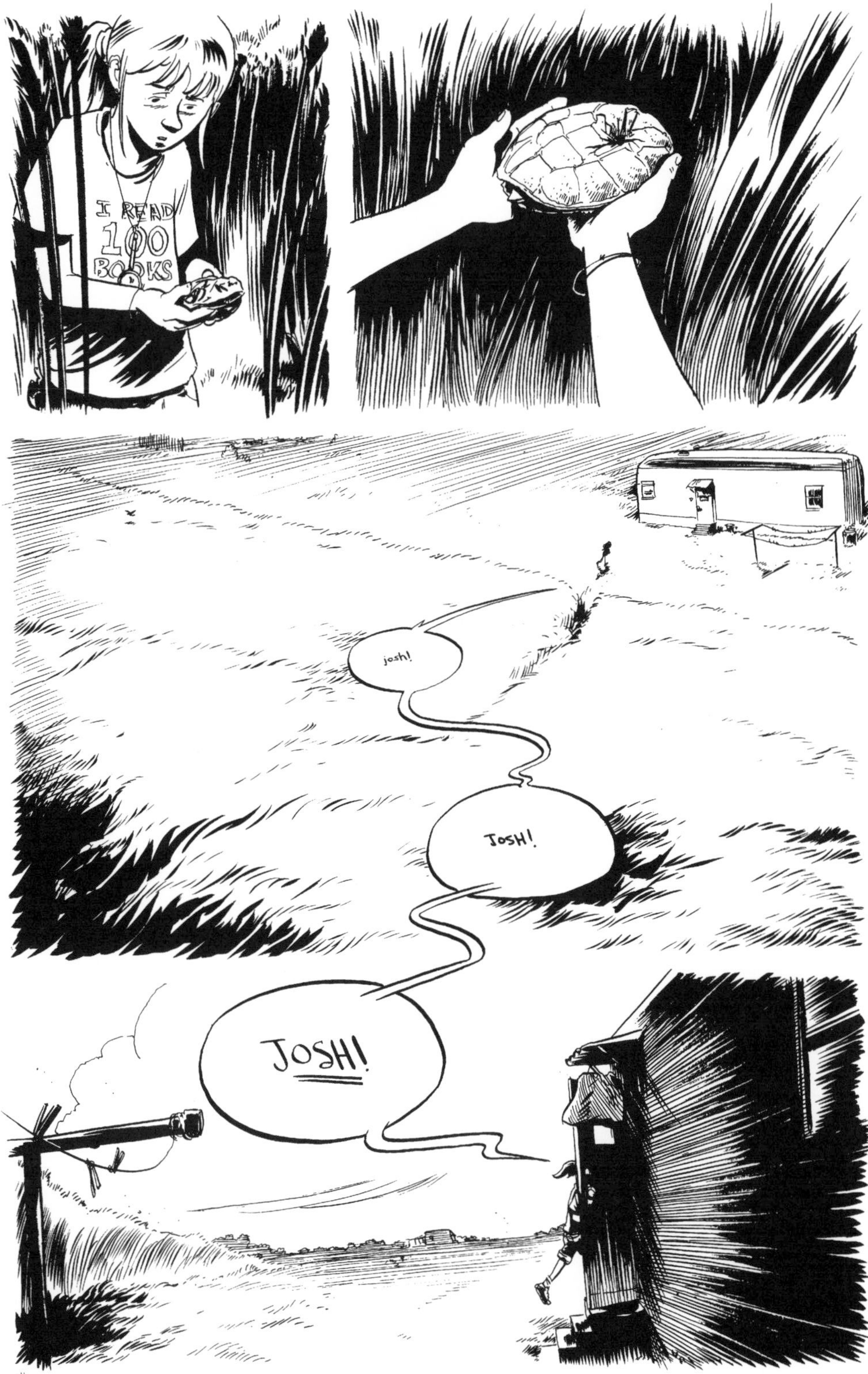
I READ 100 BOOKS
josh!
JOSH!
JOSH!

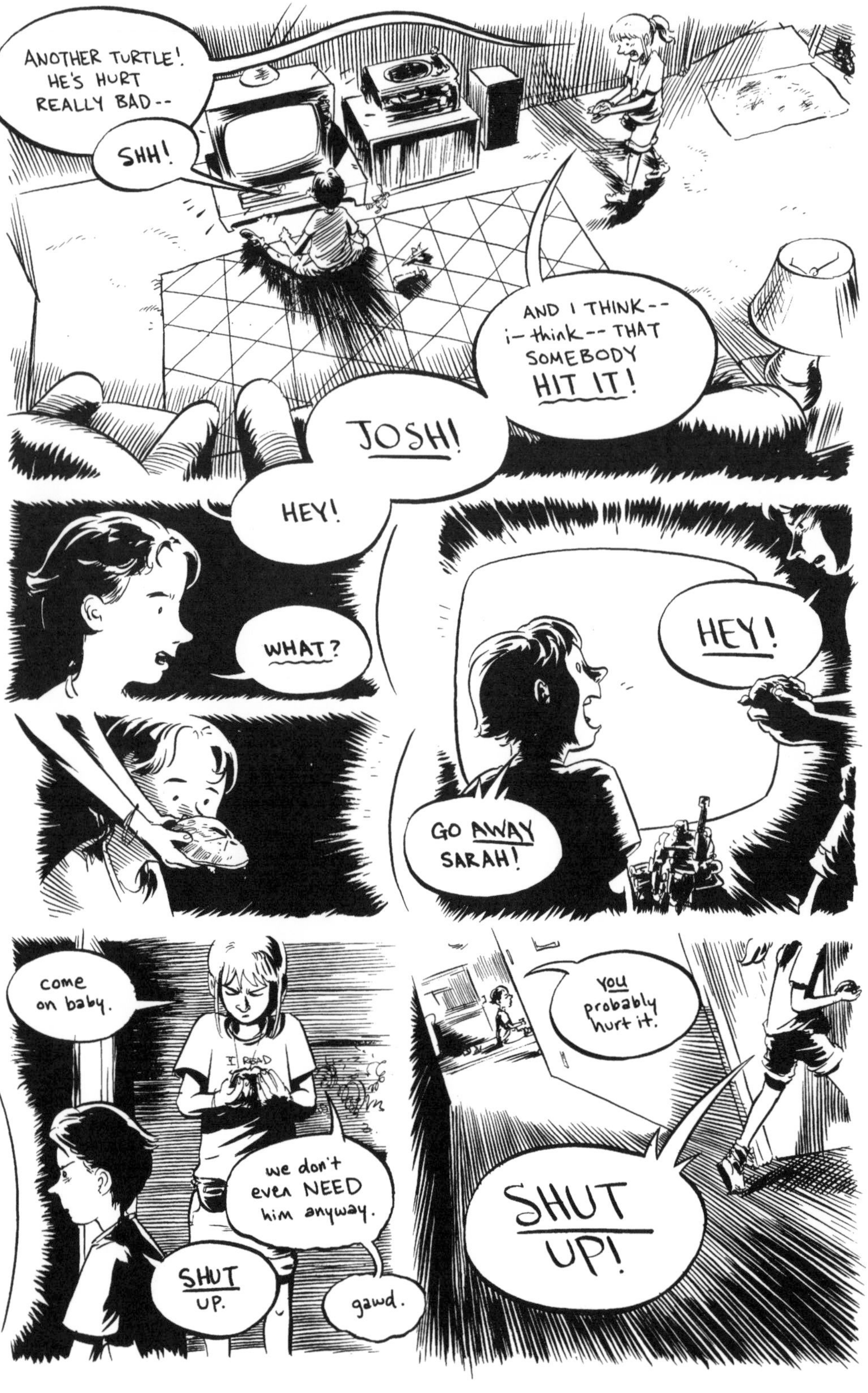

ANOTHER TURTLE! HE'S HURT REALLY BAD--
SHH!
AND I THINK-- i--think-- THAT SOMEBODY HIT IT!
JOSH!
HEY!
WHAT?
HEY!
GO AWAY SARAH!
come on baby.
we don't even NEED him anyway.
SHUT UP.
gawd.
YOU probably hurt it.
SHUT UP!

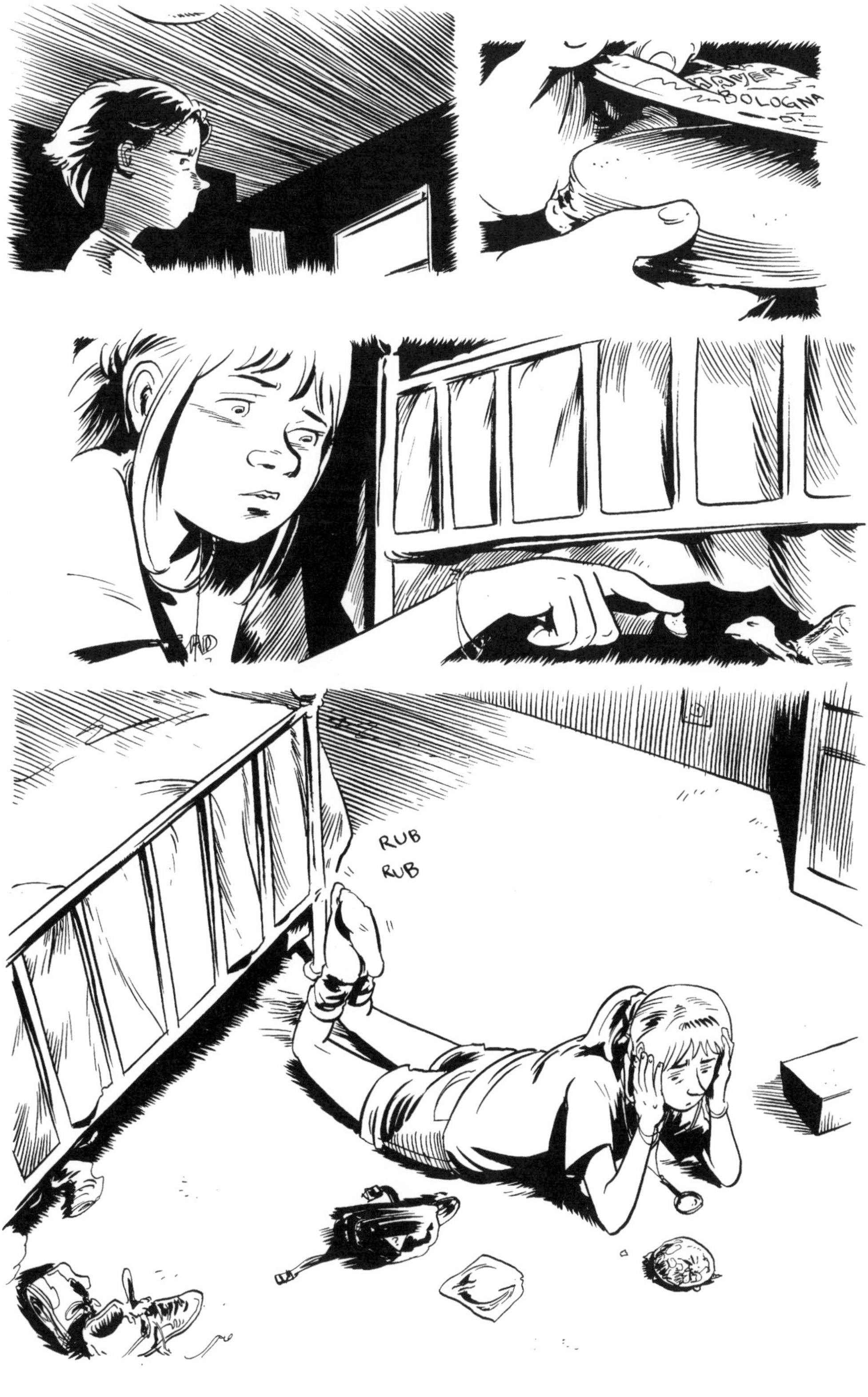
BOLOGNA
RUB
RUB

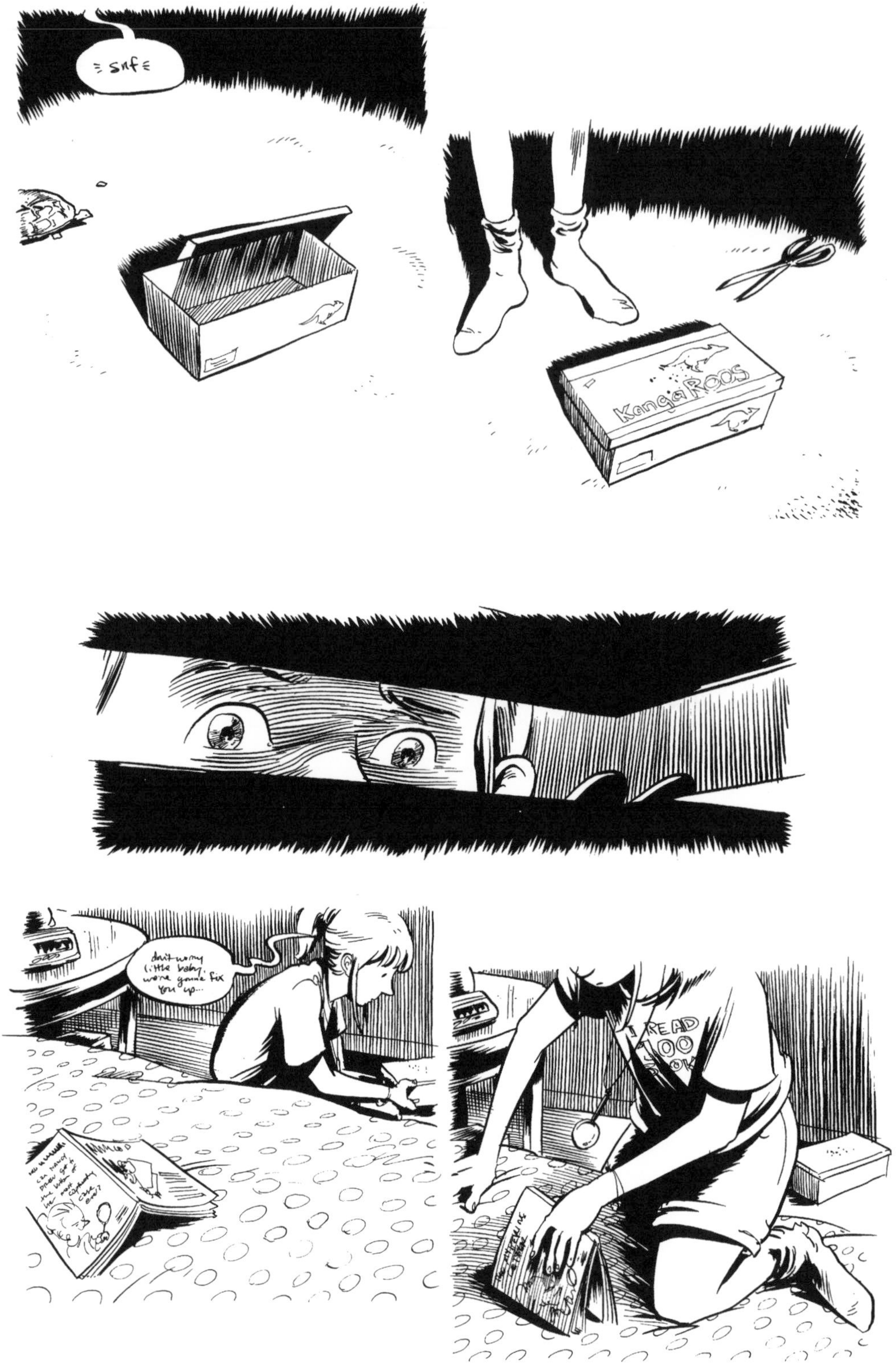
snf
KangaROOS
don't worry little baby, we're gonna fix you up...

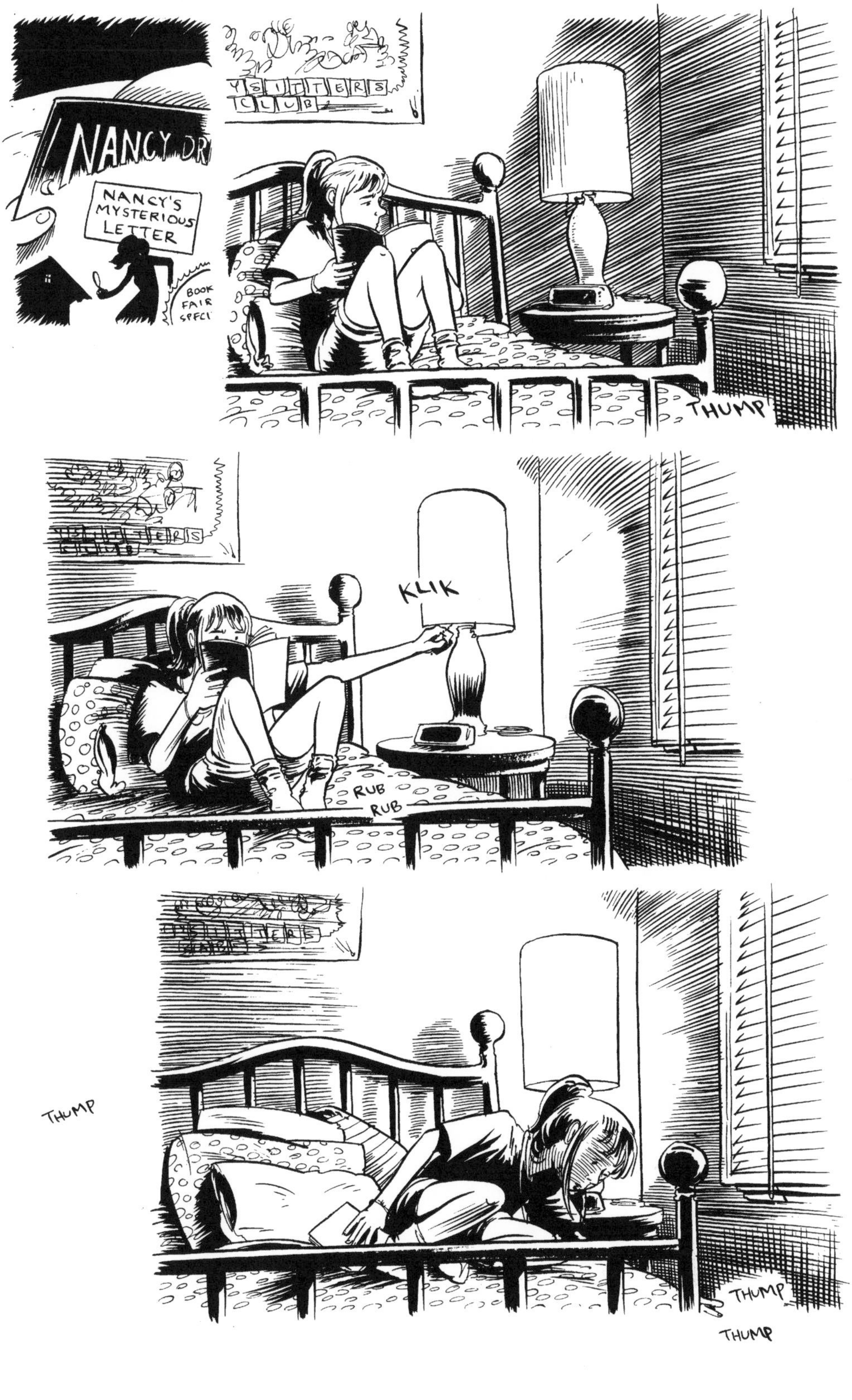
NANCY DR
NANCY'S MYSTERIOUS LETTER
BOOK FAIR SPECI
YSITTERS CLUB
THUMP
KLIK
RUB
RUB
THUMP
THUMP
THUMP

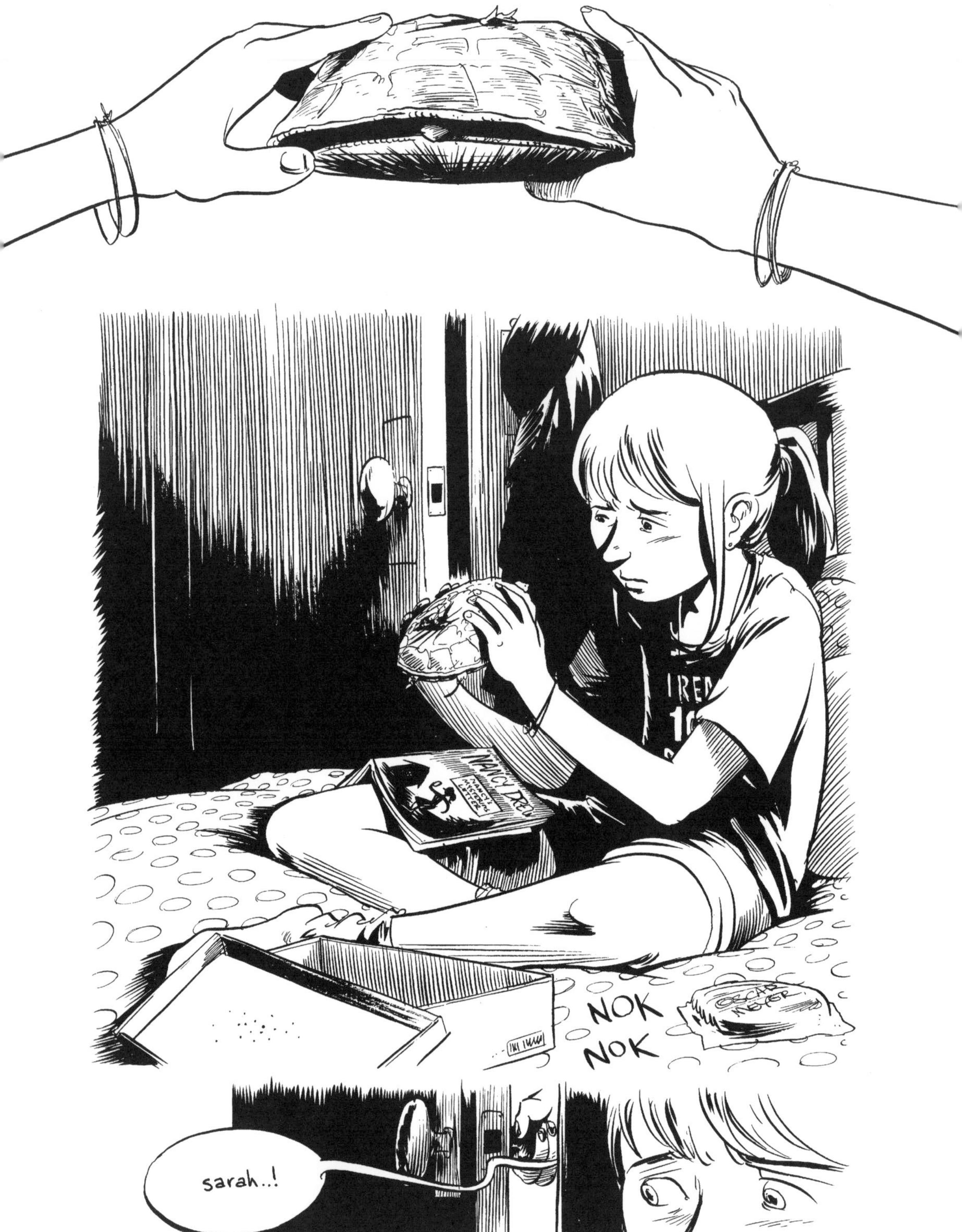
NOK
NOK
sarah..!

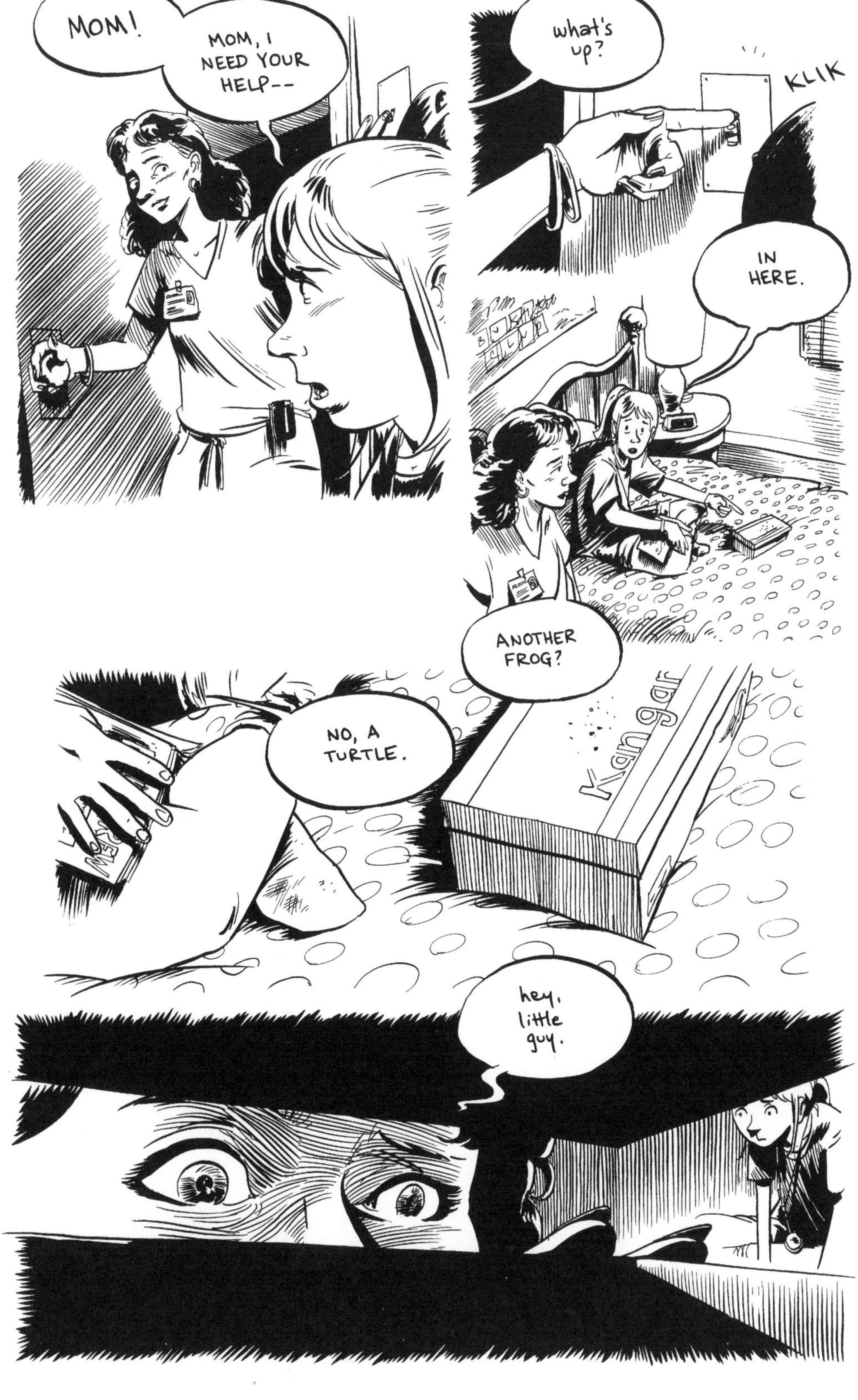
MOM!
MOM, I NEED YOUR HELP--
what's up?
KLIK
IN HERE.
ANOTHER FROG?
NO, A TURTLE.
hey, little guy.

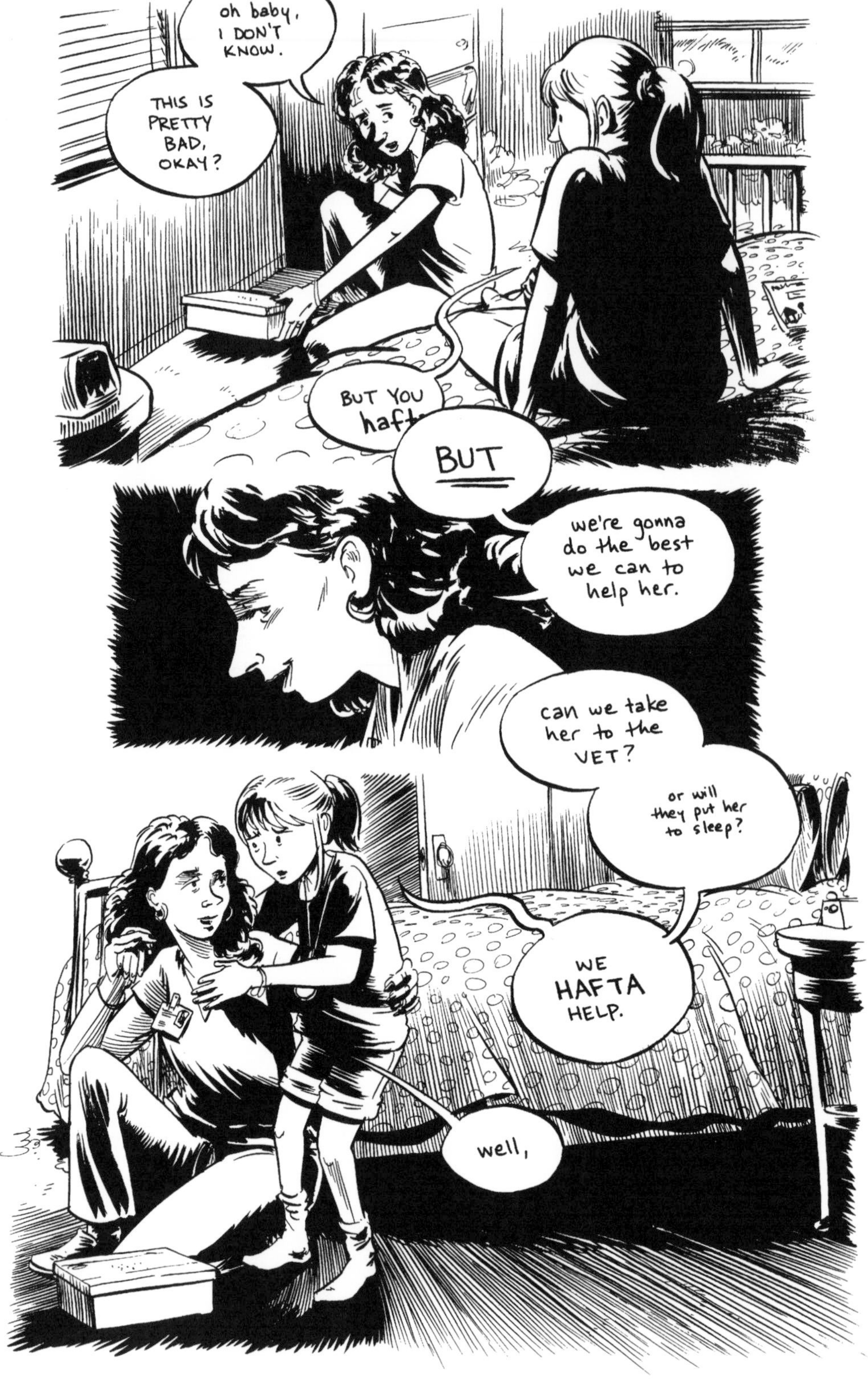
oh baby, I DON'T KNOW.
THIS IS PRETTY BAD, OKAY?
BUT YOU hafta
BUT
we're gonna do the best we can to help her.
can we take her to the VET?
or will they put her to sleep?
WE HAFTA HELP.
well,

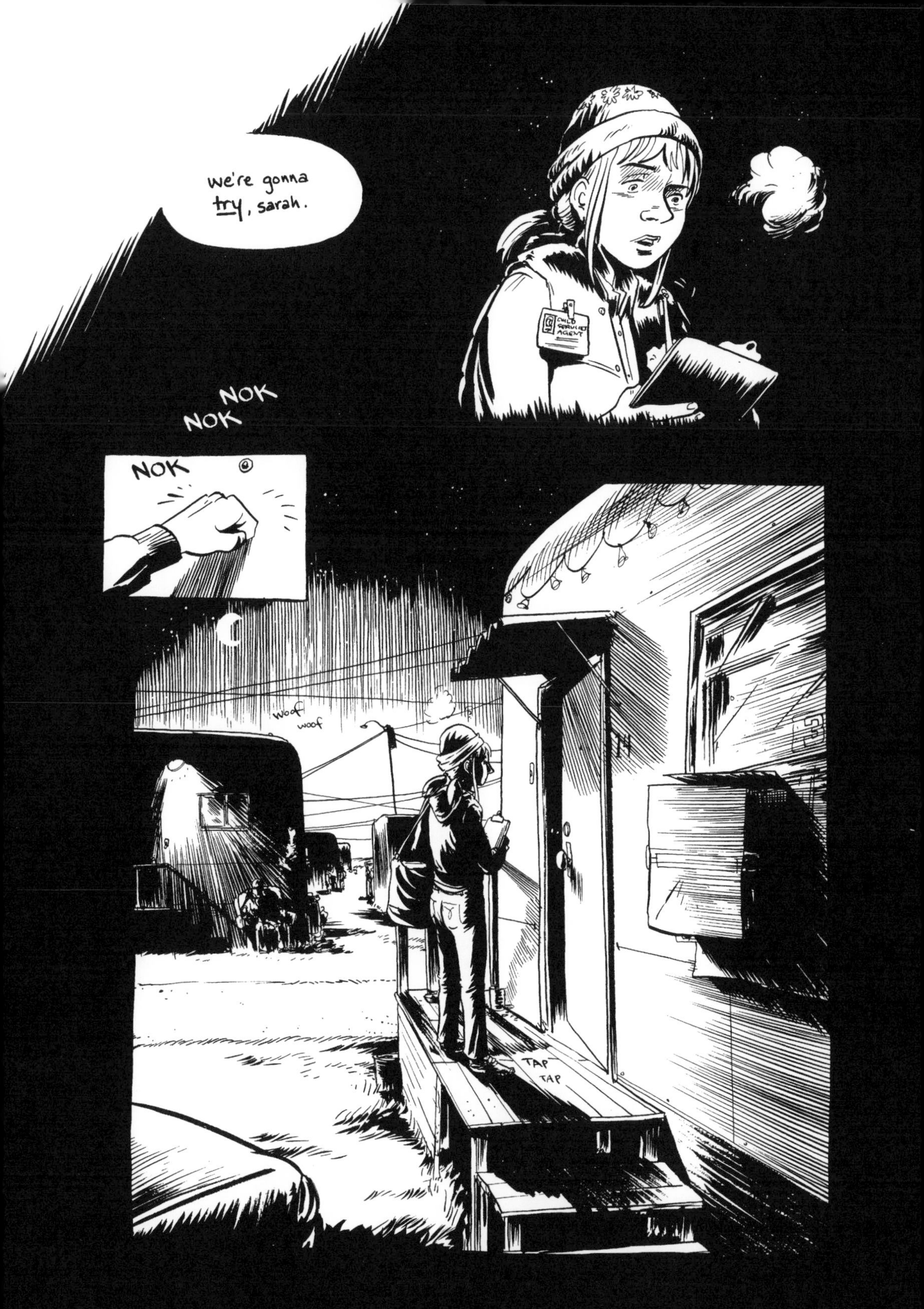
we're gonna try, sarah.
CHILD SERVICES AGENT
NOK
NOK
NOK
woof
woof
14
TAP
TAP

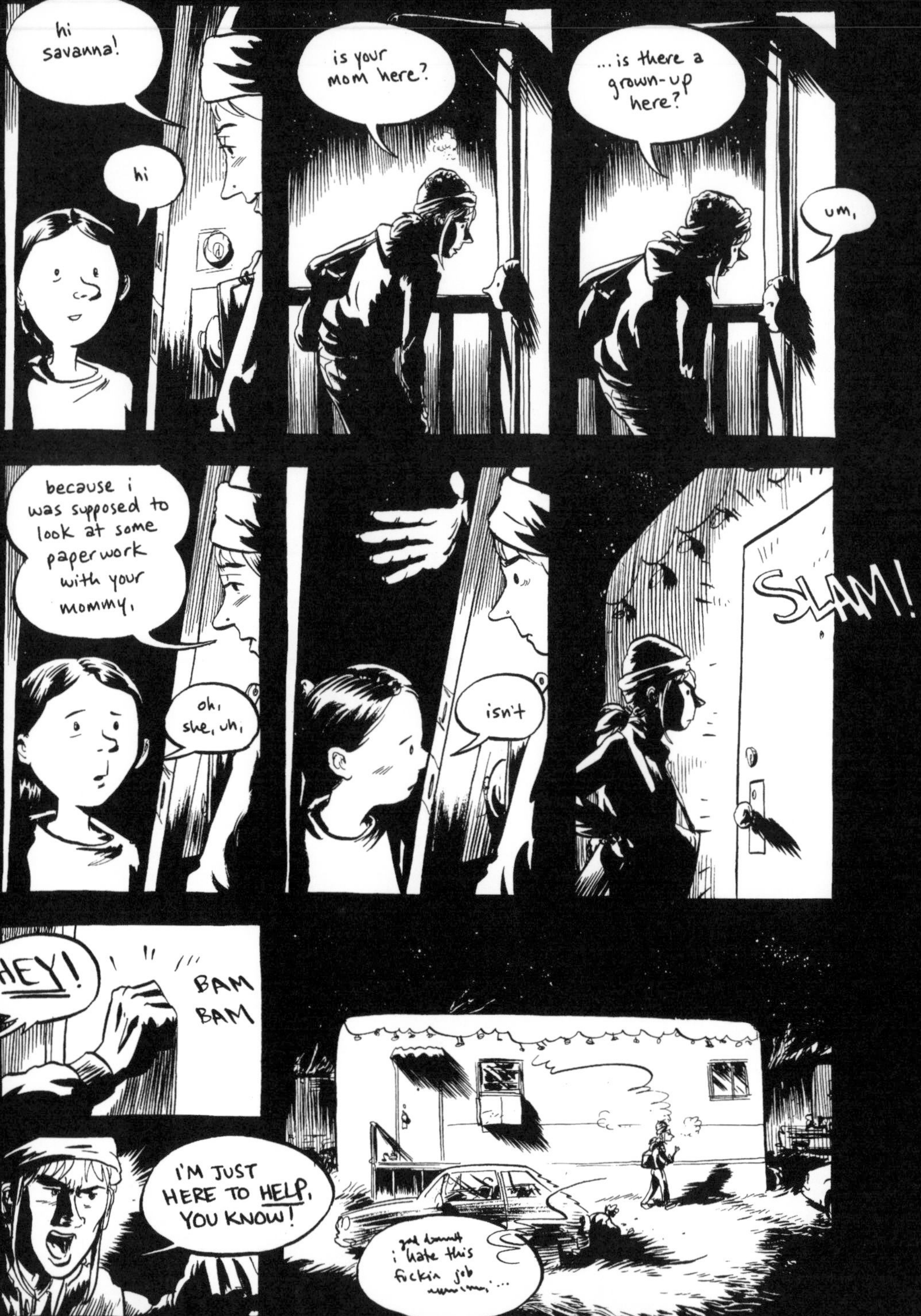
hi savanna!
hi
is your mom here?
...is there a grown-up here?
um,
because i was supposed to look at some paperwork with your mommy,
oh, she, uh,
isn't
SLAM!
HEY!
BAM BAM
I'M JUST HERE TO HELP, YOU KNOW!
god dammit
i hate this fuckin job
...

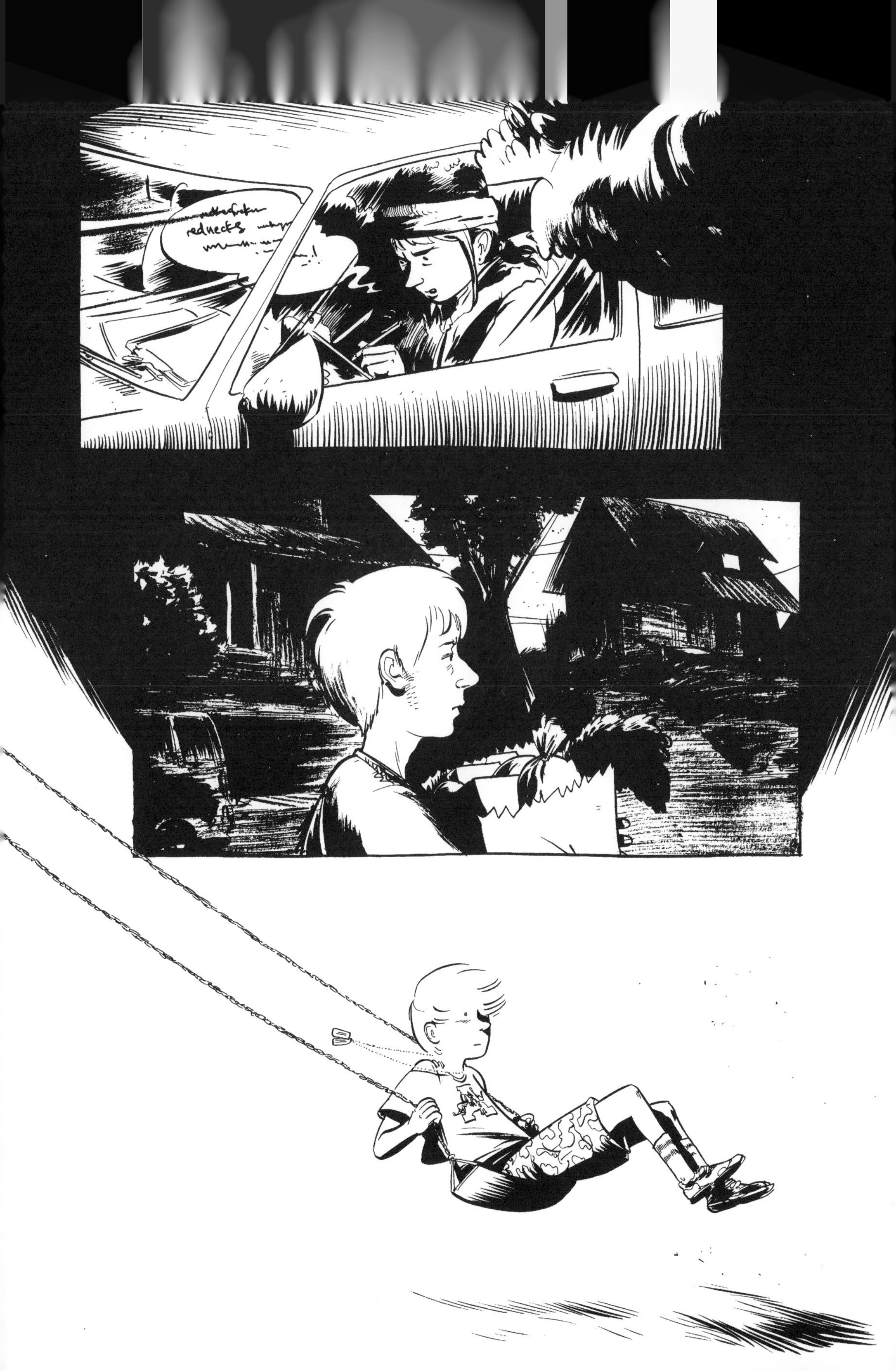
rednecks

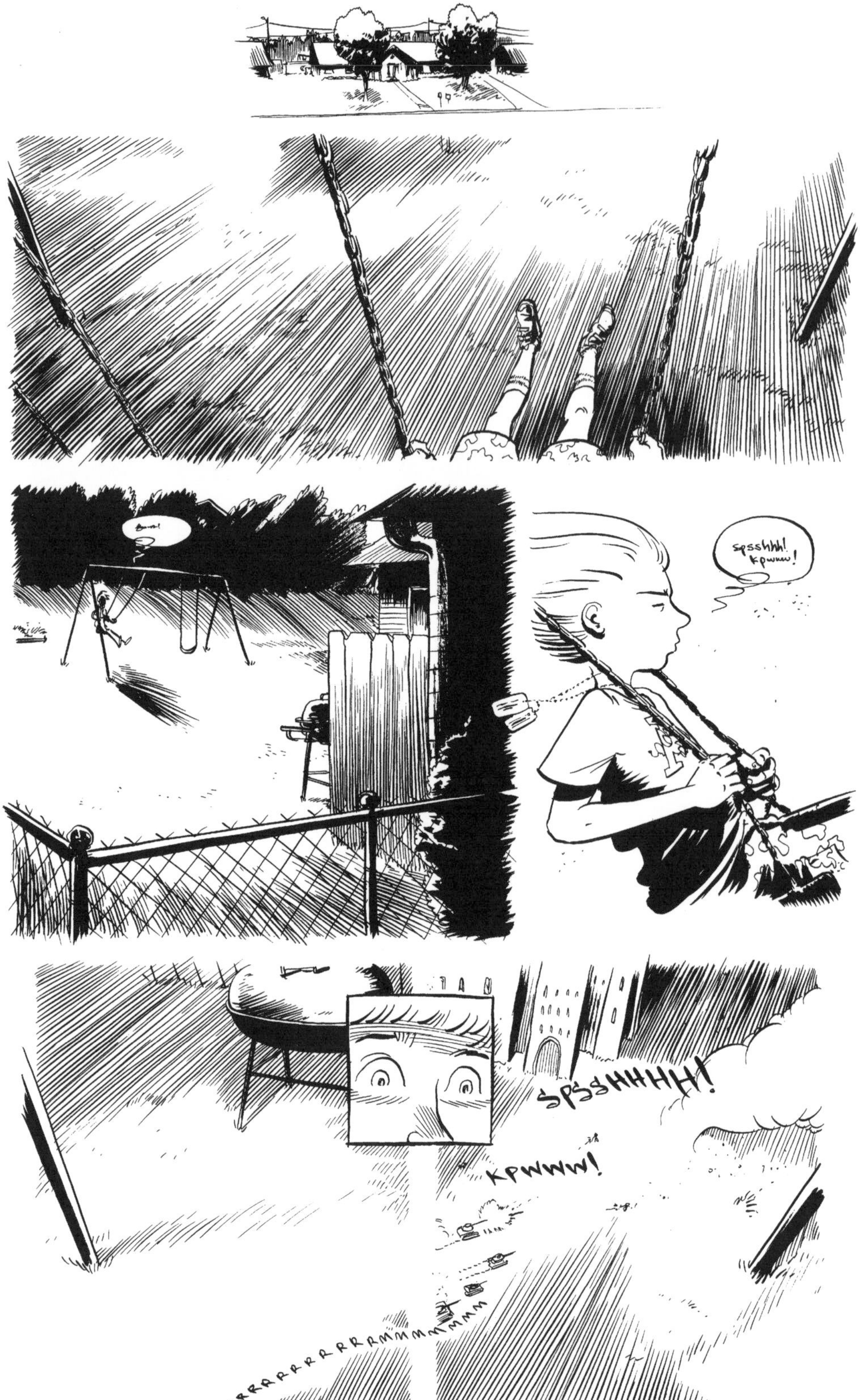
spsshhh!
kpwww!
SPSSHHHH!
KPWWW!
rRRRRRRRRRRRMMMMMMMMMM

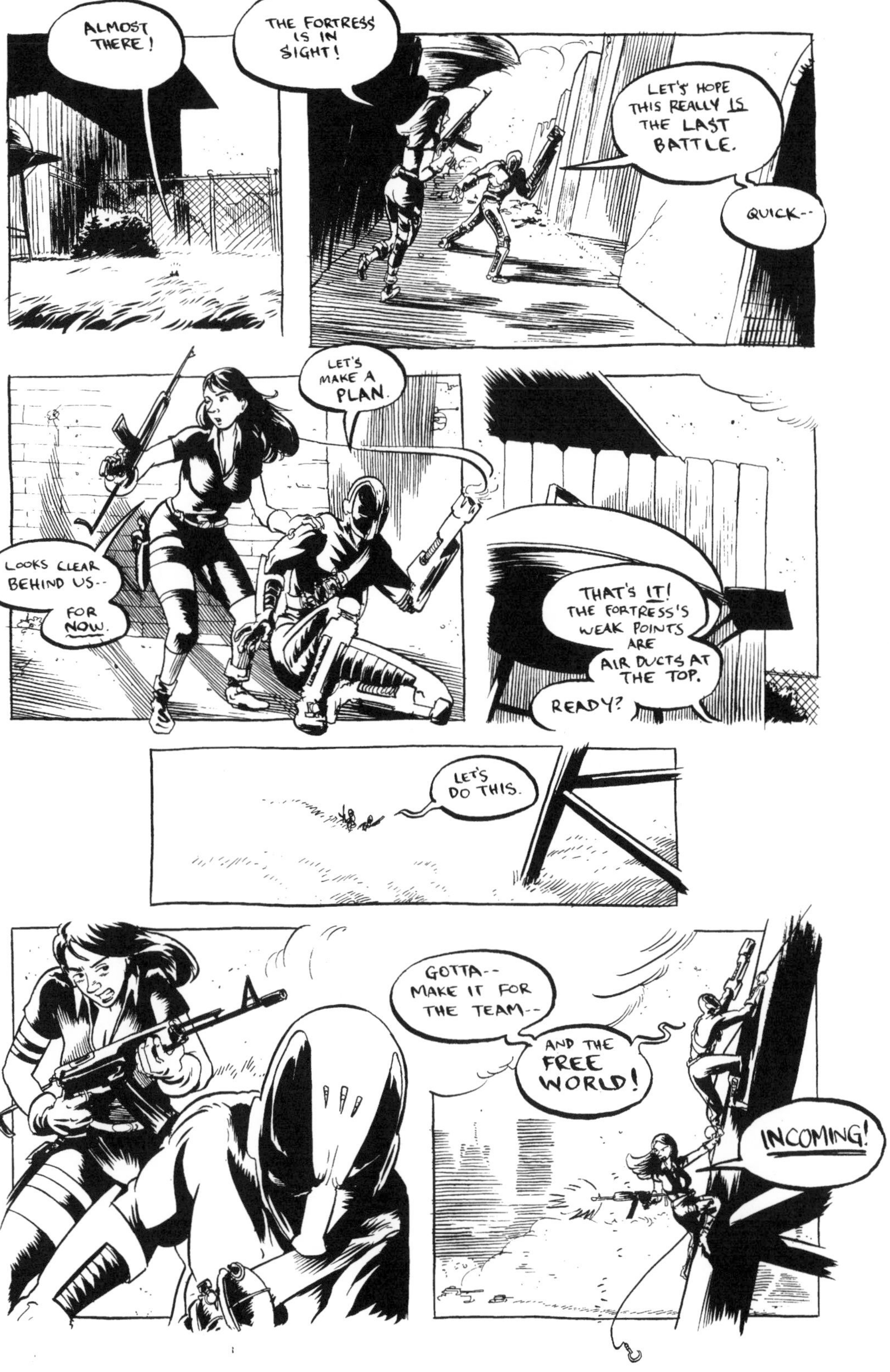
ALMOST THERE!
THE FORTRESS IS IN SIGHT!
LET'S HOPE THIS REALLY IS THE LAST BATTLE.
QUICK--
LET'S MAKE A PLAN.
LOOKS CLEAR BEHIND US--
FOR NOW.
THAT'S IT! THE FORTRESS'S WEAK POINTS ARE AIR DUCTS AT THE TOP.
READY?
LET'S DO THIS.
GOTTA-- MAKE IT FOR THE TEAM--
AND THE FREE WORLD!
INCOMING!

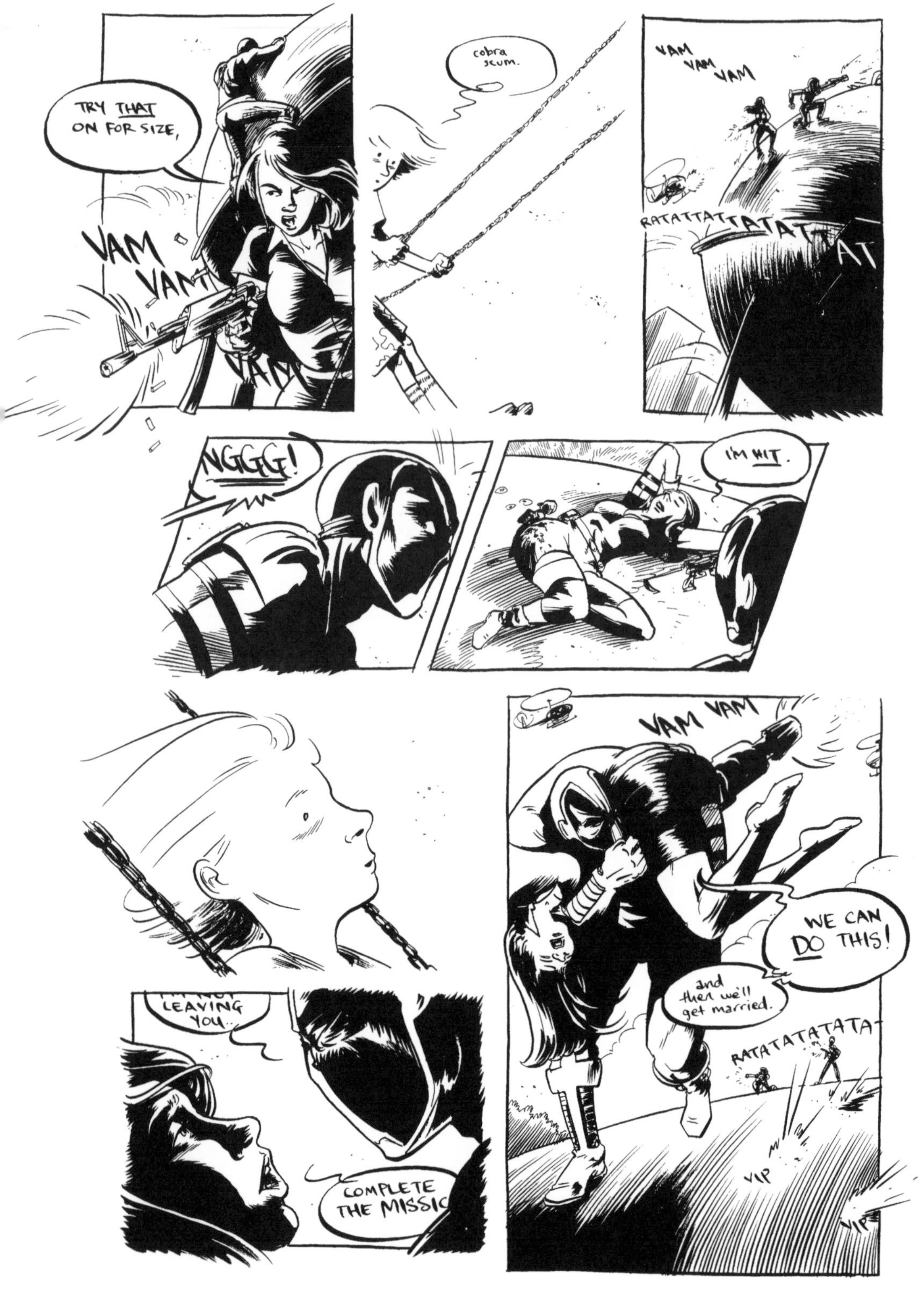
TRY THAT ON FOR SIZE,
VAM VAM VAM
cobra scum.
VAM VAM VAM
RATATTAT TATAT AT
NGGG!
I'M HIT.
LEAVING YOU..
COMPLETE THE MISSI
VAM VAM
WE CAN DO THIS!
and then we'll get married.
RATATATATATA
VIP
VIP

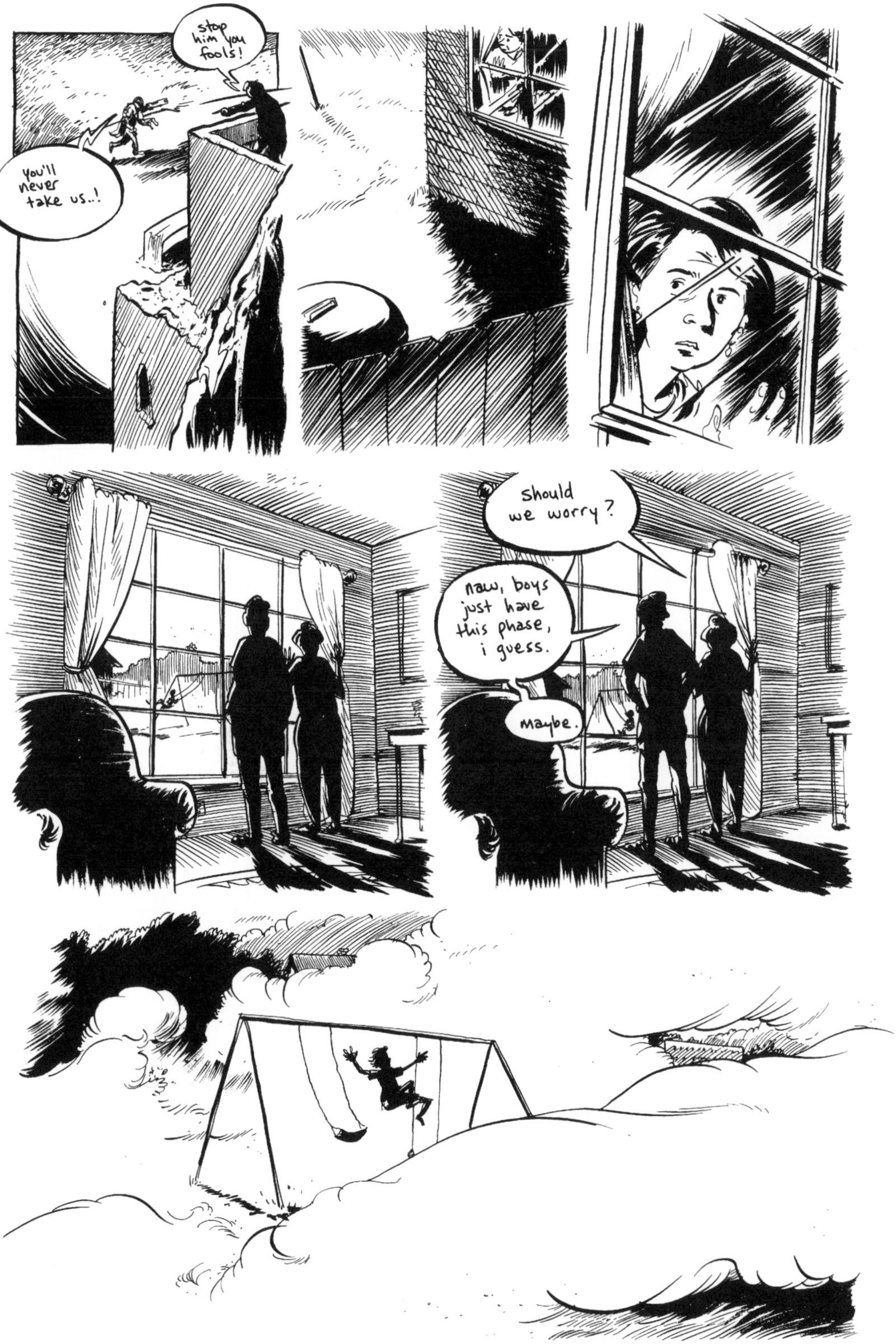
stop him you fools!
you'll never take us..!
should we worry?
naw, boys just have this phase, i guess.
maybe.

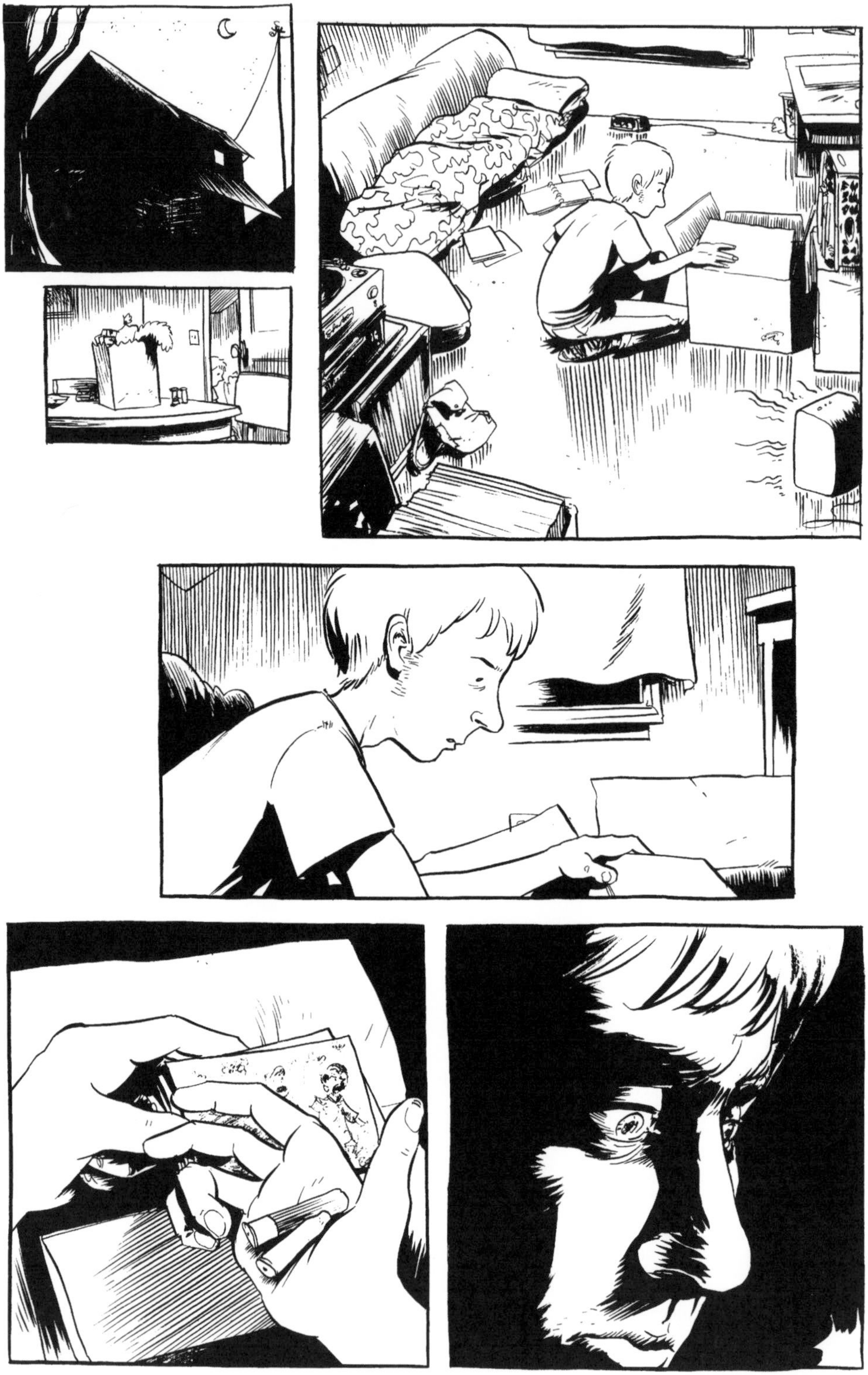

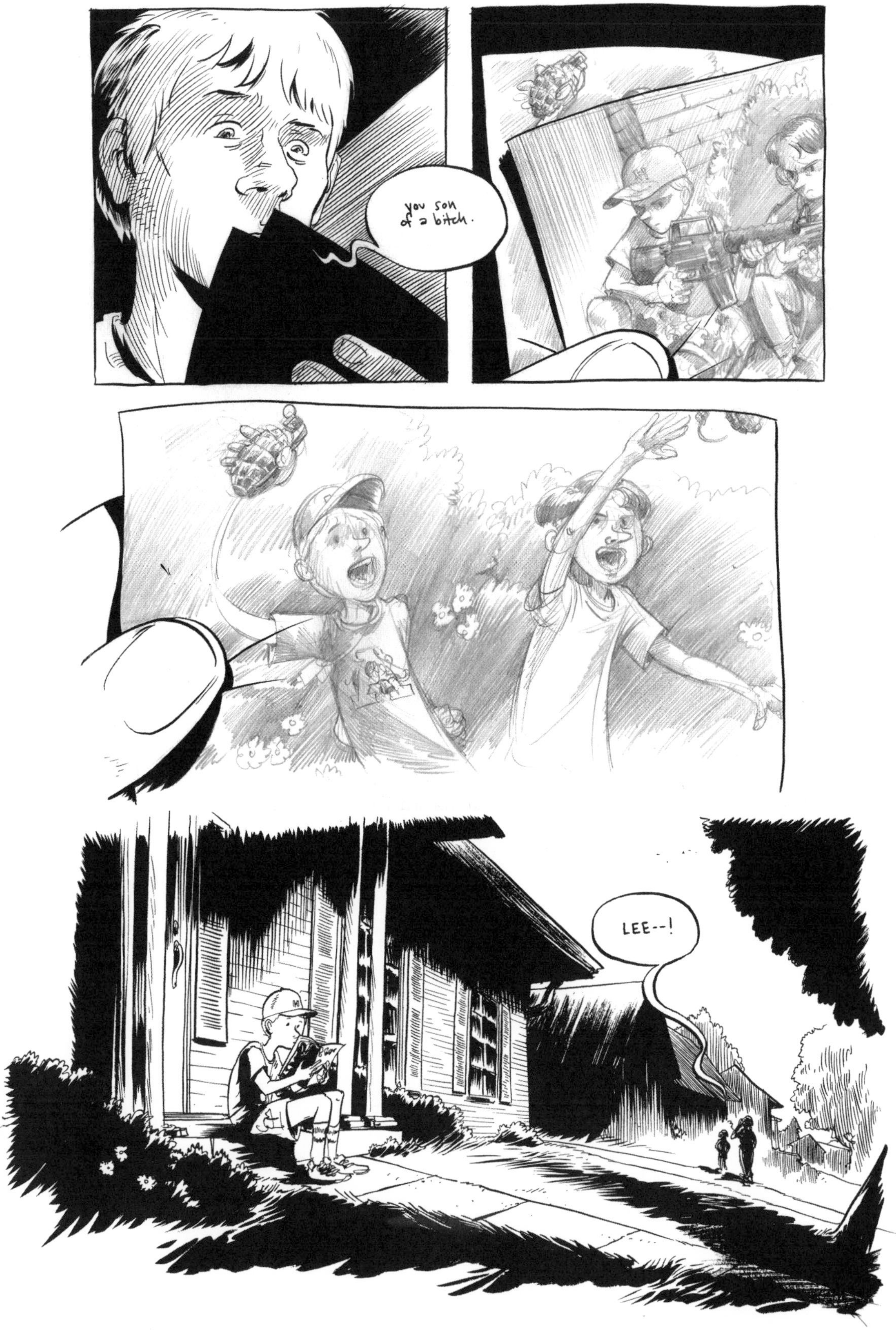
you son of a bitch.
LEE--!

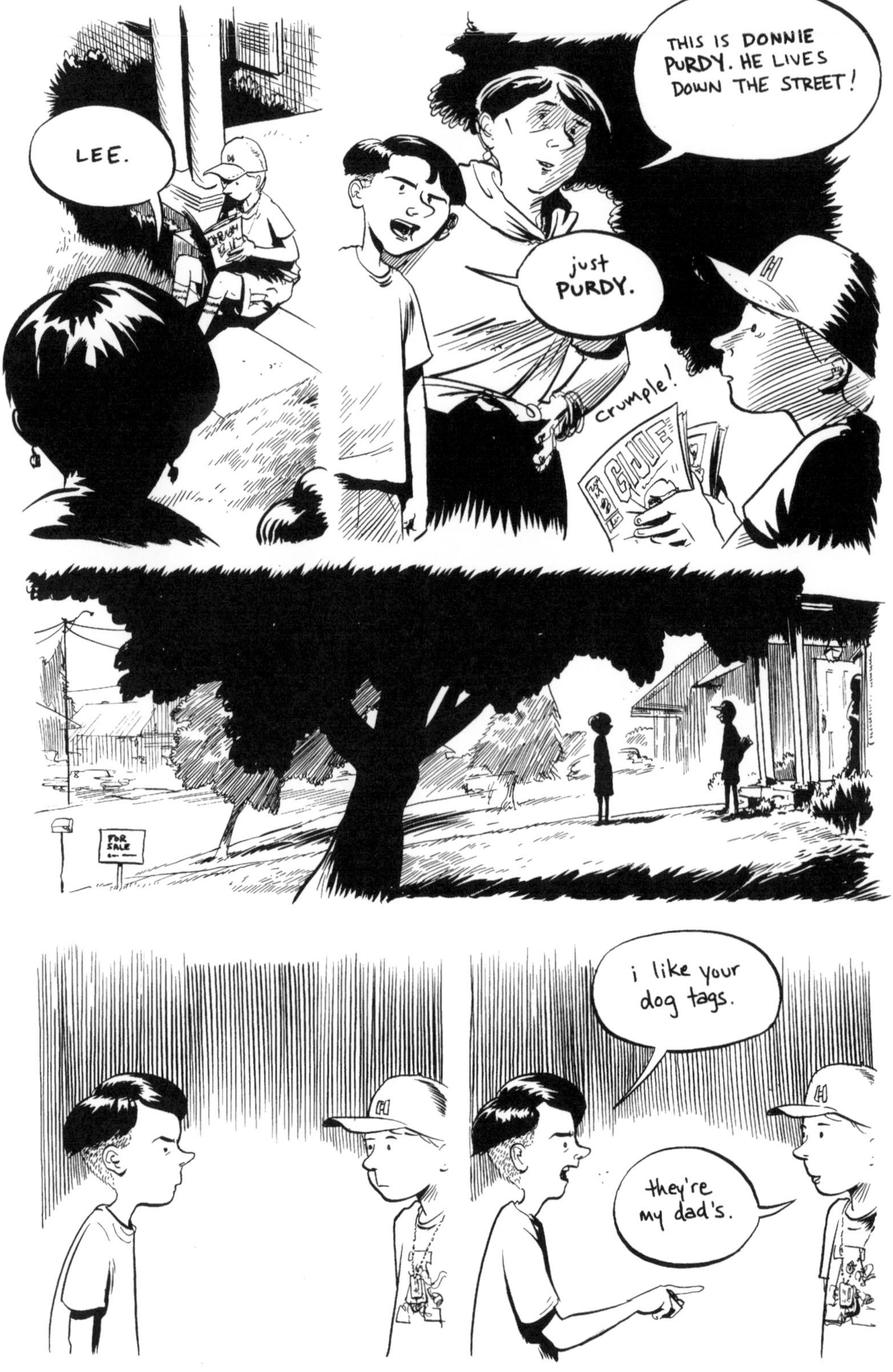
LEE.
THIS IS DONNIE PURDY. HE LIVES DOWN THE STREET!
just PURDY.
Crumple!
FOR SALE
i like your dog tags.
they're my dad's.

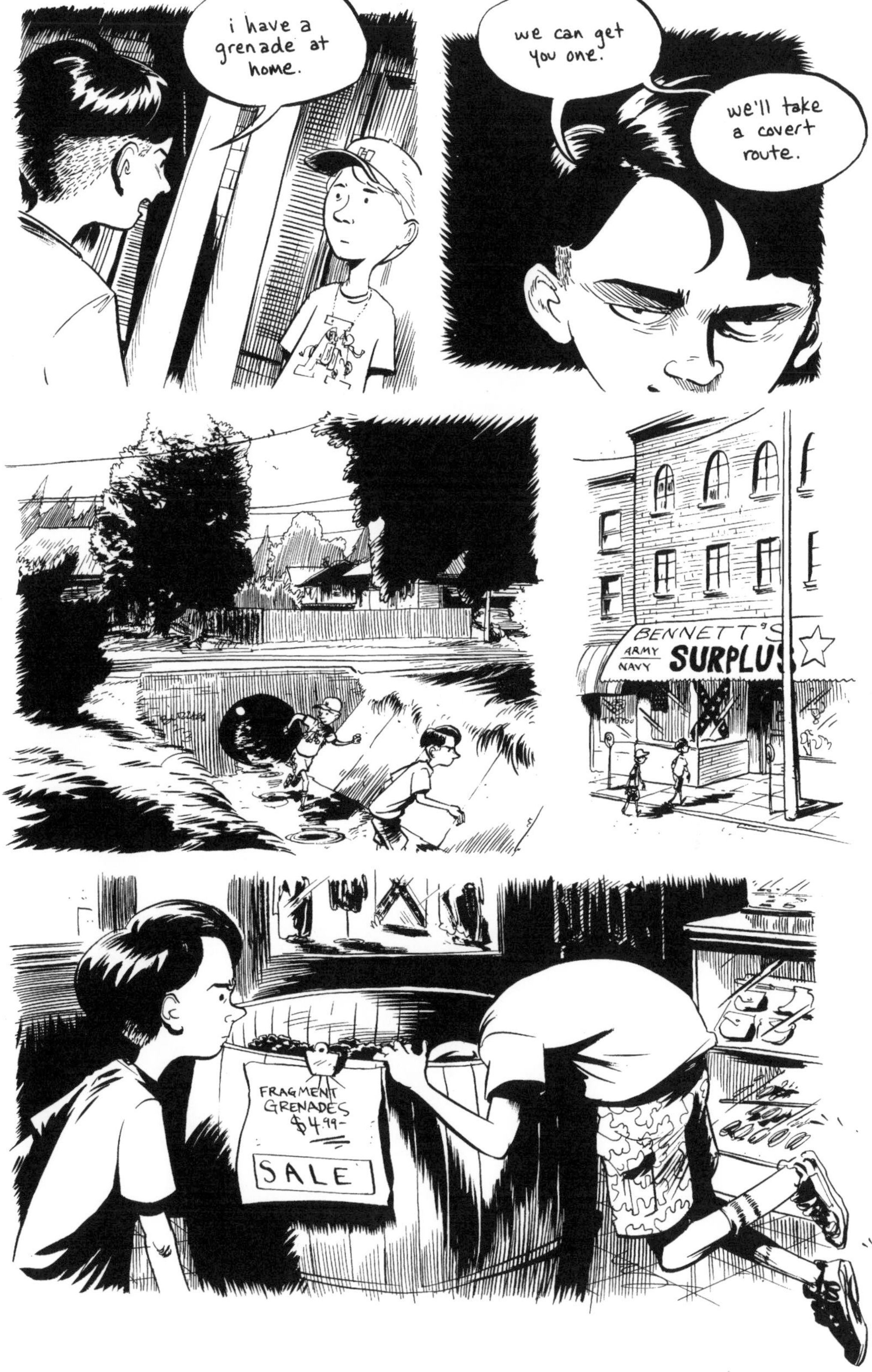
i have a grenade at home.
we can get you one.
we'll take a covert route.
BENNETT'S
ARMY
NAVY
SURPLUS
FRAGMENT GRENADES $4.99-
SALE

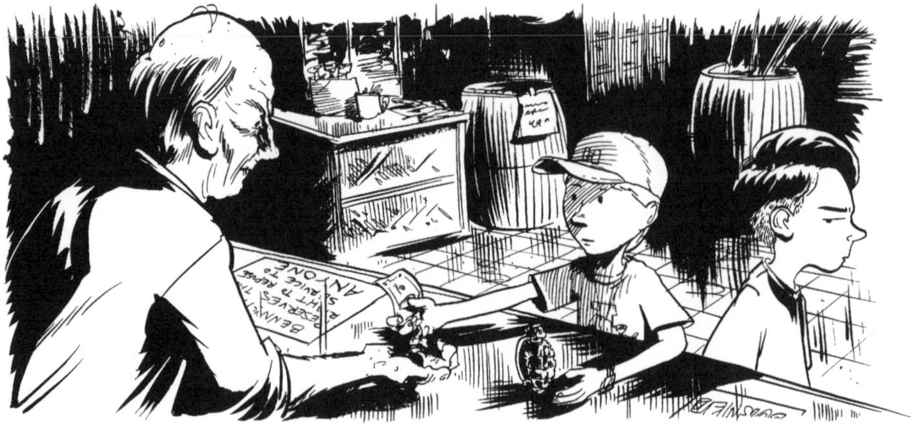
ANYONE

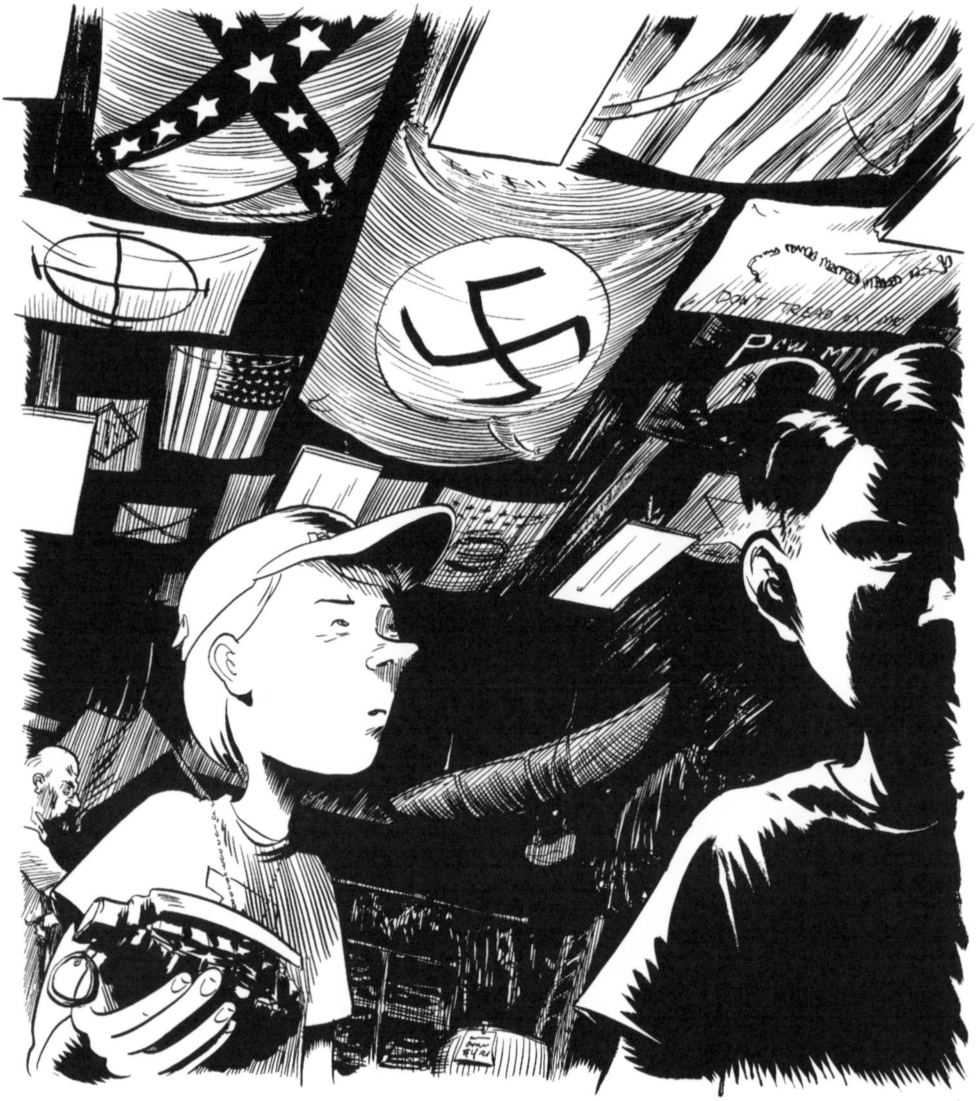
DON'T TREAD ON ME

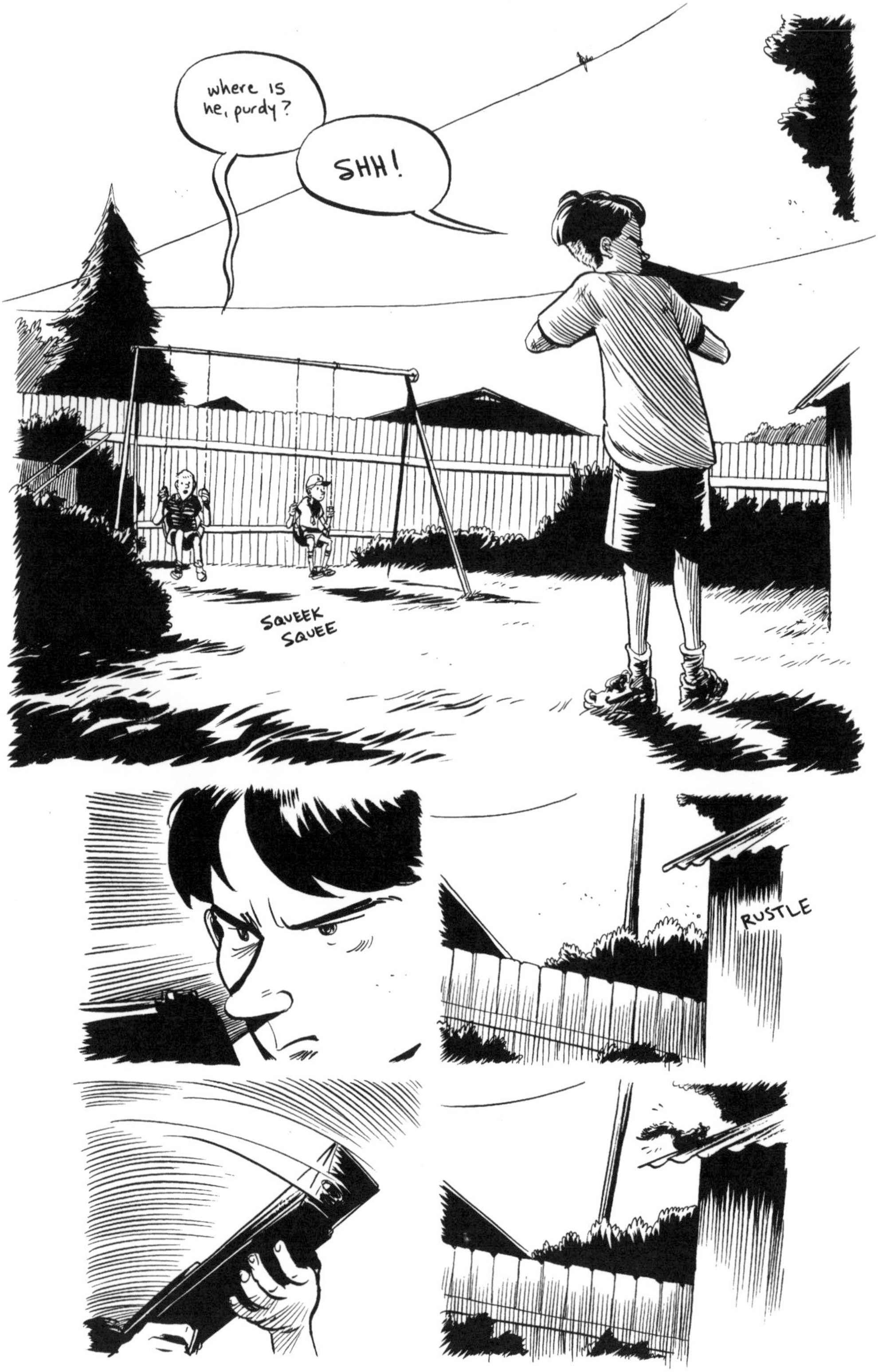
where is he, purdy?
SHH!
SQUEEK SQUEE
RUSTLE

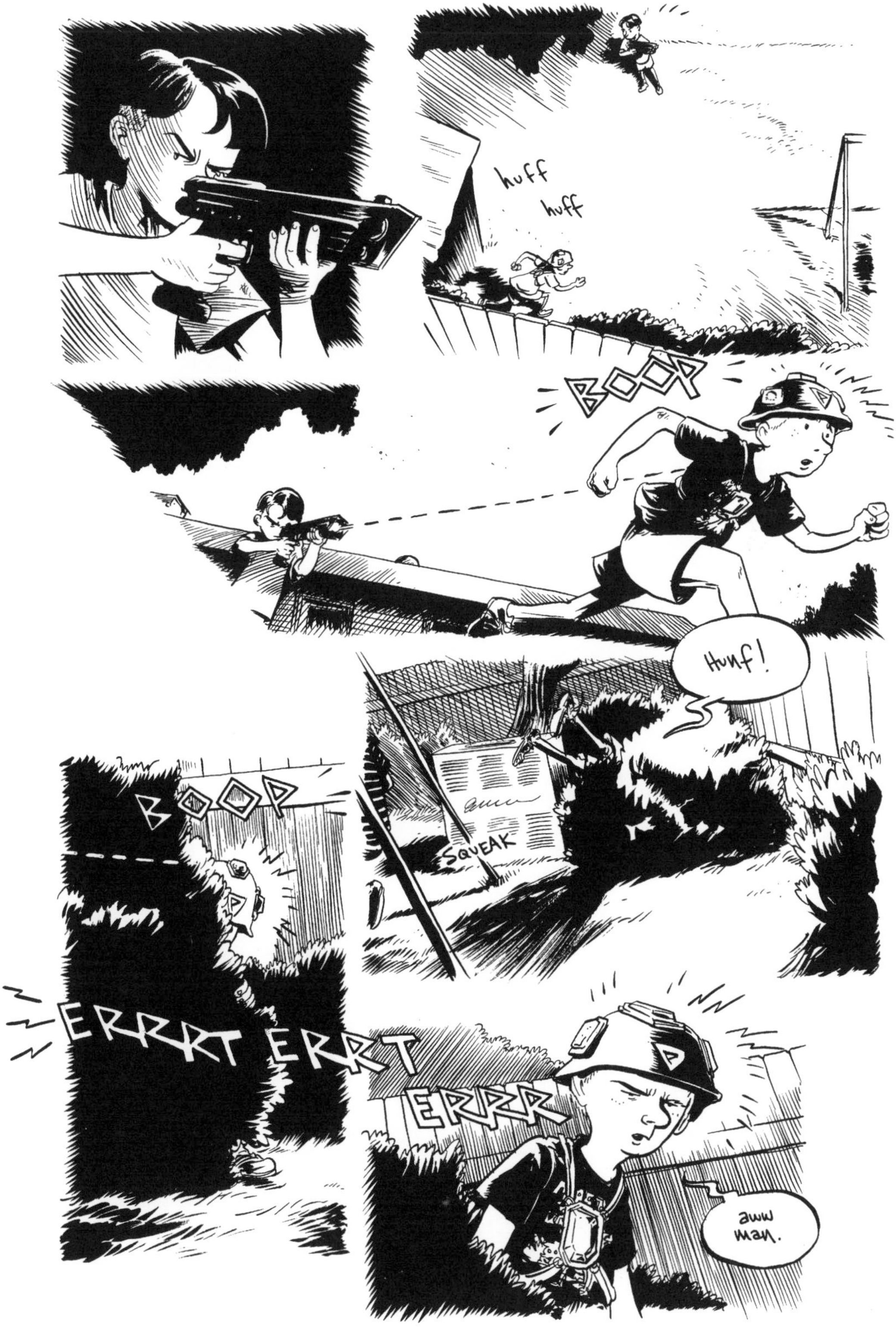
huff
huff
BOOP
Hunf!
SQUEAK
BOOP
ERRRT ERRT
ERRR
aww man.

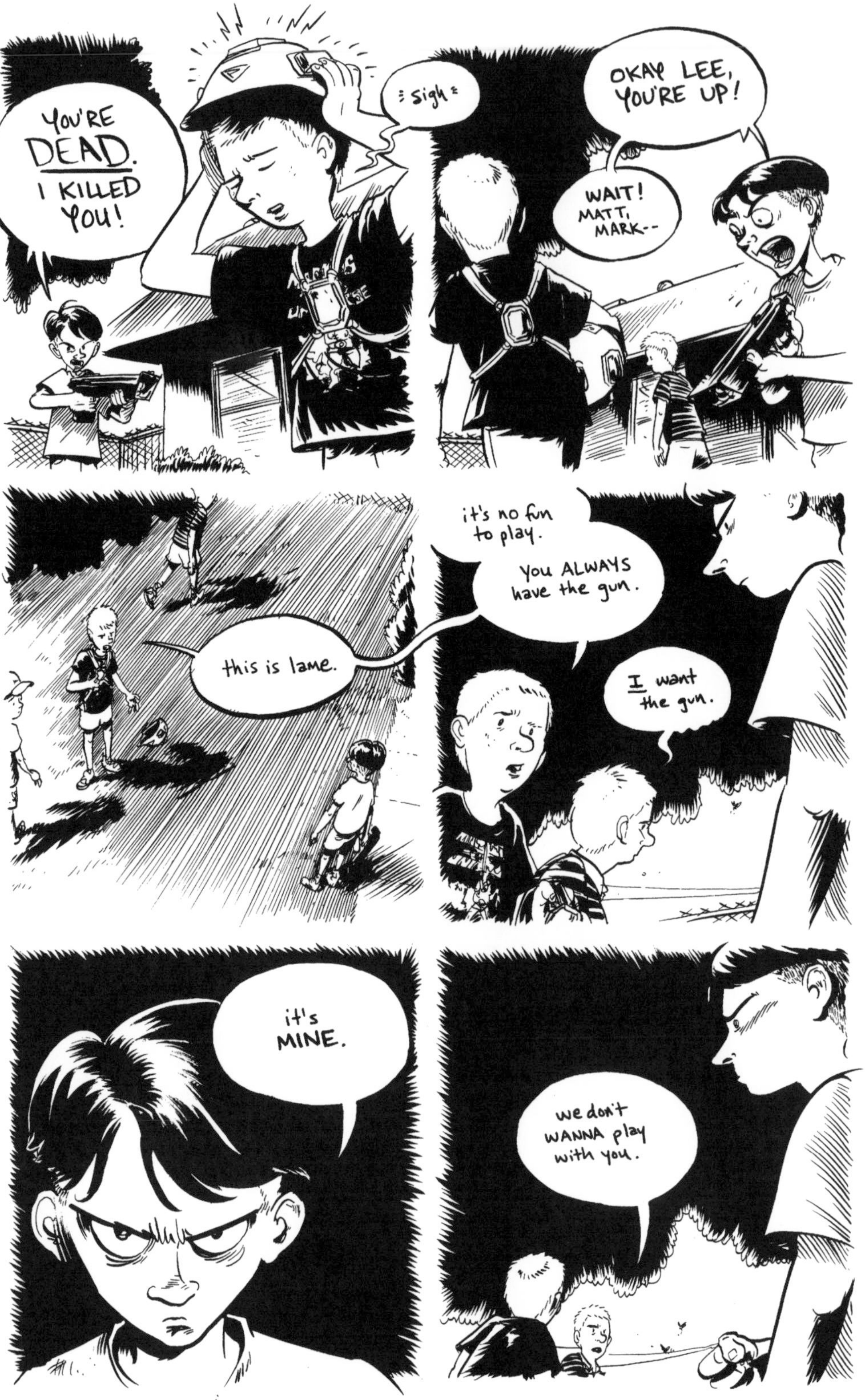
YOU'RE DEAD. I KILLED YOU!
sigh
OKAY LEE, YOU'RE UP!
WAIT! MATT, MARK--
this is lame.
it's no fun to play.
You ALWAYS have the gun.
I want the gun.
it's MINE.
we don't WANNA play with you.

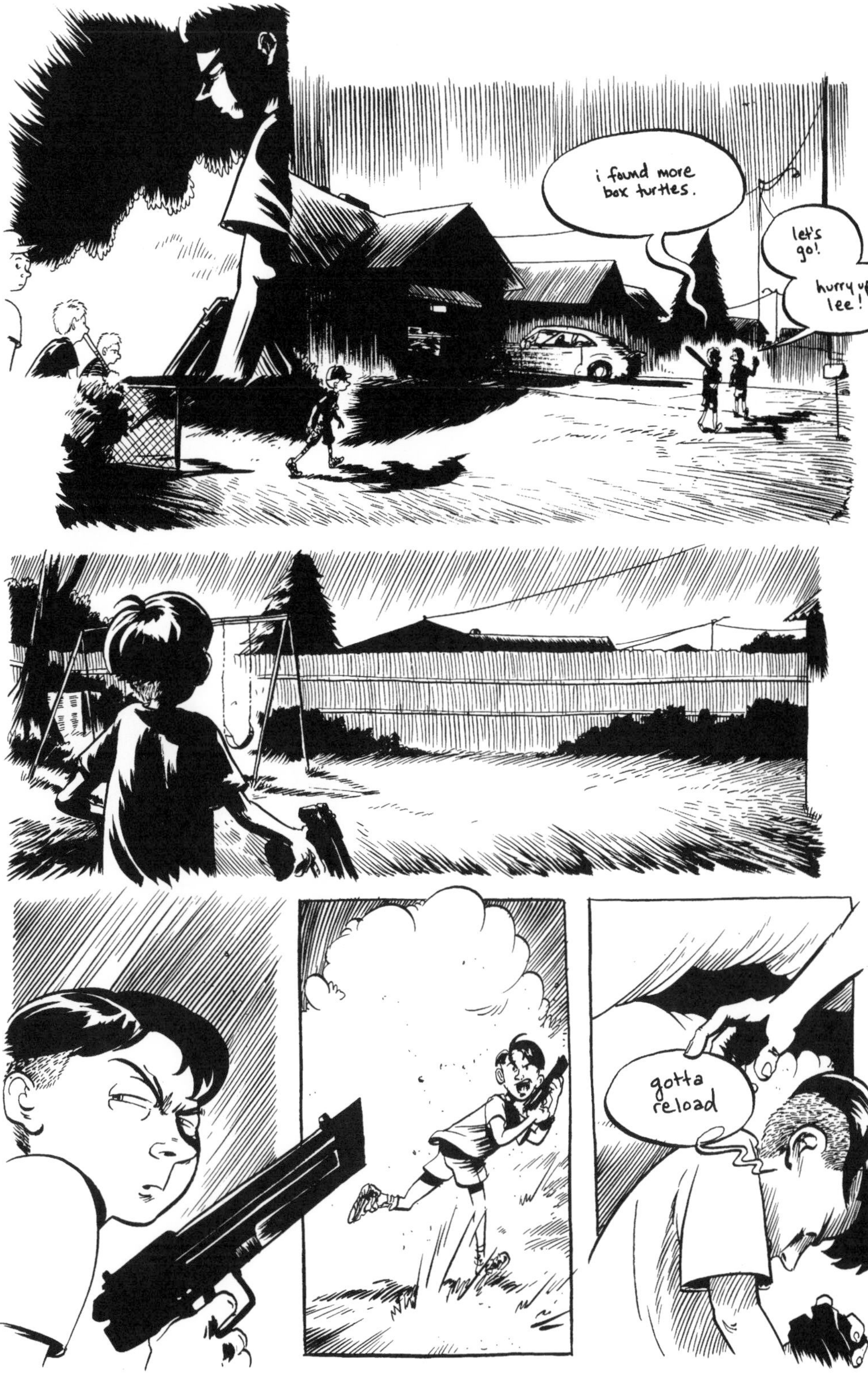
i found more box turtles.
let's go!
hurry up, lee!
gotta reload

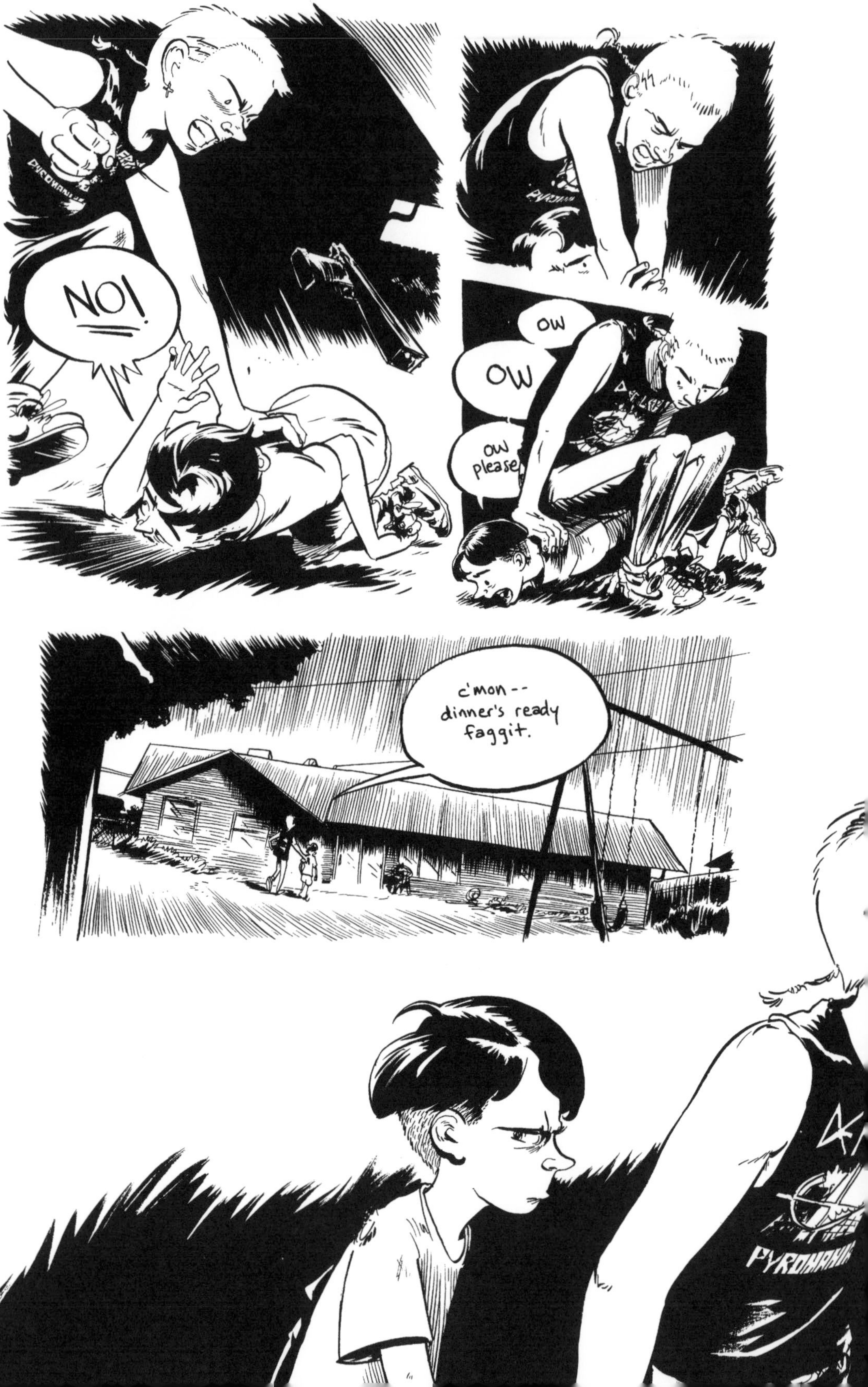
NO!
ow
OW
ow please
c'mon -- dinner's ready faggit.

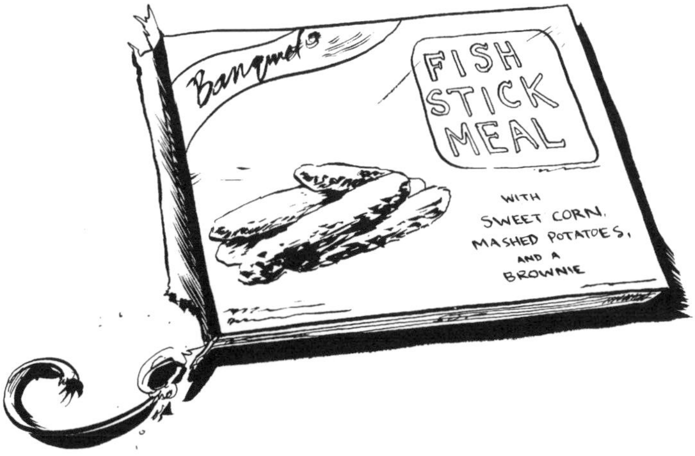
Banquet®
FISH STICK MEAL
WITH SWEET CORN, MASHED POTATOES, AND A BROWNIE

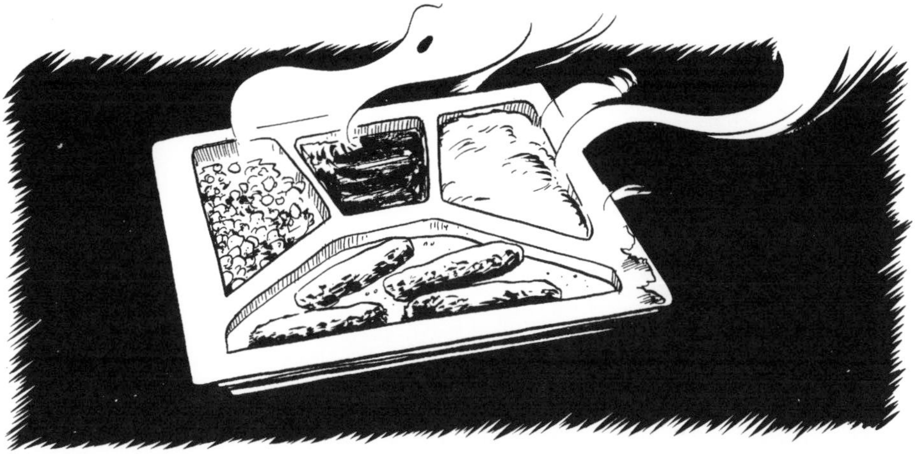

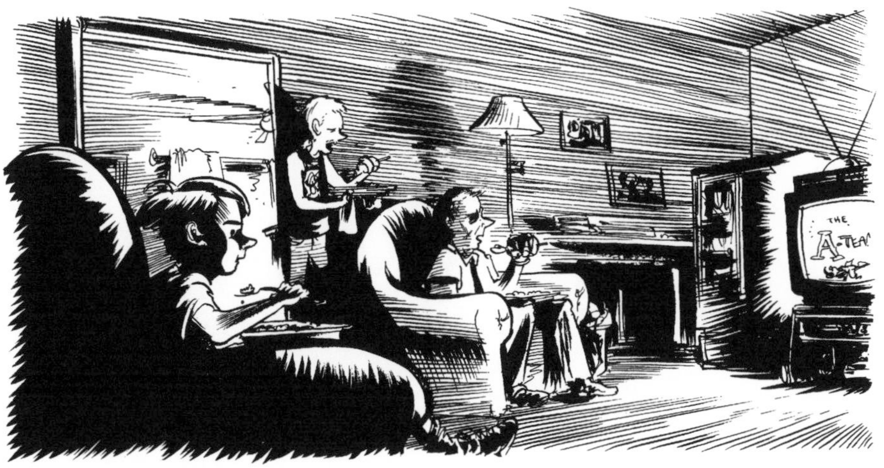
THE

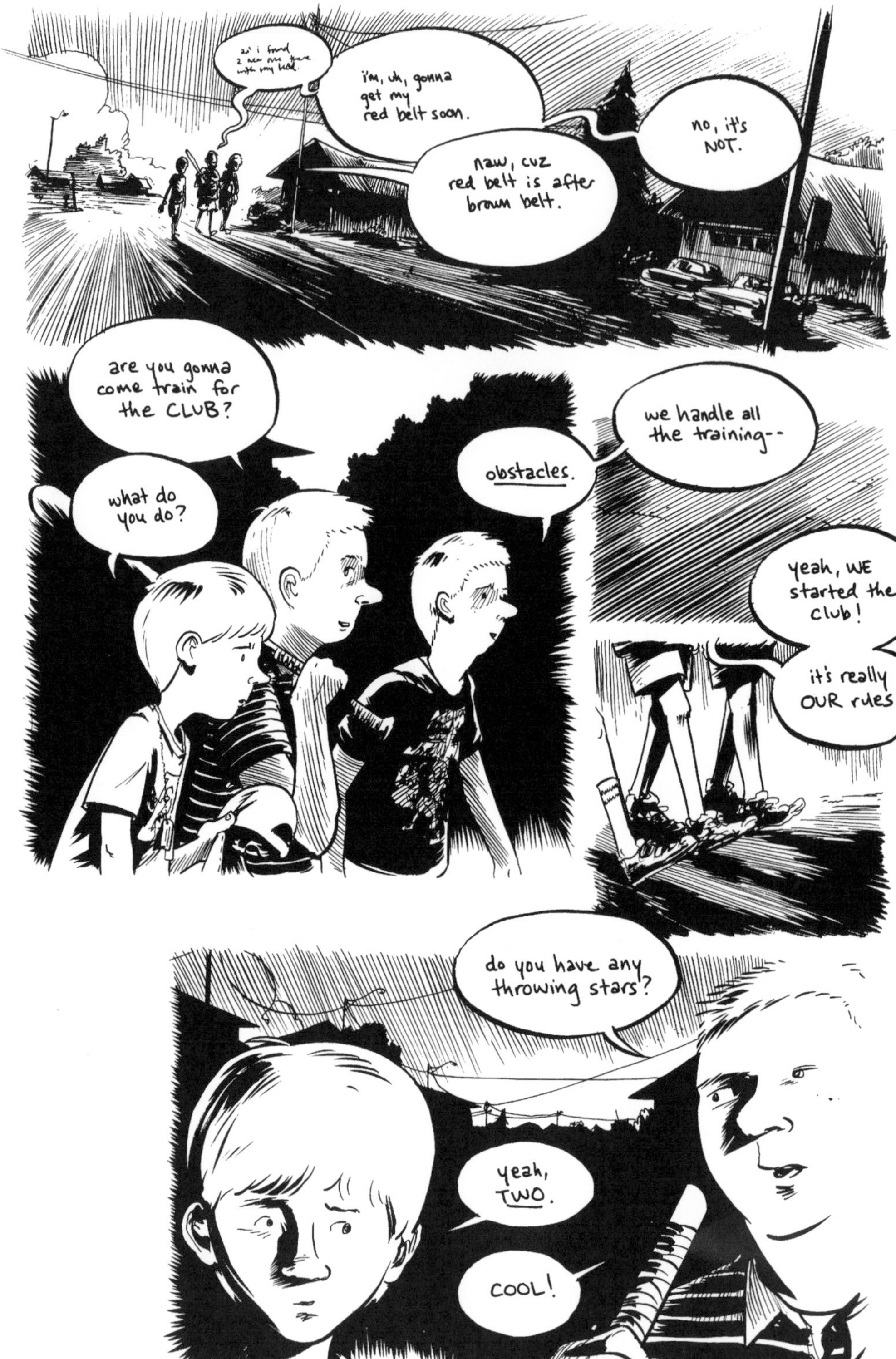

an' i found 2 new ones there with my dad.
i'm, uh, gonna get my red belt soon.
naw, cuz red belt is after brown belt.
no, it's NOT.
are you gonna come train for the CLUB?
what do you do?
obstacles.
we handle all the training--
yeah, WE started the club!
it's really OUR rules.
do you have any throwing stars?
yeah, TWO.
COOL!

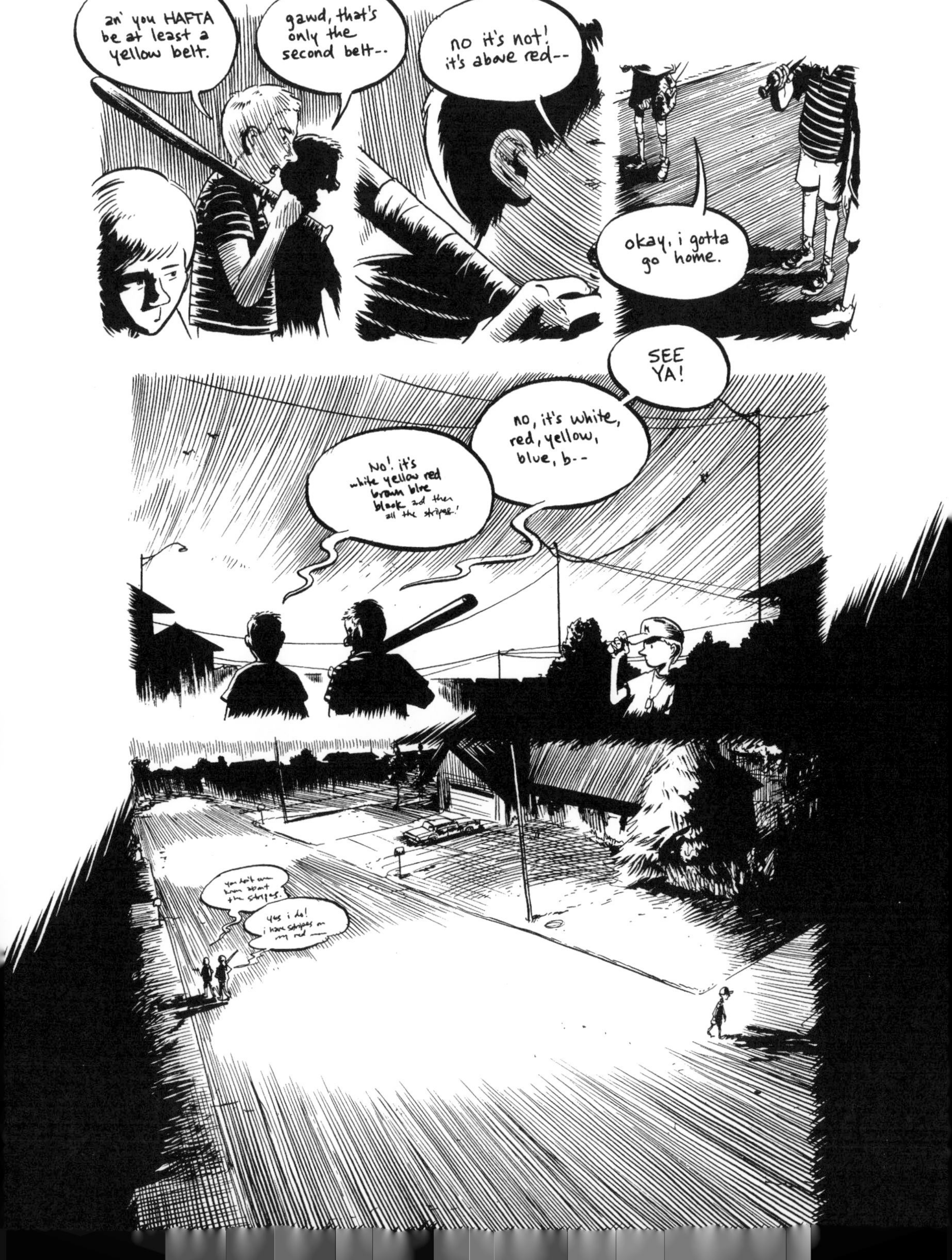
an' you HAFTA be at least a yellow belt.
gawd, that's only the second belt--
no it's not! it's above red--
okay, i gotta go home.
SEE YA!
no, it's white, red, yellow, blue, b--
No! it's white yellow red brown blue black and then all the stripes!
You don't even know about the stripes.
Yes i do! i have stripes on my red ——

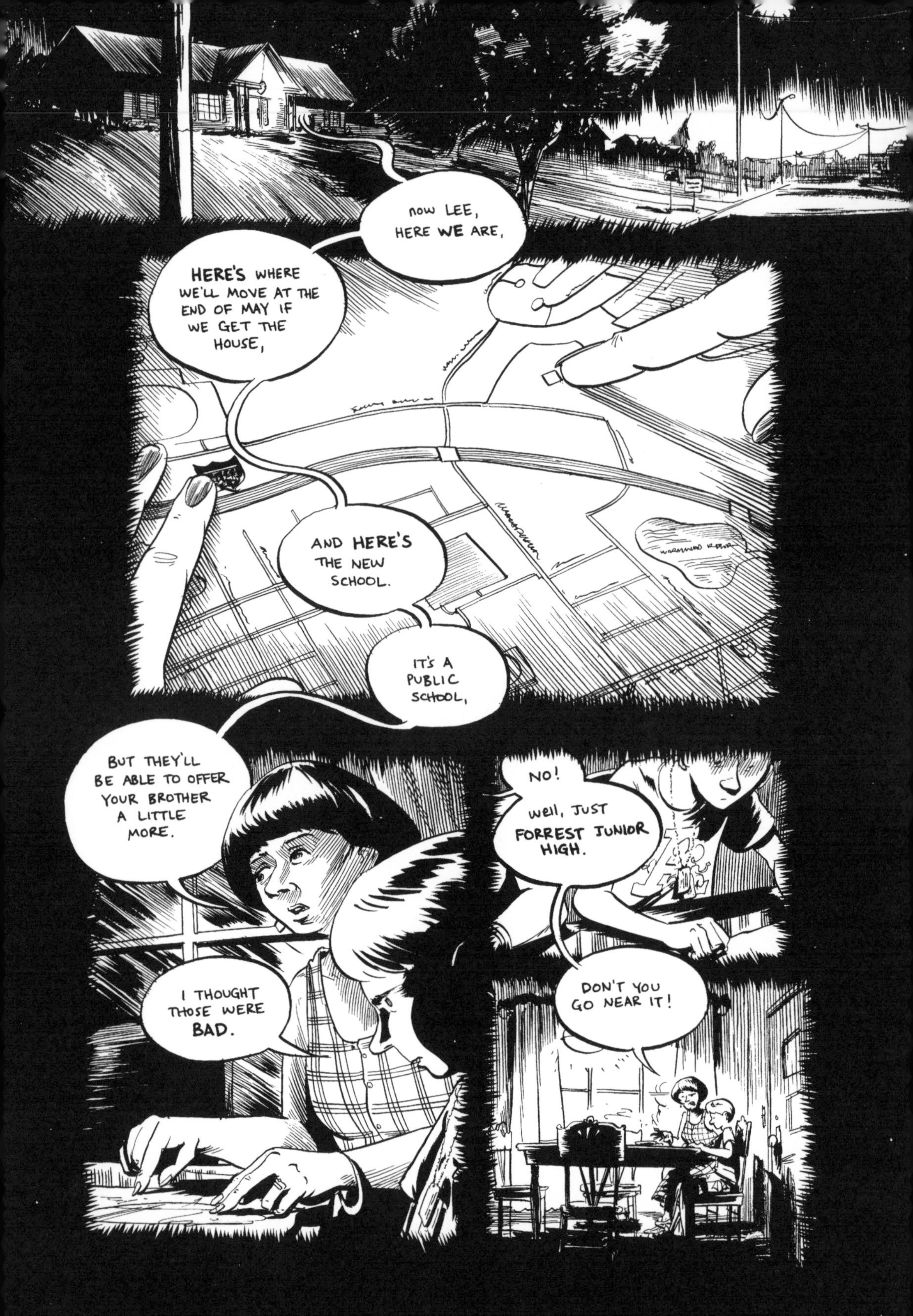
now LEE,
HERE WE ARE,
HERE'S WHERE WE'LL MOVE AT THE END OF MAY IF WE GET THE HOUSE,
AND HERE'S THE NEW SCHOOL.
IT'S A PUBLIC SCHOOL,
BUT THEY'LL BE ABLE TO OFFER YOUR BROTHER A LITTLE MORE.
I THOUGHT THOSE WERE BAD.
NO!
well, JUST FORREST JUNIOR HIGH.
DON'T YOU GO NEAR IT!

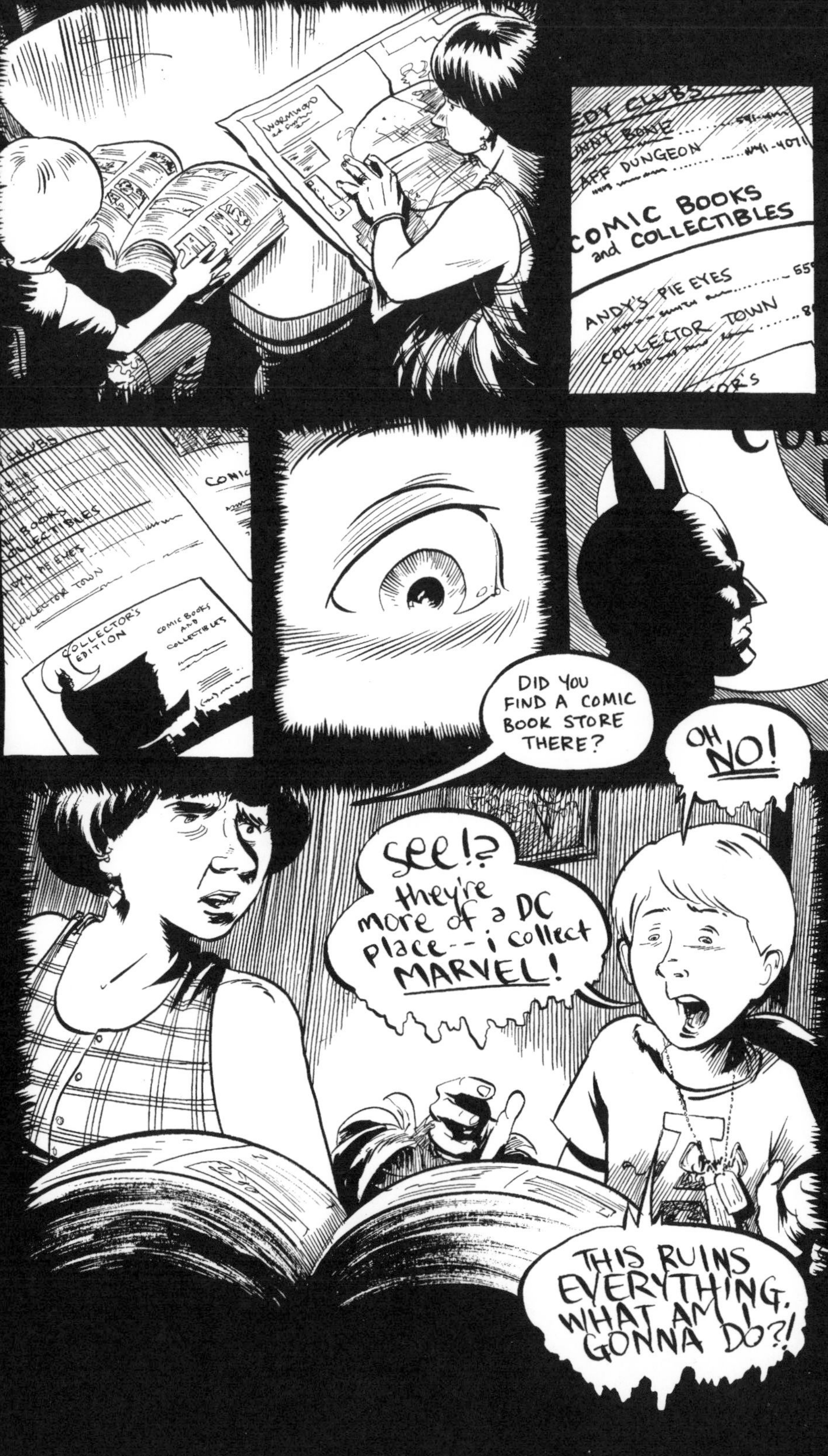
COMIC BOOKS and COLLECTIBLES
ANDY'S PIE EYES
COLLECTOR TOWN
COLLECTOR'S EDITION
COMIC BOOKS AND COLLECTIBLES
DID YOU FIND A COMIC BOOK STORE THERE?
OH NO!
SEE!? THEY'RE MORE OF A DC PLACE--I COLLECT MARVEL!
THIS RUINS EVERYTHING. WHAT AM I GONNA DO?!

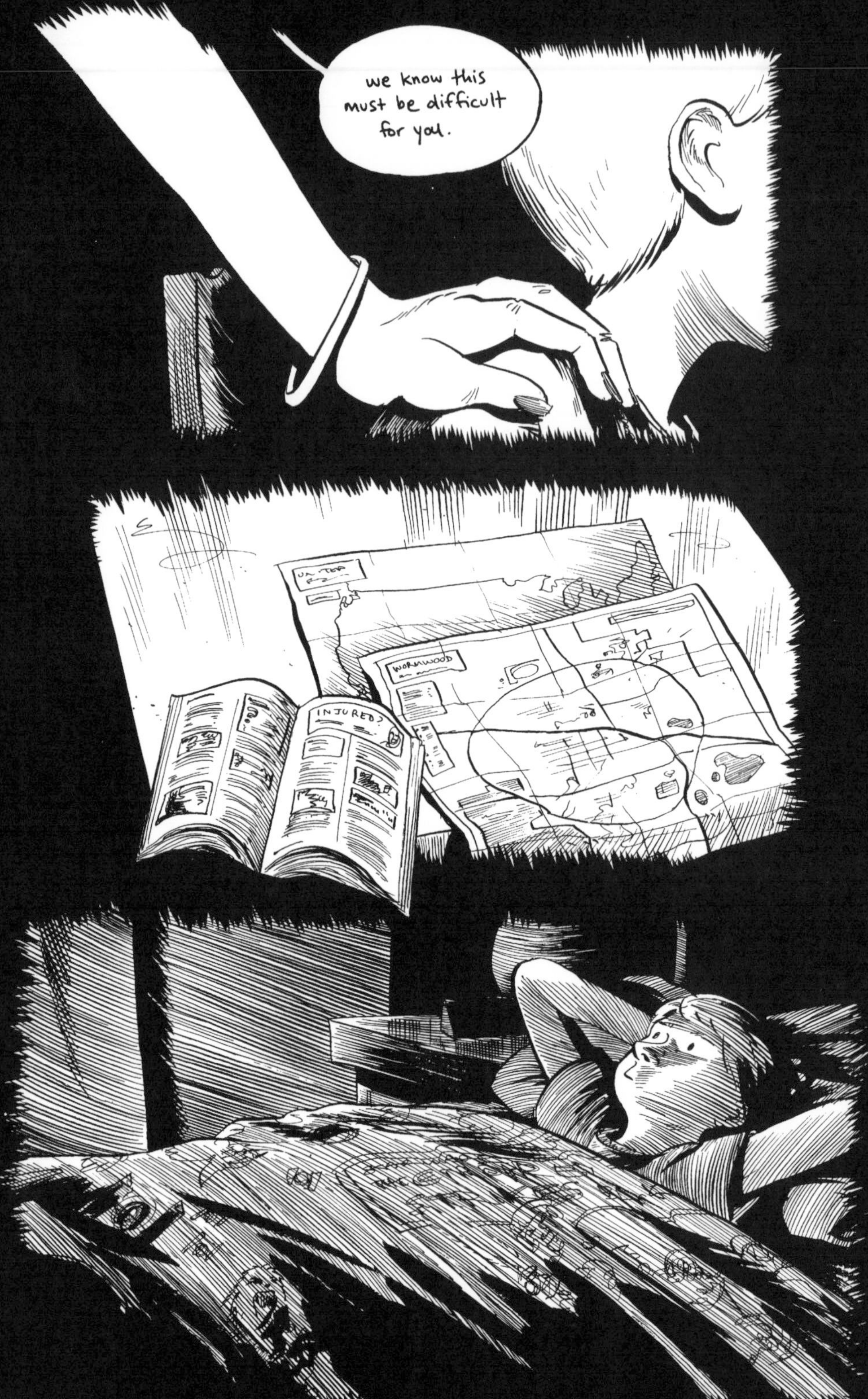
we know this must be difficult for you.
WORMWOOD
INJURED?

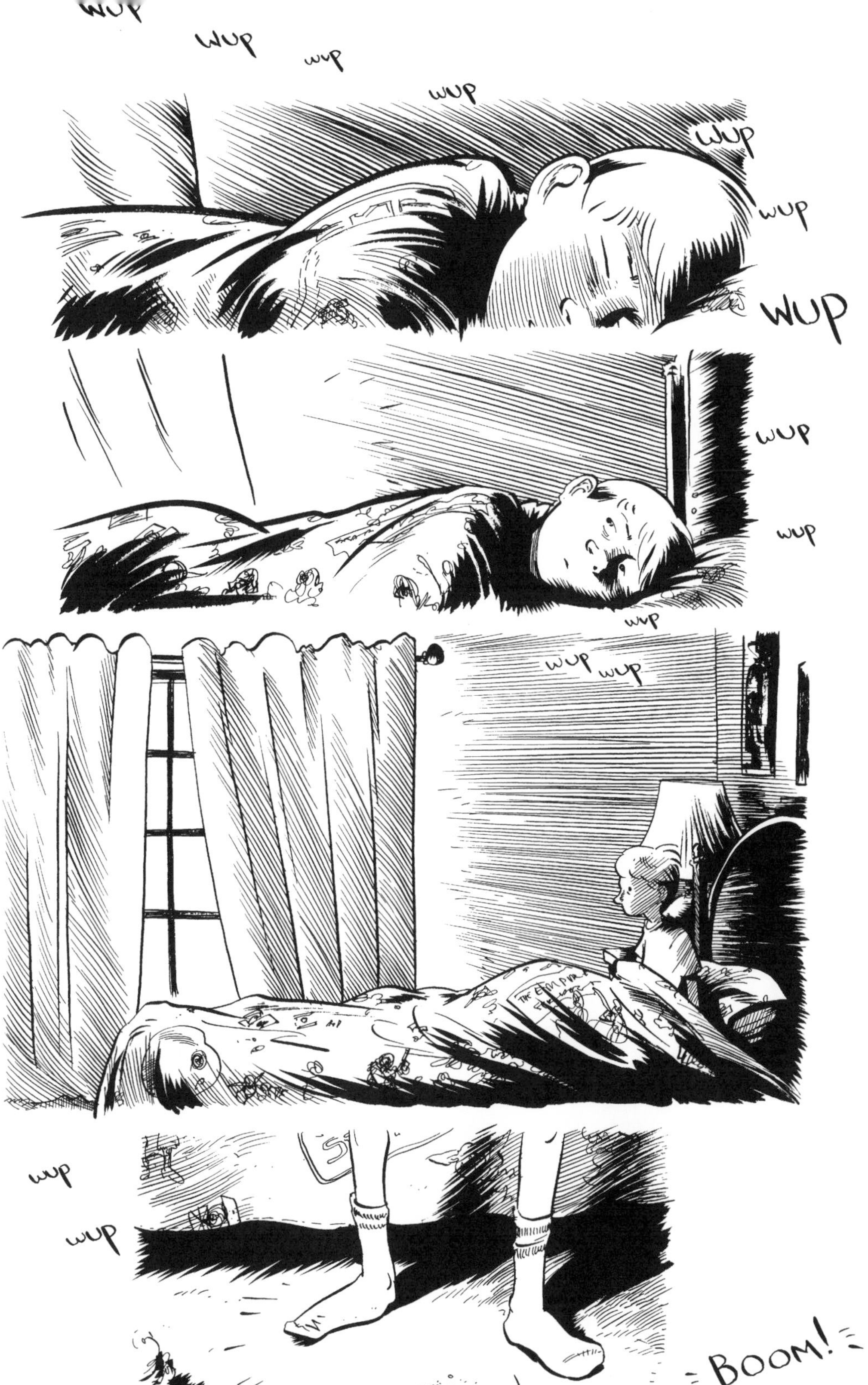
WUP
WUP
WUP
WUP
WUP
WUP
WUP
WUP
WUP
WUP
WUP
WUP
WUP
WUP
BOOM!

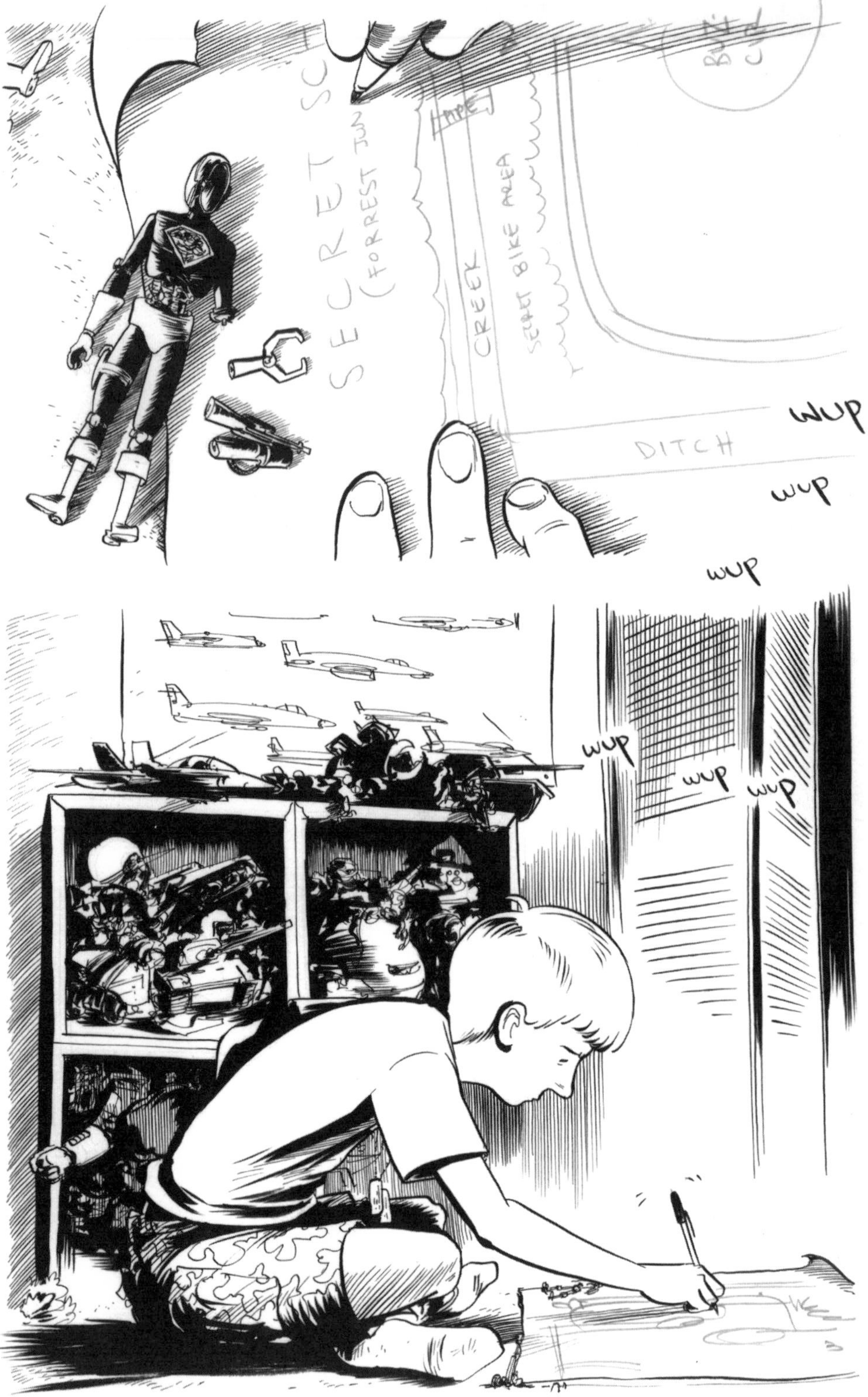
SECCRET SC
(FORREST JUN
PIPE
CREEK
SECRET BIKE AREA
DITCH
WUP
wup
wup
wup
wup
wup

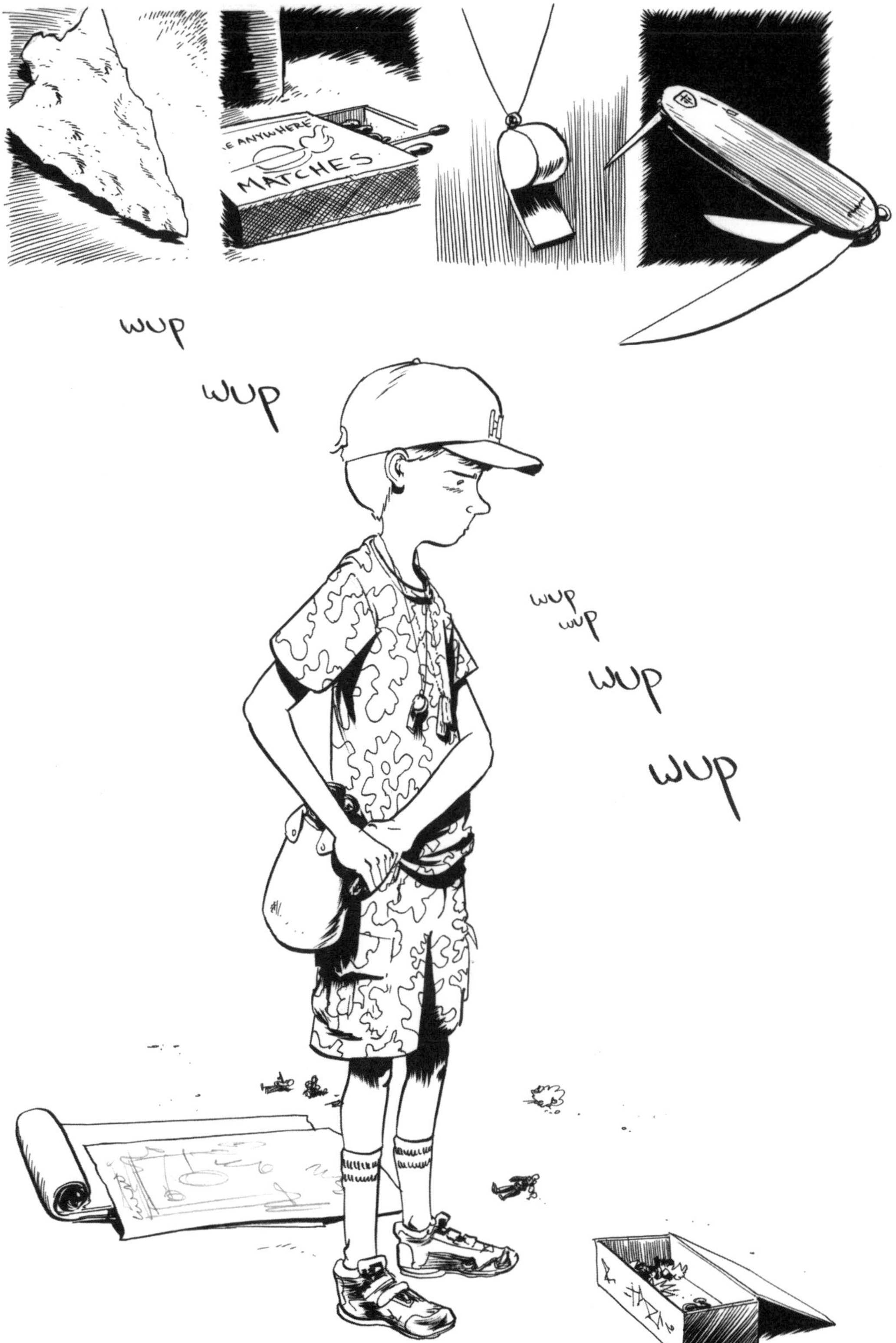

ANYWHERE
MATCHES
WUP
WUP
WUP
WUP
WUP
WUP

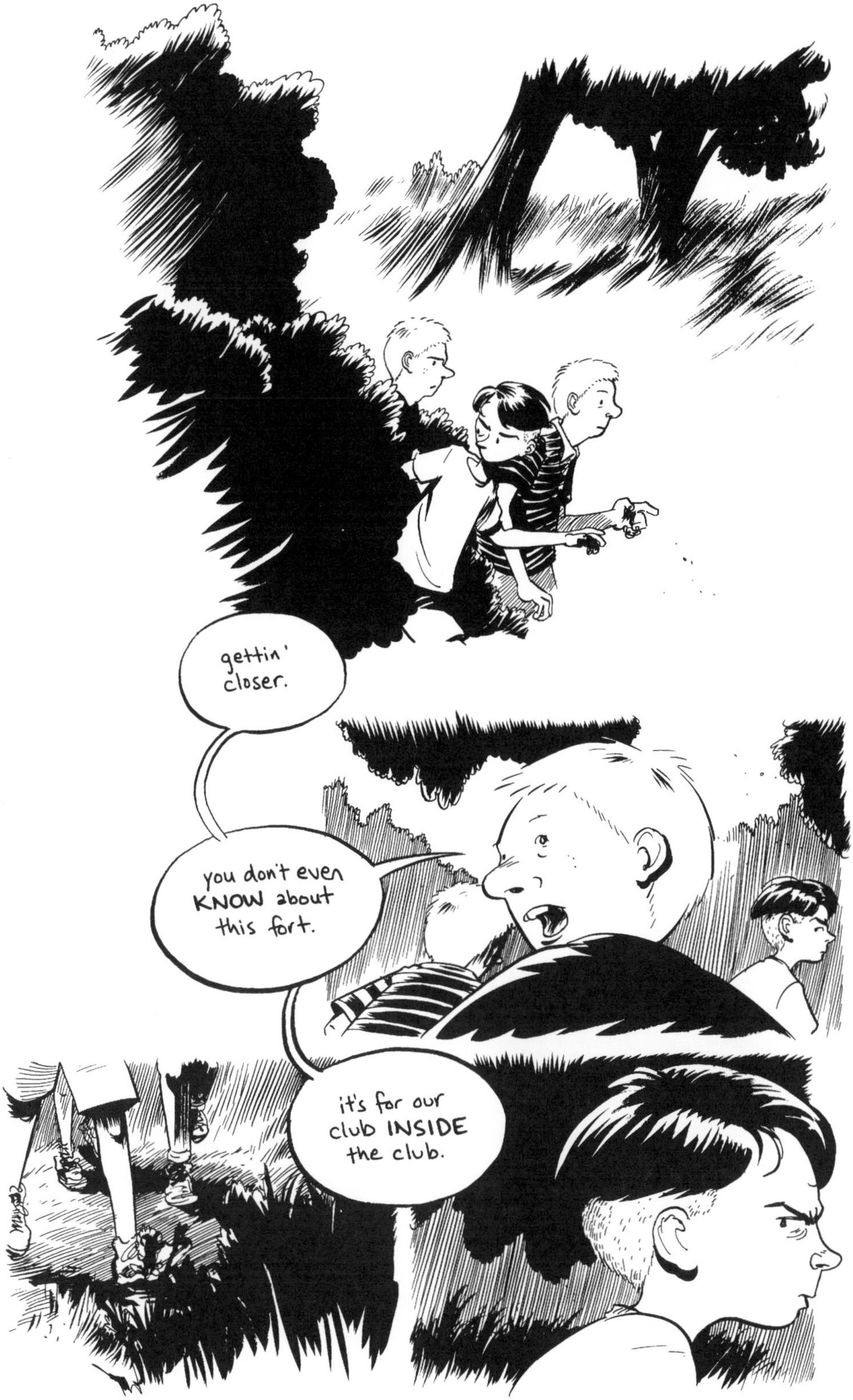
gettin' closer.
you don't even KNOW about this fort.
it's for our club INSIDE the club.

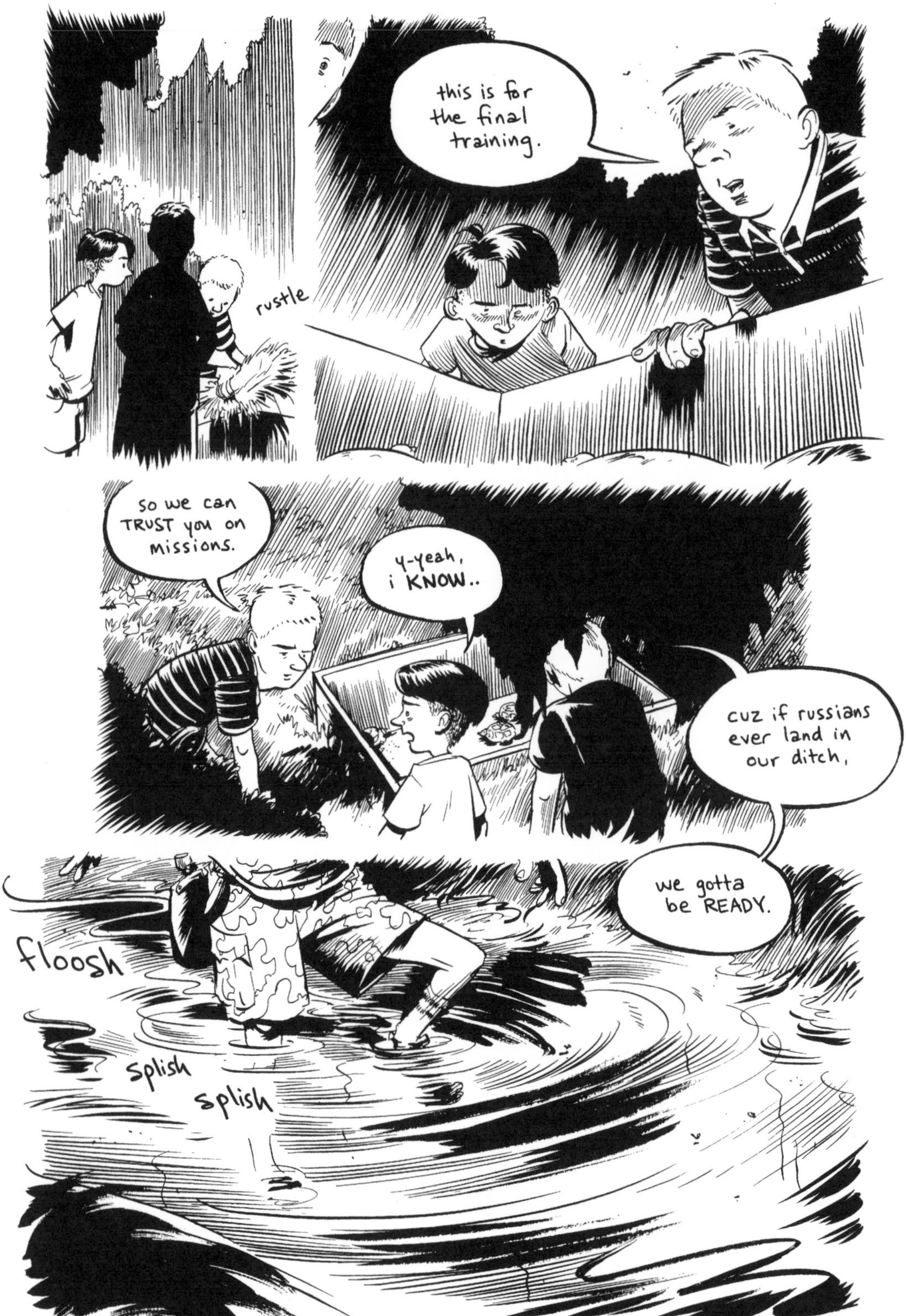
rustle
this is for the final training.
so we can TRUST you on missions.
y-yeah, i KNOW..
cuz if russians ever land in our ditch,
we gotta be READY.
floosh
splish
splish

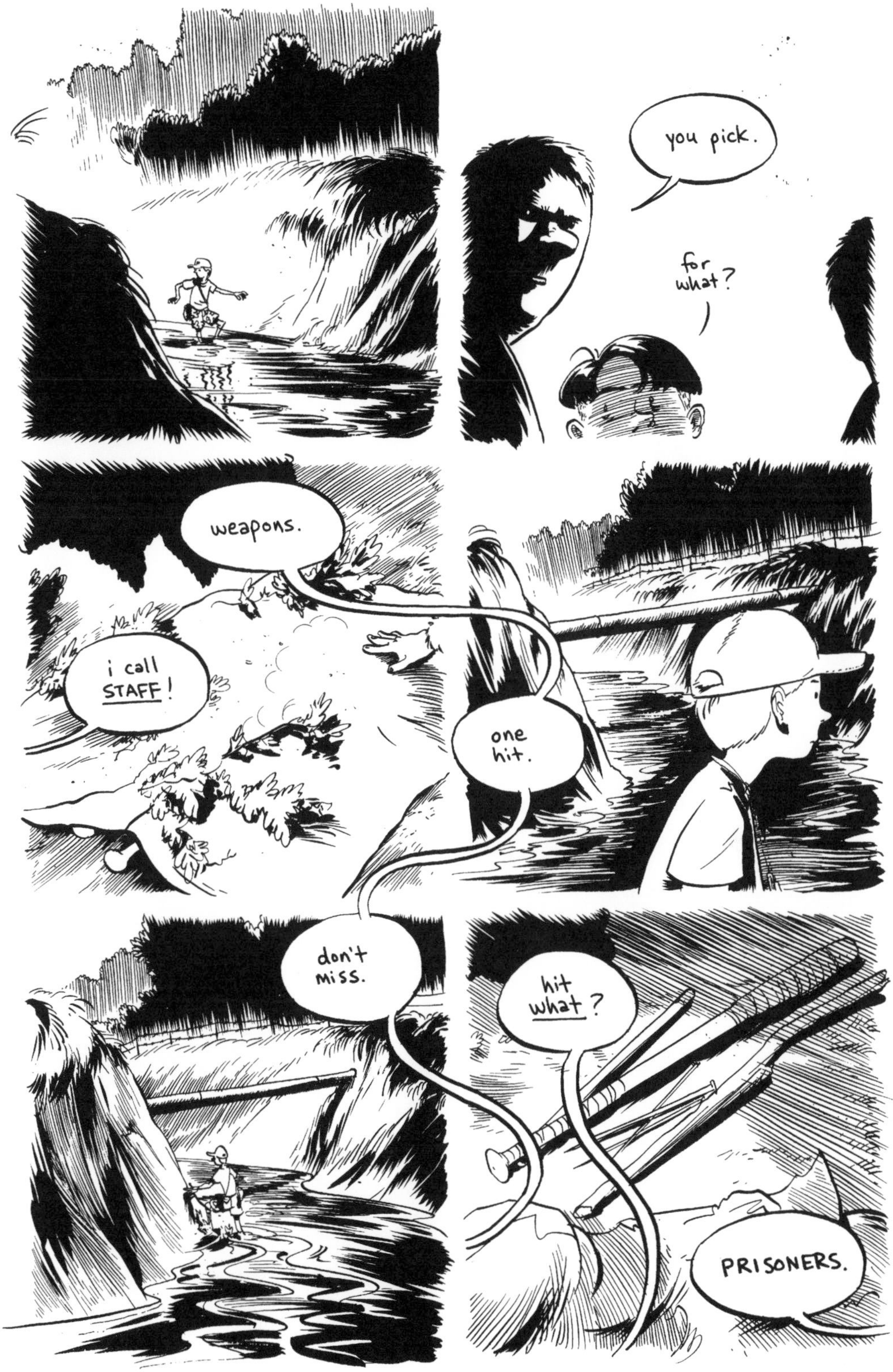
you pick.
for what?
weapons.
i call STAFF!
one hit.
don't miss.
hit what?
PRISONERS.

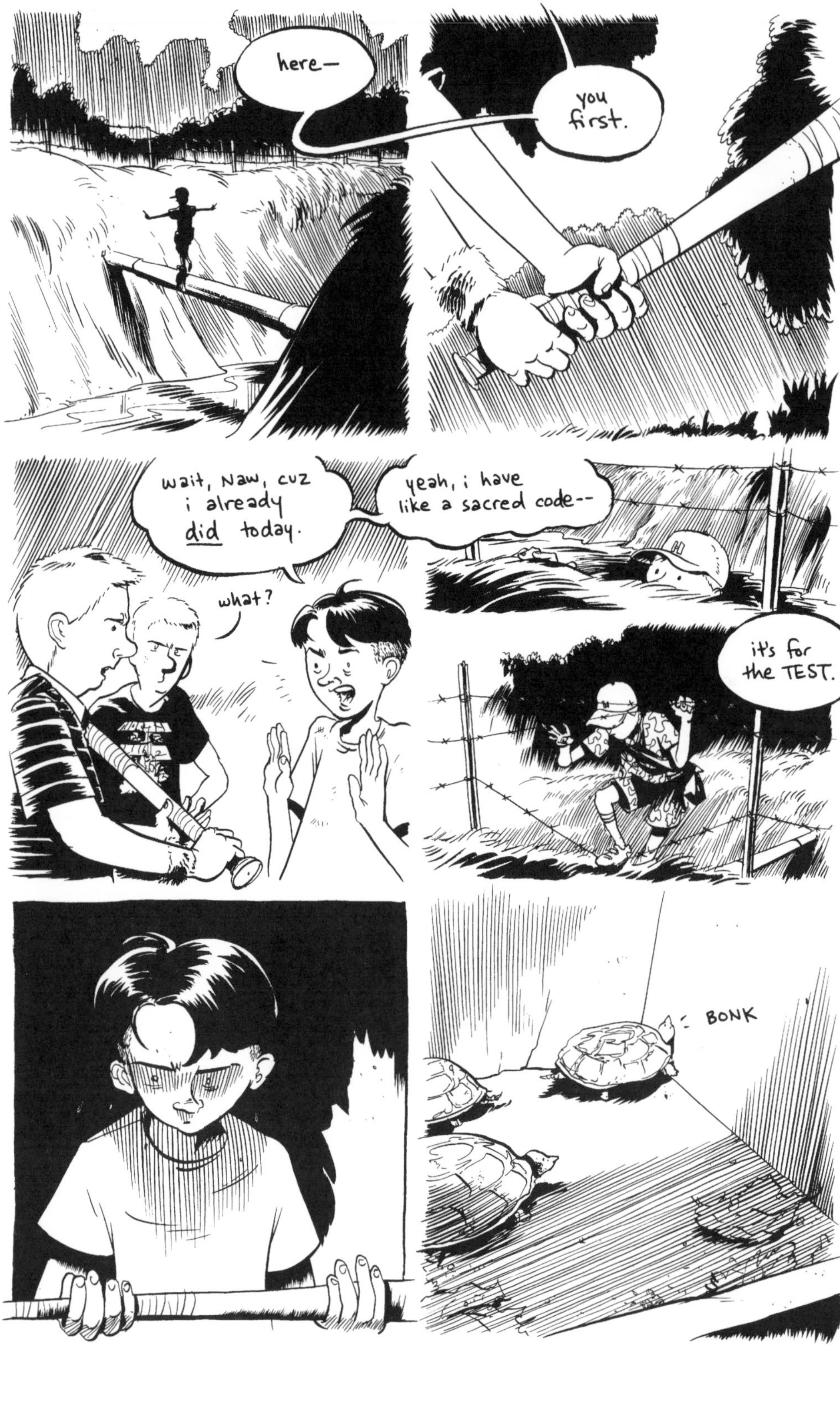
here—
you first.
wait, Naw, cuz i already did today.
yeah, i have like a sacred code--
what?
it's for the TEST.
BONK

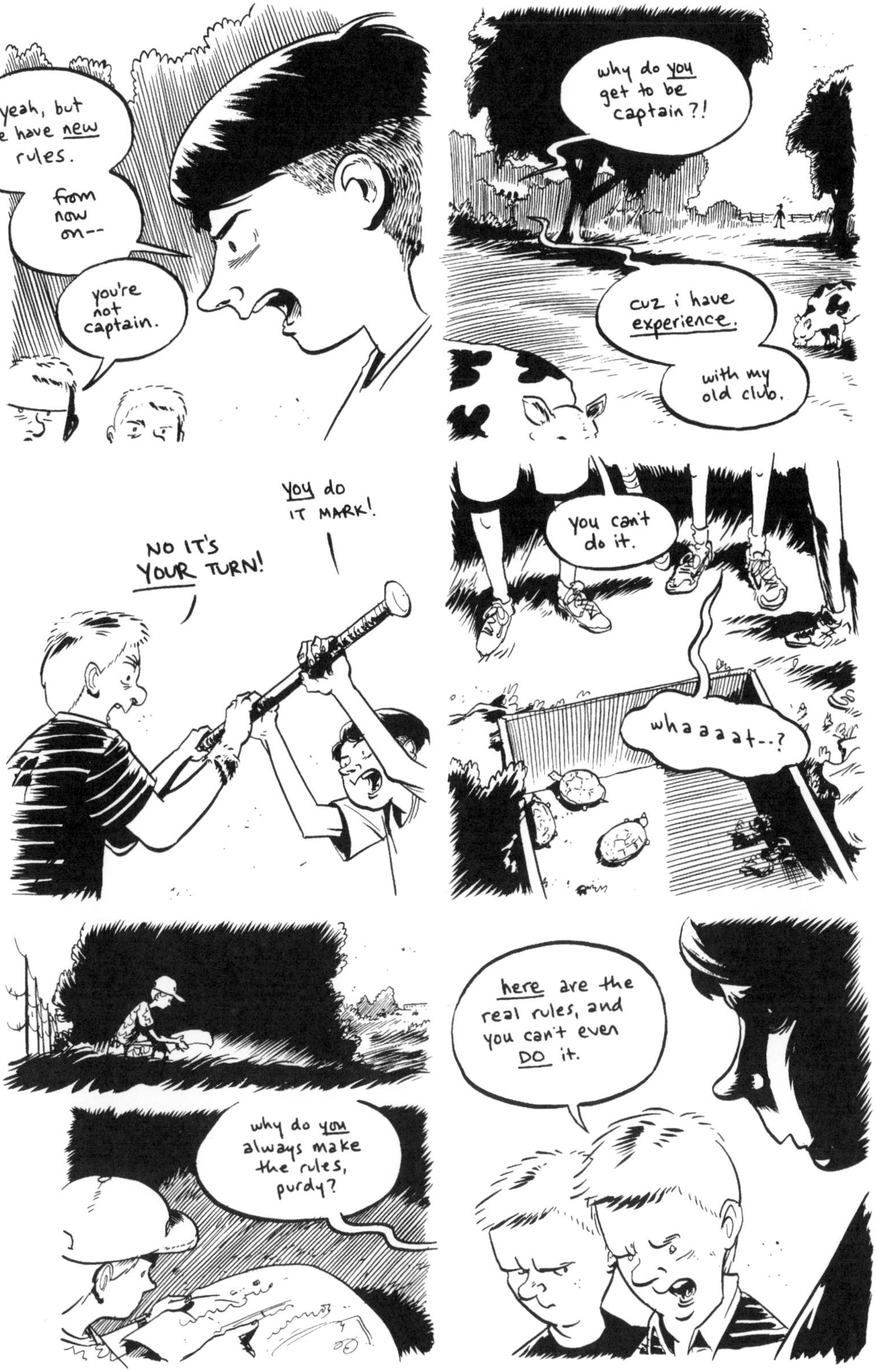
yeah, but we have new rules.
from now on--
you're not captain.
why do you get to be captain?!
cuz i have experience.
with my old club.
NO IT'S YOUR TURN!
YOU do IT MARK!
you can't do it.
whaaaat--?
why do you always make the rules, purdy?
here are the real rules, and you can't even DO it.

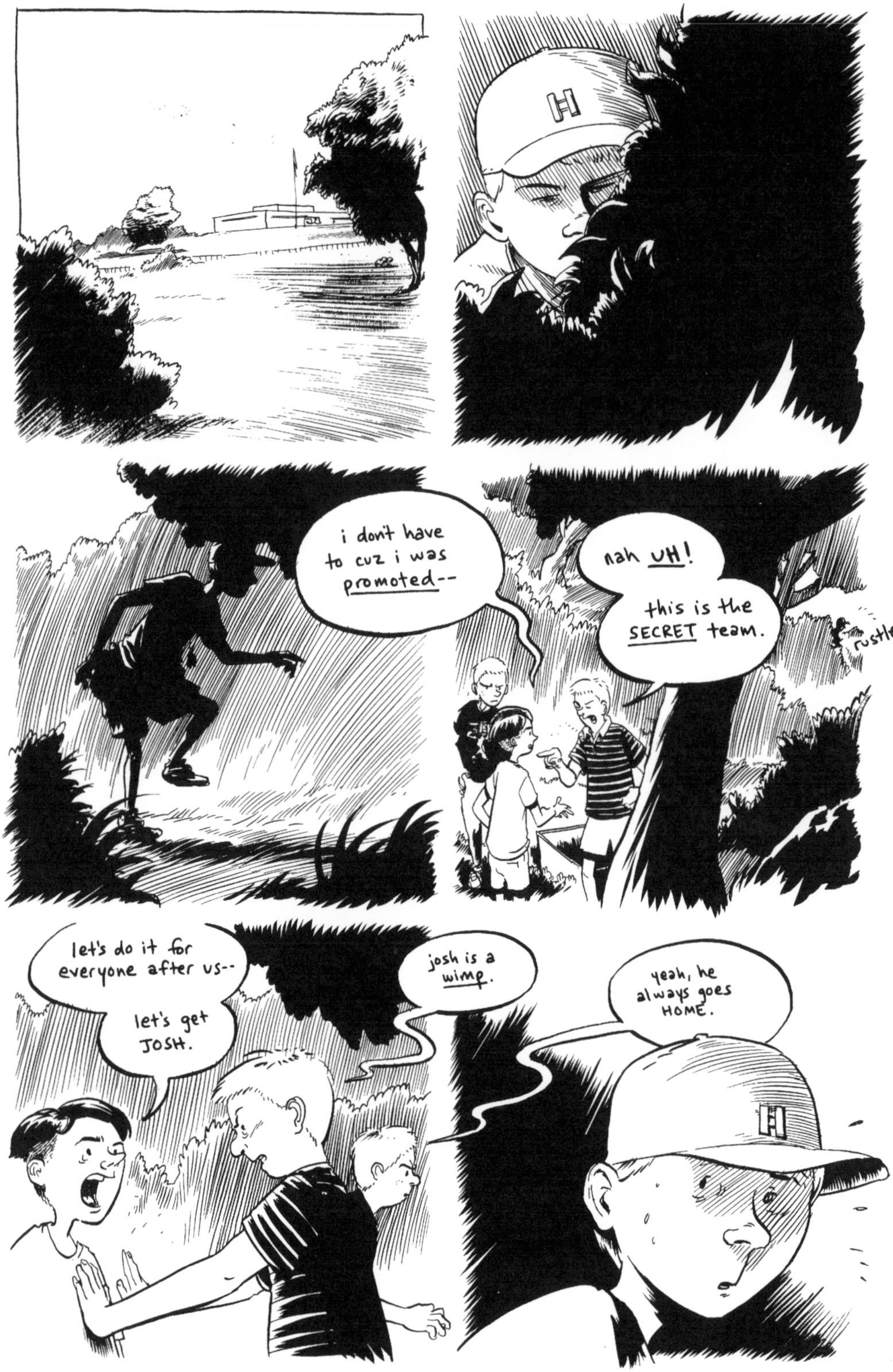
i don't have to cuz i was promoted--
nah UH!
this is the SECRET team.
rustle
let's do it for everyone after us--
let's get JOSH.
josh is a wimp.
yeah, he always goes HOME.

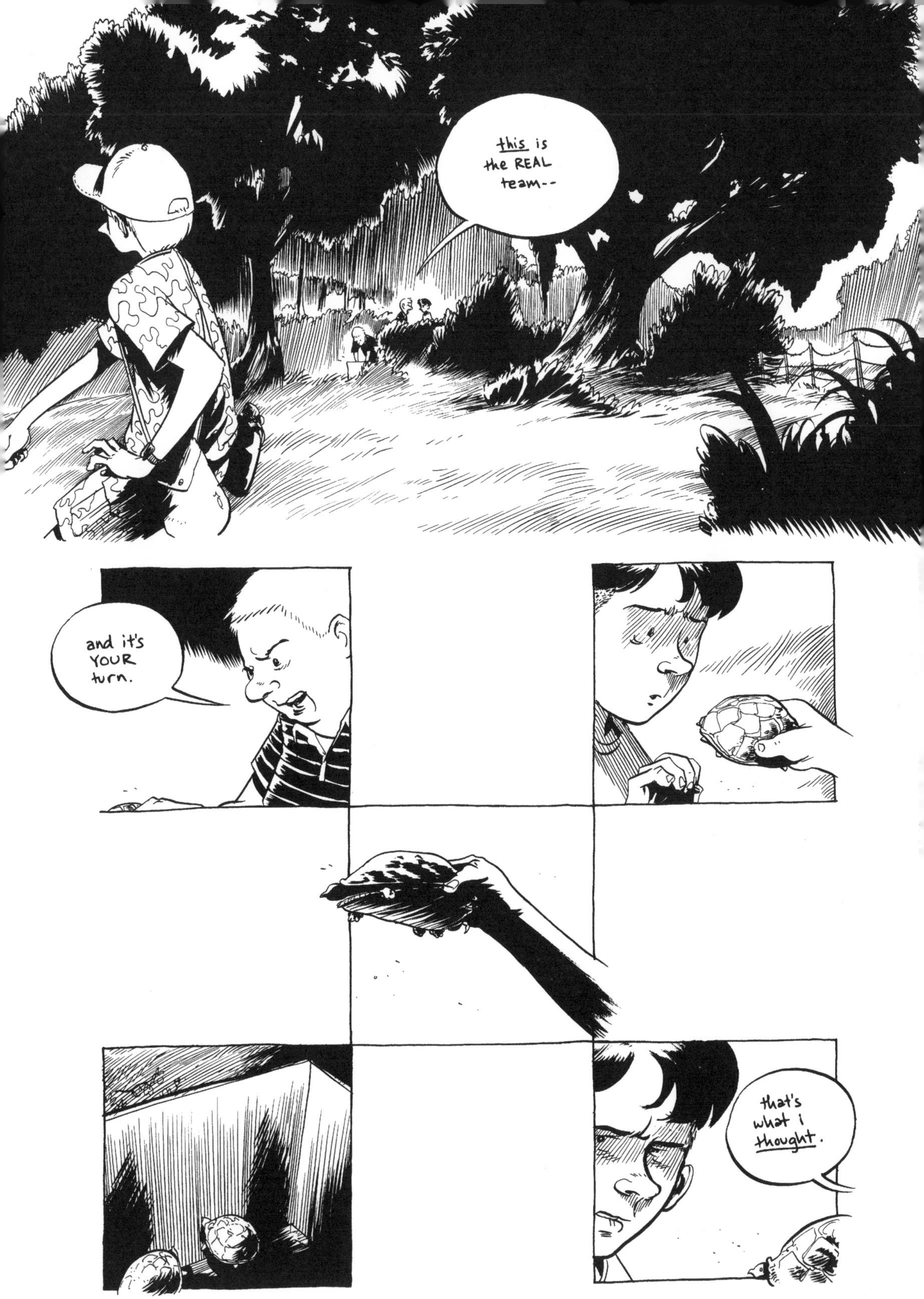
this is the REAL team--
and it's YOUR turn.
that's what i thought.

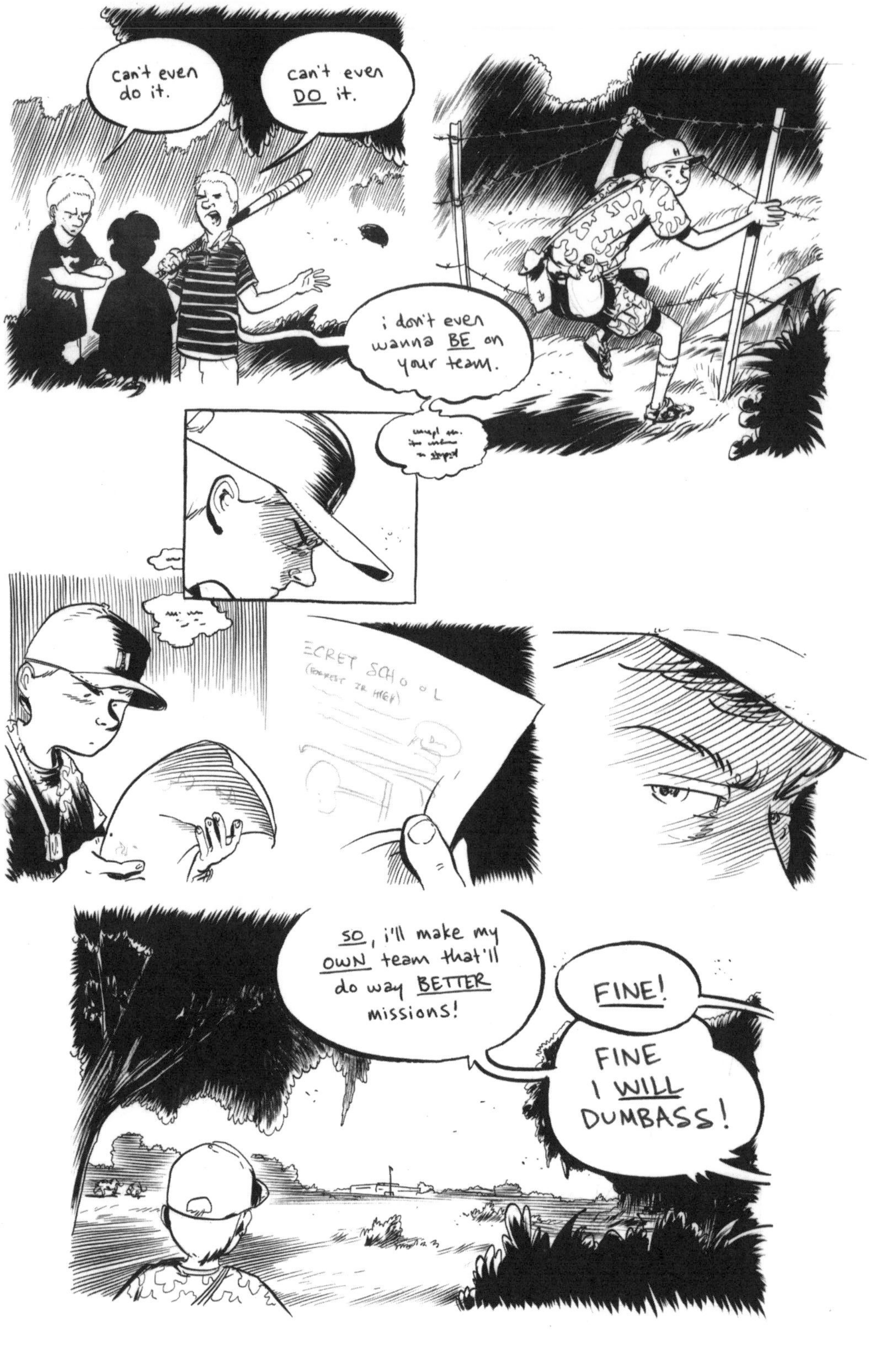
can't even do it.
can't even DO it.
i don't even wanna BE on your team.
SO, i'll make my OWN team that'll do way BETTER missions!
FINE!
FINE I WILL DUMBASS!

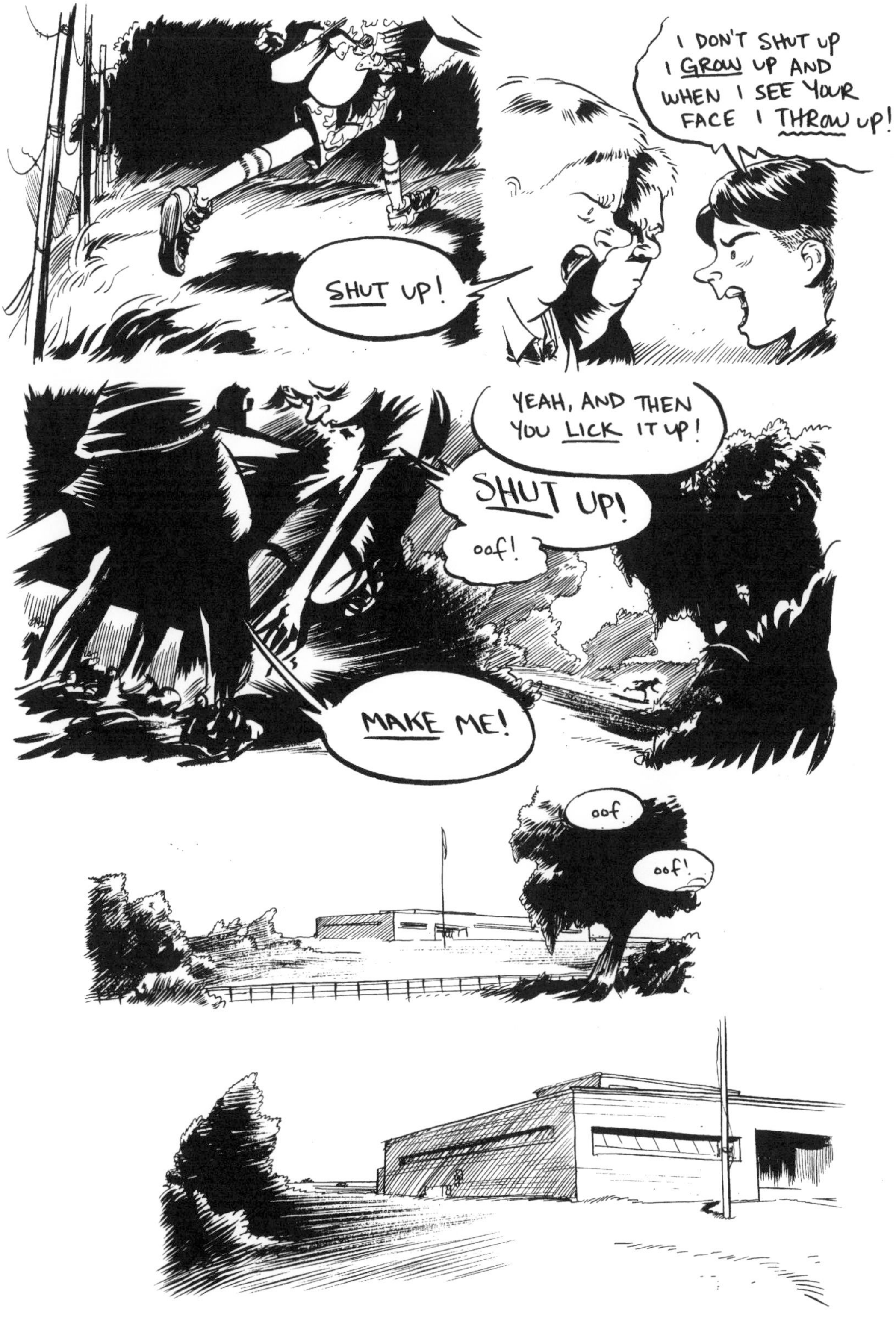
I DON'T SHUT UP
I GROW UP AND
WHEN I SEE YOUR
FACE I THROW UP!
SHUT UP!
YEAH, AND THEN
YOU LICK IT UP!
SHUT UP!
oof!
MAKE ME!
oof
oof!

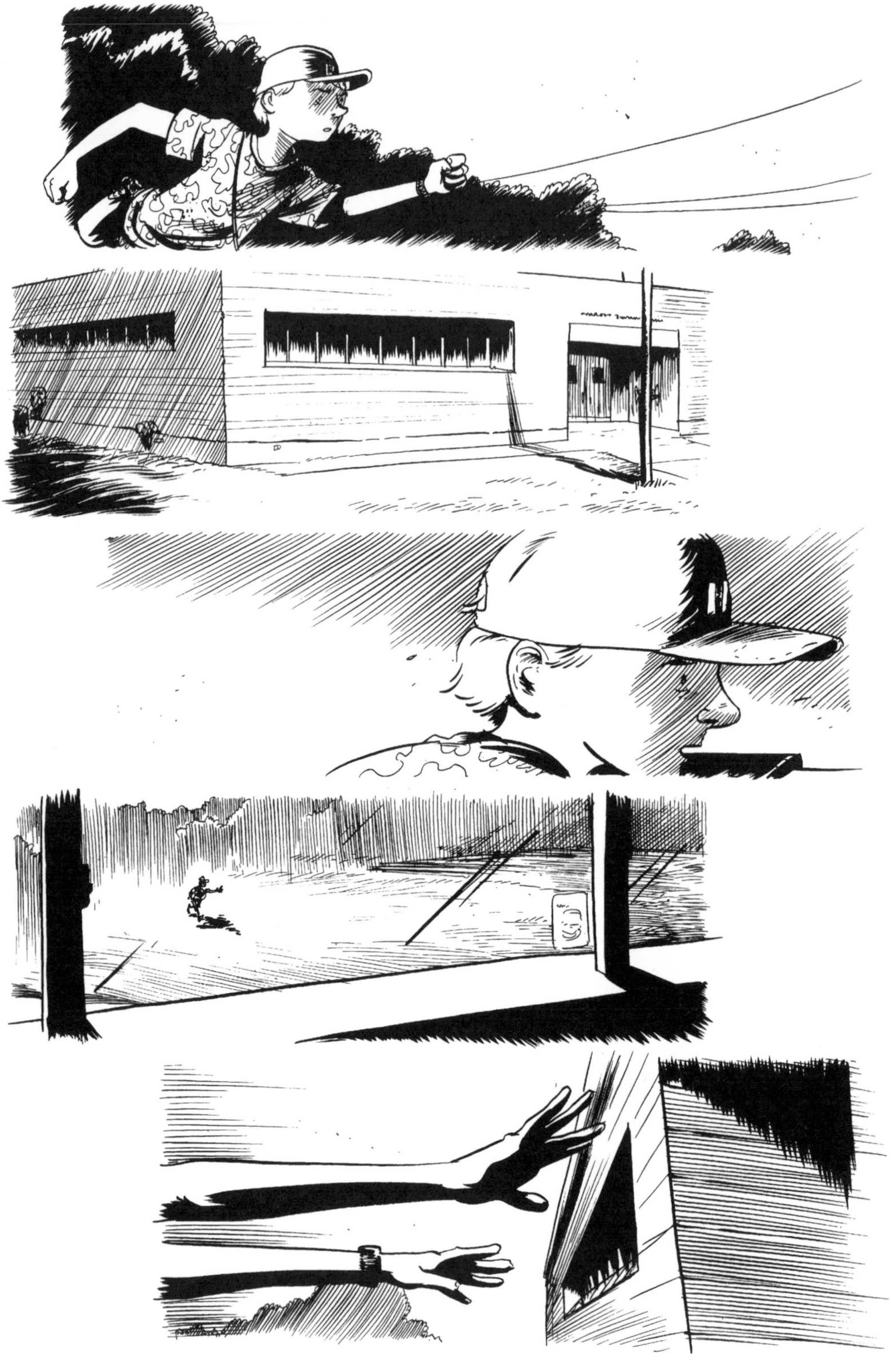

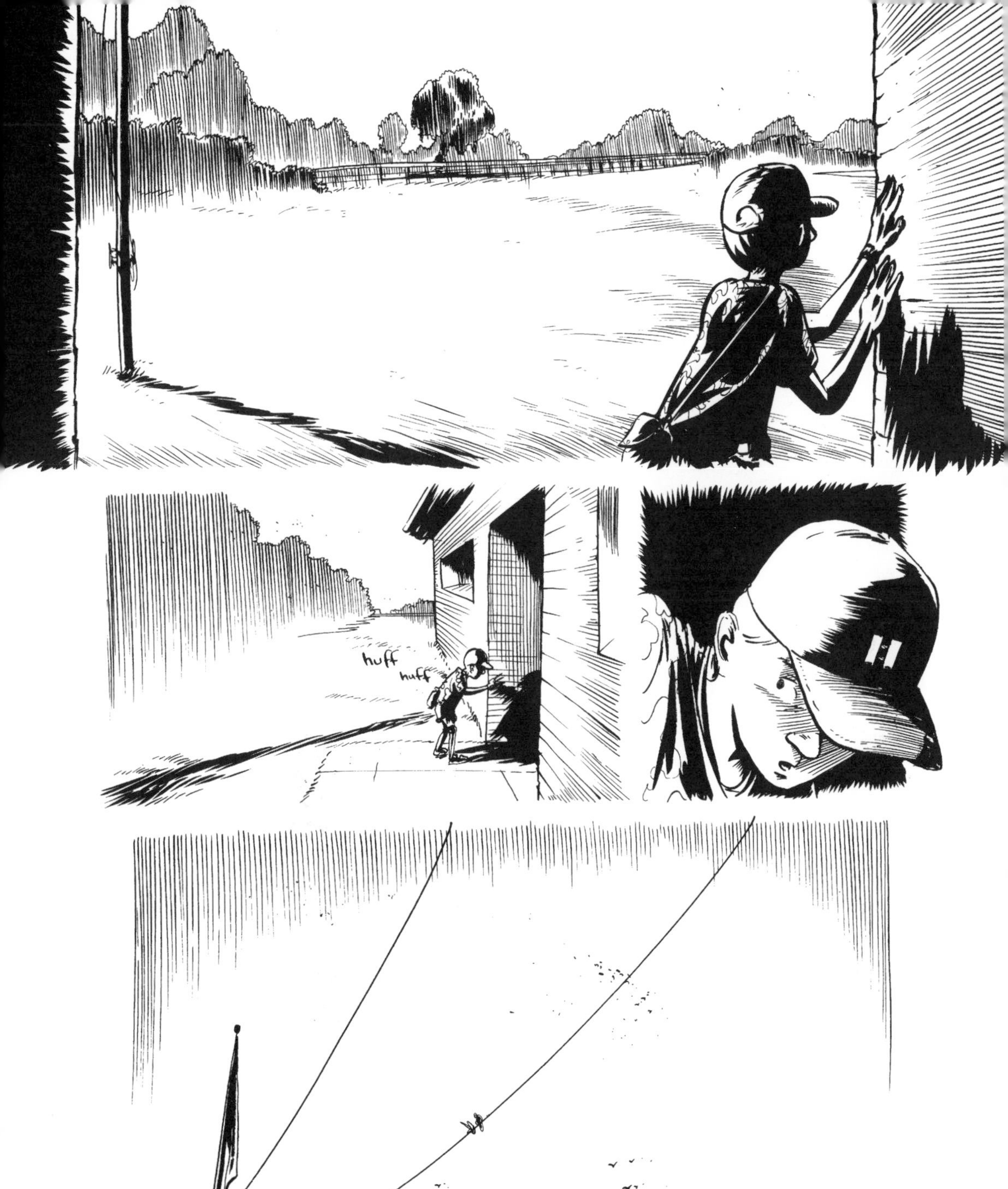
huff
huff
wup wup
wup

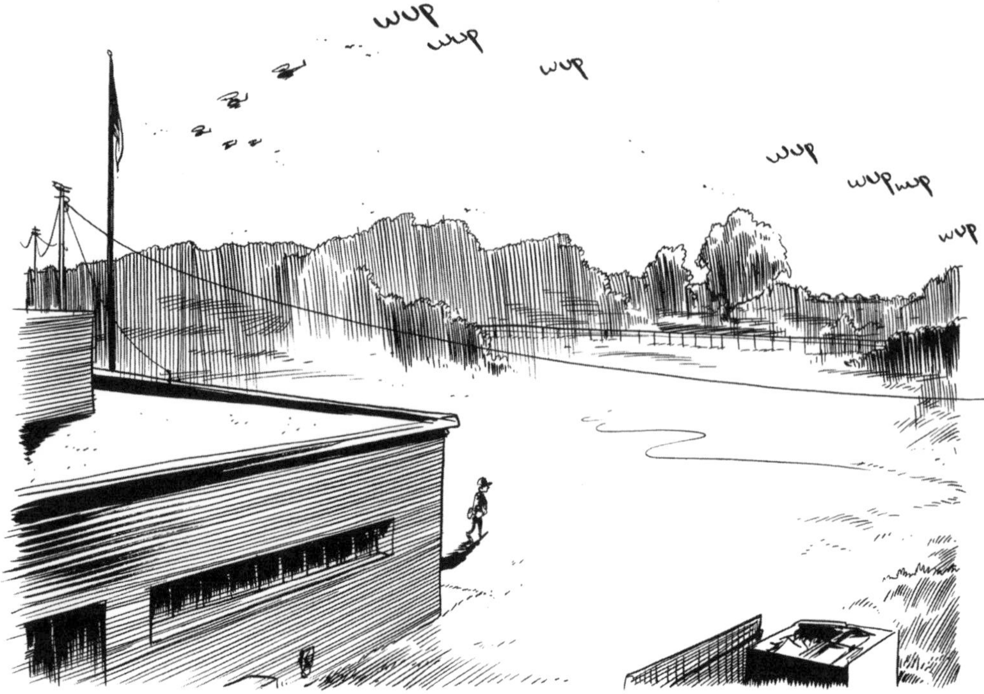

WUP
WUP
WUP
WUP
WUPWUP
WUP

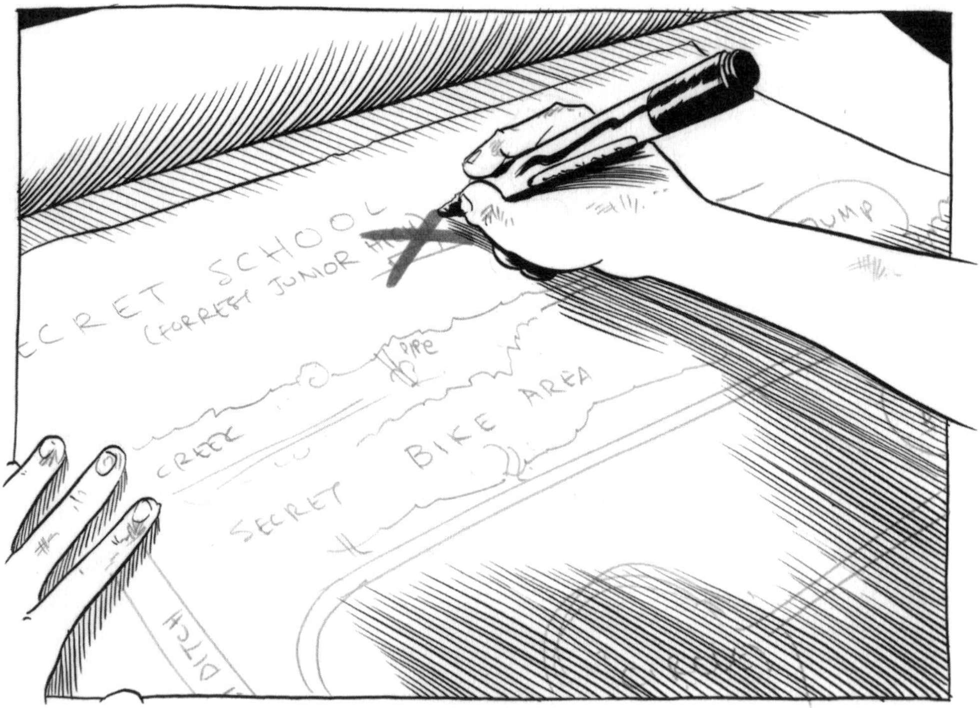

ECRET SCHOOL
(FORREST JUNIOR
PIPE
CREEK
BIKE AREA
SECRET
DITCH
DUMP

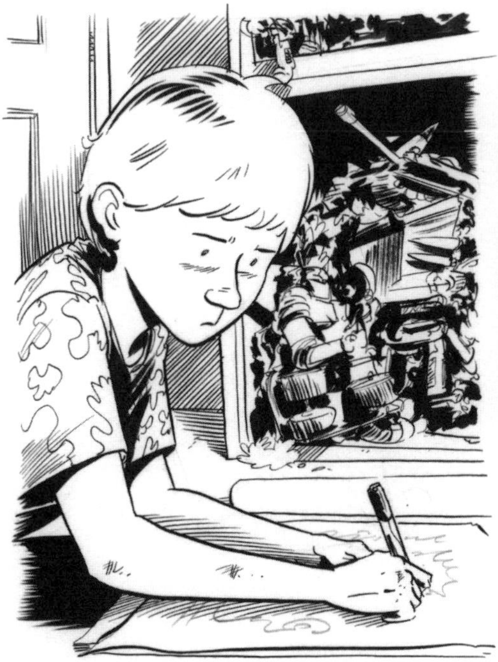

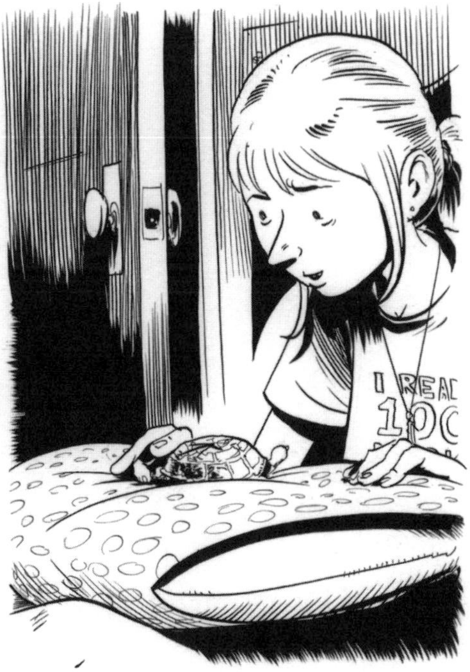

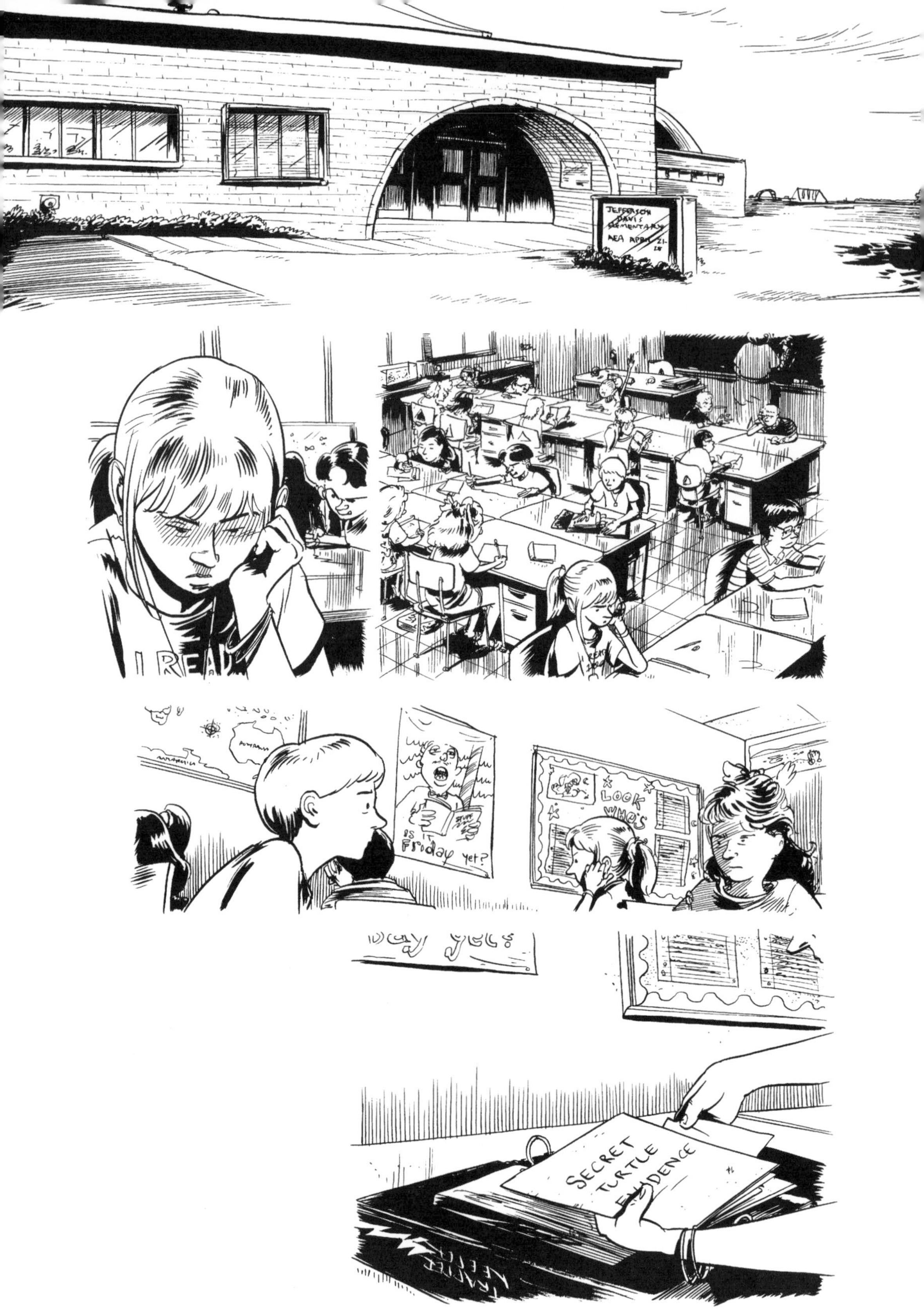
JEFFERSON DAVIS ELEMENTARY
IS IT Friday yet?
LOOK WHO'S
SECRET TURTLE EVIDENCE

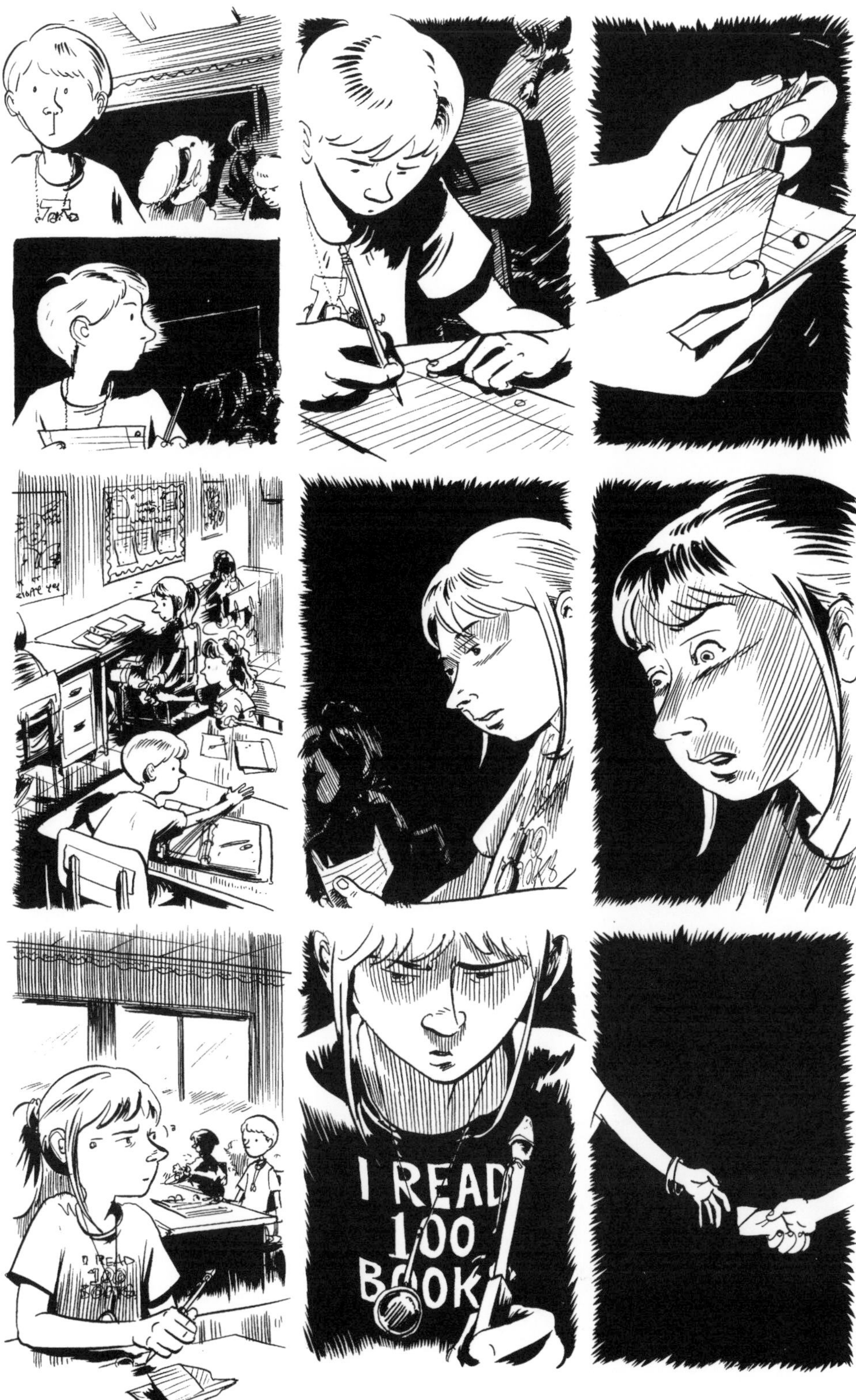
I READ 100 BOOKS

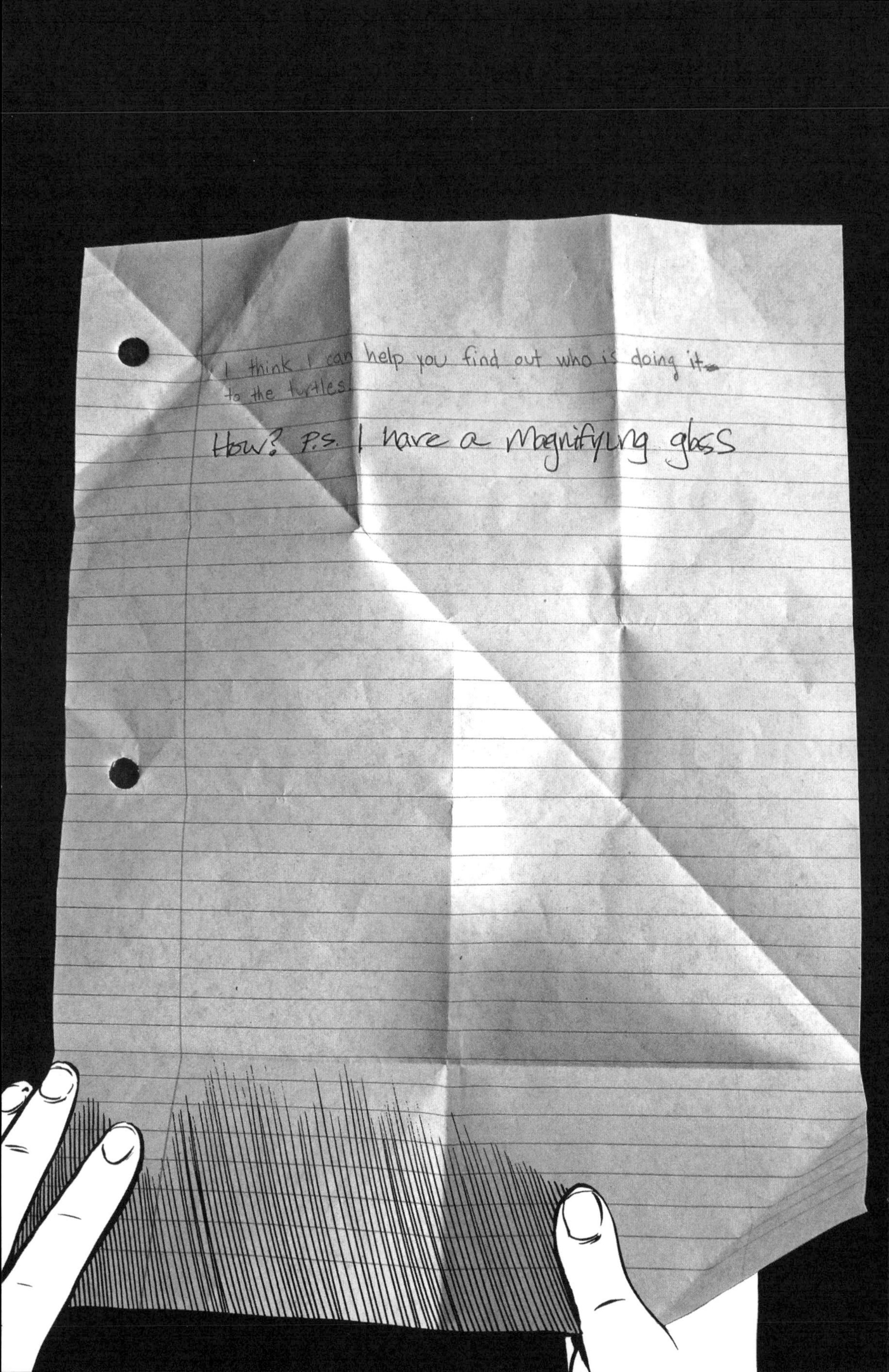

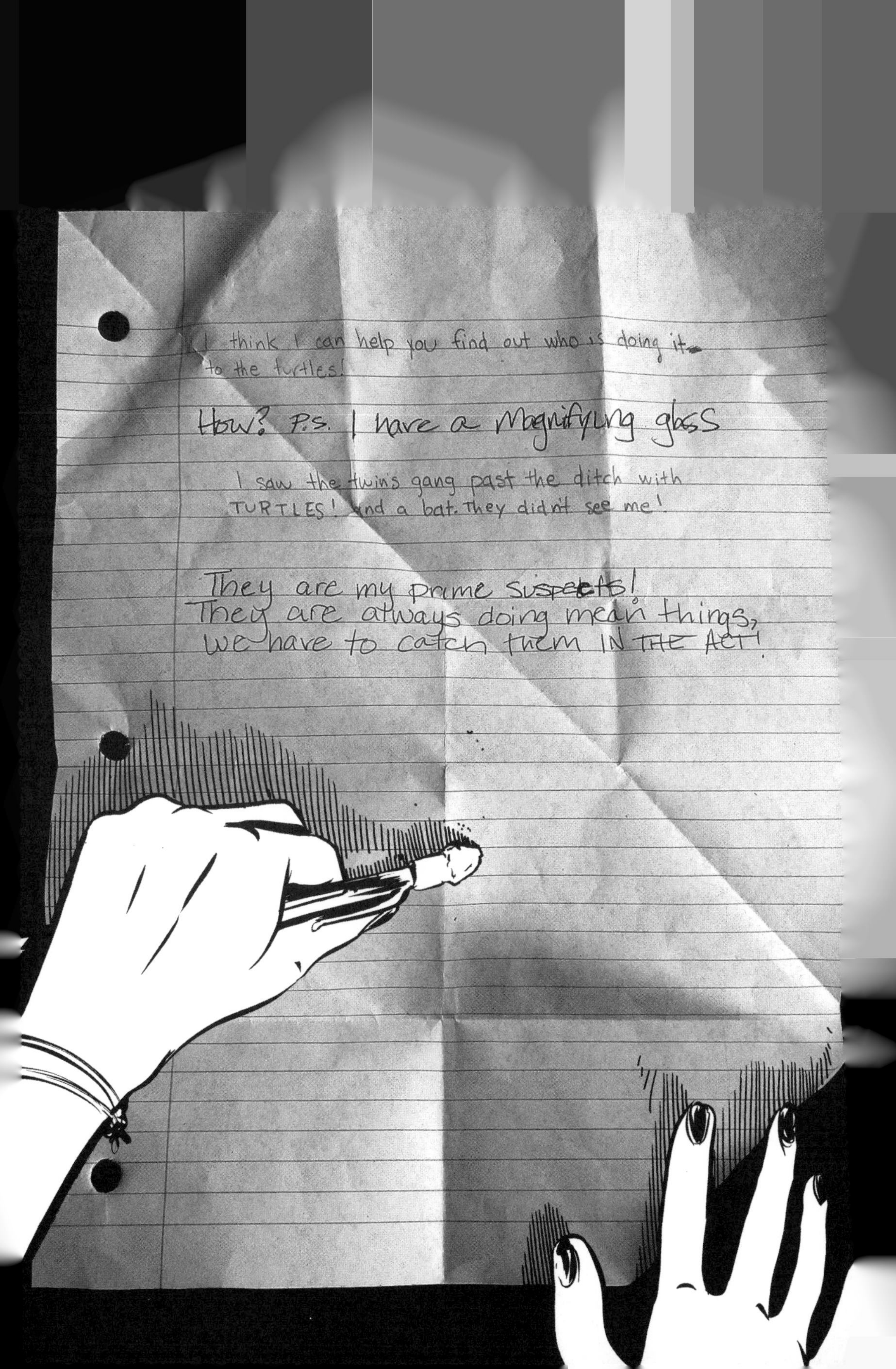
I think I can help you find out who is doing it to the turtles!
How? P.S. I have a Magnifying glass
I saw the twin's gang past the ditch with TURTLES! And a bat. They didn't see me!
They are my prime suspects!
They are always doing mean things, We have to catch them IN THE ACT!

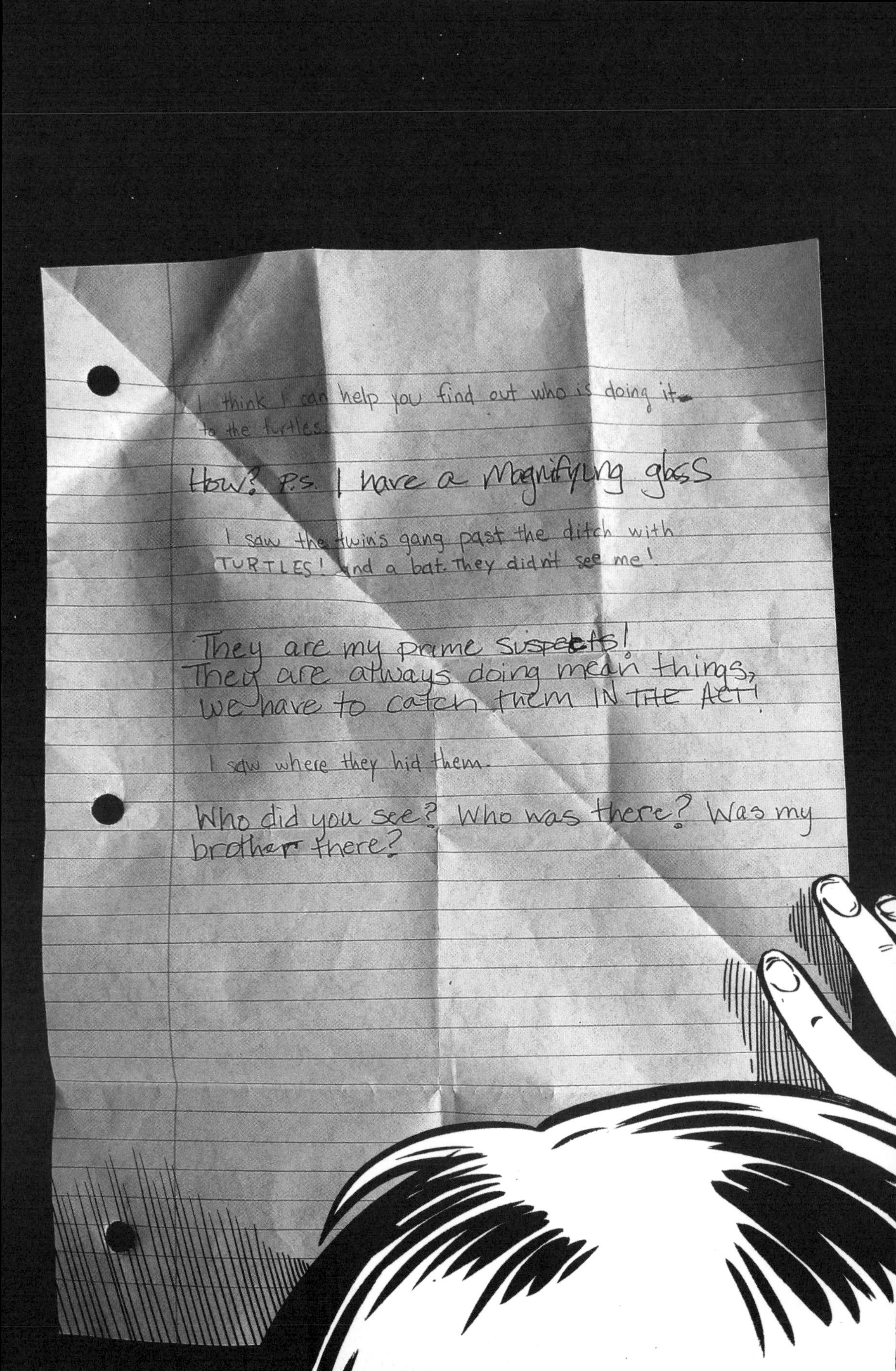

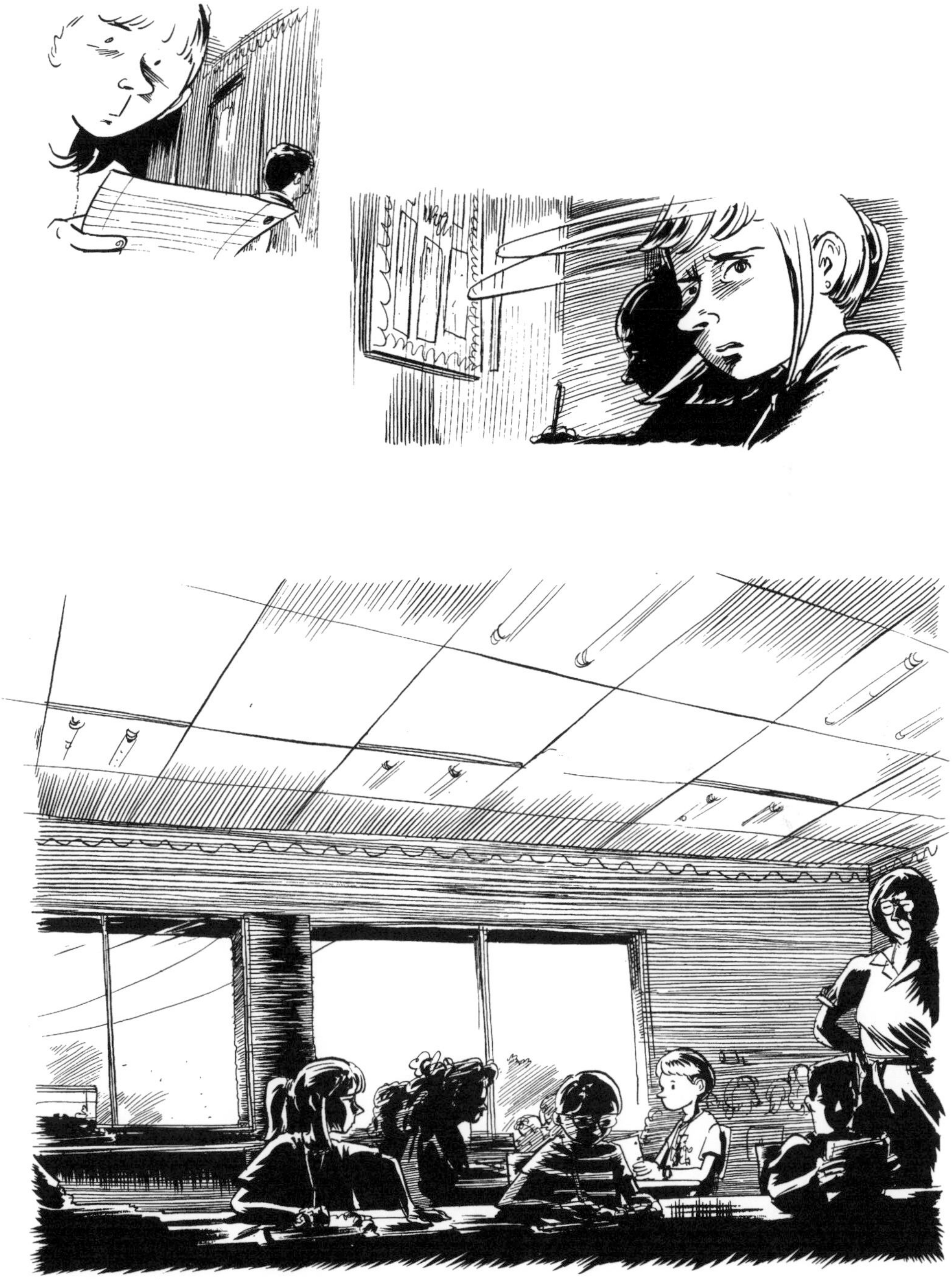

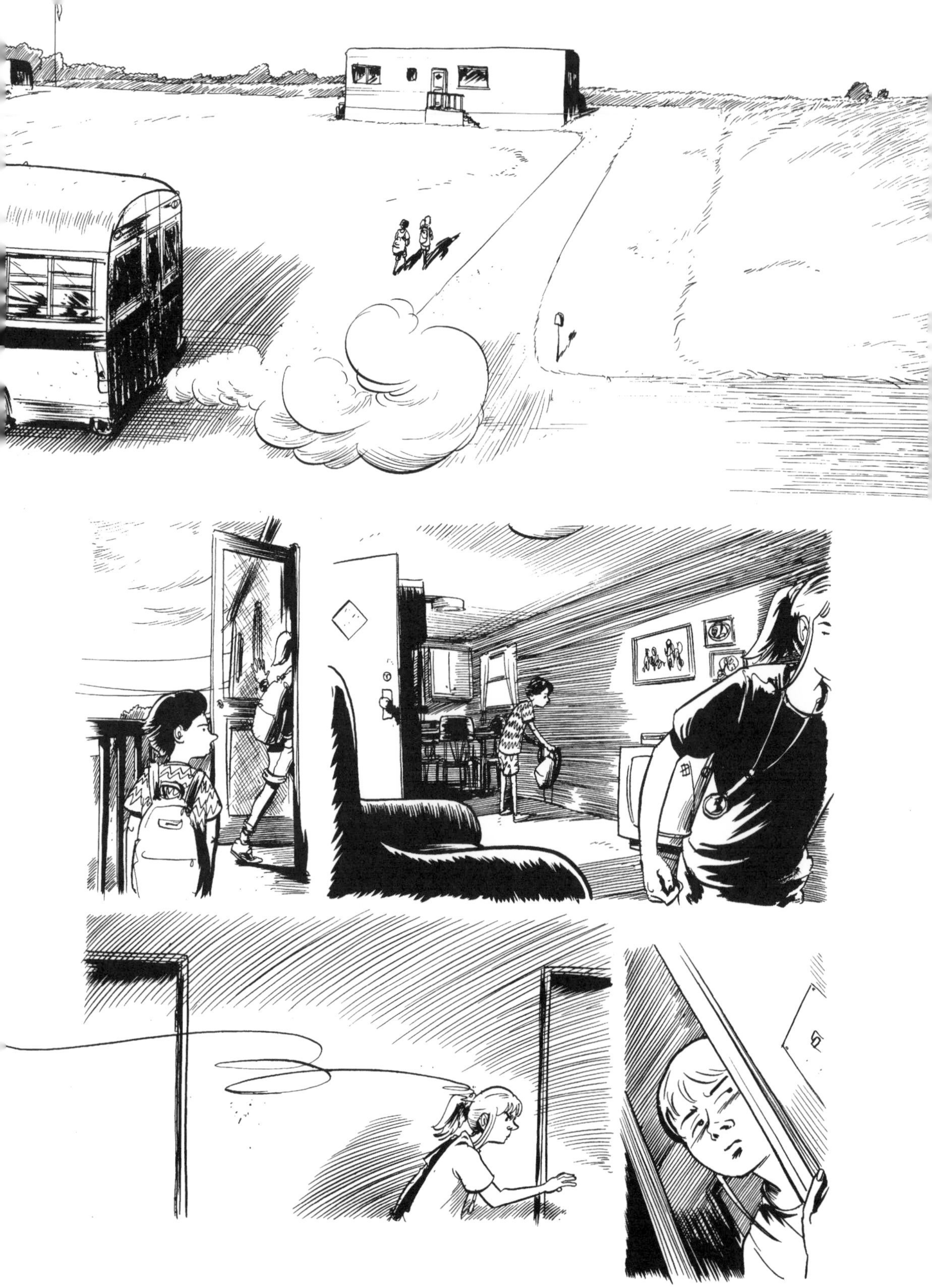

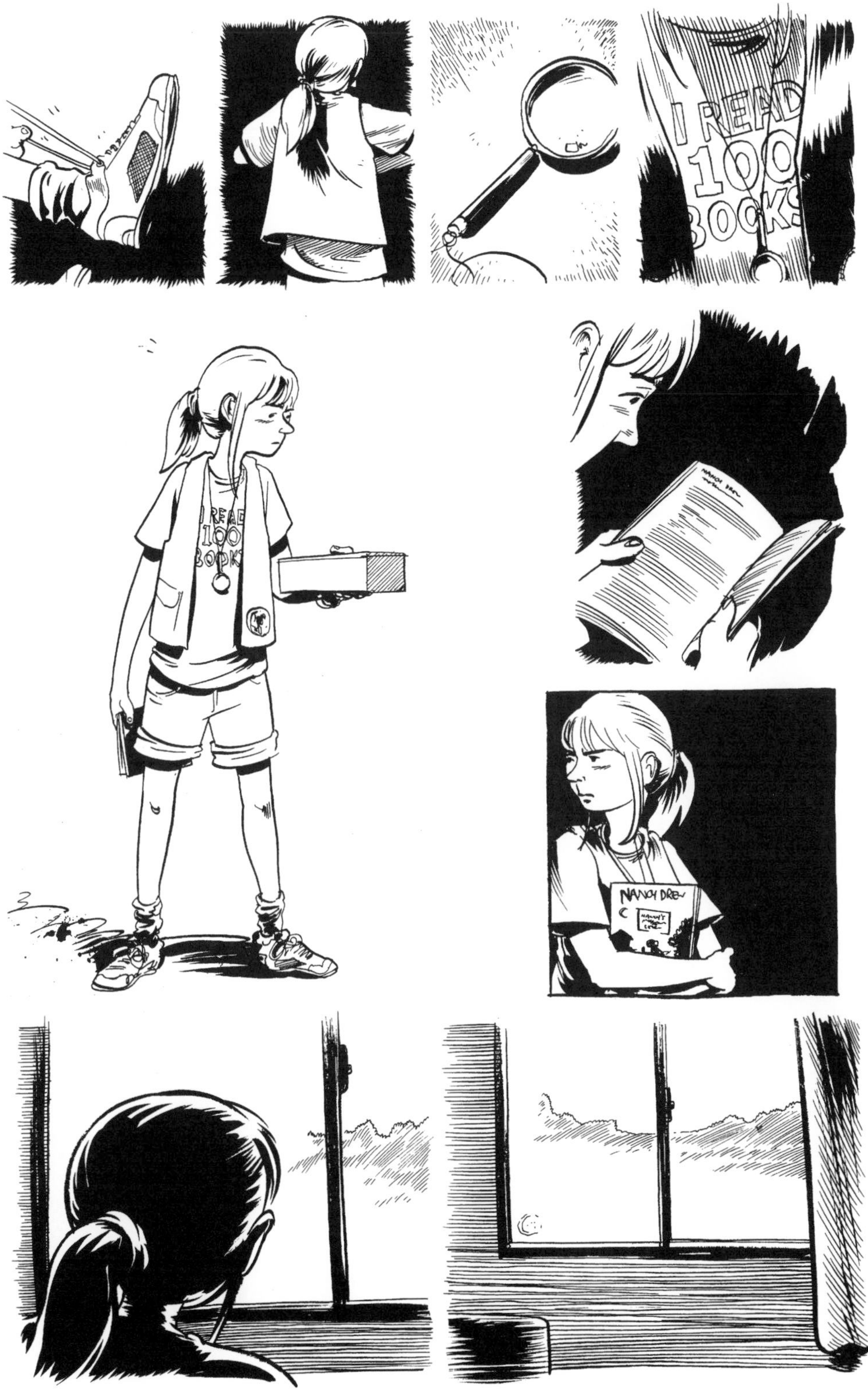
I READ 100 BOOKS

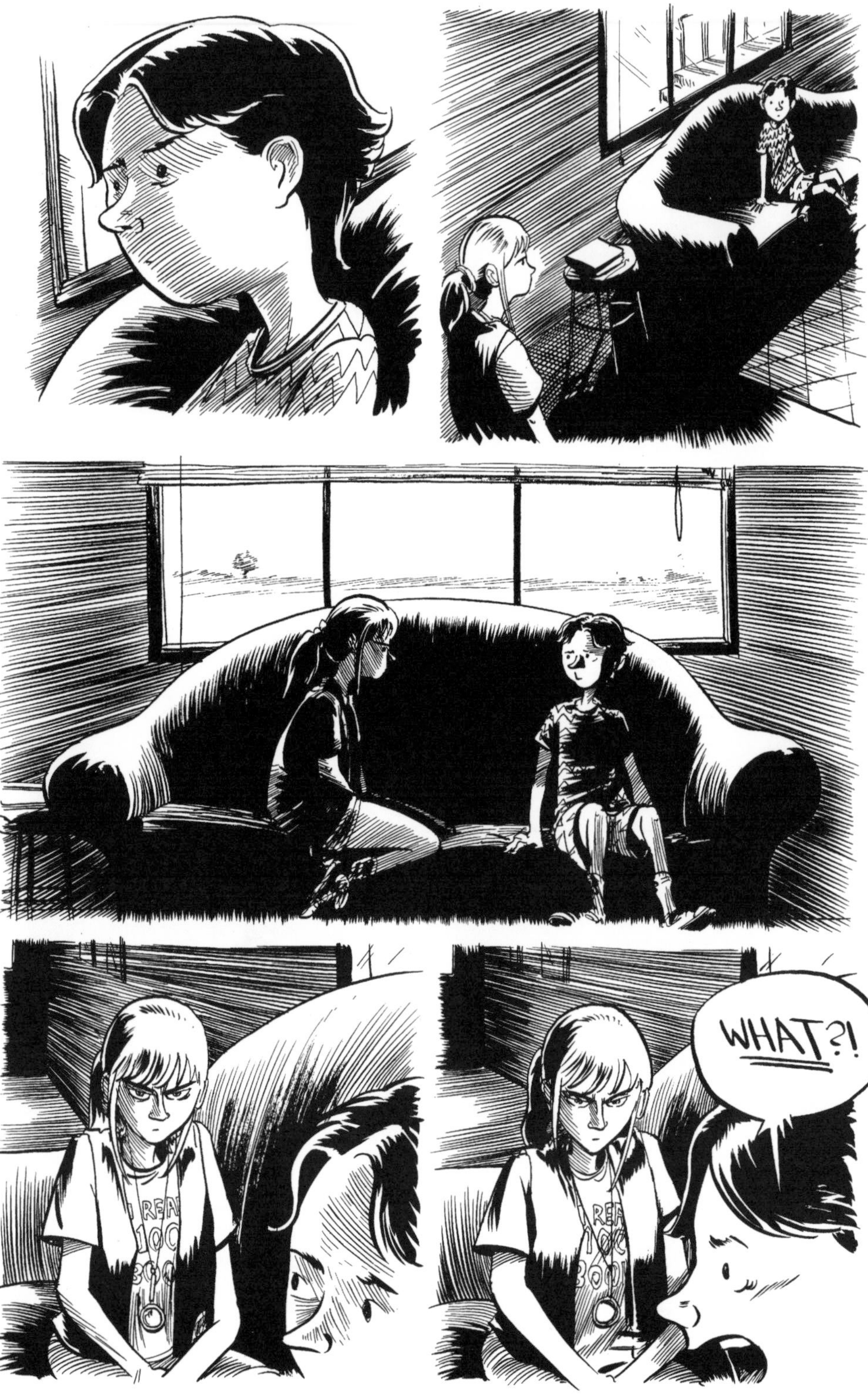
WHAT?!

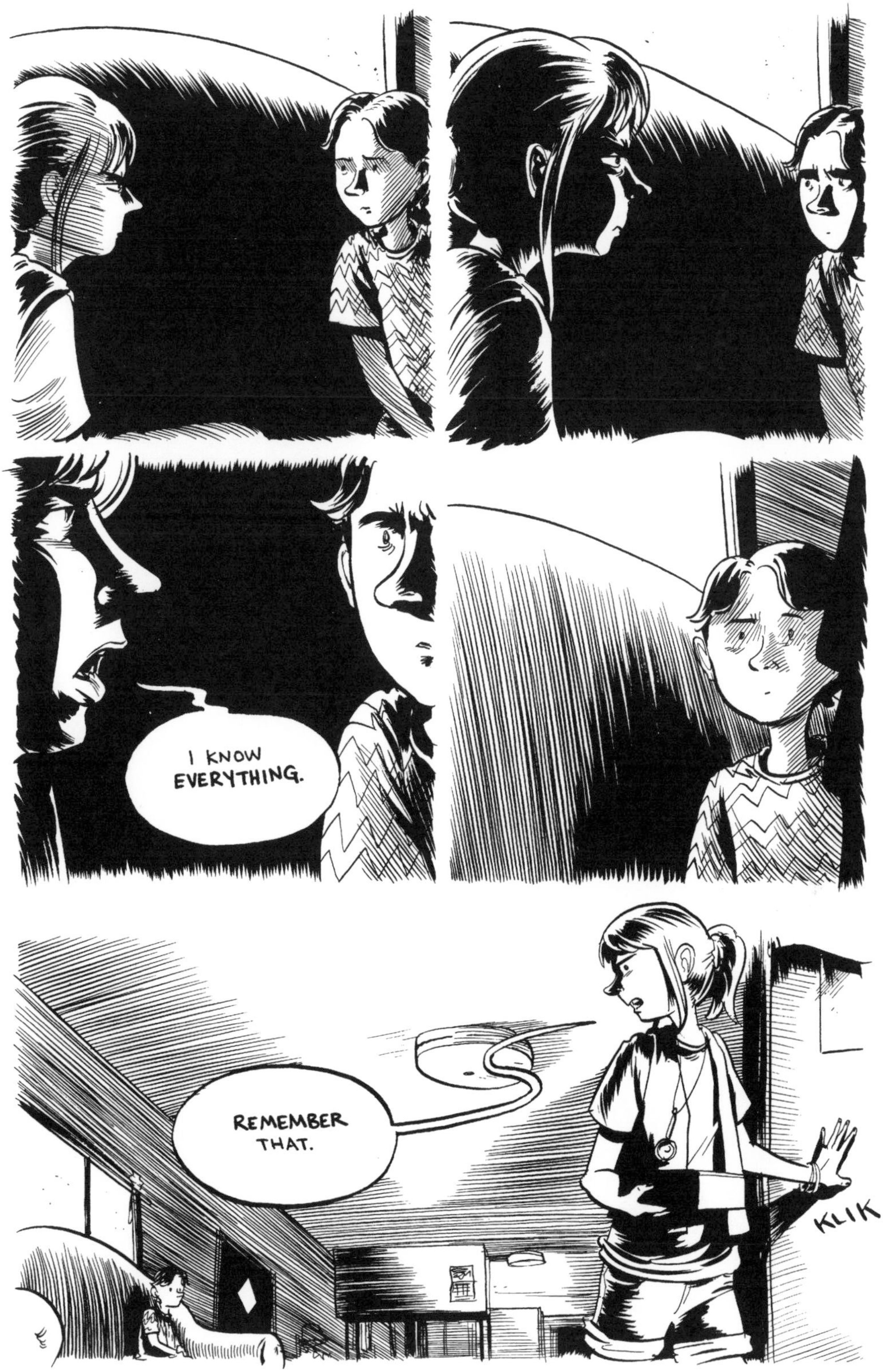
I KNOW EVERYTHING.
REMEMBER THAT.
KLIK

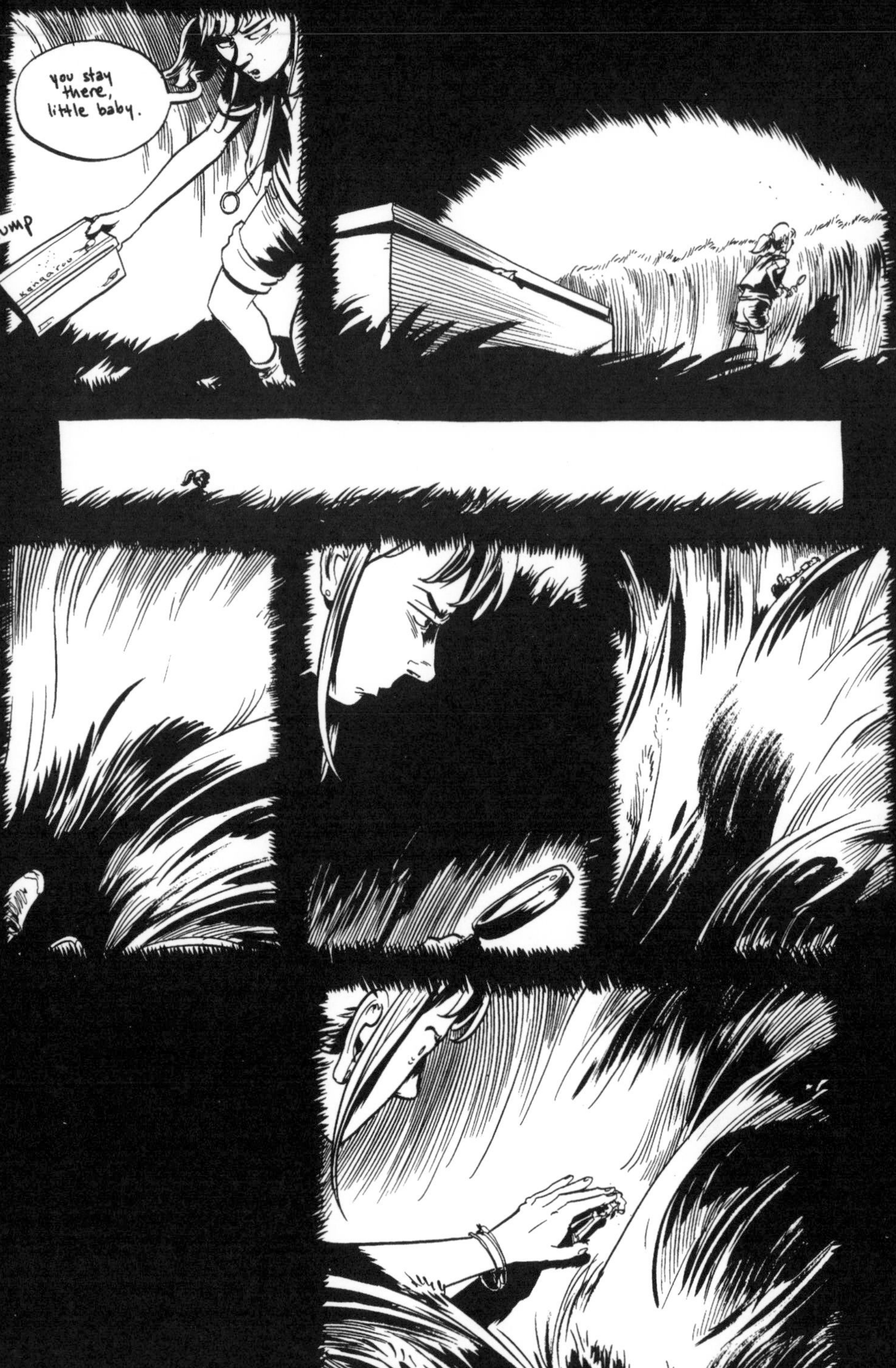
you stay there, little baby.
thump
kangaroo

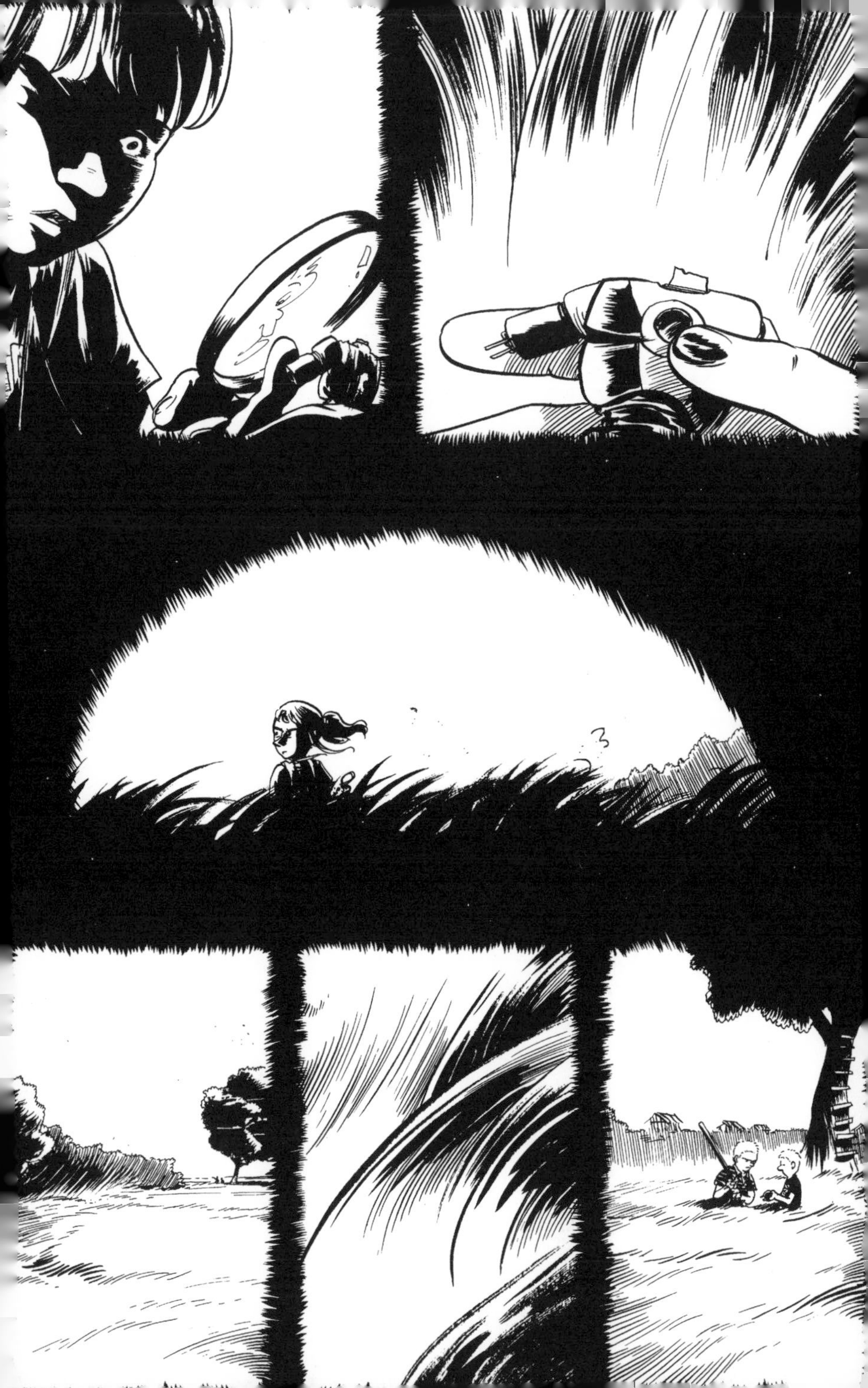

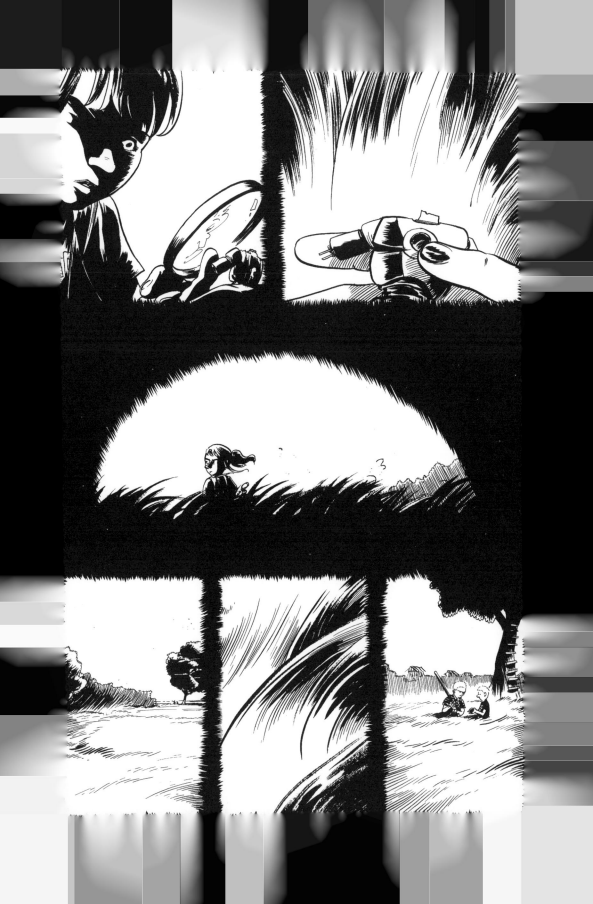

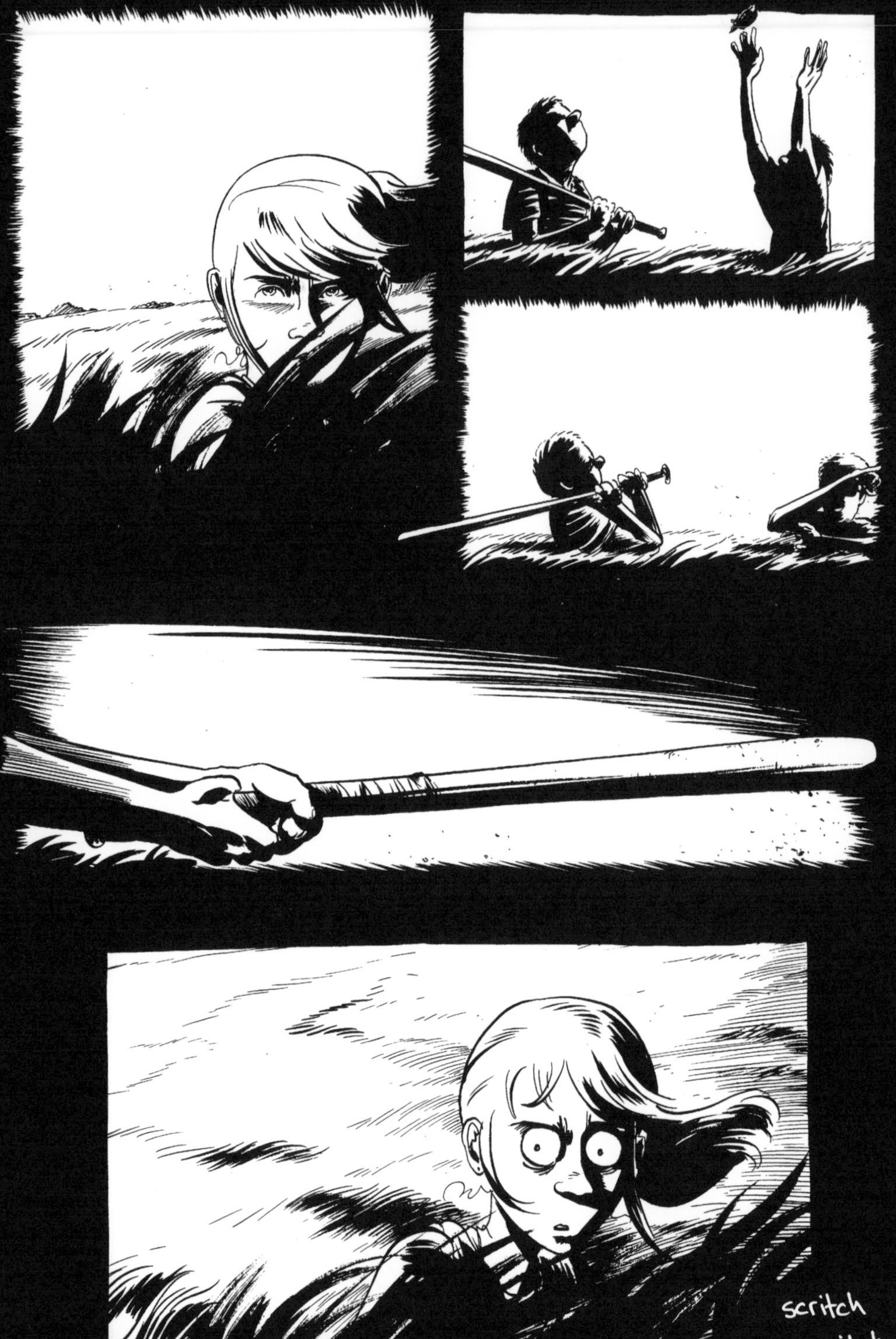
scritch
scritch

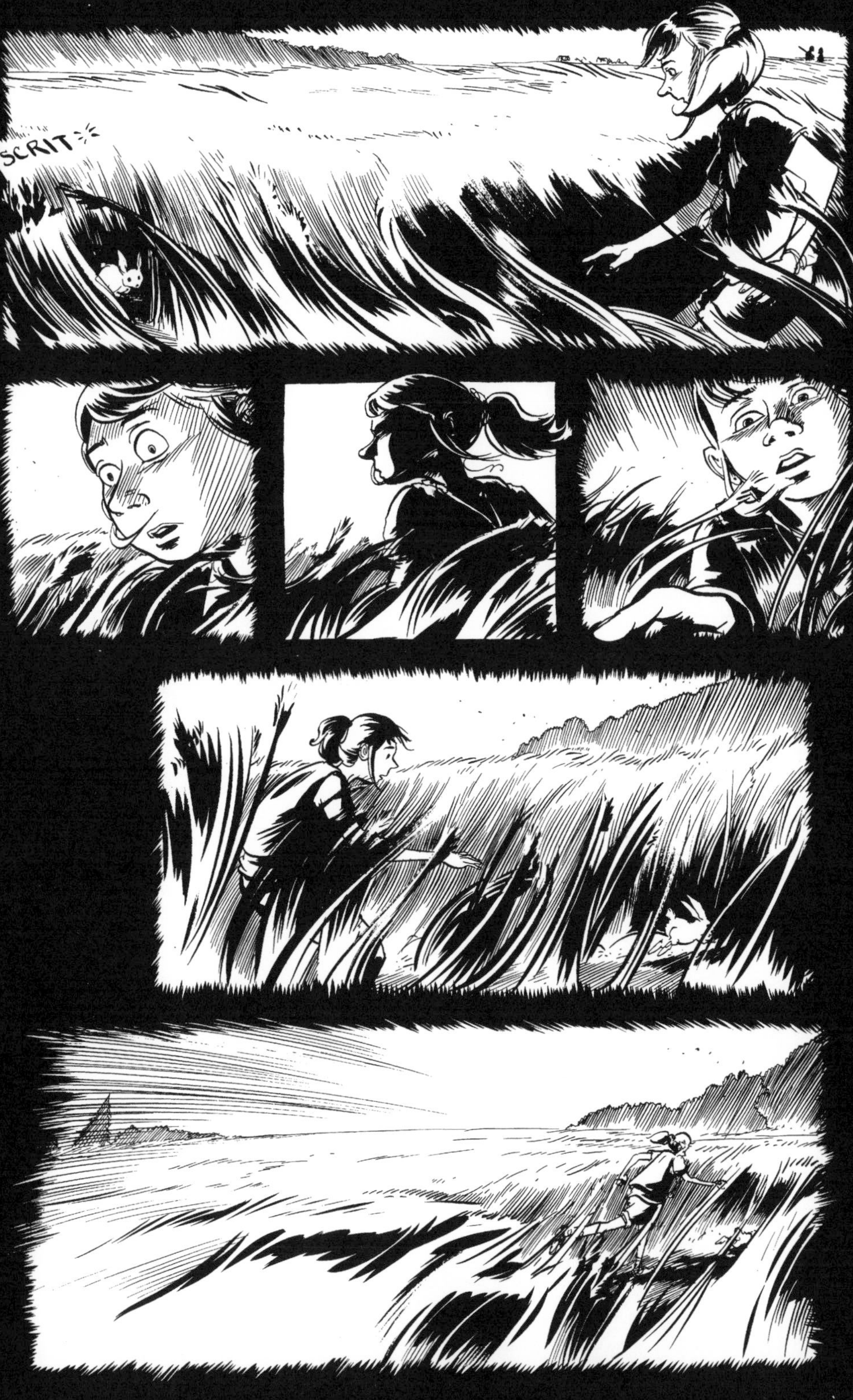
SCRIT

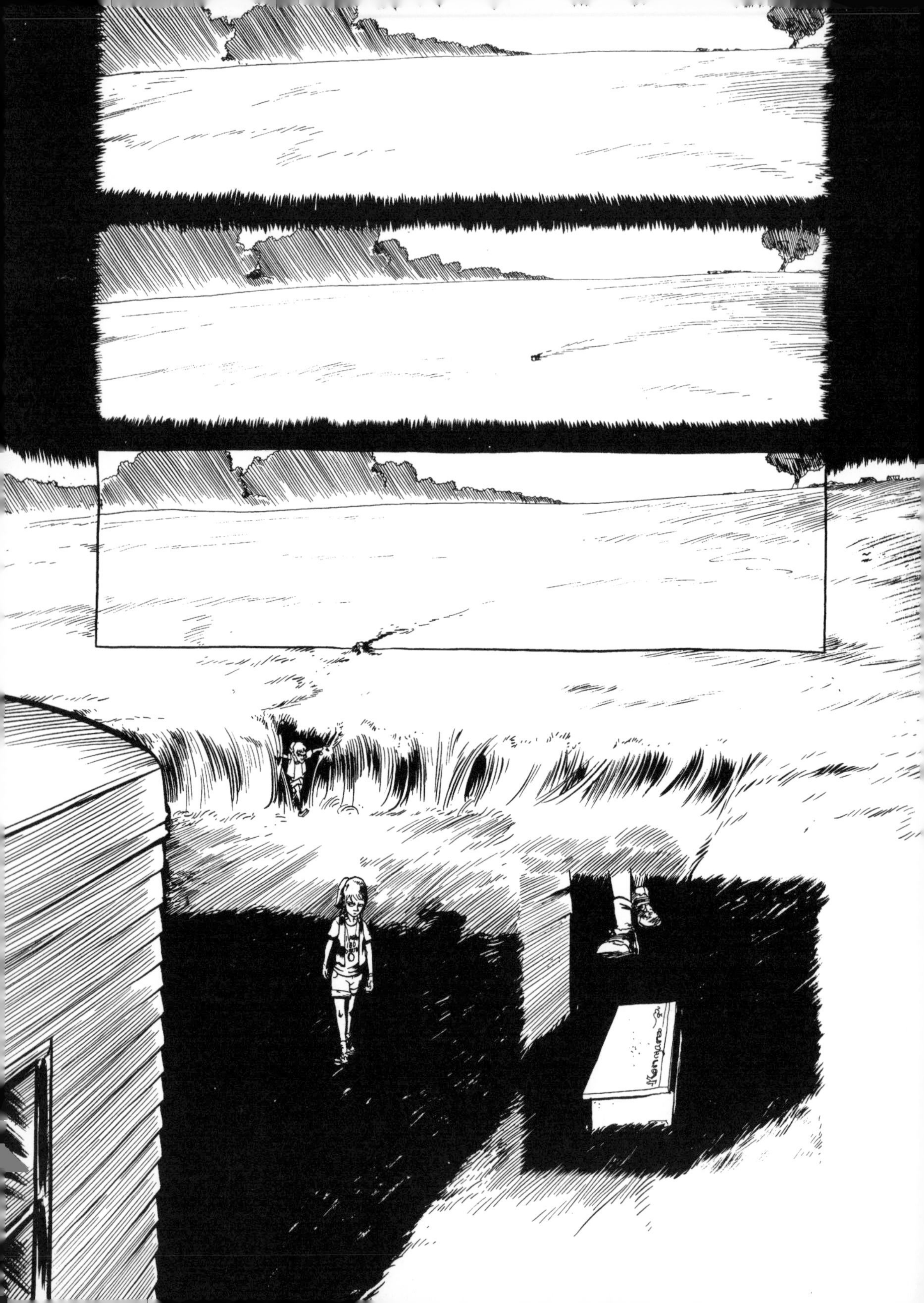

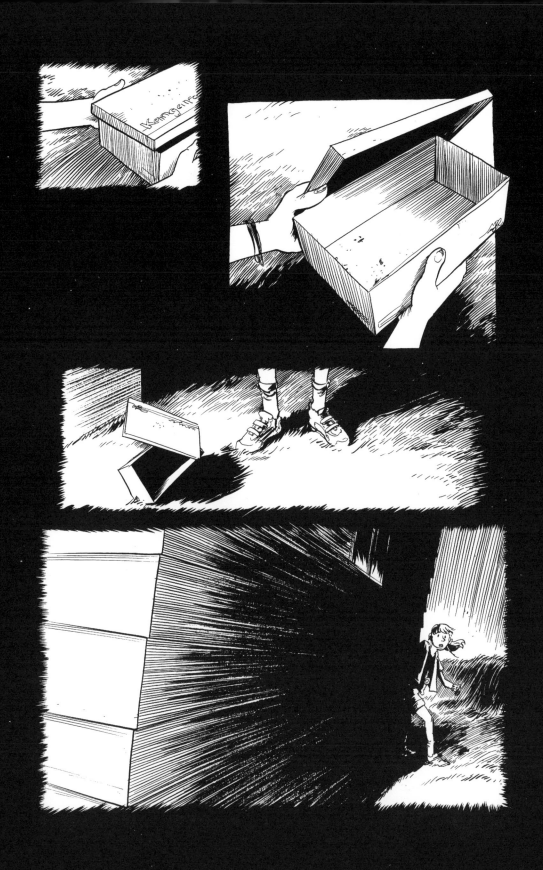

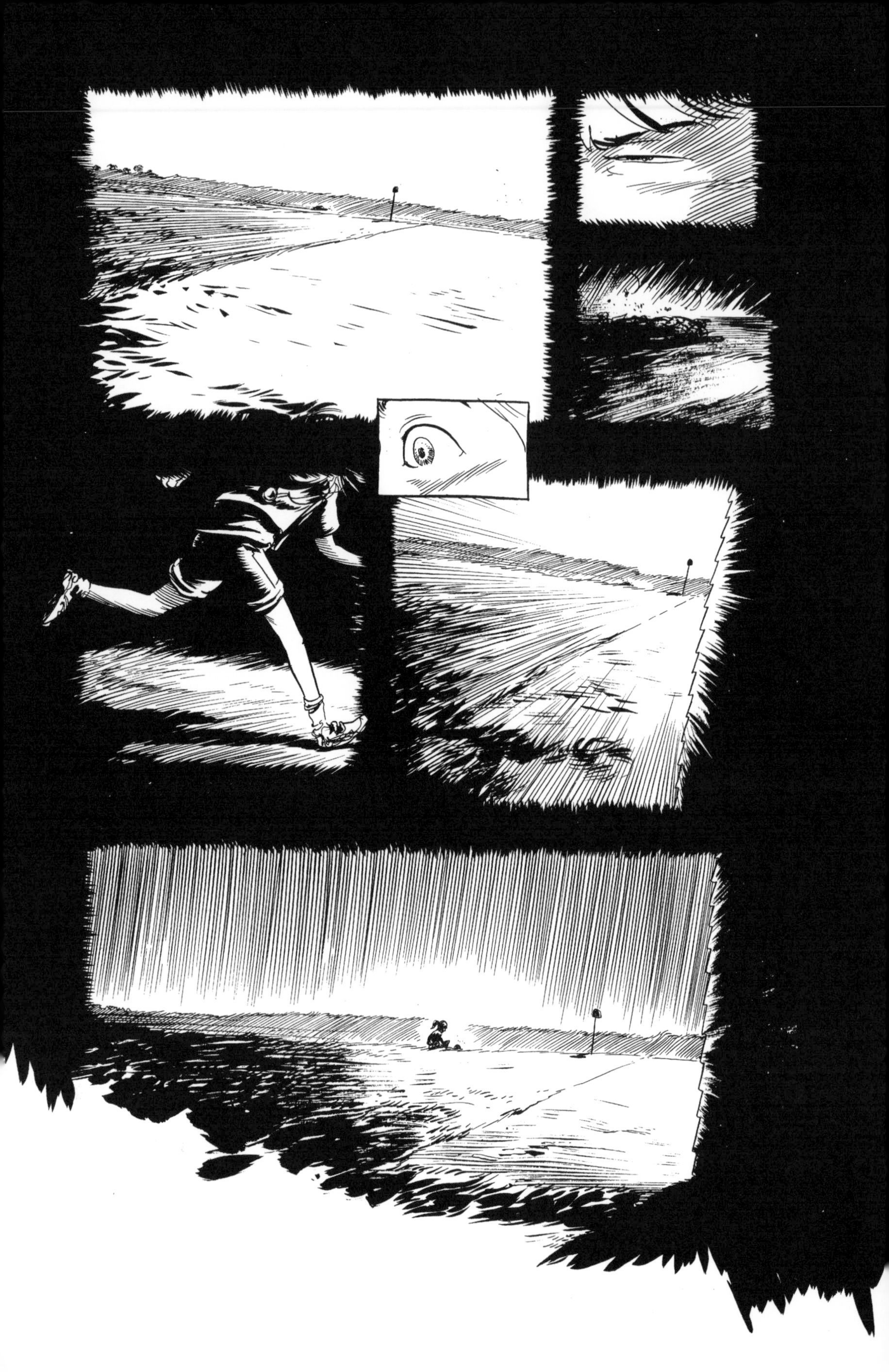

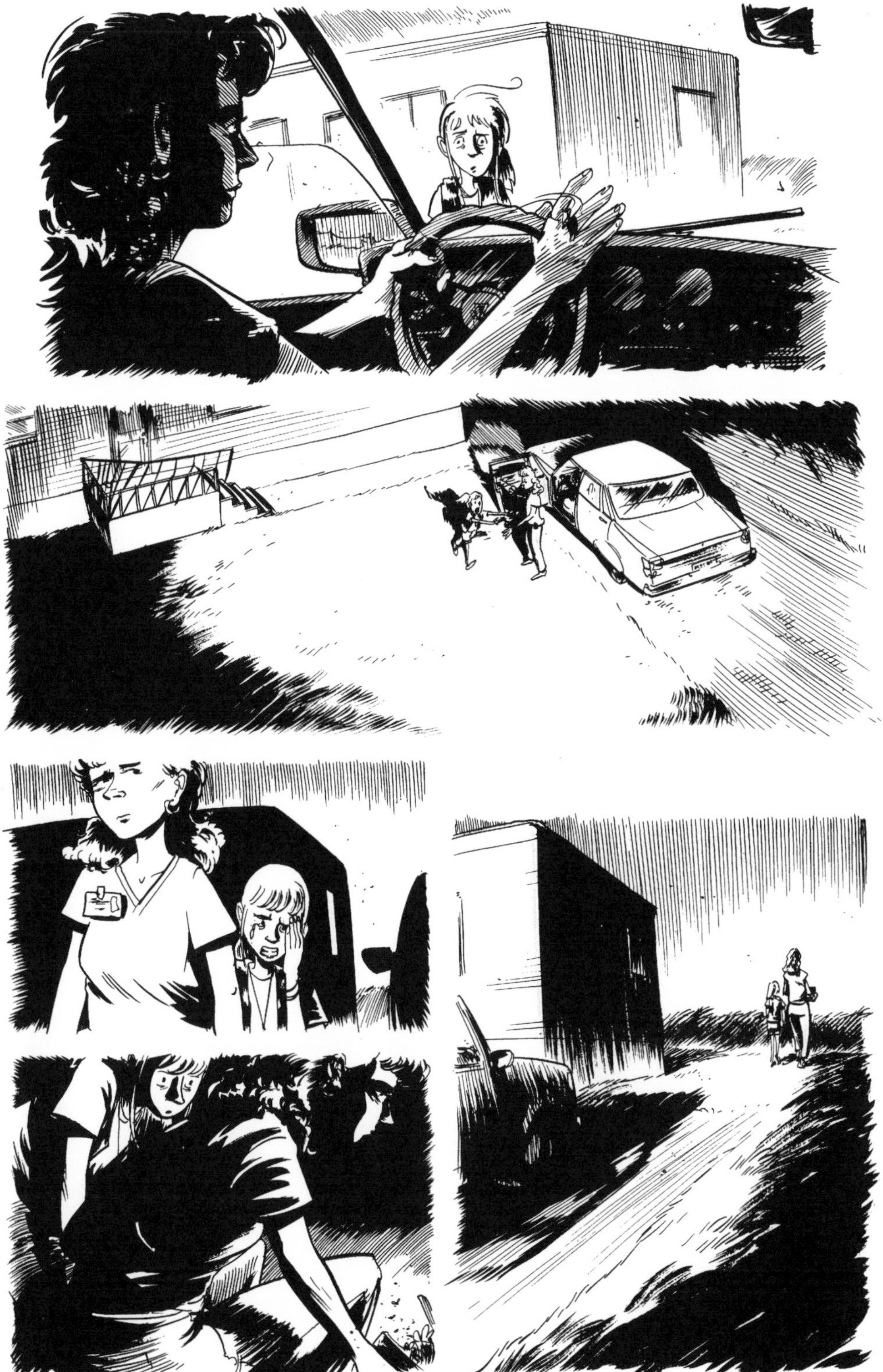

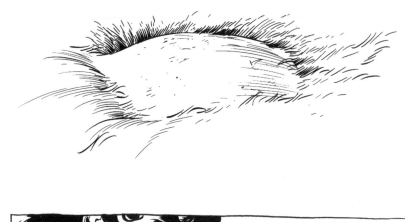

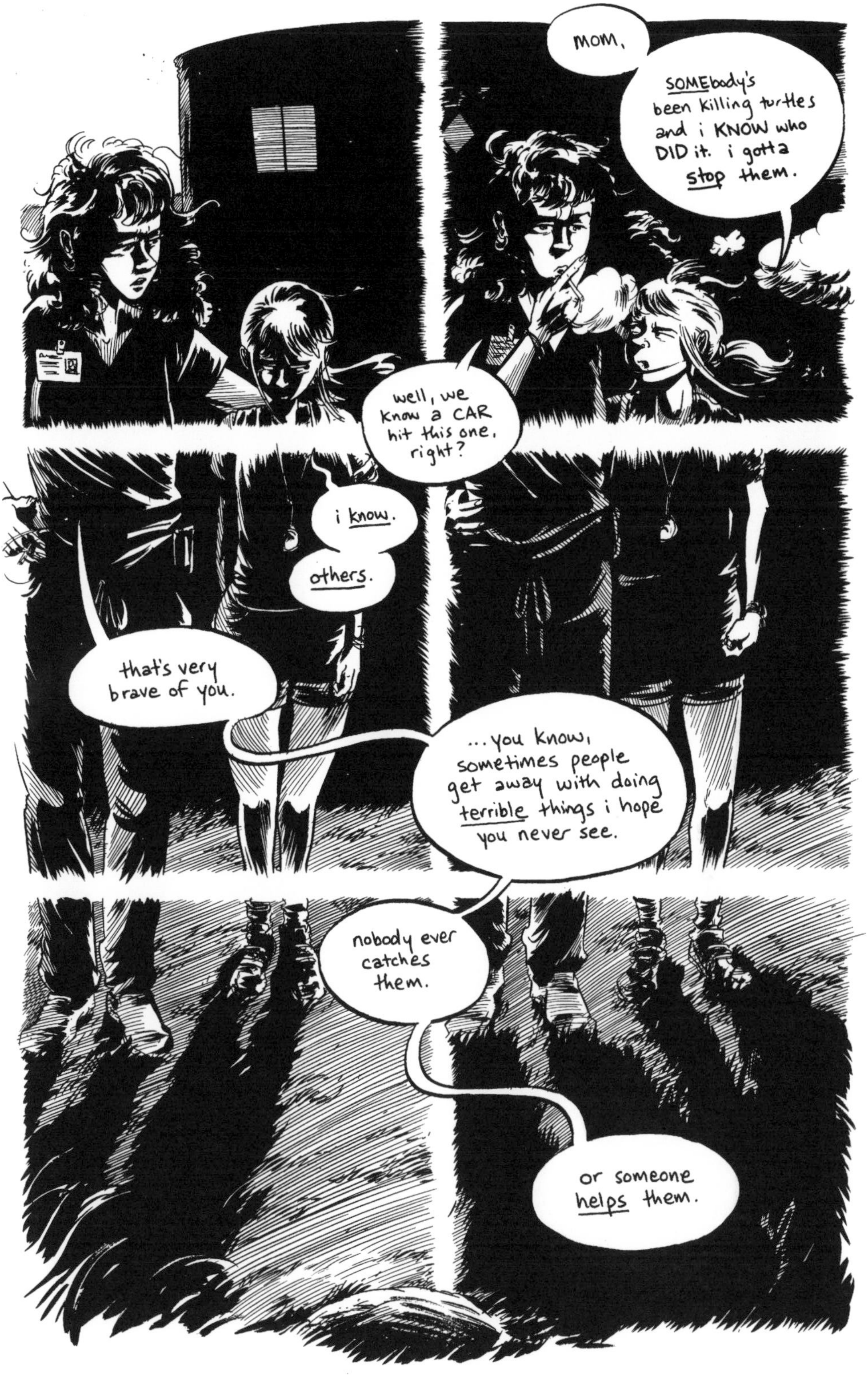

mom,
SOMEbody's been killing turtles and i KNOW who DID it. i gotta stop them.
well, we know a CAR hit this one, right?
i know.
others.
that's very brave of you.
...you know, sometimes people get away with doing terrible things i hope you never see.
nobody ever catches them.
or someone helps them.

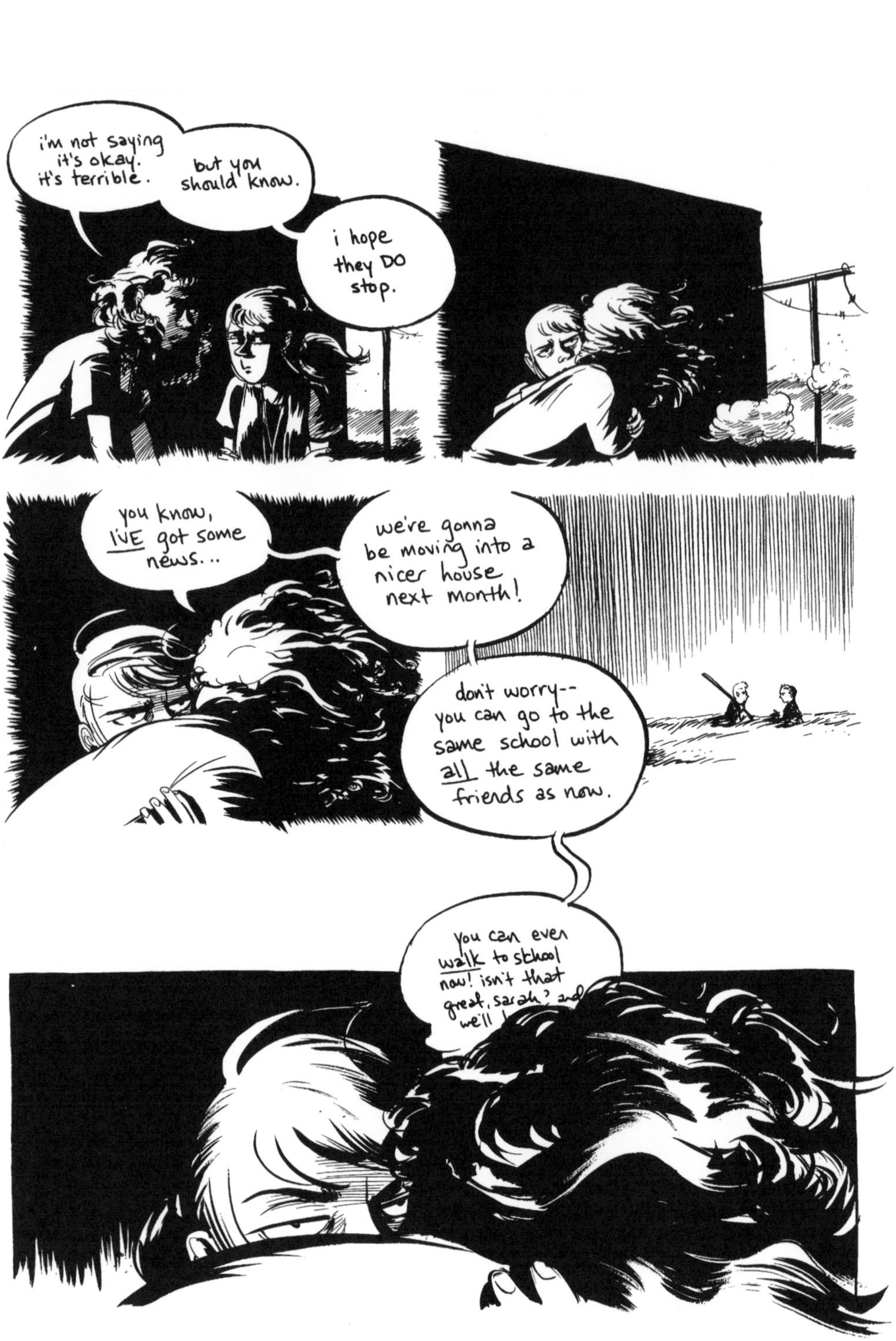
i'm not saying it's okay. it's terrible.
but you should know.
i hope they DO stop.
you know, I'VE got some news...
we're gonna be moving into a nicer house next month!
don't worry-- you can go to the same school with all the same friends as now.
you can even walk to school now! isn't that great, sarah? and we'll

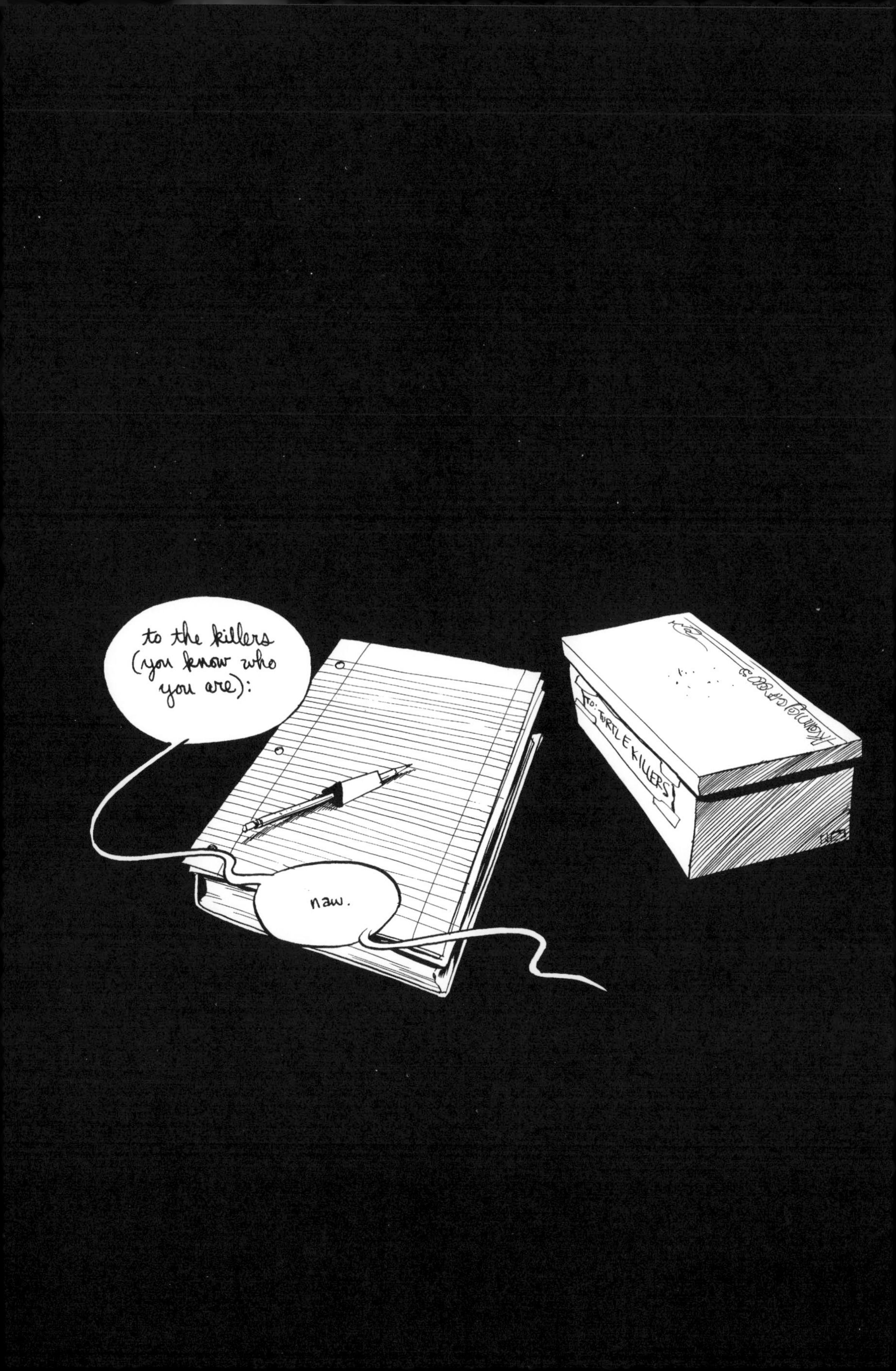
to the killers (you know who you are):
naw.
TO: TURTLE KILLERS

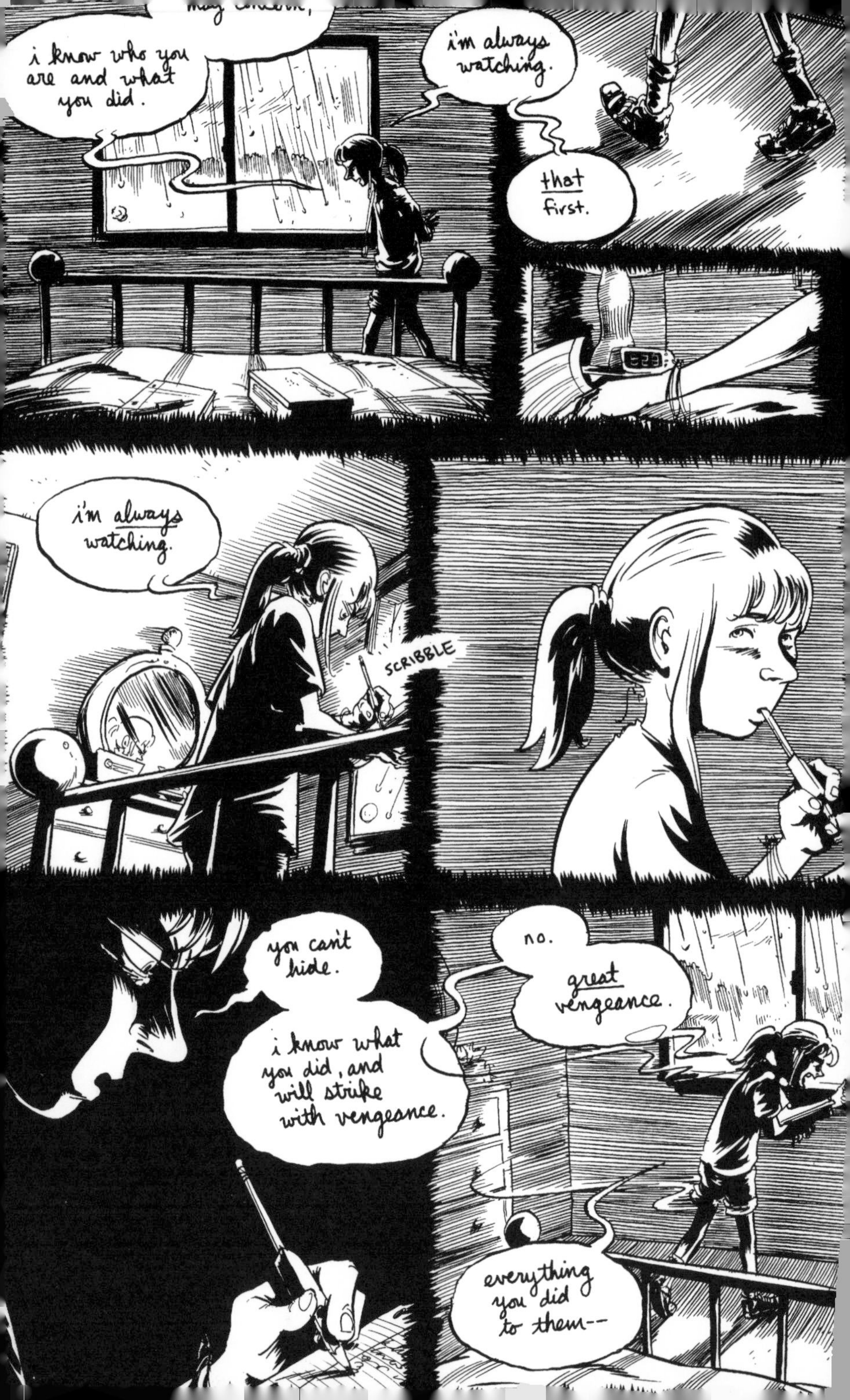
i know who you are and what you did.
i'm always watching.
that first.
i'm always watching.
SCRIBBLE
you can't hide.
i know what you did, and will strike with vengeance.
no.
great vengeance.
everything you did to them--

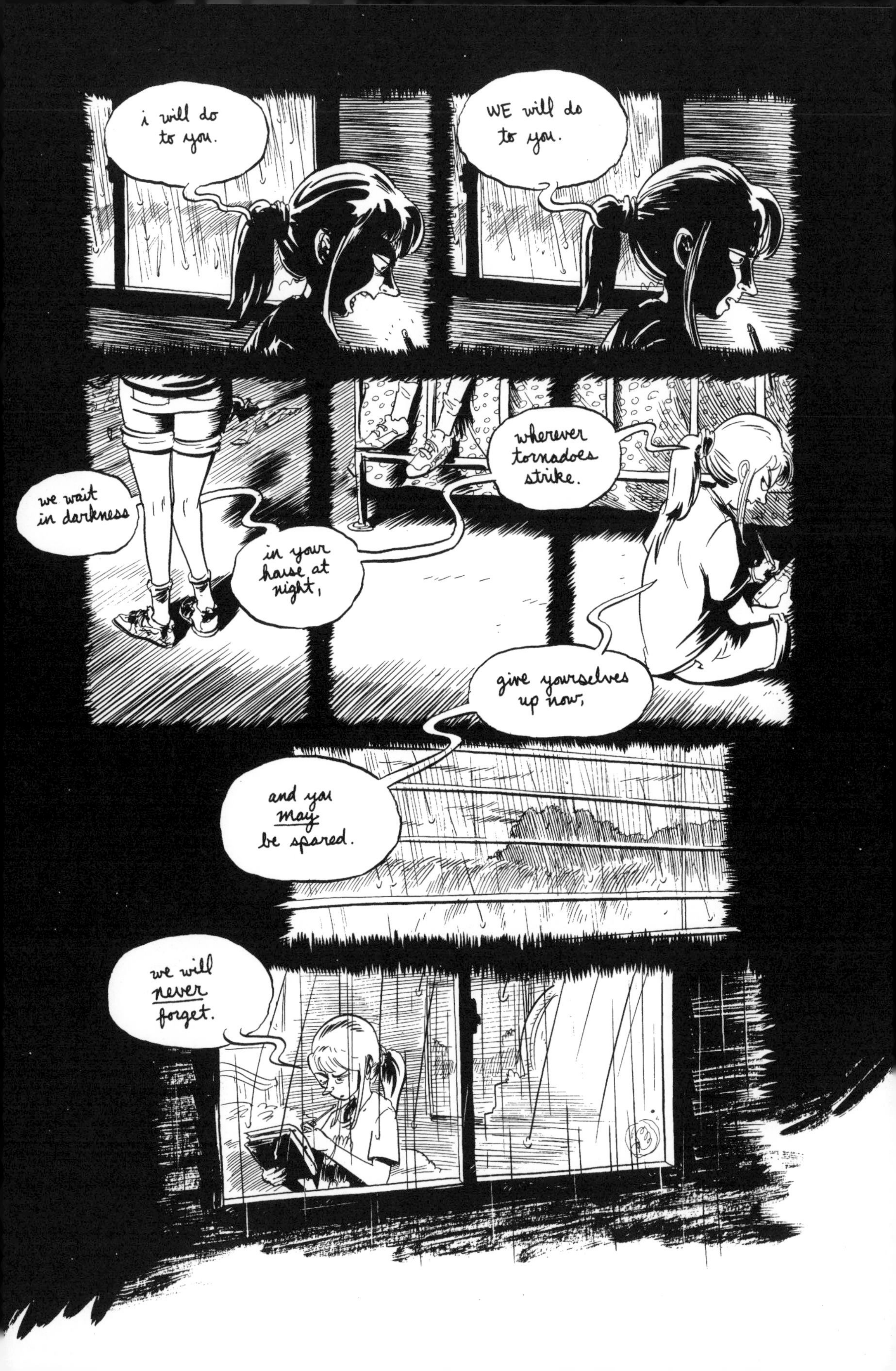
i will do to you.
WE will do to you.
we wait in darkness
in your house at night,
wherever tornadoes strike.
give yourselves up now,
and you may be spared.
we will never forget.

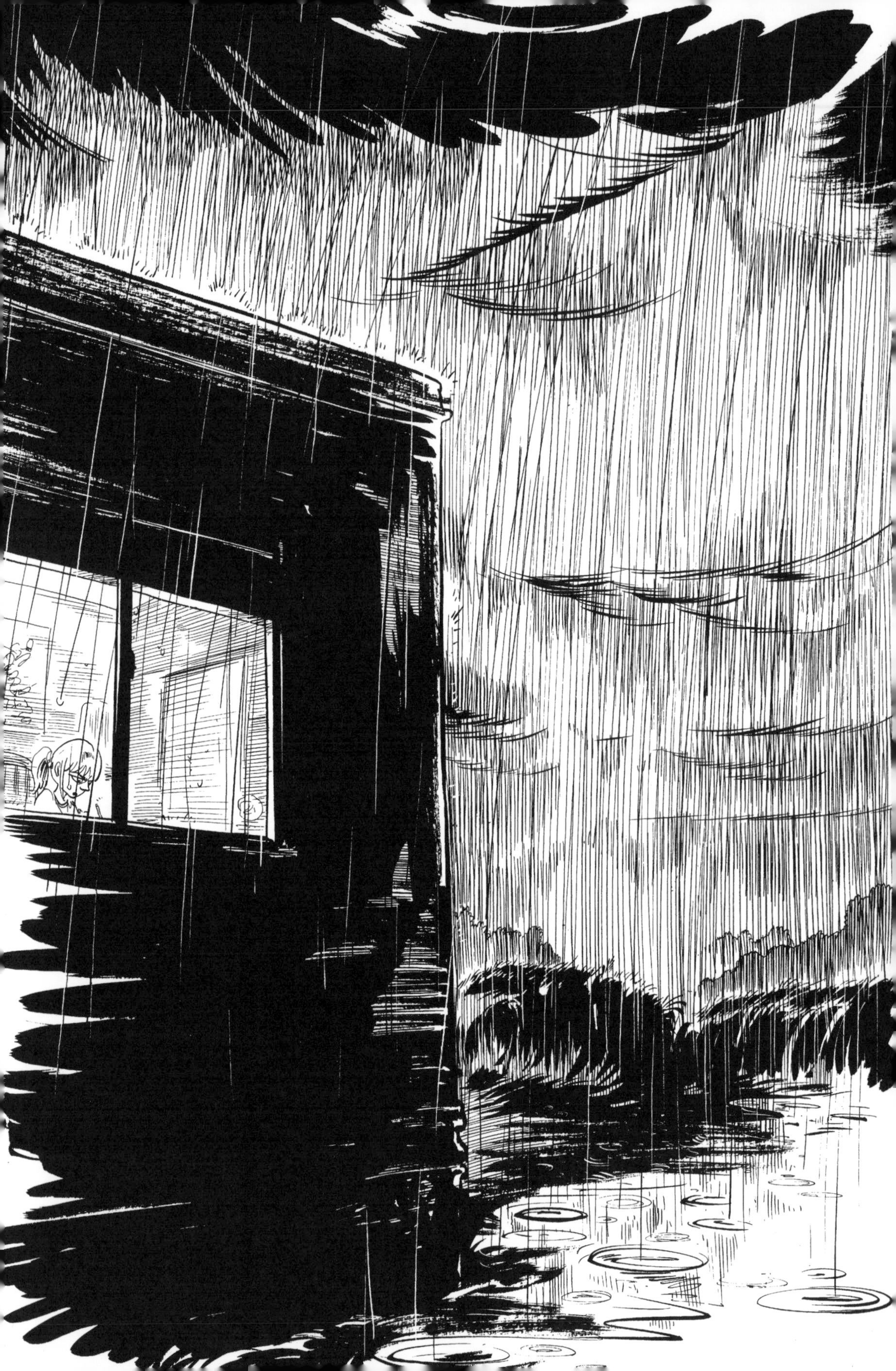

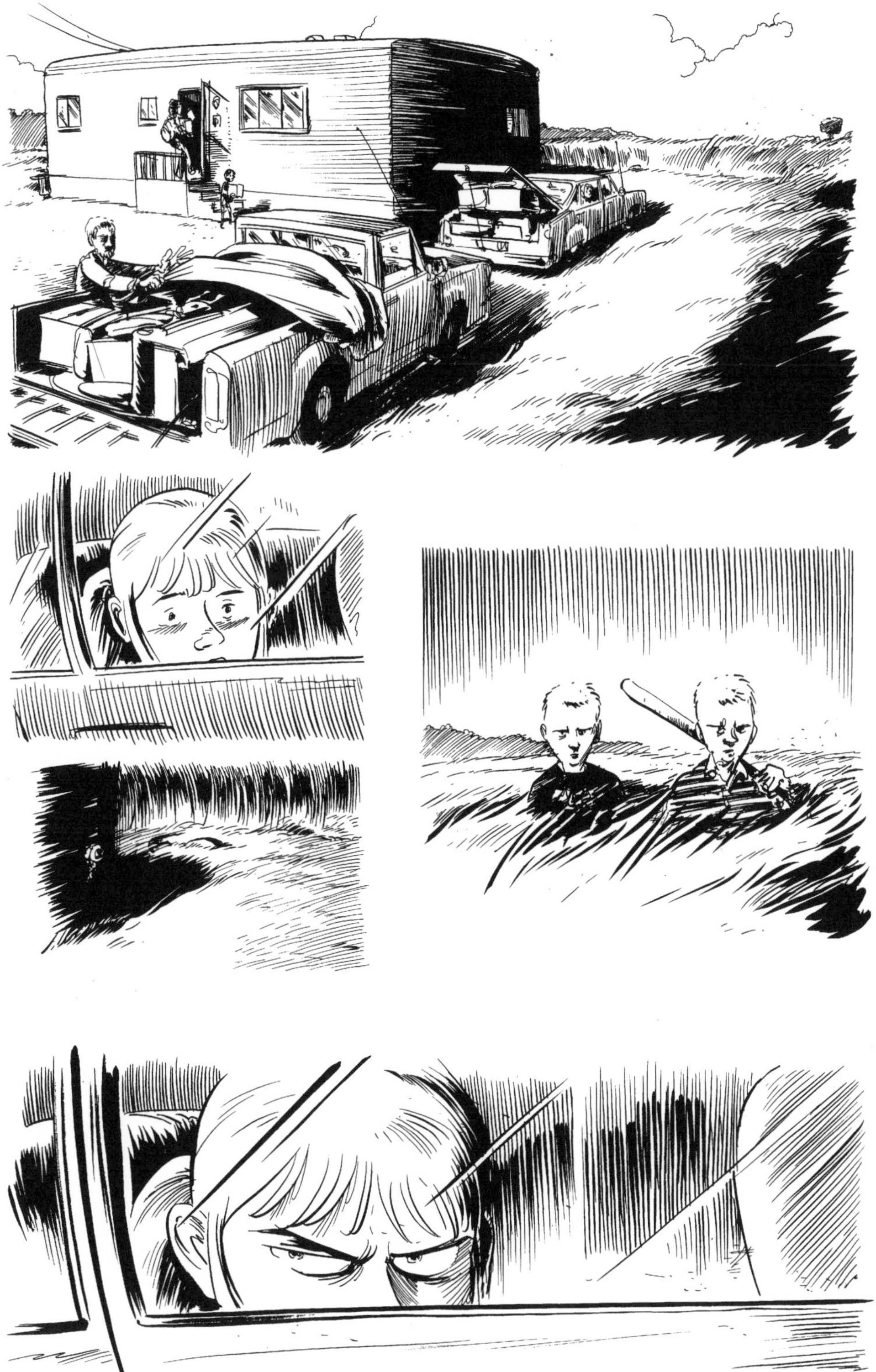

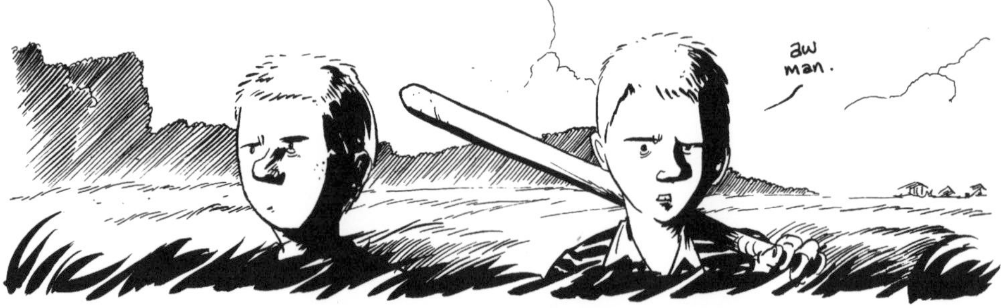
aw man.

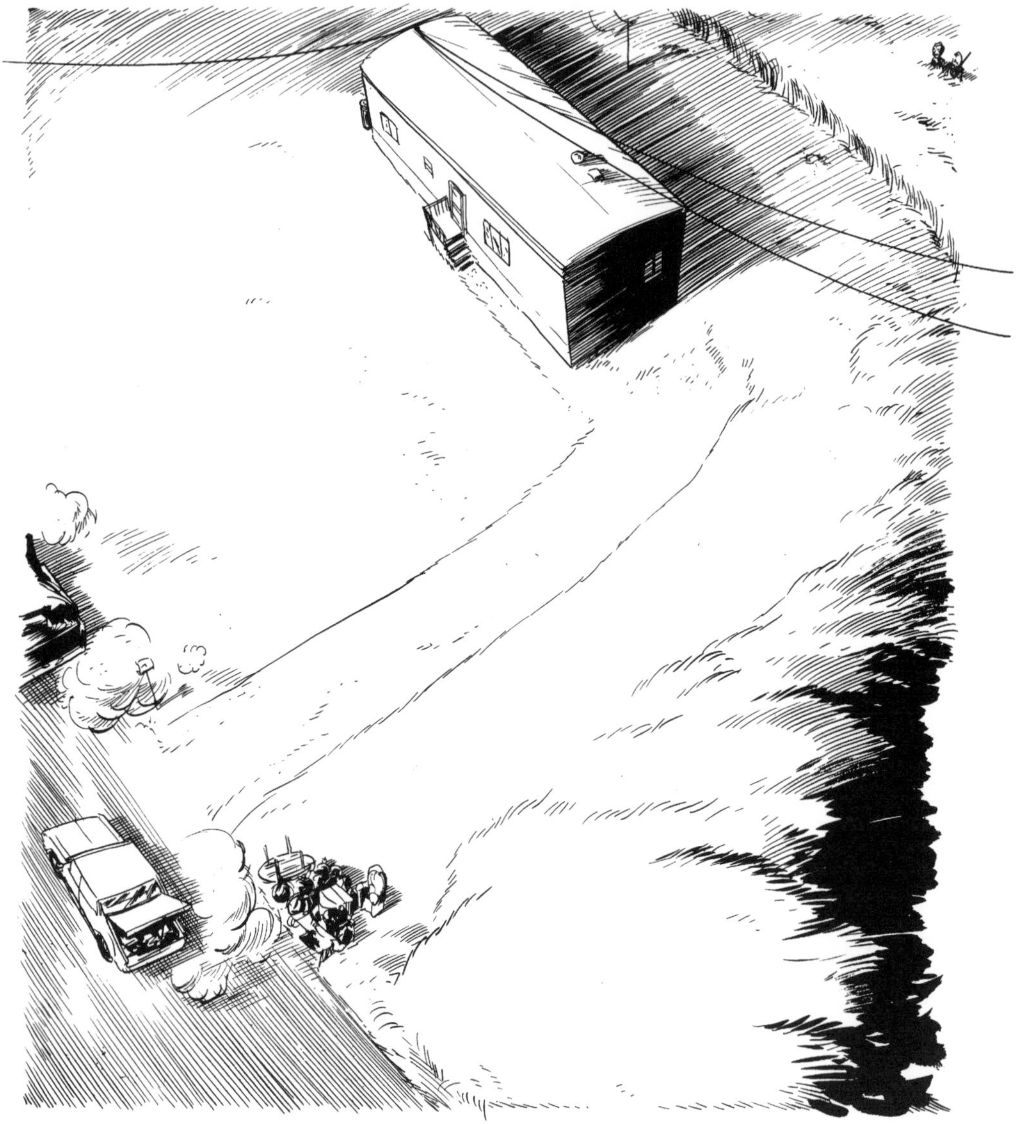

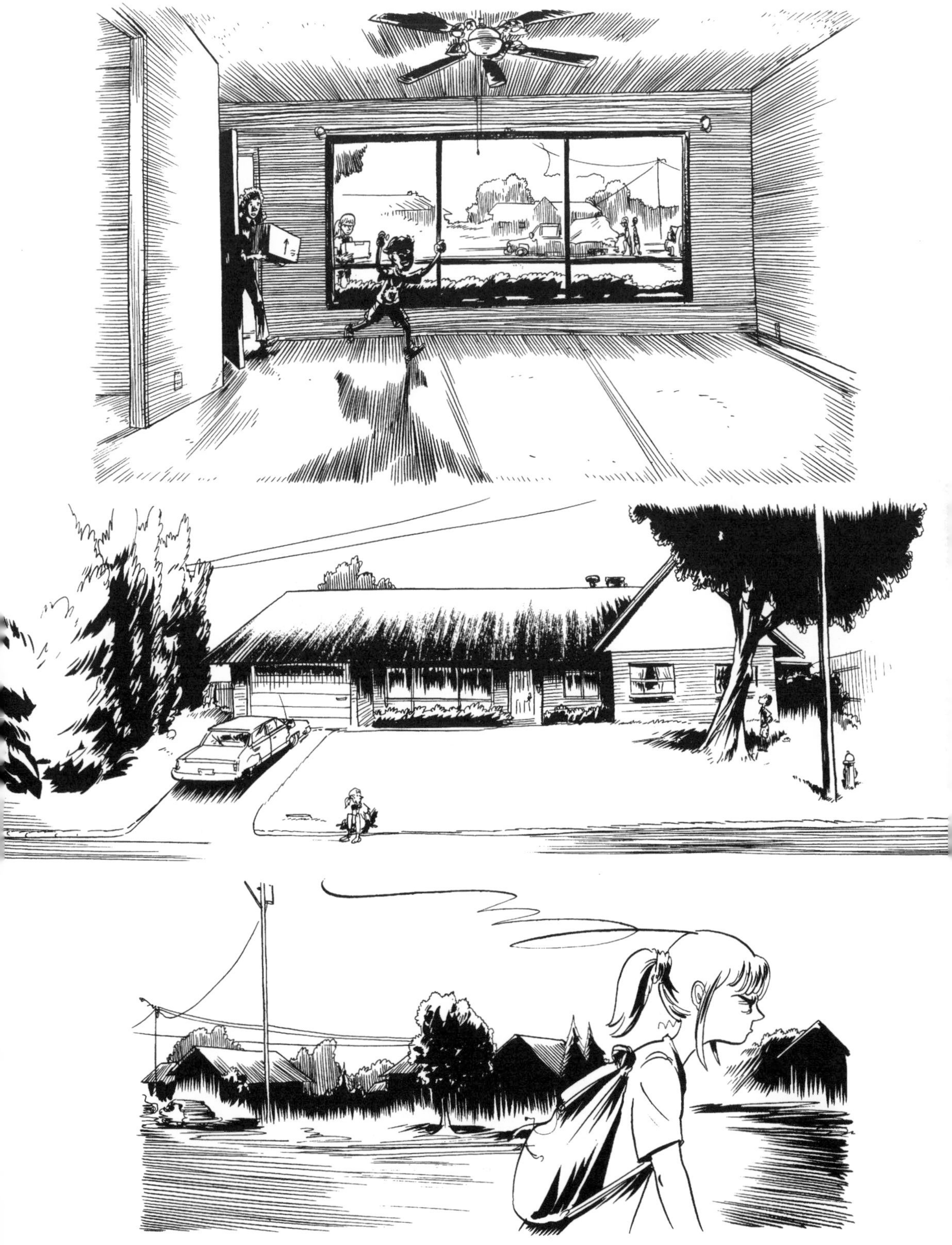

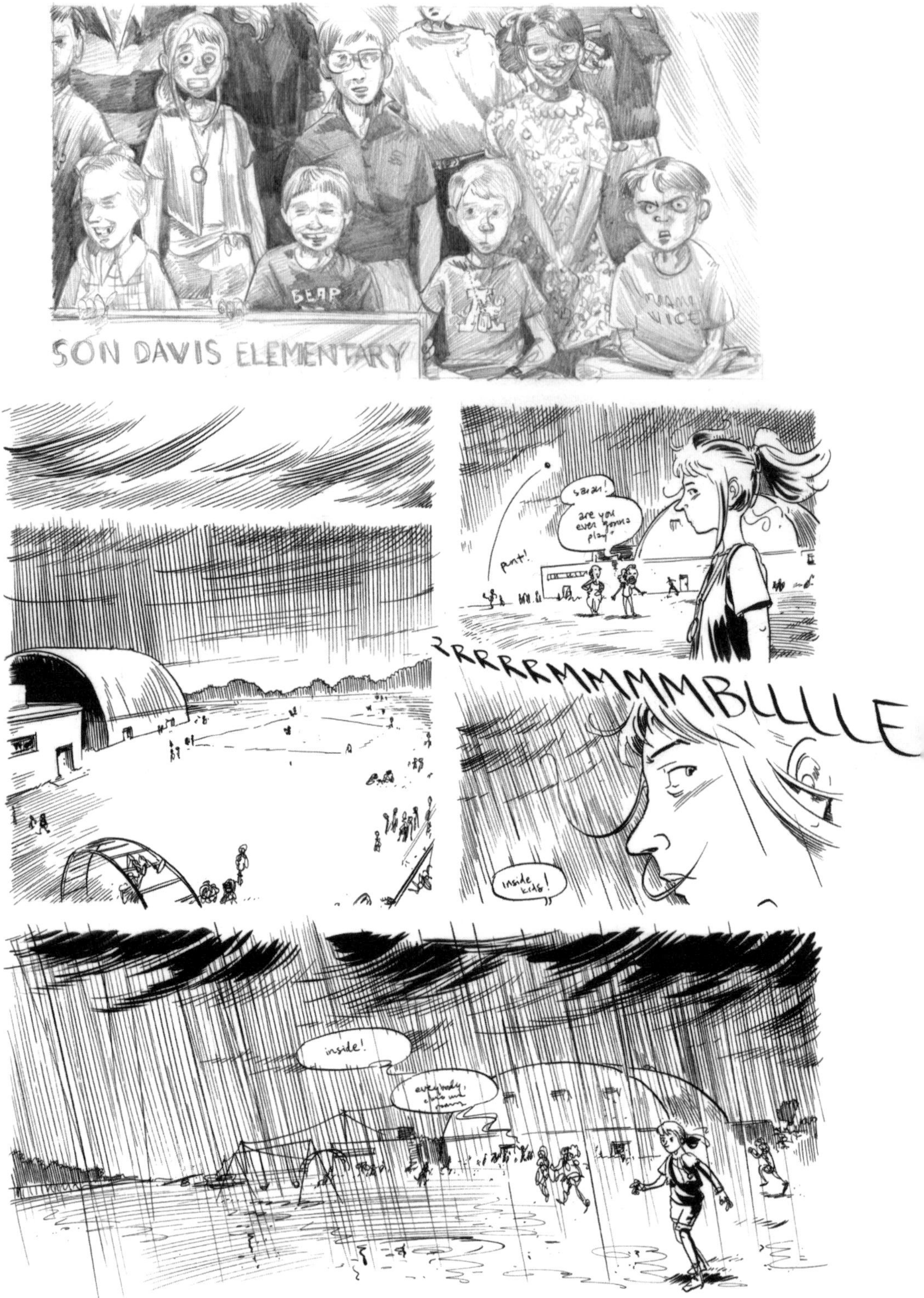
SON DAVIS ELEMENTARY
BEAR
MIAMI VICE
sarah!
are you ever gonna play?
punt!
RRRRRMMMMBLLLLE
inside kids!
inside!
everybody,

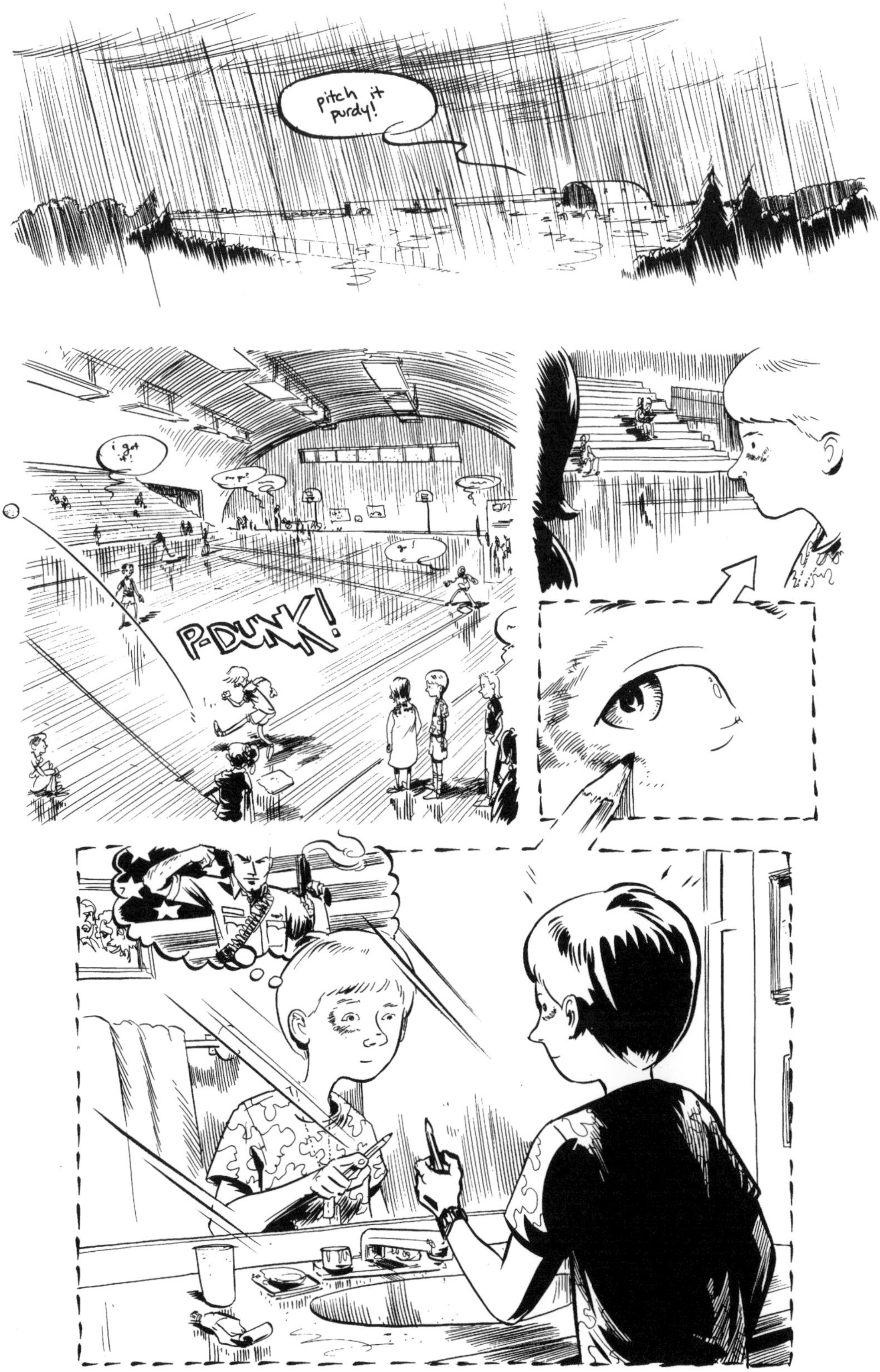
pitch it purdy!
i got it!
P-DUNK!

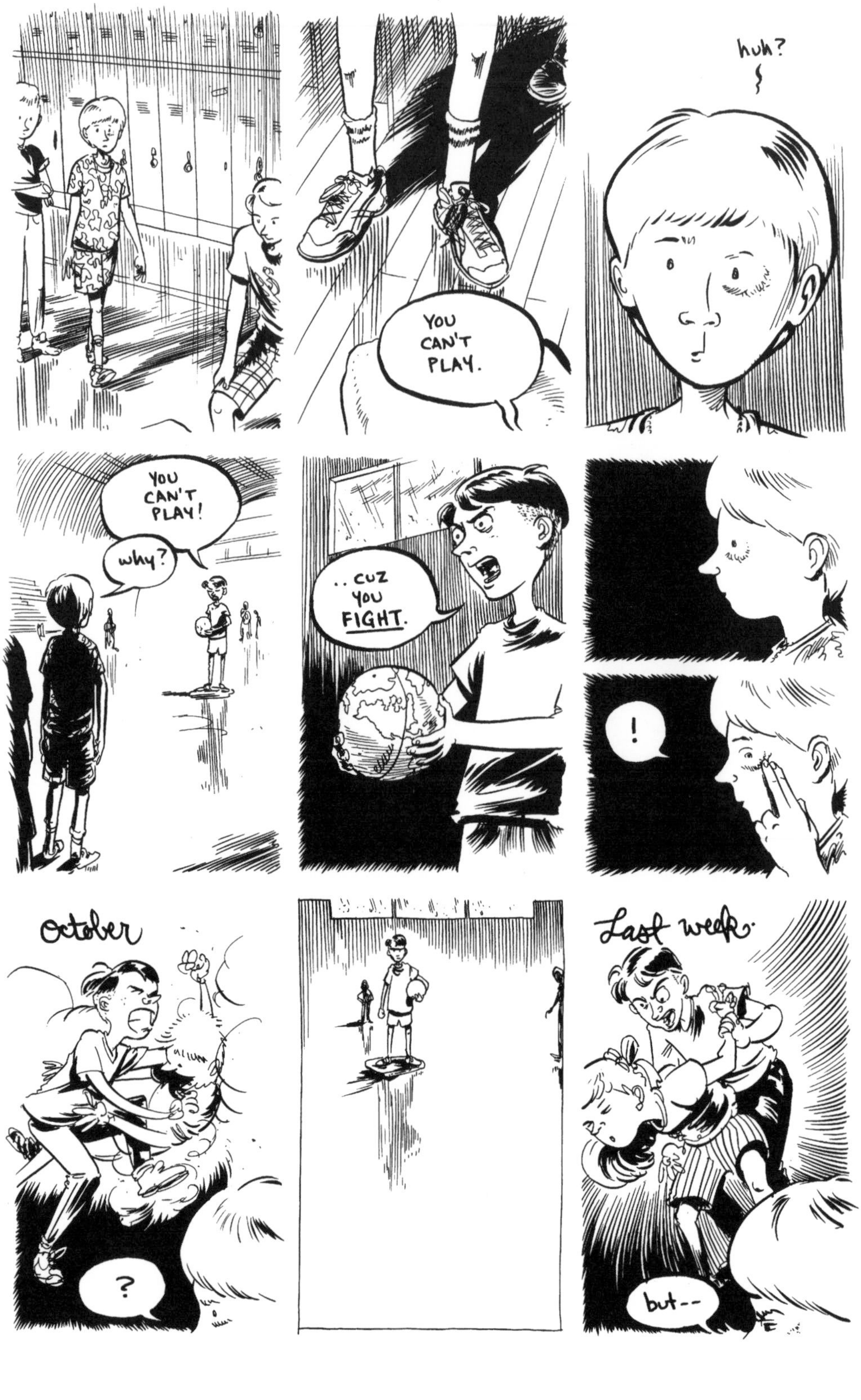
YOU CAN'T PLAY.
huh?
YOU CAN'T PLAY!
why?
..CUZ YOU FIGHT.
!
October
?
Last week.
but--

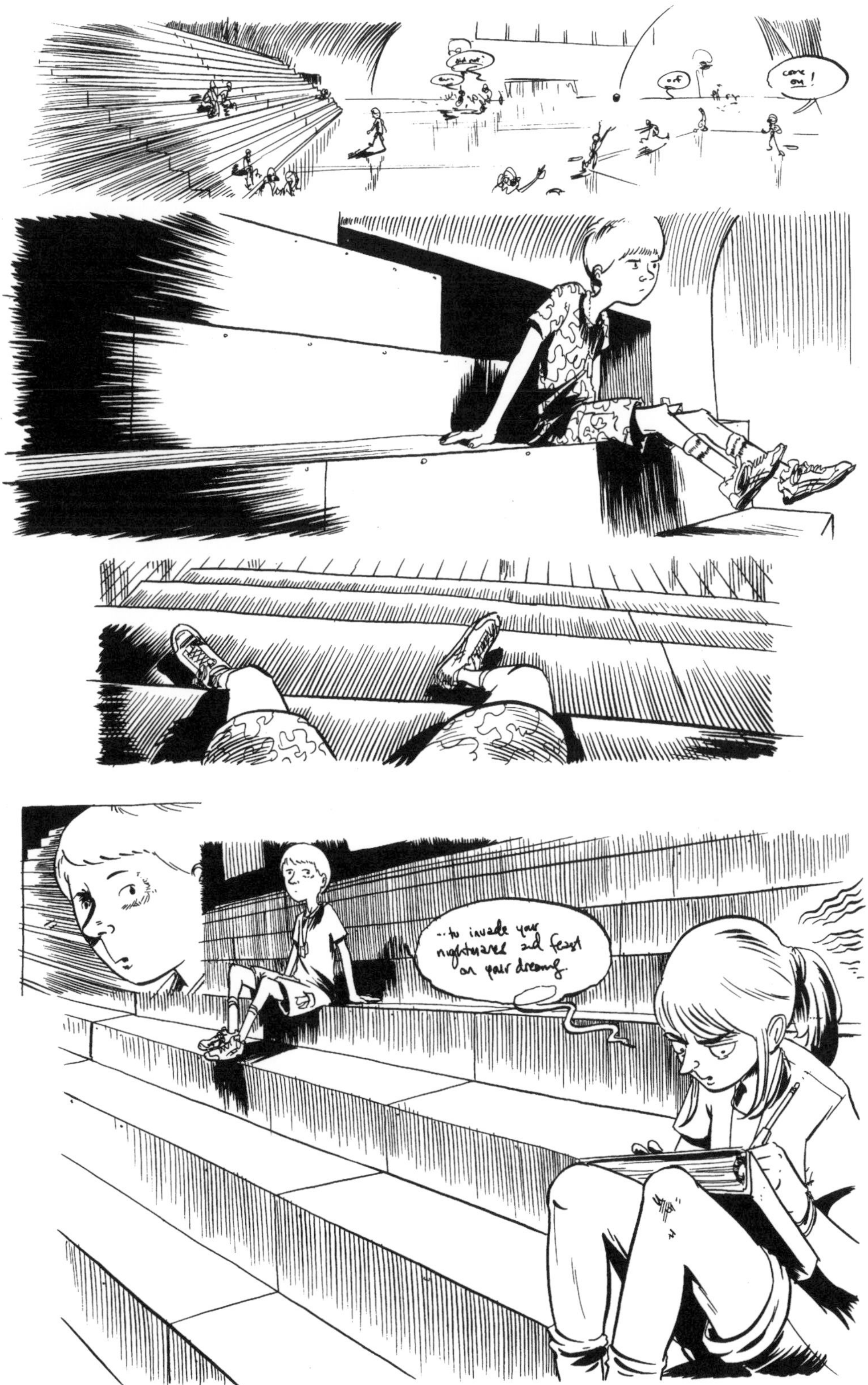
come on!
...to invade your nightmares and feast on your dreams.

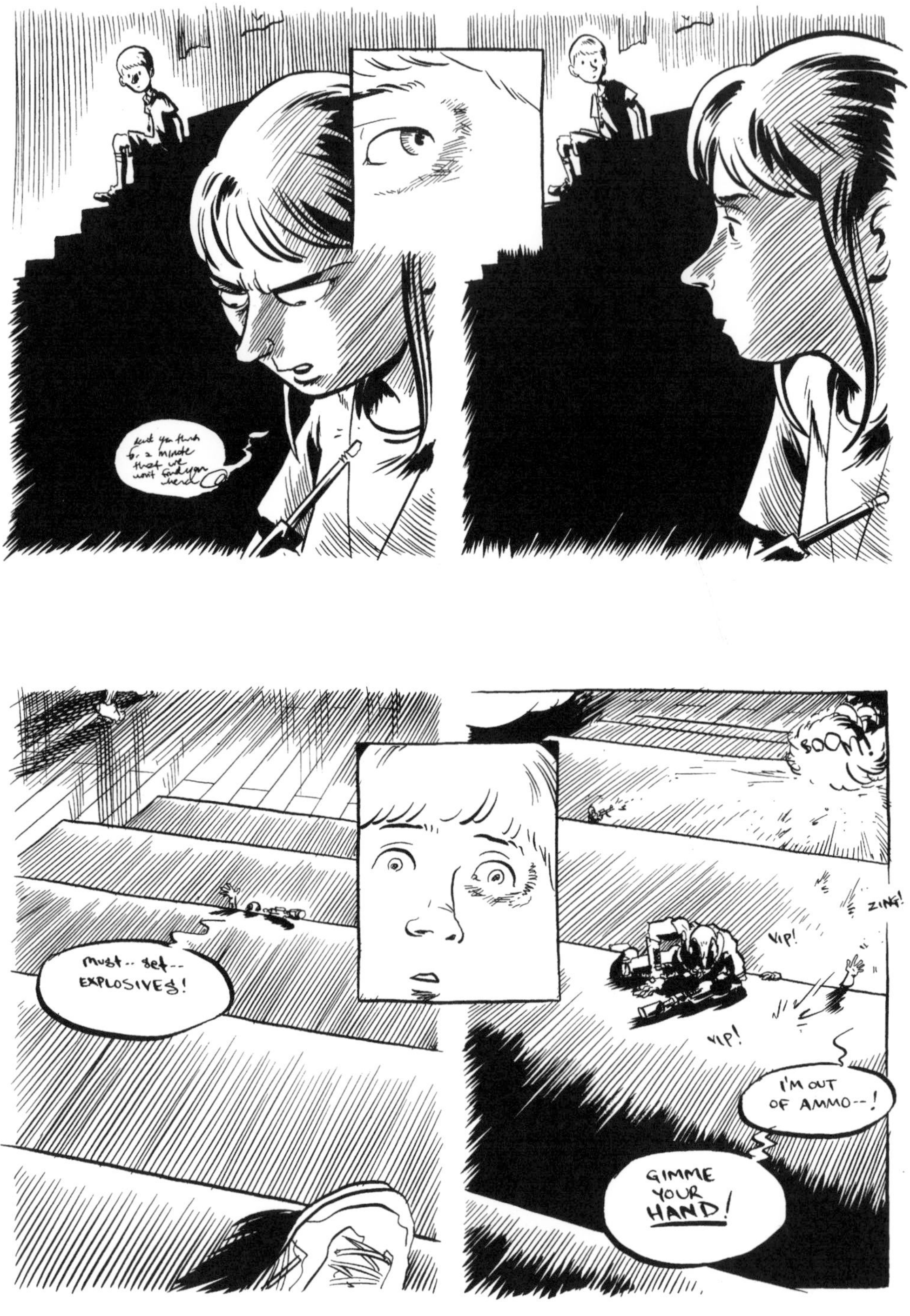
must-- set-- EXPLOSIVES!
BOOM!
ZING!
YIP!
YIP!
I'M OUT OF AMMO--!
GIMME YOUR HAND!

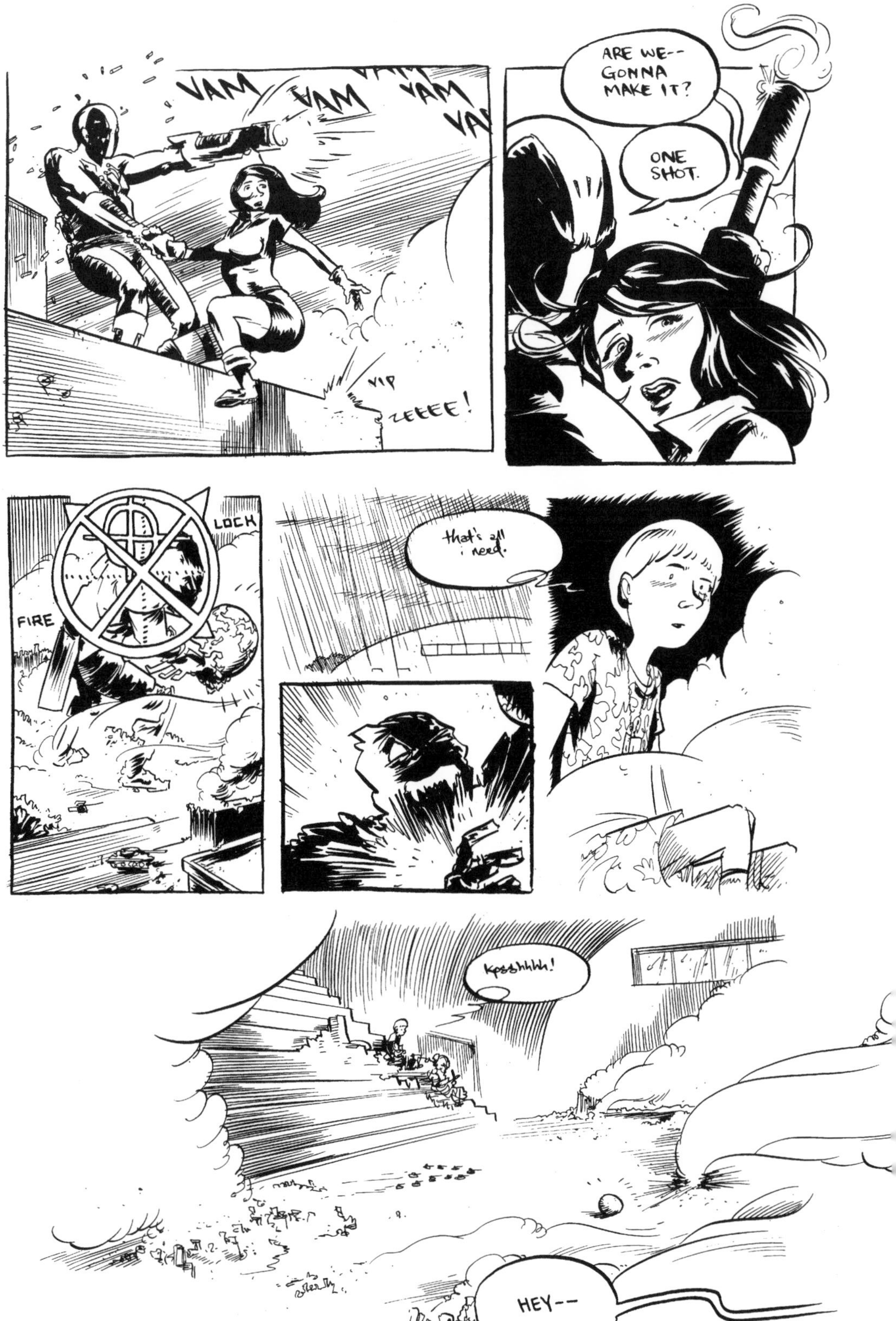
VAM
VAM
VAM
VAM
VIP
ZEEEE!
ARE WE--
GONNA
MAKE IT?
ONE
SHOT.
LOCK
FIRE
that's all
i need.
Kpssshhhh!
HEY--

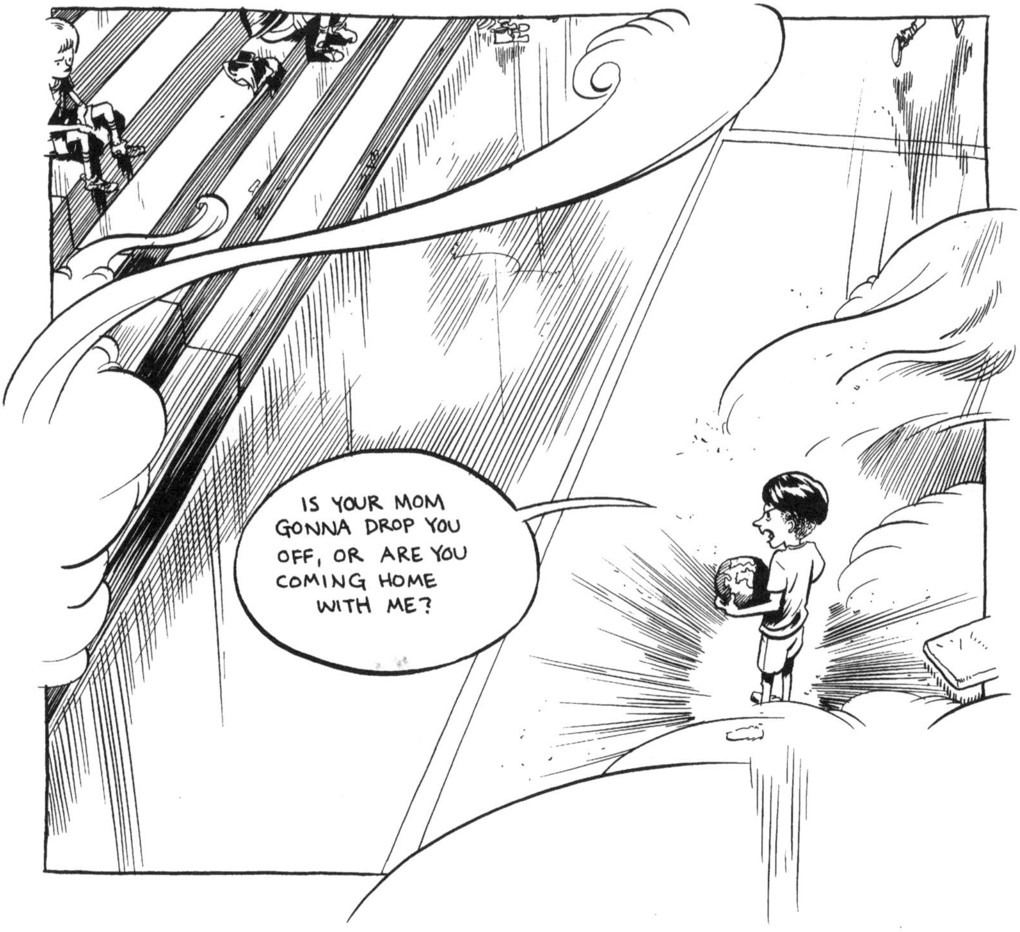
IS YOUR MOM GONNA DROP YOU OFF, OR ARE YOU COMING HOME WITH ME?

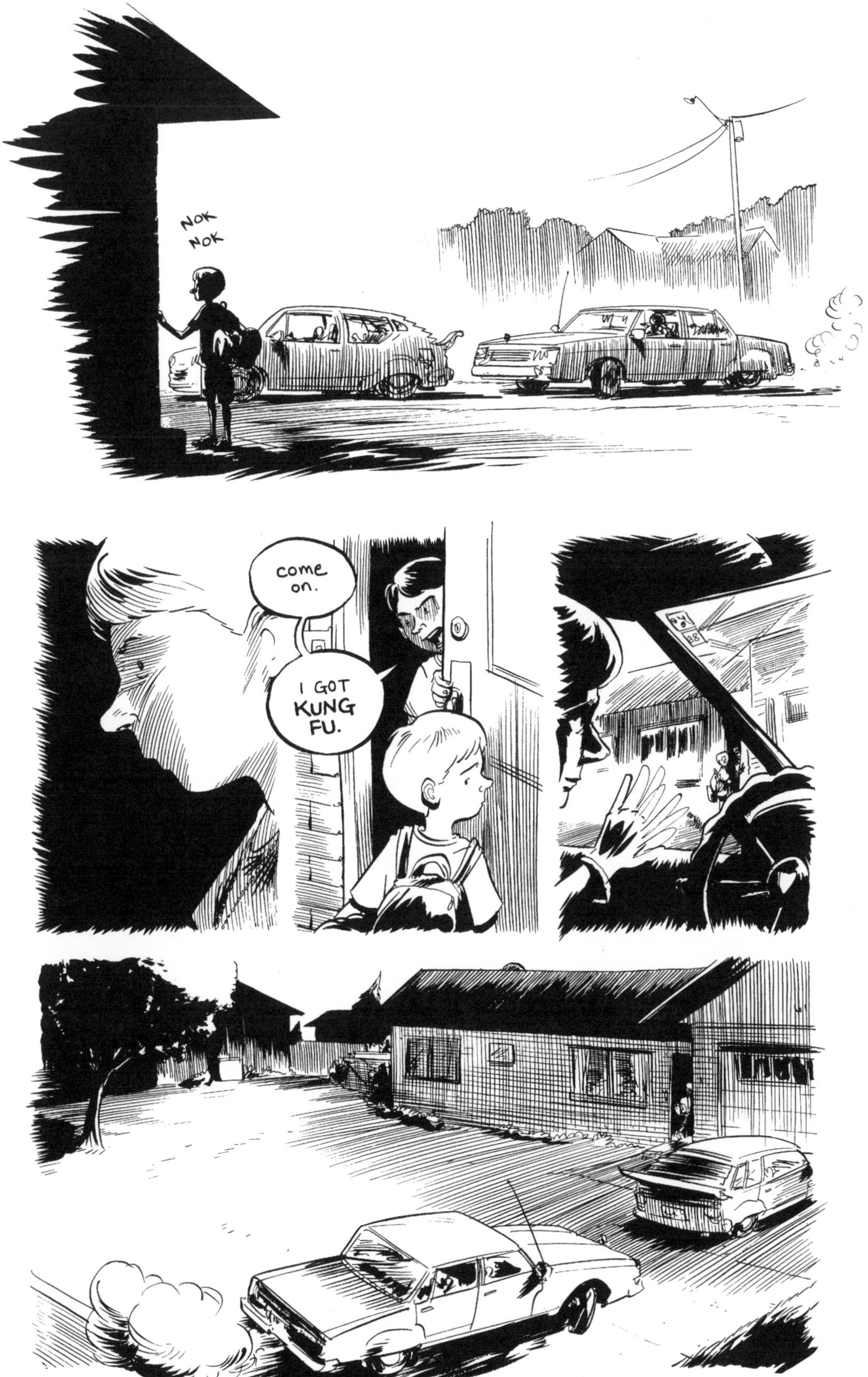
NOK
NOK
come on.
I GOT KUNG FU.

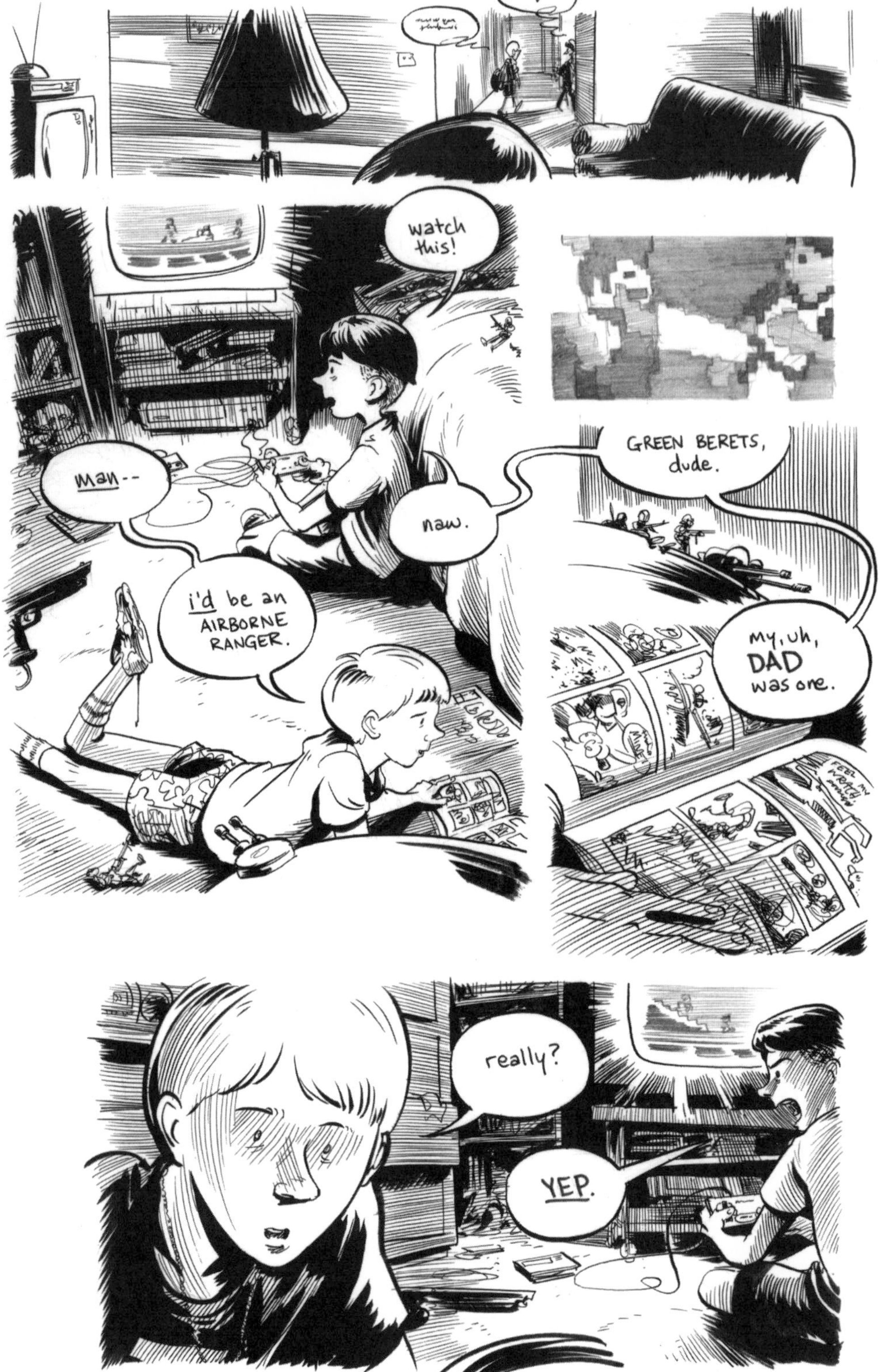
watch this!
man--
naw.
GREEN BERETS, dude.
i'd be an AIRBORNE RANGER.
my, uh, DAD was one.
really?
YEP.

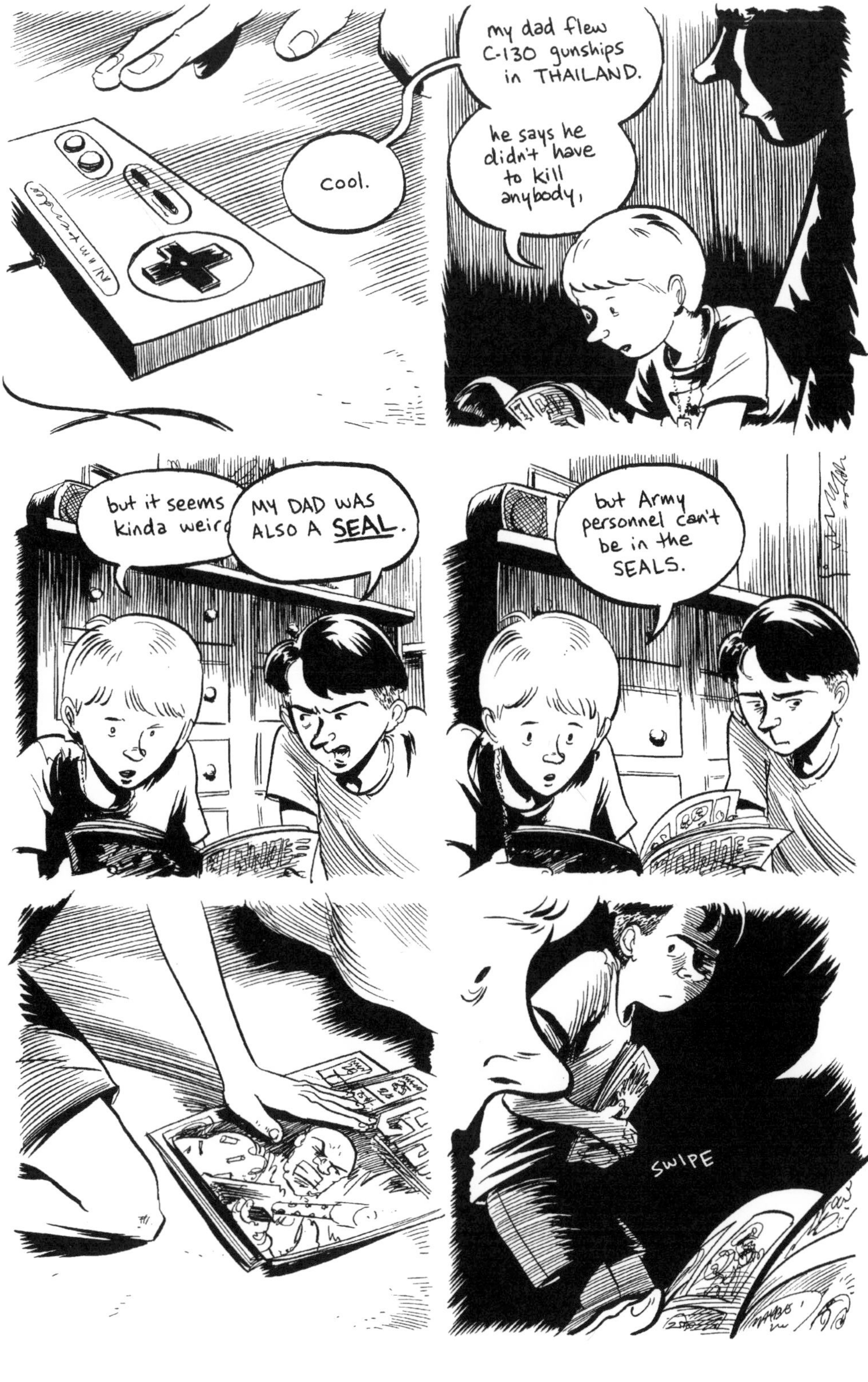

cool.
my dad flew C-130 gunships in THAILAND.
he says he didn't have to kill anybody,
but it seems kinda weird
MY DAD WAS ALSO A SEAL.
but Army personnel can't be in the SEALS.
SWIPE

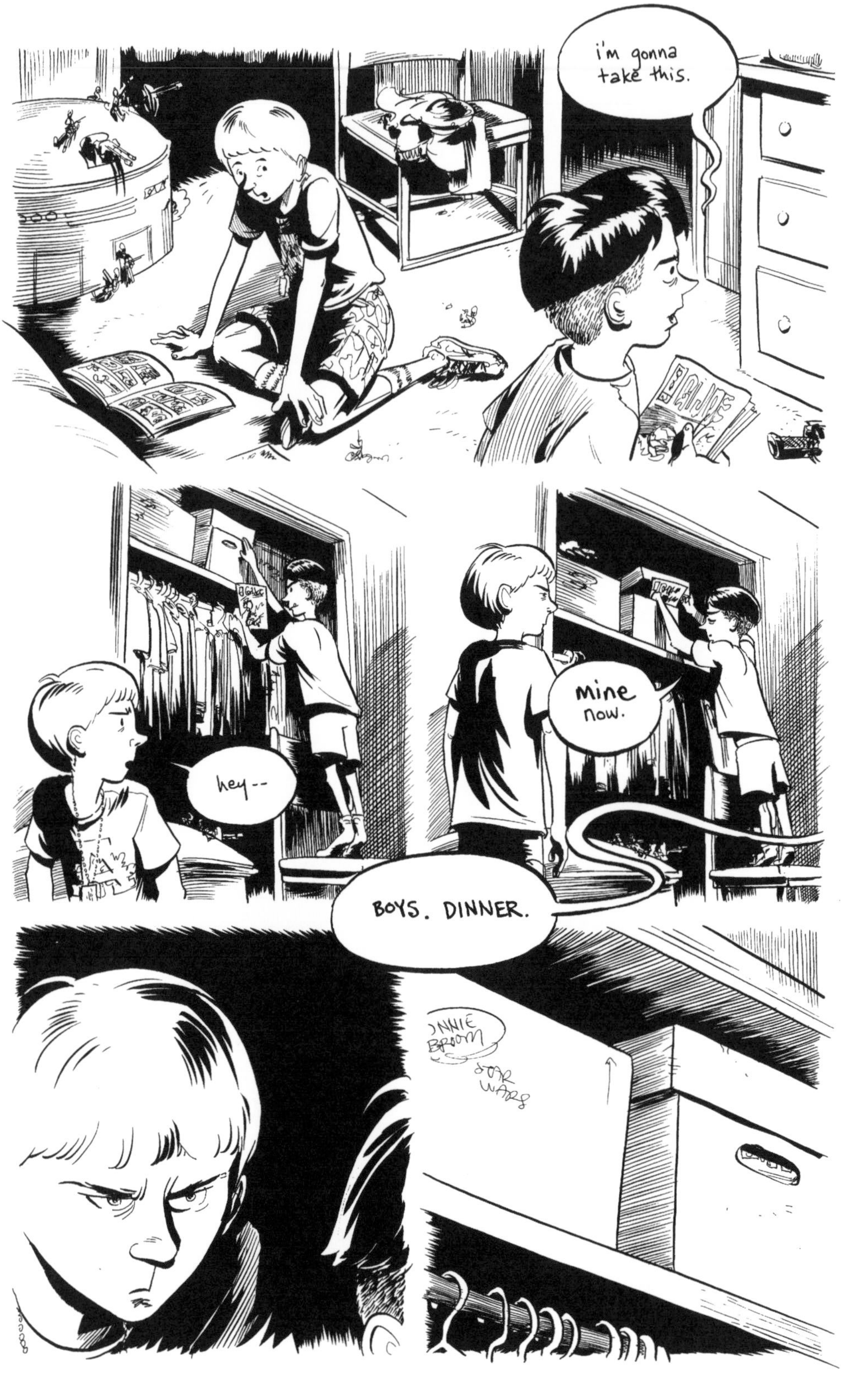
i'm gonna take this.
hey--
mine now.
BOYS. DINNER.

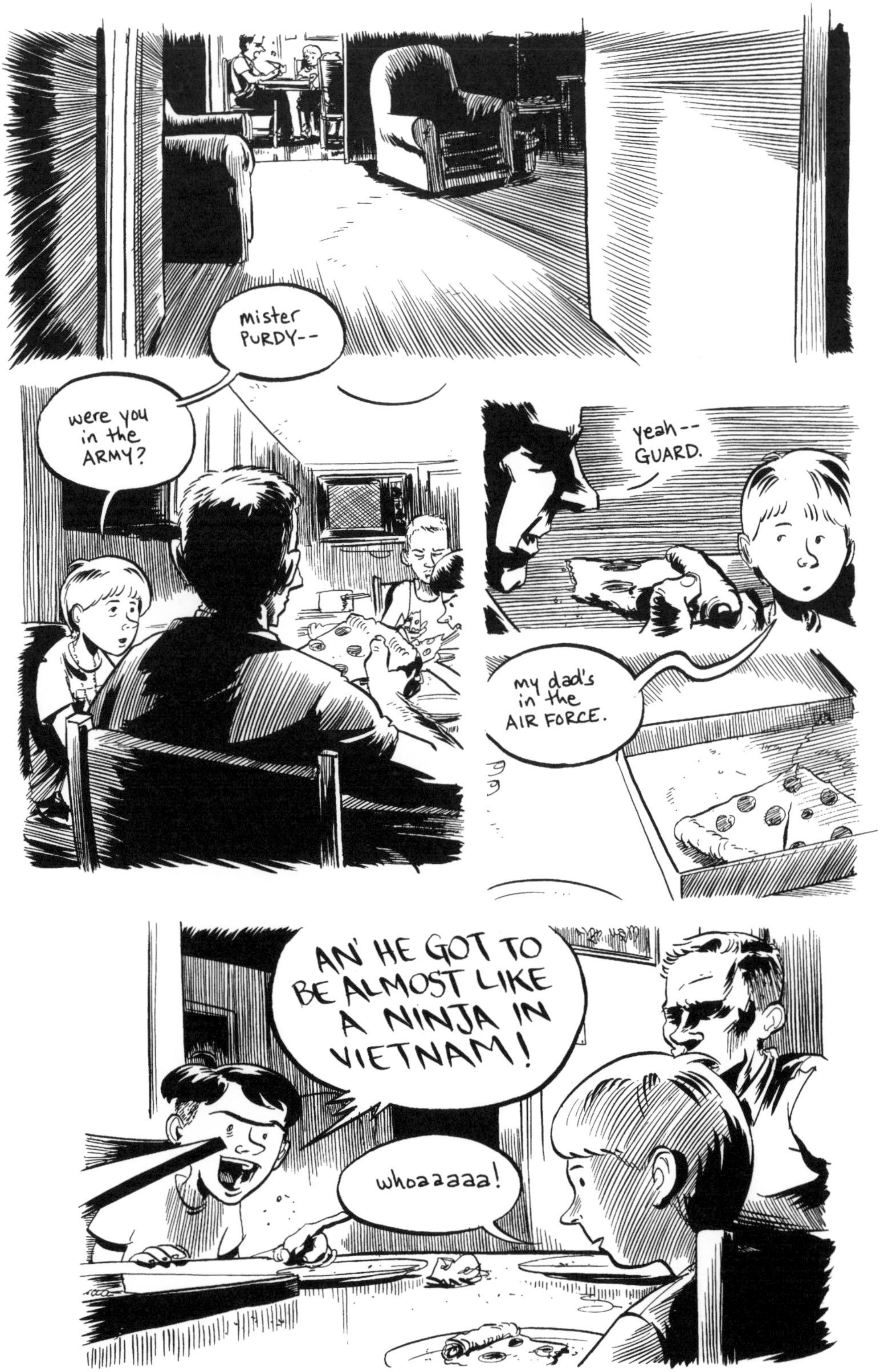
mister PURDY--
were you in the ARMY?
yeah-- GUARD.
my dad's in the AIR FORCE.
AN' HE GOT TO BE ALMOST LIKE A NINJA IN VIETNAM!
whoaaaaa!

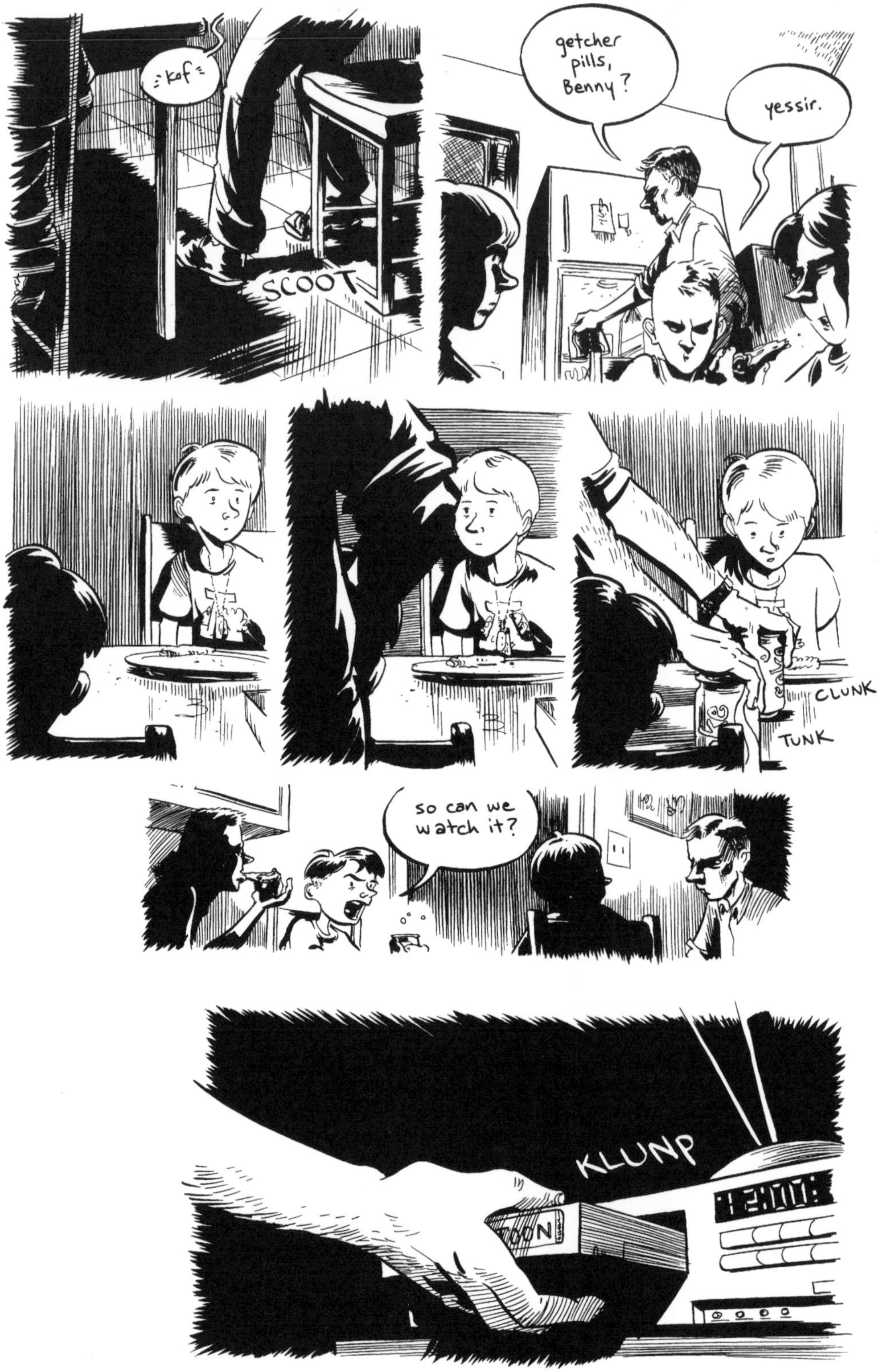
kof
SCOOT
getcher pills, Benny?
yessir.
CLUNK
TUNK
so can we watch it?
KLUNP
TOON

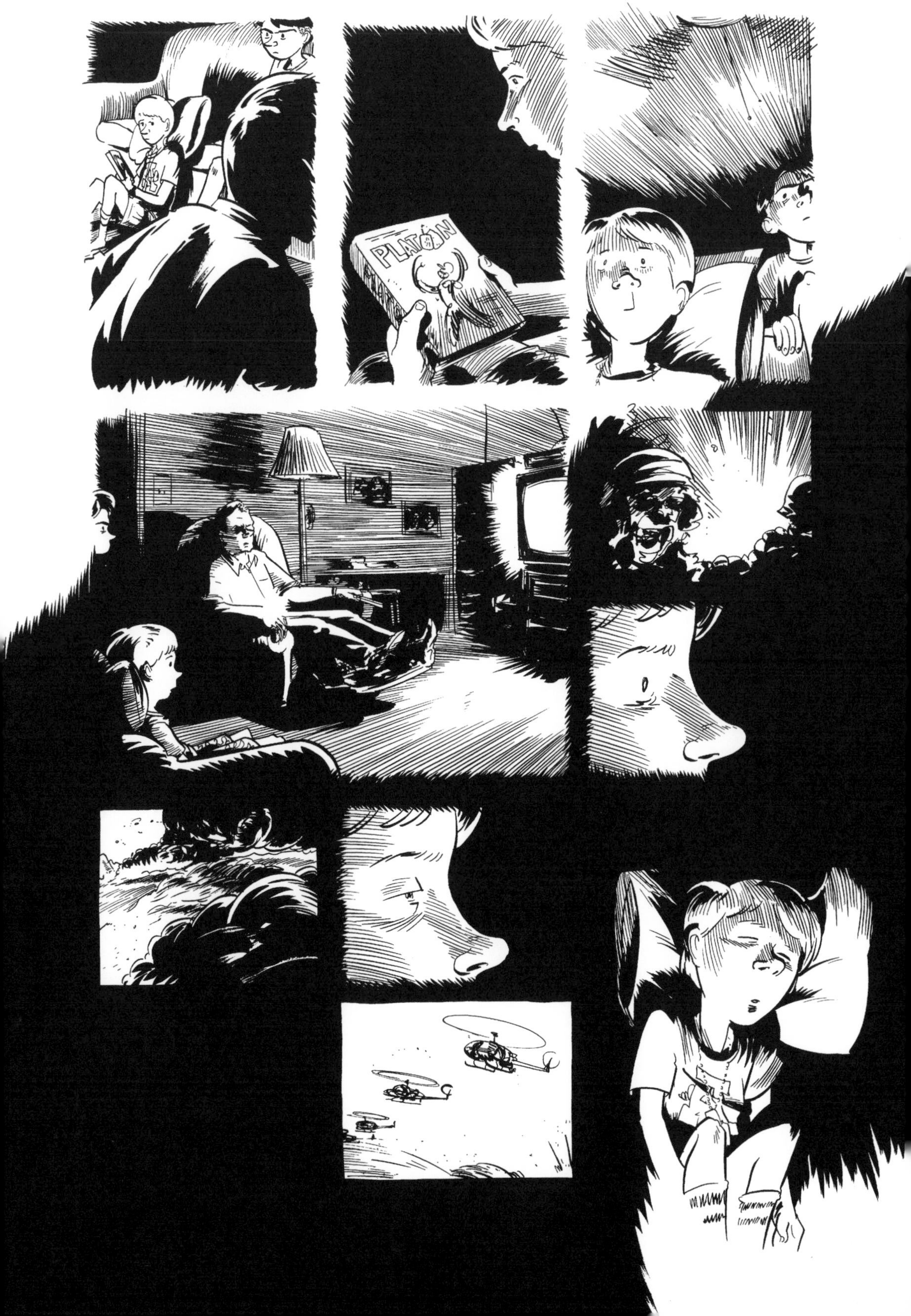
PLATÓN

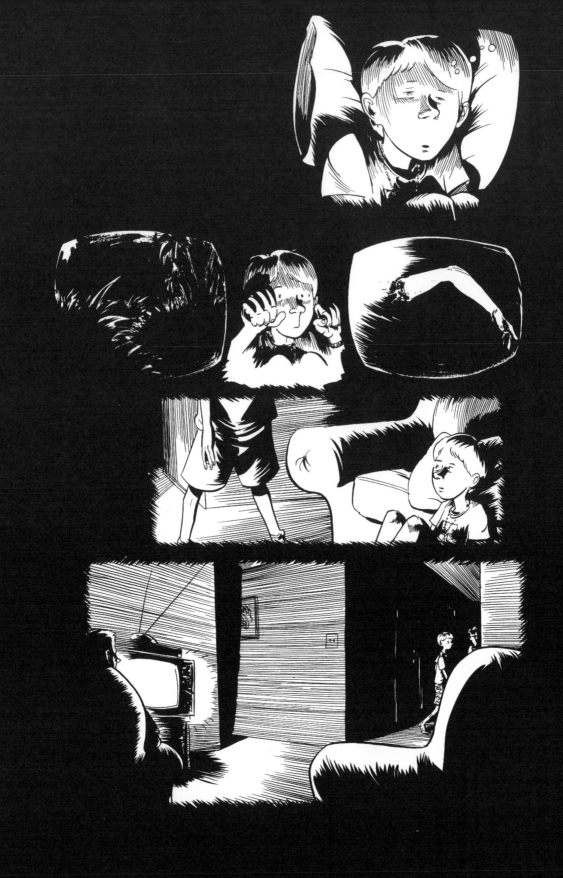

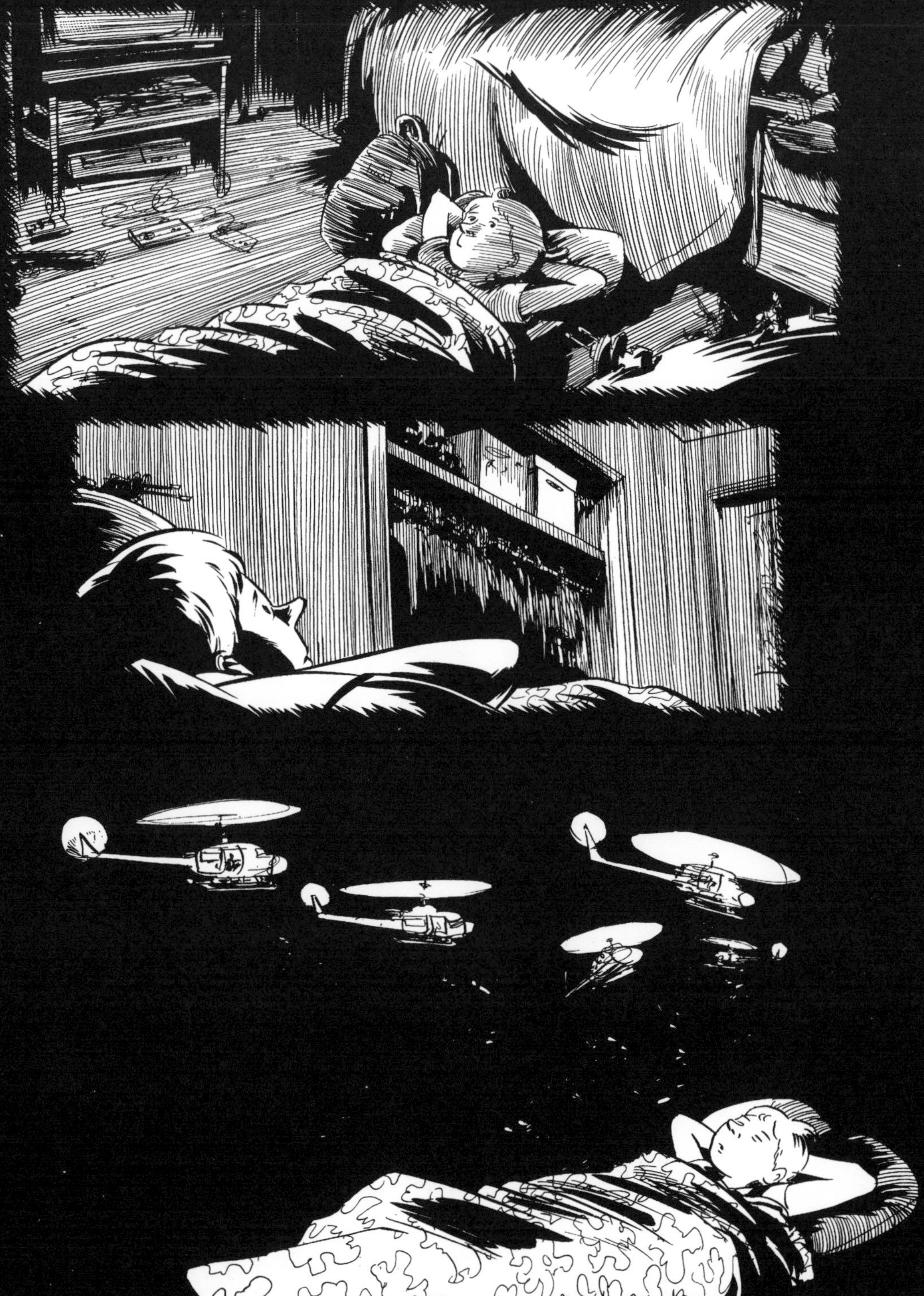

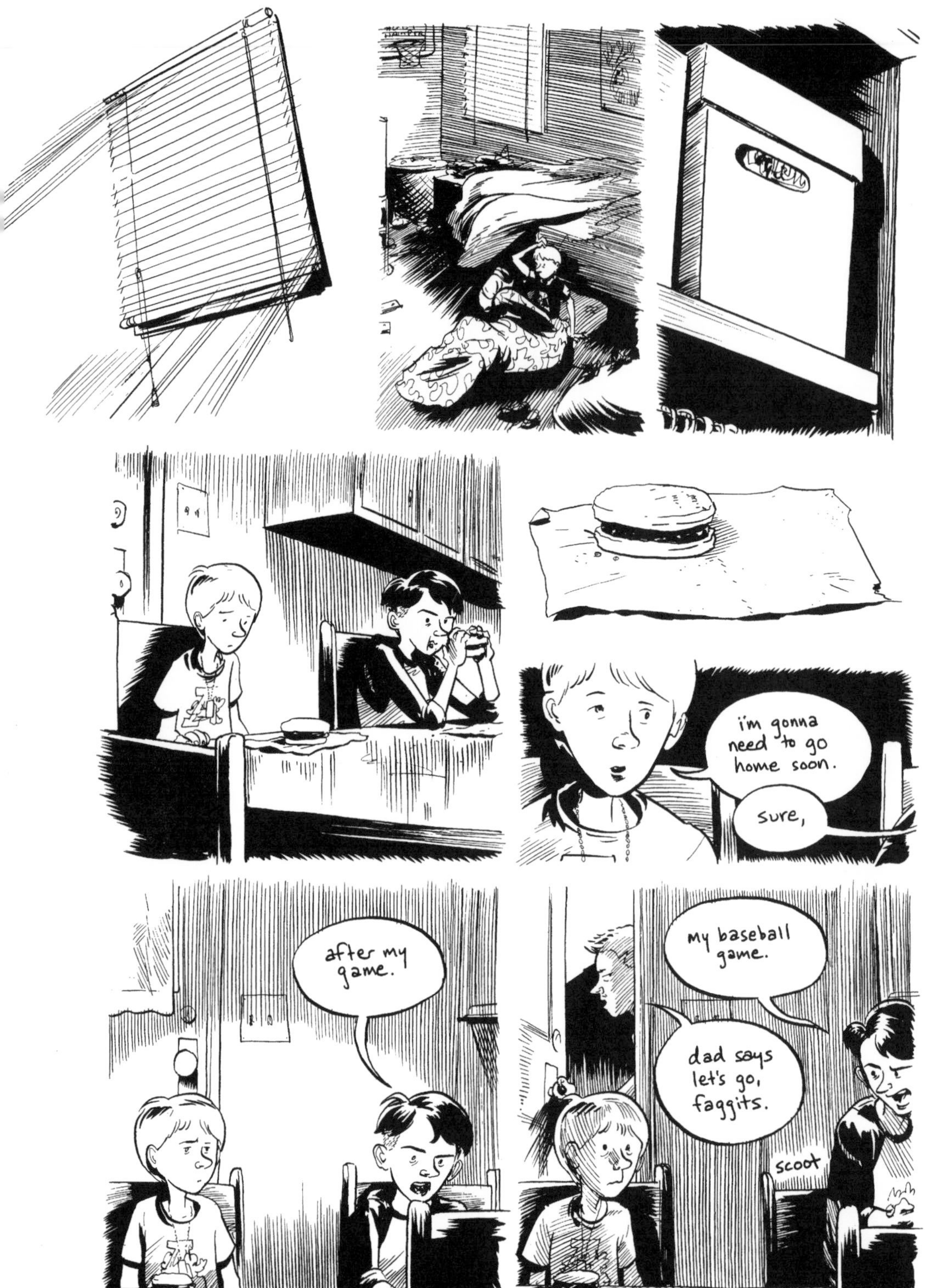
i'm gonna need to go home soon.
sure,
after my game.
my baseball game.
dad says let's go, faggits.
scoot

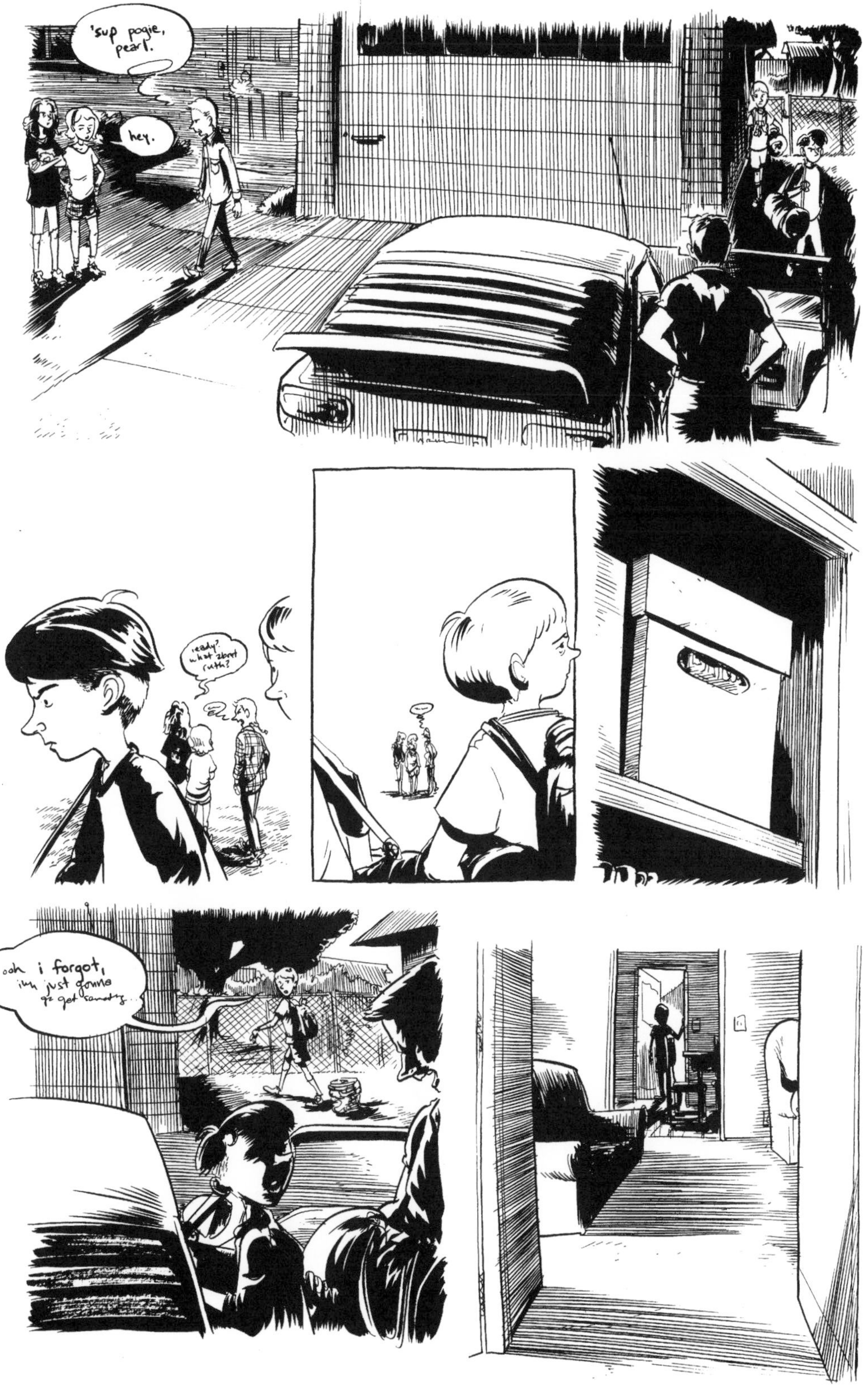
'sup pogie, pearl.
hey.
ready? what about ruth?
ooh i forgot, im just gonna go get something...

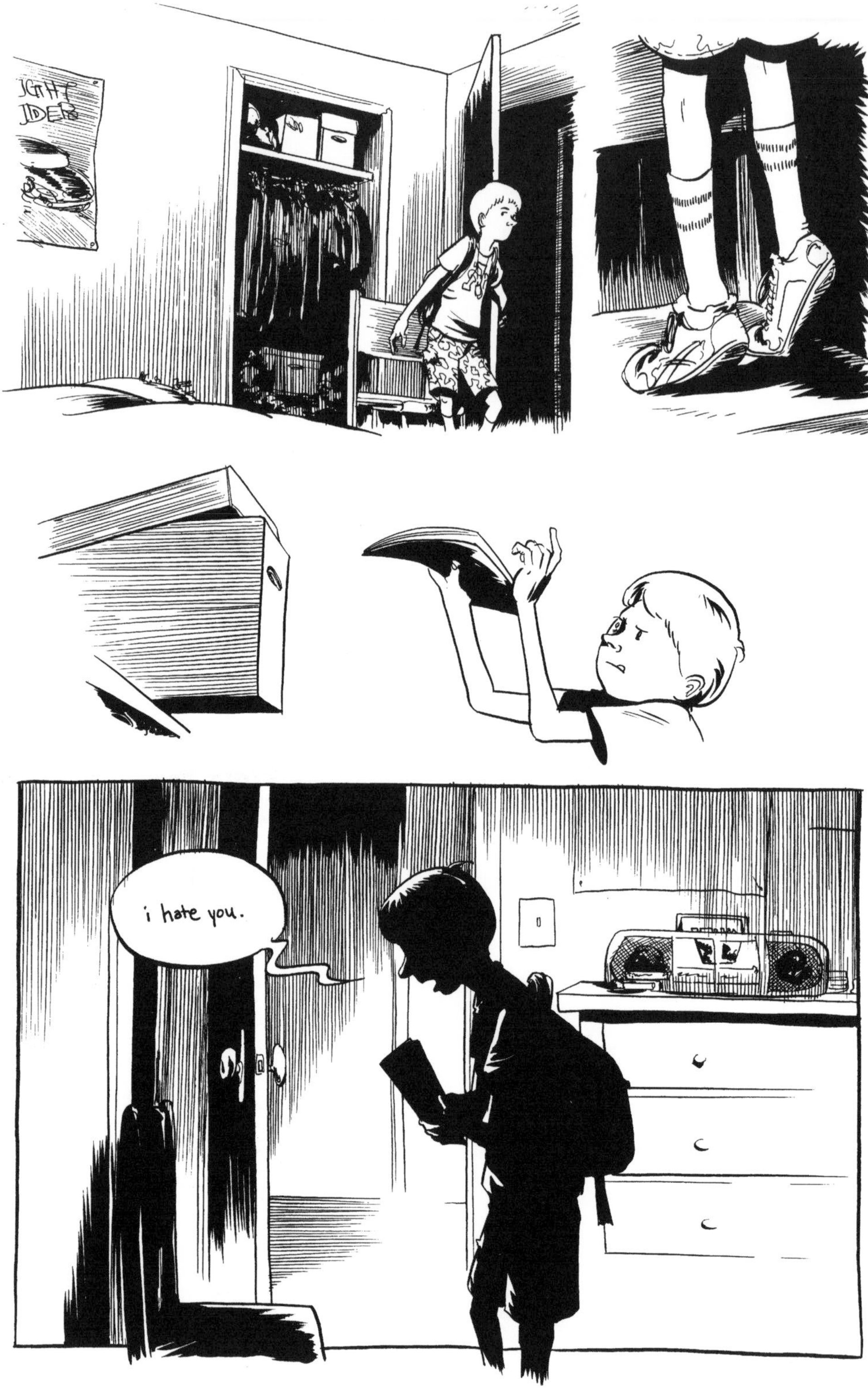
i hate you.

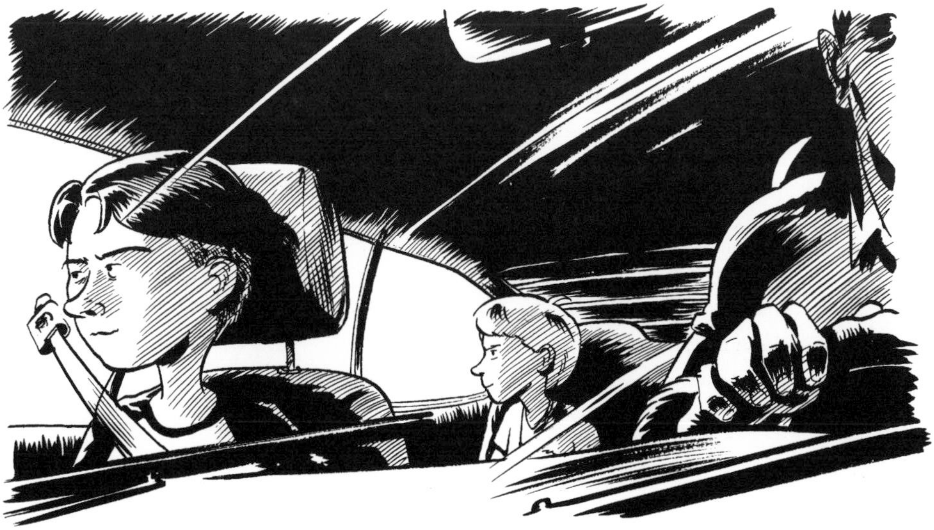

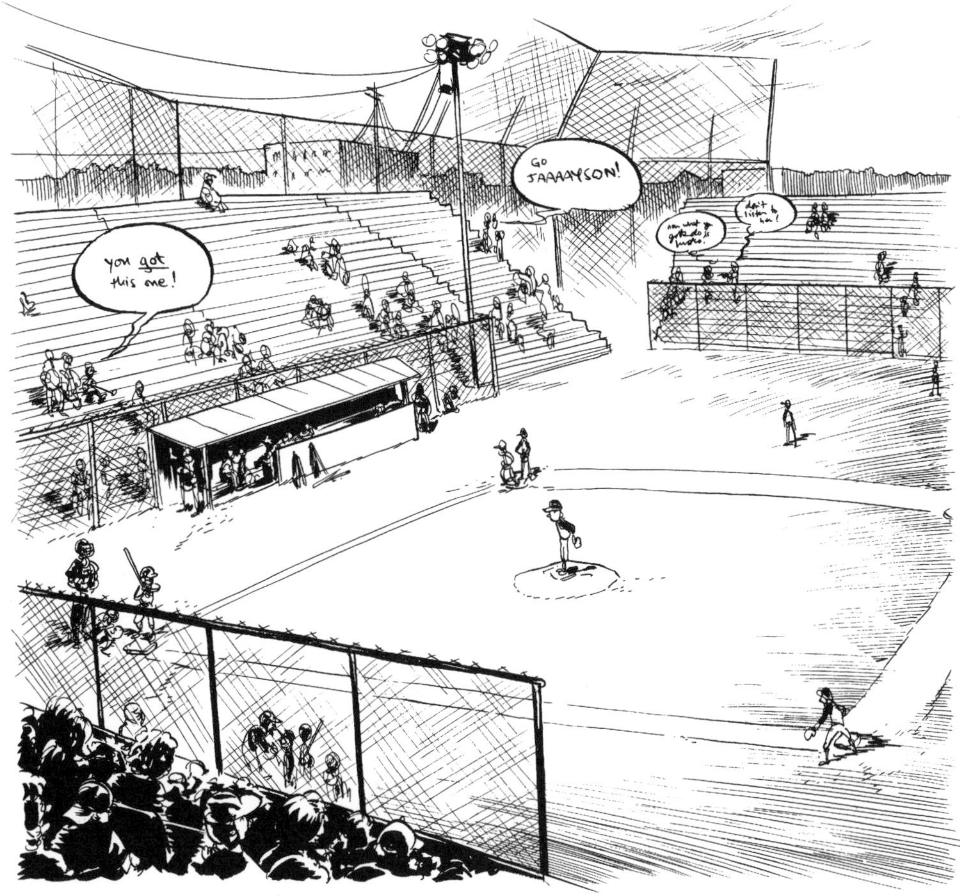
you got this one!
GO JAAAAYSON!
don't listen to him!

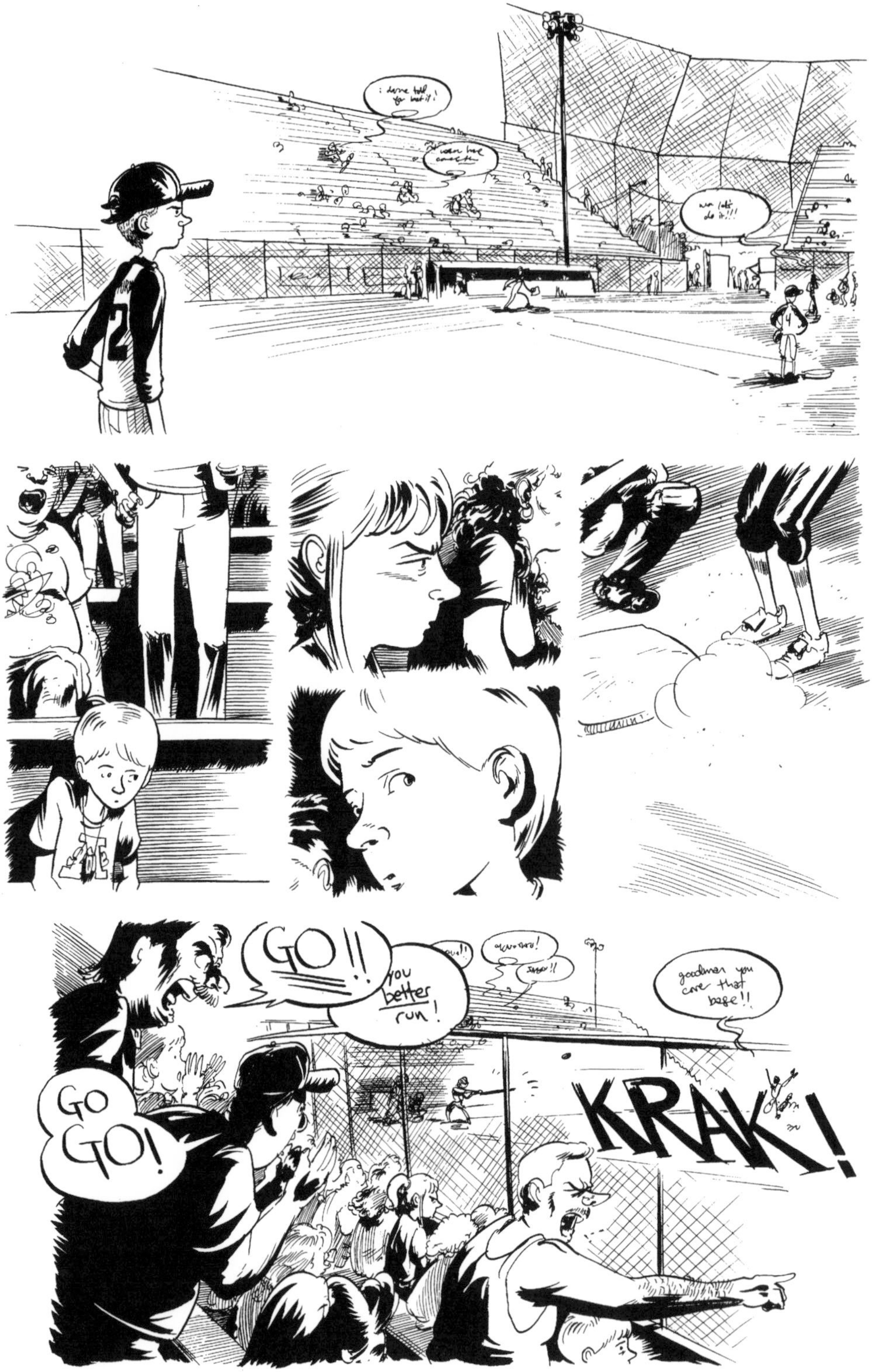
now let's do it!!!
GO!!
you better run!
goodman you cove that base!!
GO GO!
KRAK!

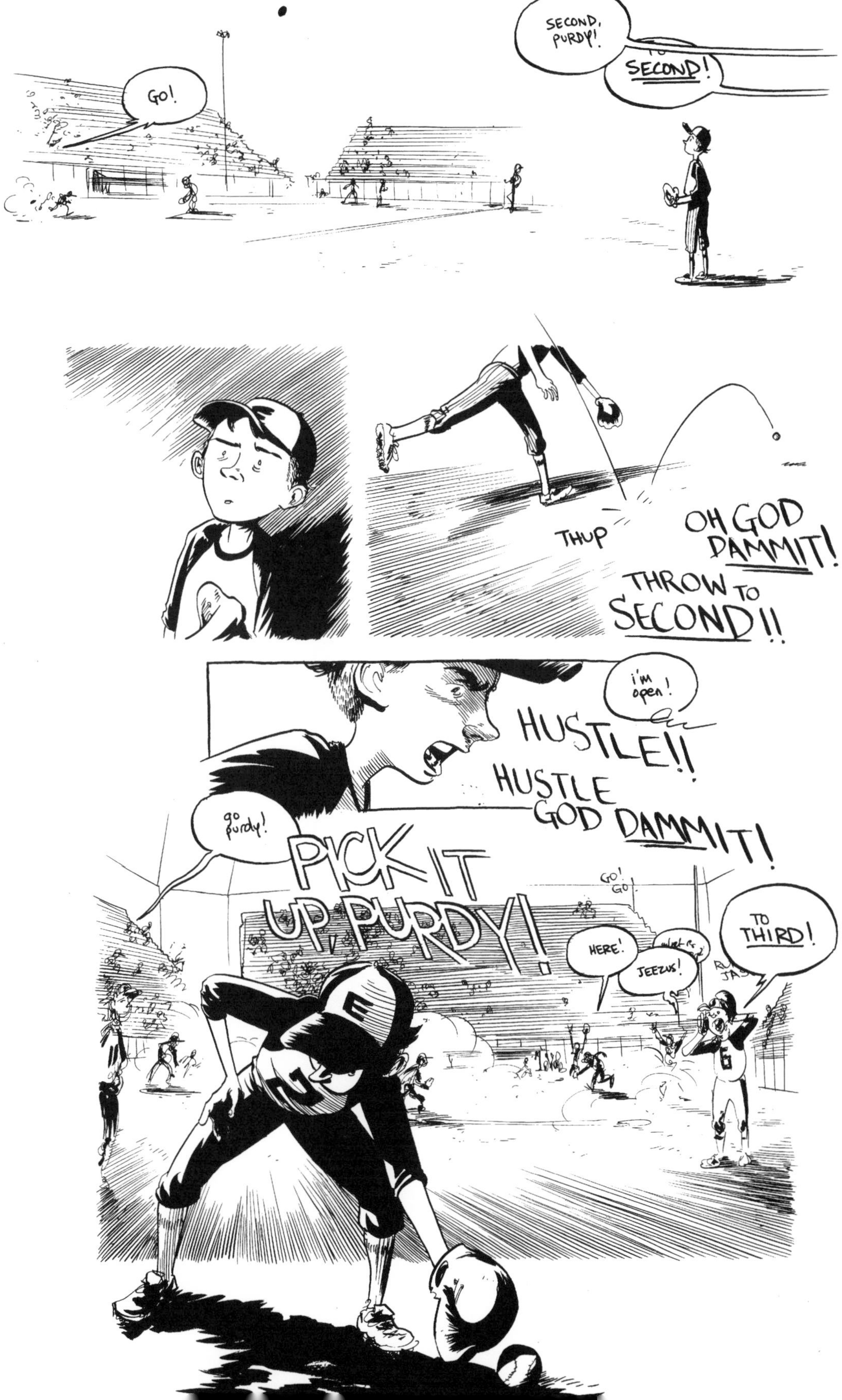
Go!
SECOND, PURDY!
TO SECOND!
THUP
OH GOD DAMMIT!
THROW TO SECOND!!
i'm open!
HUSTLE!!
HUSTLE GOD DAMMIT!
go purdy!
PICK IT UP, PURDY!
GO! GO!
HERE!
JEEZUS!
TO THIRD!

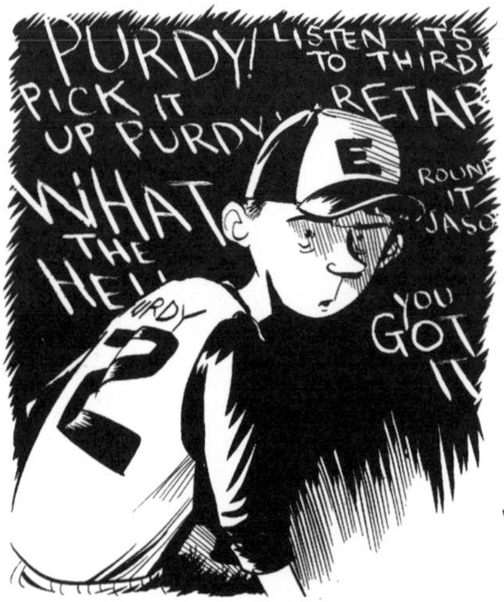
PURDY!
LISTEN IT'S TO THIRD!
PICK IT UP PURDY!
RETAR
WHAT THE HEL
ROUND IT JASO
YOU GOT IT

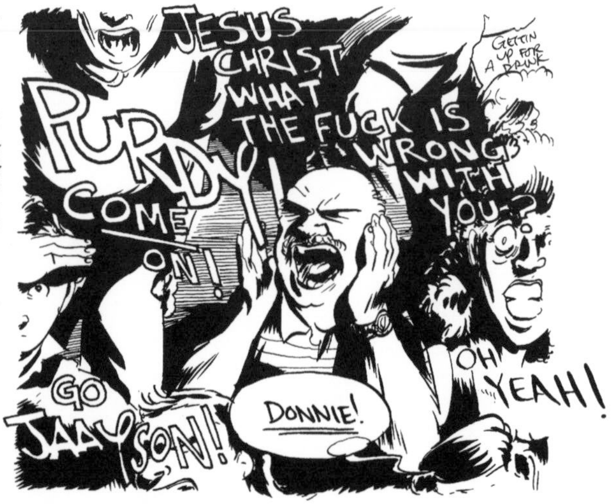
JESUS CHRIST WHAT THE FUCK IS WRONG WITH YOU?
GETTIN UP FOR A DRINK
PURDY!
COME ON!
GO JAAYSON!
DONNIE!
OH YEAH!

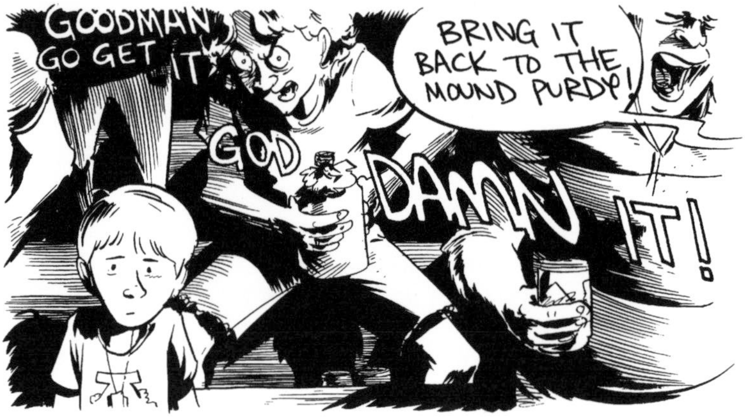
GOODMAN GO GET IT
BRING IT BACK TO THE MOUND PURDY!
GOD DAMN IT!

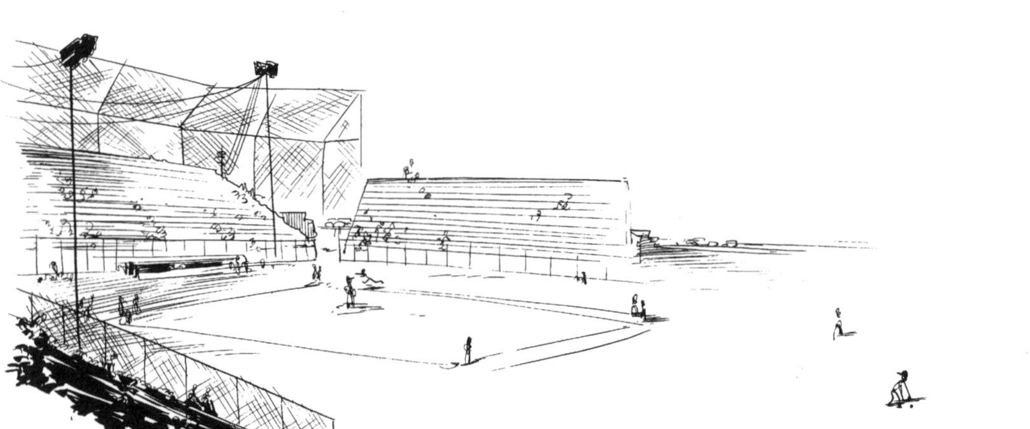

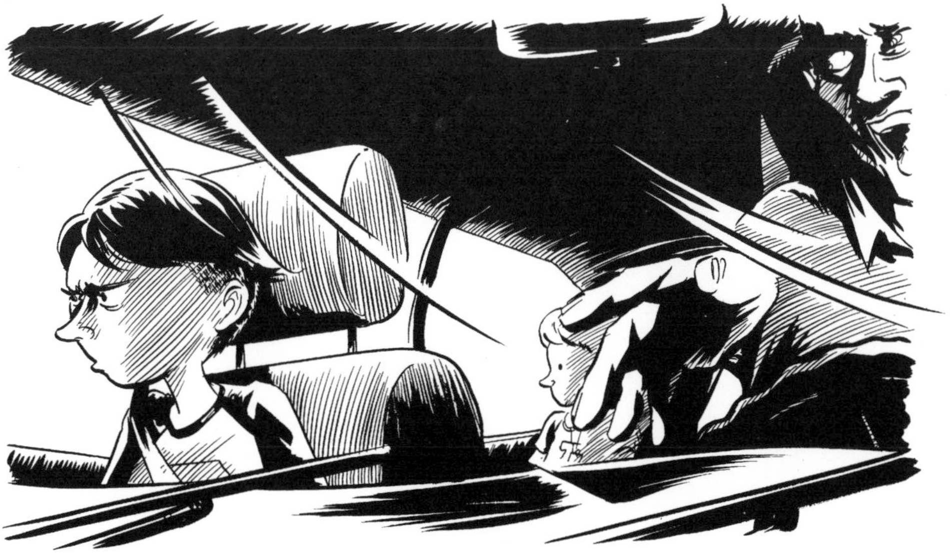

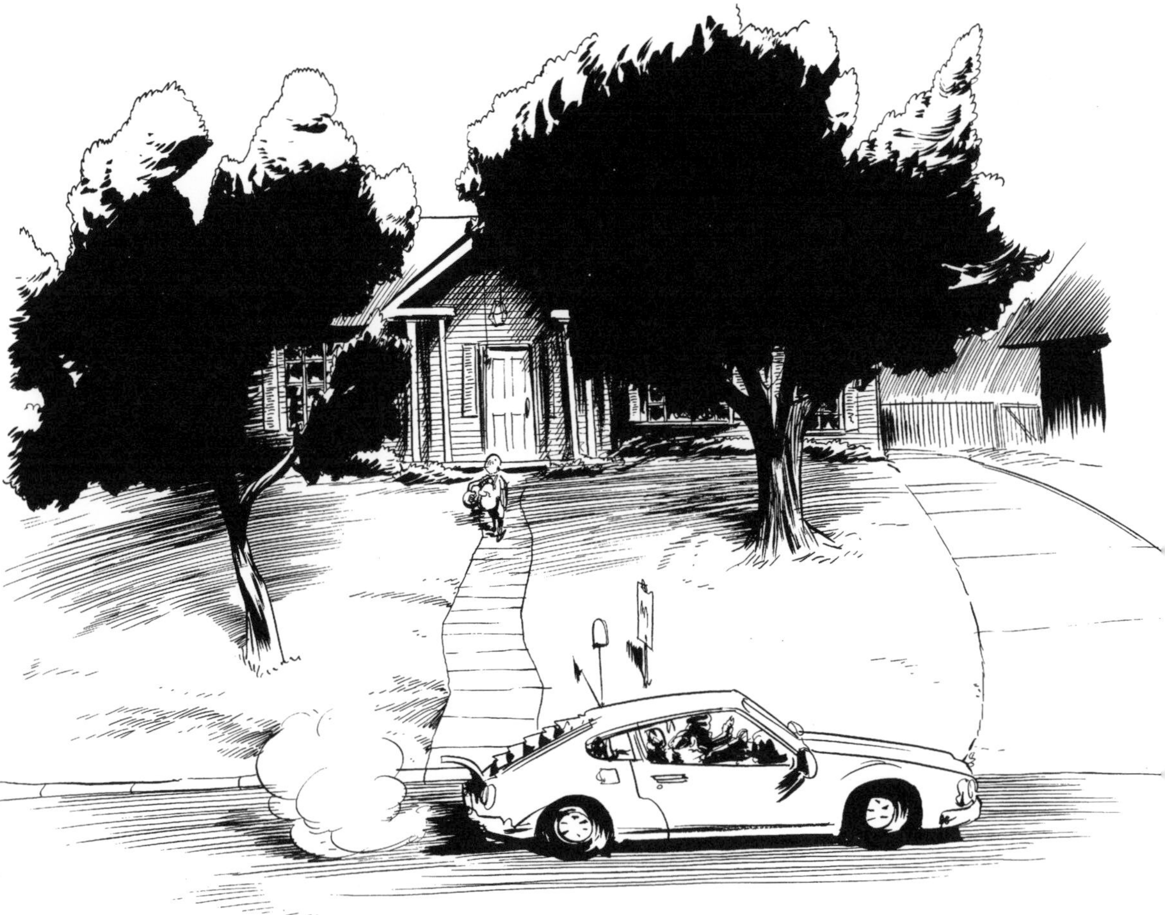

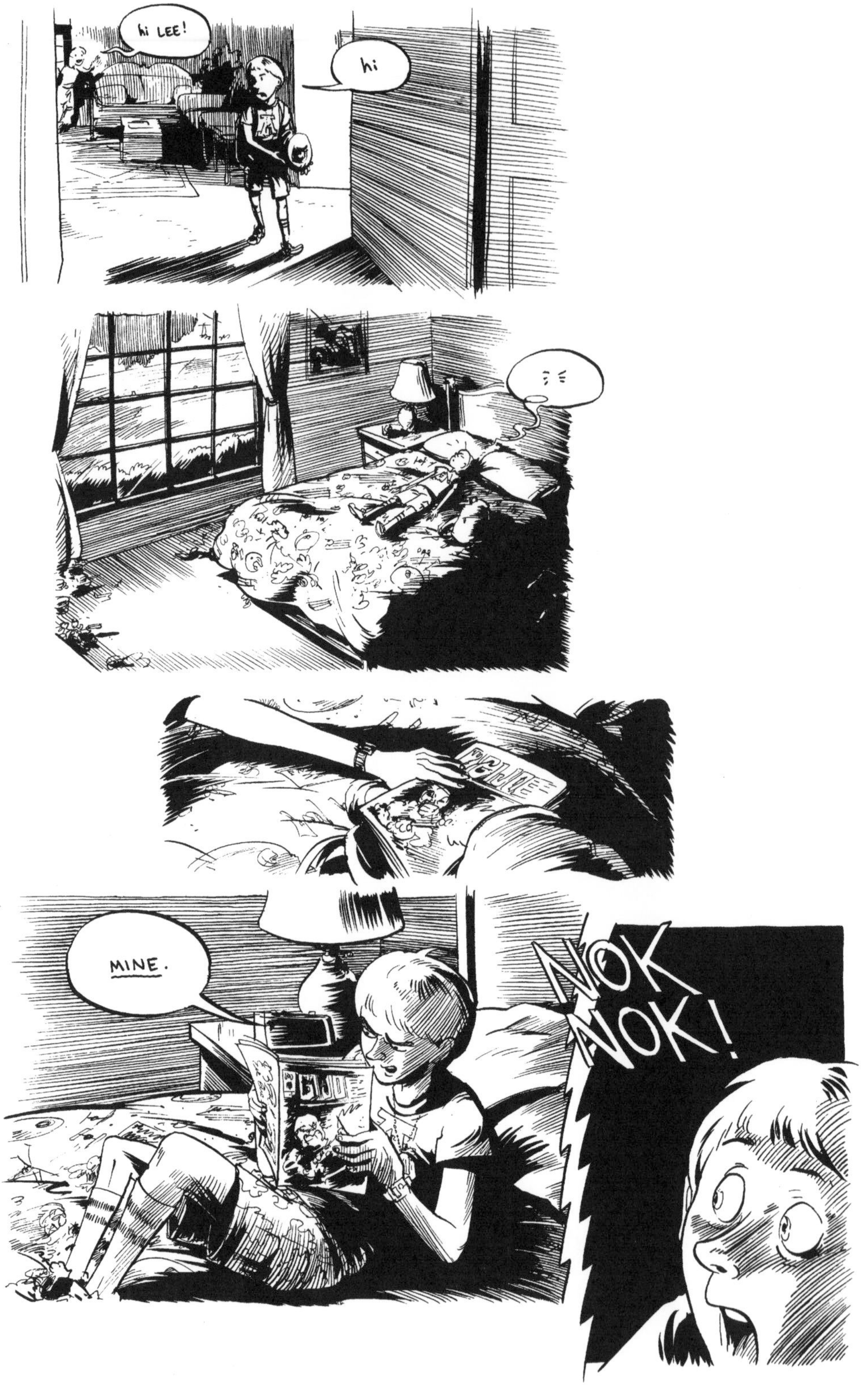

hi LEE!
hi
MINE.
NOK NOK!

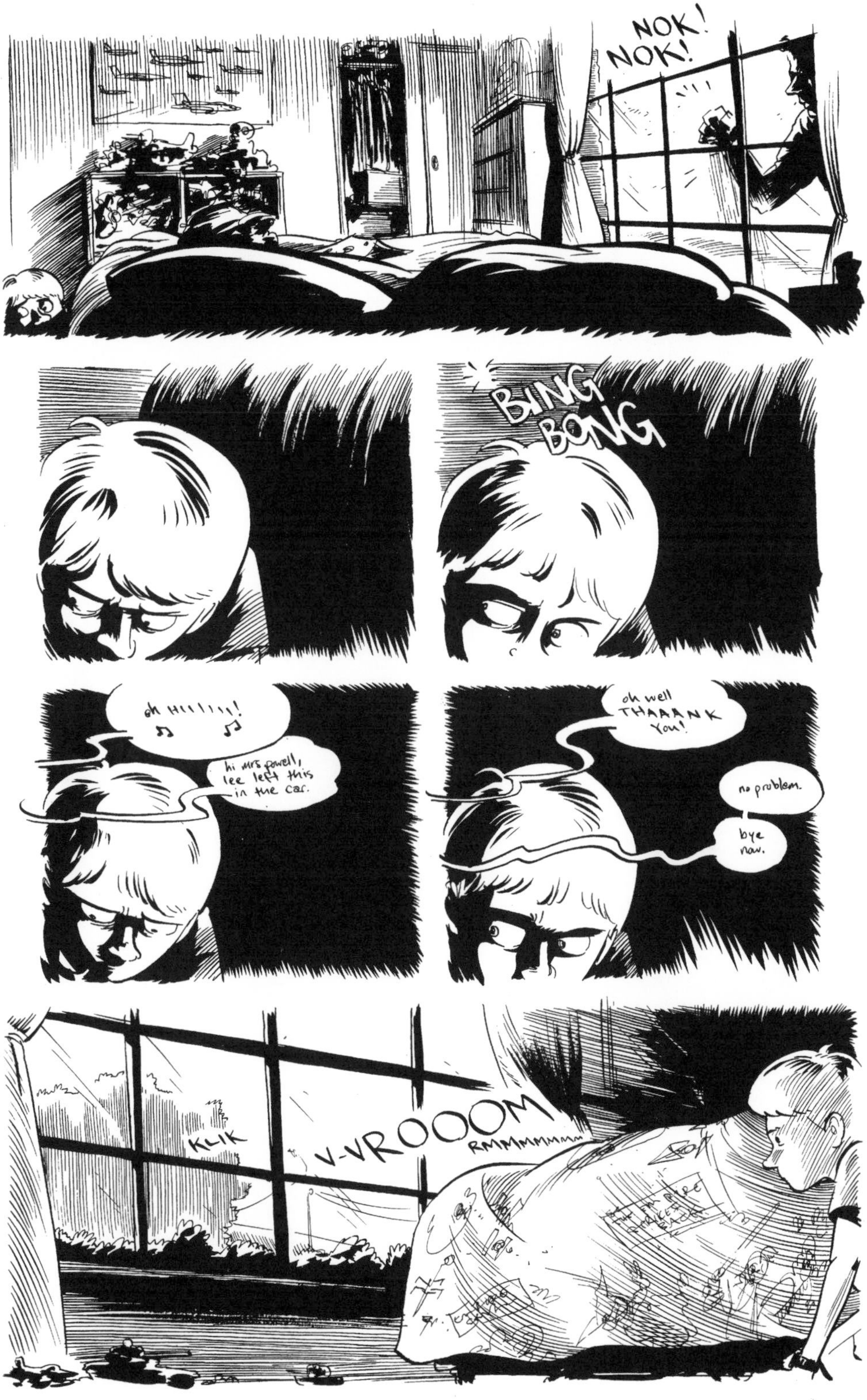
NOK! NOK!
BING BONG
oh HI!!!!!!
hi mrs powell, lee left this in the car.
oh well THAAANK You!
no problem.
bye now.
KLIK
V-VROOOM
RMMMMMMM

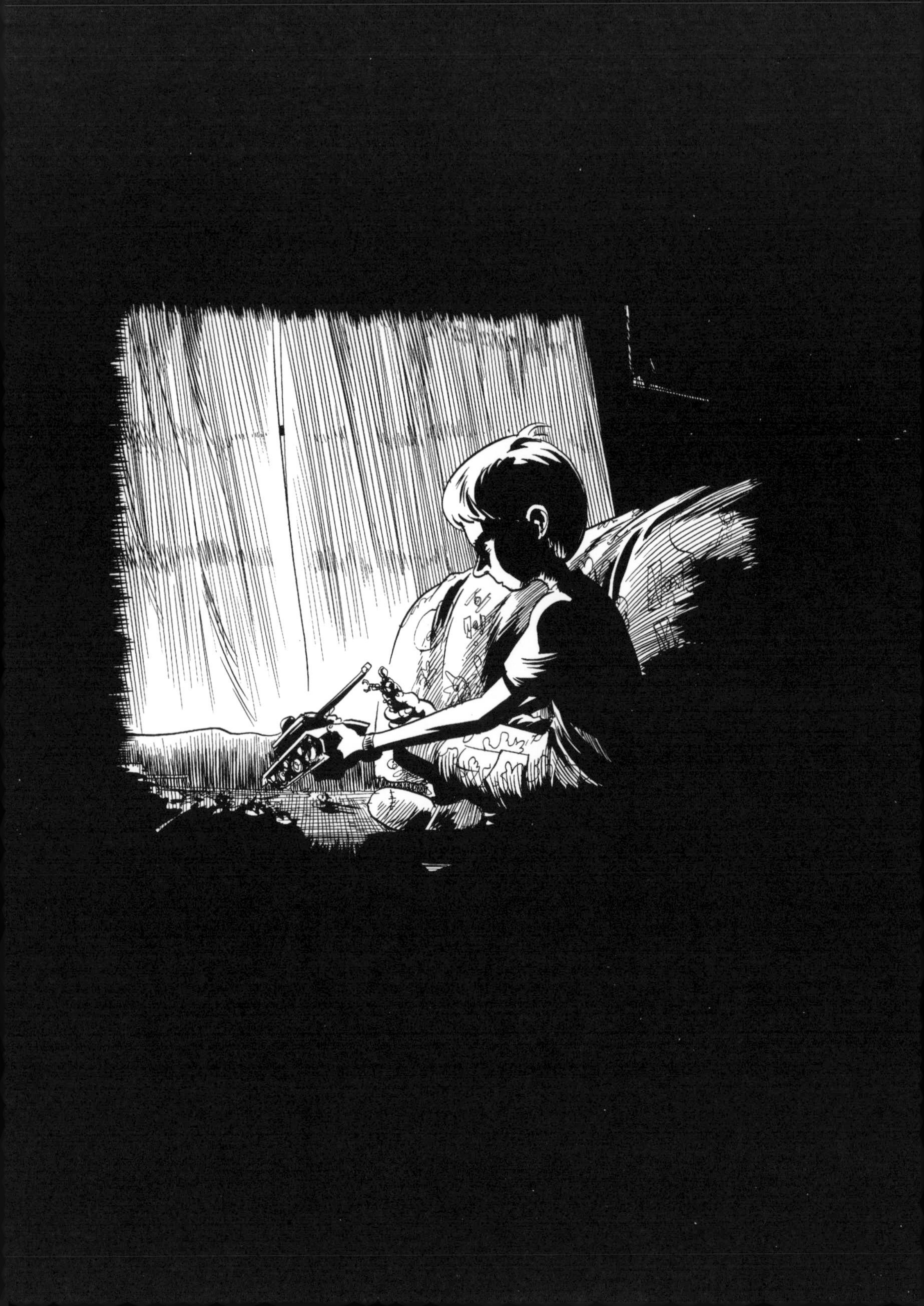

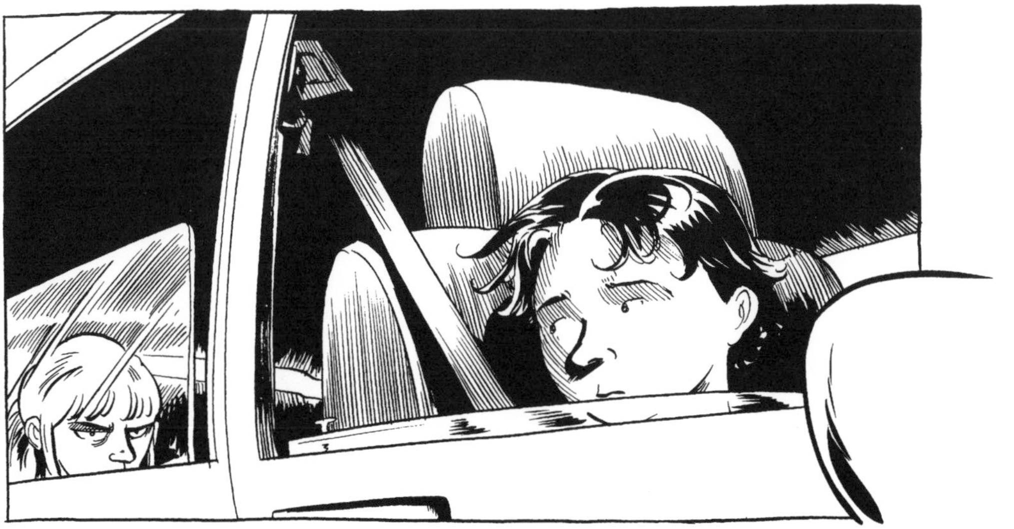
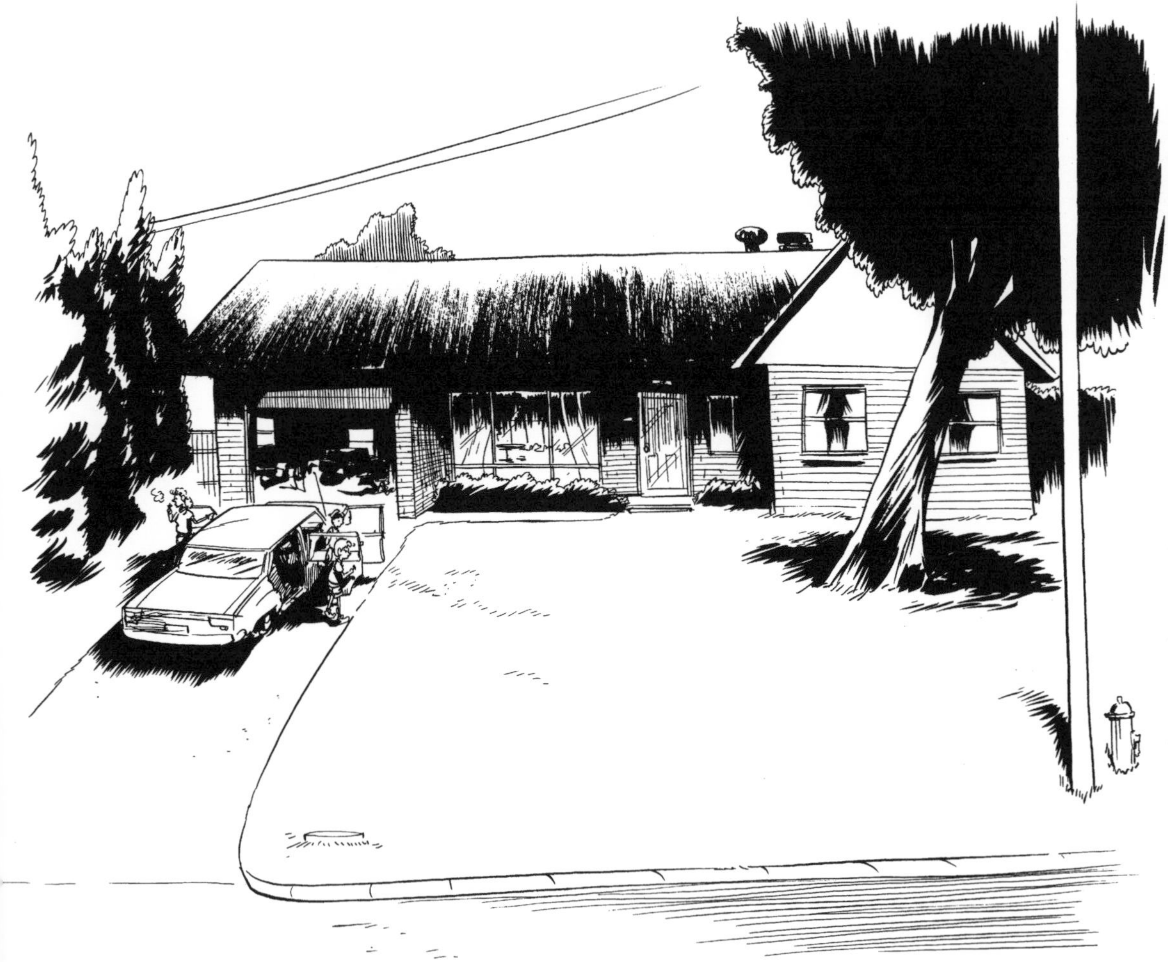

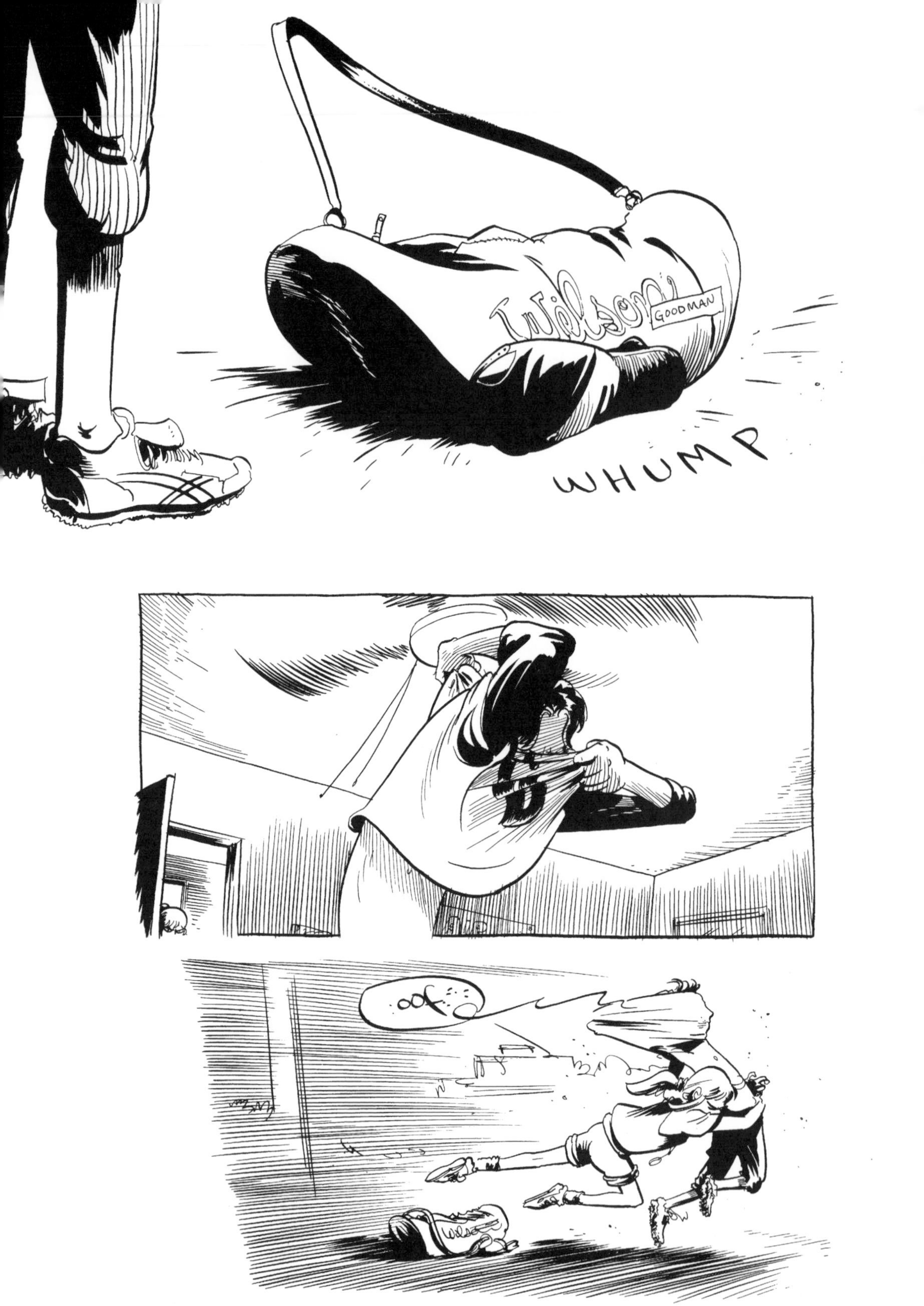
Wilson
GOODMAN
WHUMP
oof

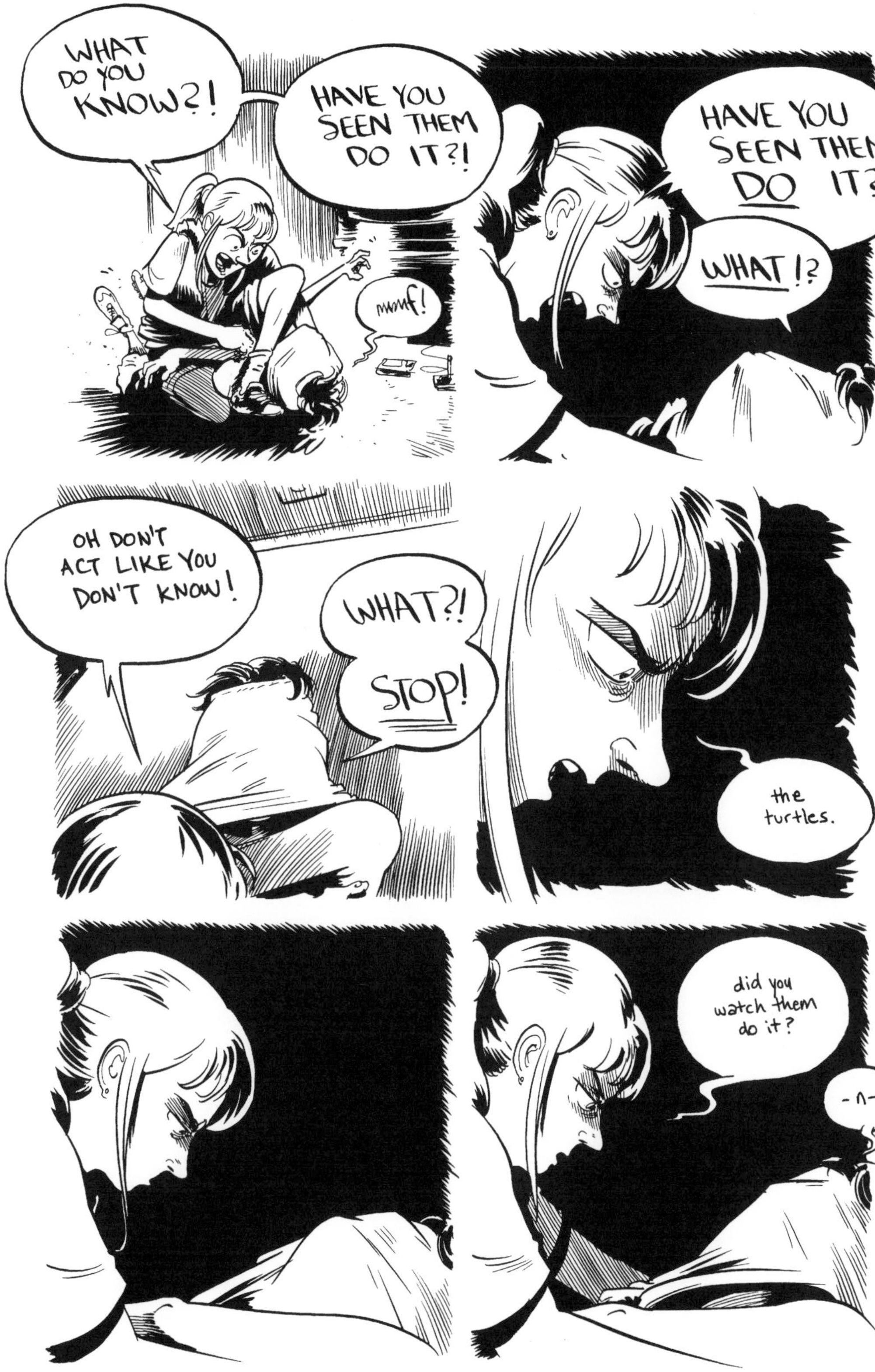
WHAT DO YOU KNOW?!
HAVE YOU SEEN THEM DO IT?!
mmf!
HAVE YOU SEEN THEM DO IT?!!
WHAT!?
OH DON'T ACT LIKE YOU DON'T KNOW!
WHAT?!
STOP!
the turtles.
did you watch them do it?
-n-

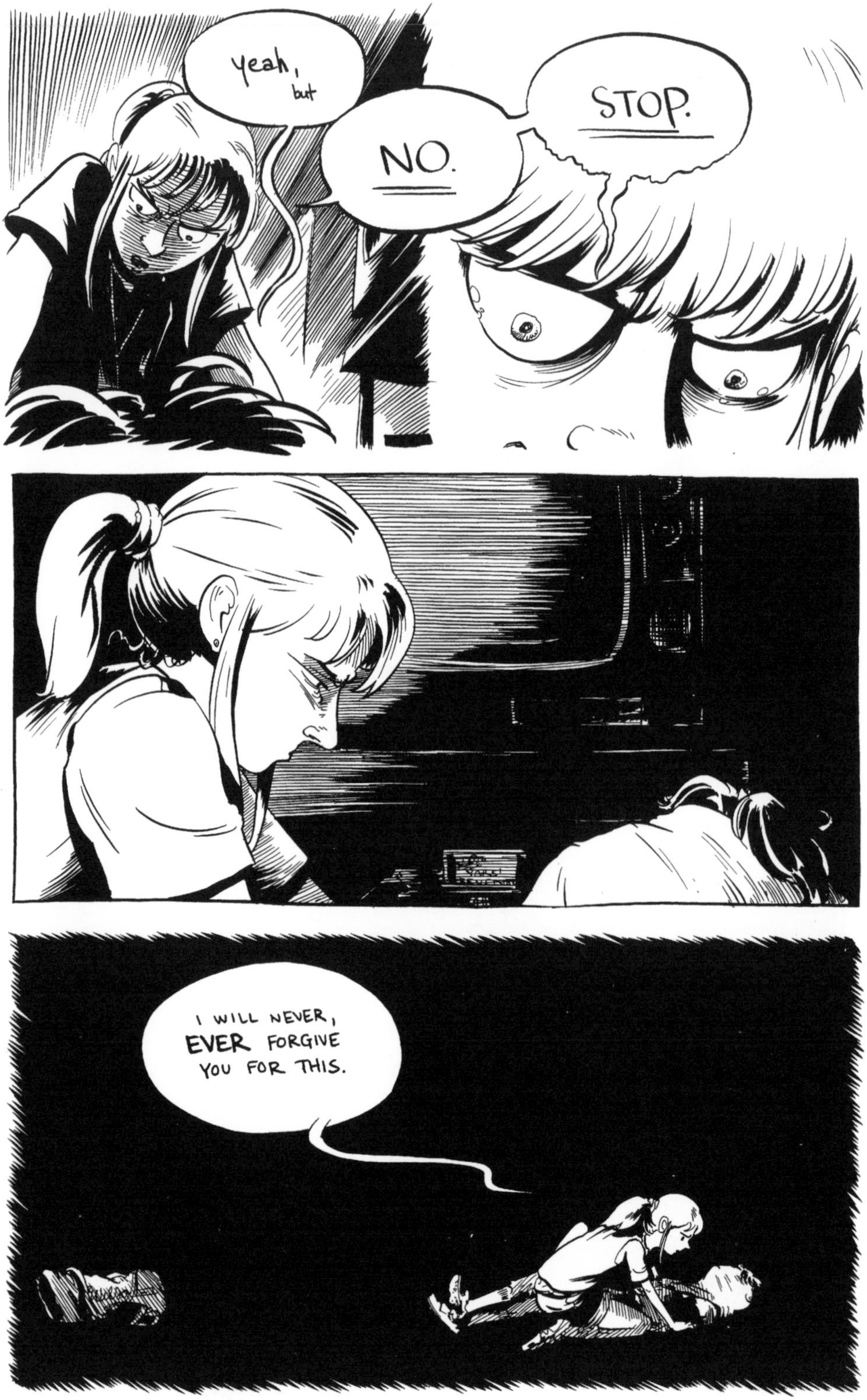
yeah, but
NO.
STOP.
I WILL NEVER, EVER FORGIVE YOU FOR THIS.

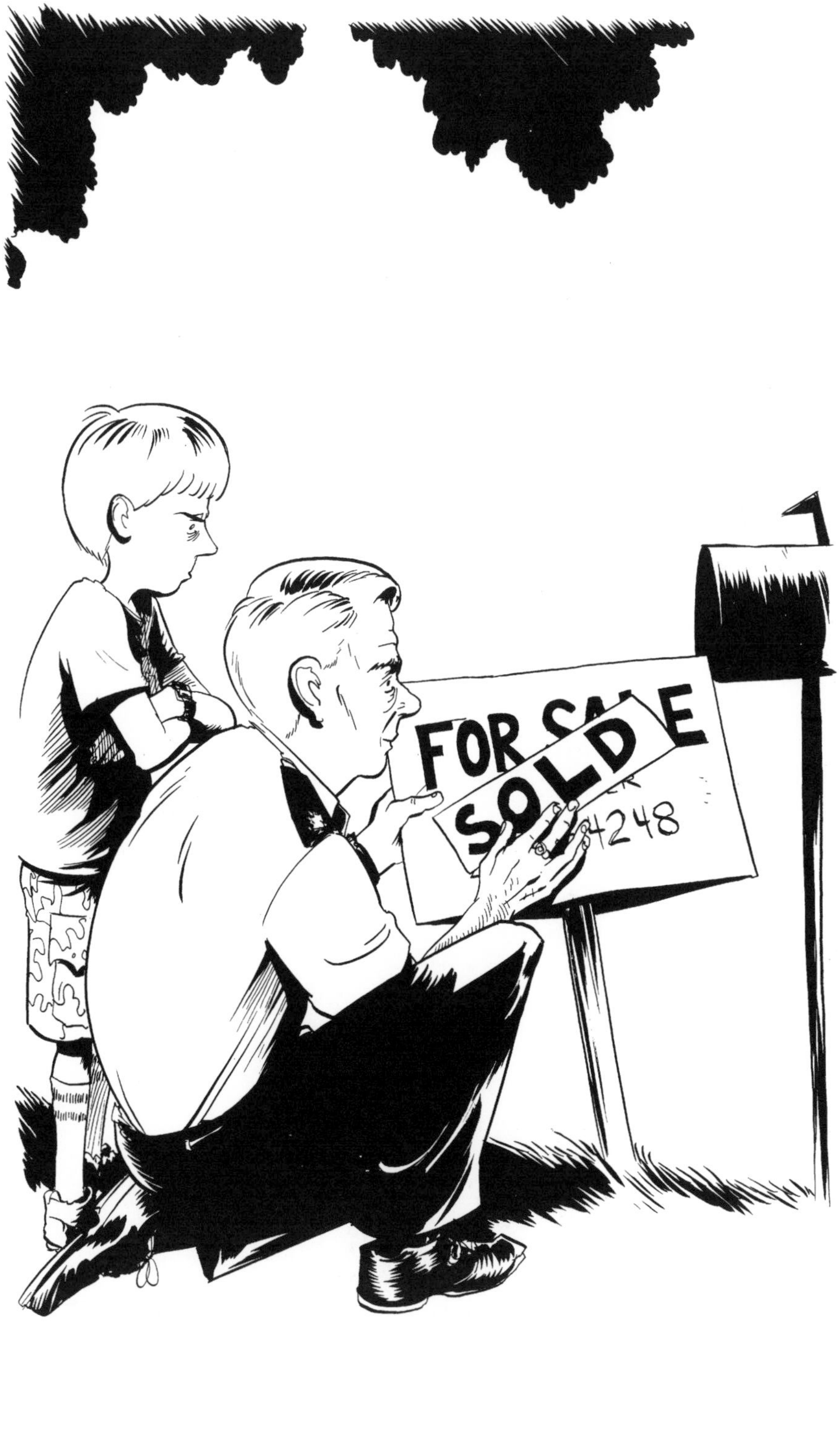

FOR SA E
SOLD
4248

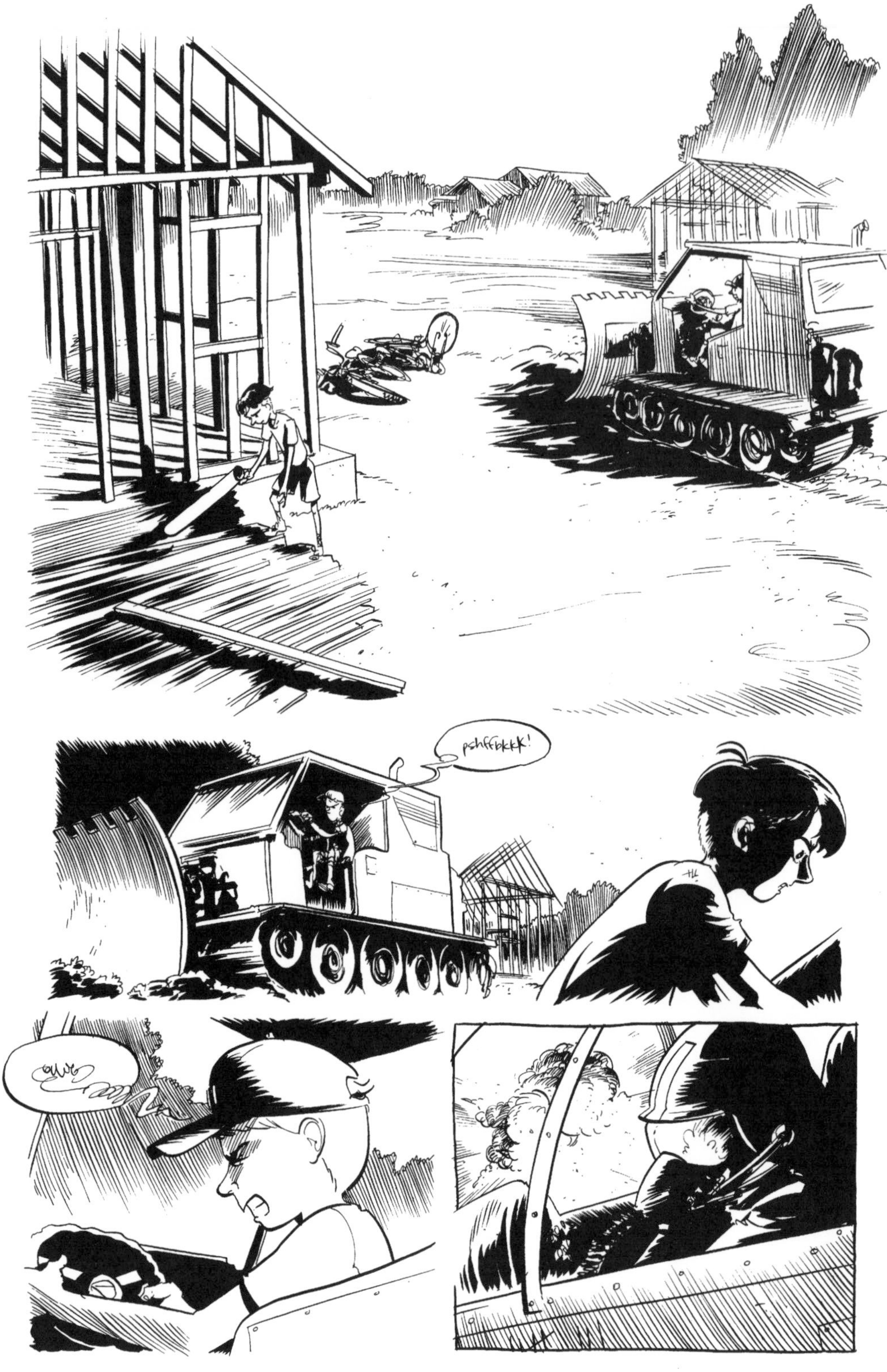
pshffbkkk!

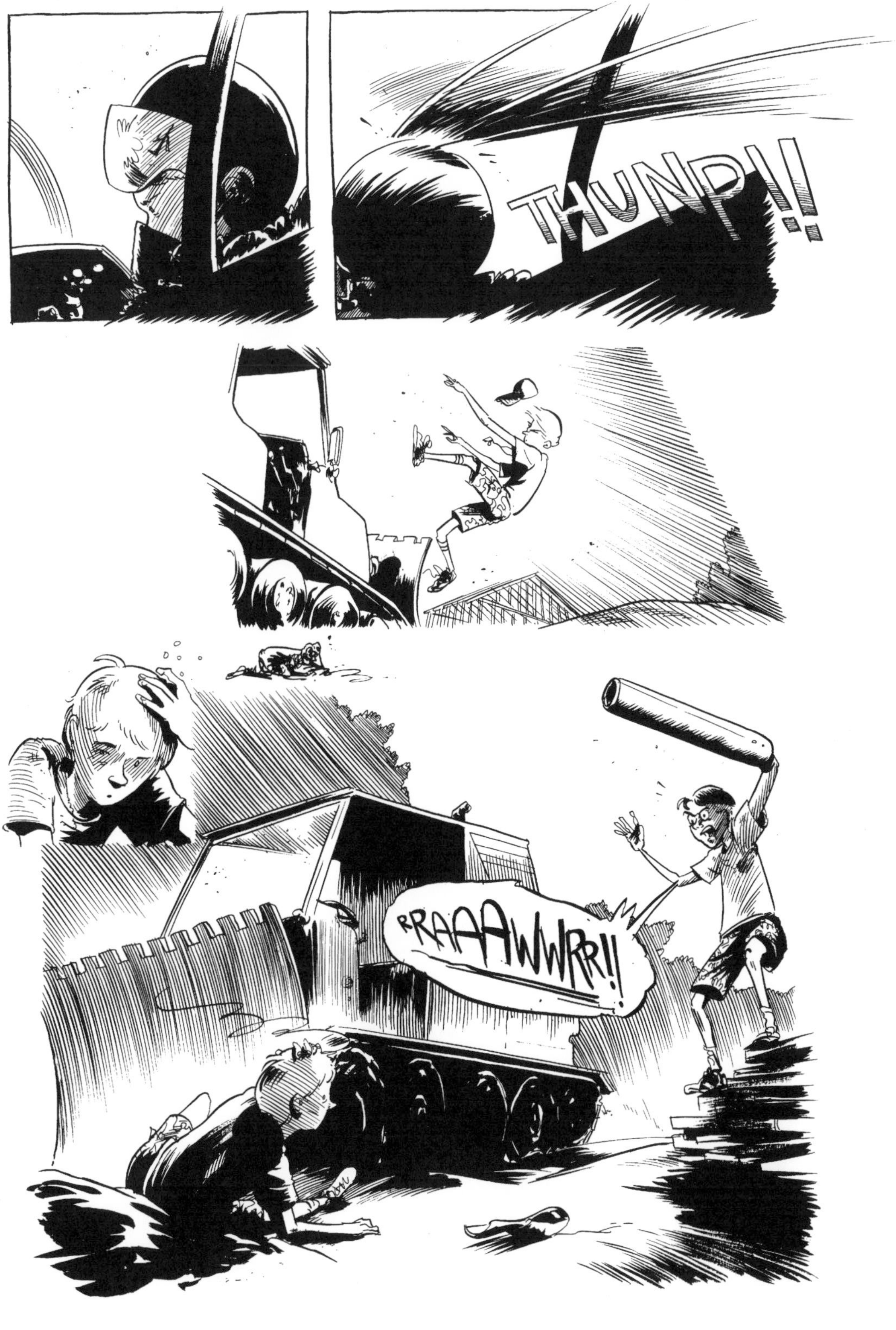
THUNP!!
RRAAAWWRRR!!

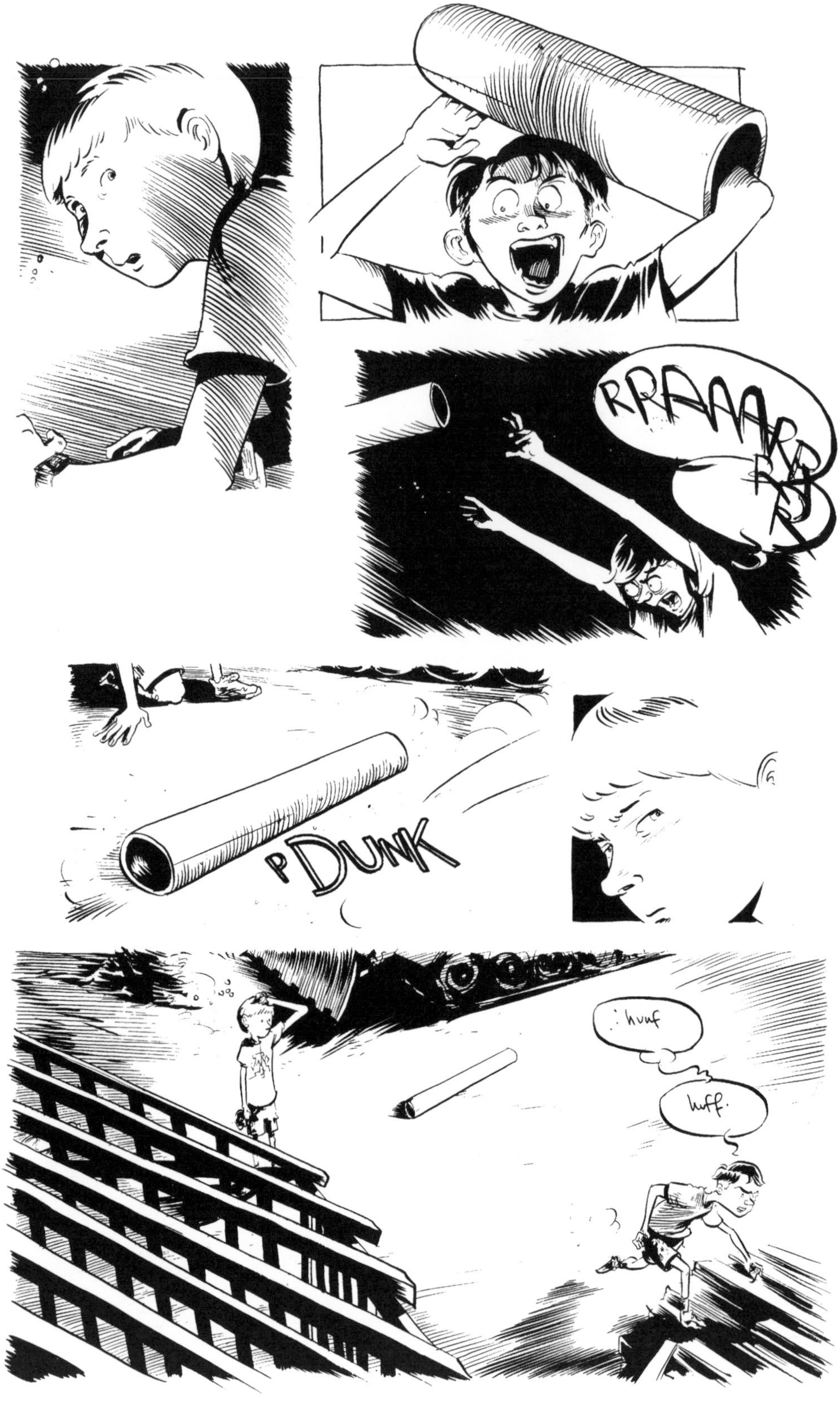
RRAAARR RRR
PDUNK
:. hunf
huff.

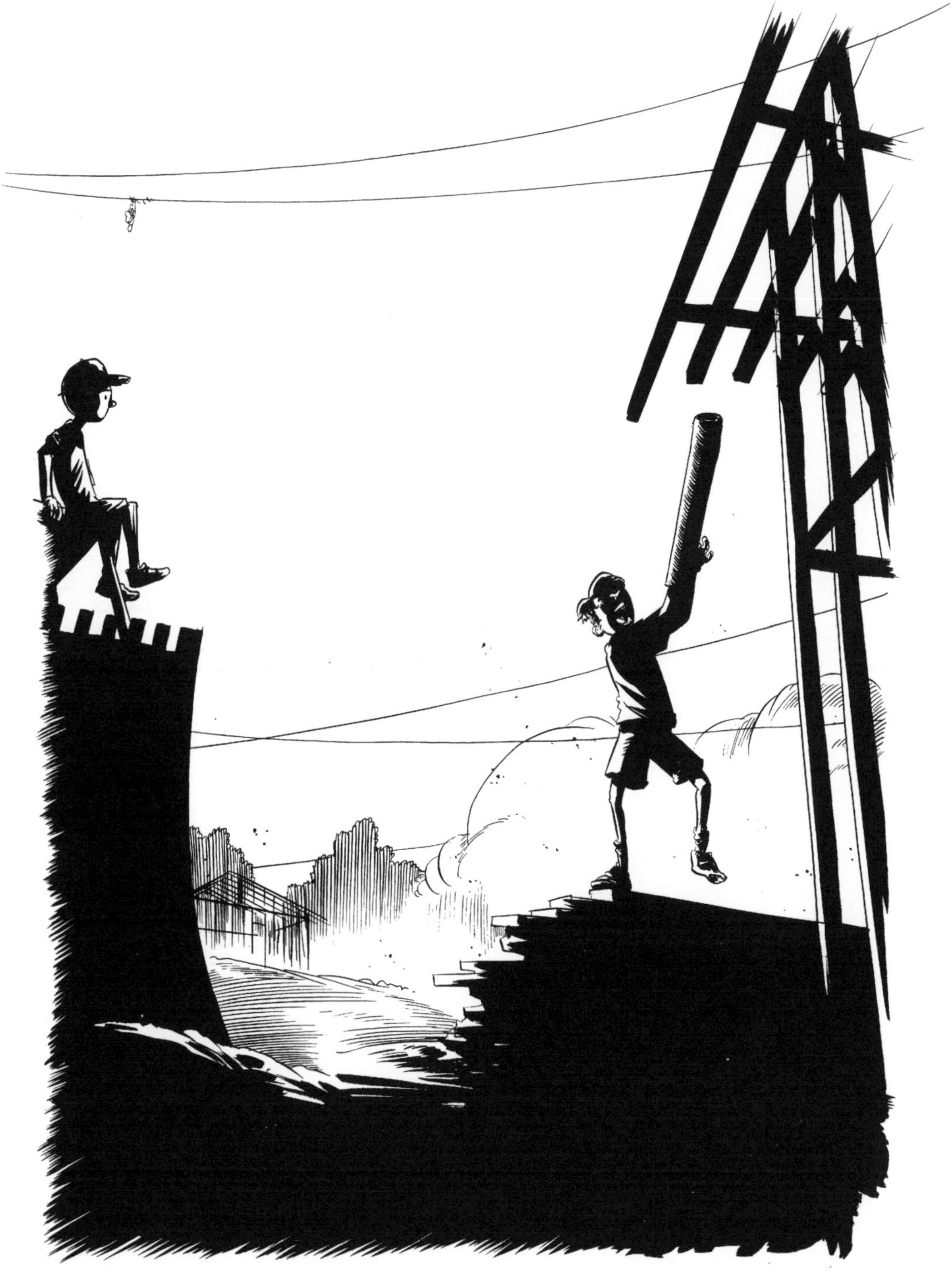

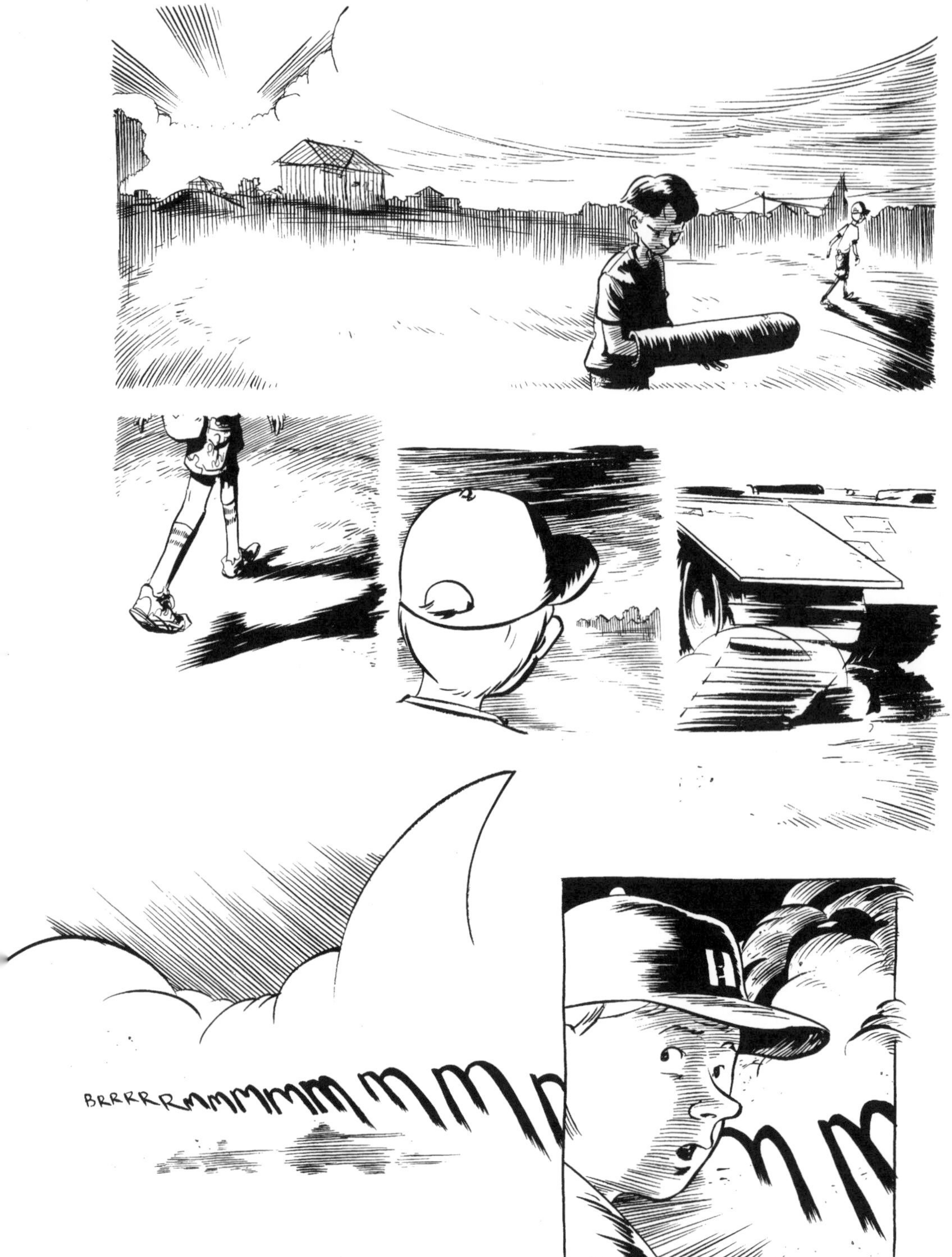
BRRRRRMMMMMMMMMMMM

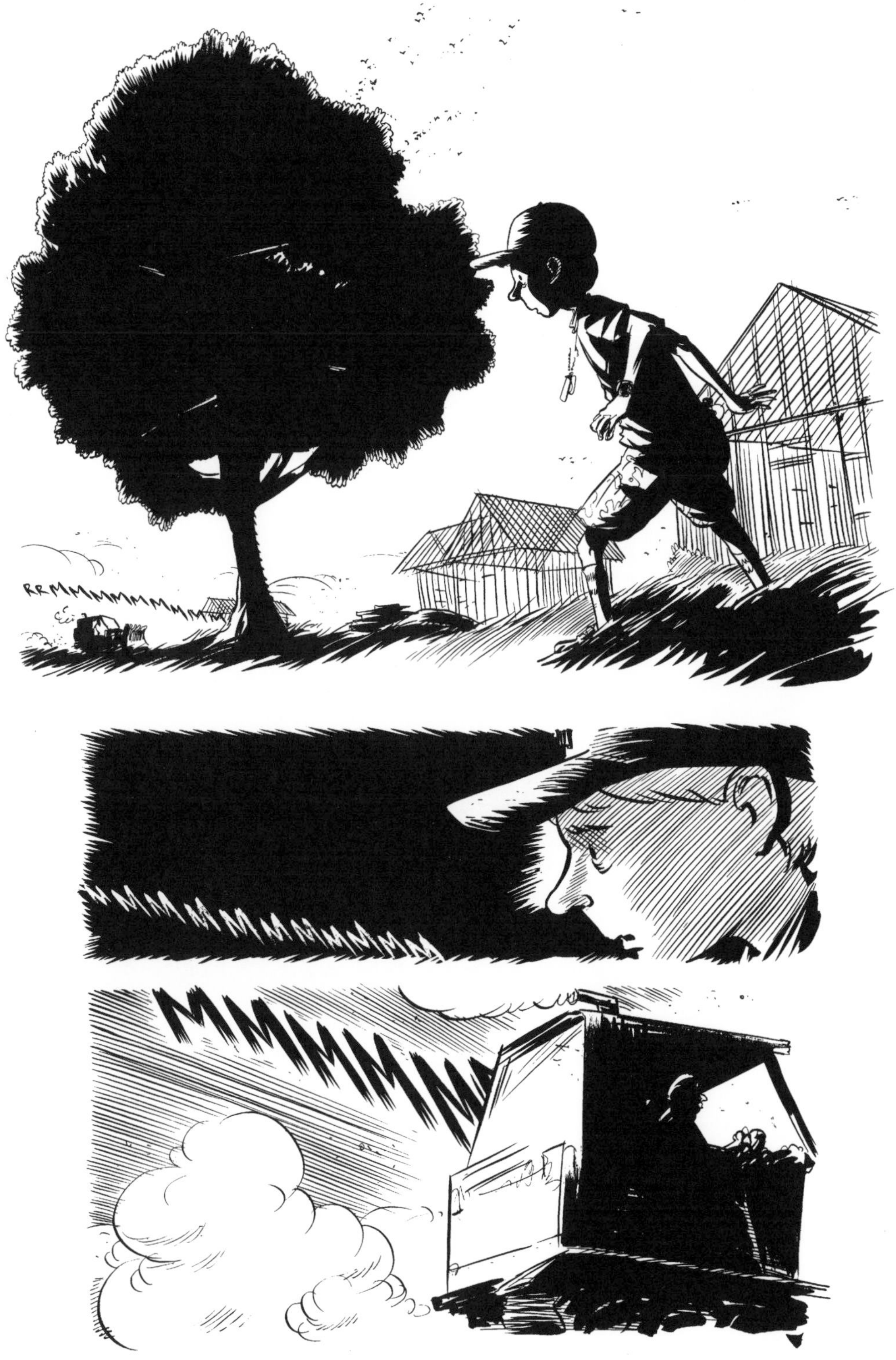

RRMMMMMMMMMMM
MMMMMMMMMMMMMM
MMMMMM

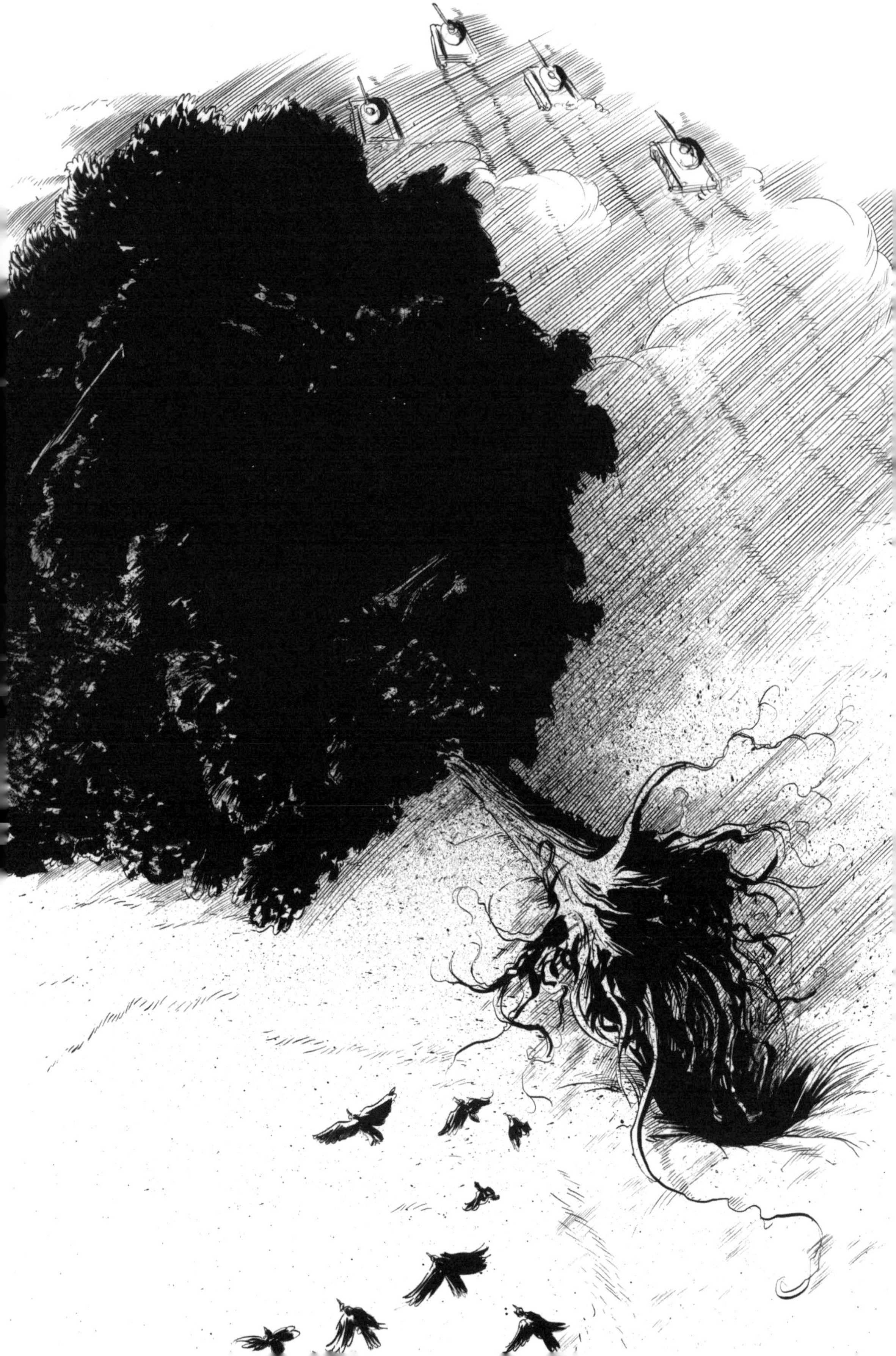

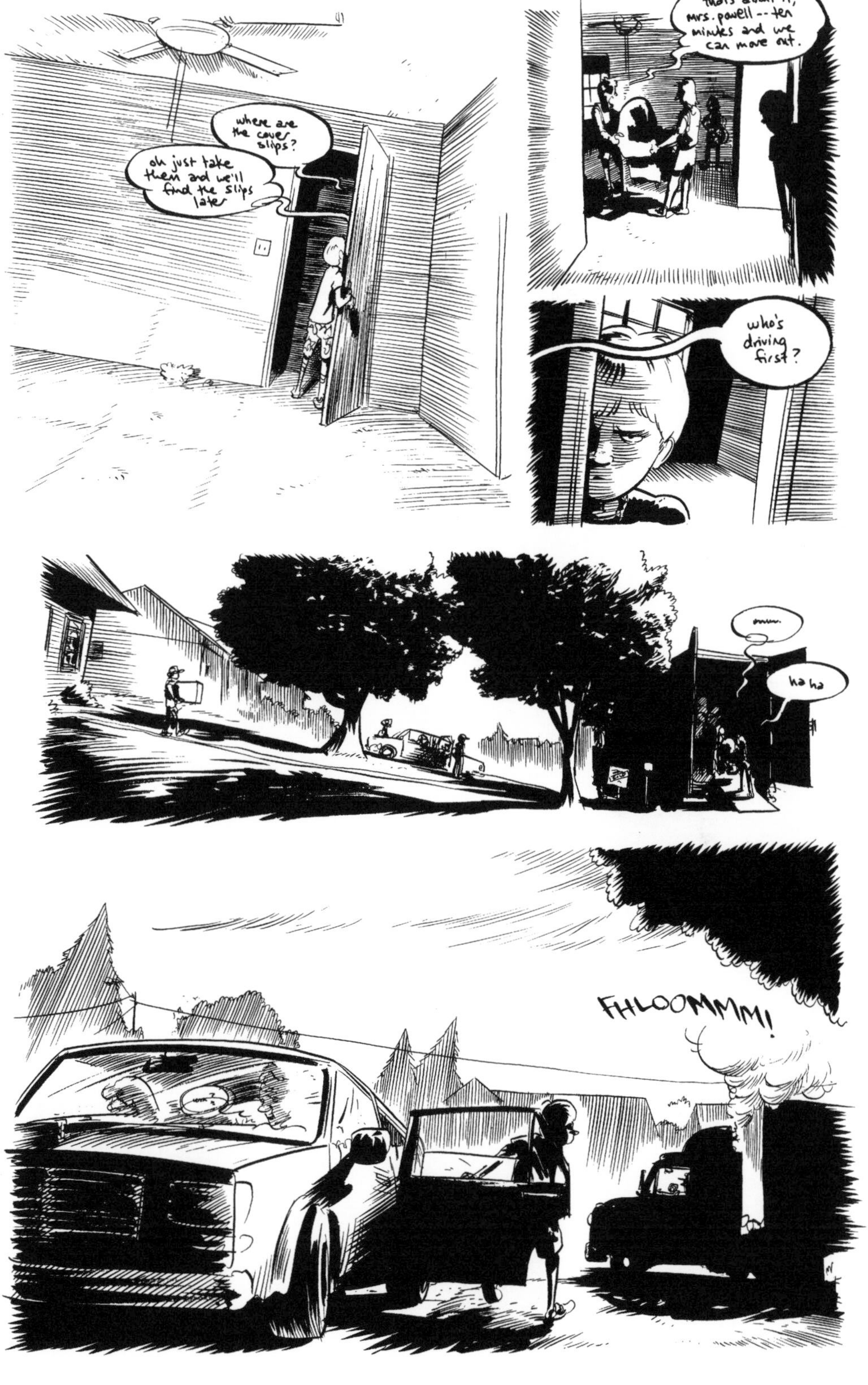
where are the cover slips?
oh just take them and we'll find the slips later
that's about it, mrs. powell -- ten minutes and we can move out.
who's driving first?
mmm.
ha ha
FHLOOMMM!

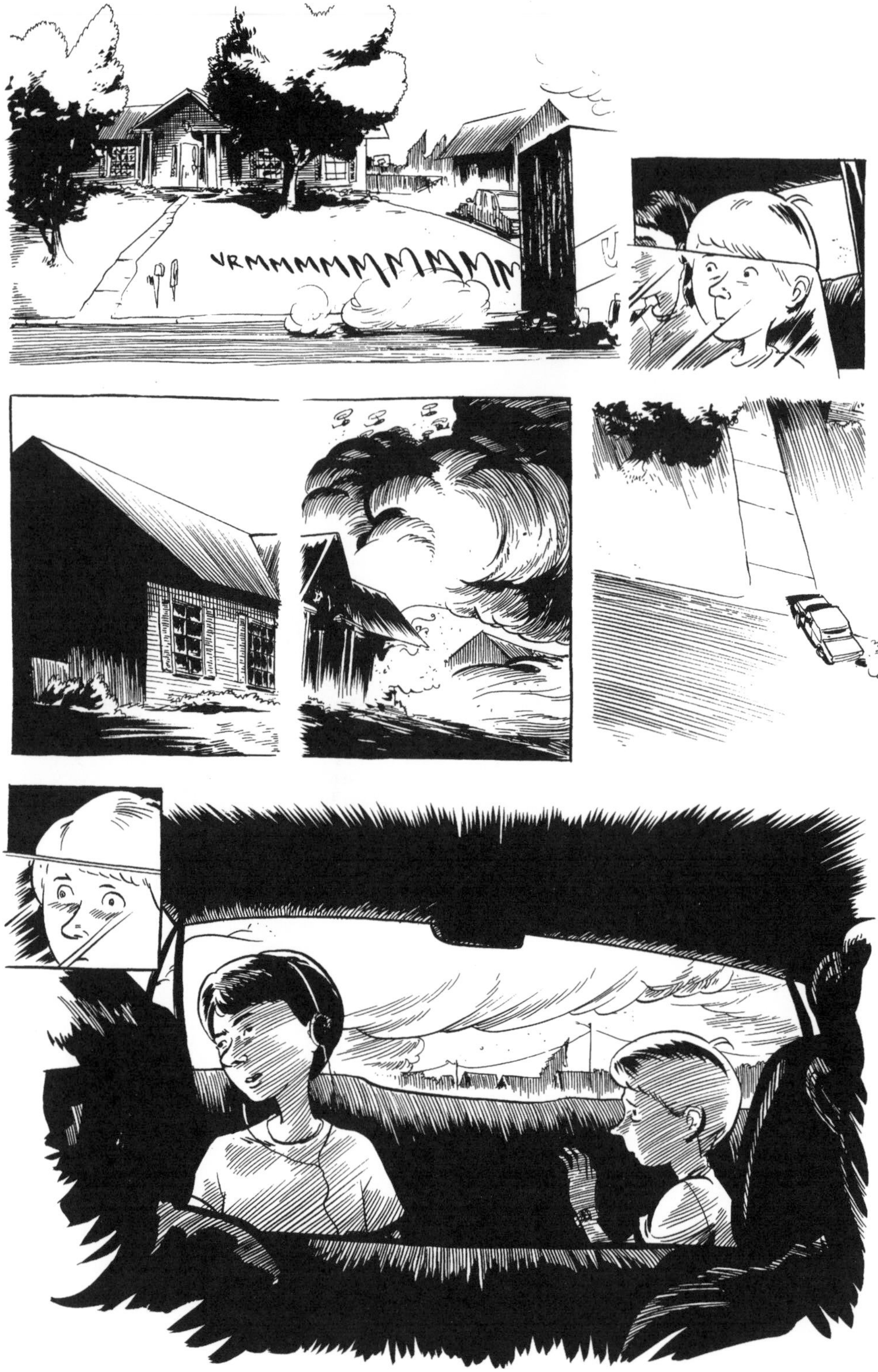
VRMMMMMMMMMMM

PART
2

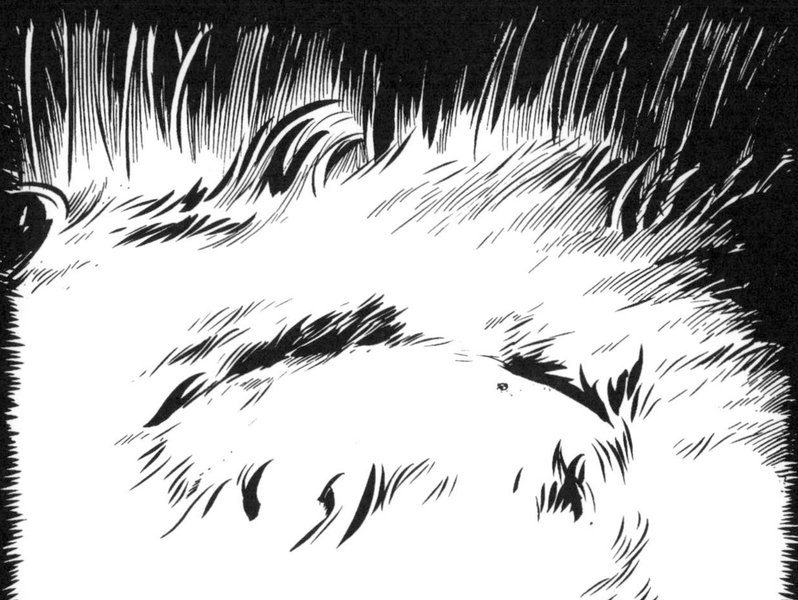

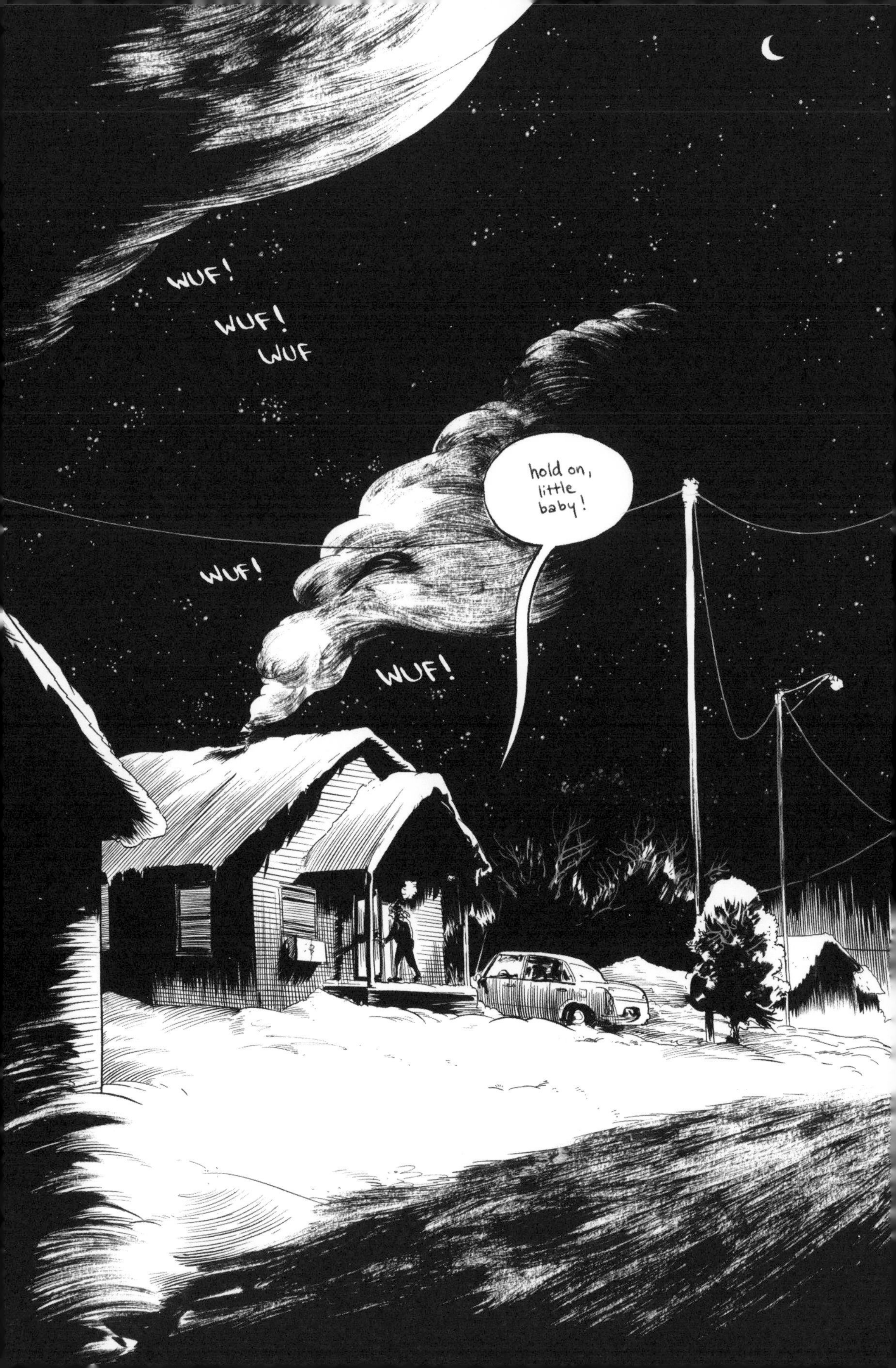
WUF!
WUF!
WUF
hold on, little baby!
WUF!
WUF!

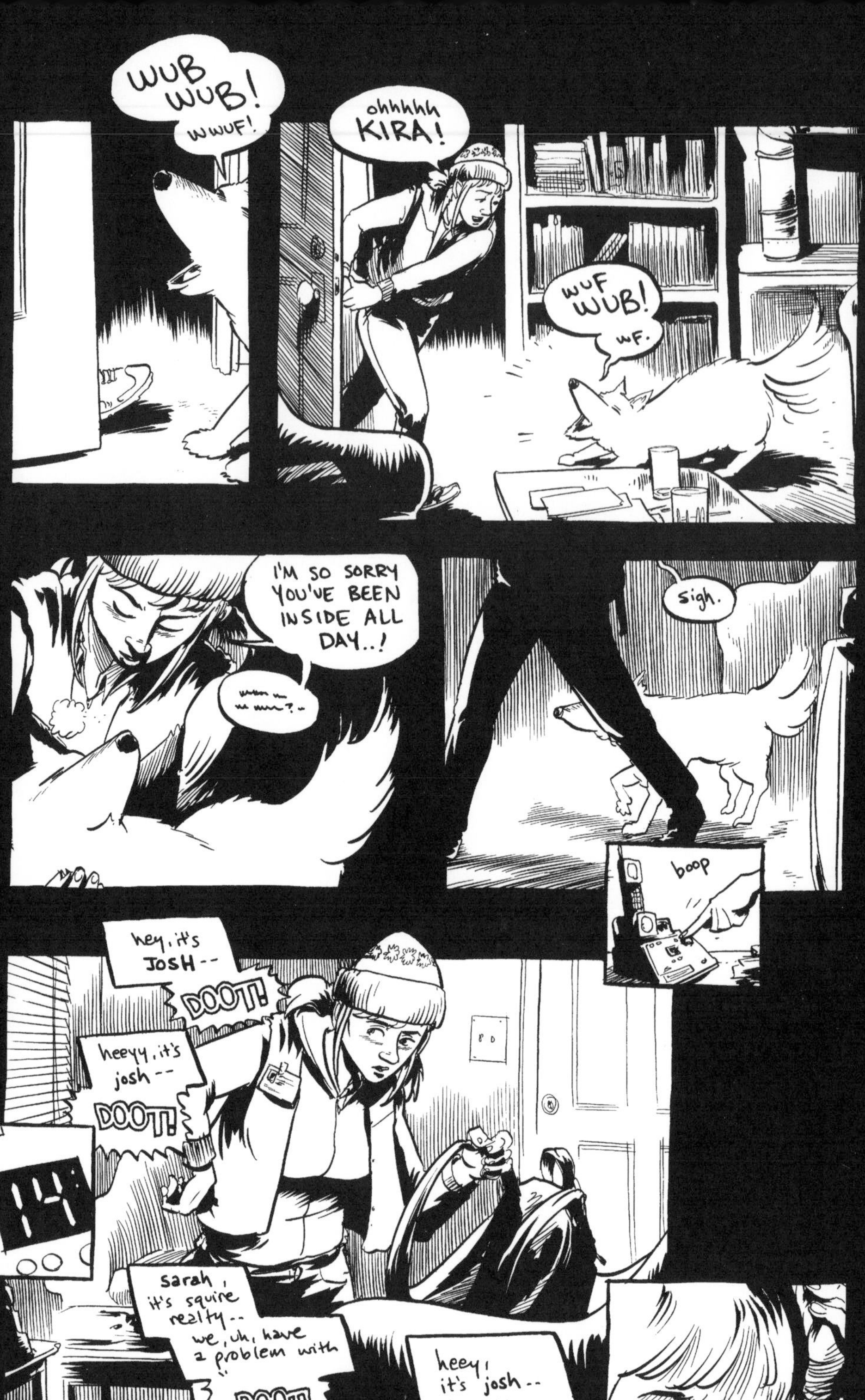
WUB WUB!
WWUF!
ohhhhh KIRA!
WUF WUB!
WF.
I'M SO SORRY YOU'VE BEEN INSIDE ALL DAY..!
sigh.
boop
hey, it's JOSH --
DOOT!
heeyy, it's josh --
DOOT!
14
sarah, it's squire realty -- we, uh, have a problem with
DOOT!
heey, it's josh -- can you please r
DOOT!

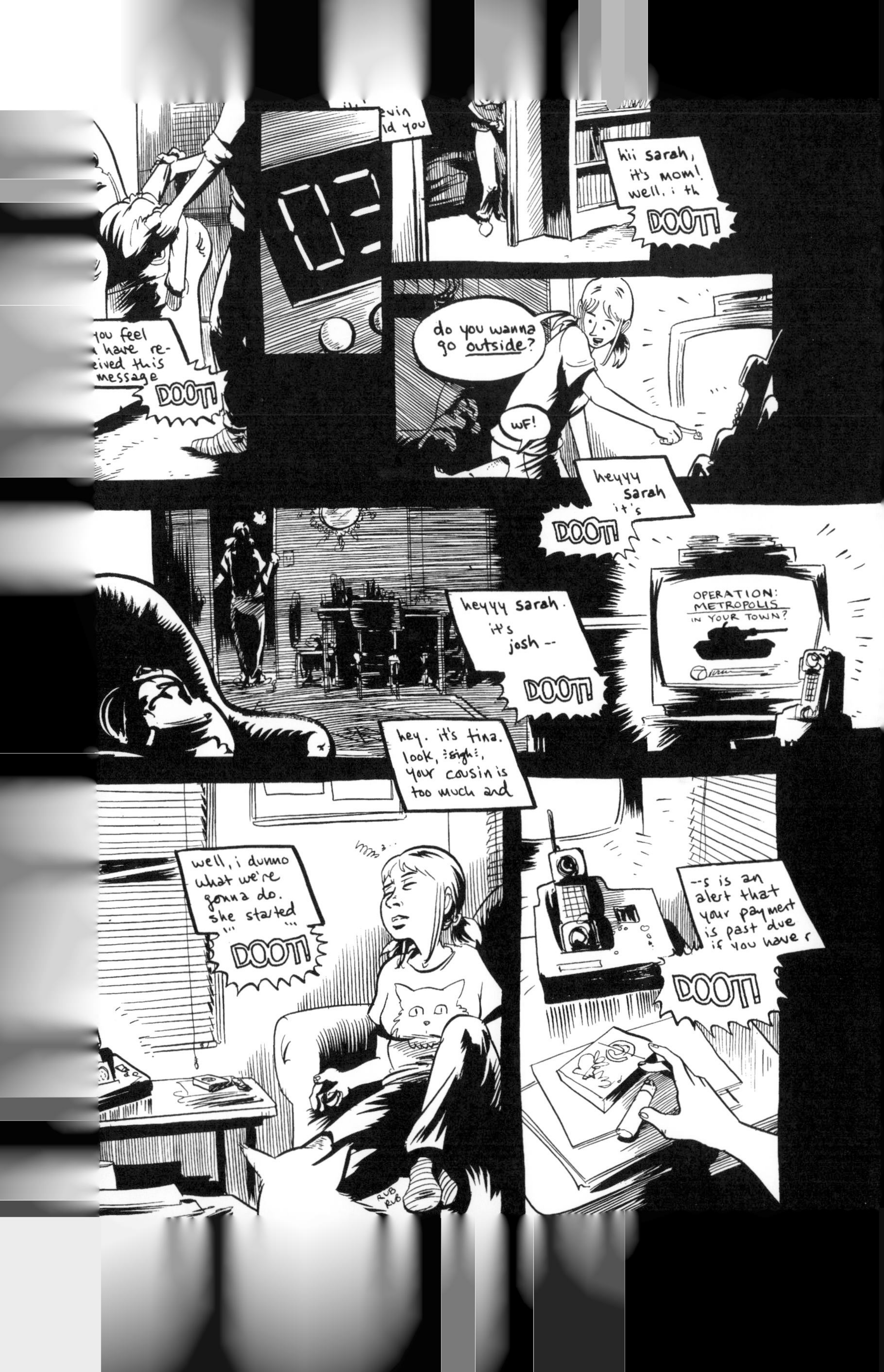

evin
ld you
you feel
n have re-
eived this
message
DOOT!
hii sarah,
it's mom!
well, i th
DOOT!
do you wanna go outside?
WF!
heyyy sarah it's
DOOT!
heyyy sarah. it's josh --
DOOT!
OPERATION: METROPOLIS IN YOUR TOWN?
hey. it's tina. look, sigh, your cousin is too much and
well, i dunno what we're gonna do. she started ... ...
DOOT!
--s is an alert that your payment is past due if you have r
DOOT!
RUB RUB

ya know, it's like the world opened up my mouth and took a BIG FAT SHIT in it.
sigh
big fat shit.

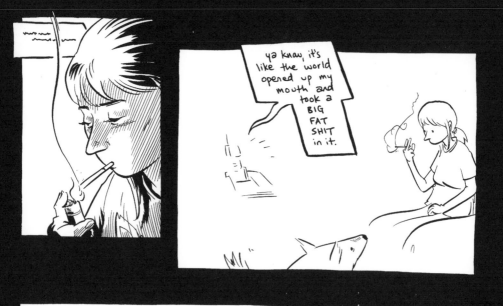

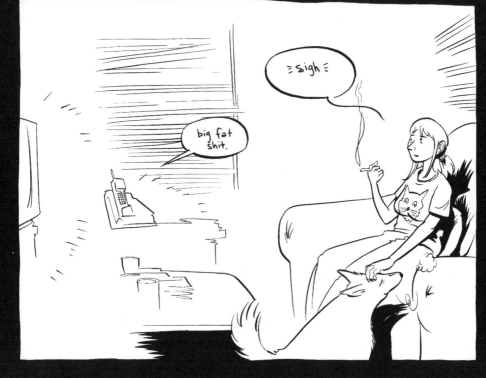

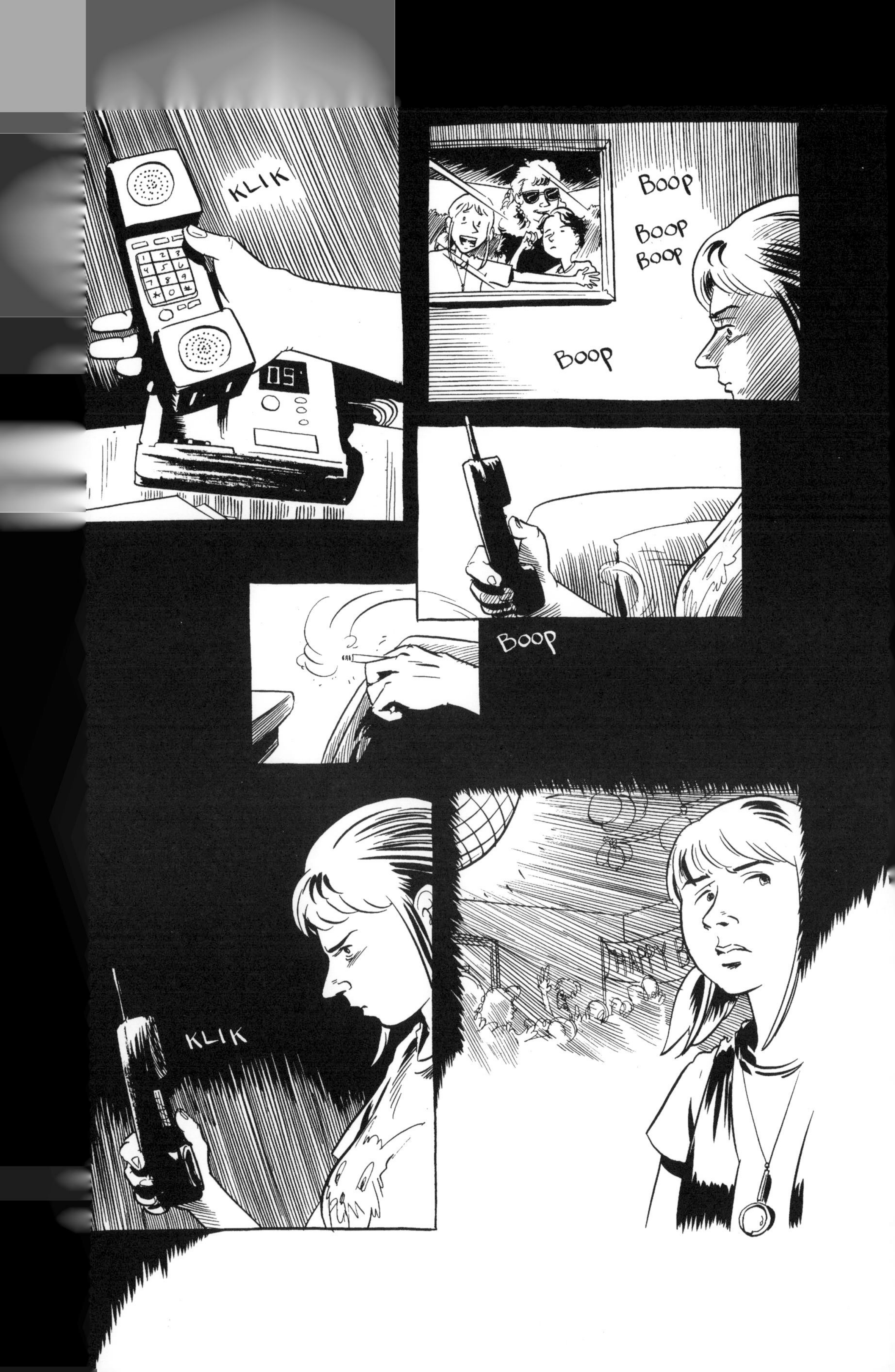
KLIK
Boop
Boop
Boop
Boop
Boop
KLIK

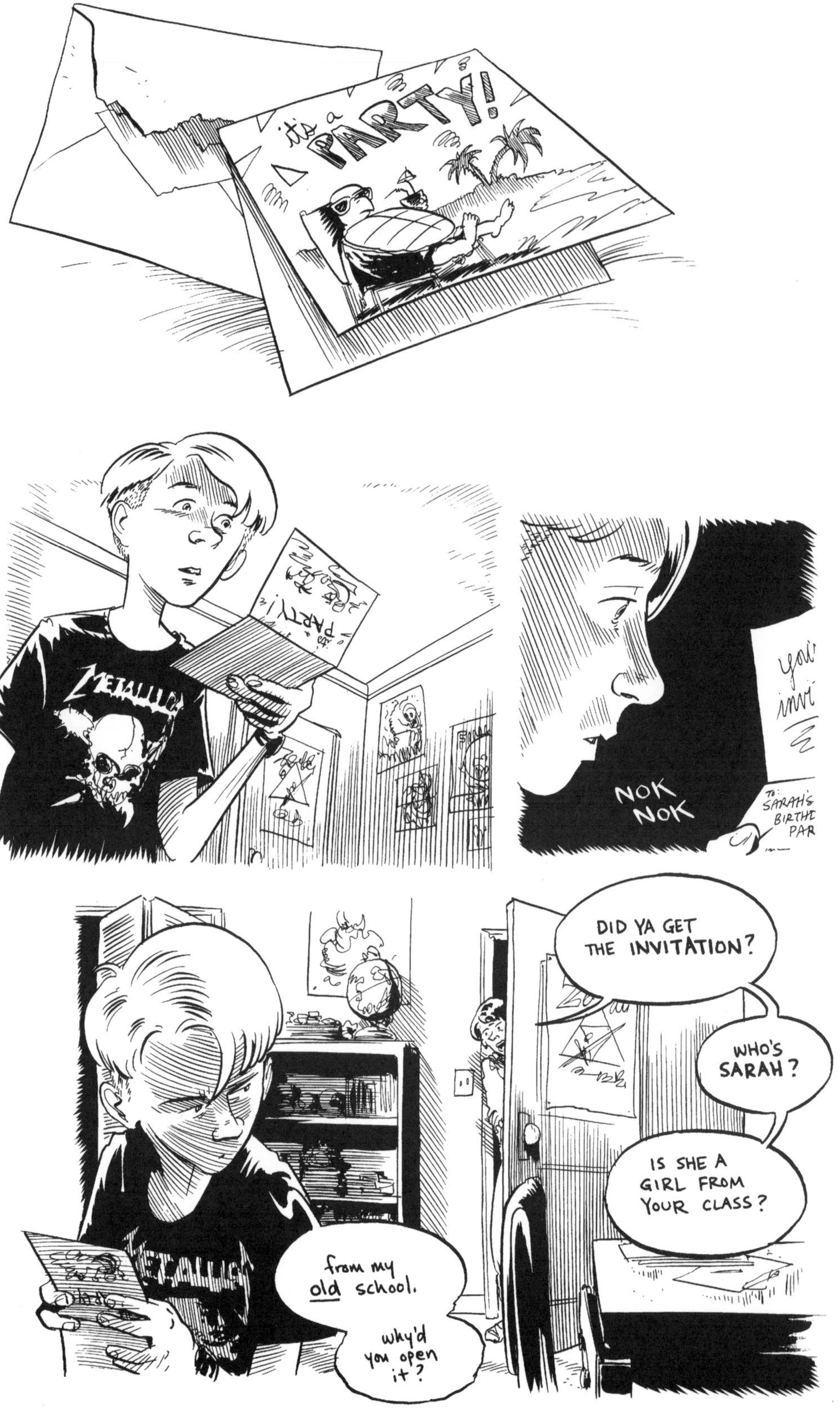
it's a PARTY!
METALLICA
NOK NOK
TO: SARAH'S
DID YA GET THE INVITATION?
WHO'S SARAH?
IS SHE A GIRL FROM YOUR CLASS?
from my old school.
why'd you open it?

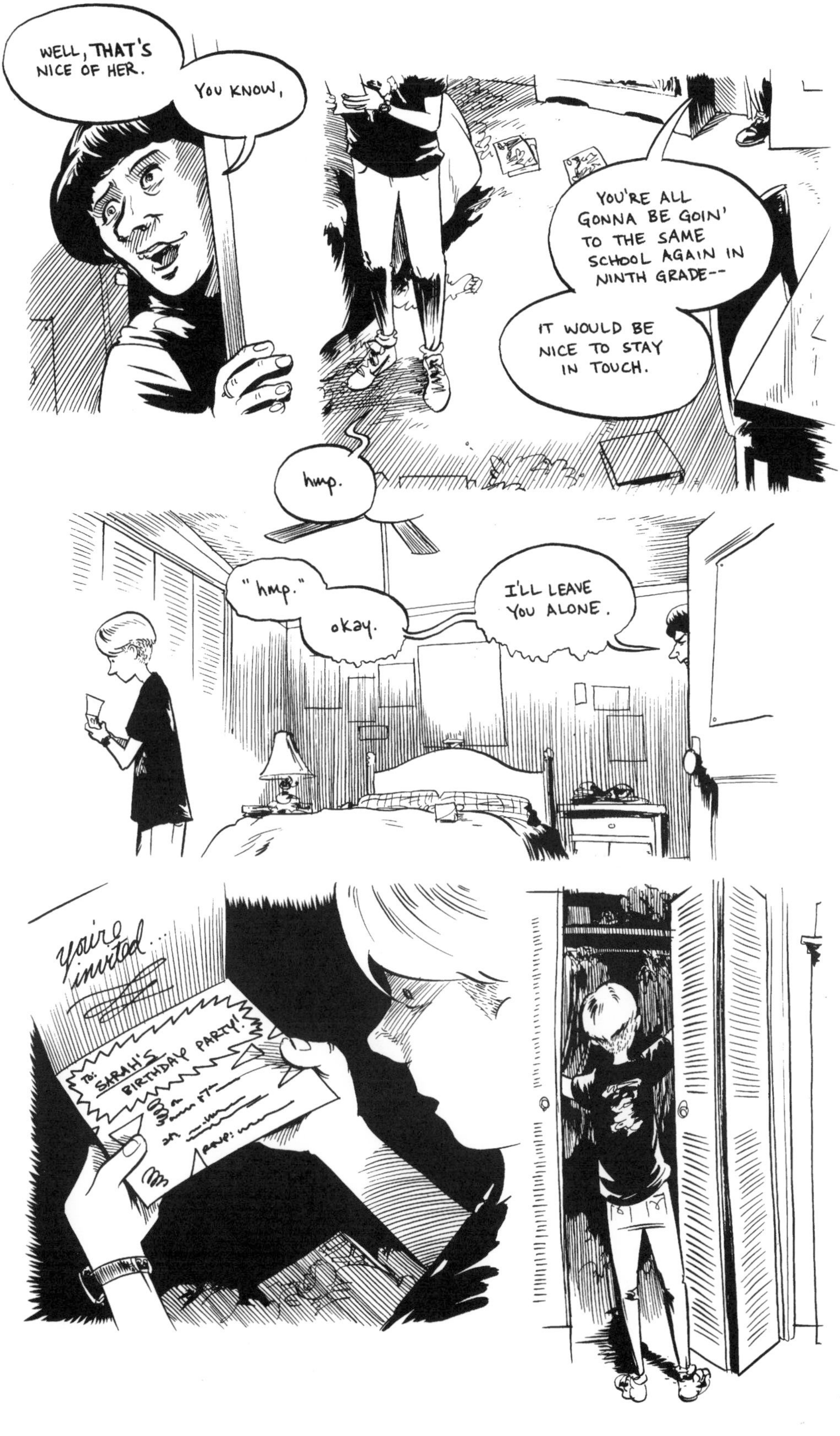
WELL, THAT'S NICE OF HER.
YOU KNOW,
YOU'RE ALL GONNA BE GOIN' TO THE SAME SCHOOL AGAIN IN NINTH GRADE--
IT WOULD BE NICE TO STAY IN TOUCH.
hmp.
"hmp." okay.
I'LL LEAVE YOU ALONE.
you're invited...
TO: SARAH'S BIRTHDAY PARTY!

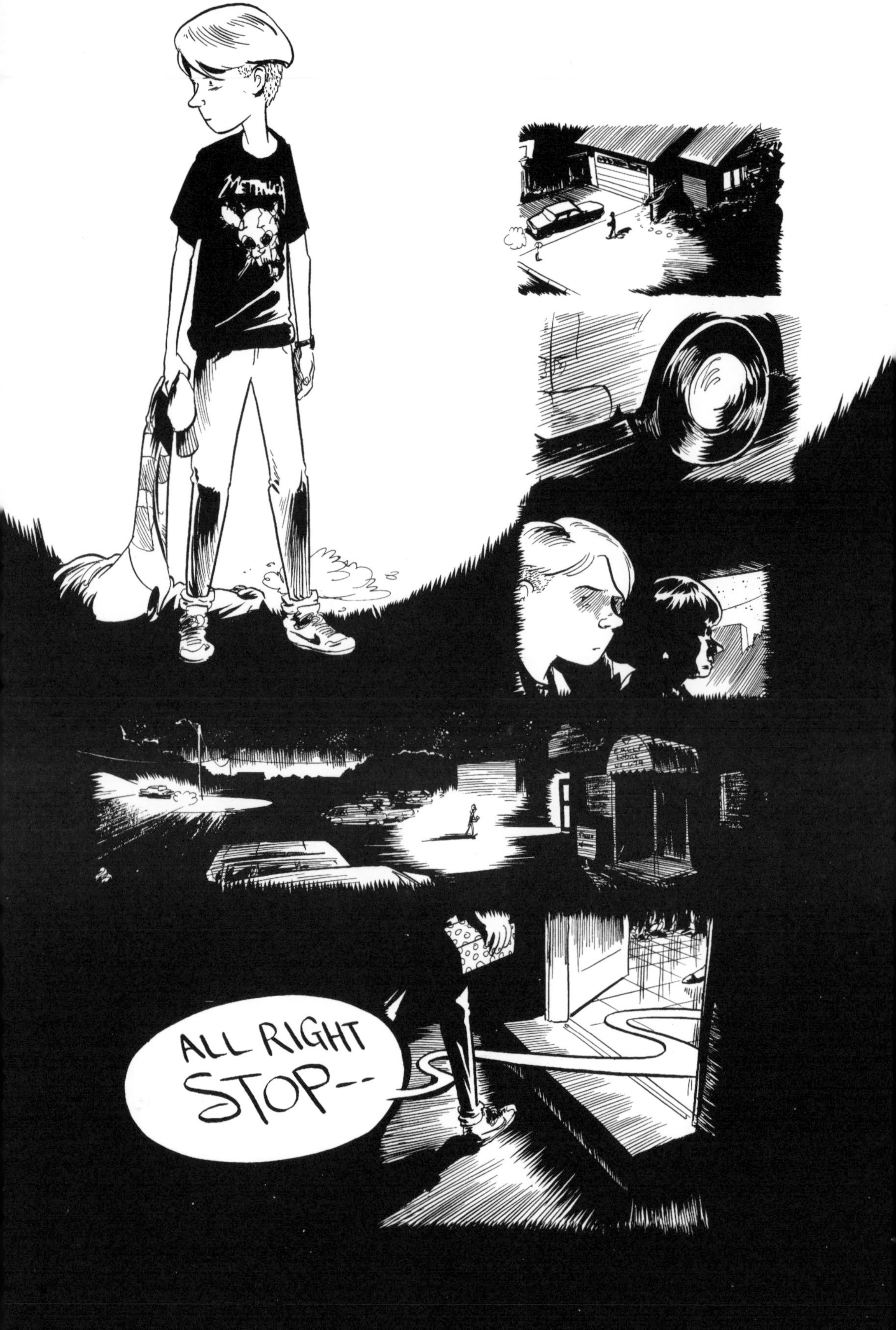
METALLICA
ALL RIGHT STOP--

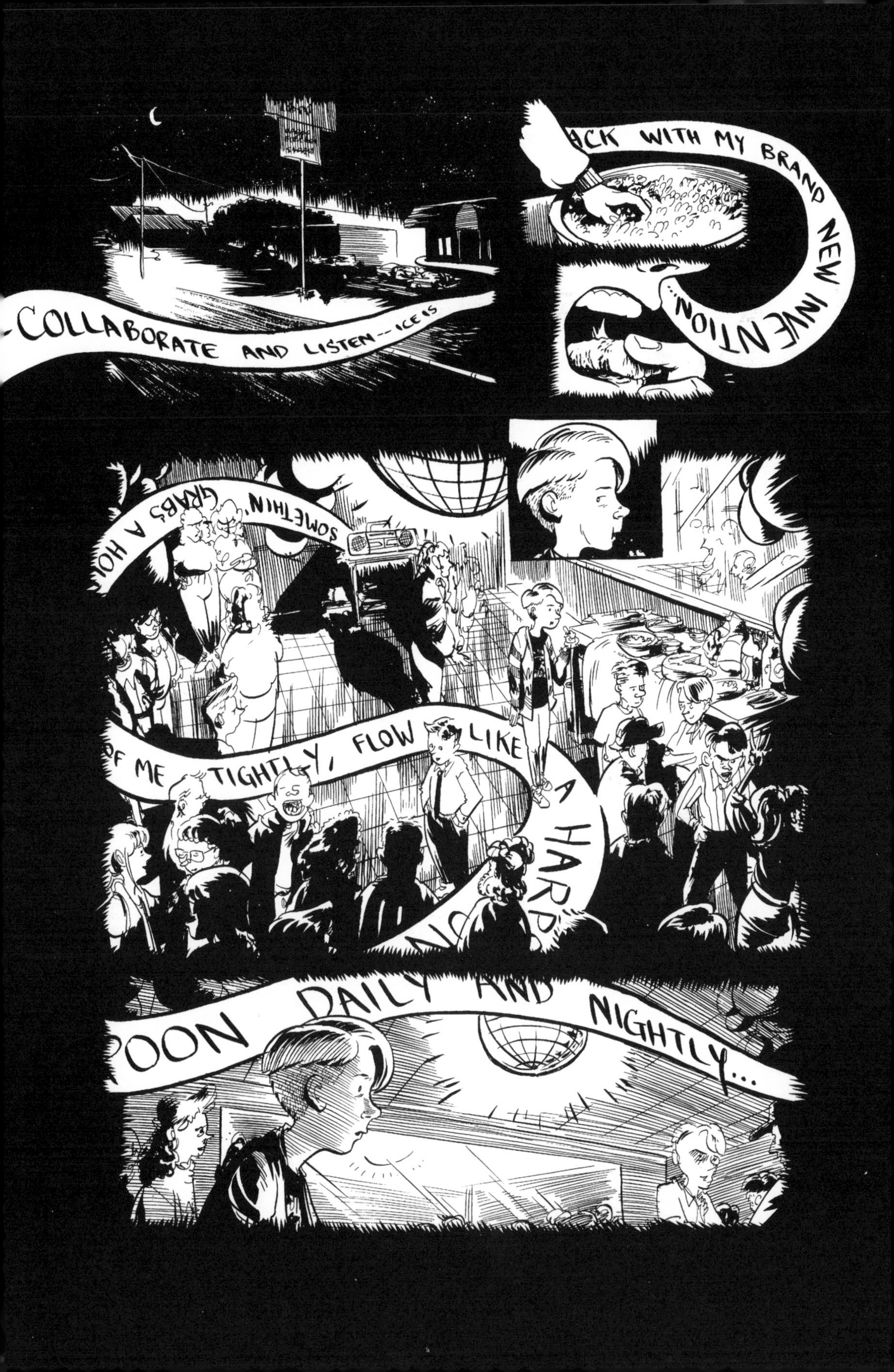
-COLLABORATE AND LISTEN--ICE IS
ACK WITH MY BRAND NEW INVENTION...
SOMETHIN', GRABS A HOL
OF ME TIGHTLY, FLOW LIKE A HARPOON
POON DAILY AND NIGHTLY...

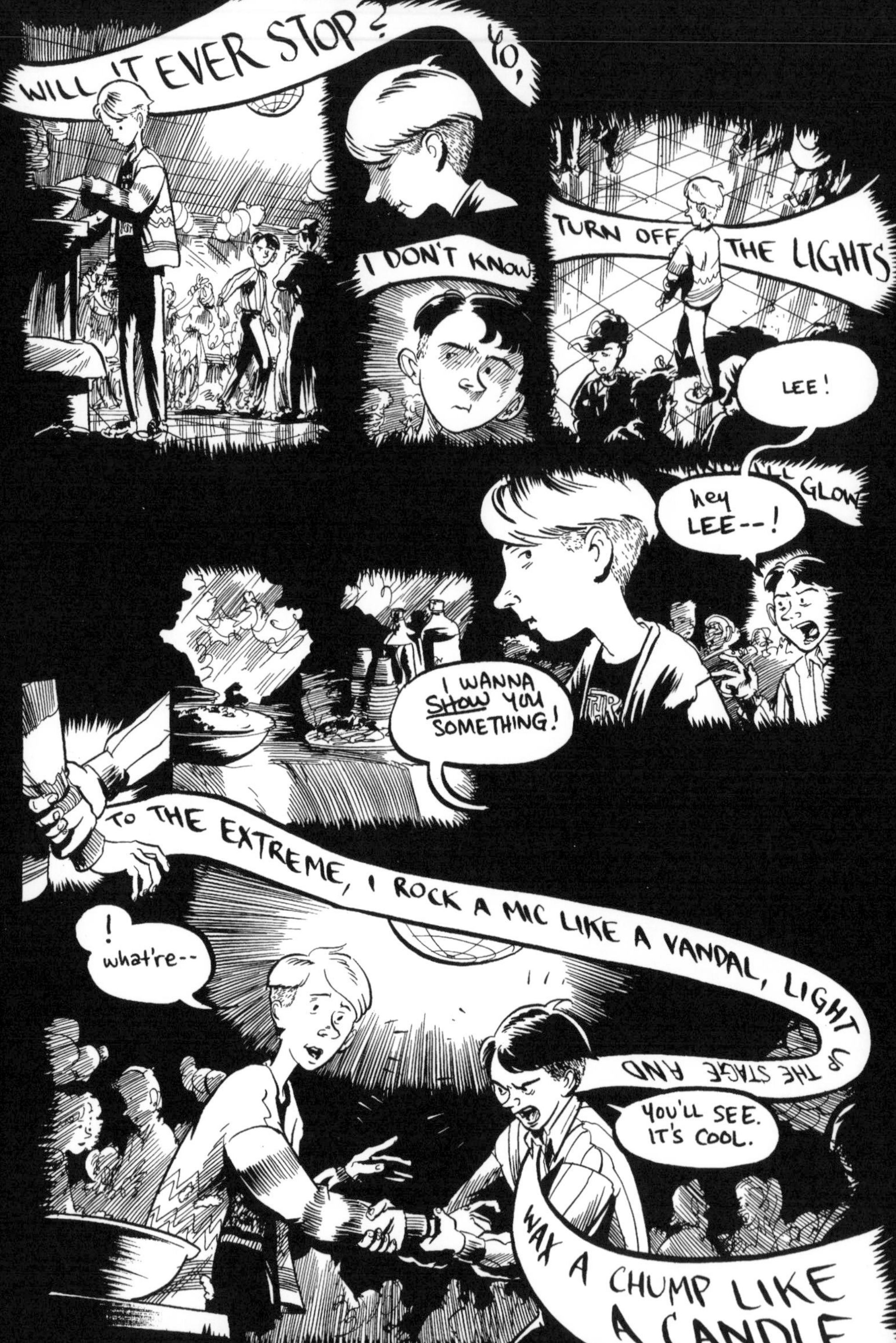
WILL IT EVER STOP?
YO,
I DON'T KNOW
TURN OFF THE LIGHTS
LEE!
hey LEE--!
I WANNA SHOW YOU SOMETHING!
TO THE EXTREME, I ROCK A MIC LIKE A VANDAL, LIGHT UP THE STAGE AND
! what're--
YOU'LL SEE. IT'S COOL.
WAX A CHUMP LIKE A CANDLE.

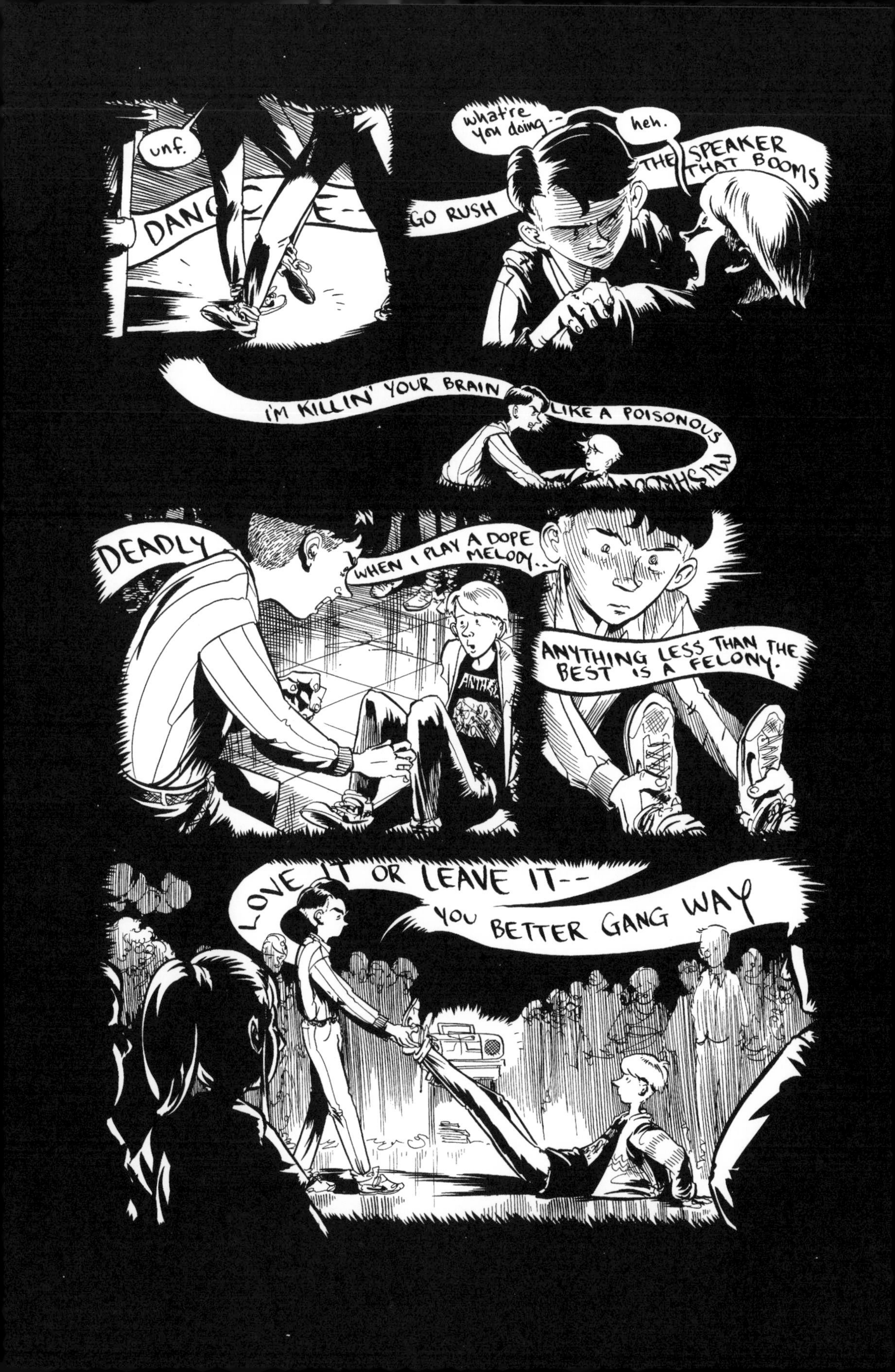
unf.
DANCE--
what're you doing--
heh.
GO RUSH
THE SPEAKER THAT BOOMS
I'M KILLIN' YOUR BRAIN
LIKE A POISONOUS MUSHROOM
DEADLY
WHEN I PLAY A DOPE MELODY..
ANYTHING LESS THAN THE BEST IS A FELONY.
LOVE IT OR LEAVE IT--
YOU BETTER GANG WAY

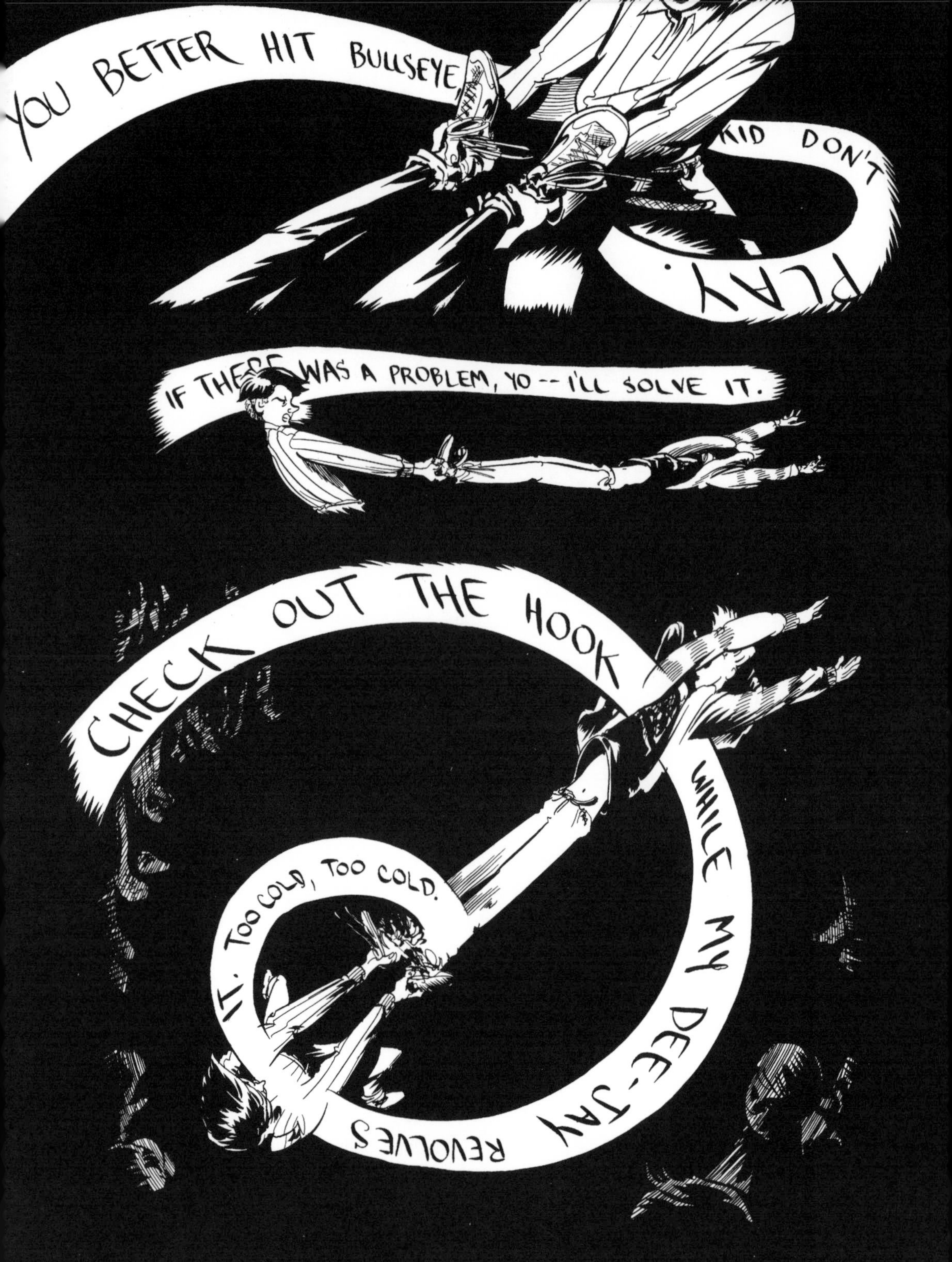
YOU BETTER HIT BULLSEYE, KID DON'T PLAY.
IF THERE WAS A PROBLEM, YO -- I'LL SOLVE IT.
CHECK OUT THE HOOK WHILE MY DEE-JAY REVOLVES IT. TOO COLD, TOO COLD.

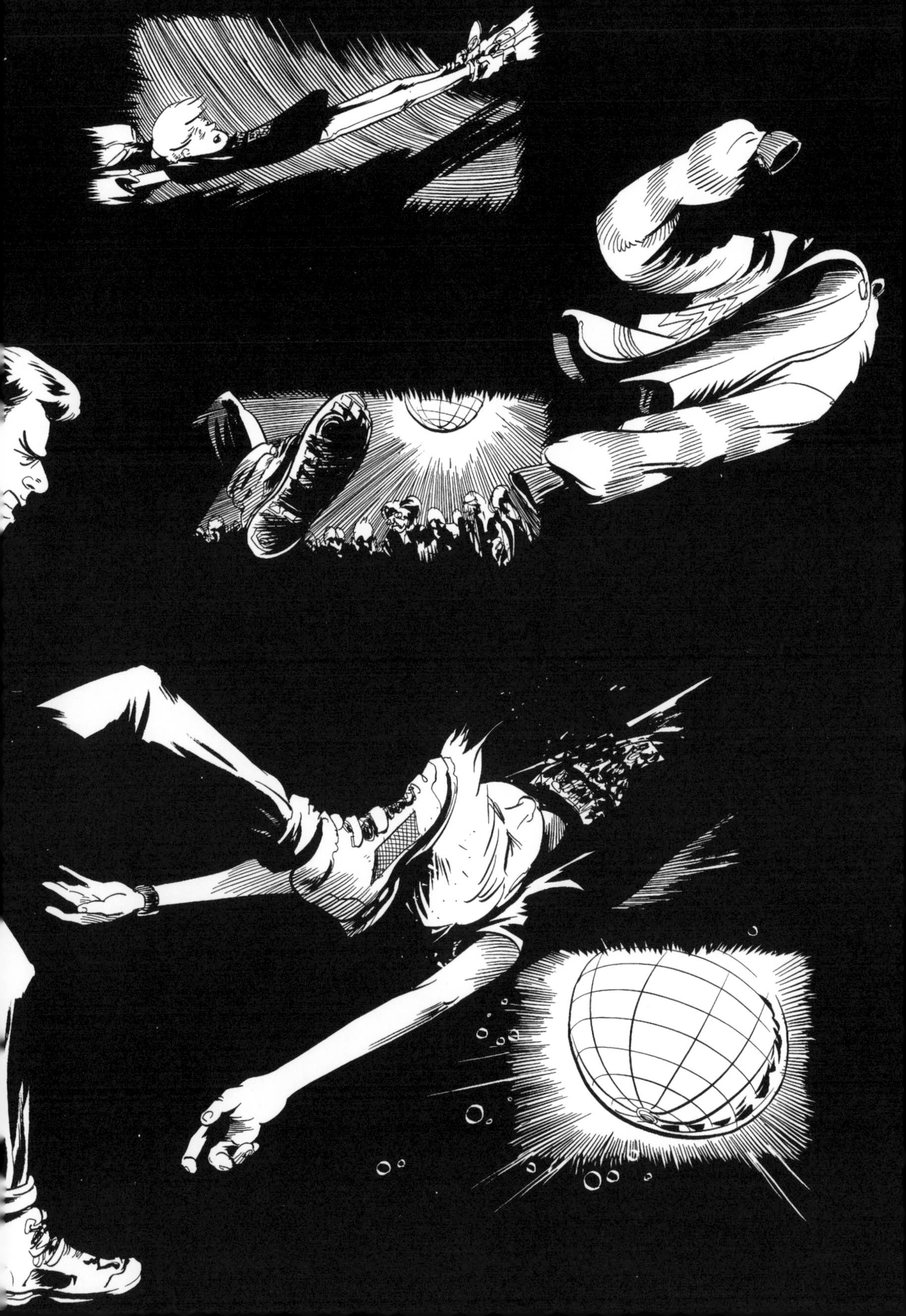

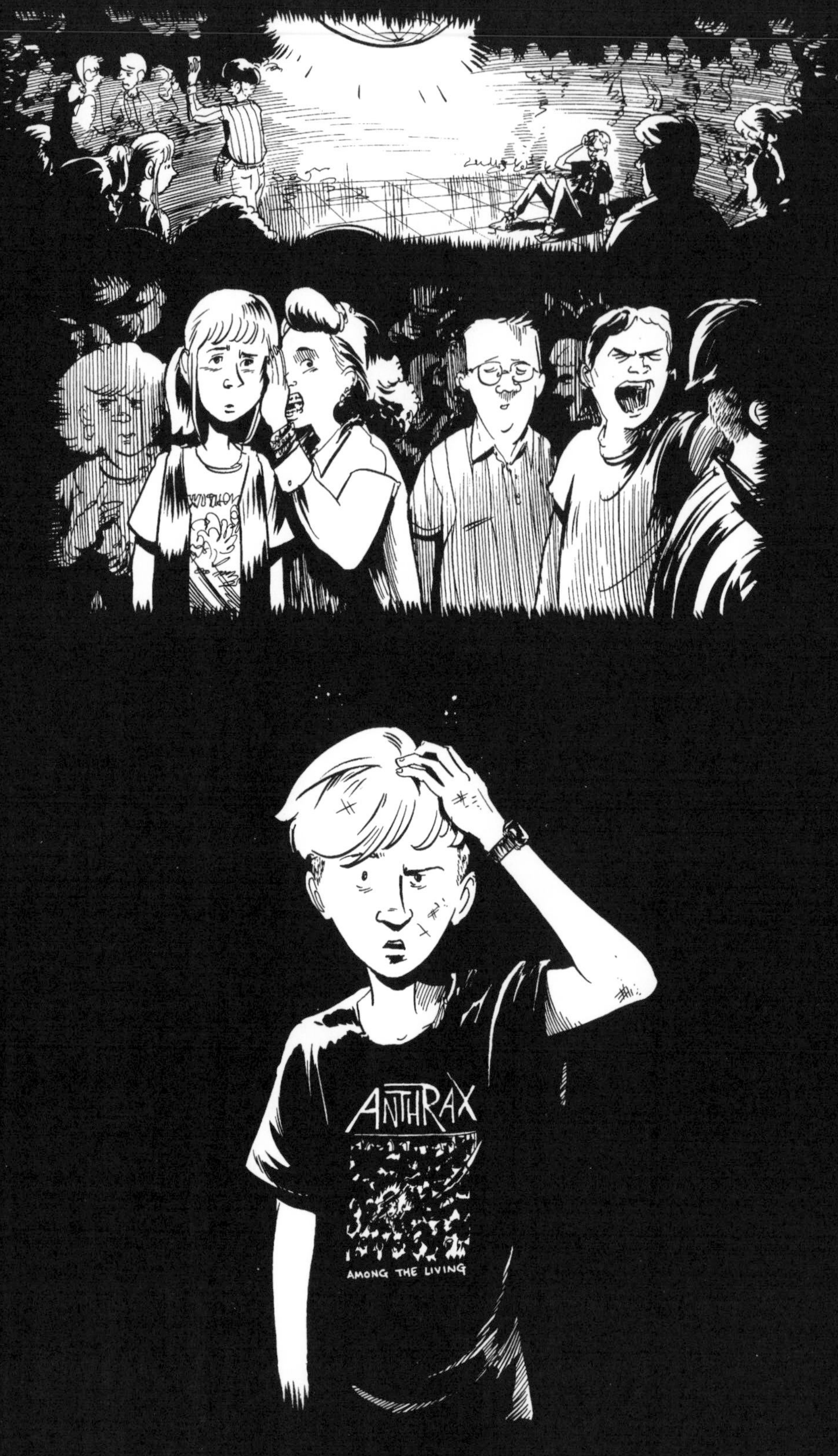
ANTHRAX
AMONG THE LIVING

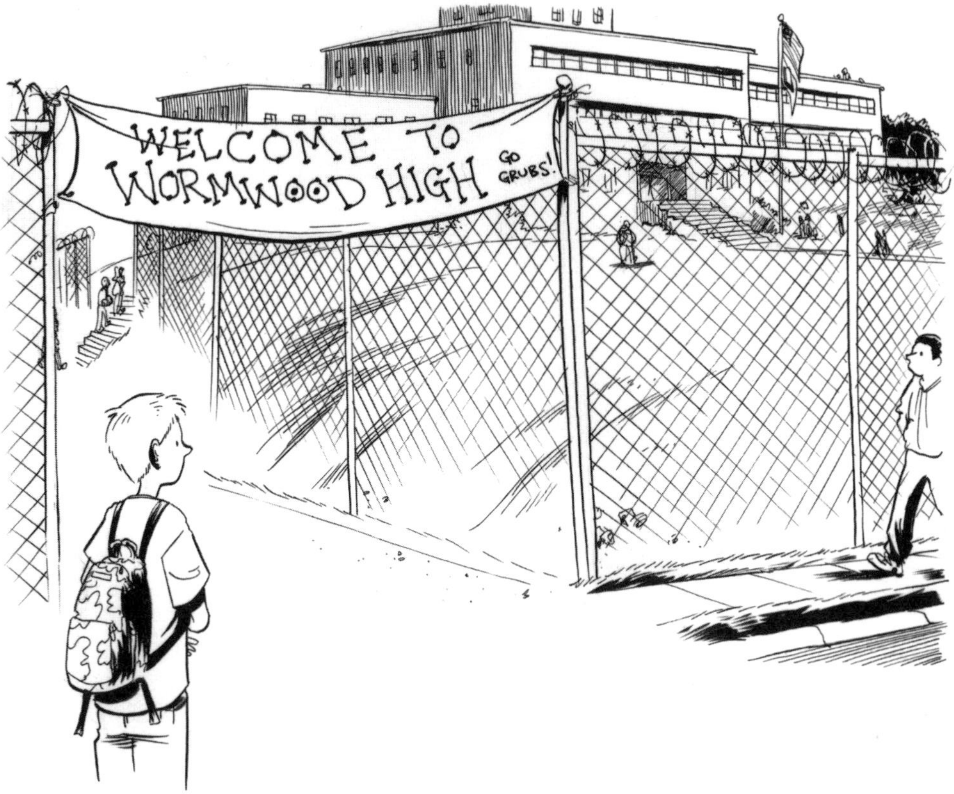
WELCOME TO
WORMWOOD HIGH
GO GRUBS!

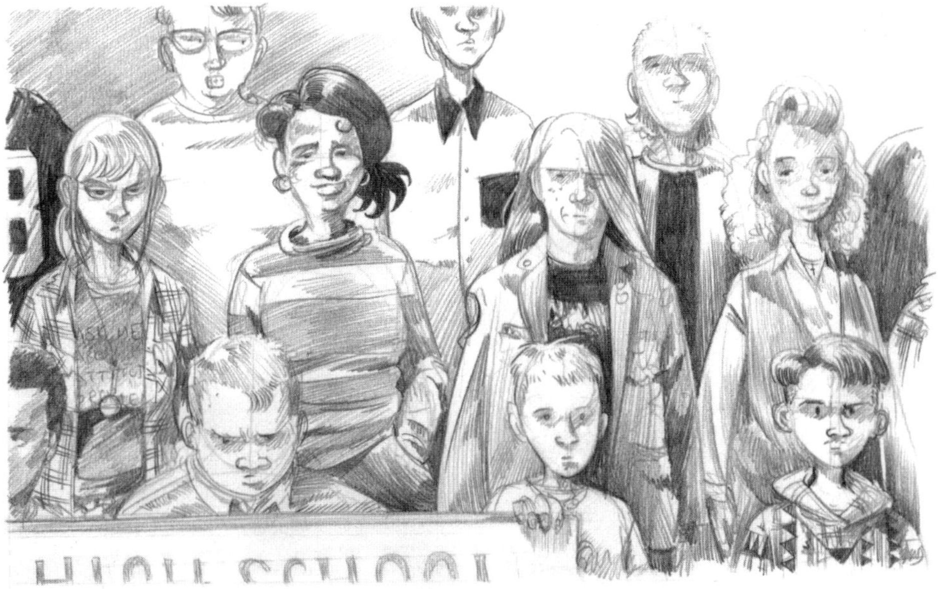

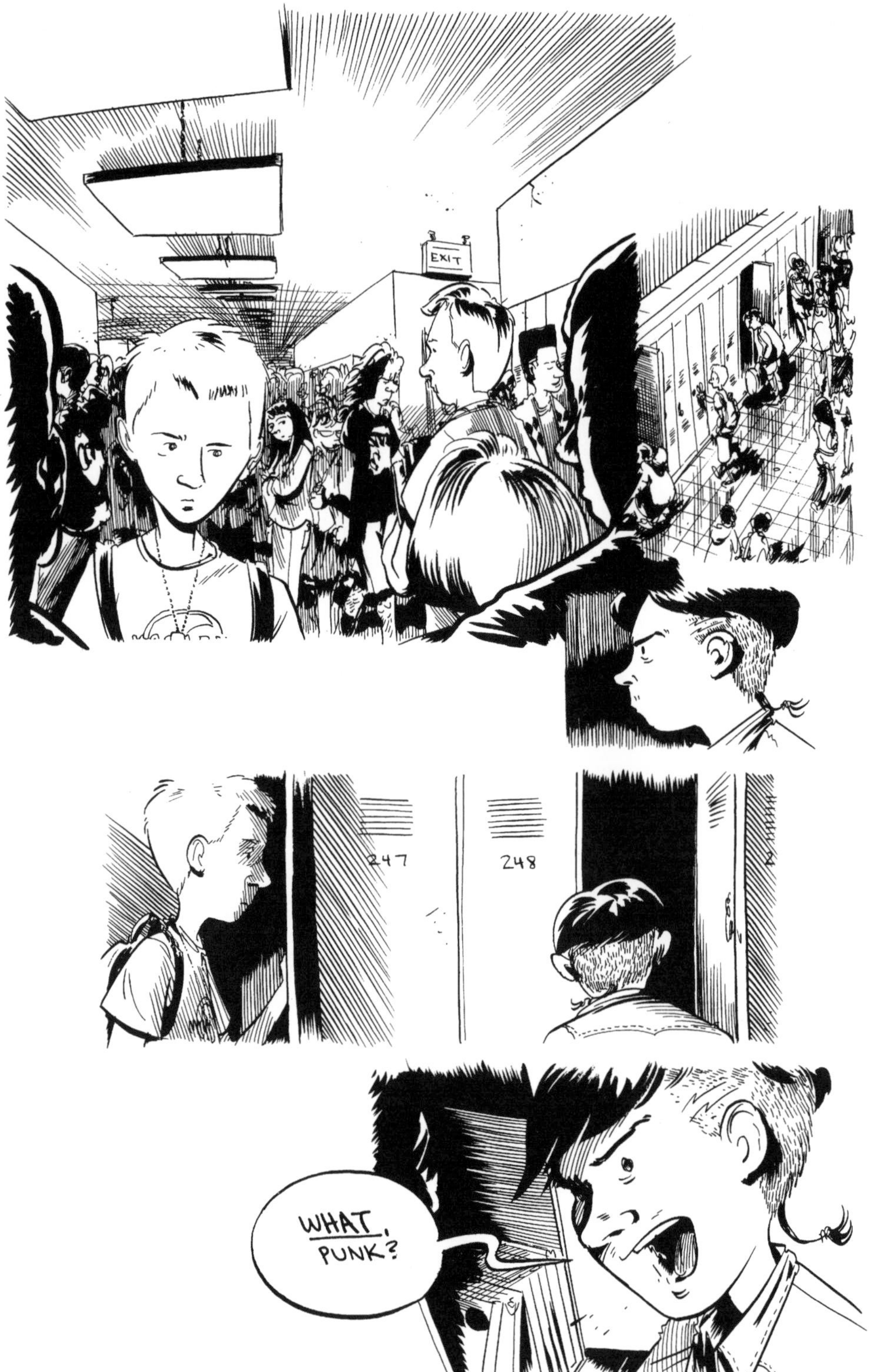
EXIT
247
248
WHAT, PUNK?

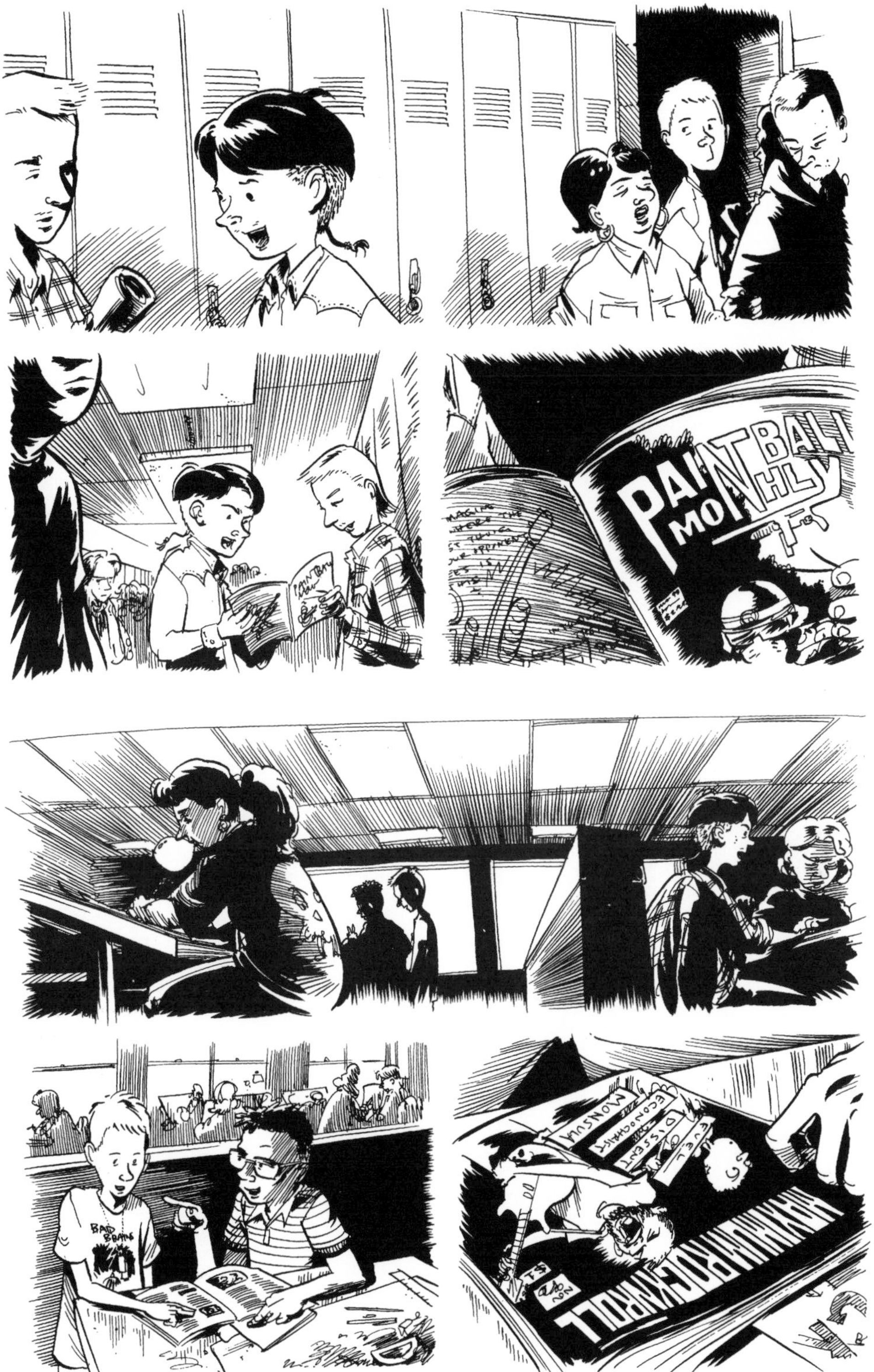
BAD BRAINS

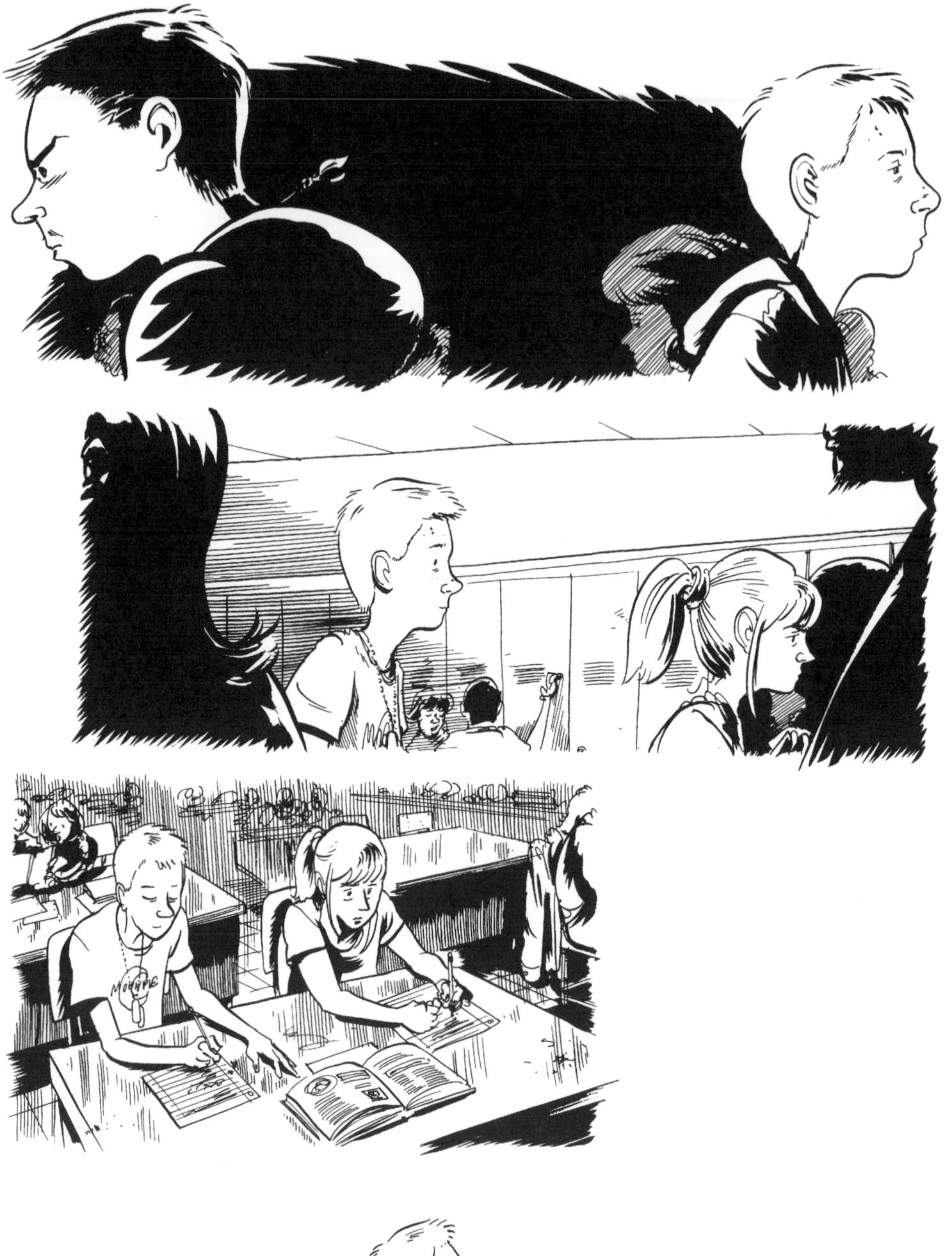

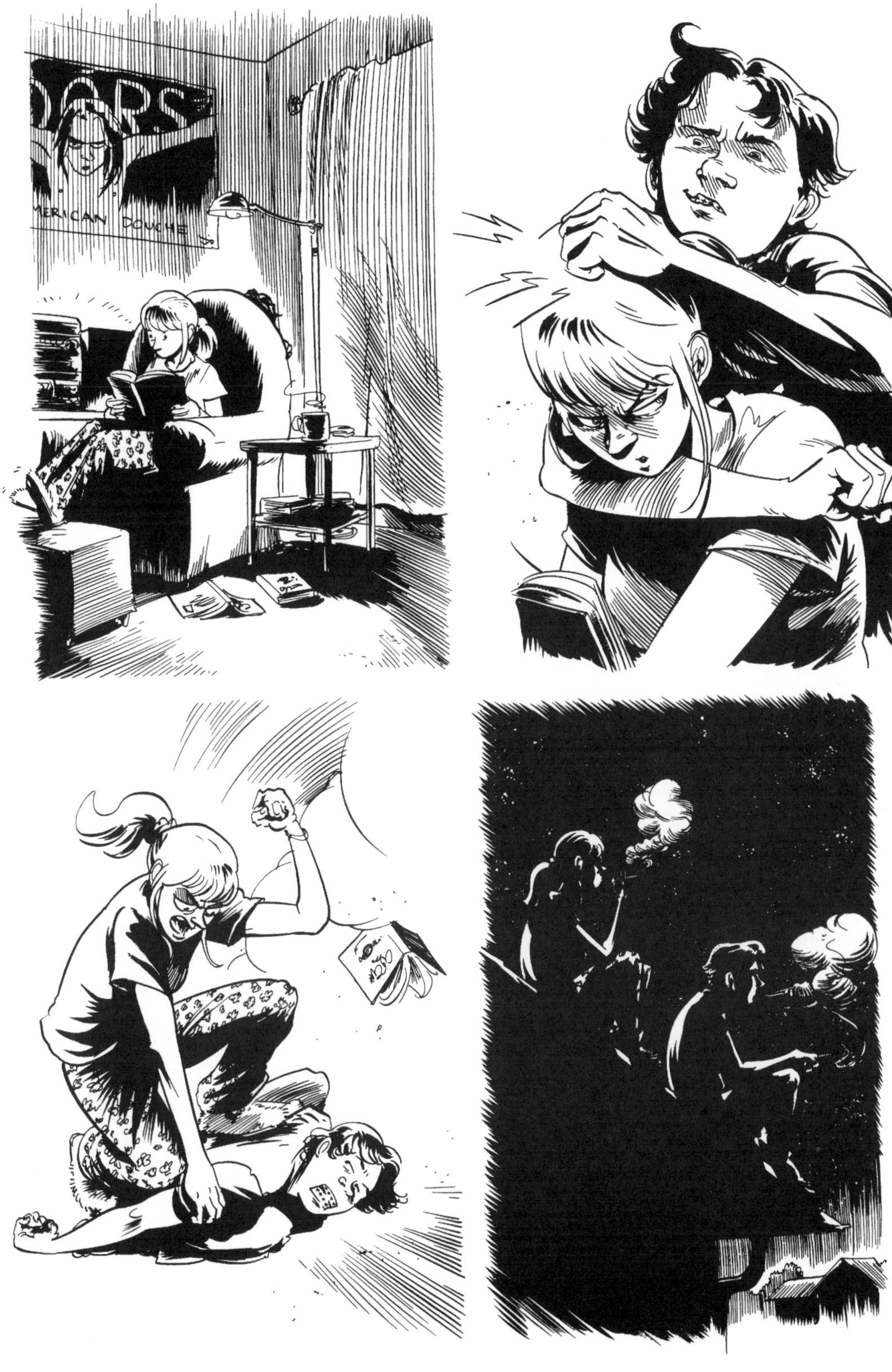
MERICAN DOUCHE

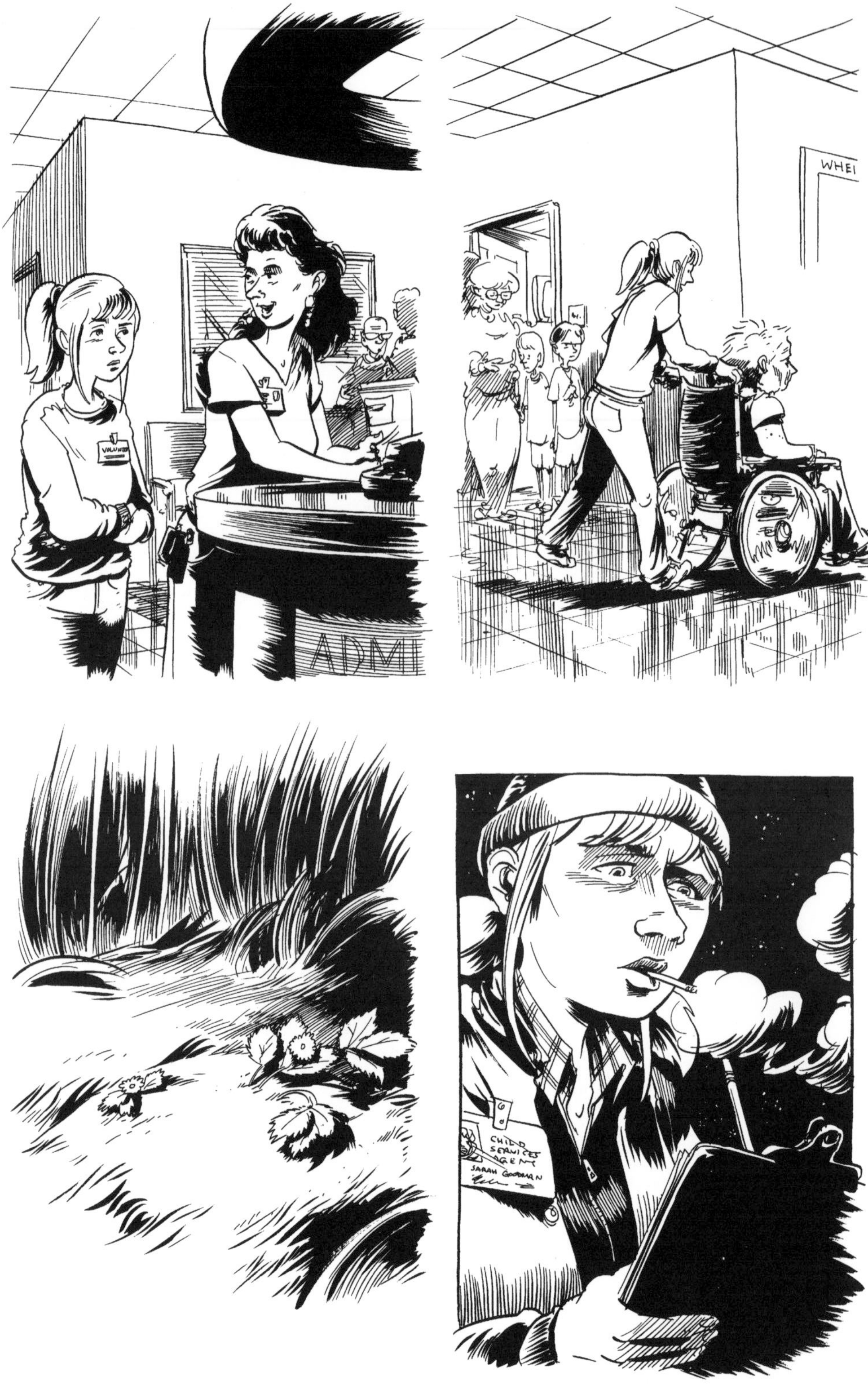
CHILD SERVICES AGENT
SARAH GOODMAN

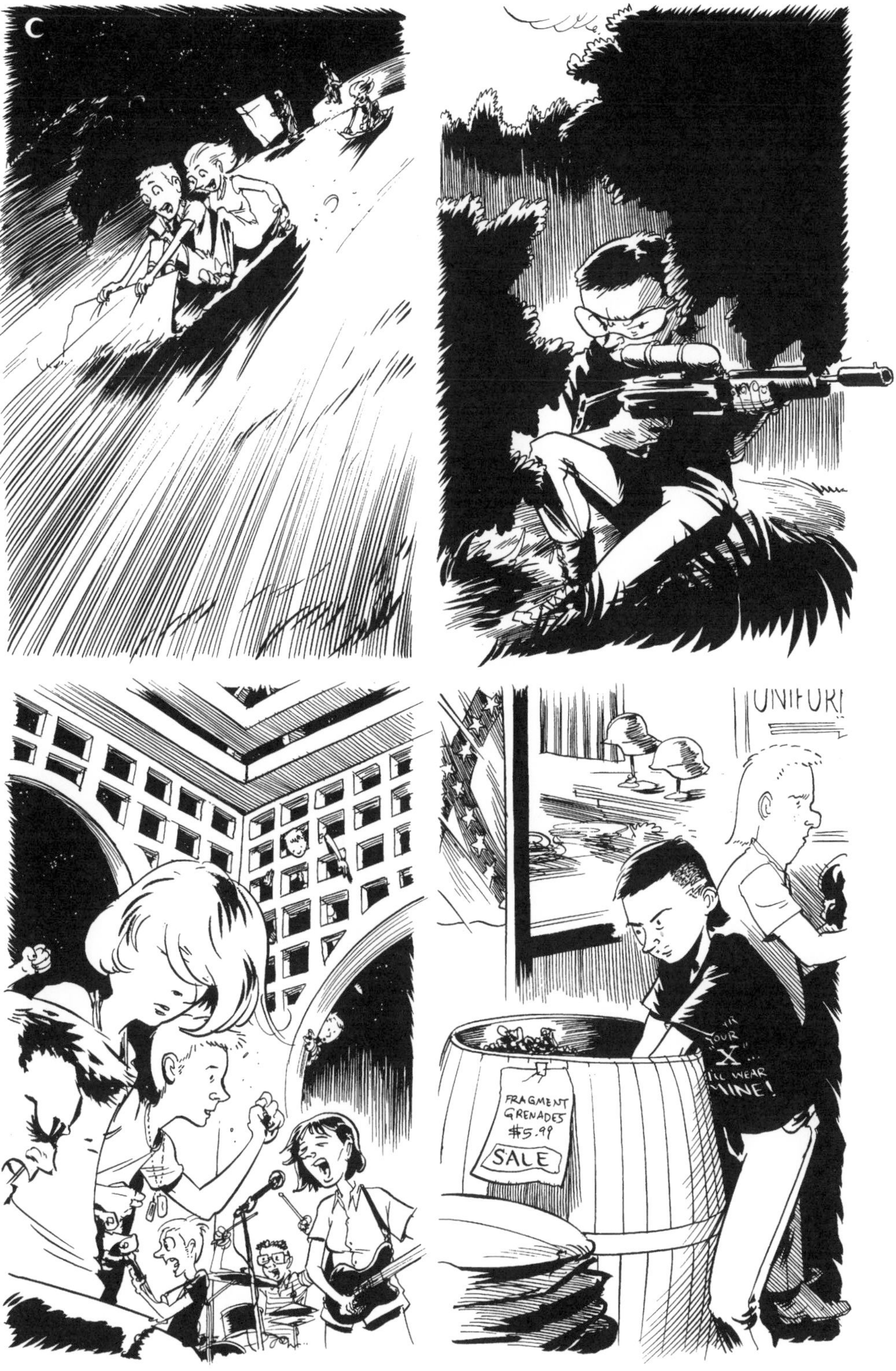
FRAGMENT
GRENADES
$5.99
SALE
YOUR
X...
WEAR

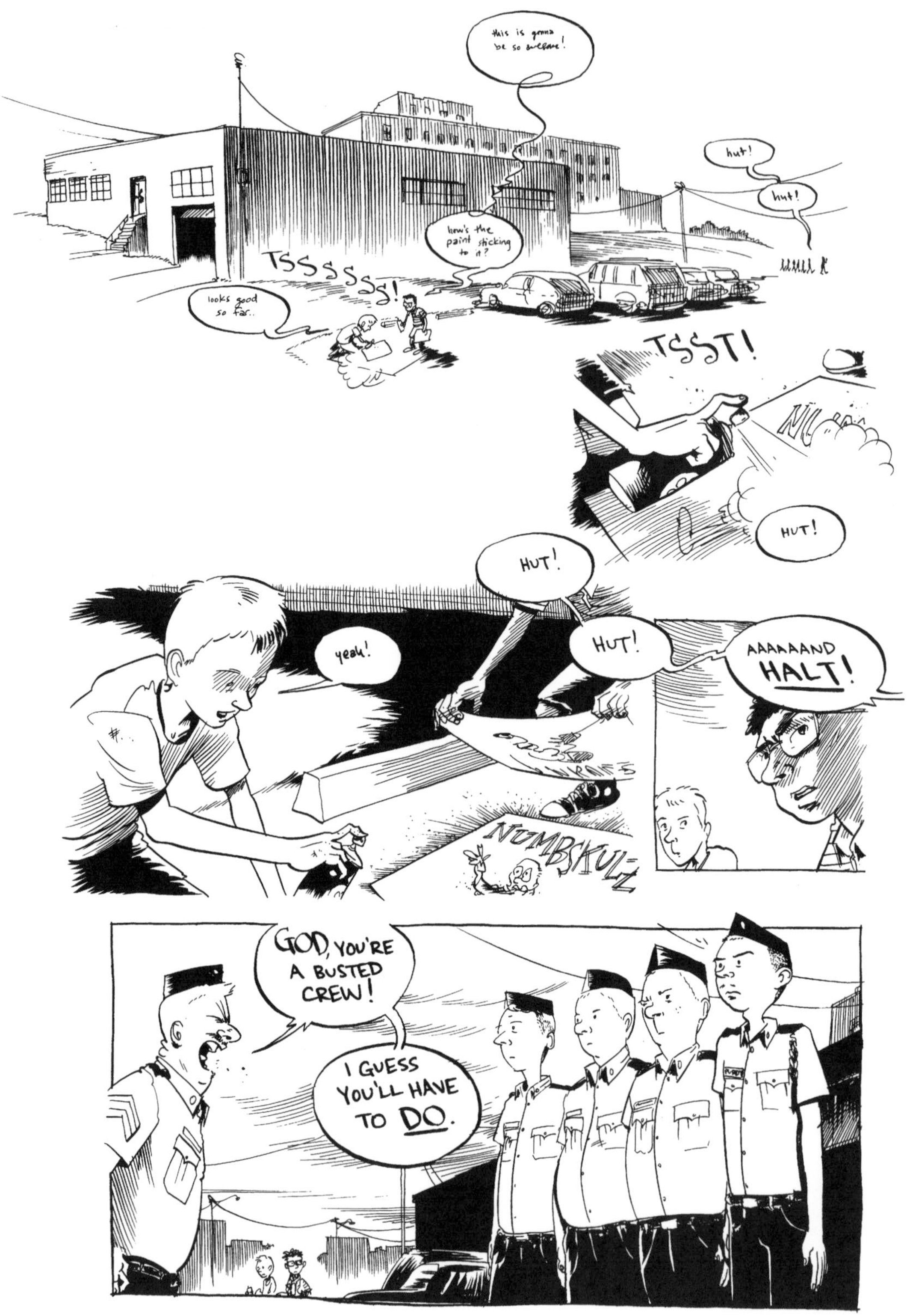
this is gonna be so awesome!
hut!
hut!
how's the paint sticking to it?
TSSSSSS!
looks good so far..
TSSST!
HUT!
HUT!
yeah!
HUT!
AAAAAAND HALT!
NUMBSKULZ
GOD, YOU'RE A BUSTED CREW!
I GUESS YOU'LL HAVE TO DO.

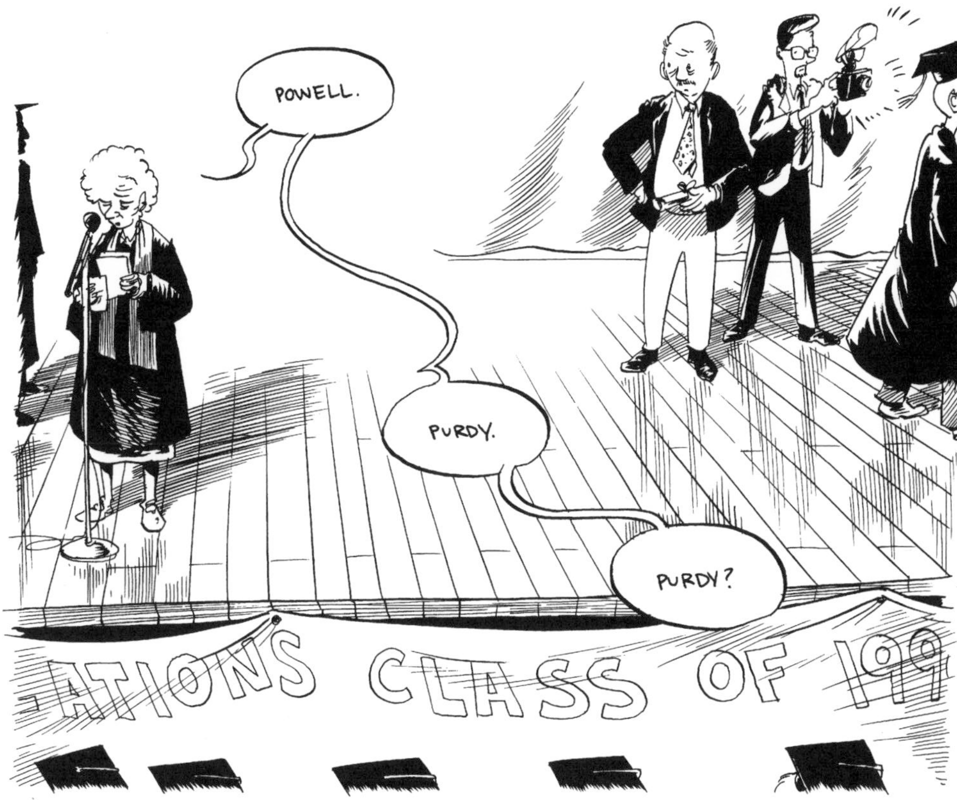
POWELL.
PURDY.
PURDY?
ATIONS CLASS OF 199

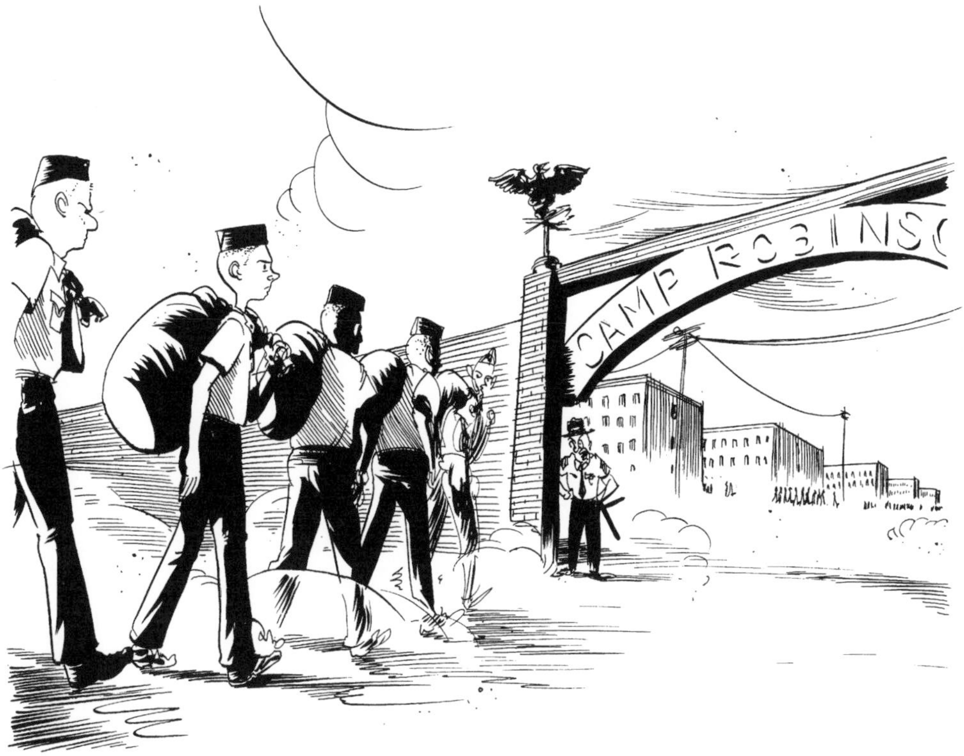
CAMP ROBINSO

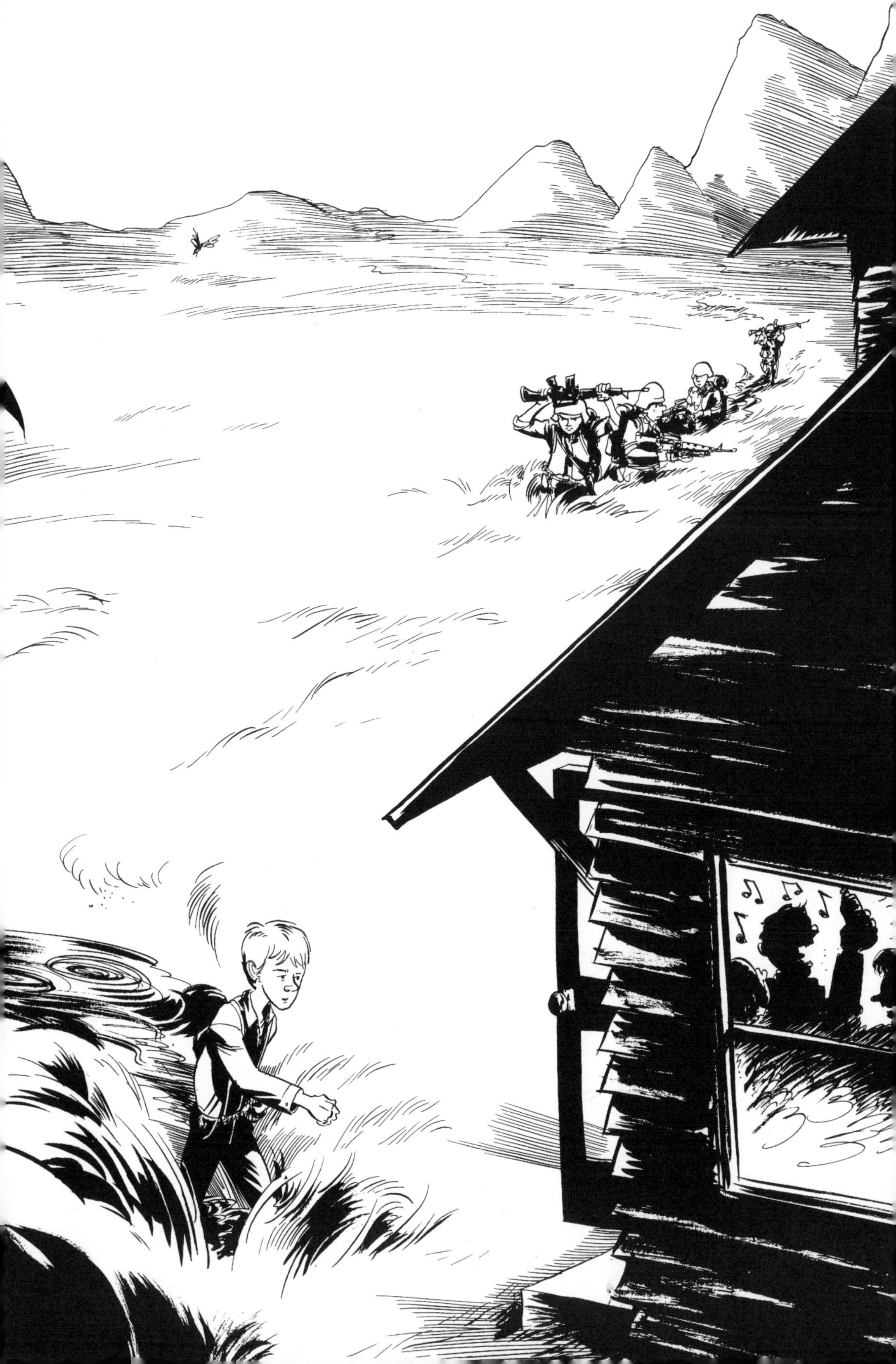

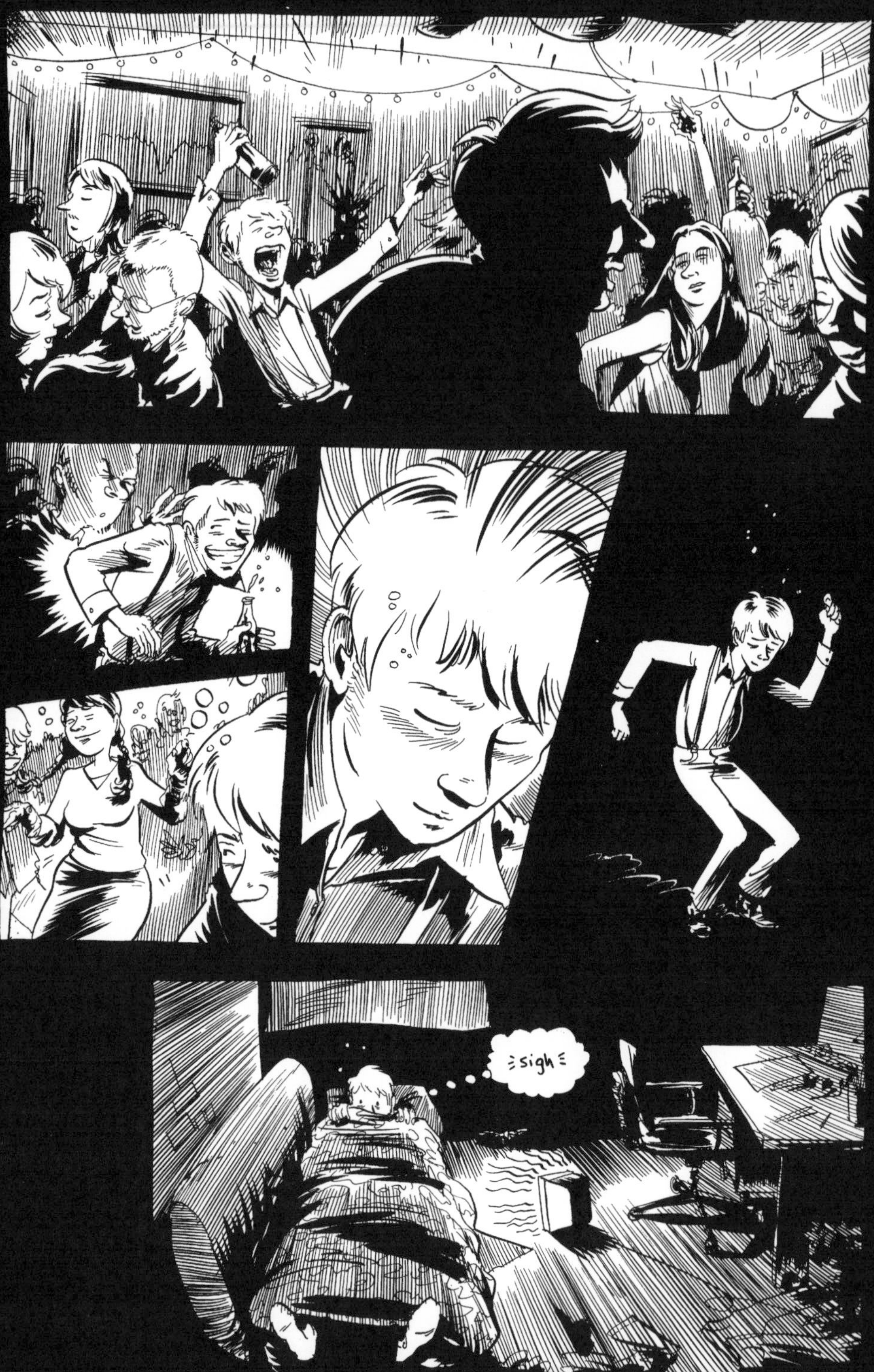
sigh

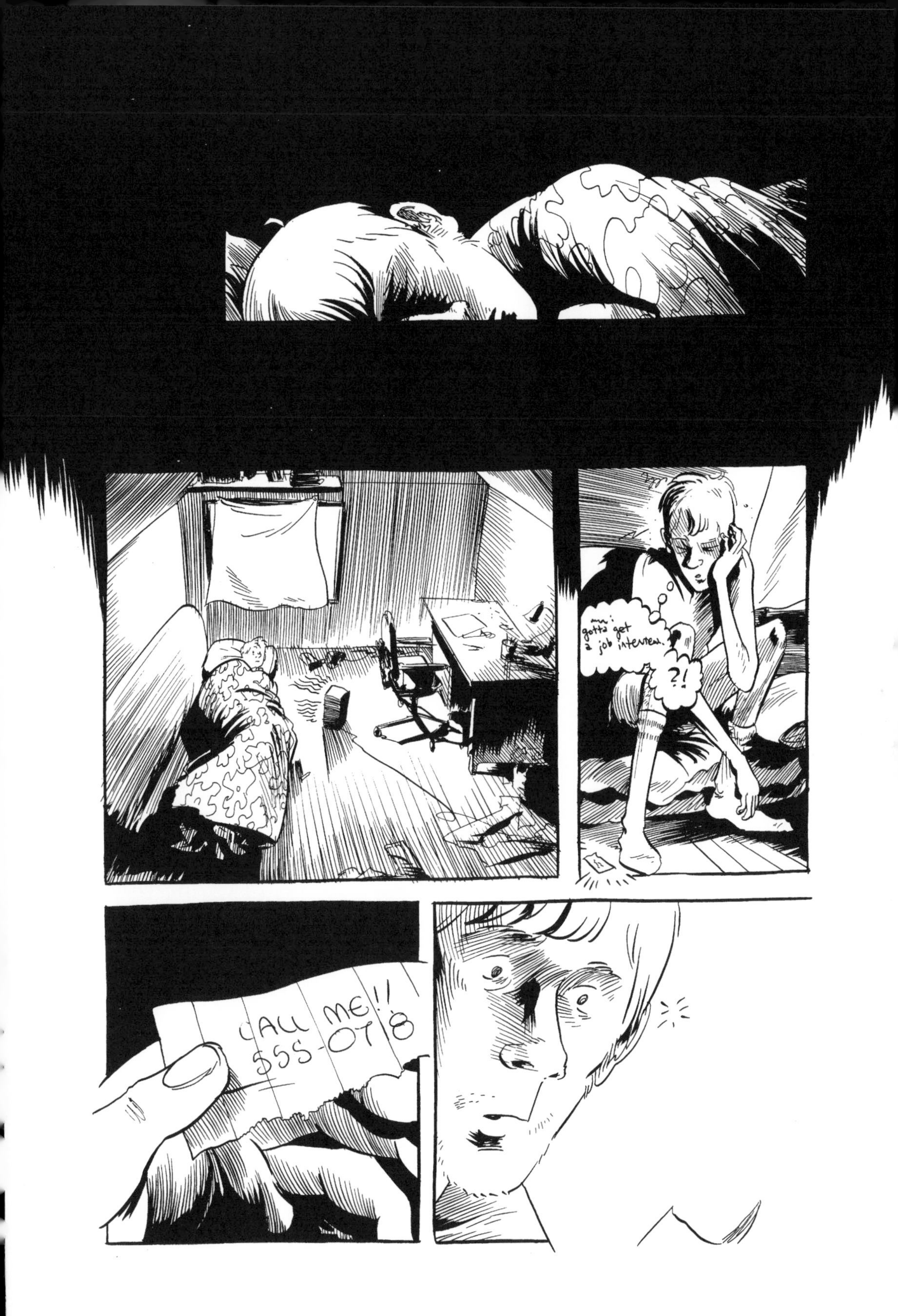
mm:
gotta get a job interview.
?!
CALL ME!!
555-0718

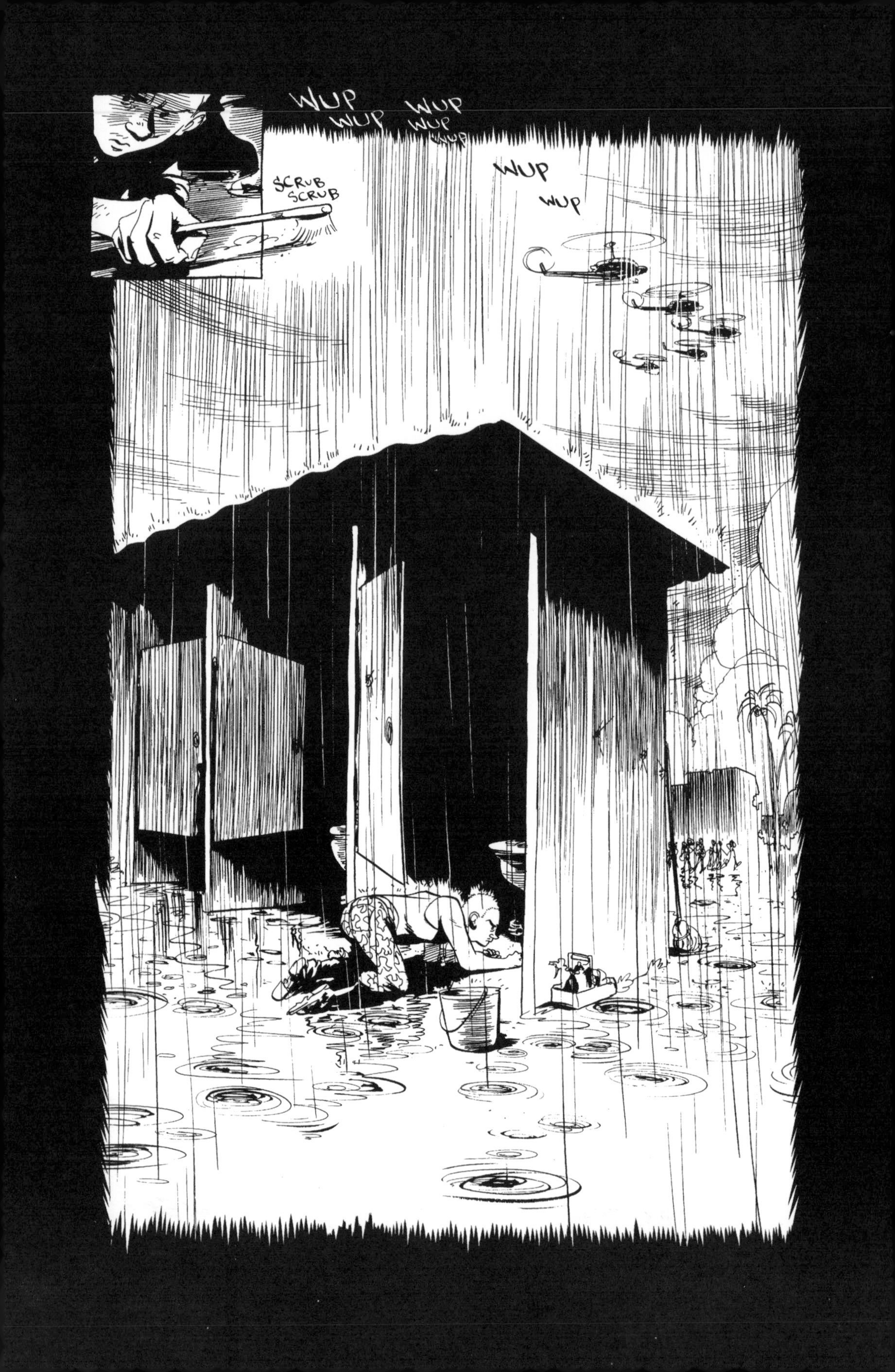
WUP WUP WUP
WUP WUP
SCRUB SCRUB
WUP
WUP

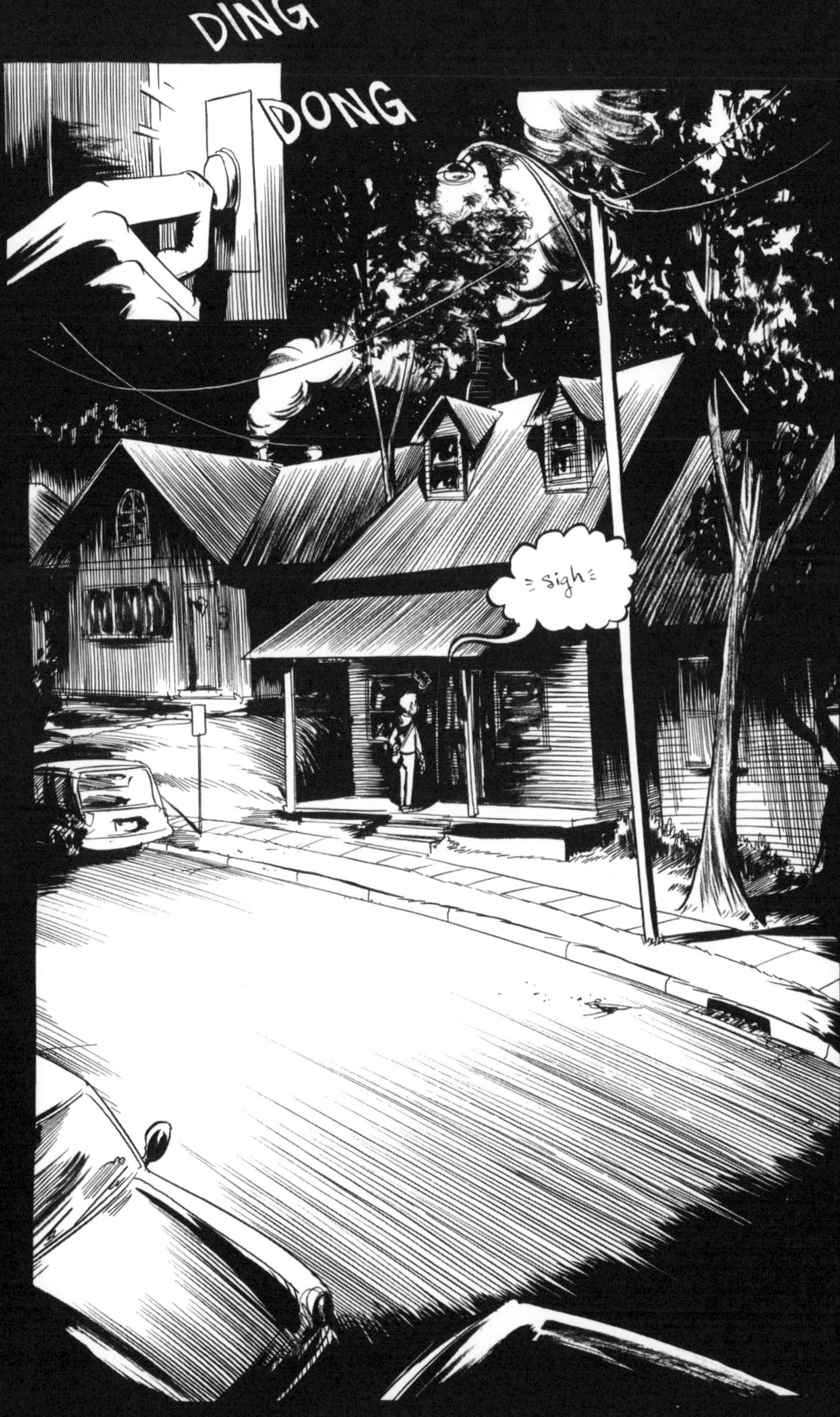
DING
DONG
sigh

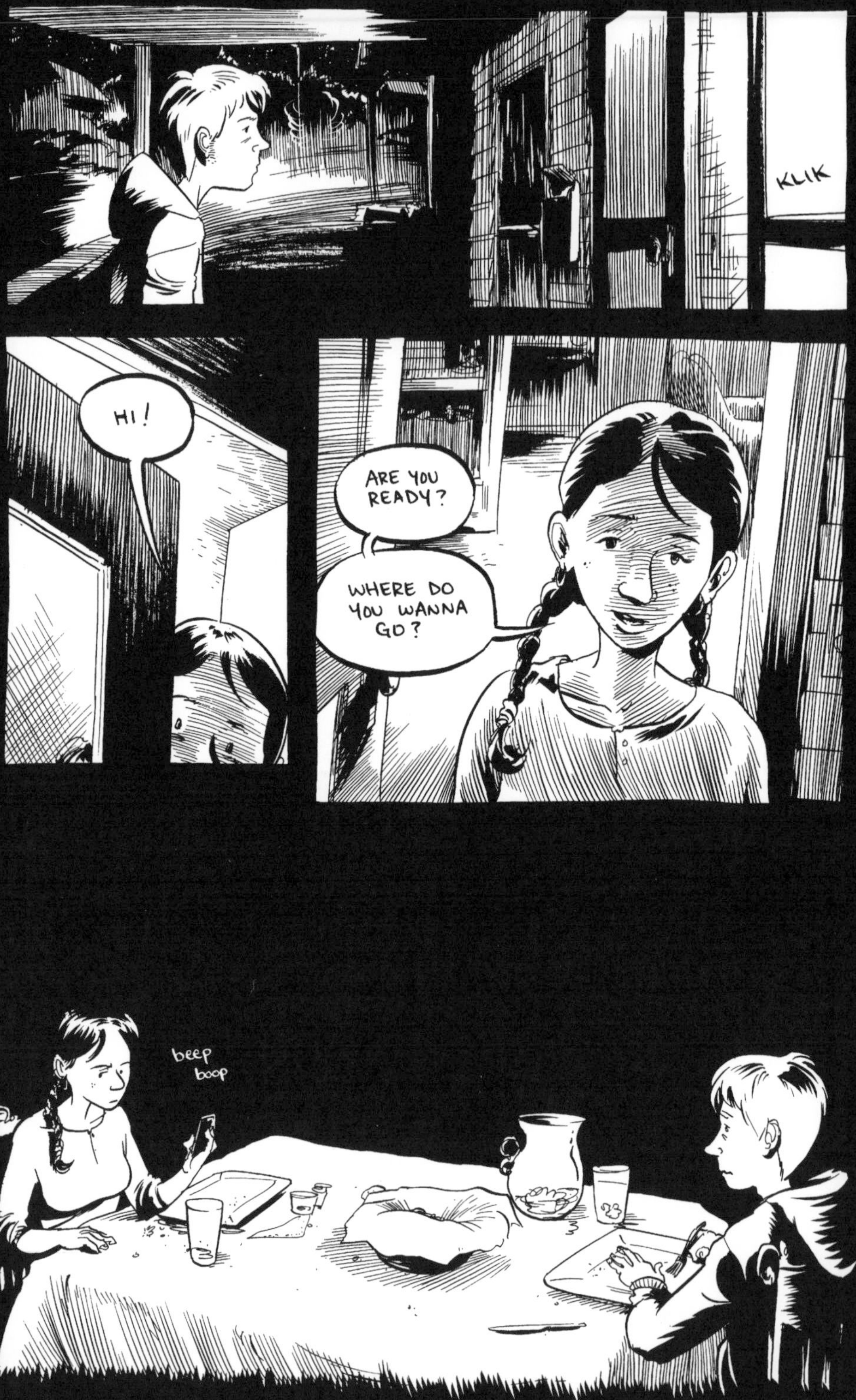
KLIK
HI!
ARE YOU READY?
WHERE DO YOU WANNA GO?
beep boop

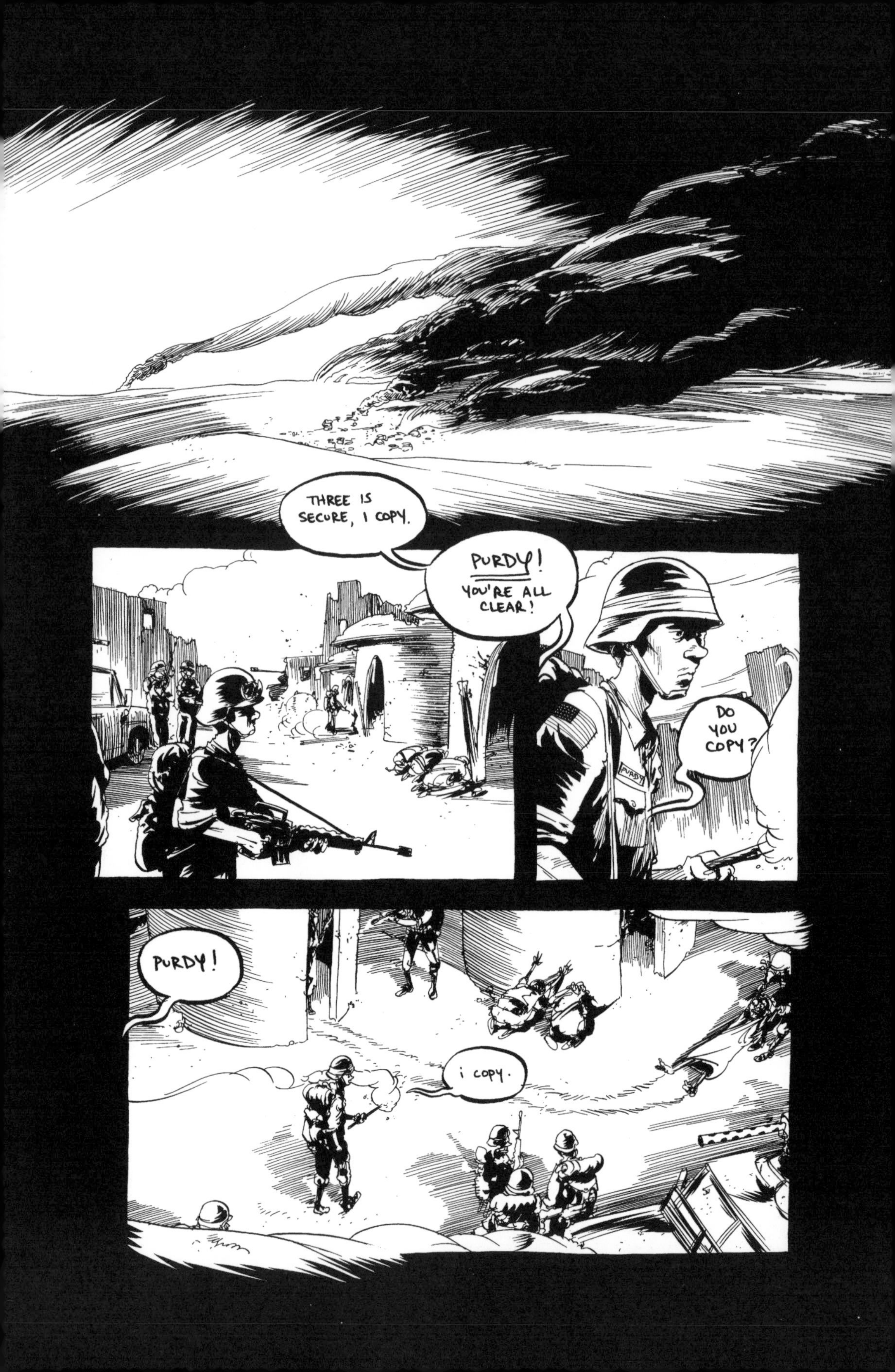
THREE IS SECURE, I COPY.
PURDY! YOU'RE ALL CLEAR!
DO YOU COPY?
PURDY!
i copy.

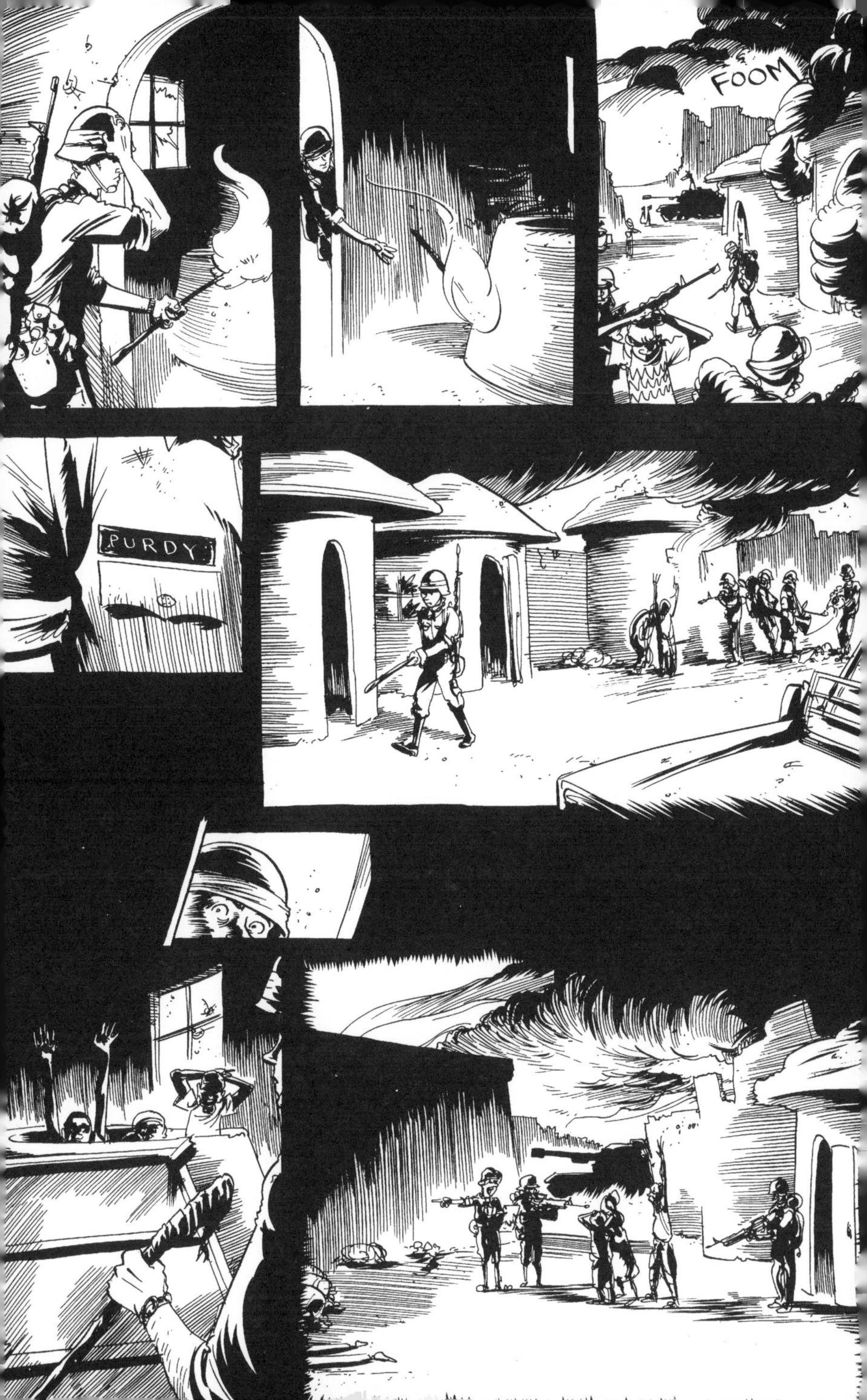
FOOM
PURDY

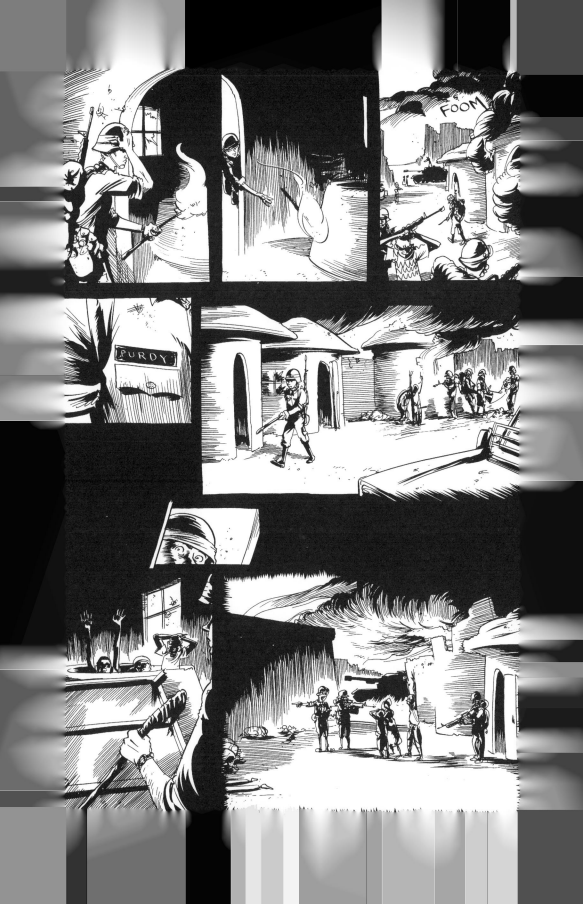

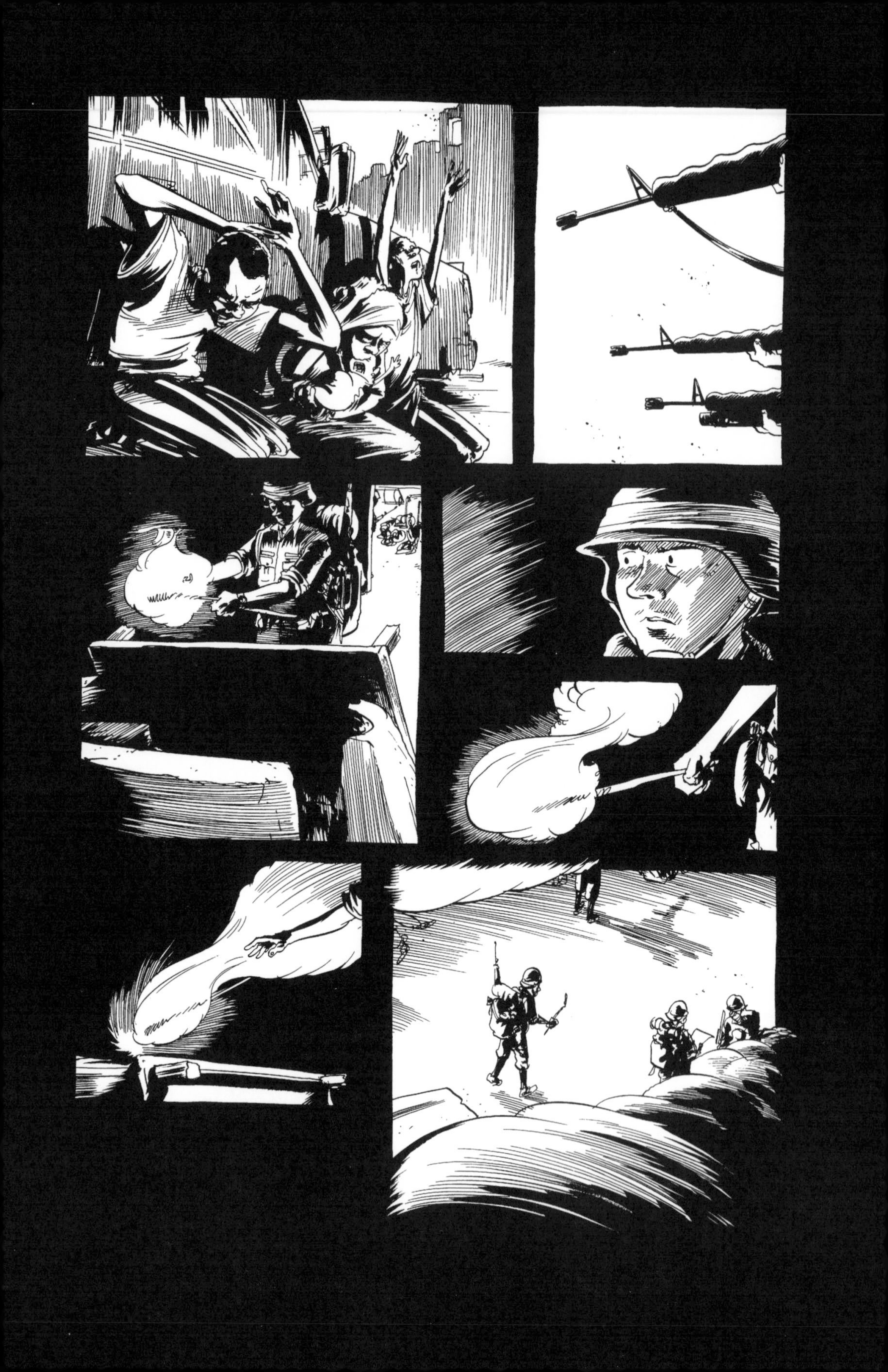

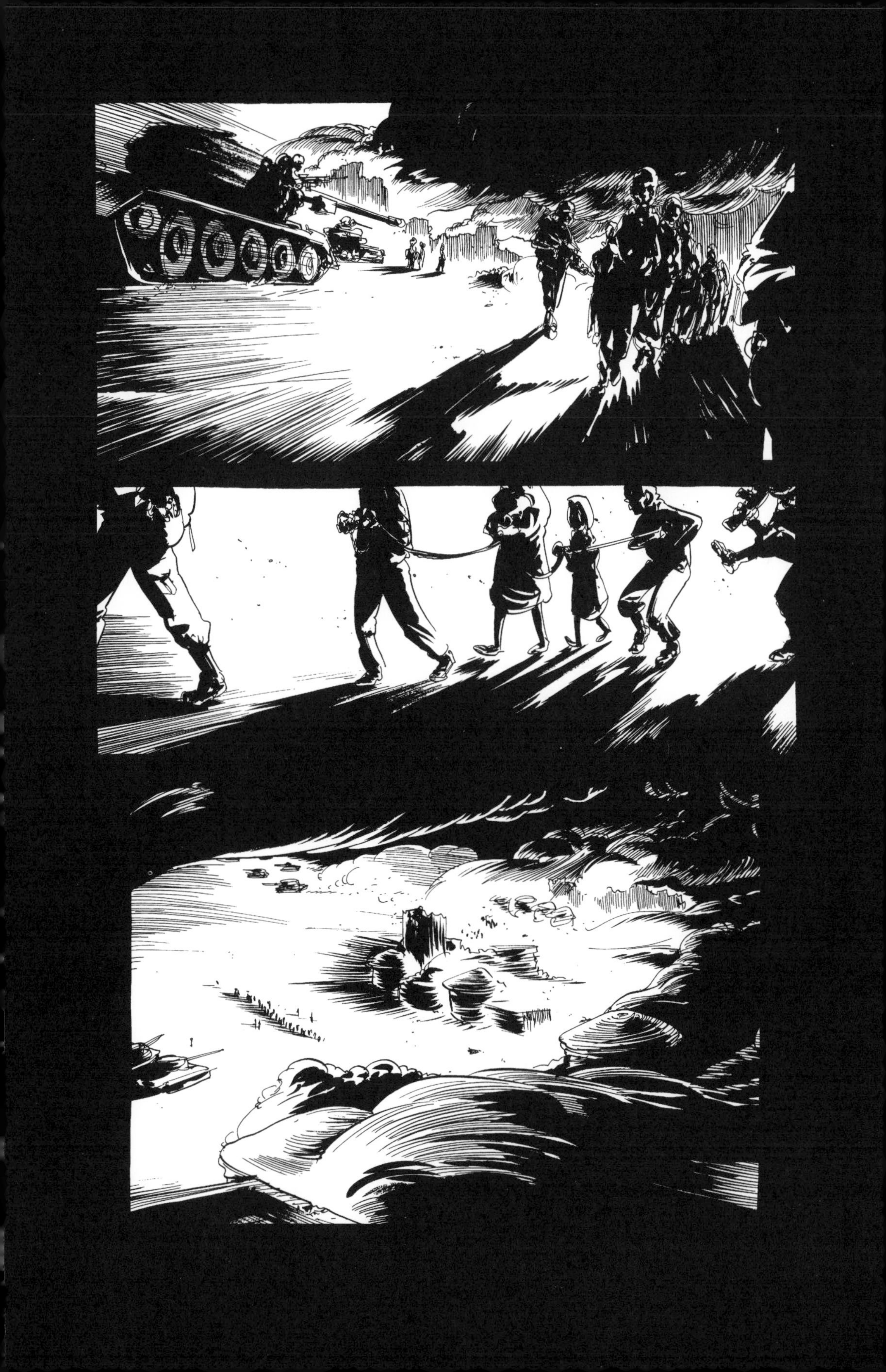

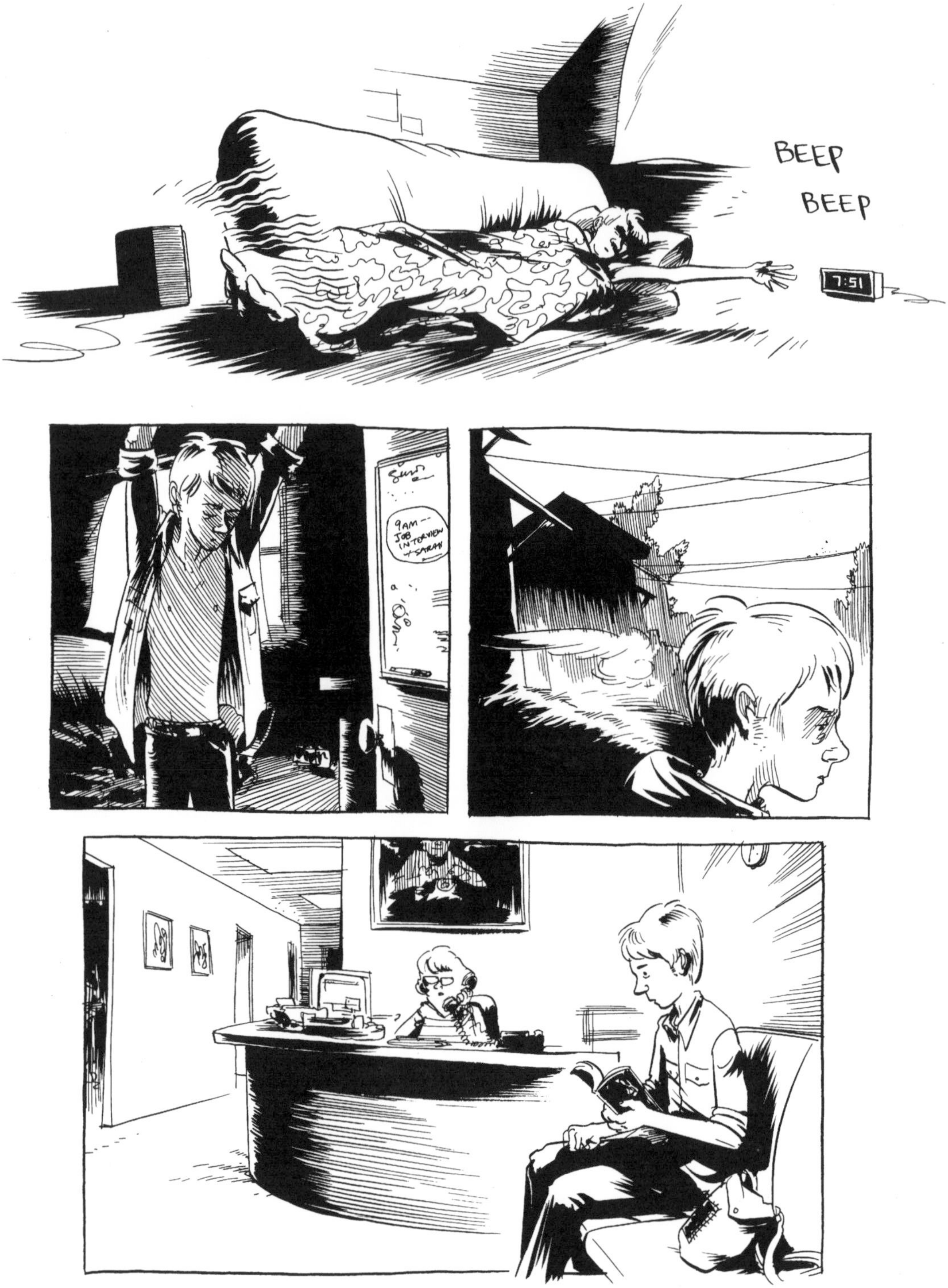
BEEP
BEEP
7:51
9AM --
JOB
INTERVIEW
w/ SARAH

BEEP
BEEP
BEEP

7:51

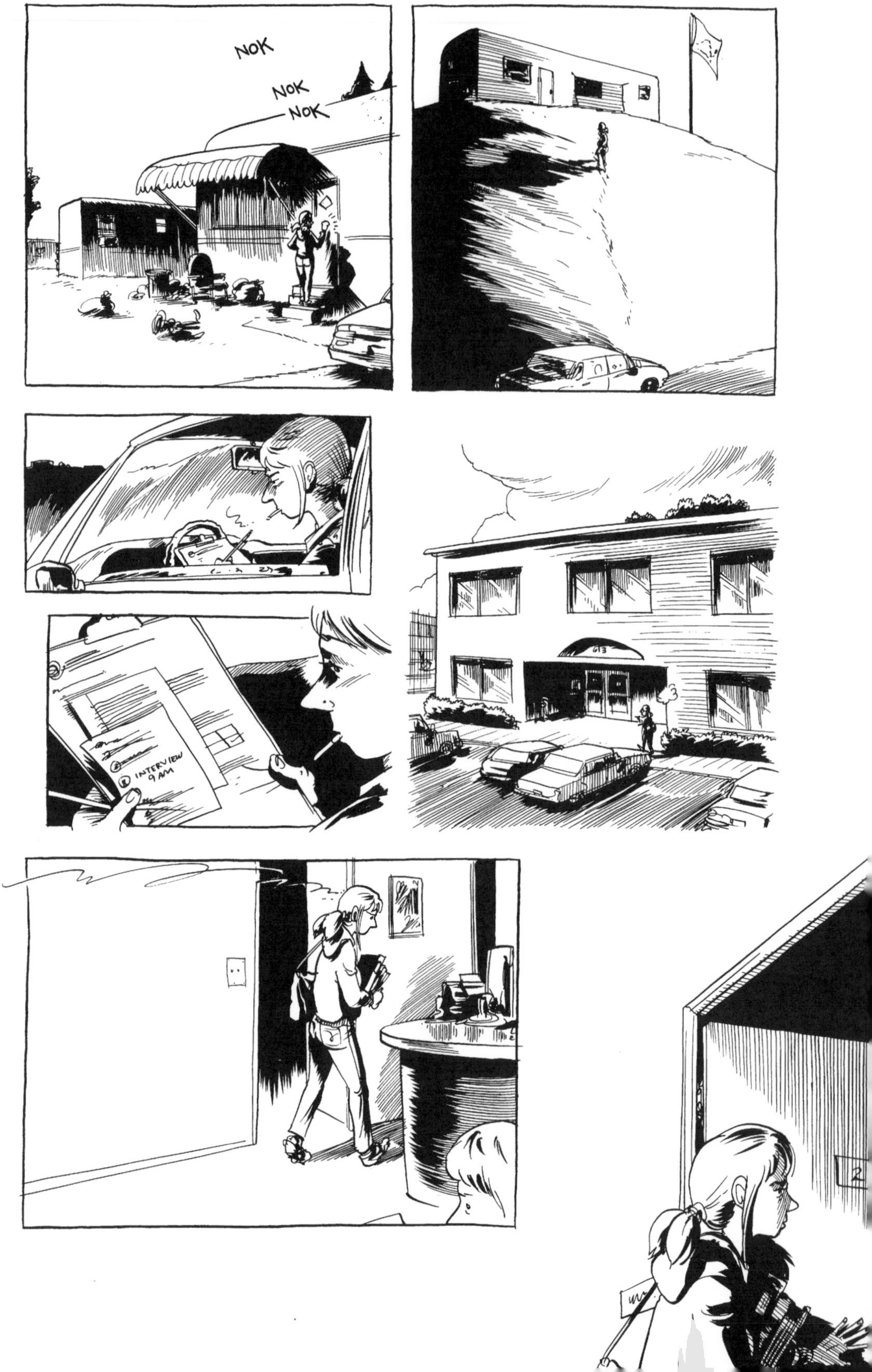
NOK
NOK
NOK
INTERVIEW 9 AM

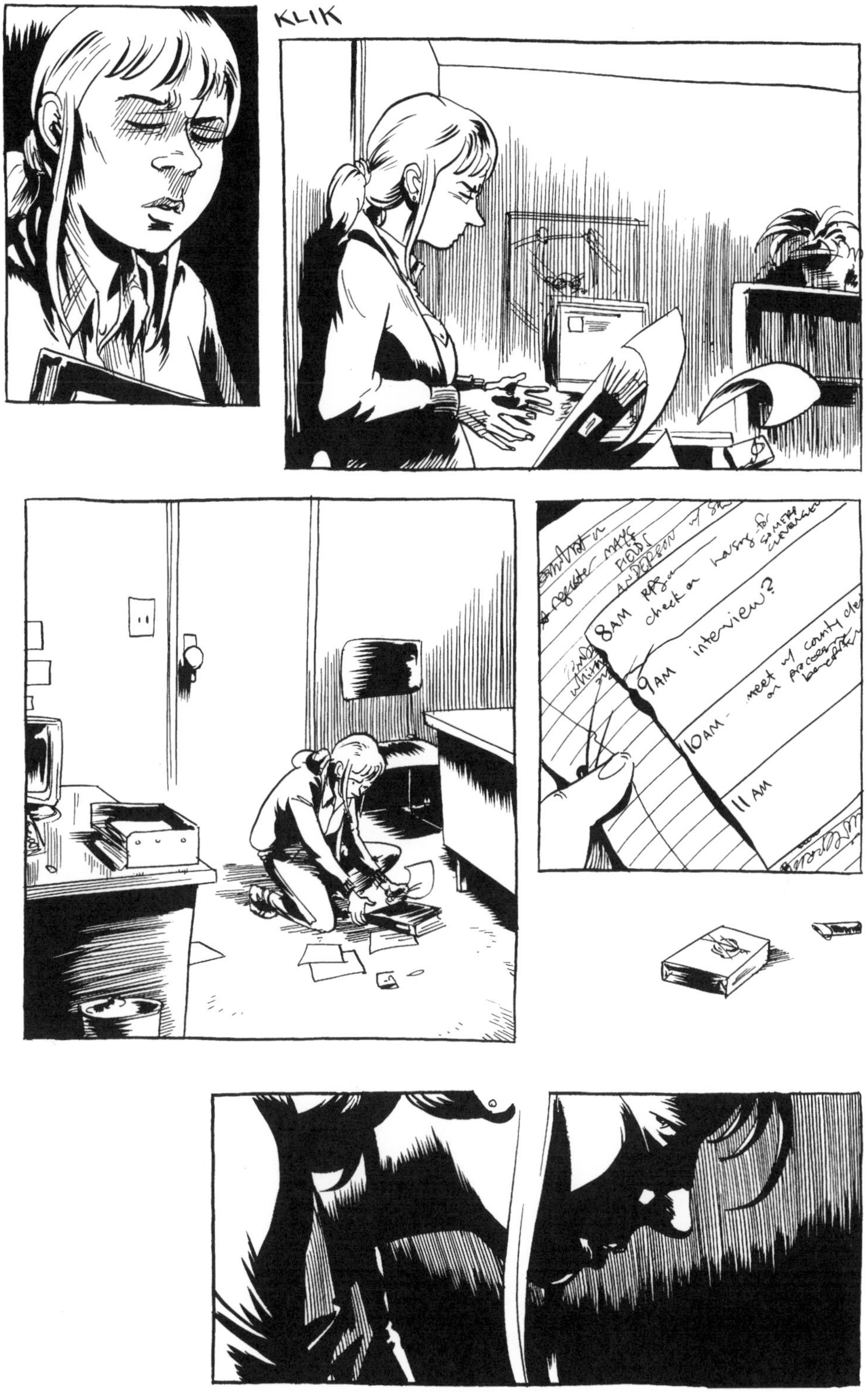
KLIK
8AM
interview?
9AM
10AM
11 AM

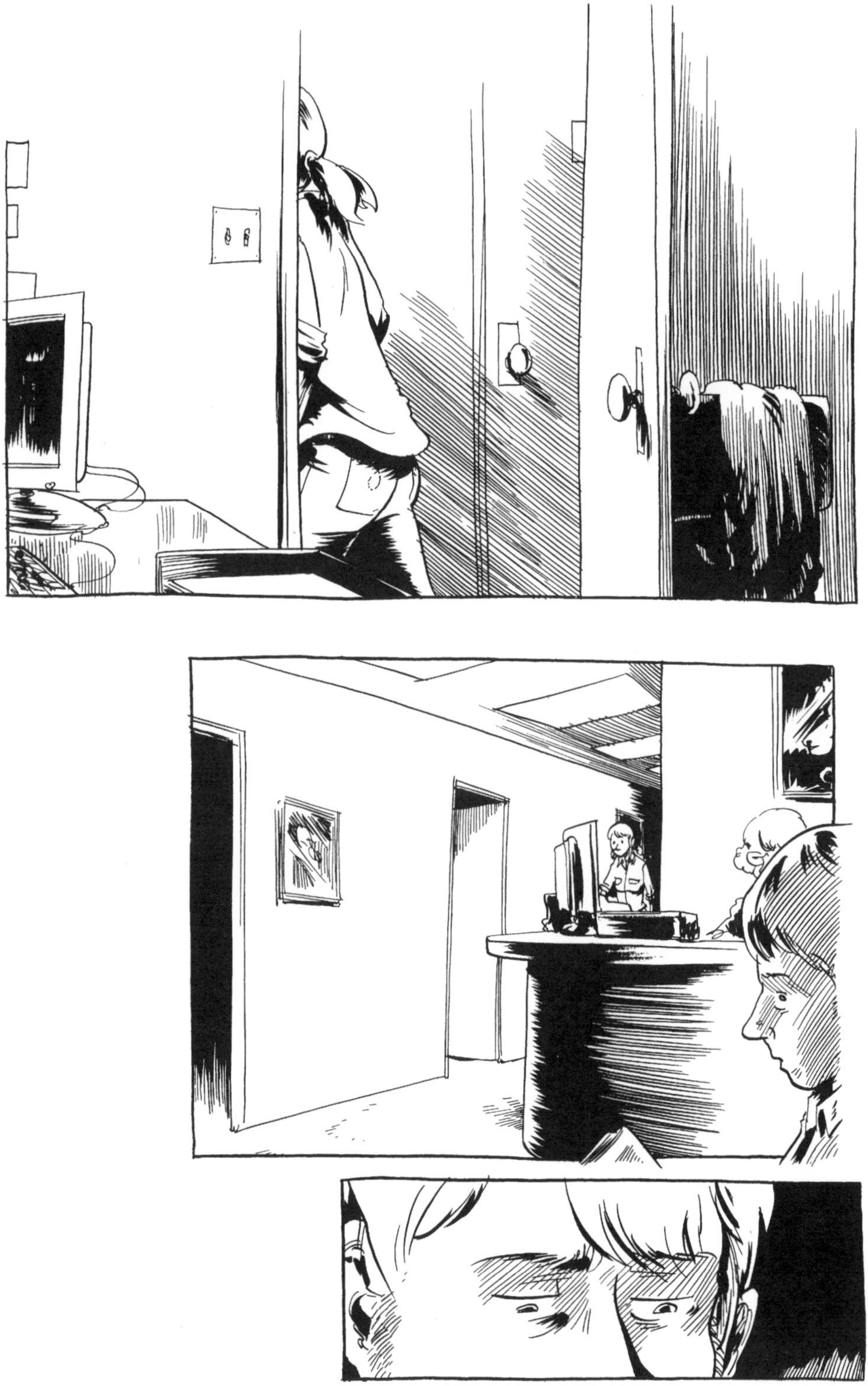

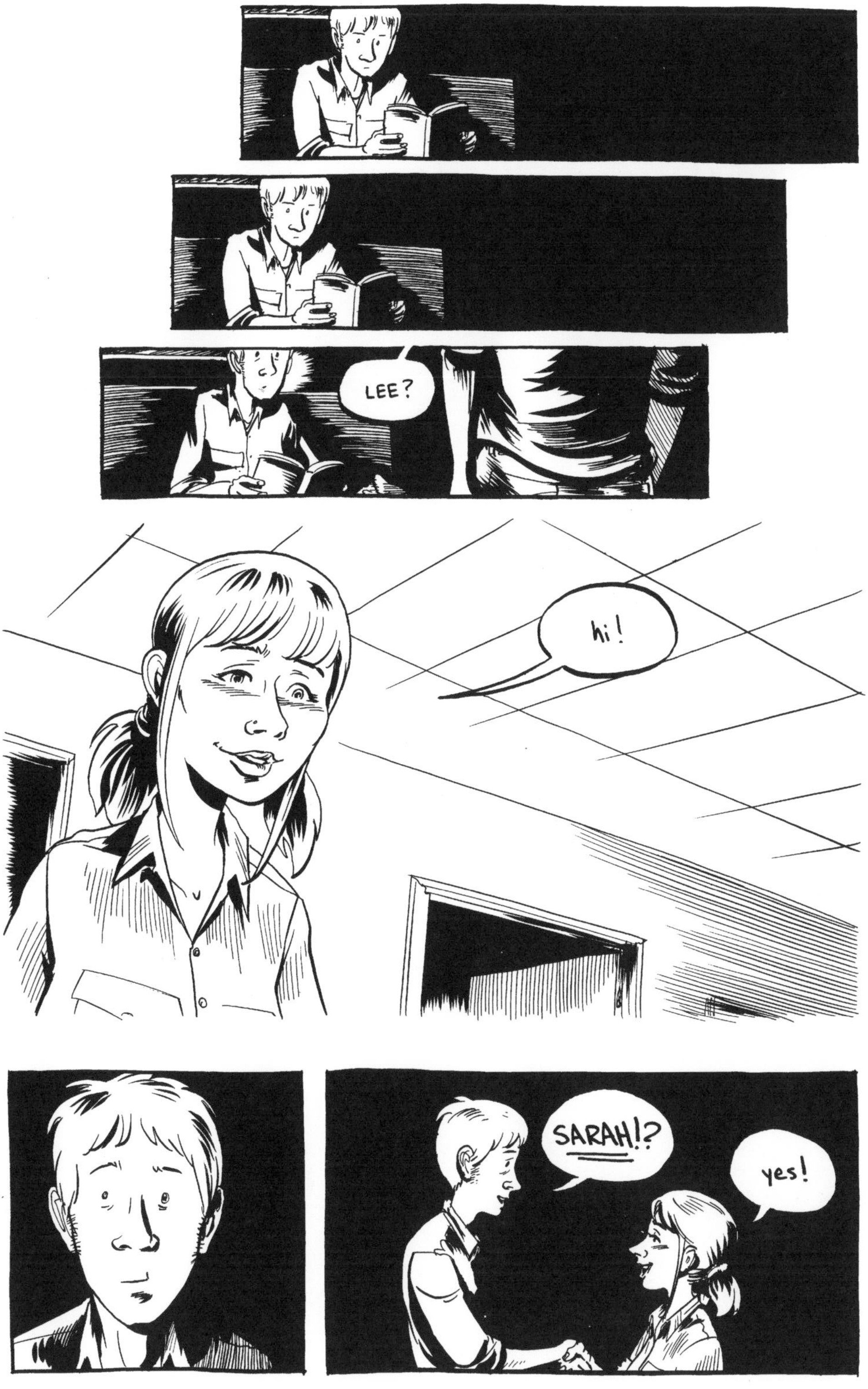
LEE?
hi!
SARAH!?
yes!

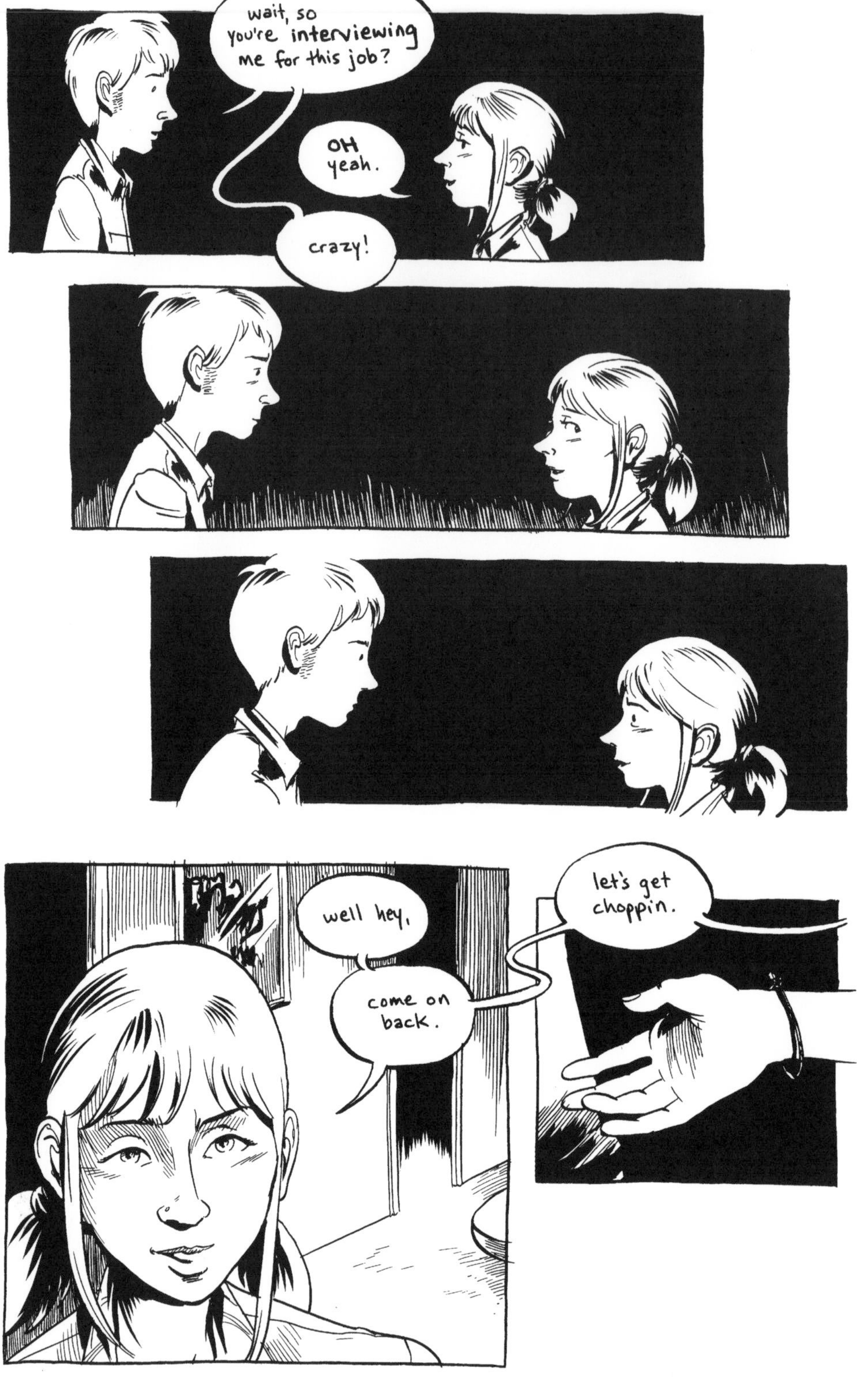
wait, so you're interviewing me for this job?
OH yeah.
crazy!
well hey,
come on back.
let's get choppin.

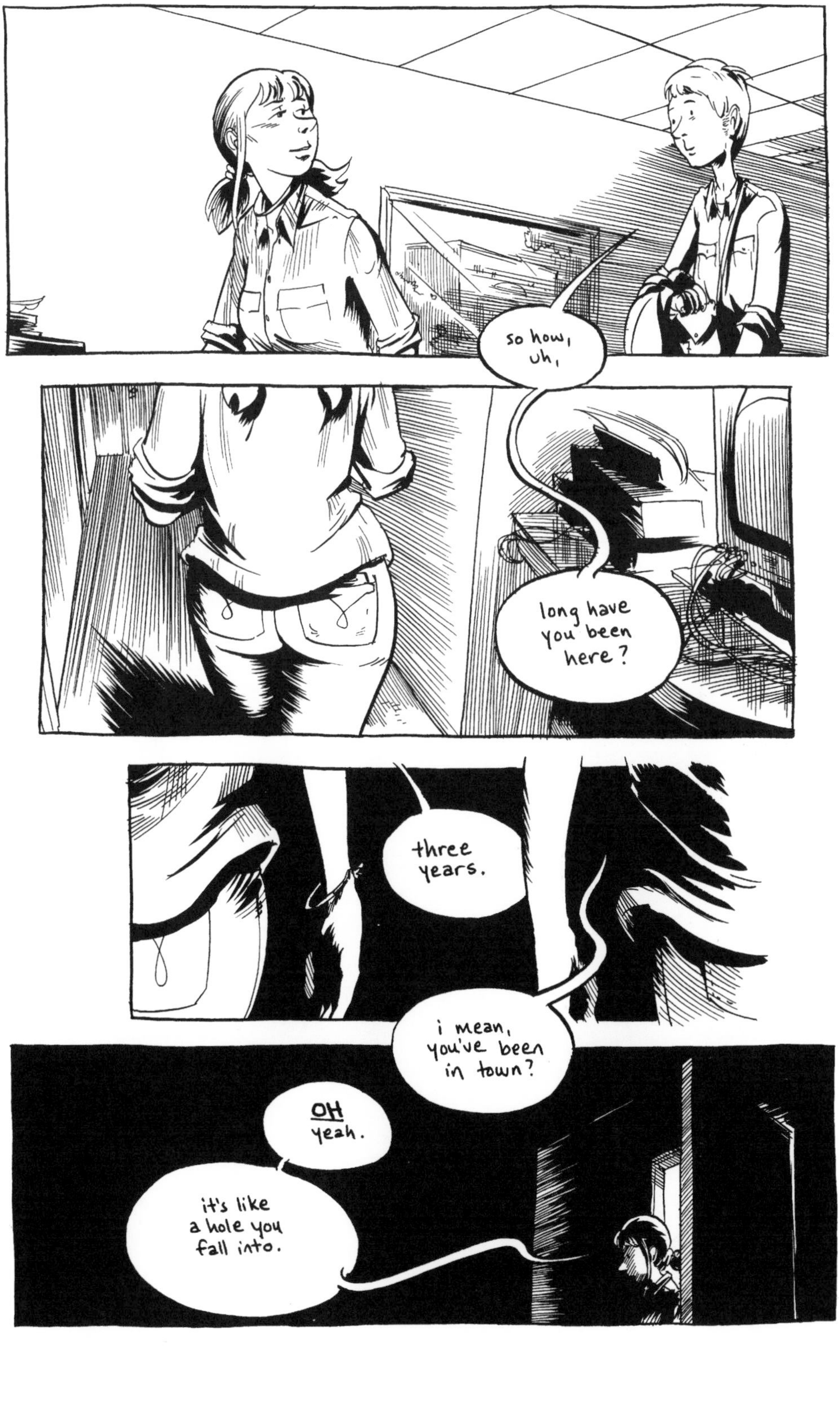
so how, uh,
long have you been here?
three years.
i mean, you've been in town?
OH yeah.
it's like a hole you fall into.

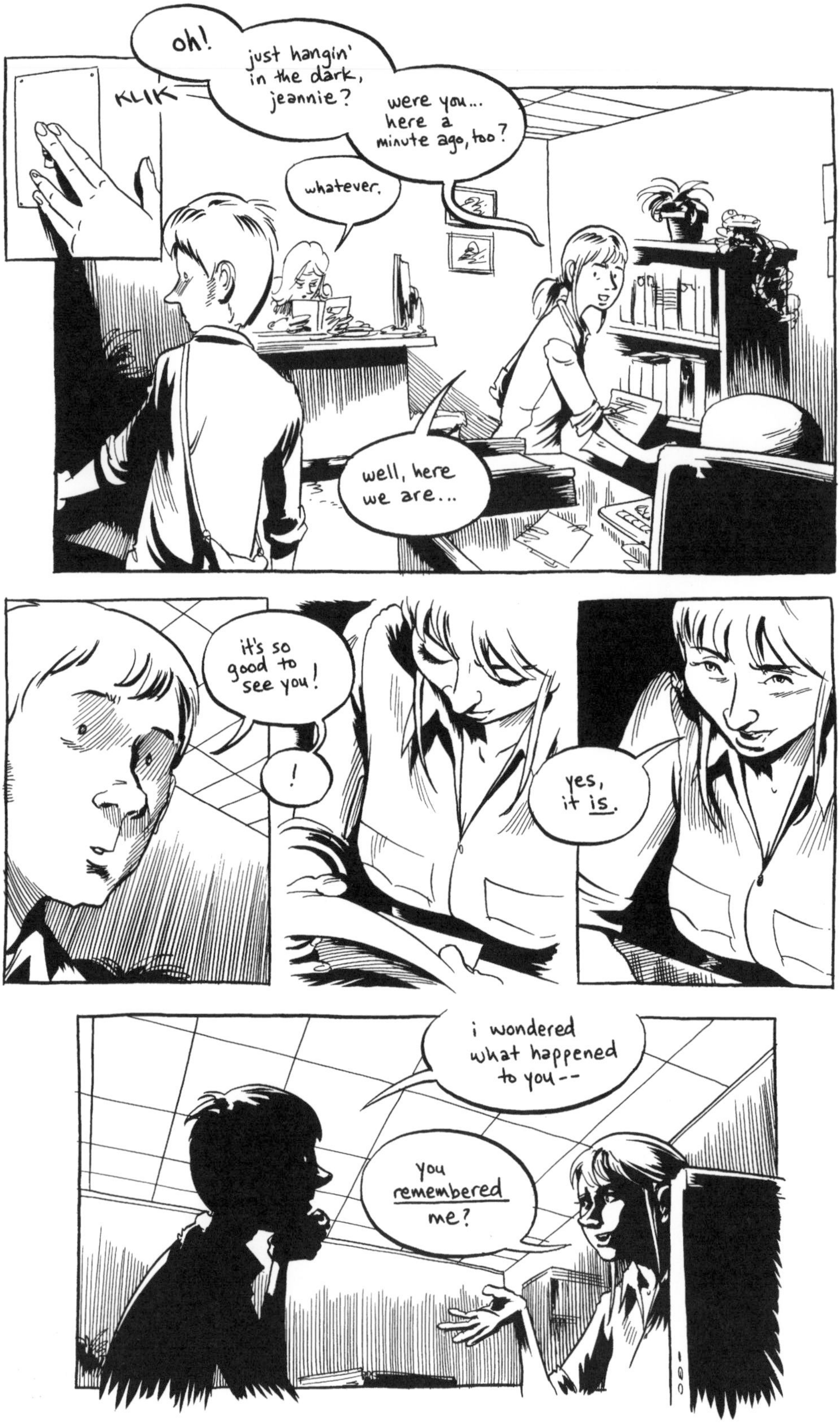
oh!
KLIK
just hangin' in the dark, jeannie?
were you... here a minute ago, too?
whatever.
well, here we are...
it's so good to see you!
!
yes, it is.
i wondered what happened to you--
you remembered me?

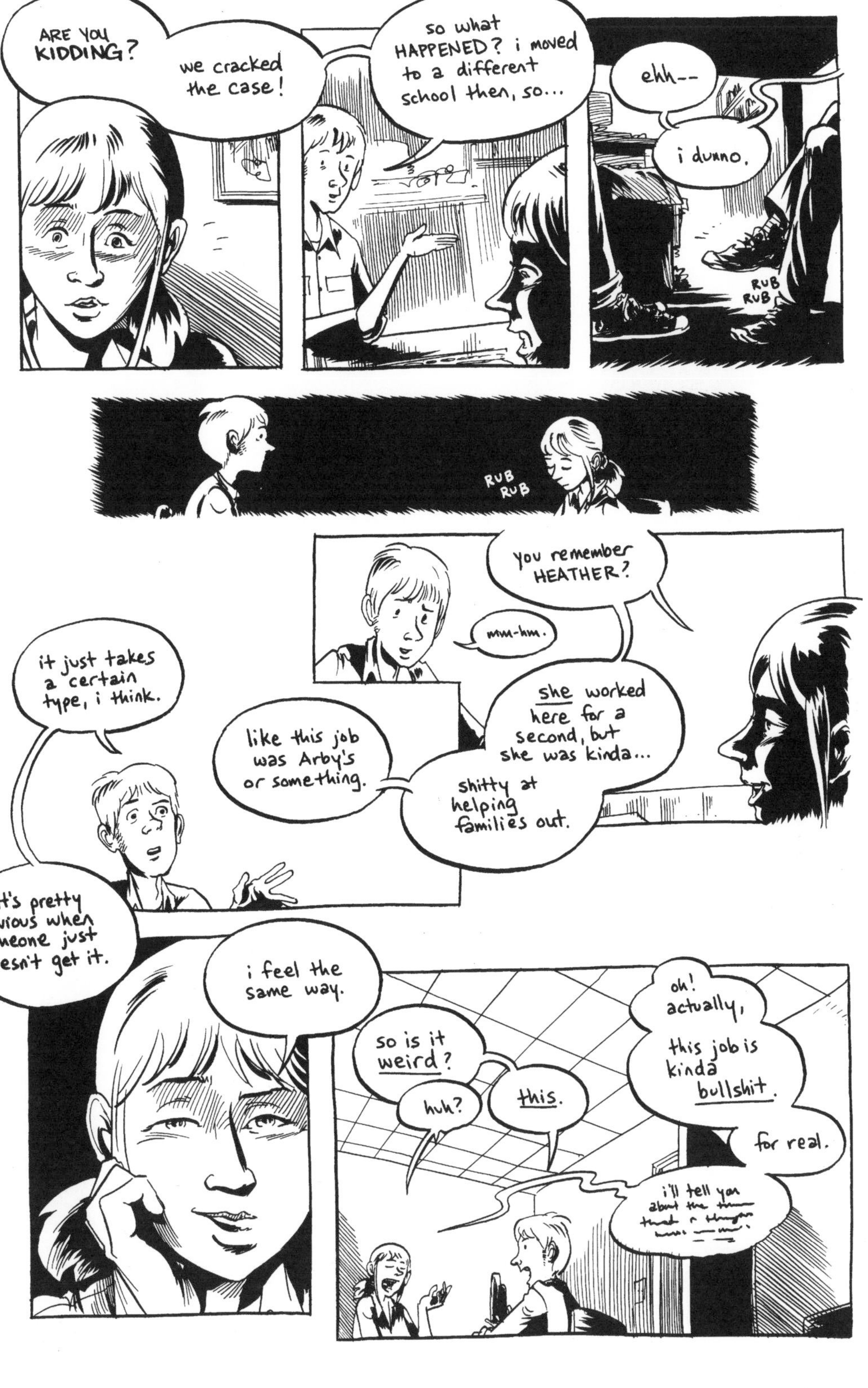
ARE YOU KIDDING?
we cracked the case!
so what HAPPENED? i moved to a different school then, so...
ehh--
i dunno.
RUB RUB
RUB RUB
you remember HEATHER?
mm-hm.
she worked here for a second, but she was kinda...
shitty at helping families out.
like this job was Arby's or something.
it just takes a certain type, i think.
it's pretty obvious when someone just doesn't get it.
i feel the same way.
so is it weird?
huh?
this.
oh! actually,
this job is kinda bullshit.
for real.
i'll tell you about the

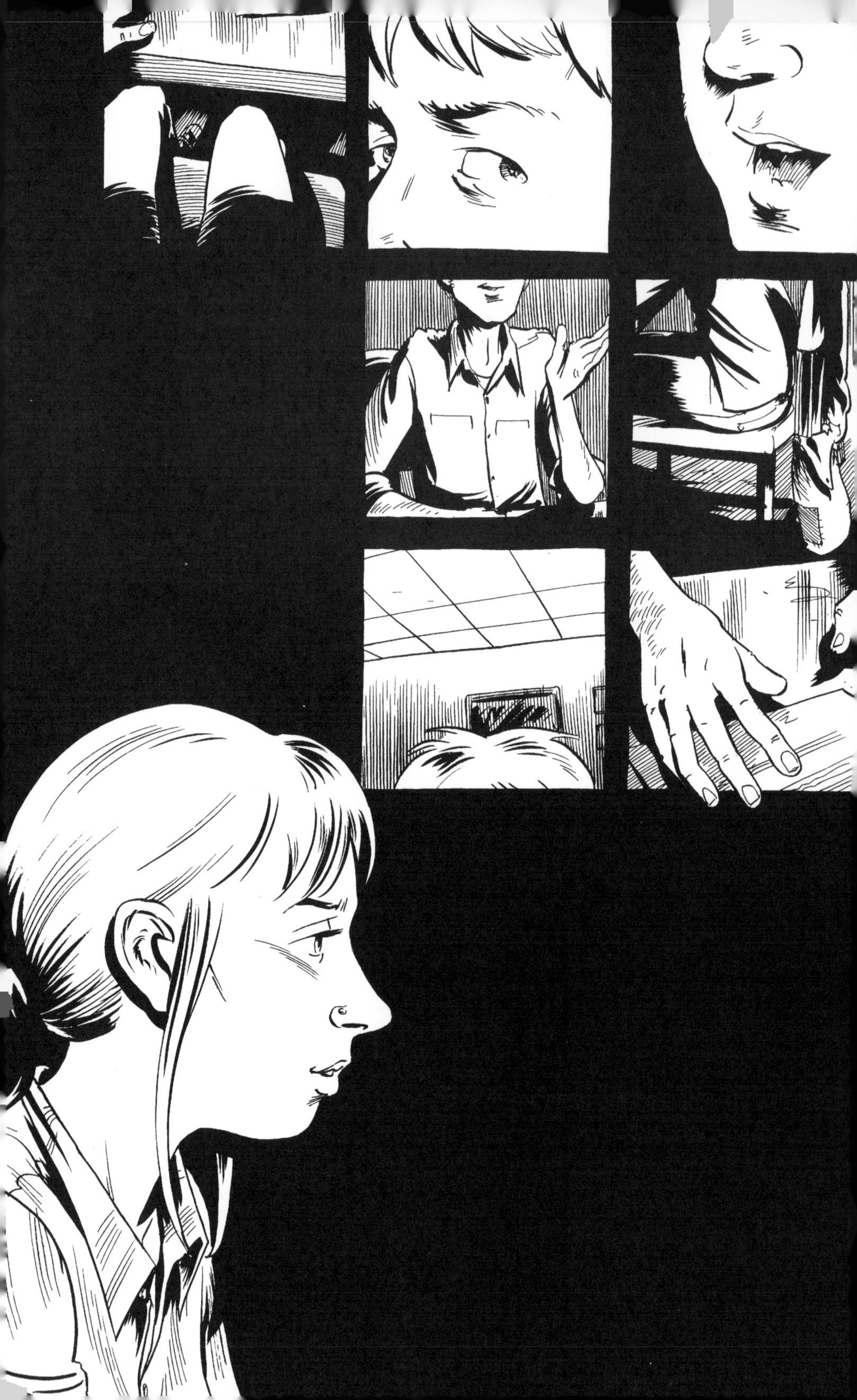

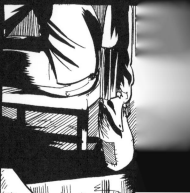

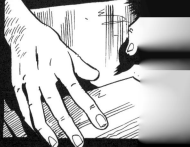

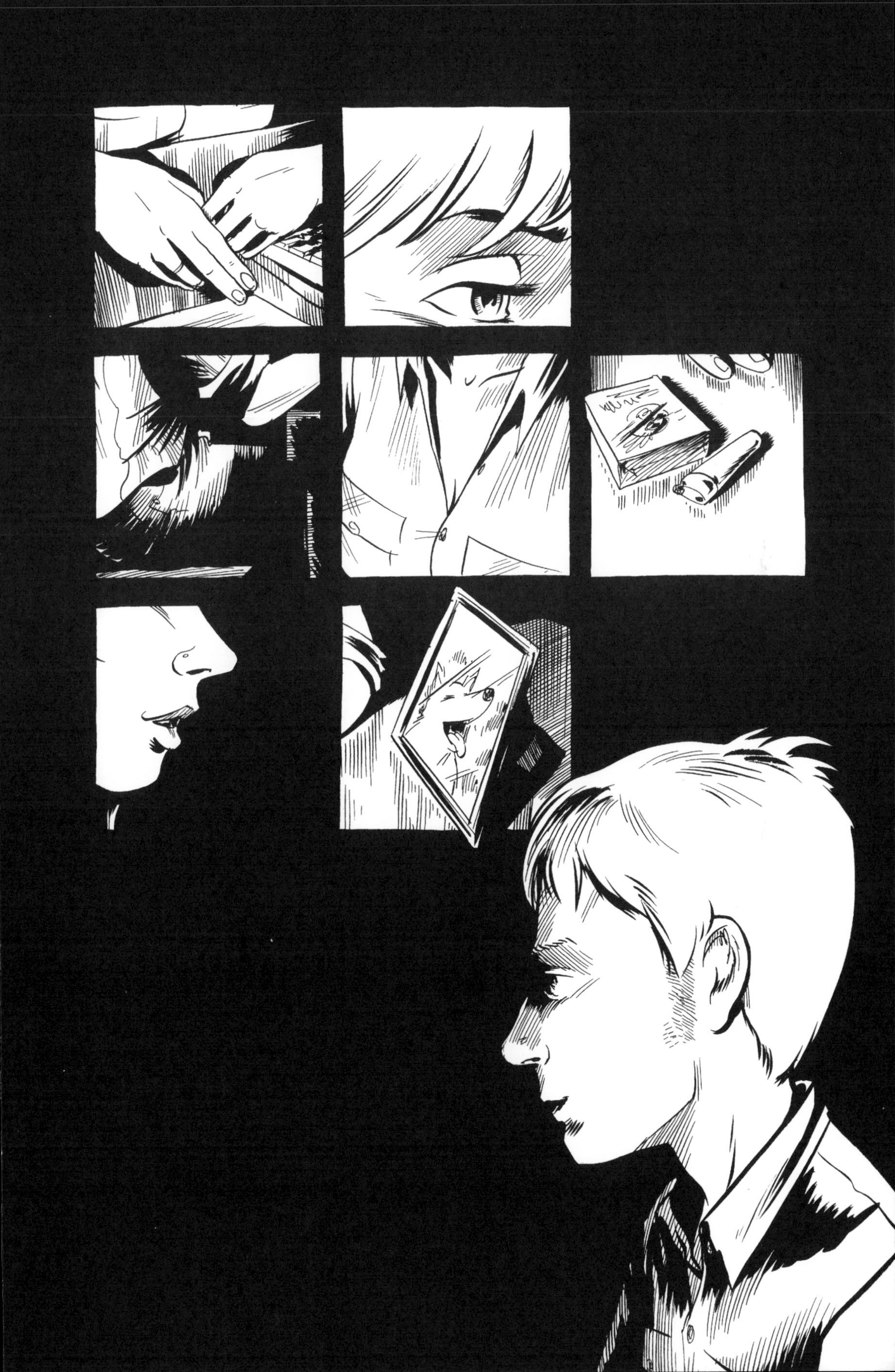

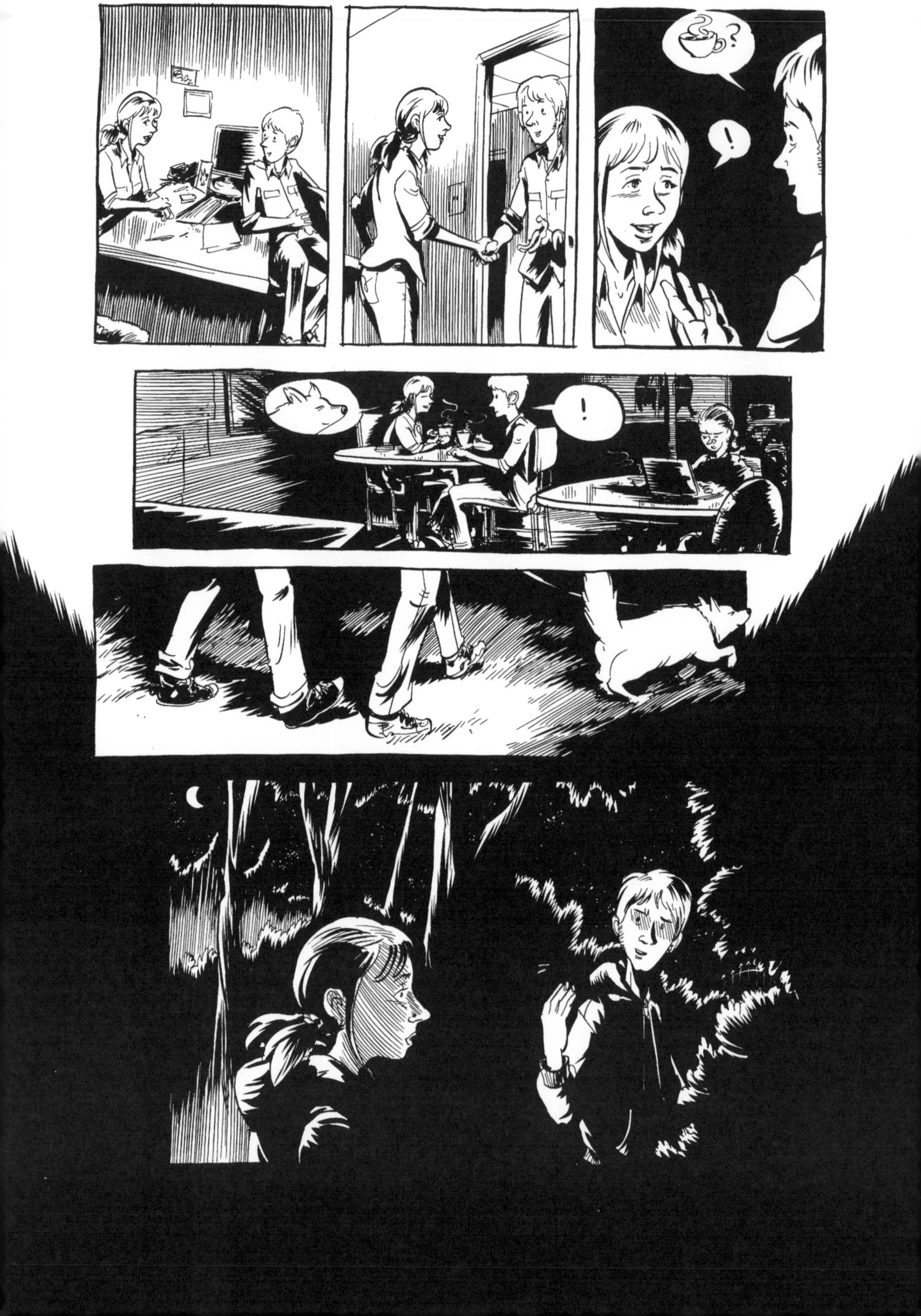

?
!
!

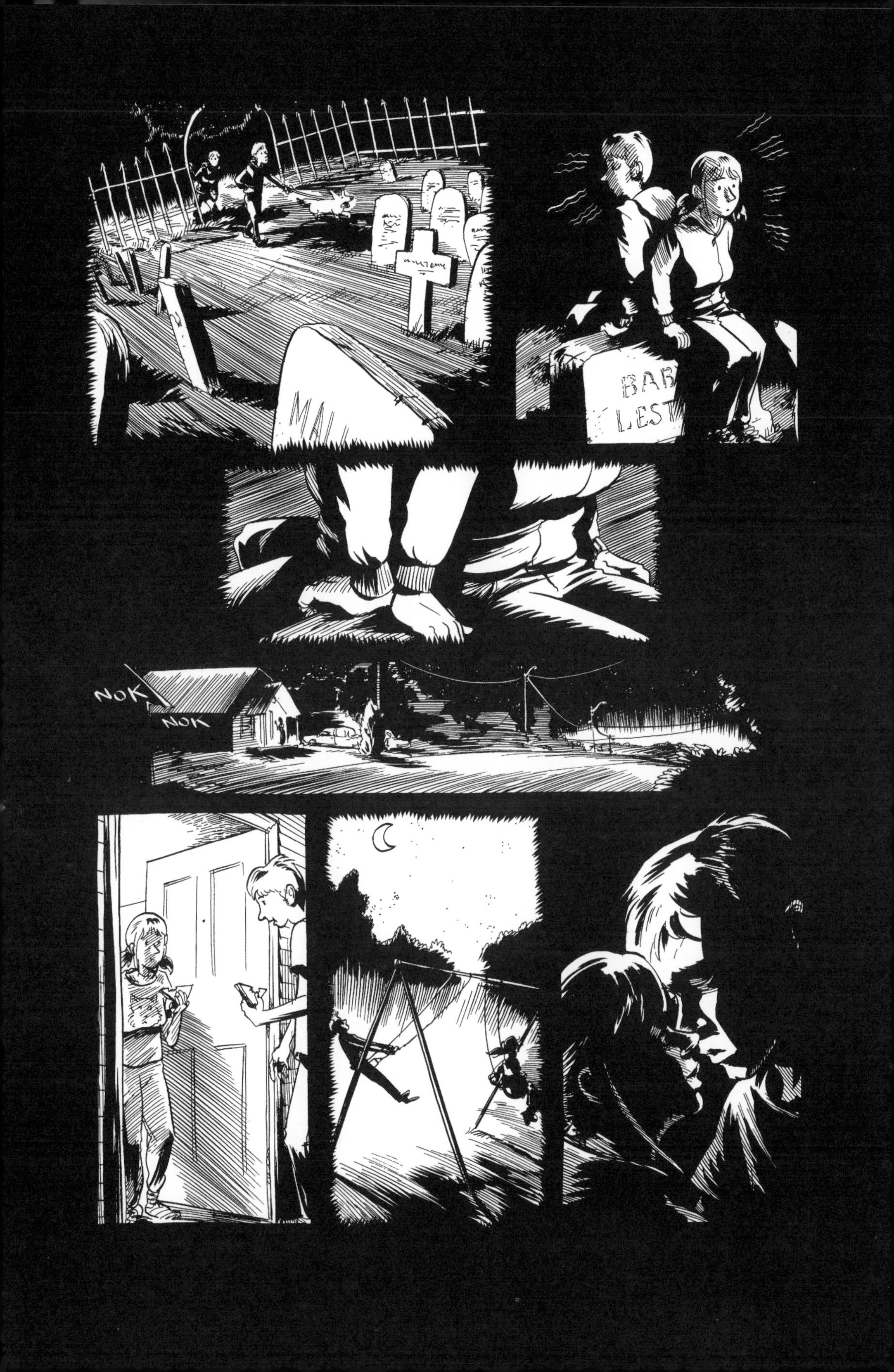
MA
BAB
LEST
NOK
NOK

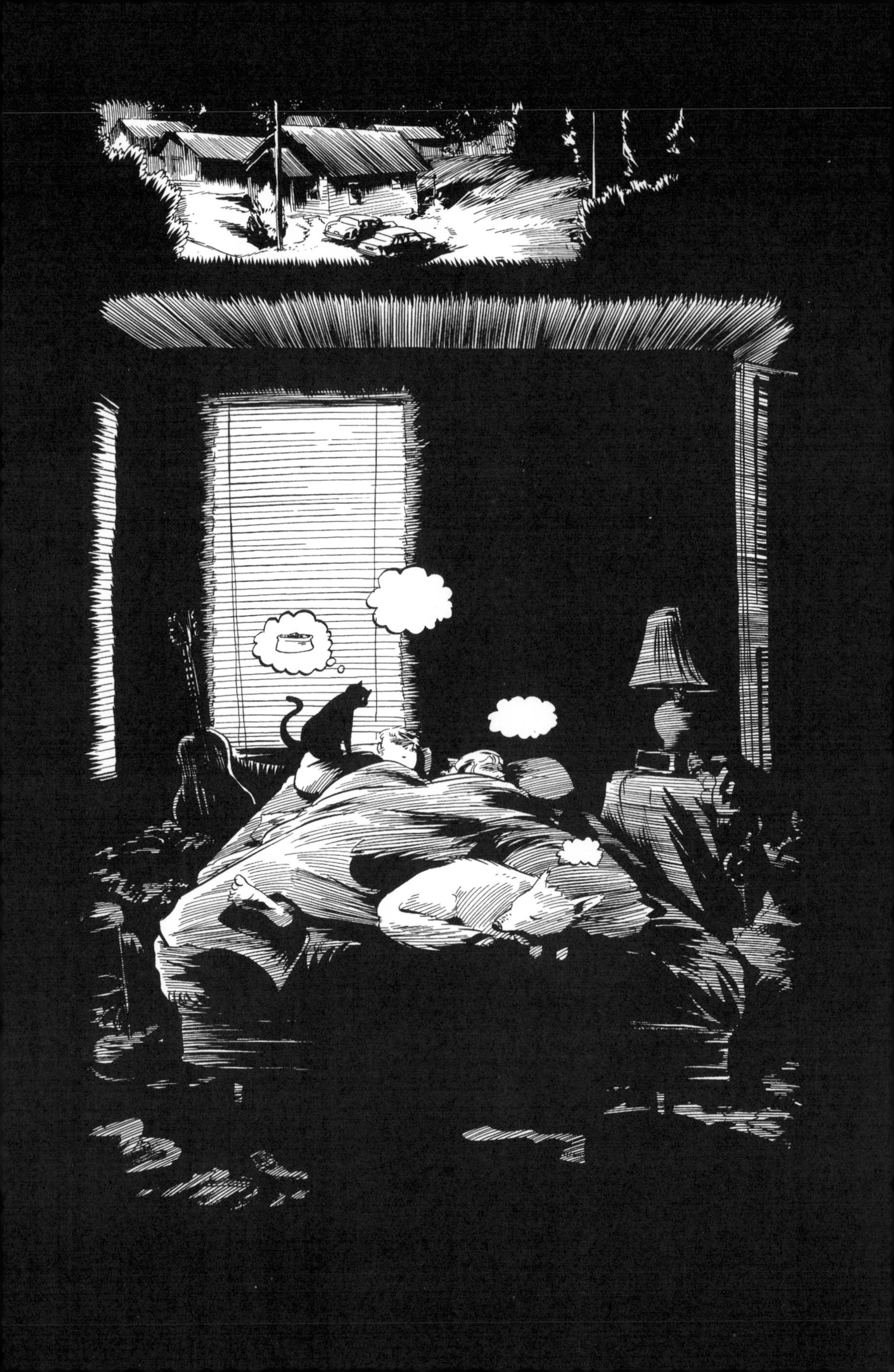

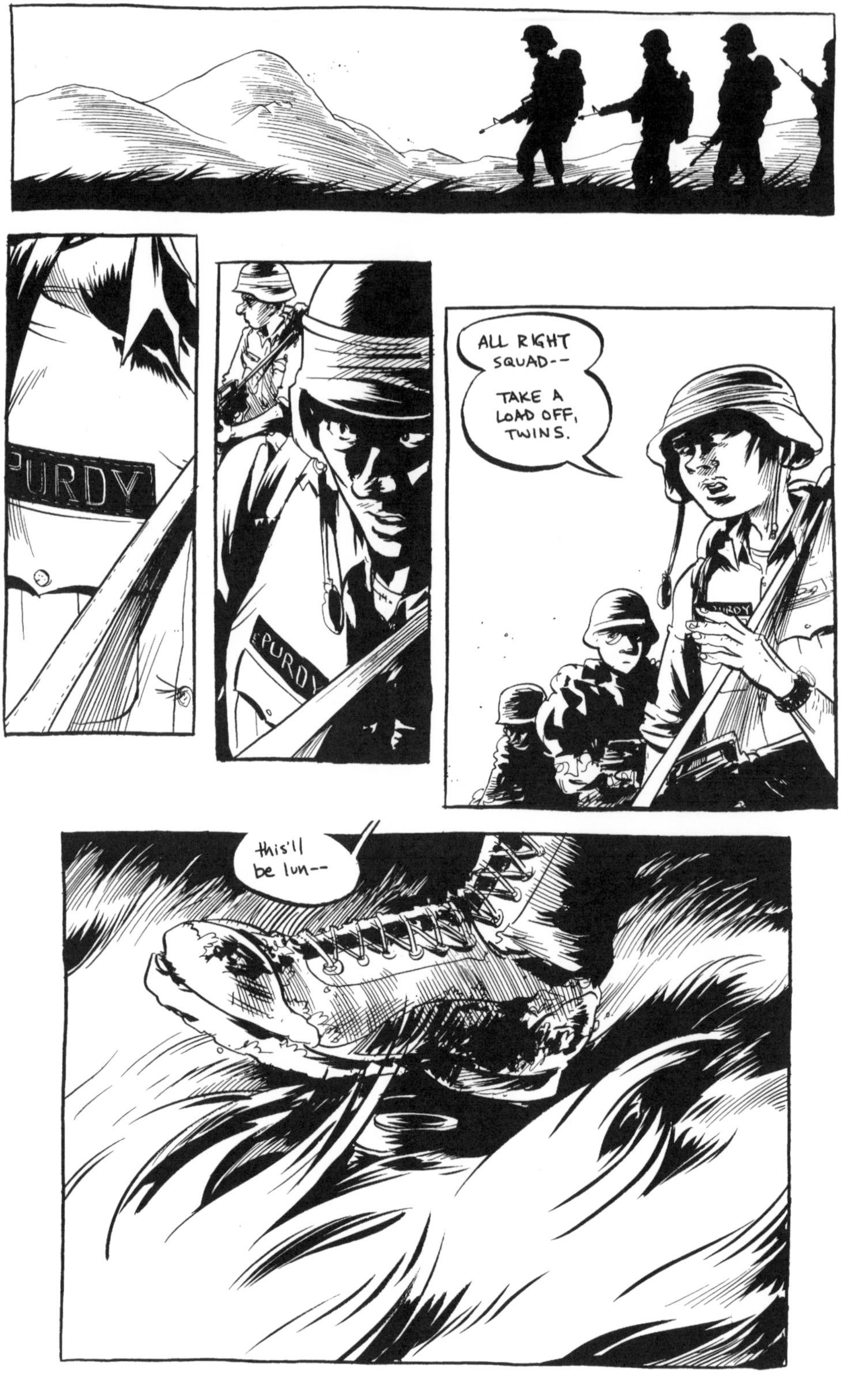
PURDY
PURDY
ALL RIGHT SQUAD--
TAKE A LOAD OFF, TWINS.
PURDY
this'll be fun--

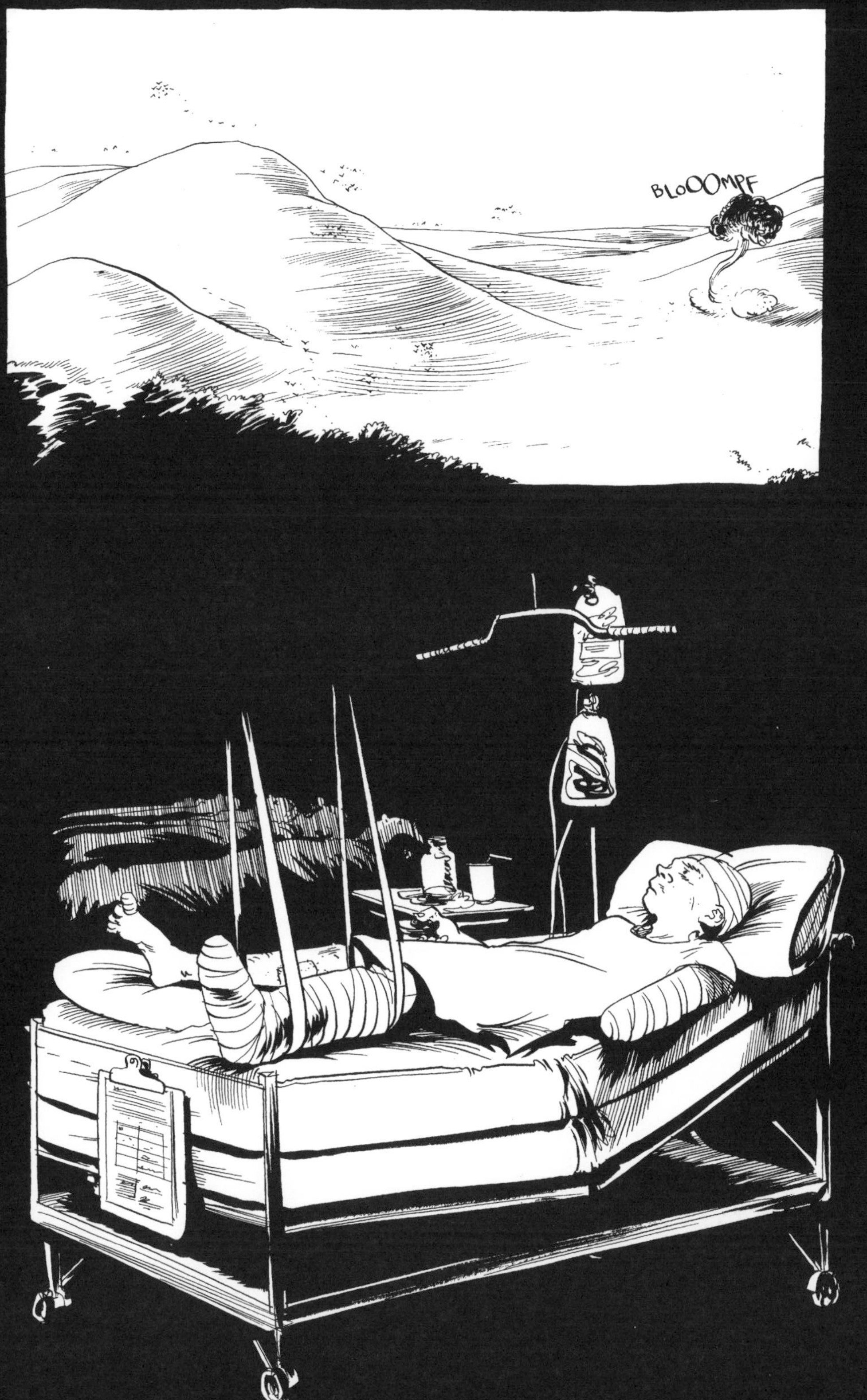
BLoOOMPF

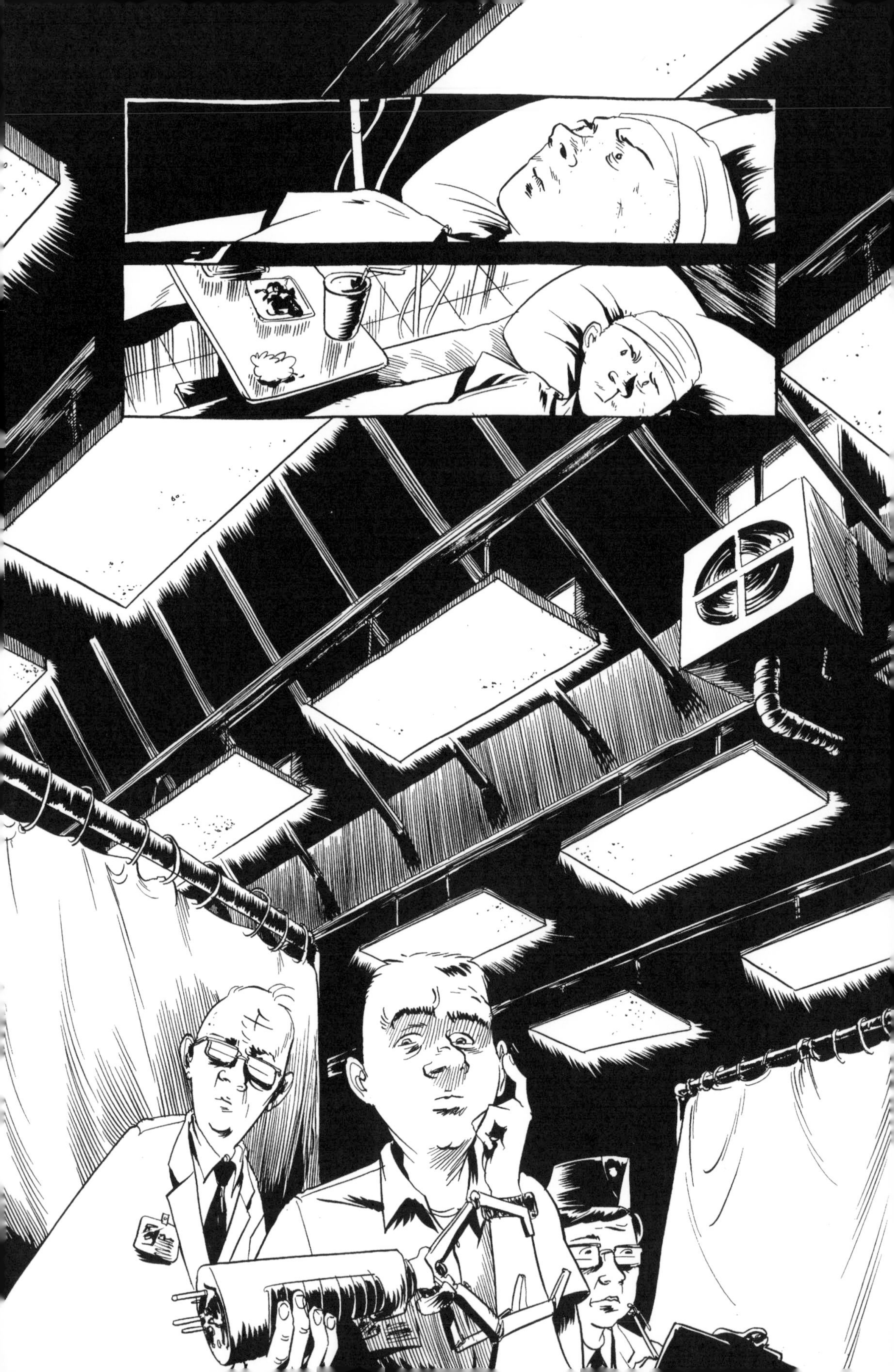

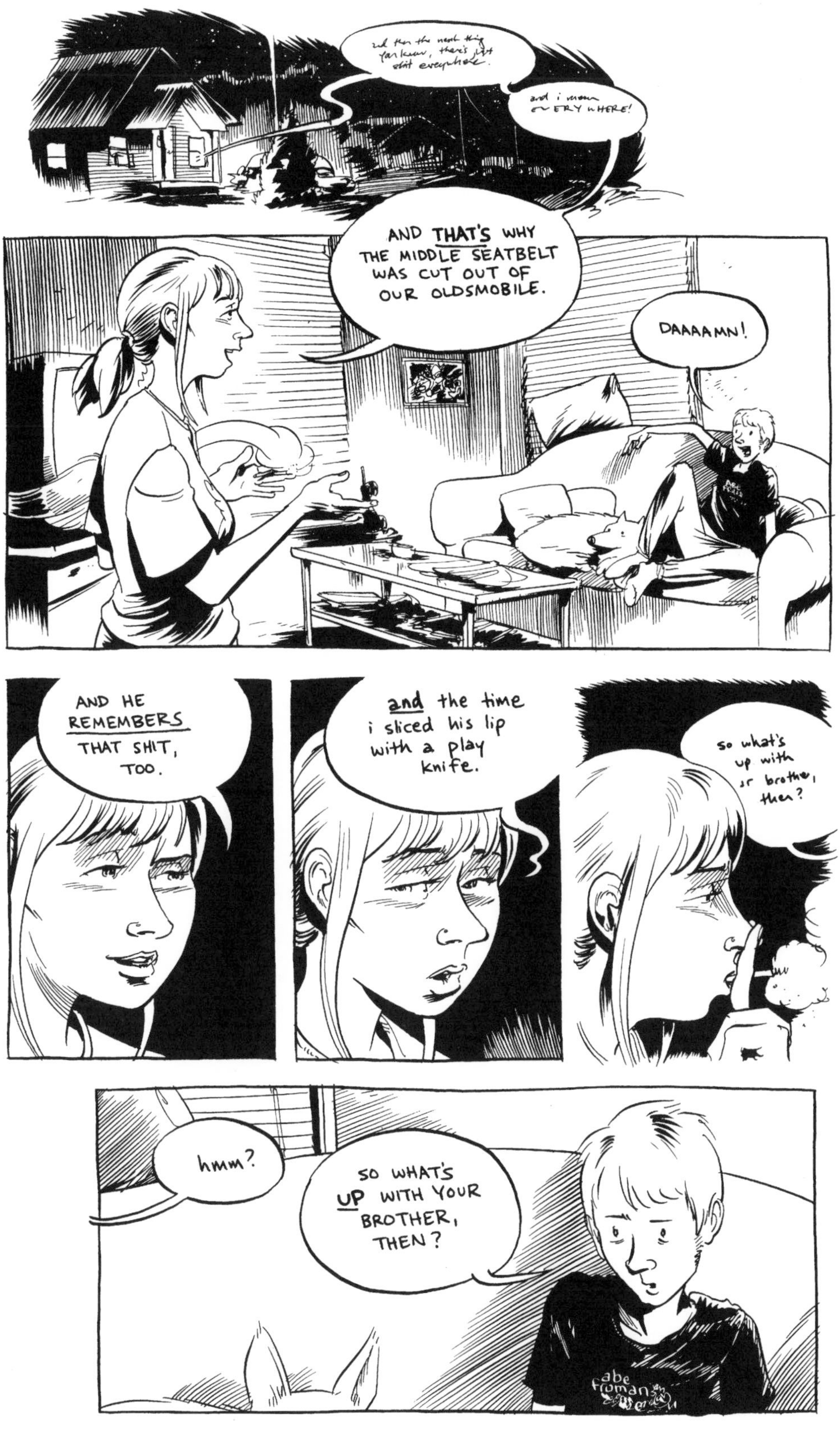
and then the next thing yaknow, there's just shit everywhere.
and i mean EVERYWHERE!
AND THAT'S WHY THE MIDDLE SEATBELT WAS CUT OUT OF OUR OLDSMOBILE.
DAAAAMN!
AND HE REMEMBERS THAT SHIT, TOO.
and the time i sliced his lip with a play knife.
so what's up with yr brother, then?
hmm?
SO WHAT'S UP WITH YOUR BROTHER, THEN?
abe froman

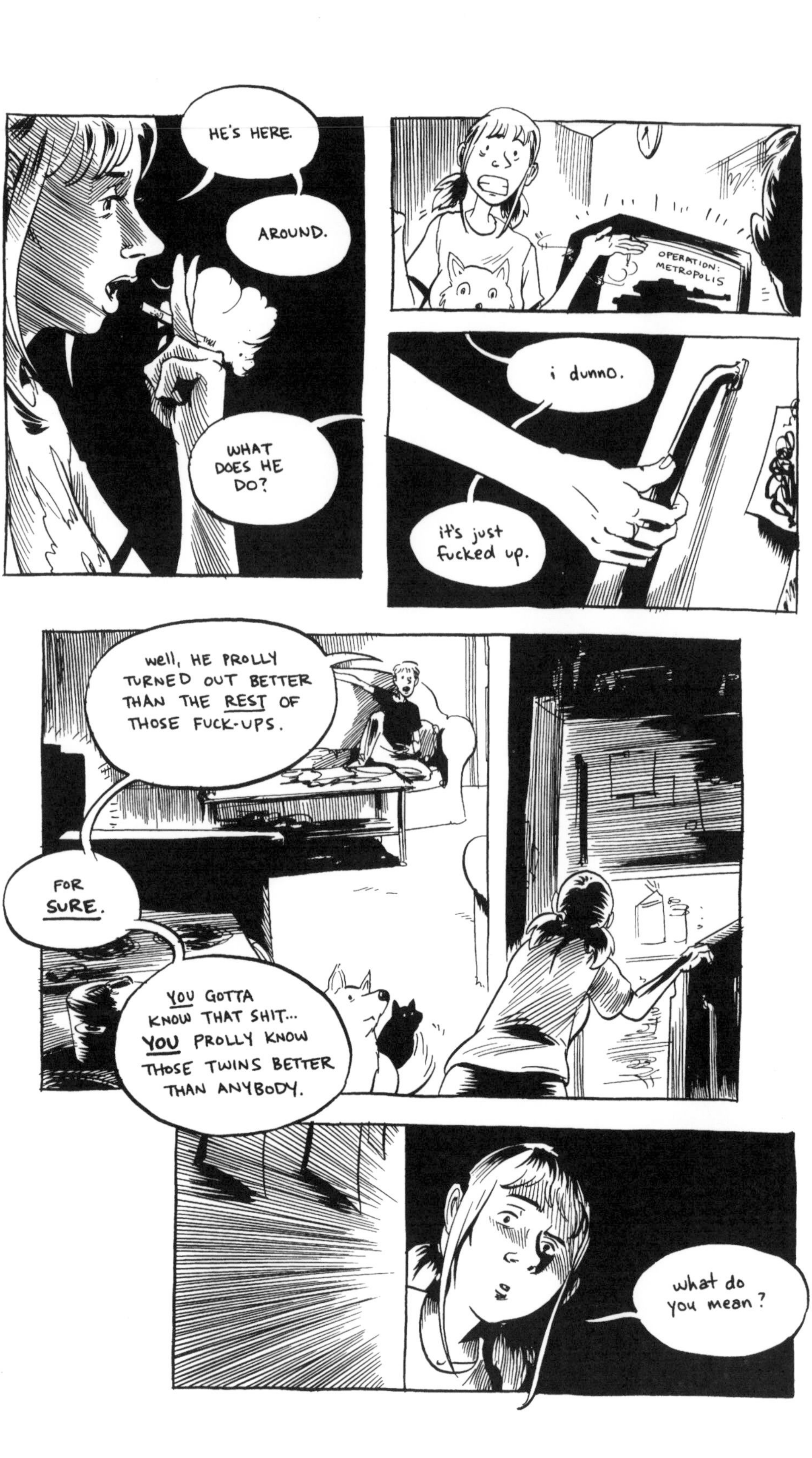
HE'S HERE.
AROUND.
WHAT DOES HE DO?
OPERATION: METROPOLIS
i dunno.
it's just fucked up.
well, HE PROLLY TURNED OUT BETTER THAN THE REST OF THOSE FUCK-UPS.
FOR SURE.
YOU GOTTA KNOW THAT SHIT... YOU PROLLY KNOW THOSE TWINS BETTER THAN ANYBODY.
what do you mean?

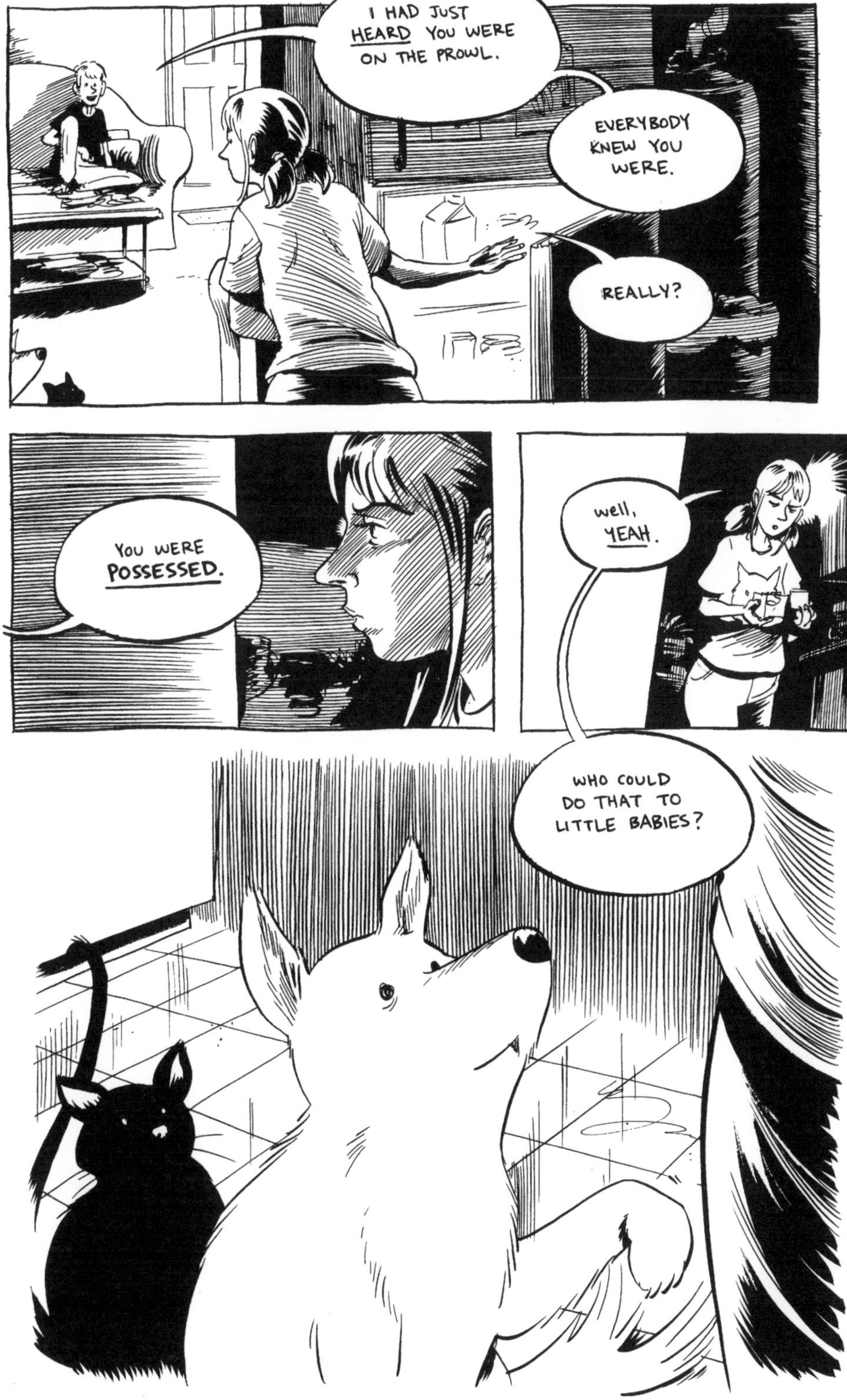
I HAD JUST HEARD YOU WERE ON THE PROWL.
EVERYBODY KNEW YOU WERE.
REALLY?
YOU WERE POSSESSED.
well, YEAH.
WHO COULD DO THAT TO LITTLE BABIES?

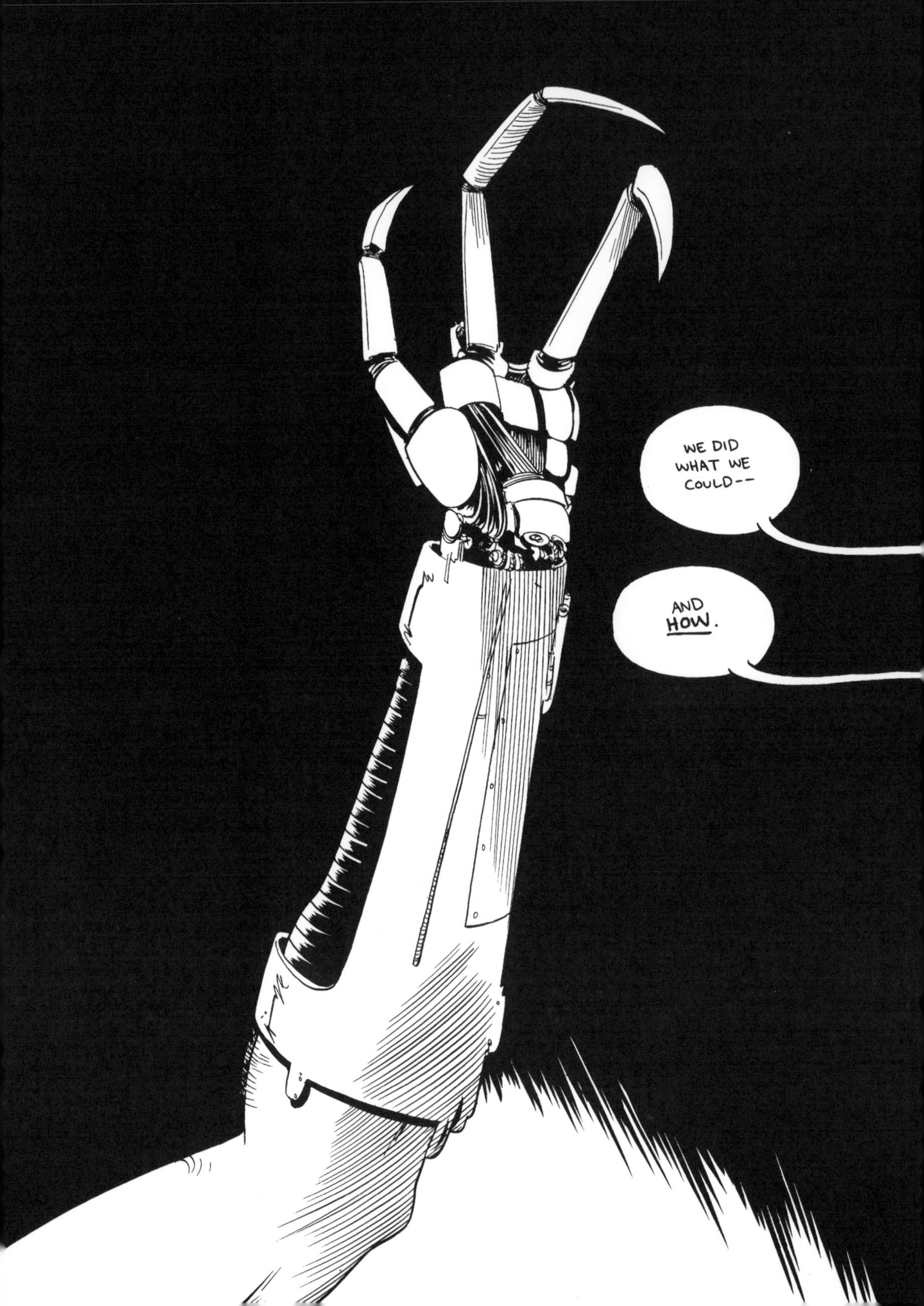
WE DID WHAT WE COULD--
AND **HOW**.

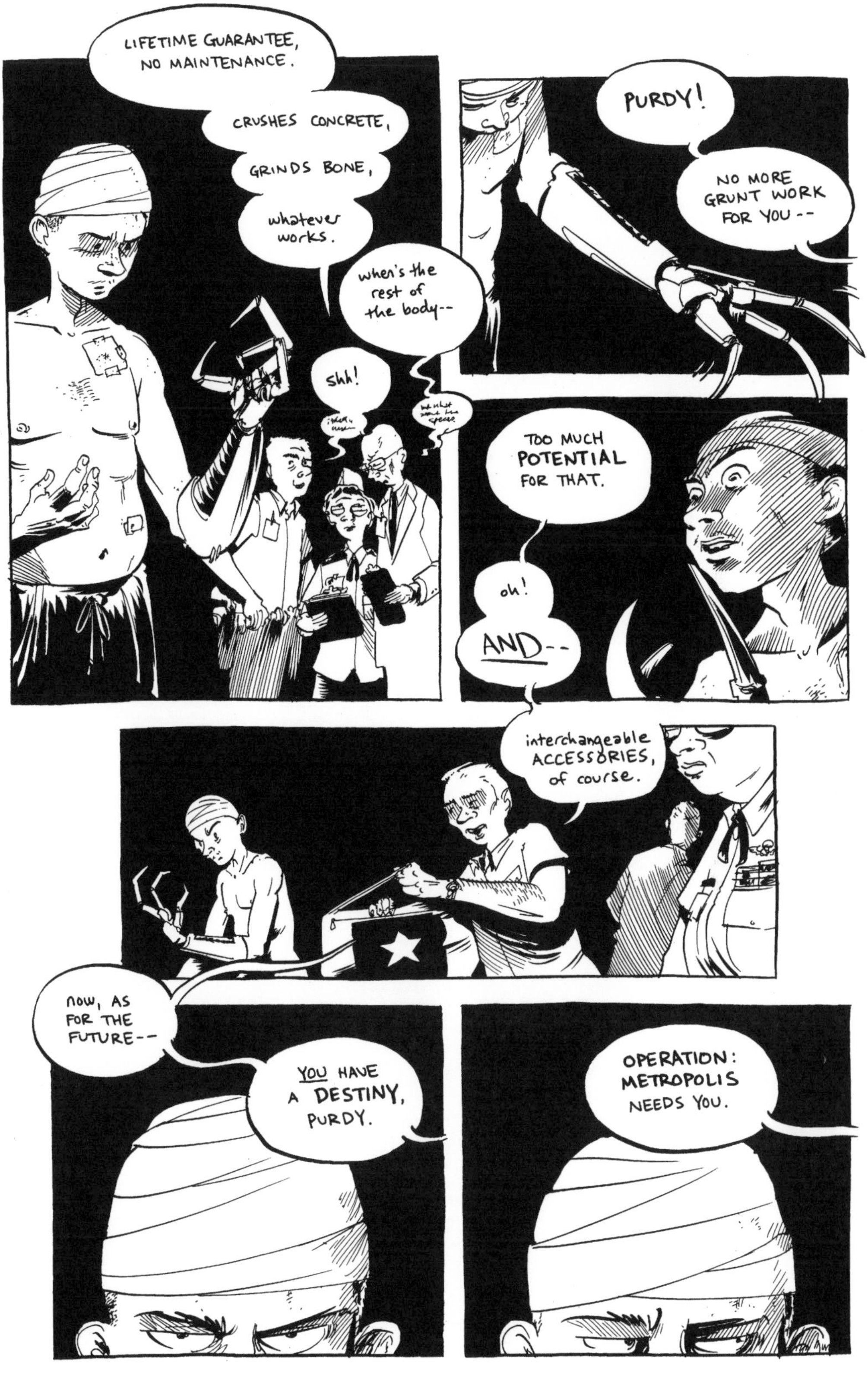
LIFETIME GUARANTEE, NO MAINTENANCE.
CRUSHES CONCRETE,
GRINDS BONE,
whatever works.
when's the rest of the body--
Shh!
PURDY!
NO MORE GRUNT WORK FOR YOU--
TOO MUCH POTENTIAL FOR THAT.
oh!
AND--
interchangeable ACCESSORIES, of course.
now, AS FOR THE FUTURE--
YOU HAVE A DESTINY, PURDY.
OPERATION: METROPOLIS NEEDS YOU.

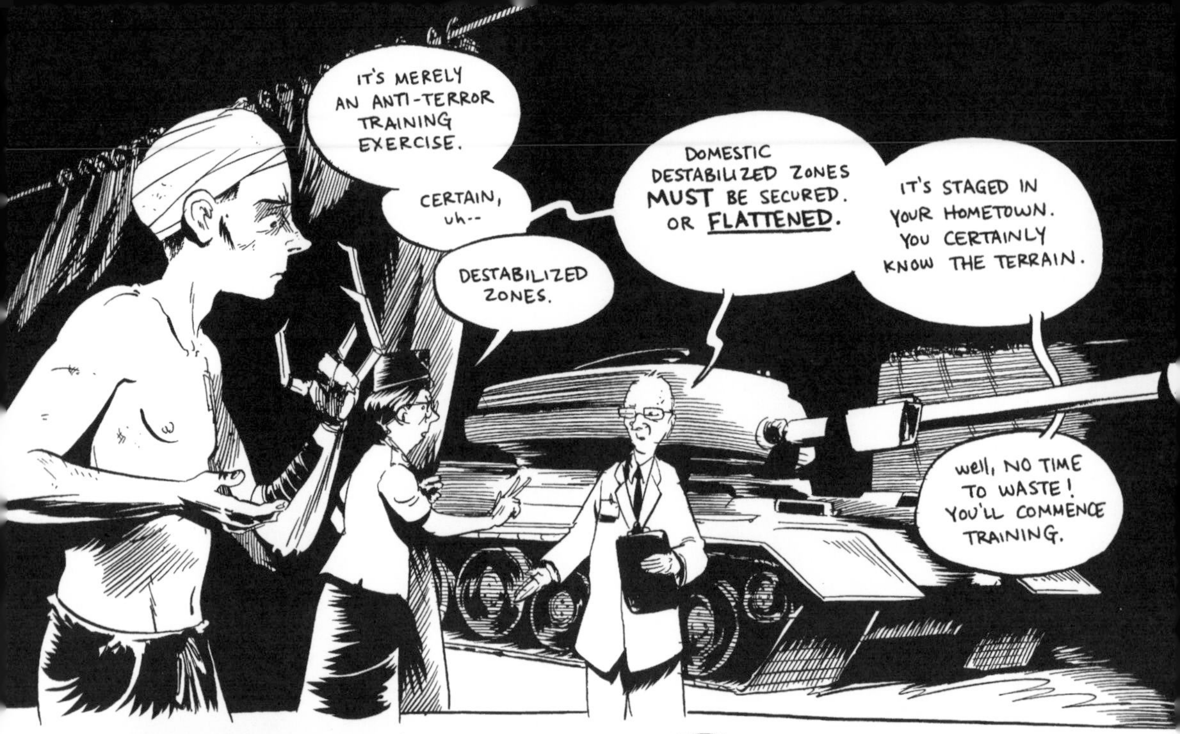
IT'S MERELY AN ANTI-TERROR TRAINING EXERCISE.
CERTAIN, uh--
DESTABILIZED ZONES.
DOMESTIC DESTABILIZED ZONES MUST BE SECURED. OR FLATTENED.
IT'S STAGED IN YOUR HOMETOWN. YOU CERTAINLY KNOW THE TERRAIN.
well, NO TIME TO WASTE! YOU'LL COMMENCE TRAINING.
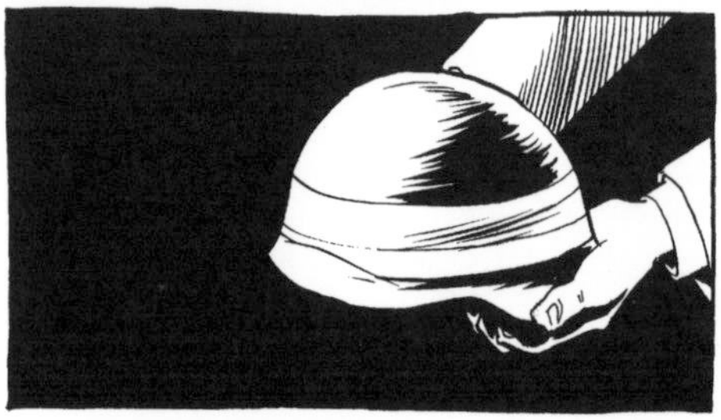
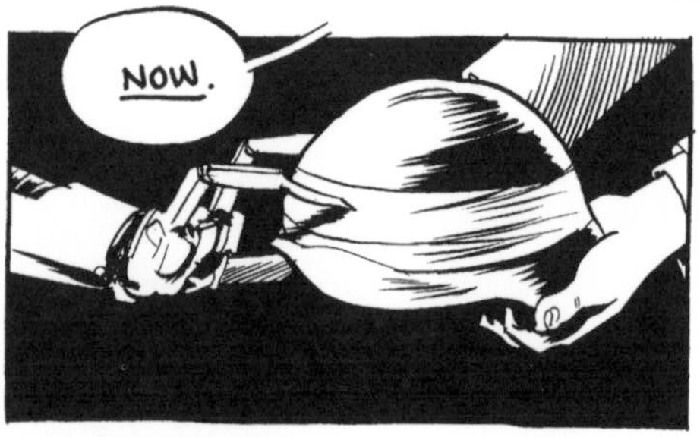
NOW.
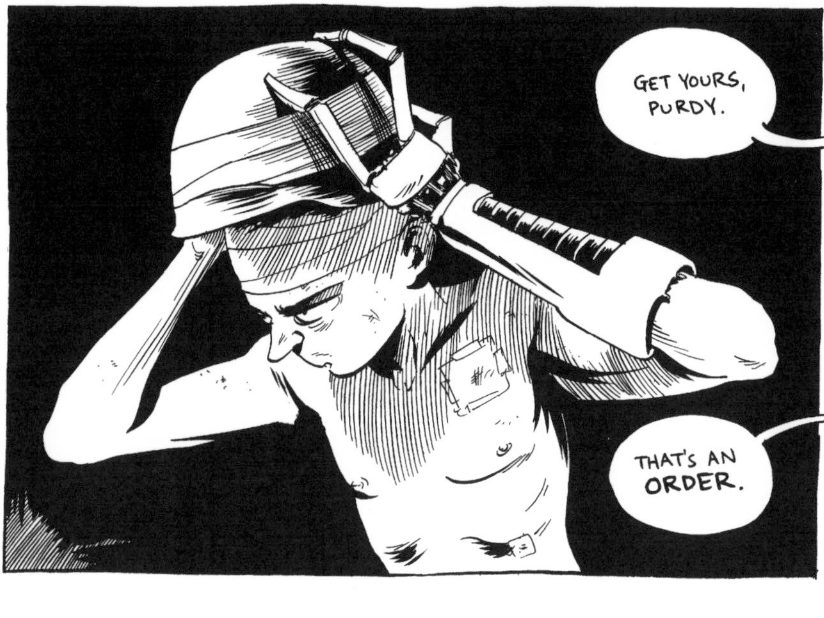
GET YOURS, PURDY.
THAT'S AN ORDER.

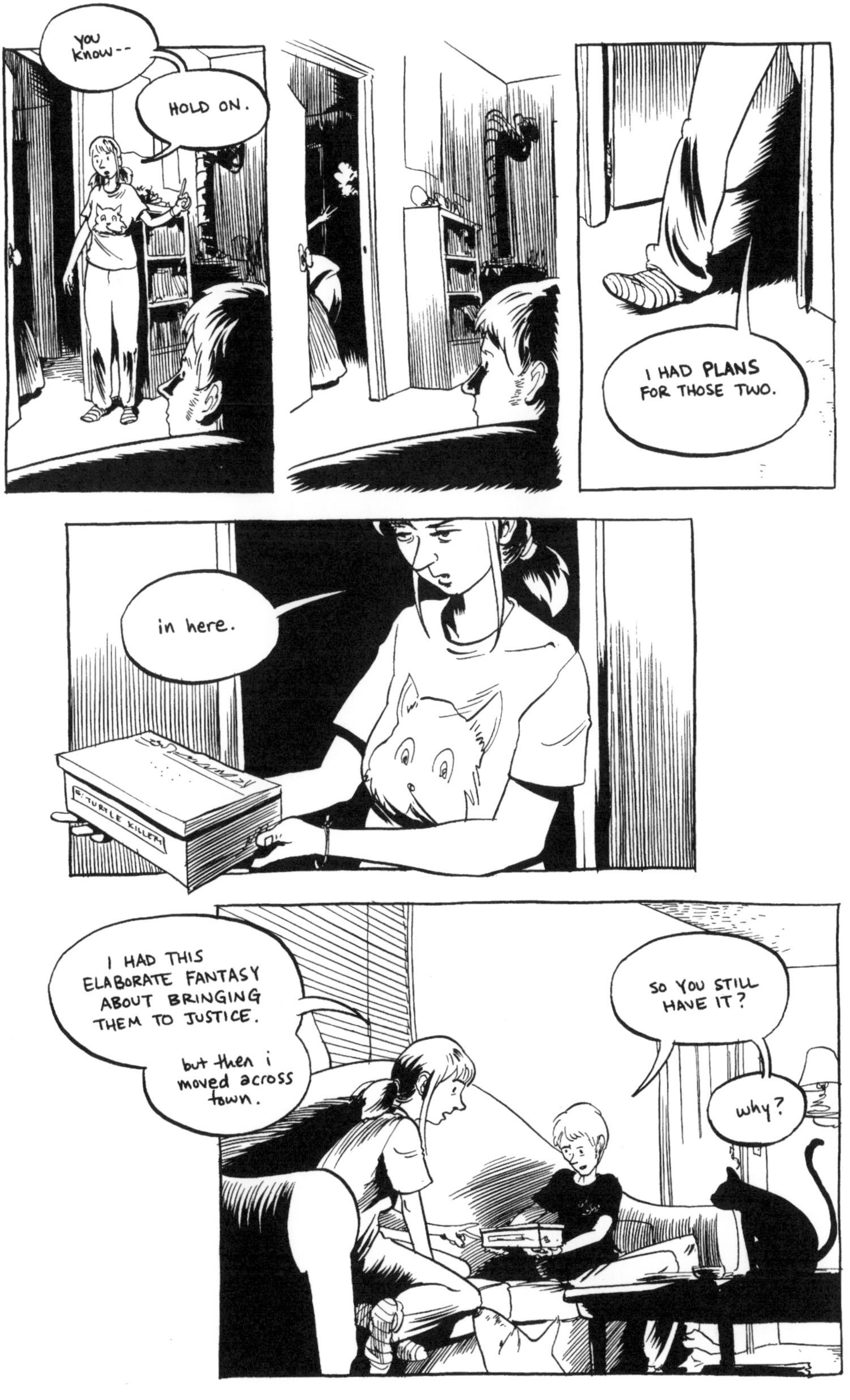
you know--
HOLD ON.
I HAD PLANS FOR THOSE TWO.
in here.
I HAD THIS ELABORATE FANTASY ABOUT BRINGING THEM TO JUSTICE.
but then i moved across town.
SO YOU STILL HAVE IT?
why?

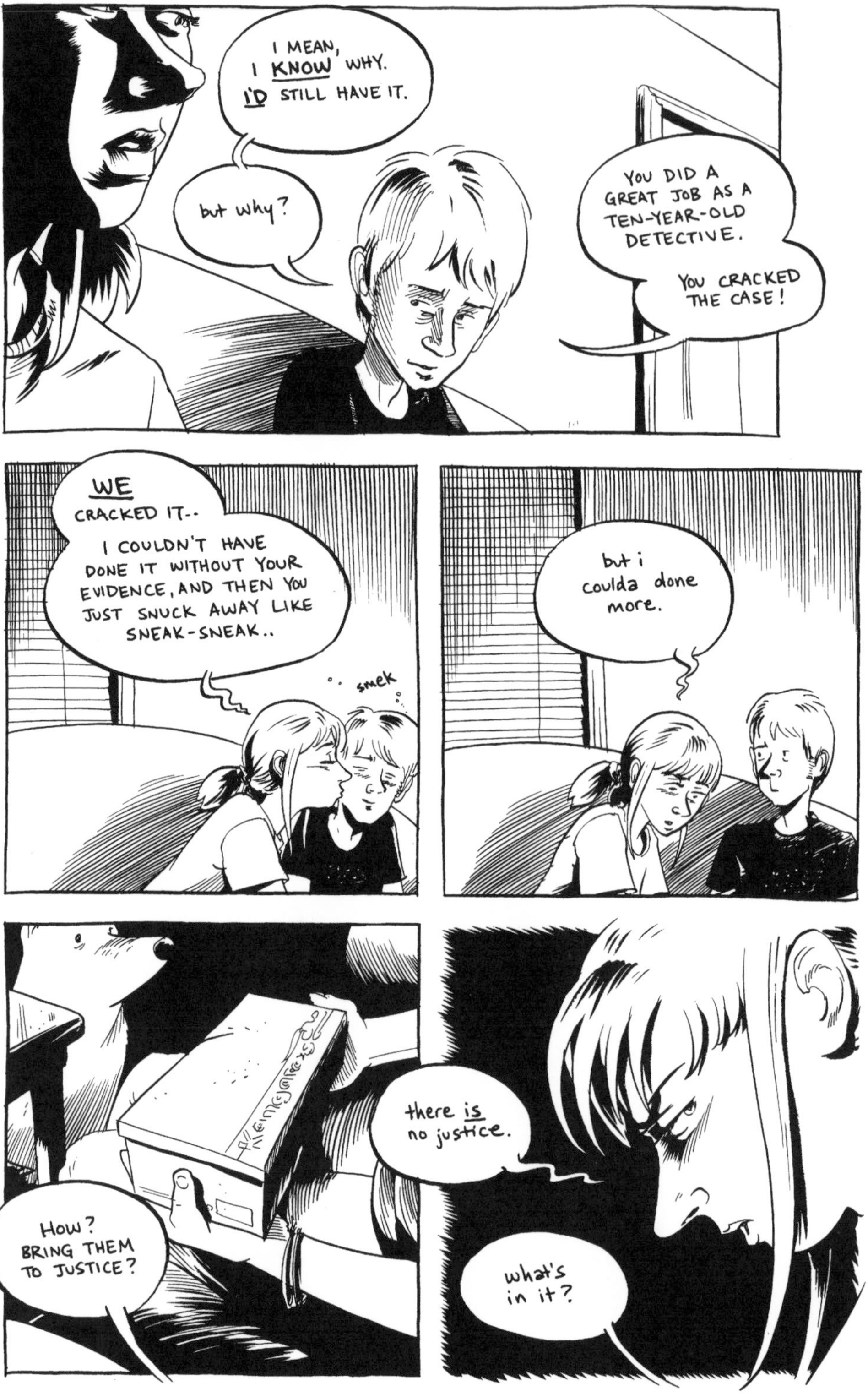
I MEAN, I KNOW WHY. I'D STILL HAVE IT.
but why?
YOU DID A GREAT JOB AS A TEN-YEAR-OLD DETECTIVE.
YOU CRACKED THE CASE!
WE CRACKED IT.. I COULDN'T HAVE DONE IT WITHOUT YOUR EVIDENCE, AND THEN YOU JUST SNUCK AWAY LIKE SNEAK-SNEAK..
smek
but i coulda done more.
How? BRING THEM TO JUSTICE?
there is no justice.
what's in it?

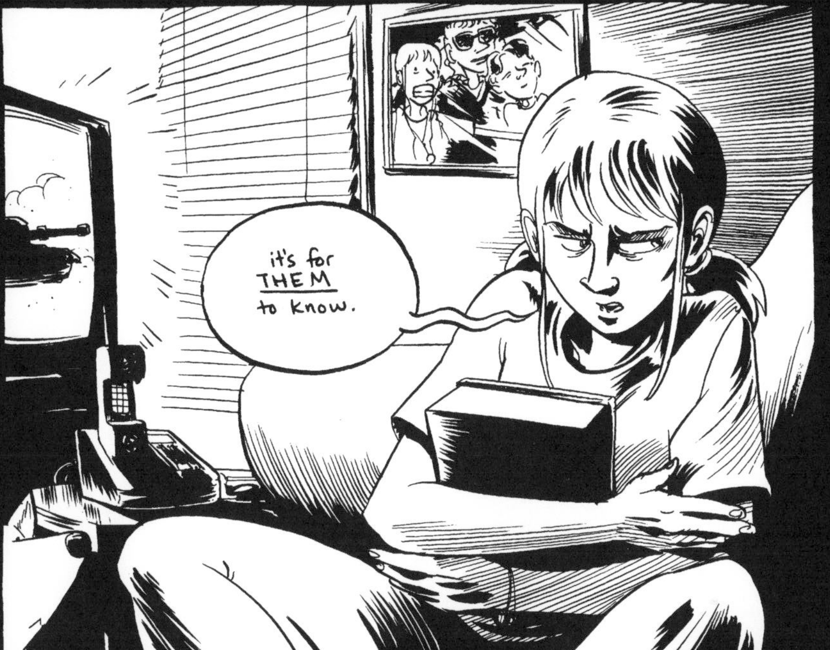
it's for THEM to know.

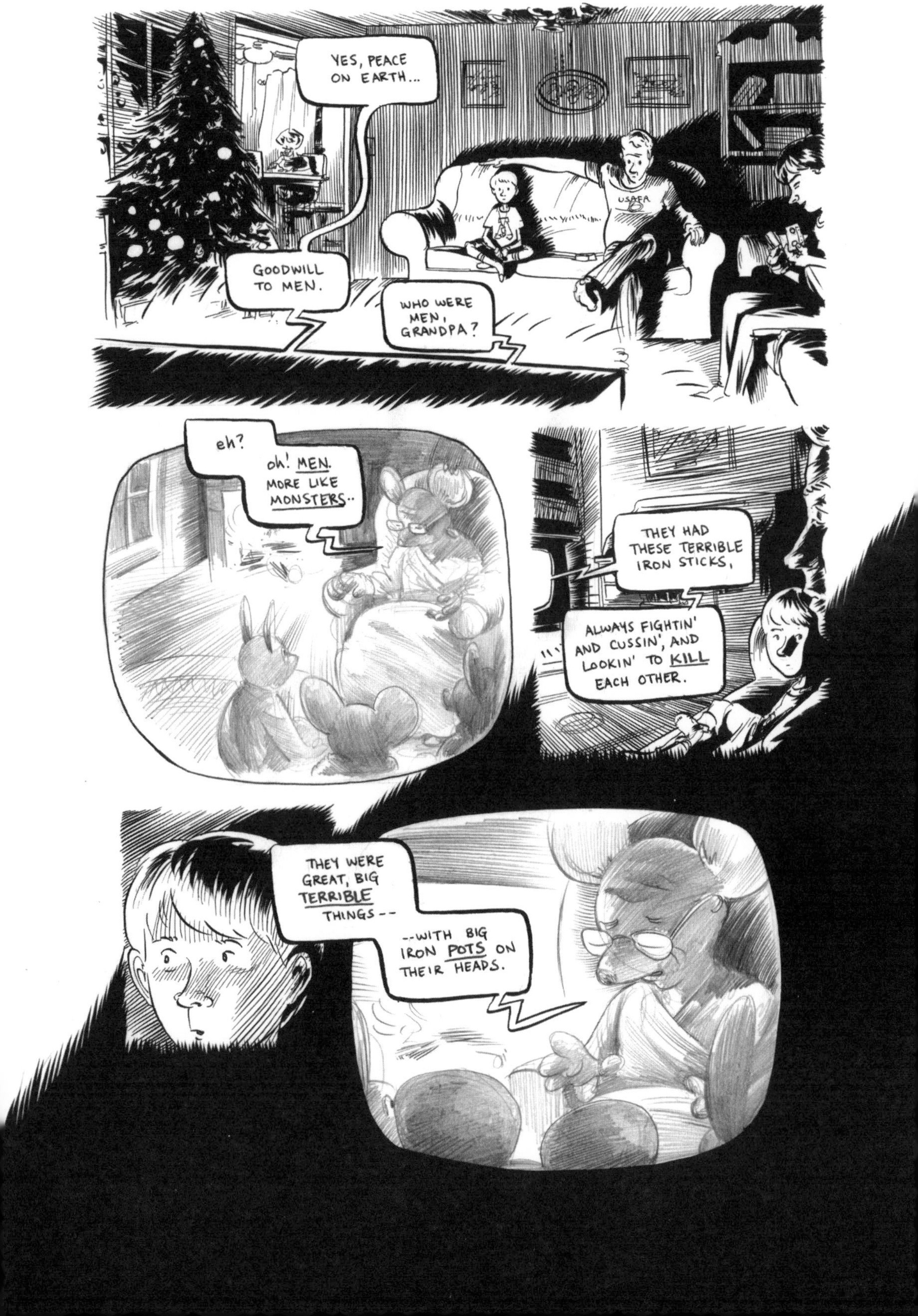
YES, PEACE ON EARTH...
GOODWILL TO MEN.
WHO WERE MEN, GRANDPA?
eh?
oh! MEN. MORE LIKE MONSTERS..
THEY HAD THESE TERRIBLE IRON STICKS,
ALWAYS FIGHTIN' AND CUSSIN', AND LOOKIN' TO KILL EACH OTHER.
THEY WERE GREAT, BIG TERRIBLE THINGS--
--WITH BIG IRON POTS ON THEIR HEADS.

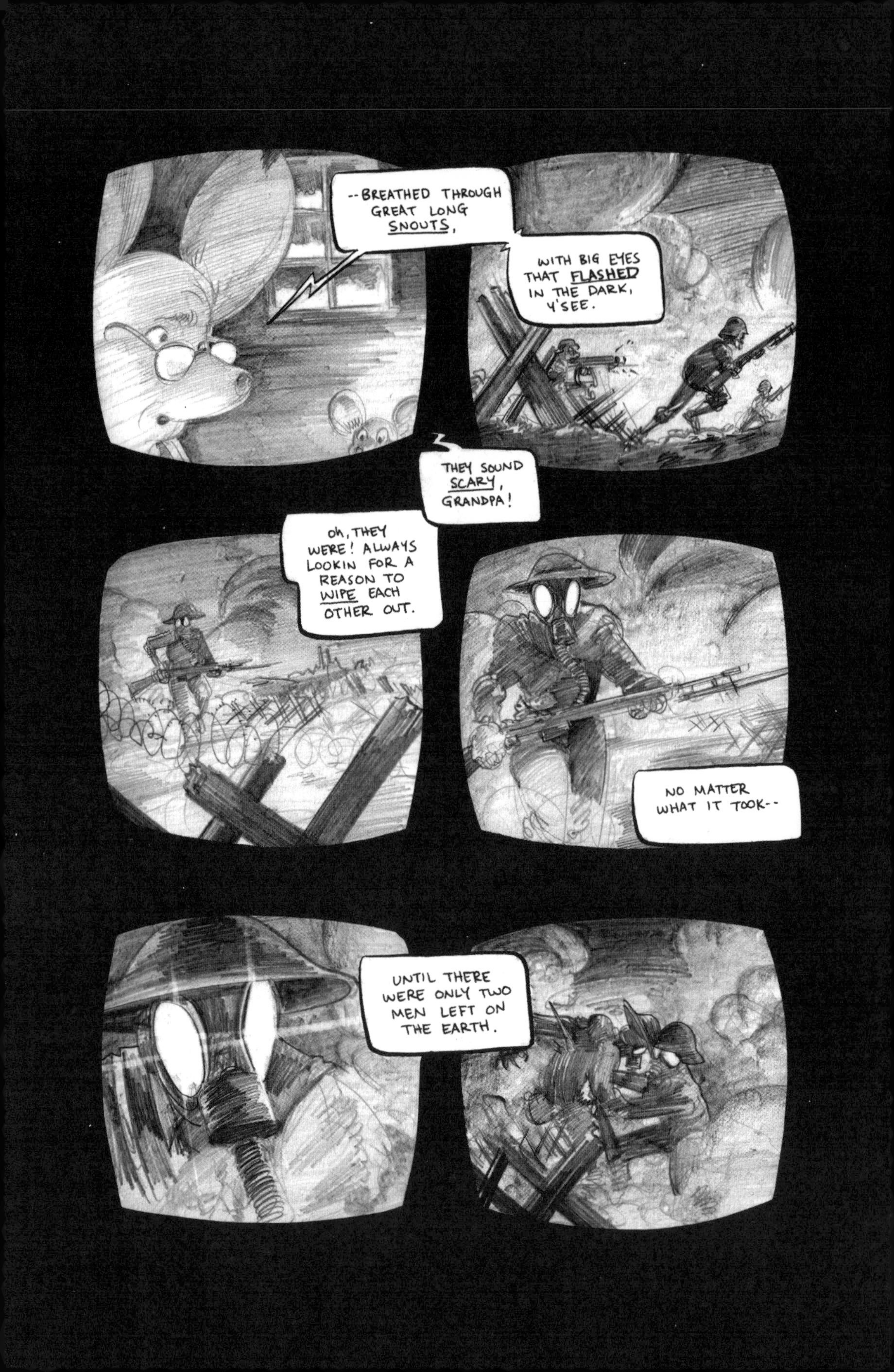
--BREATHED THROUGH GREAT LONG SNOUTS,
WITH BIG EYES THAT FLASHED IN THE DARK, Y'SEE.
THEY SOUND SCARY, GRANDPA!
OH, THEY WERE! ALWAYS LOOKIN FOR A REASON TO WIPE EACH OTHER OUT.
NO MATTER WHAT IT TOOK--
UNTIL THERE WERE ONLY TWO MEN LEFT ON THE EARTH.

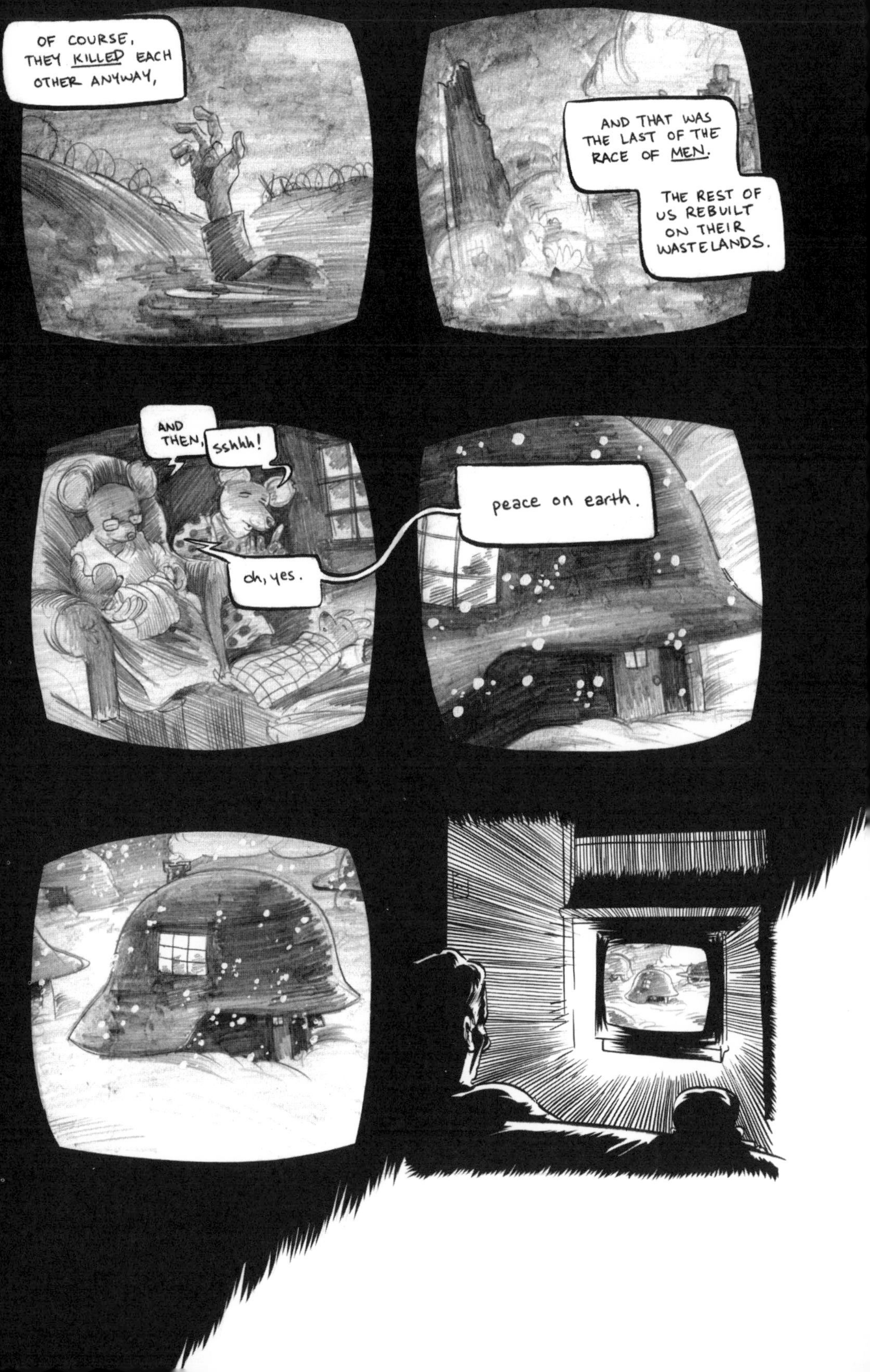
OF COURSE, THEY KILLED EACH OTHER ANYWAY,
AND THAT WAS THE LAST OF THE RACE OF MEN.
THE REST OF US REBUILT ON THEIR WASTELANDS.
AND THEN,
sshhh!
oh, yes.
peace on earth.

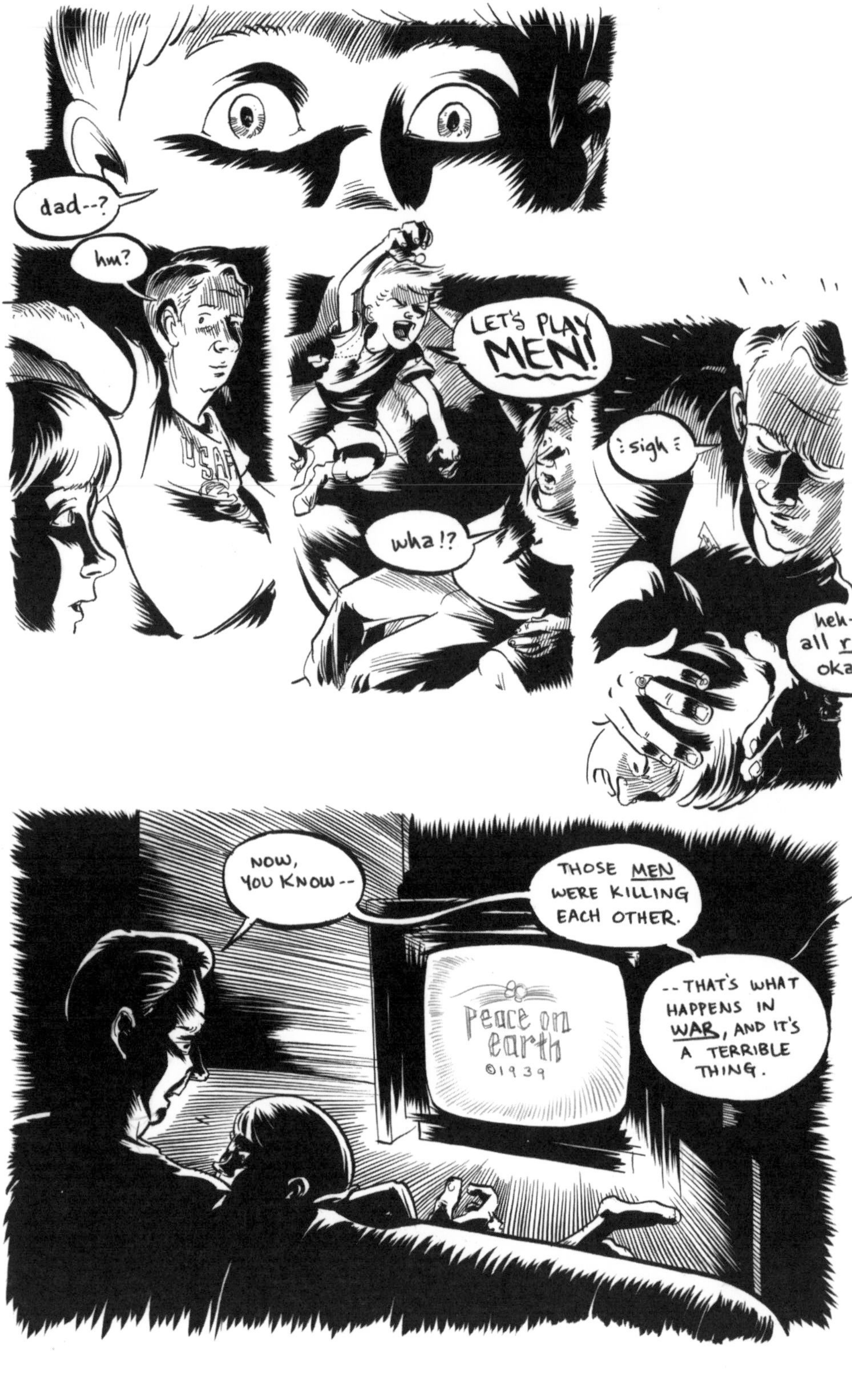
dad--?
hm?
LET'S PLAY MEN!
wha!?
sigh
heh-- all right, okay,
NOW, YOU KNOW--
THOSE MEN WERE KILLING EACH OTHER.
--THAT'S WHAT HAPPENS IN WAR, AND IT'S A TERRIBLE THING.
Peace on earth
©1939

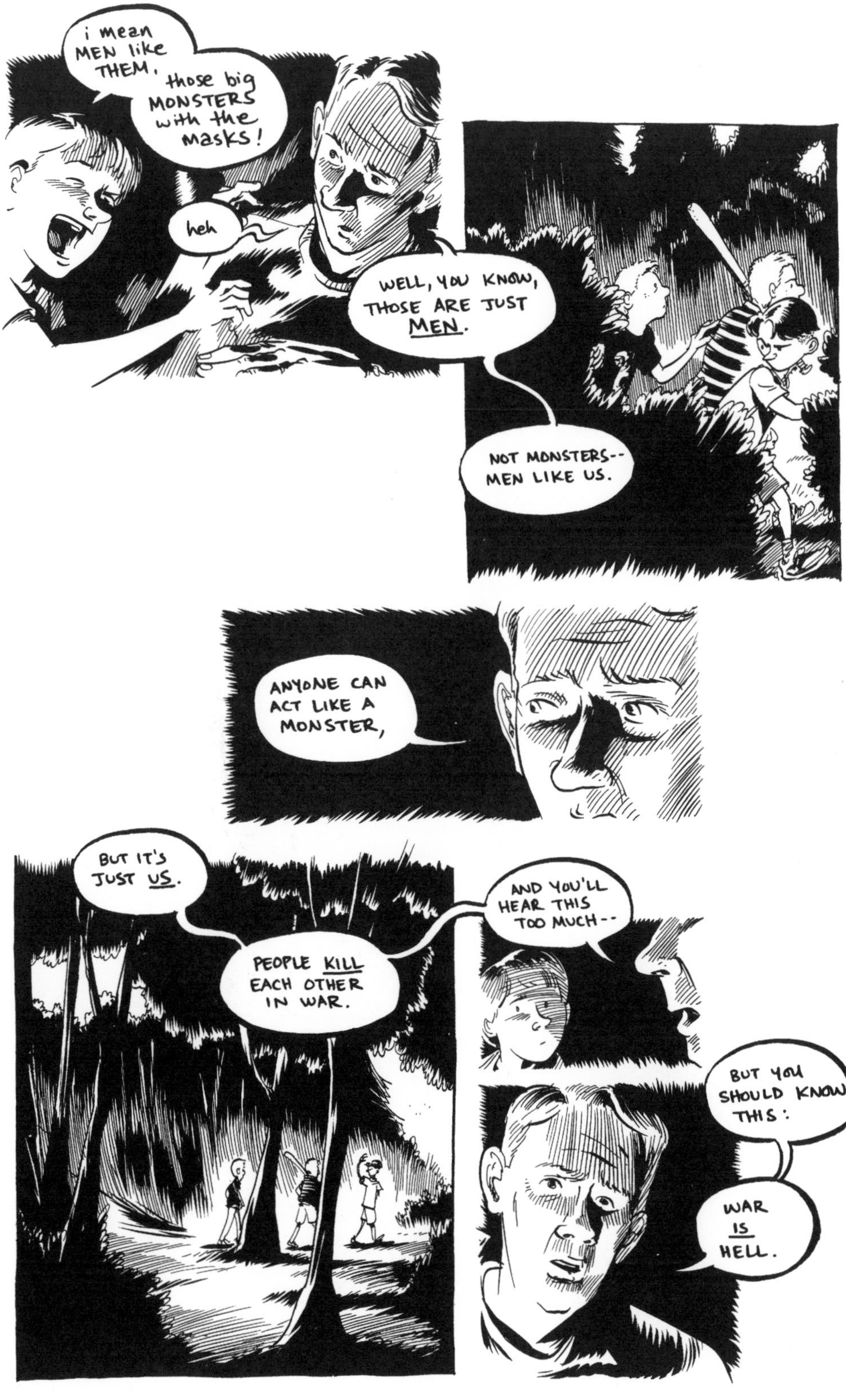
i mean MEN like THEM,
those big MONSTERS with the masks!
heh
WELL, YOU KNOW, THOSE ARE JUST MEN.
NOT MONSTERS-- MEN LIKE US.
ANYONE CAN ACT LIKE A MONSTER,
BUT IT'S JUST US.
PEOPLE KILL EACH OTHER IN WAR.
AND YOU'LL HEAR THIS TOO MUCH--
BUT YOU SHOULD KNOW THIS:
WAR IS HELL.

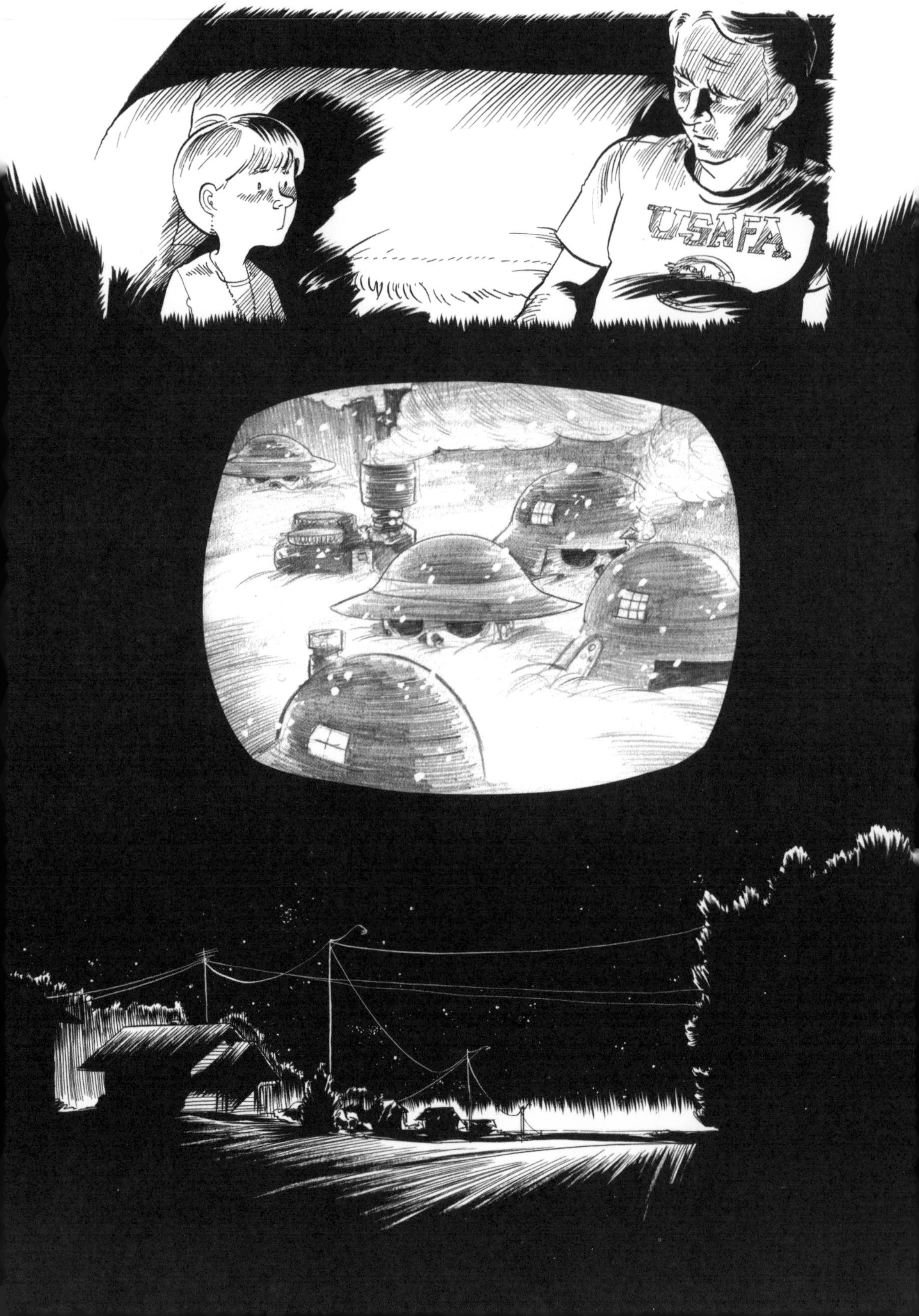
USAFA

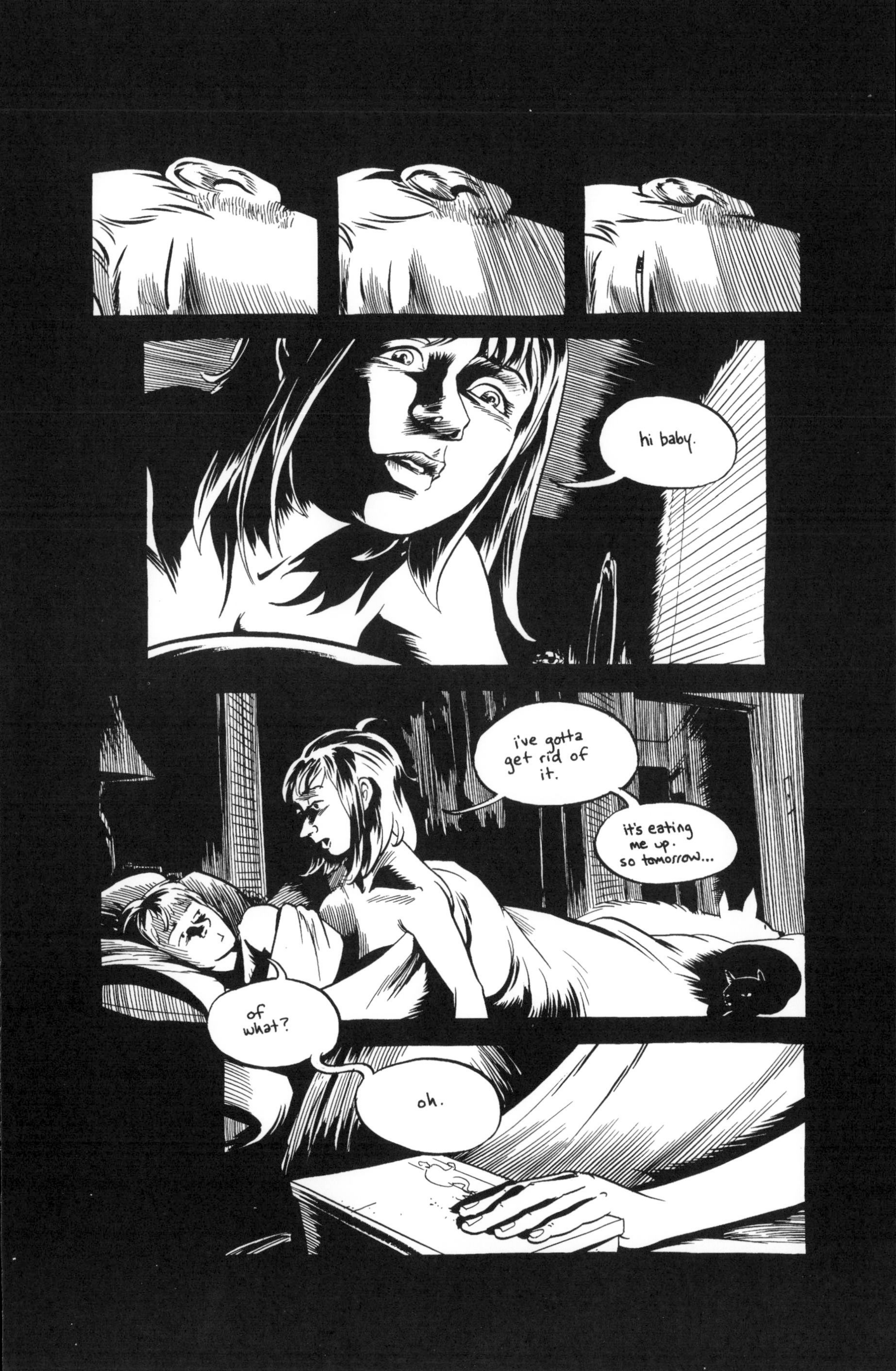
hi baby.
i've gotta get rid of it.
it's eating me up. so tomorrow...
of what?
oh.

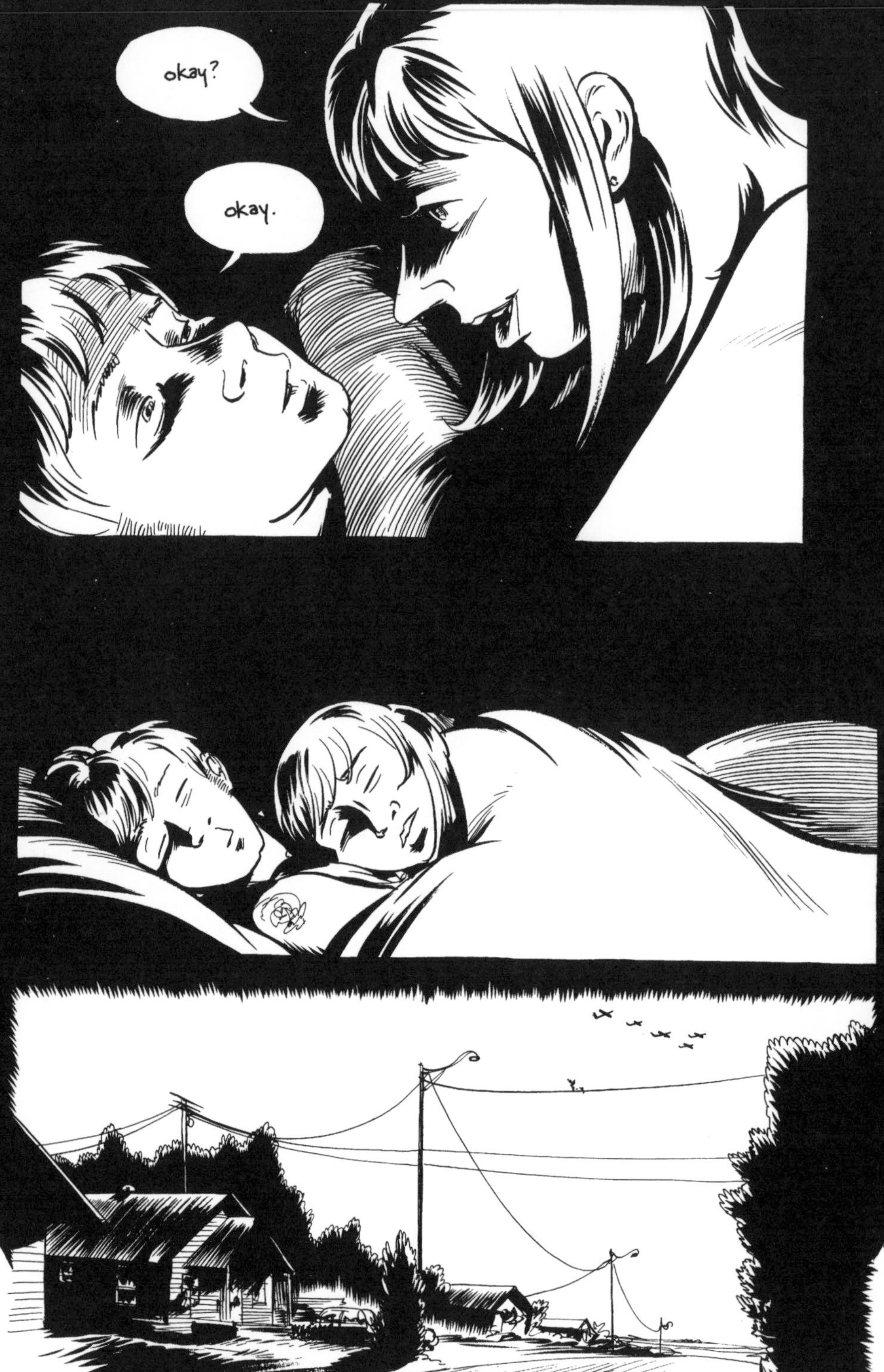
okay?
okay.

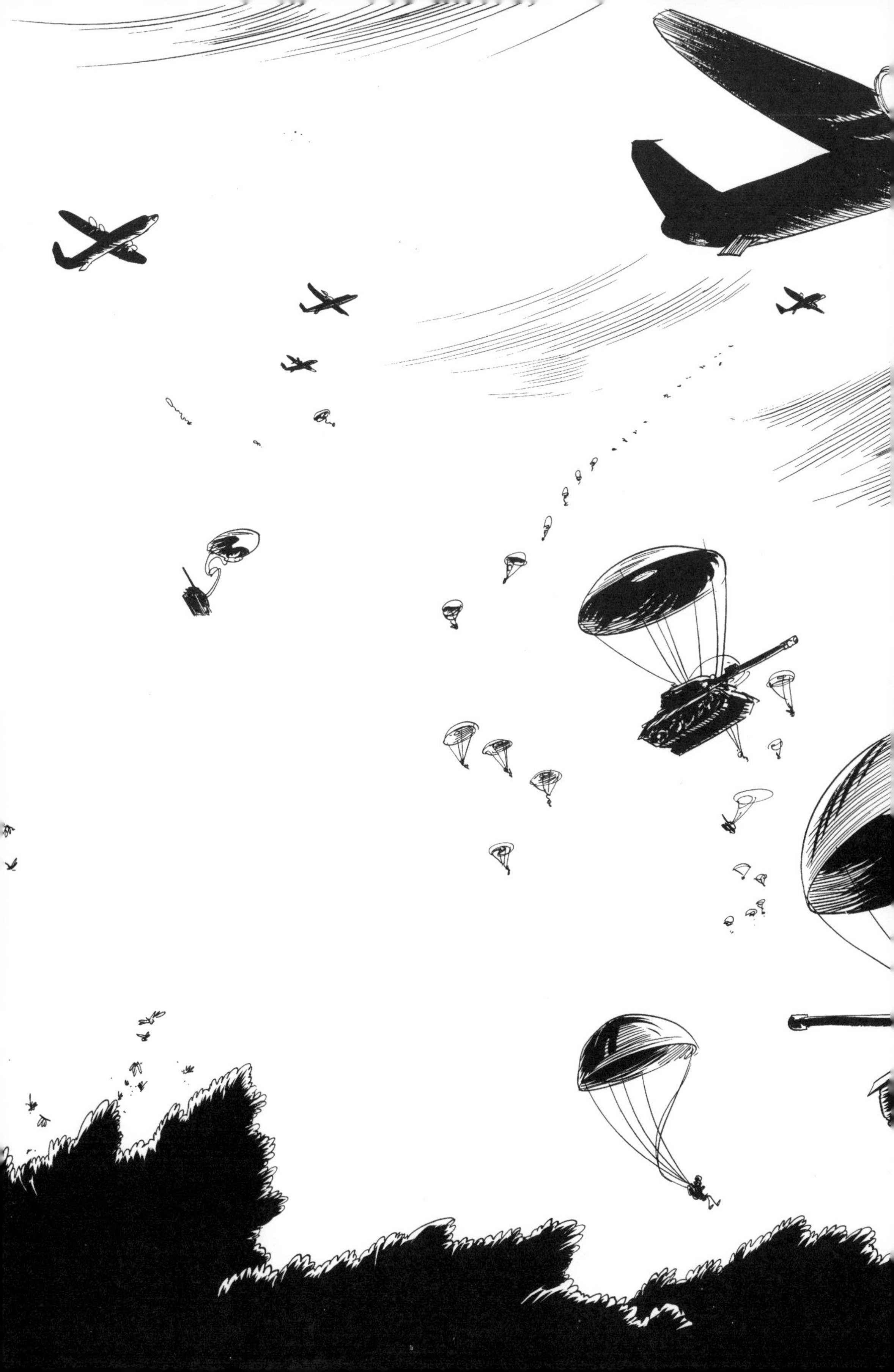

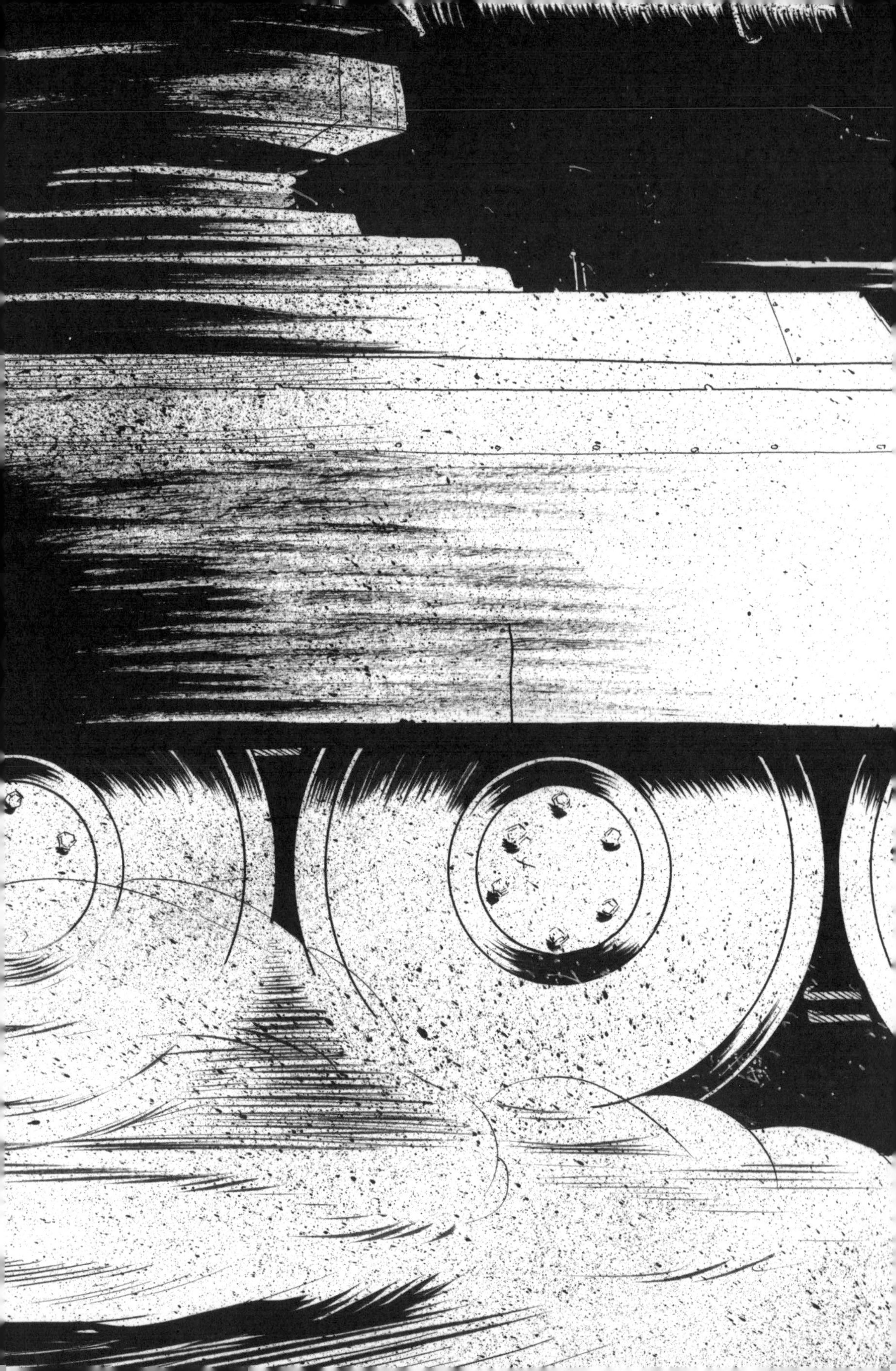

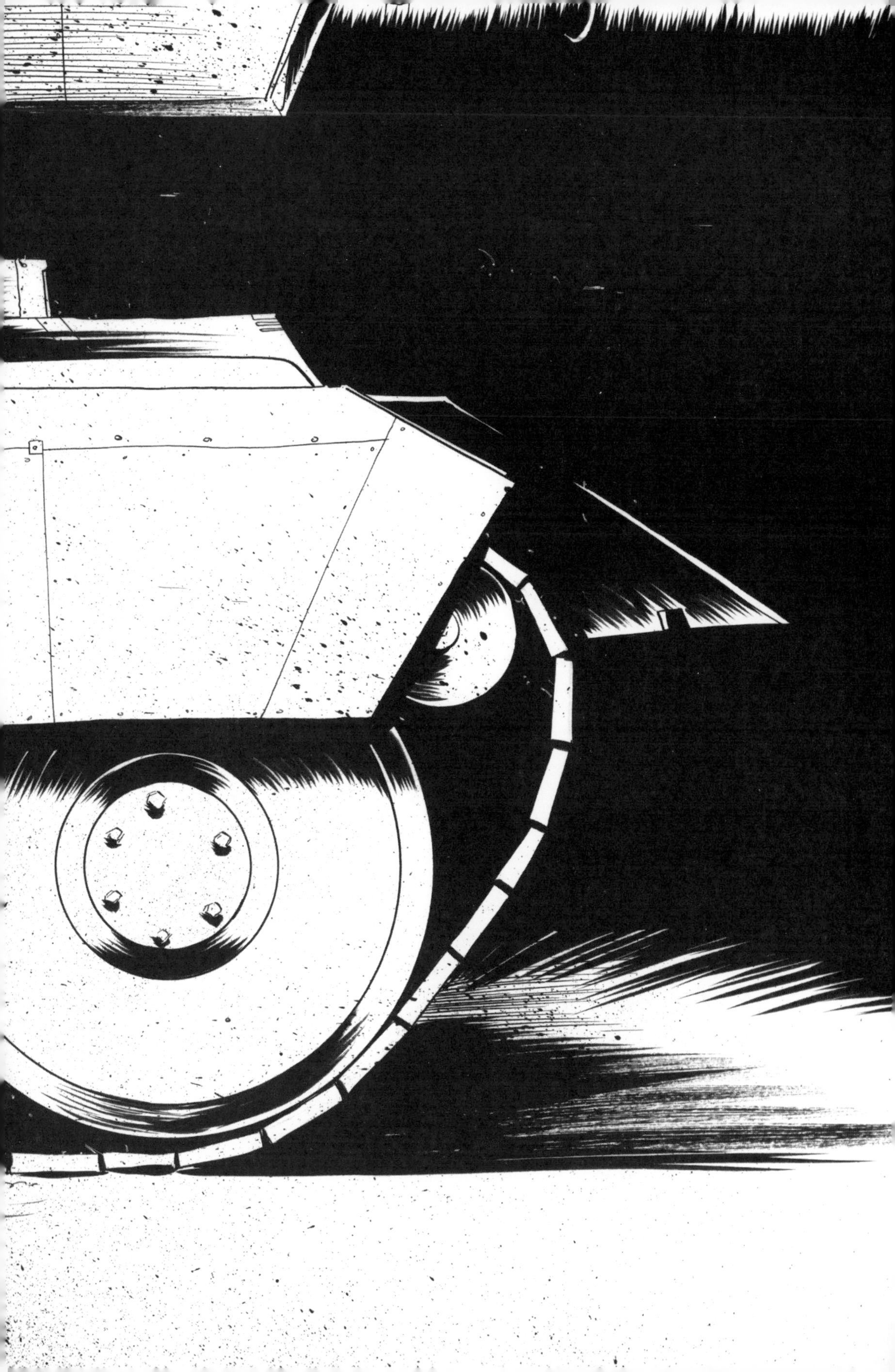

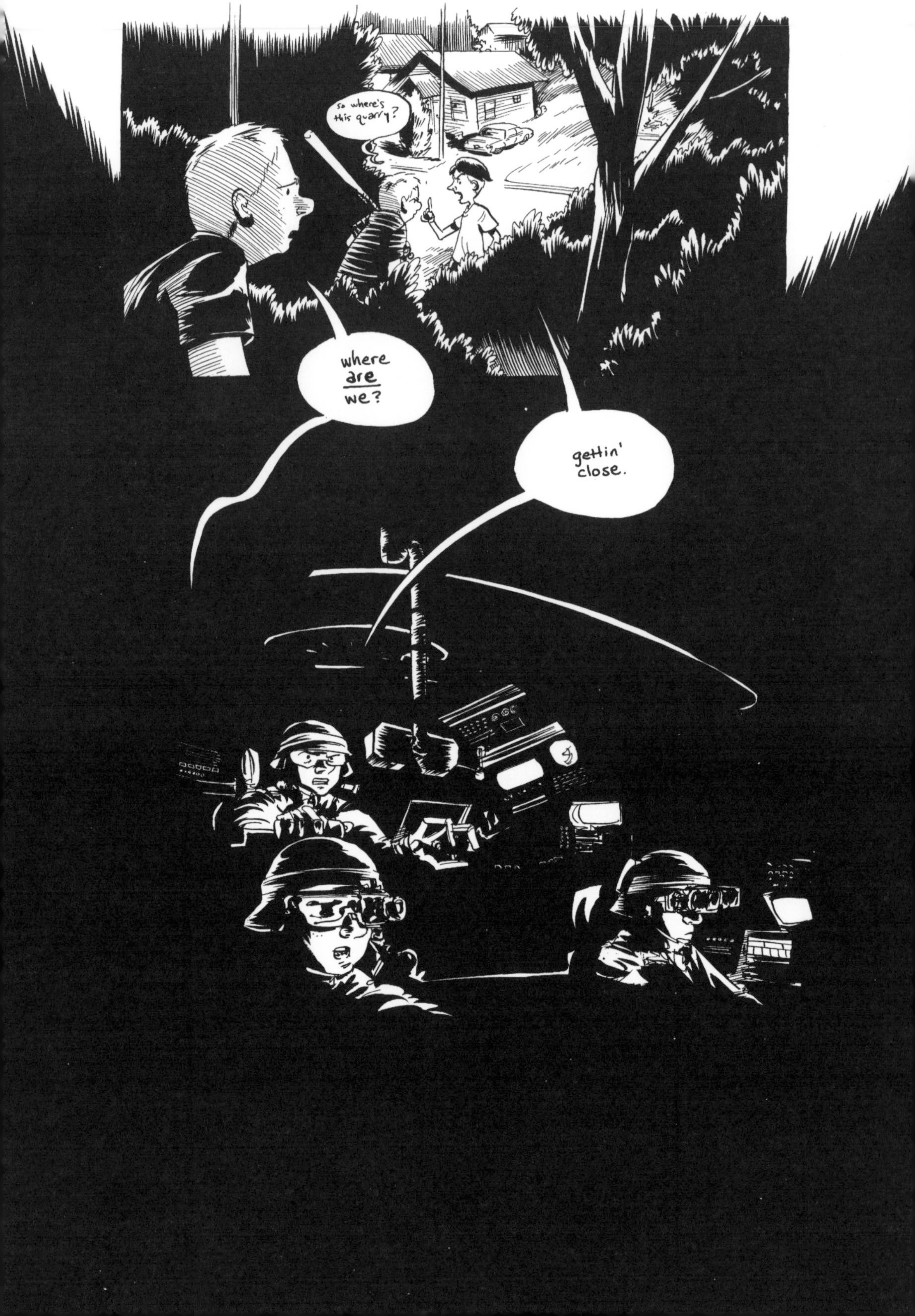
so where's this quarry?
where are we?
gettin' close.

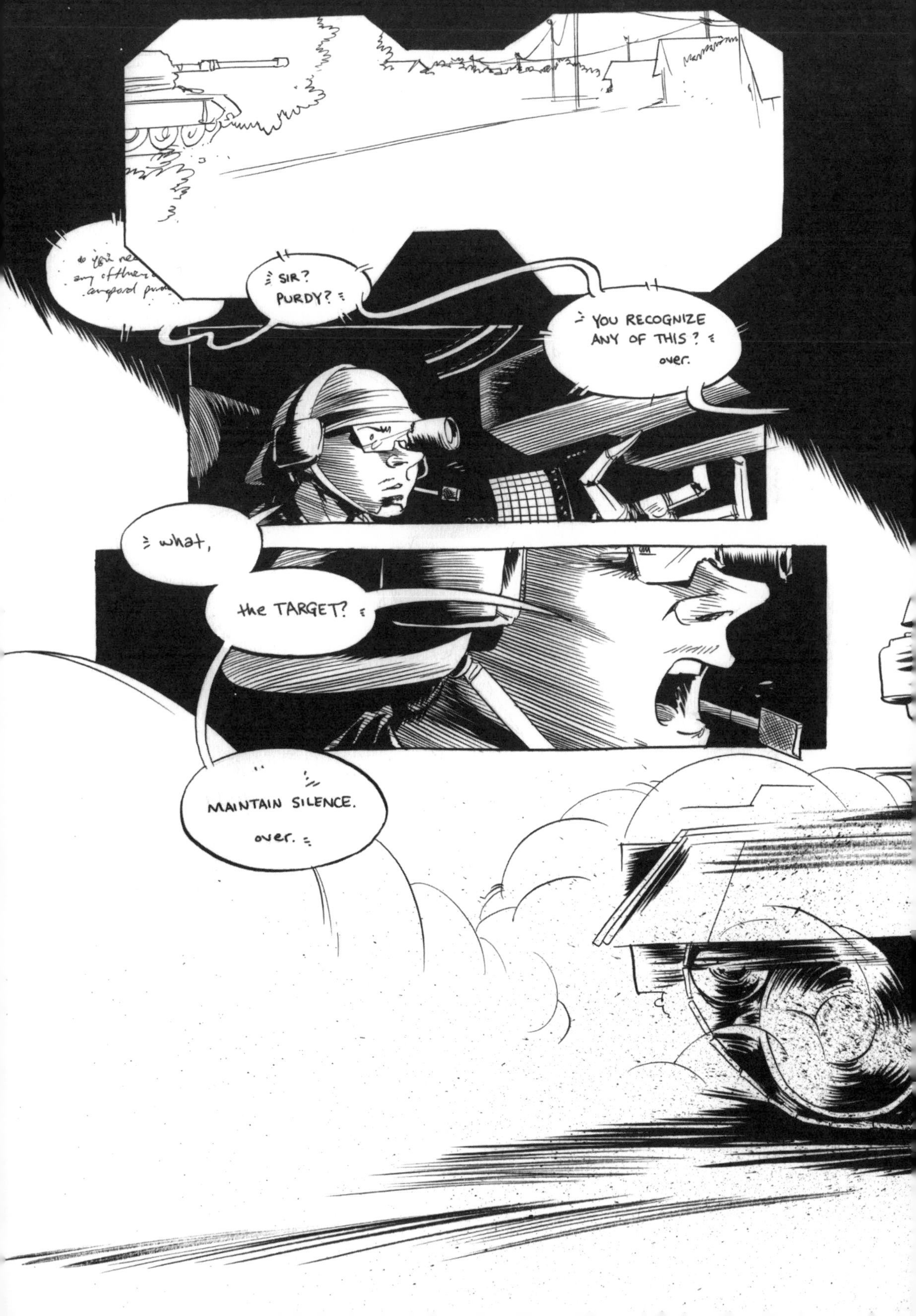
SIR? PURDY?
YOU RECOGNIZE ANY OF THIS? over.
what,
the TARGET?
MAINTAIN SILENCE. over.

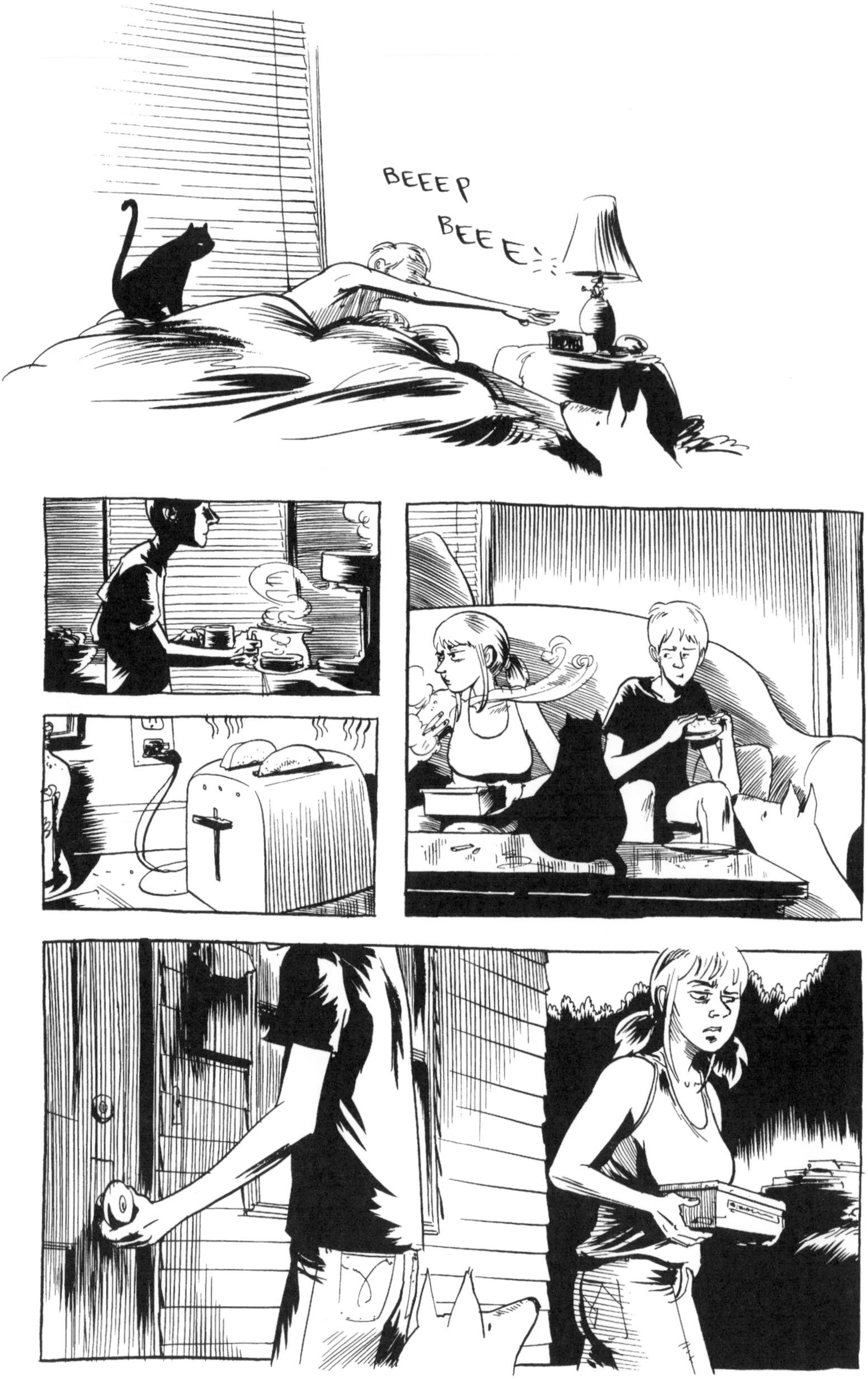
BEEEP
BEEE

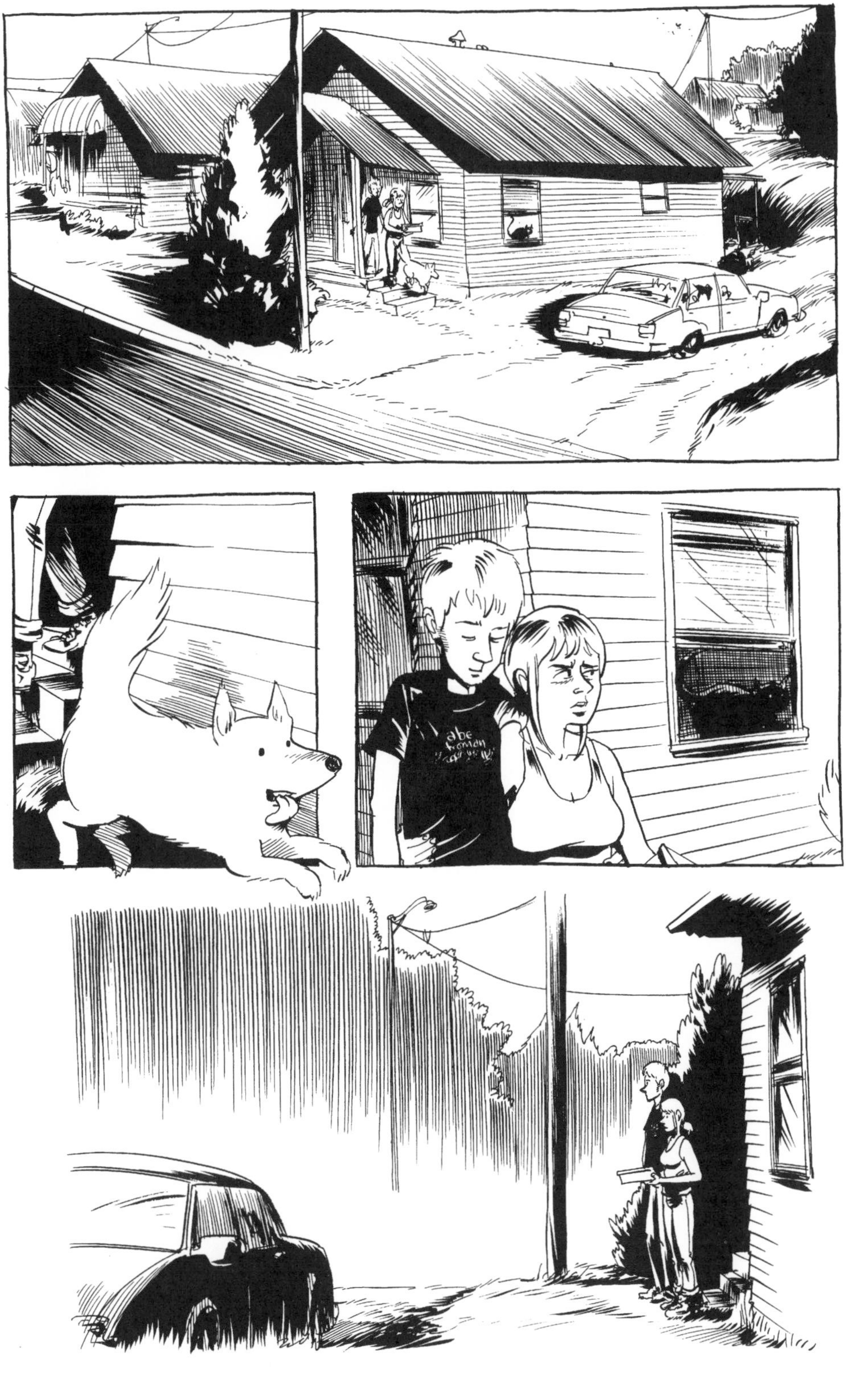
abe froman

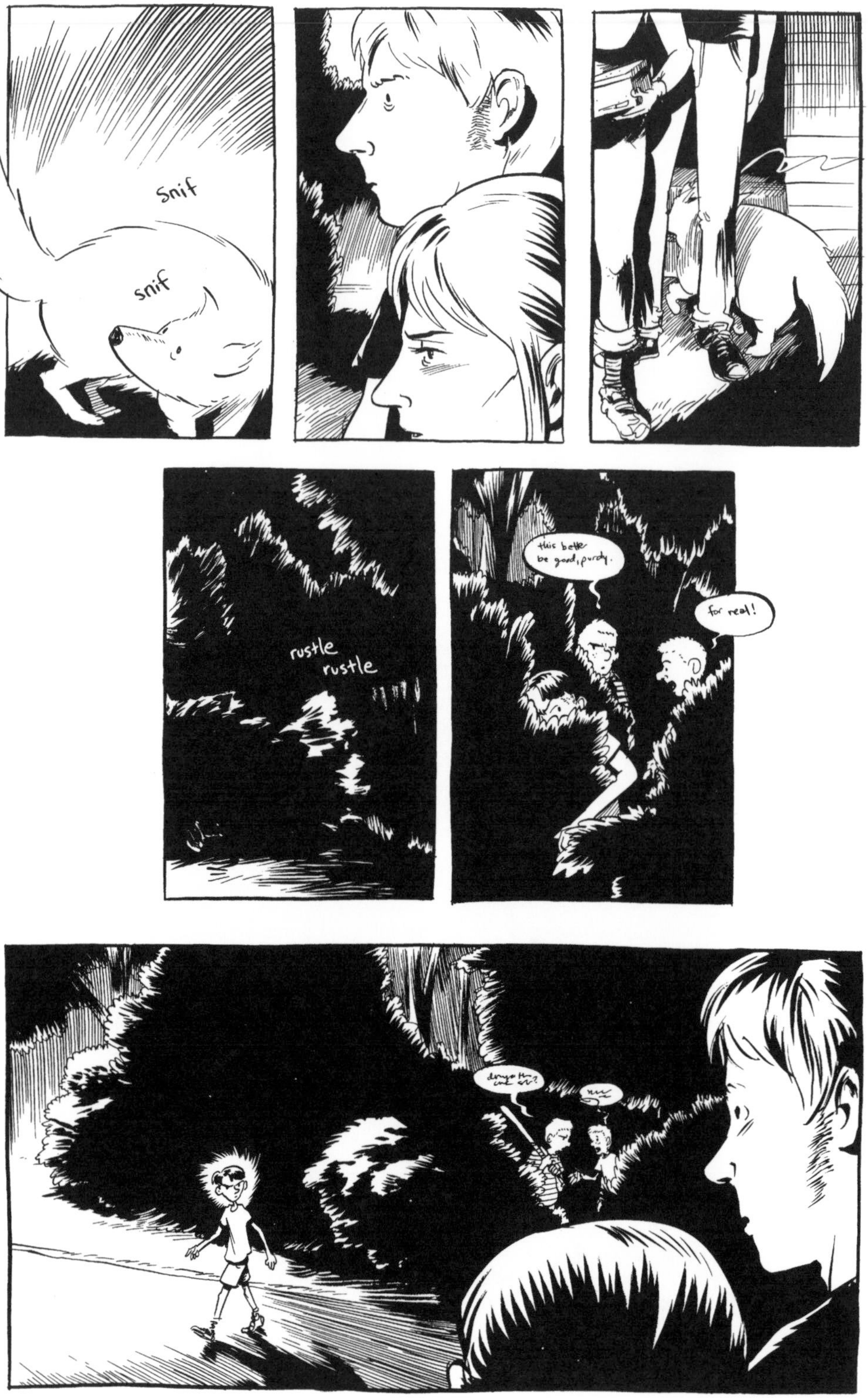
snif
snif
rustle
rustle
this better be good, purdy.
for real!

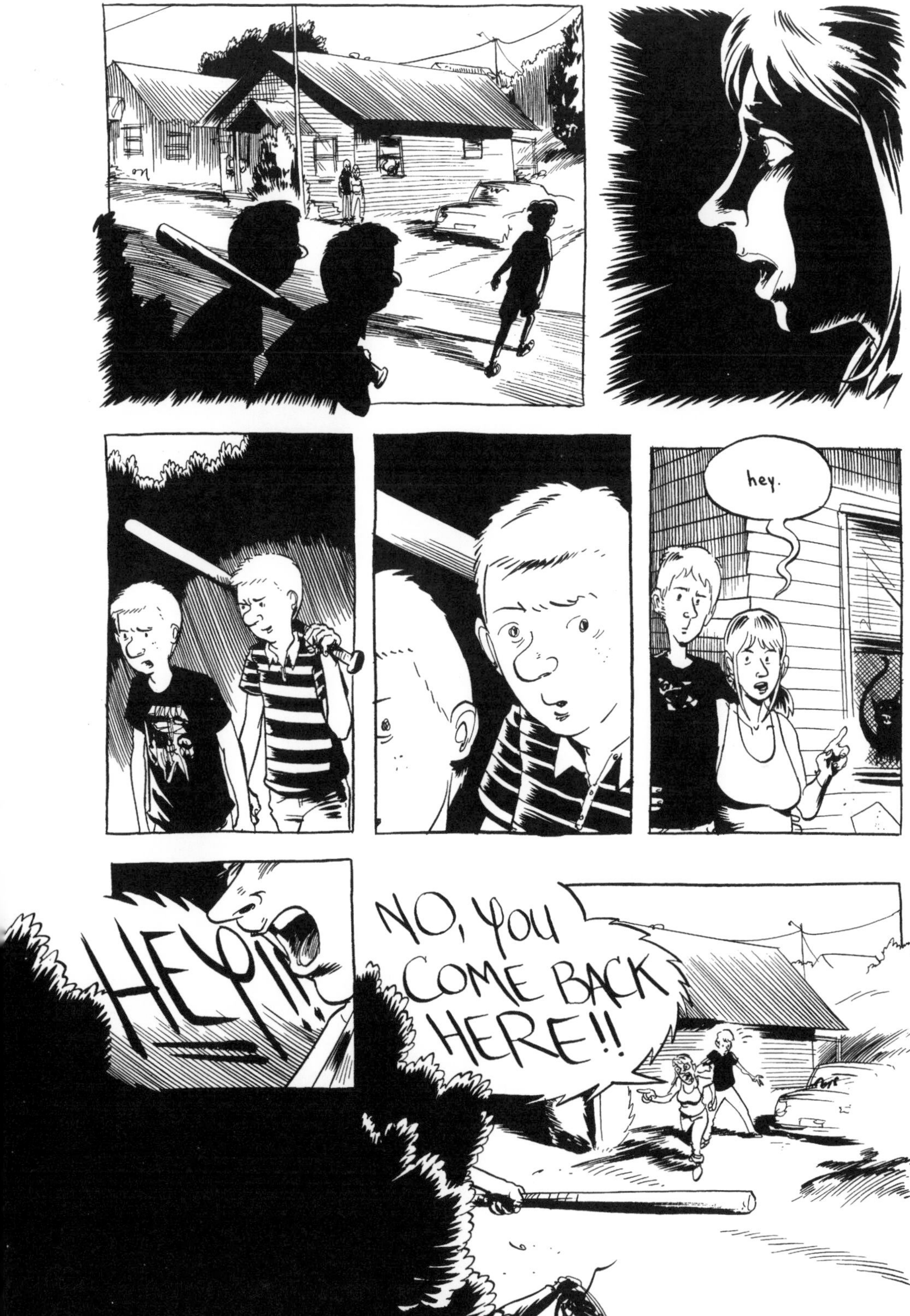
hey.
HEY!!
NO, YOU COME BACK HERE!!

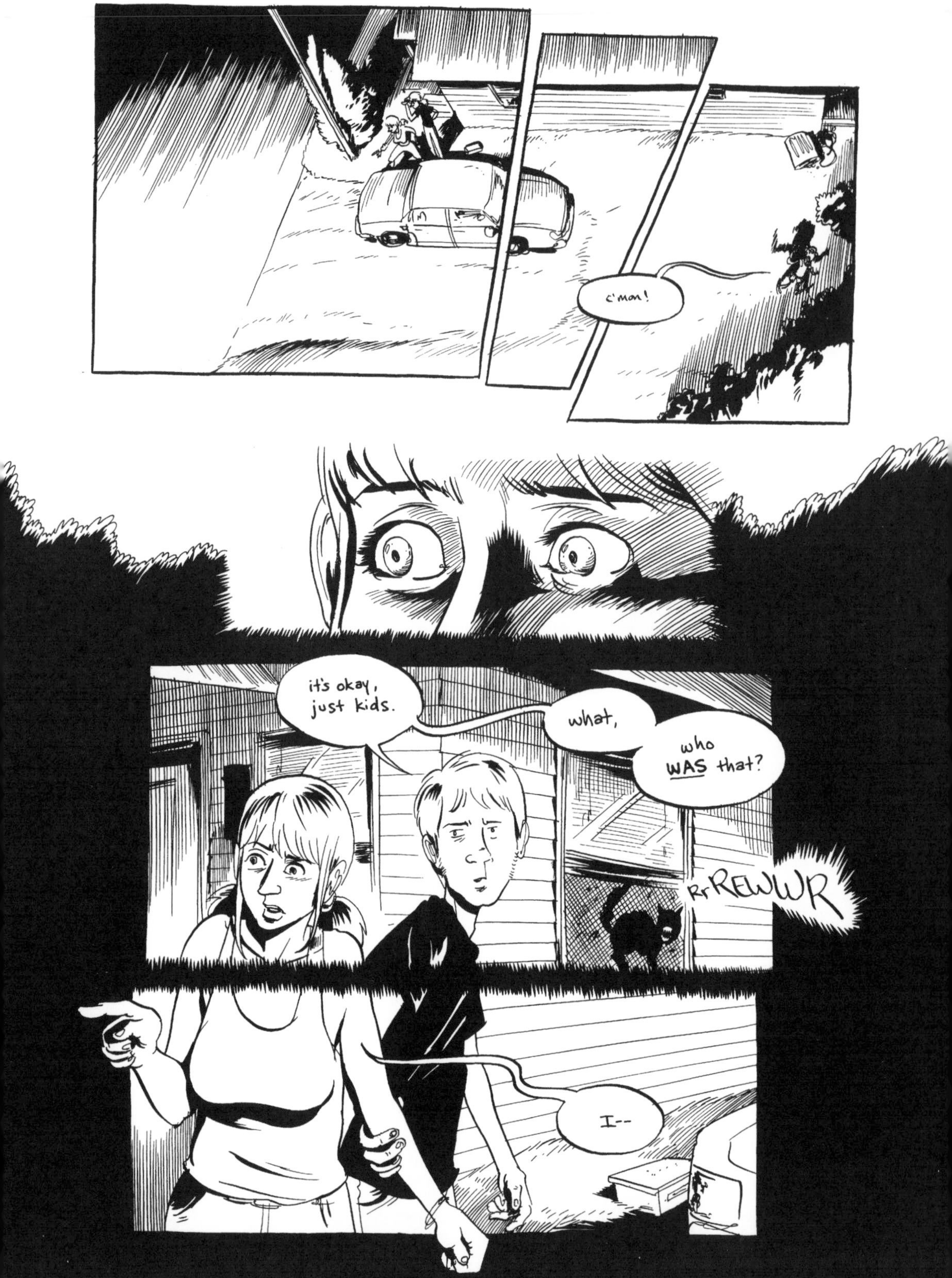
c'mon!
it's okay, just kids.
what,
who WAS that?
RrREWWR
I--

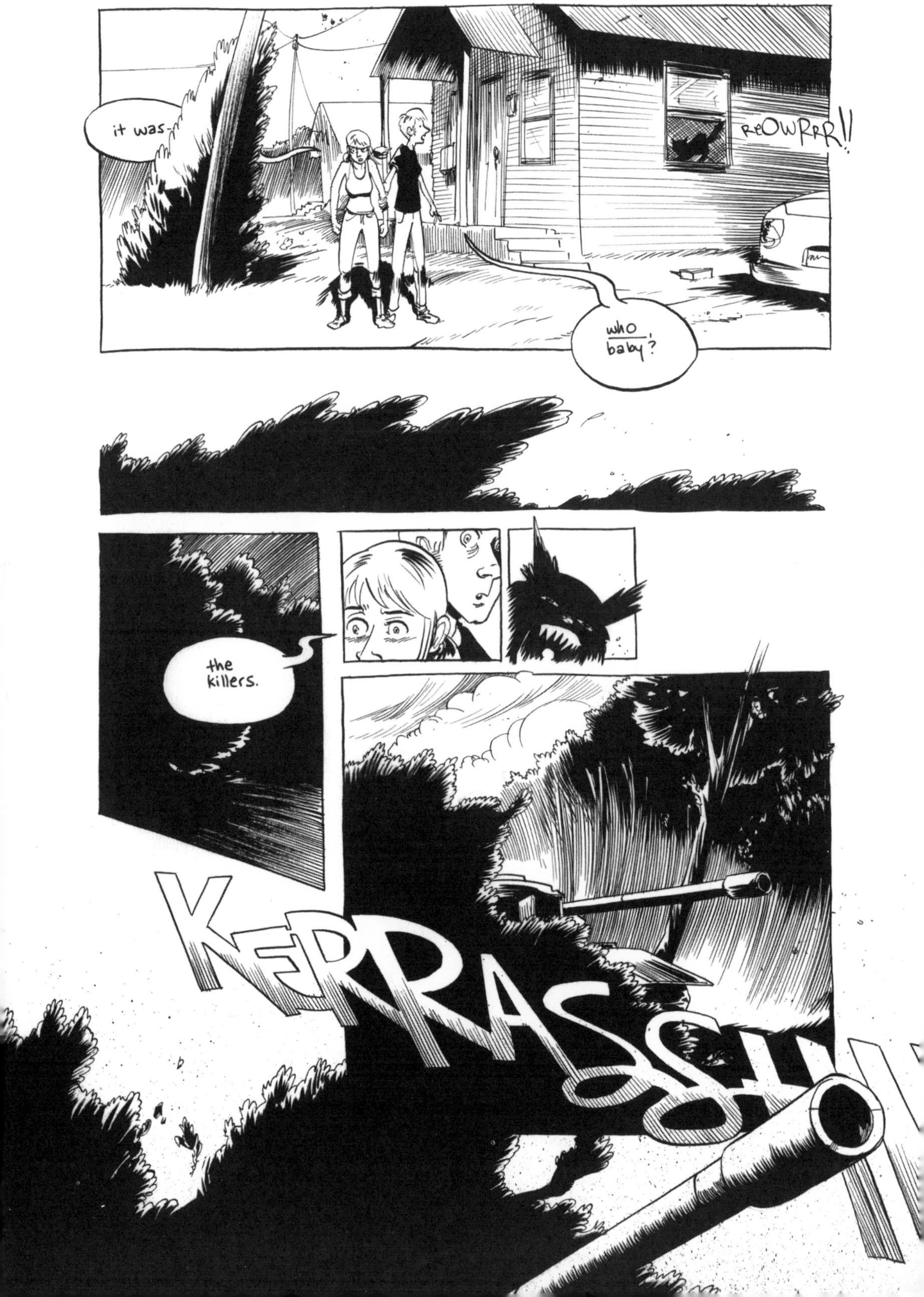

it was-
REOWRRR!!
who baby?
the killers.
KERRASSH

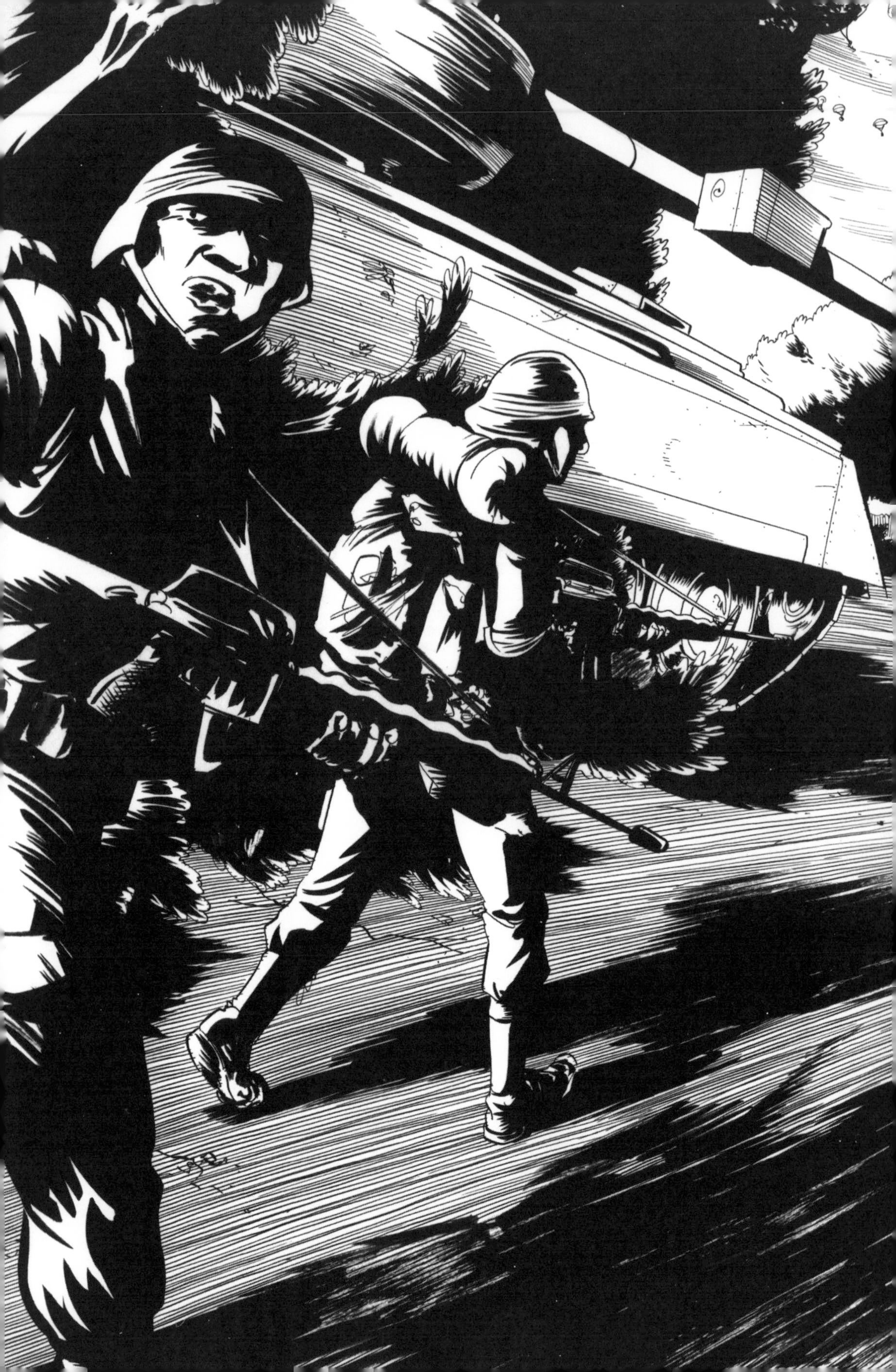

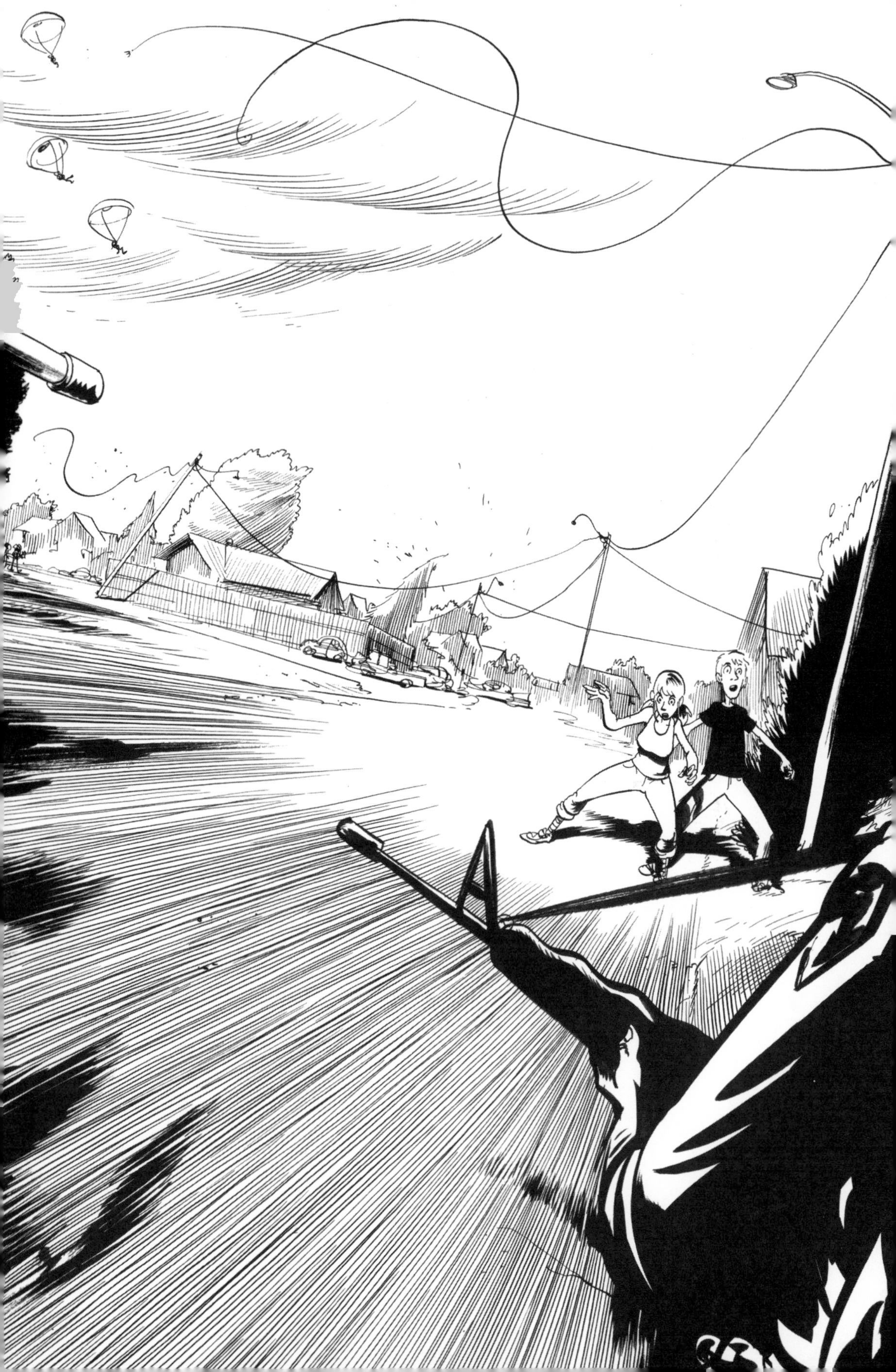

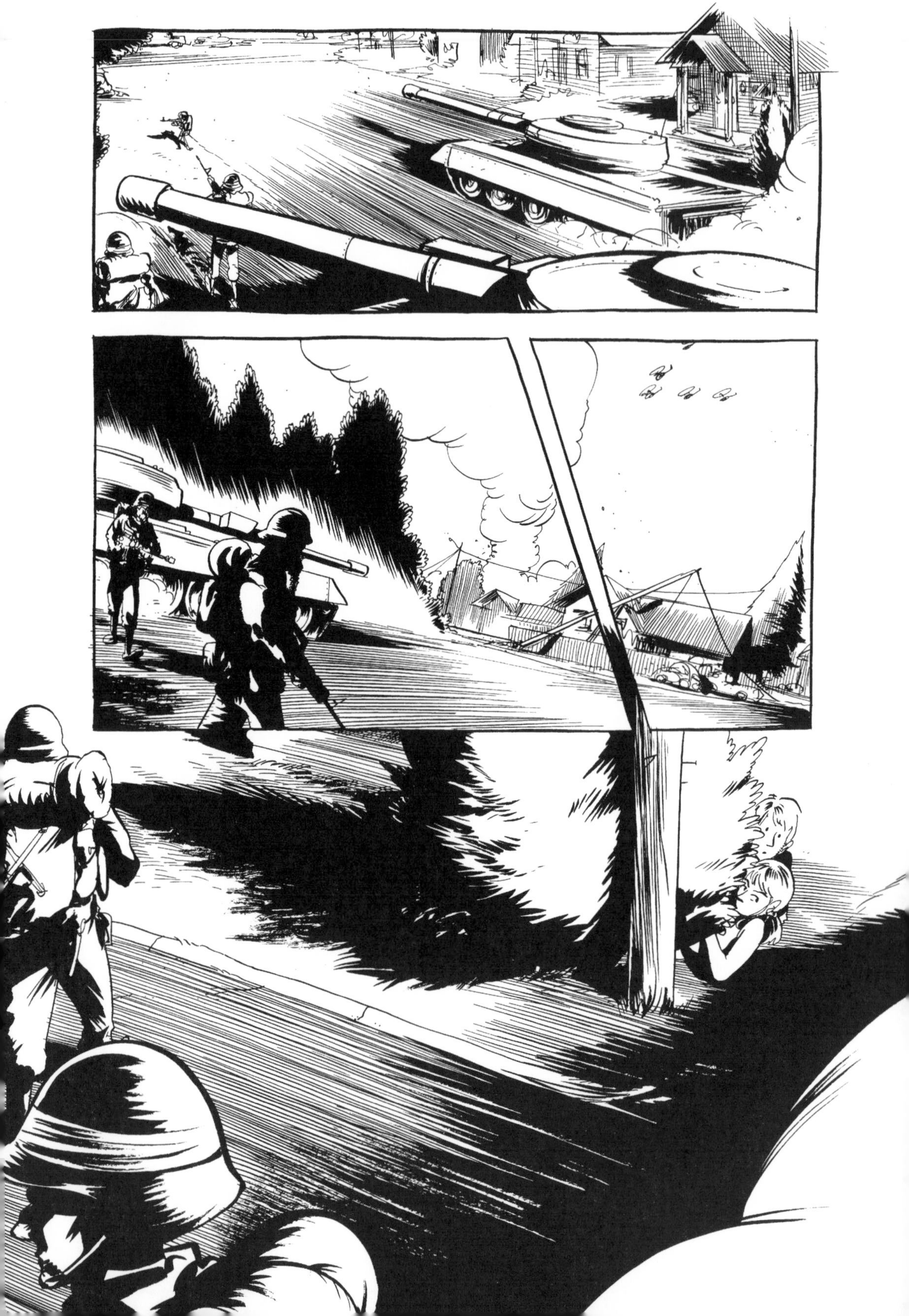

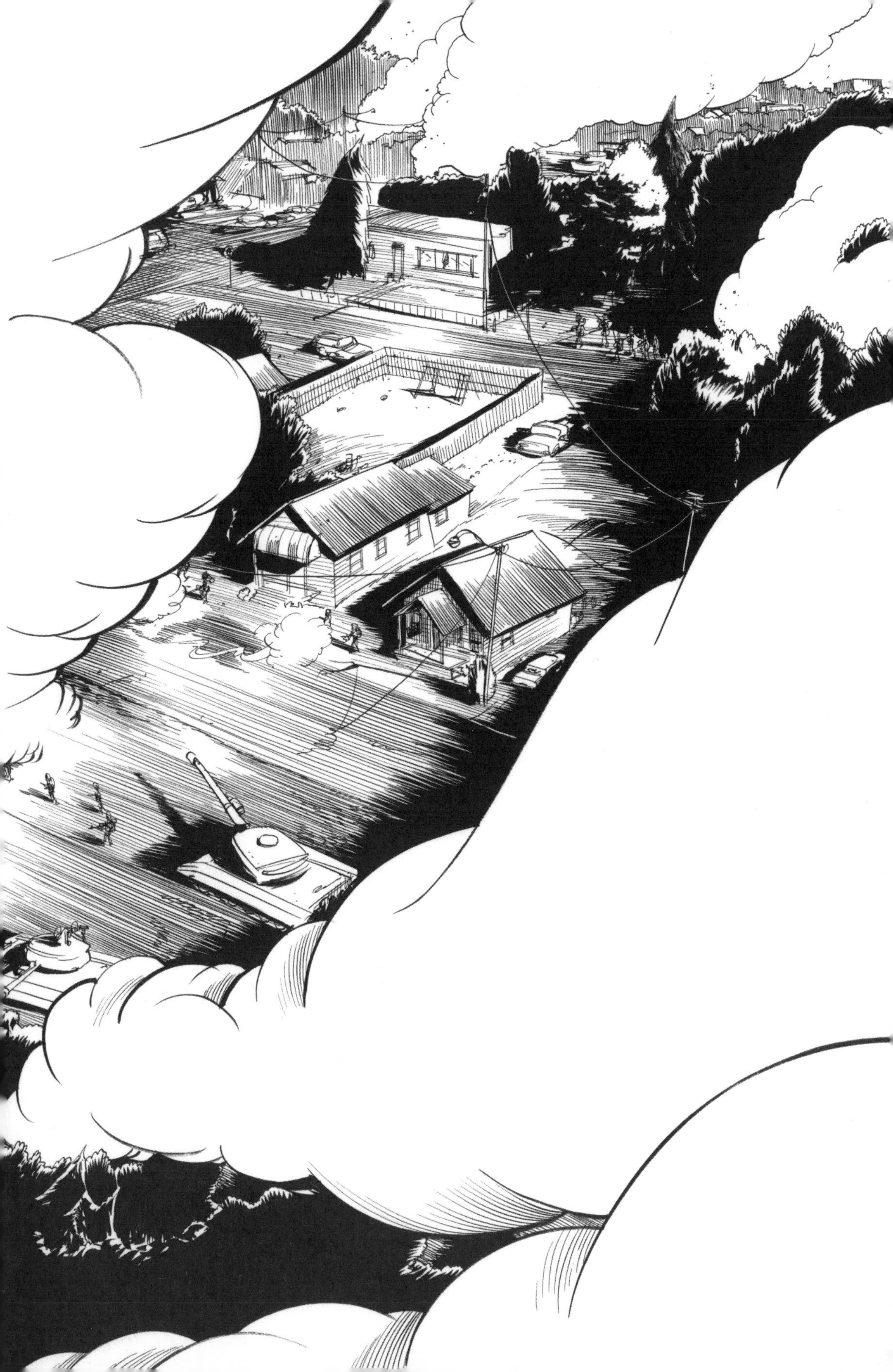

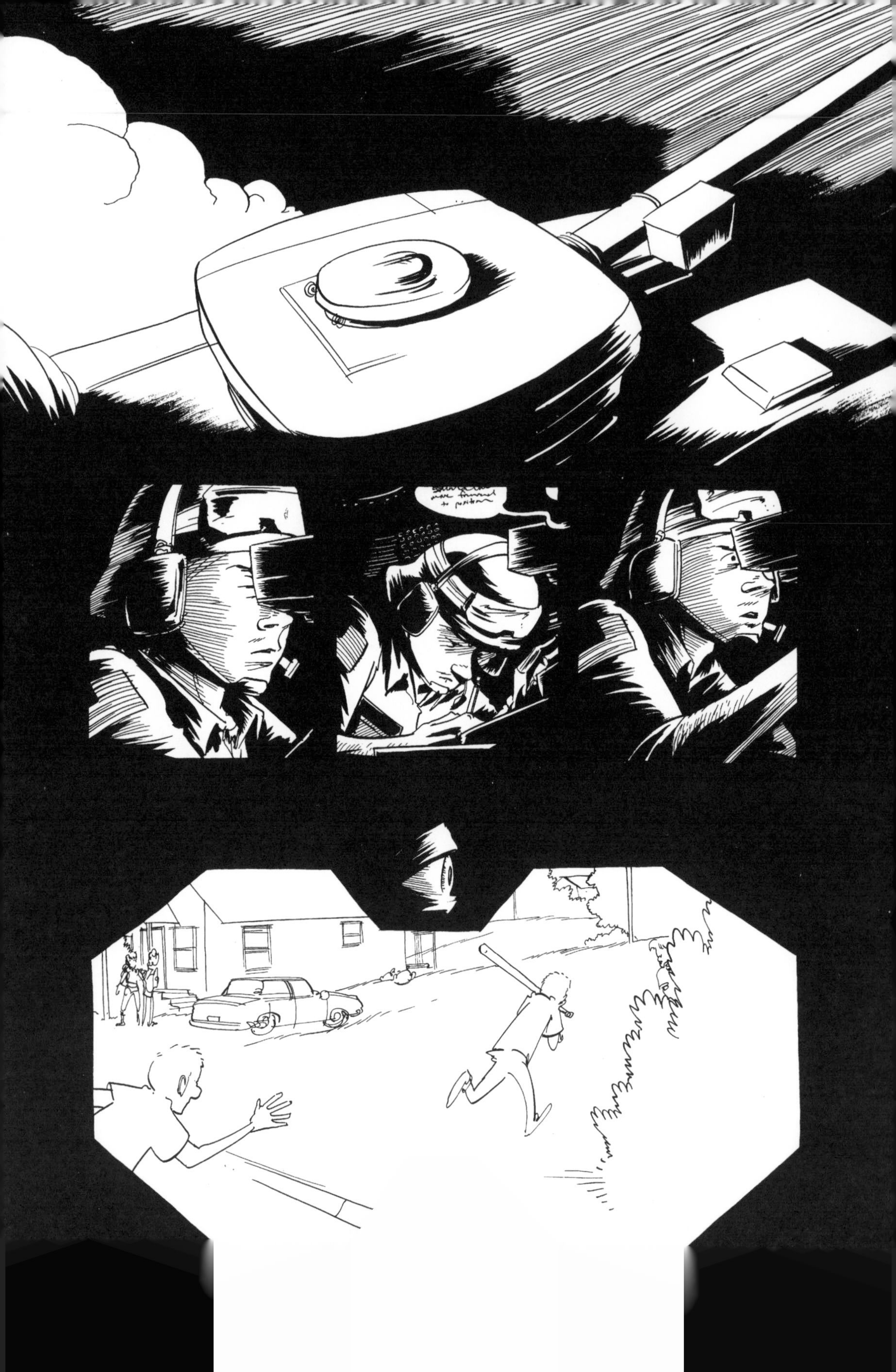
move forward to position

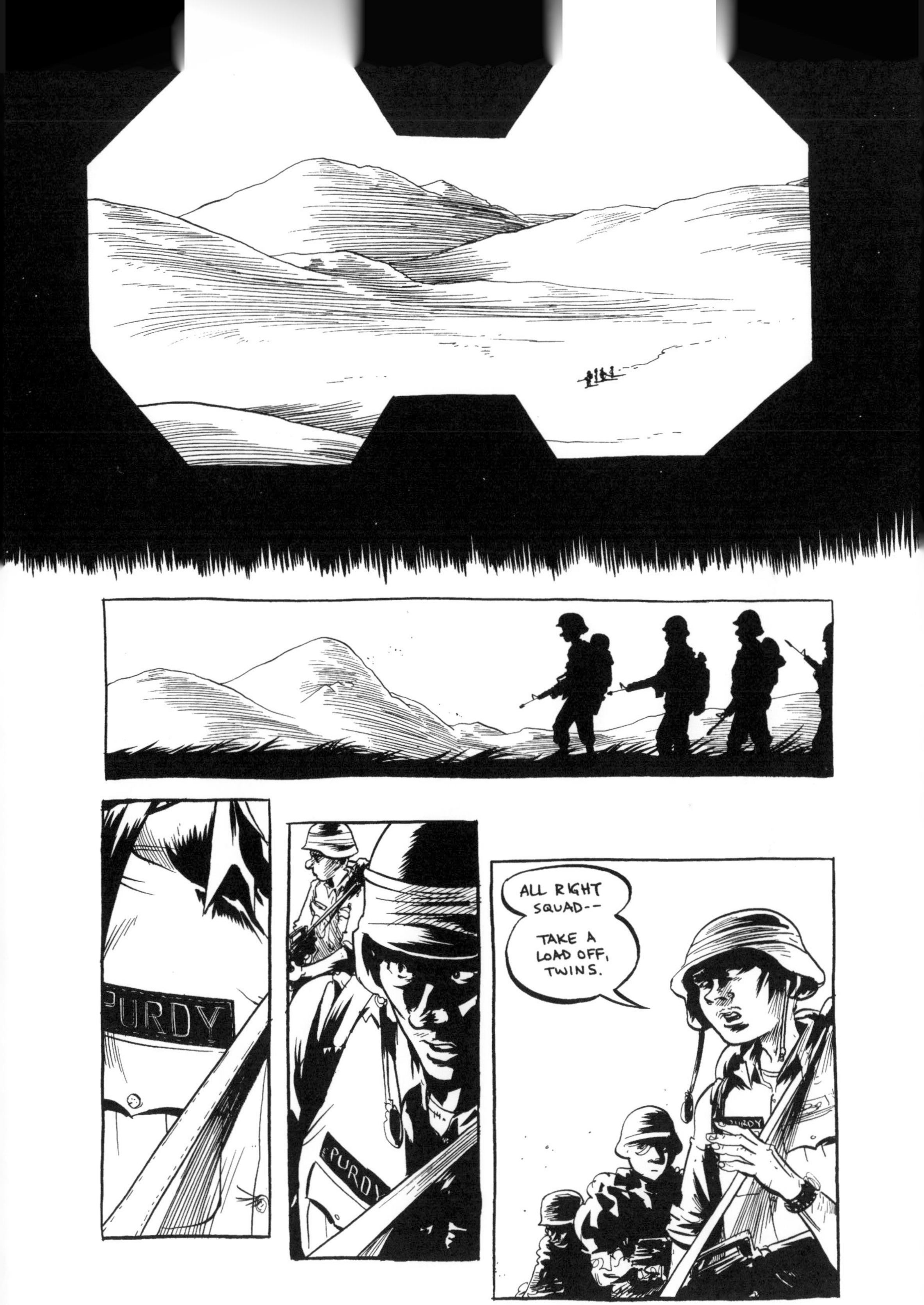
PURDY
PURDY
ALL RIGHT SQUAD--
TAKE A LOAD OFF, TWINS.
PURDY

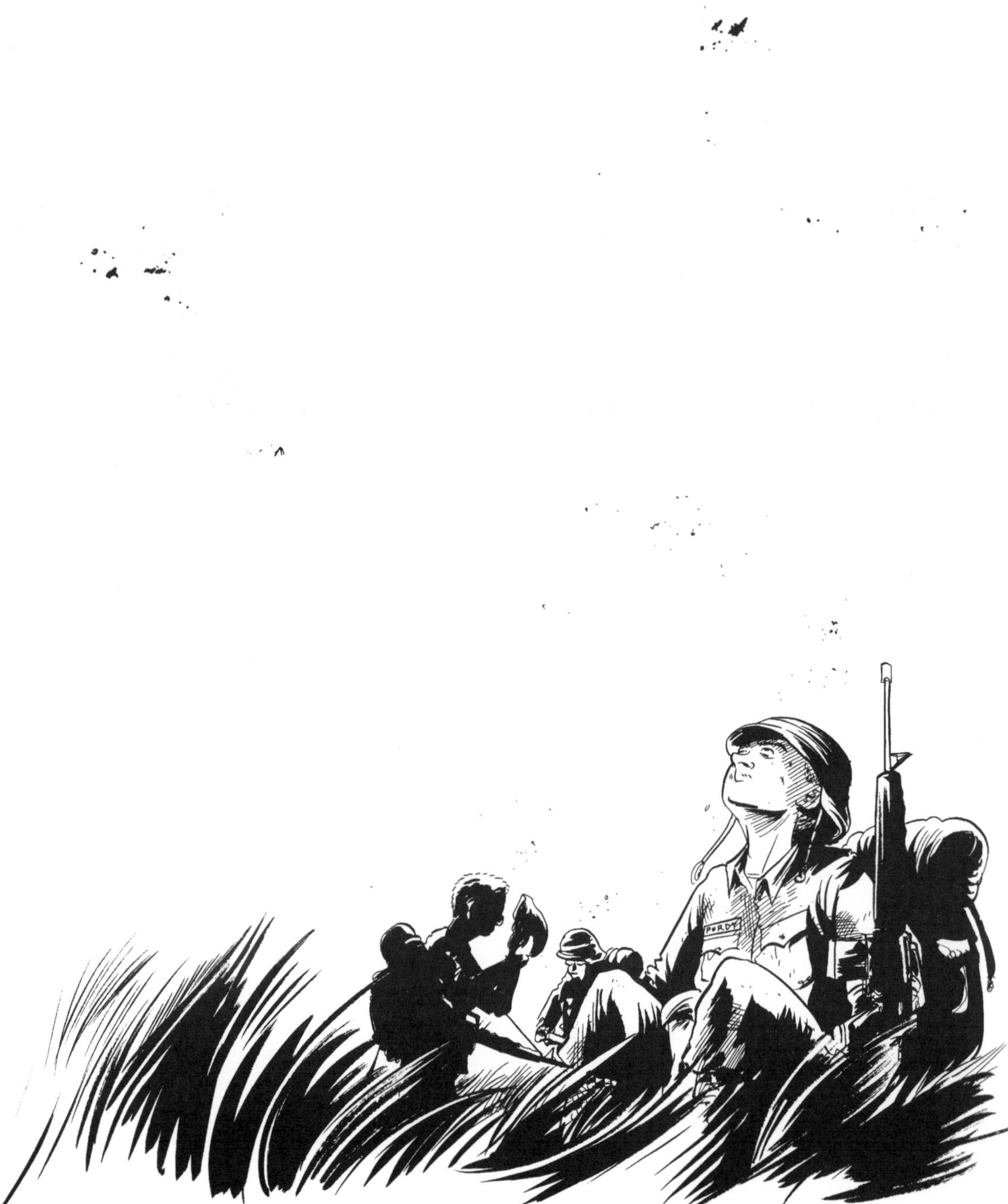
PURDY

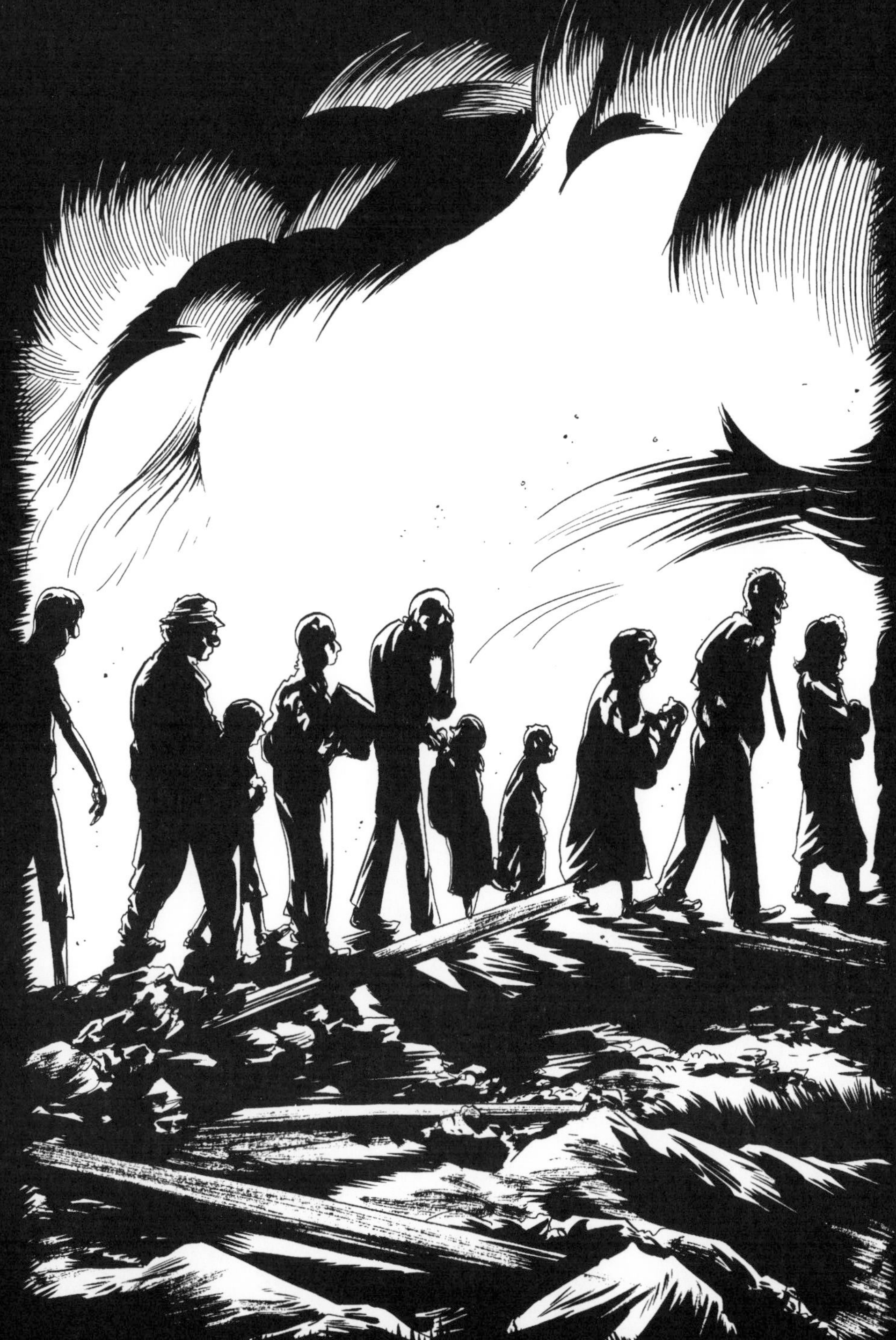

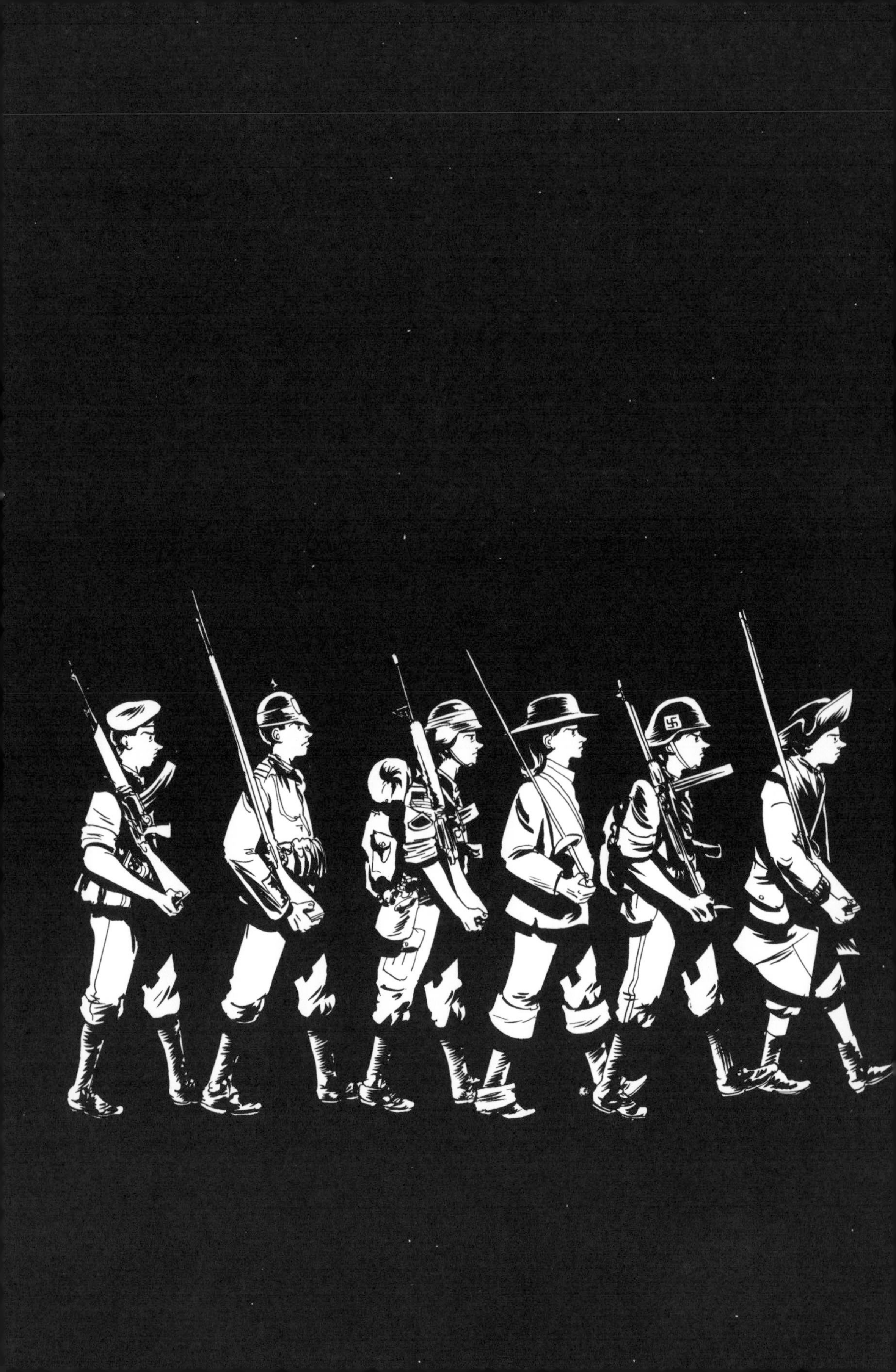

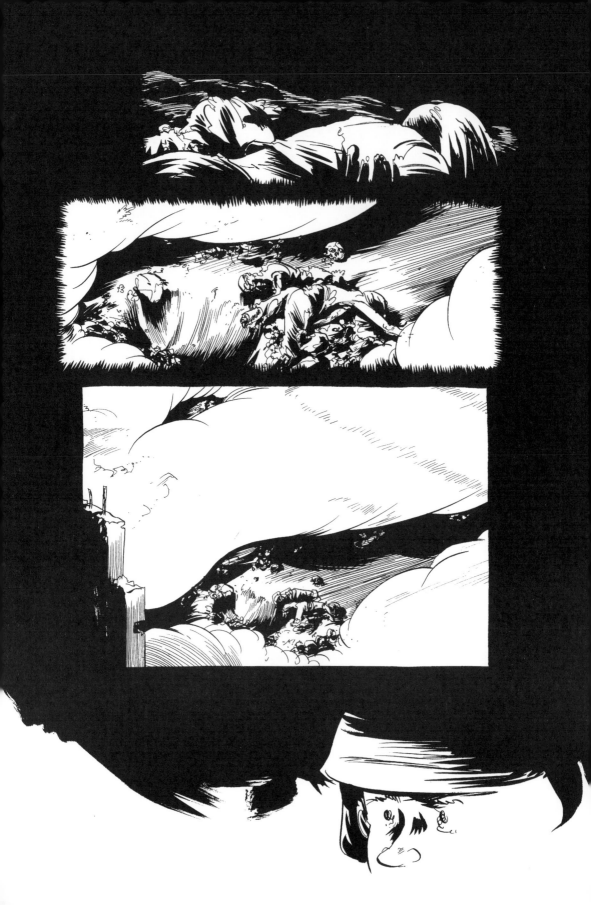

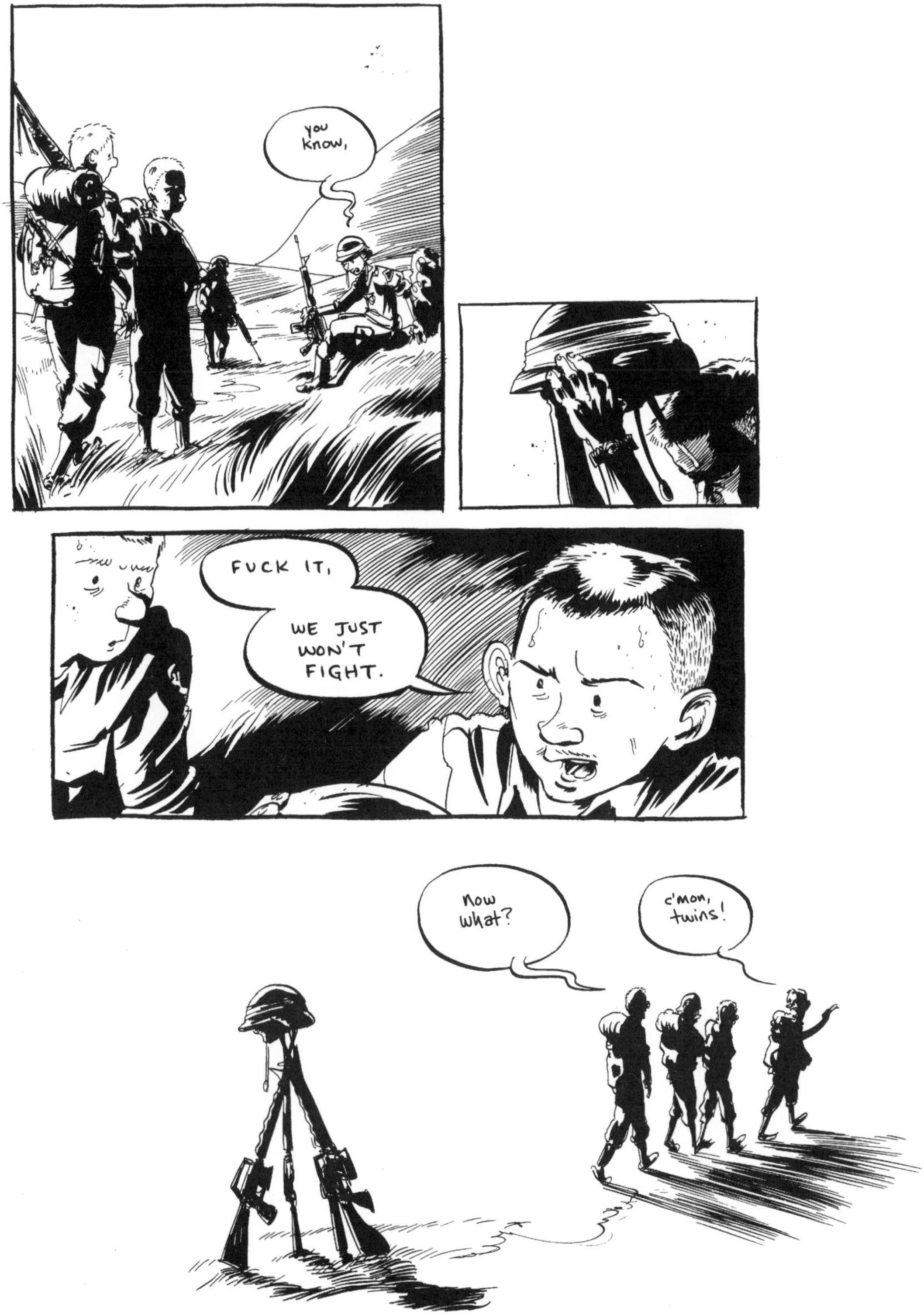
you know,
FUCK IT,
WE JUST WON'T FIGHT.
now what?
c'mon, twins!

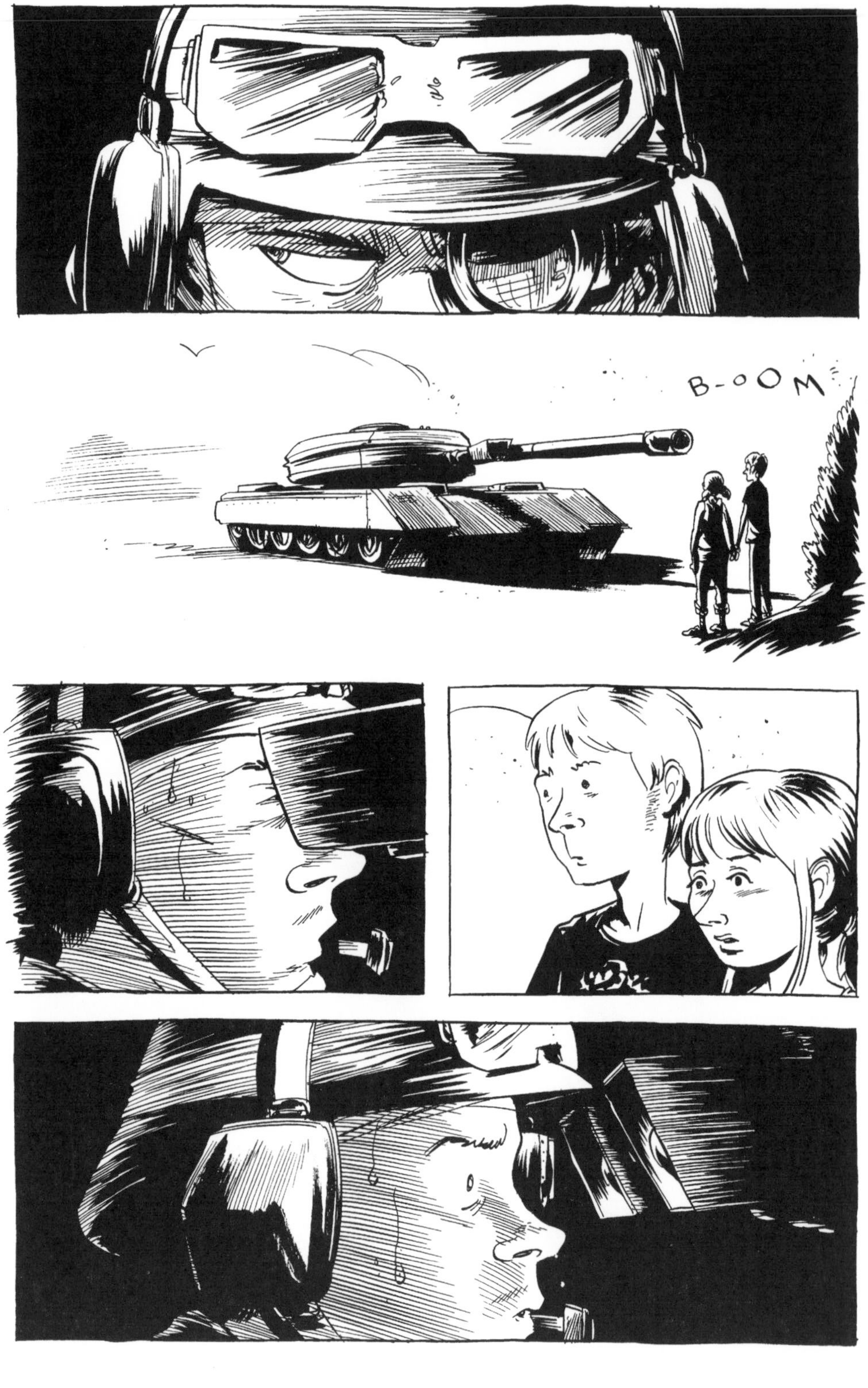
B-OOM

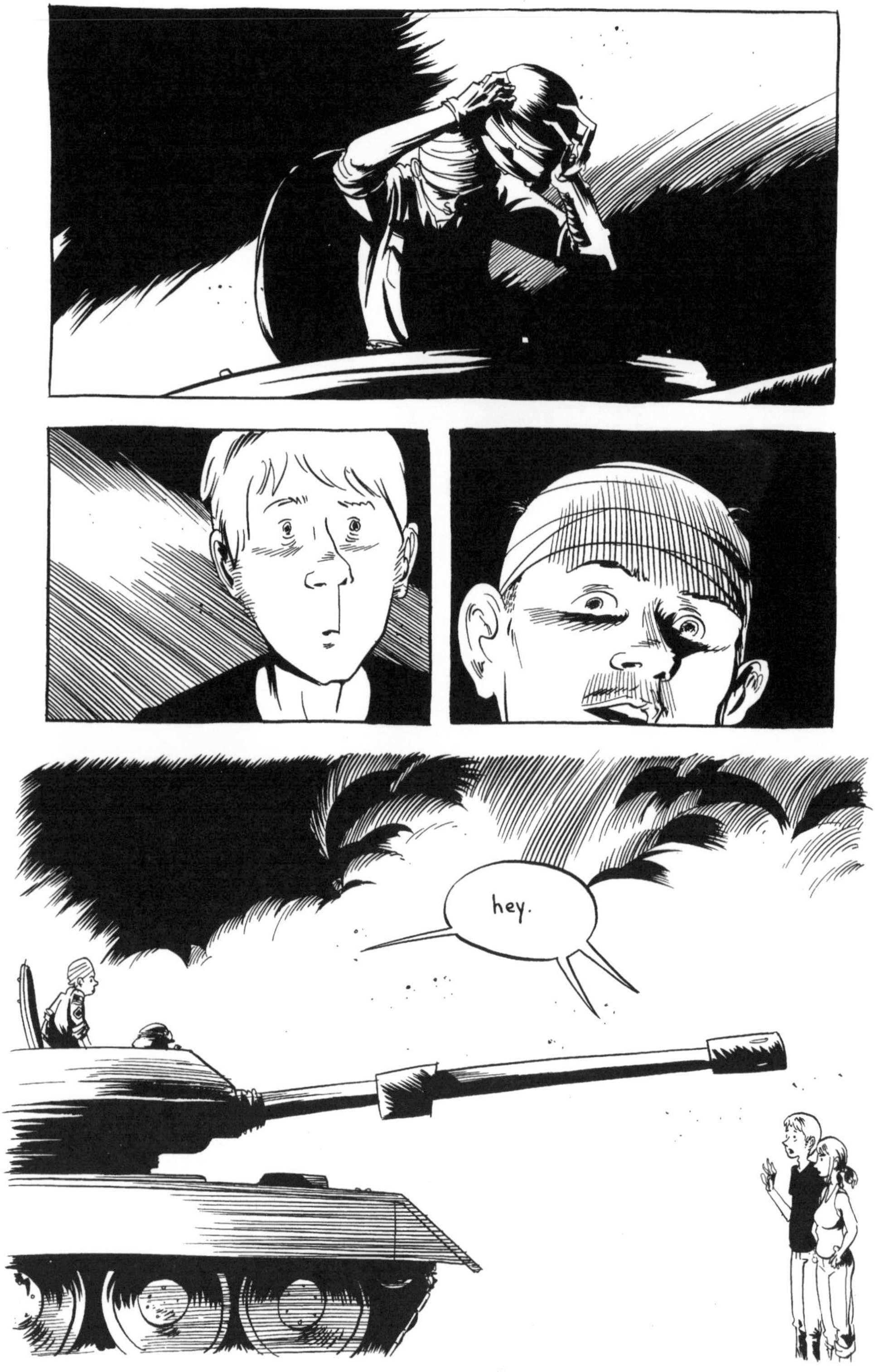
hey.

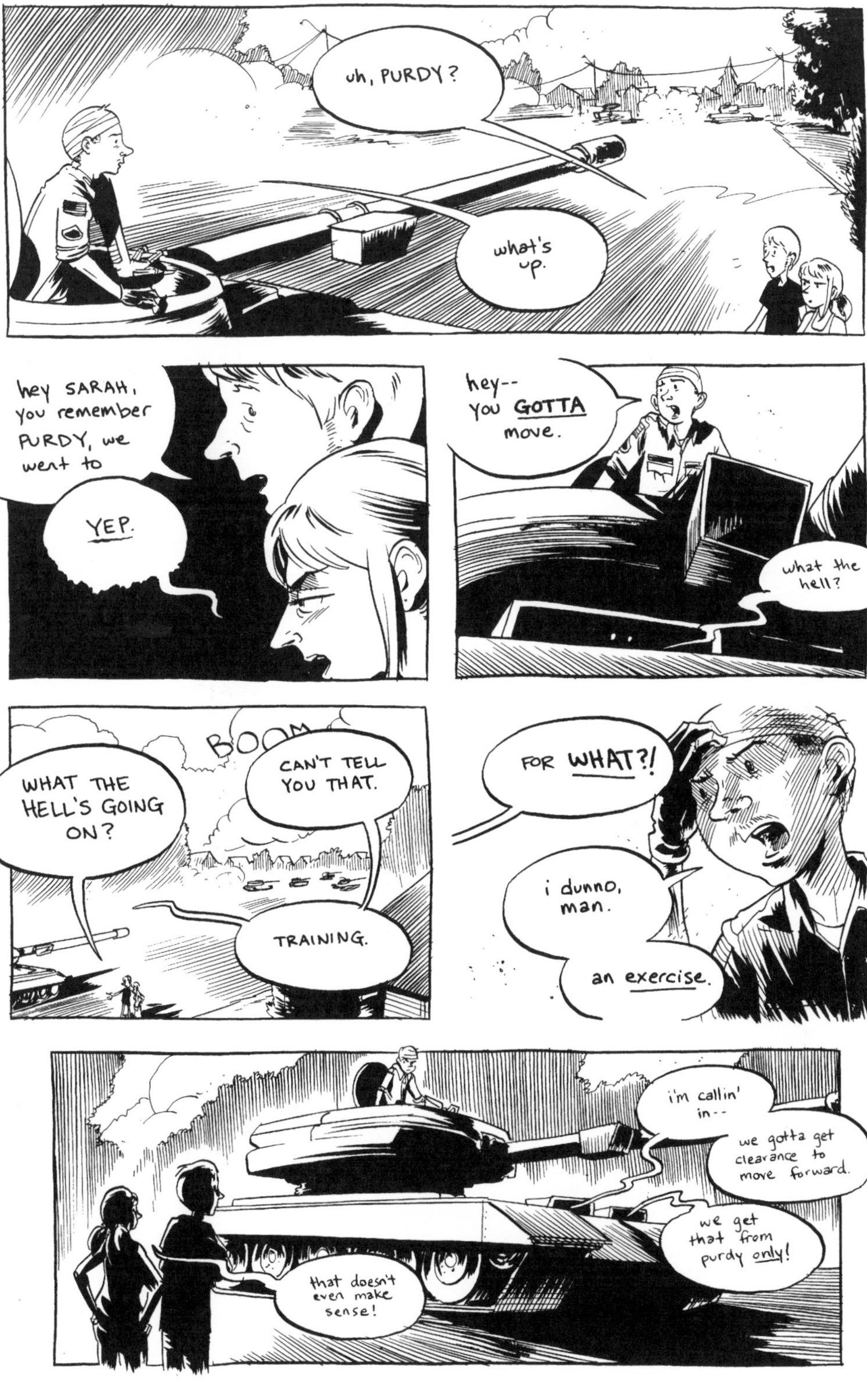
uh, PURDY?
what's up.
hey SARAH, you remember PURDY, we went to
YEP.
hey-- you GOTTA move.
what the hell?
BOOM
WHAT THE HELL'S GOING ON?
CAN'T TELL YOU THAT.
TRAINING.
FOR WHAT?!
i dunno, man.
an exercise.
i'm callin' in--
we gotta get clearance to move forward.
we get that from purdy only!
that doesn't even make sense!

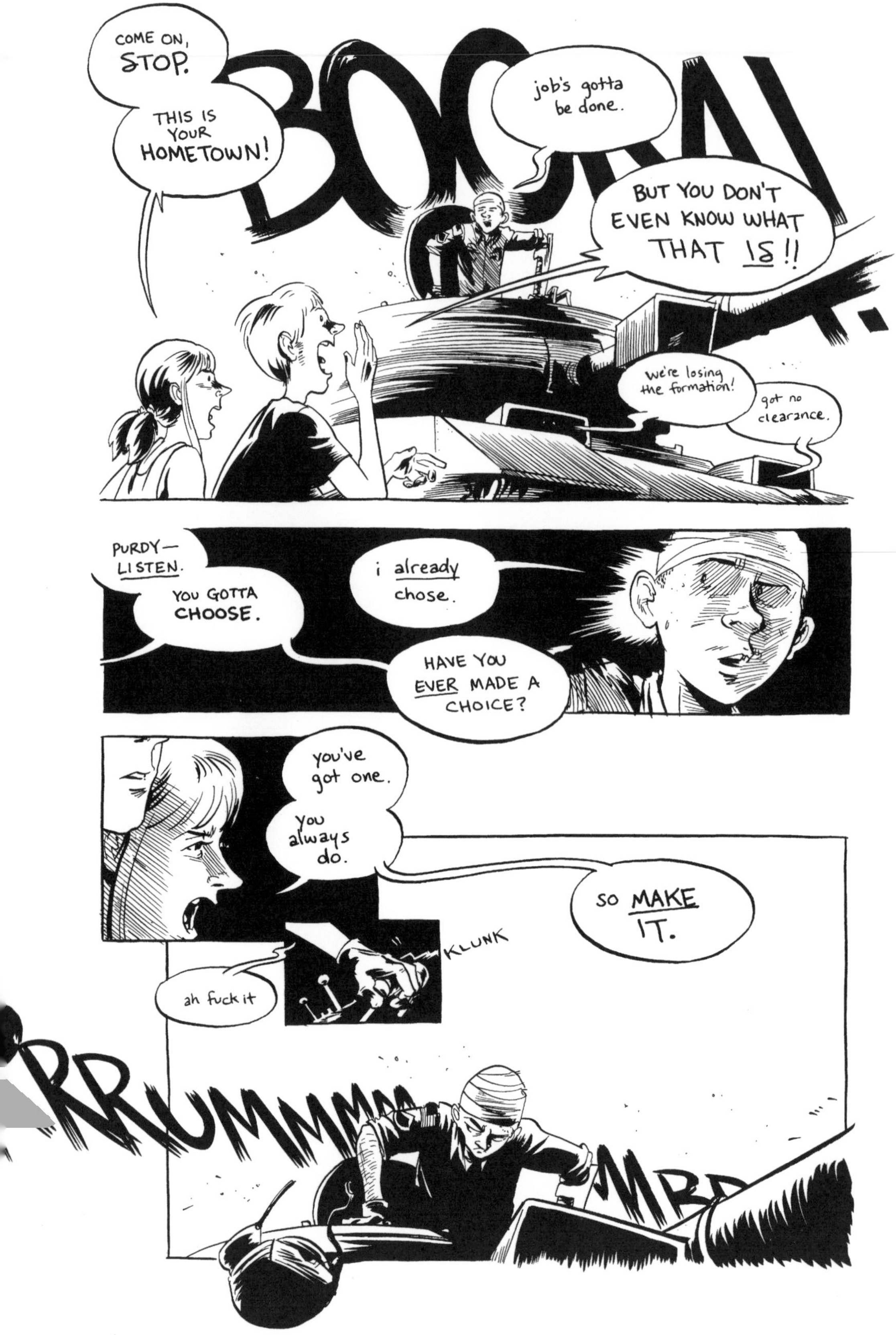
COME ON, STOP.
THIS IS YOUR HOMETOWN!
BOOM
job's gotta be done.
BUT YOU DON'T EVEN KNOW WHAT THAT IS!!
we're losing the formation!
got no clearance.
PURDY— LISTEN.
YOU GOTTA CHOOSE.
i already chose.
HAVE YOU EVER MADE A CHOICE?
you've got one.
you always do.
SO MAKE IT.
KLUNK
ah fuck it
RRUMMMM

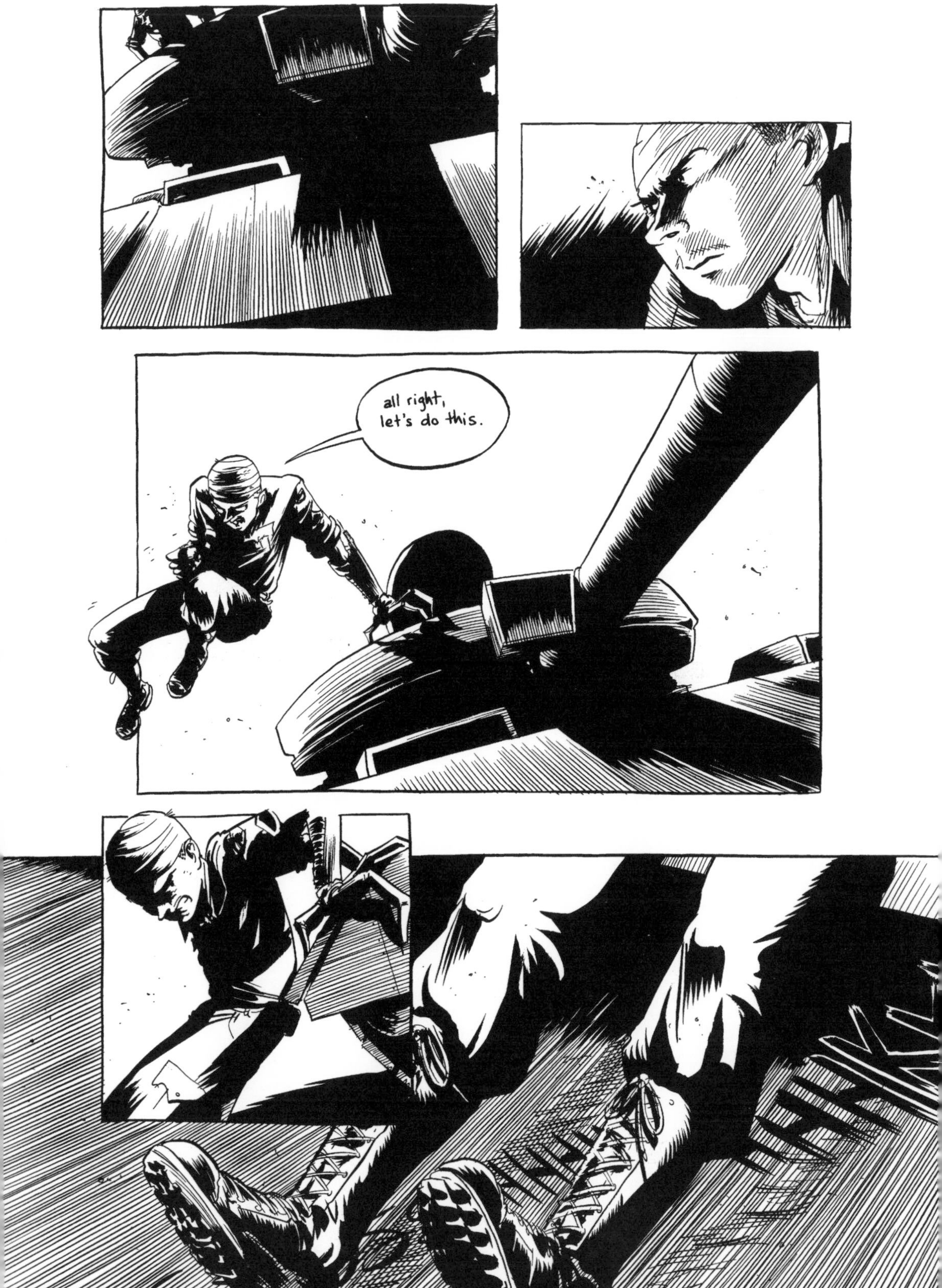
all right,
let's do this.

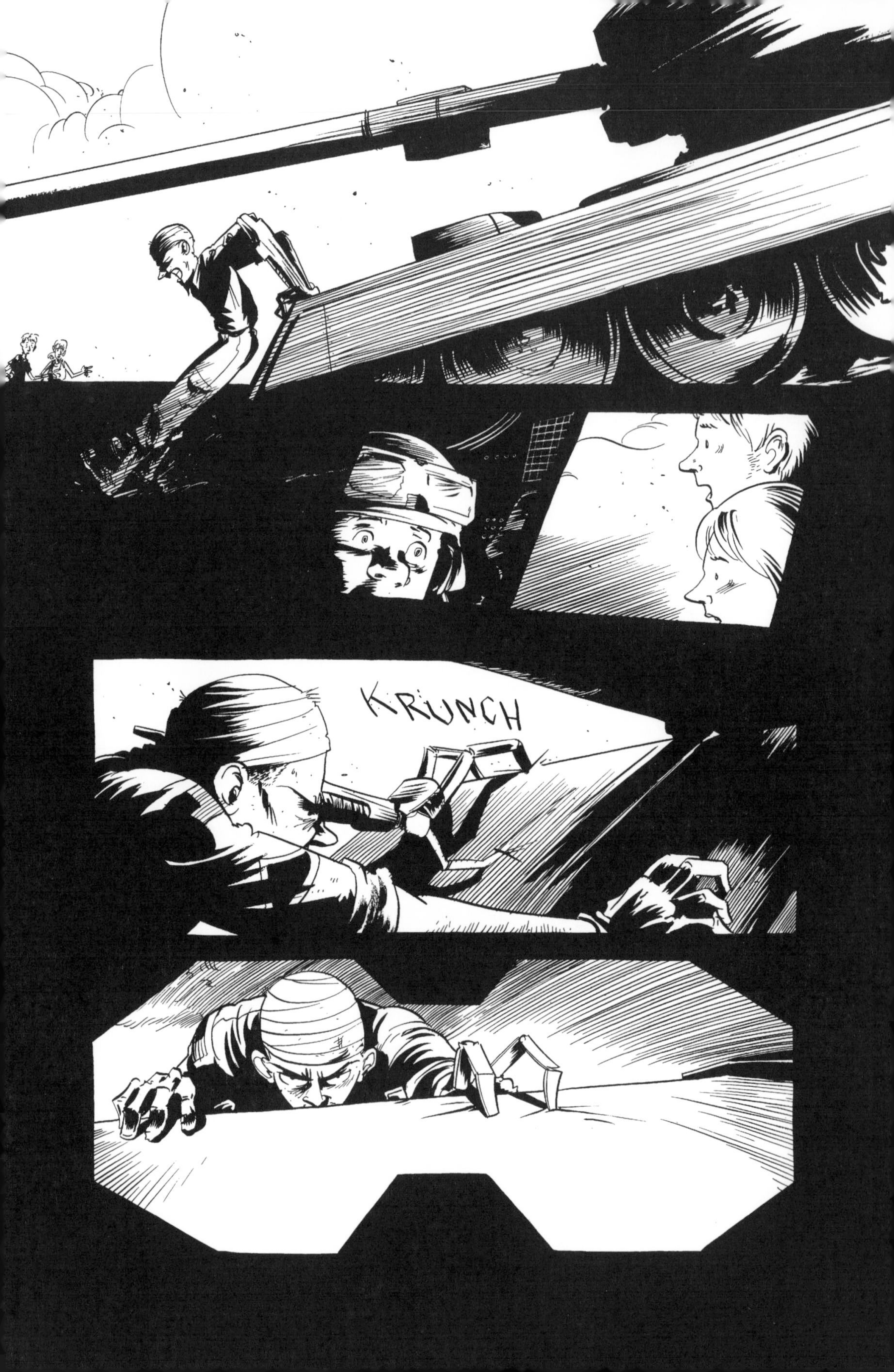
KRUNCH

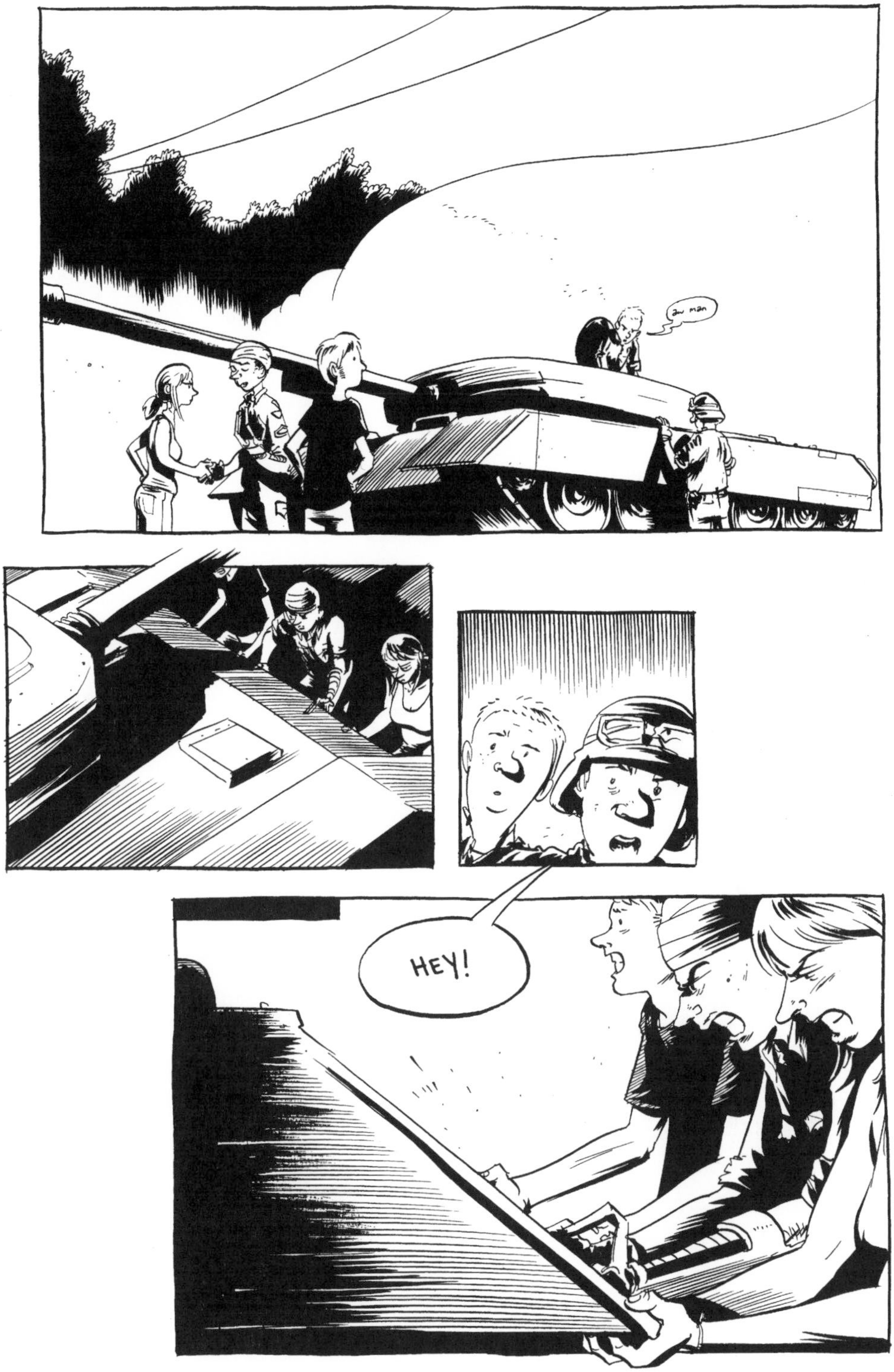
aw man
HEY!

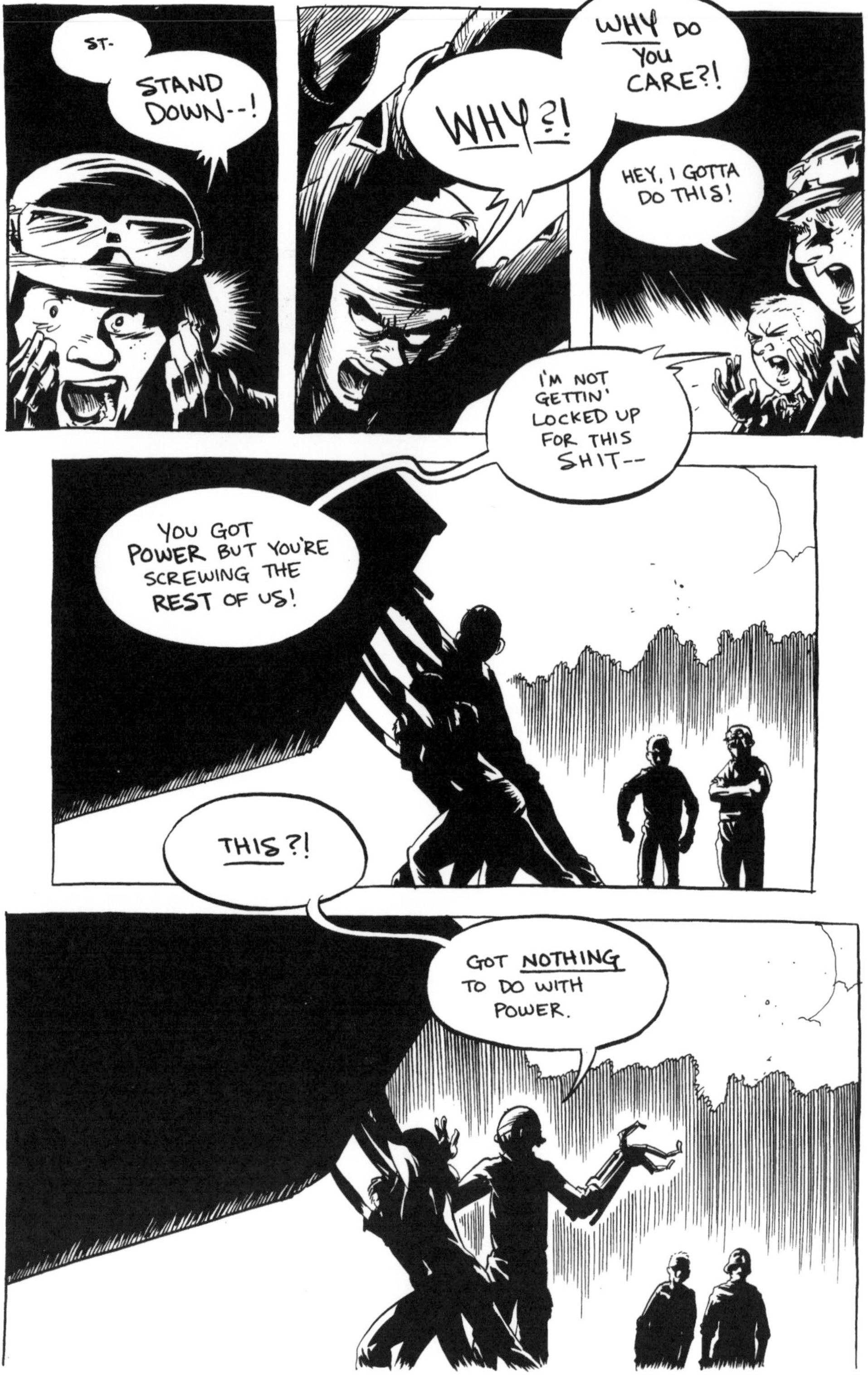
ST-
STAND DOWN--!
WHY?!
WHY DO YOU CARE?!
HEY, I GOTTA DO THIS!
I'M NOT GETTIN' LOCKED UP FOR THIS SHIT--
YOU GOT POWER BUT YOU'RE SCREWING THE REST OF US!
THIS?!
GOT NOTHING TO DO WITH POWER.

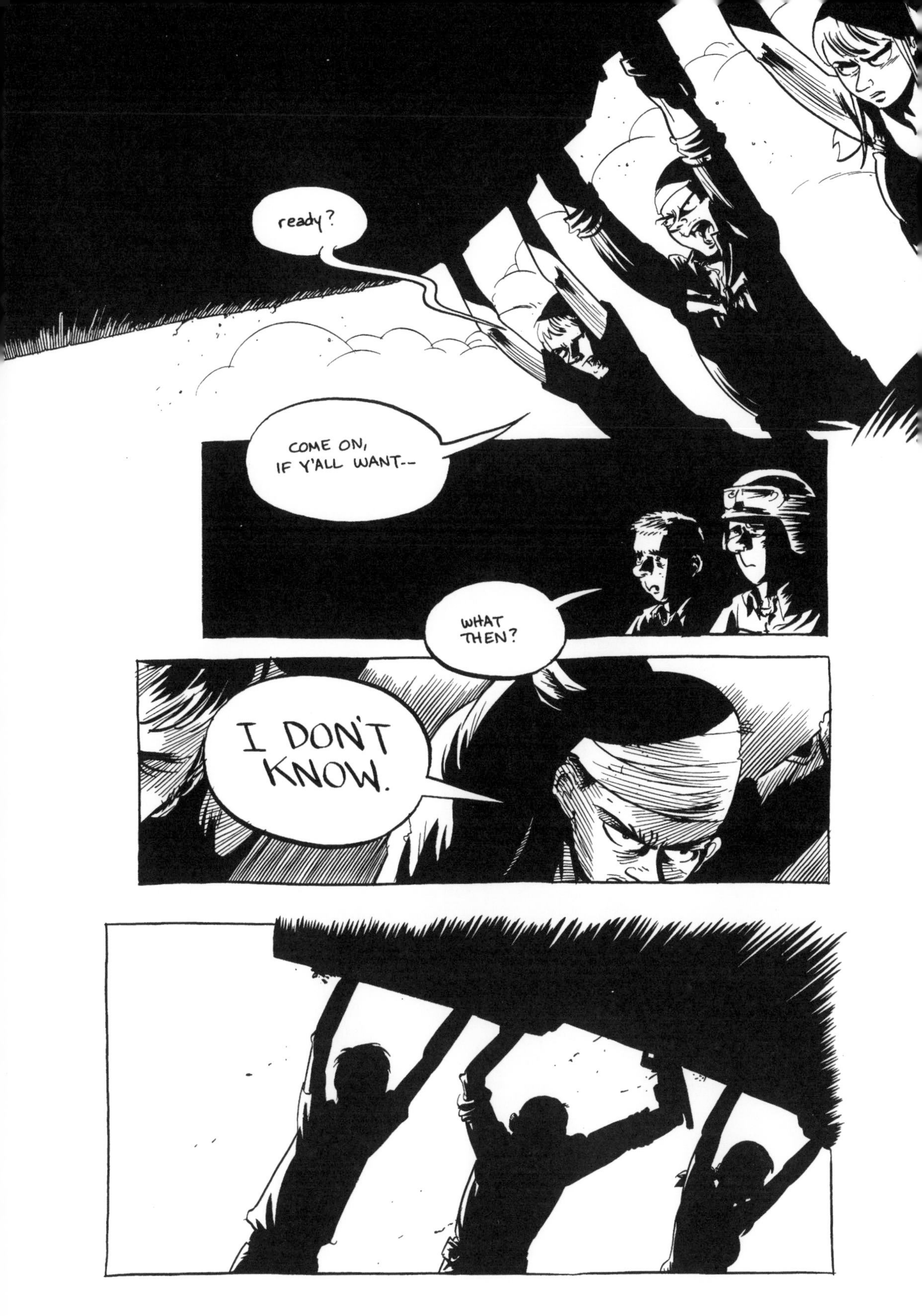
ready?
COME ON, IF Y'ALL WANT--
WHAT THEN?
I DON'T KNOW.

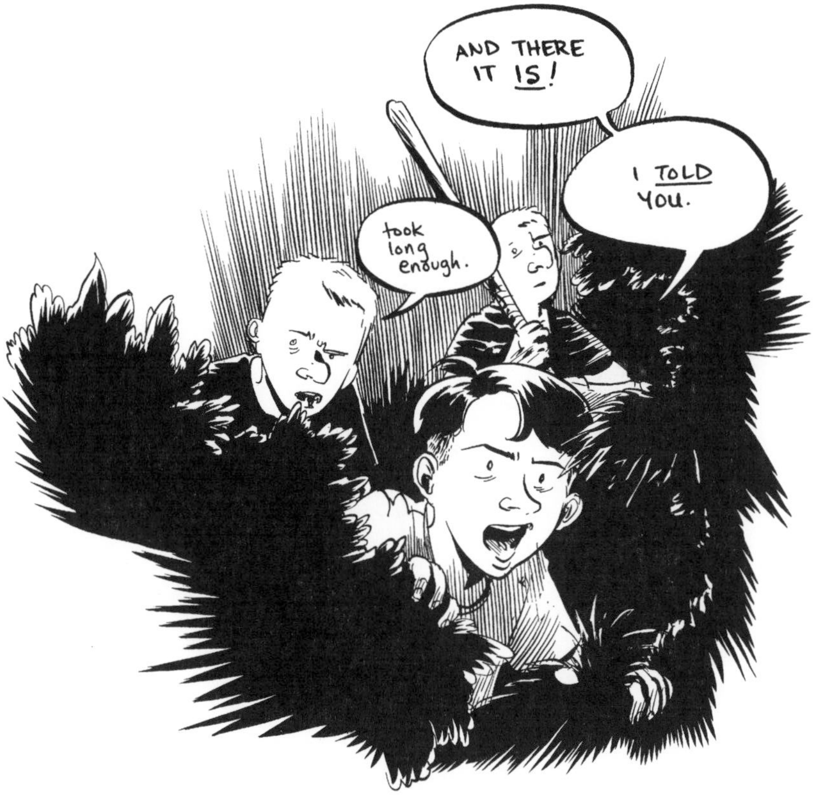
AND THERE IT IS!
I TOLD YOU.
took long enough.

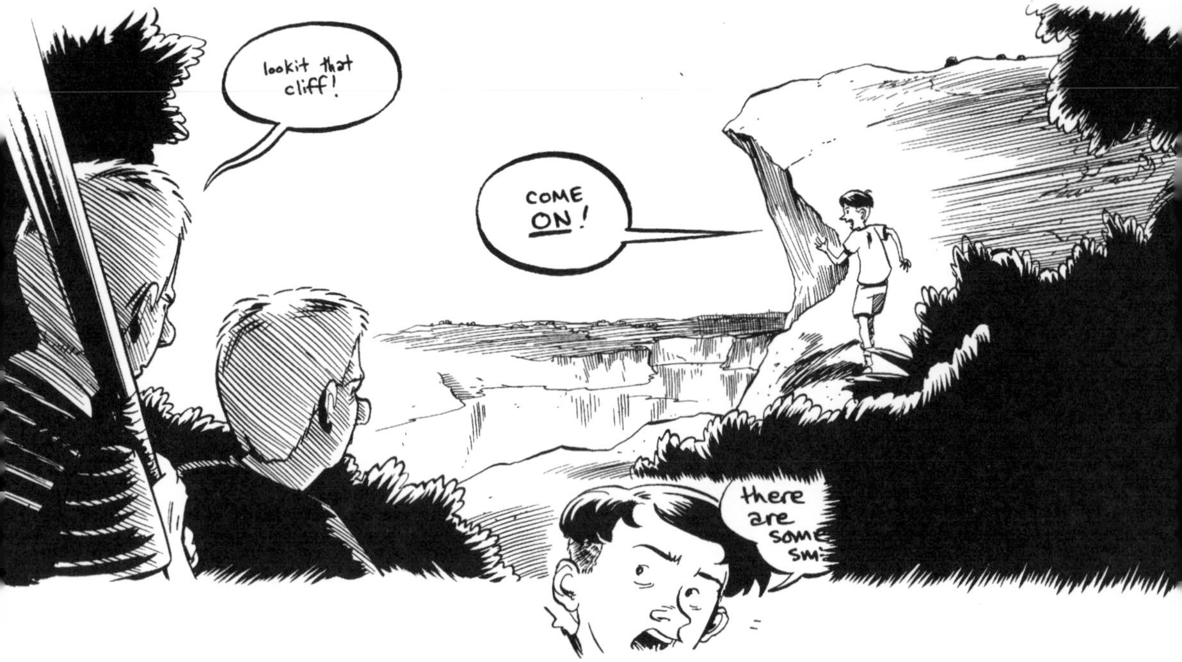
lookit that cliff!
COME ON!
there are some sm

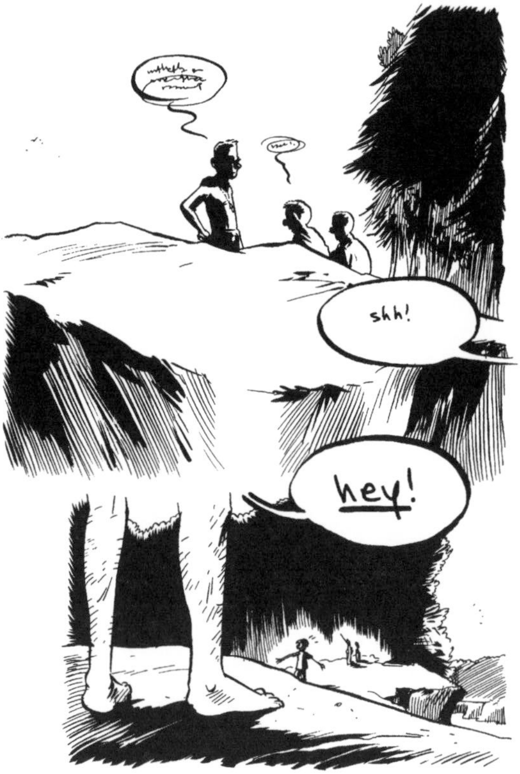
shh!
hey!

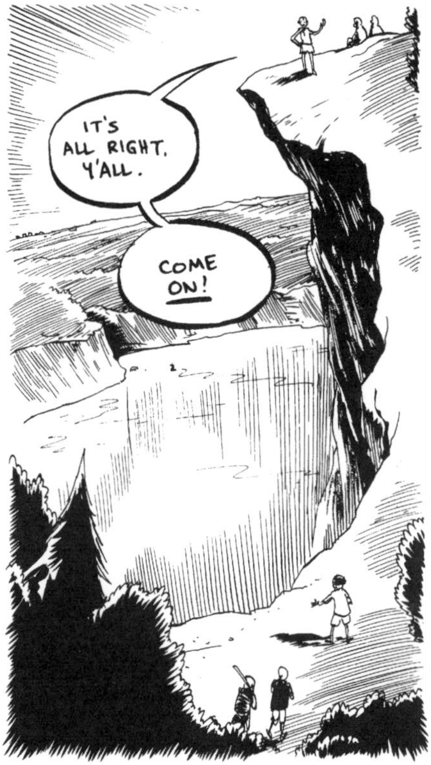
IT'S ALL RIGHT, Y'ALL.
COME ON!

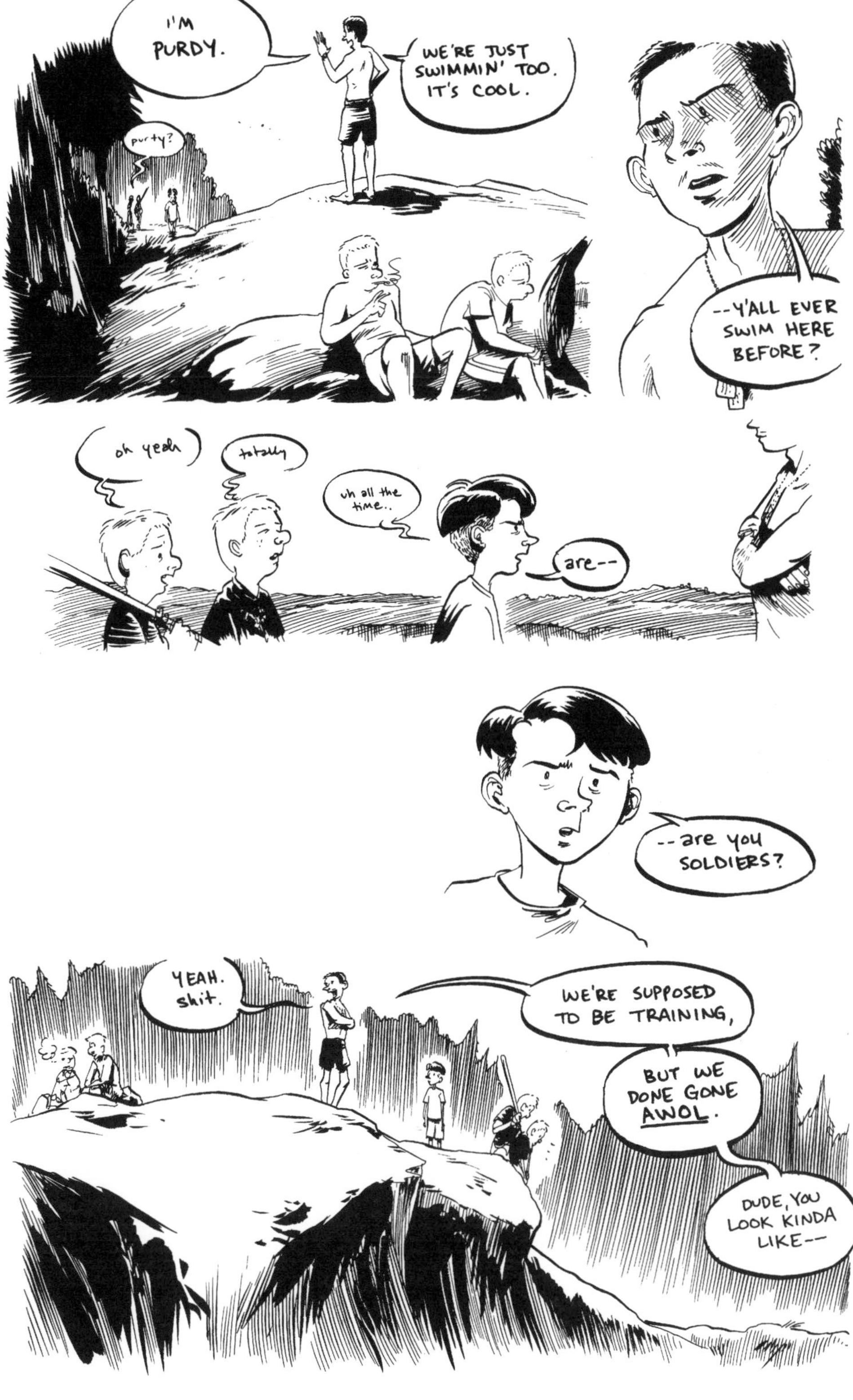
I'M PURDY.
purty?
WE'RE JUST SWIMMIN' TOO. IT'S COOL.
--Y'ALL EVER SWIM HERE BEFORE?
oh yeah
totally
uh all the time..
are--
--are you SOLDIERS?
YEAH. shit.
WE'RE SUPPOSED TO BE TRAINING,
BUT WE DONE GONE AWOL.
DUDE, YOU LOOK KINDA LIKE--

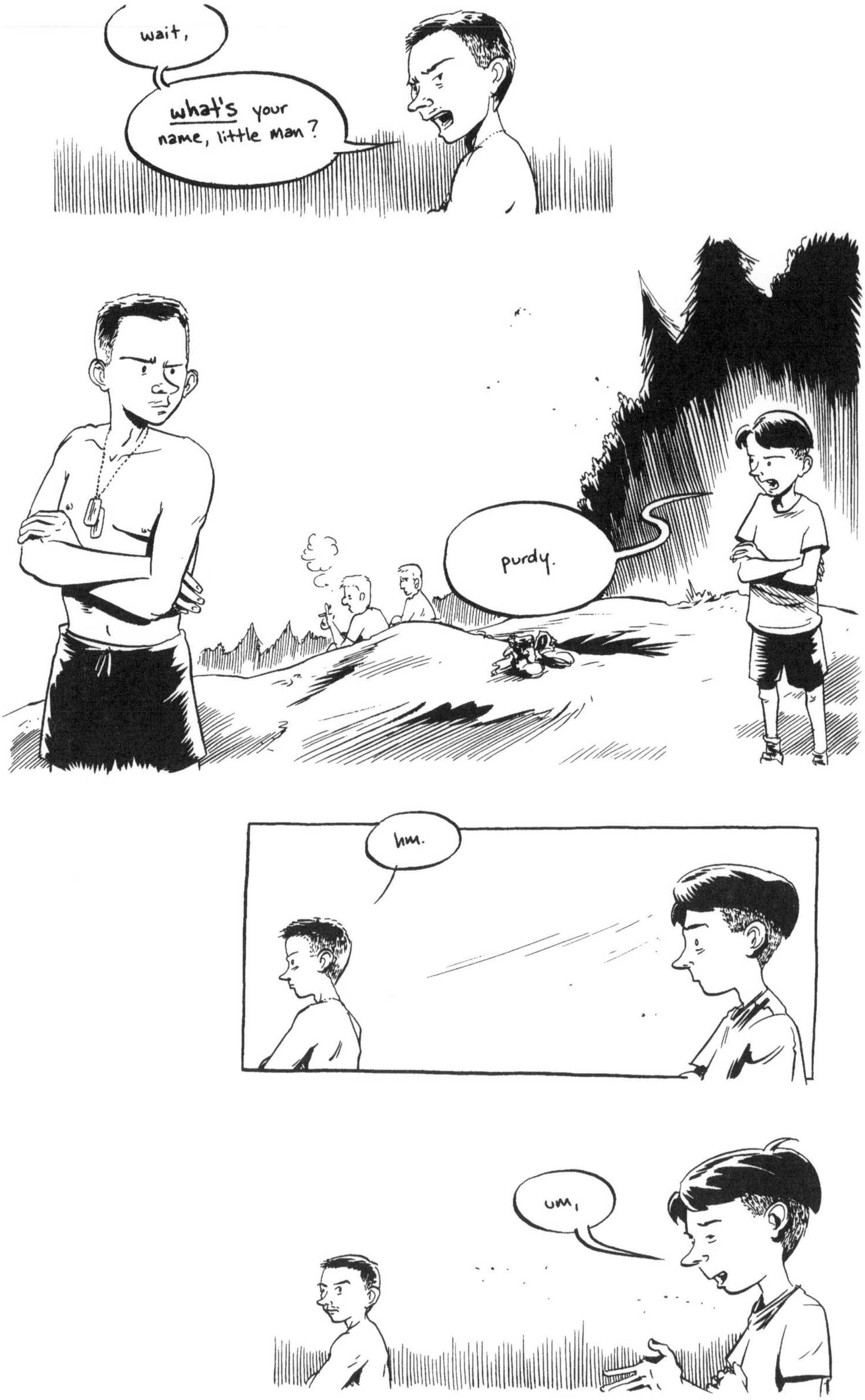
wait,
what's your name, little man?
purdy.
hm.
um,

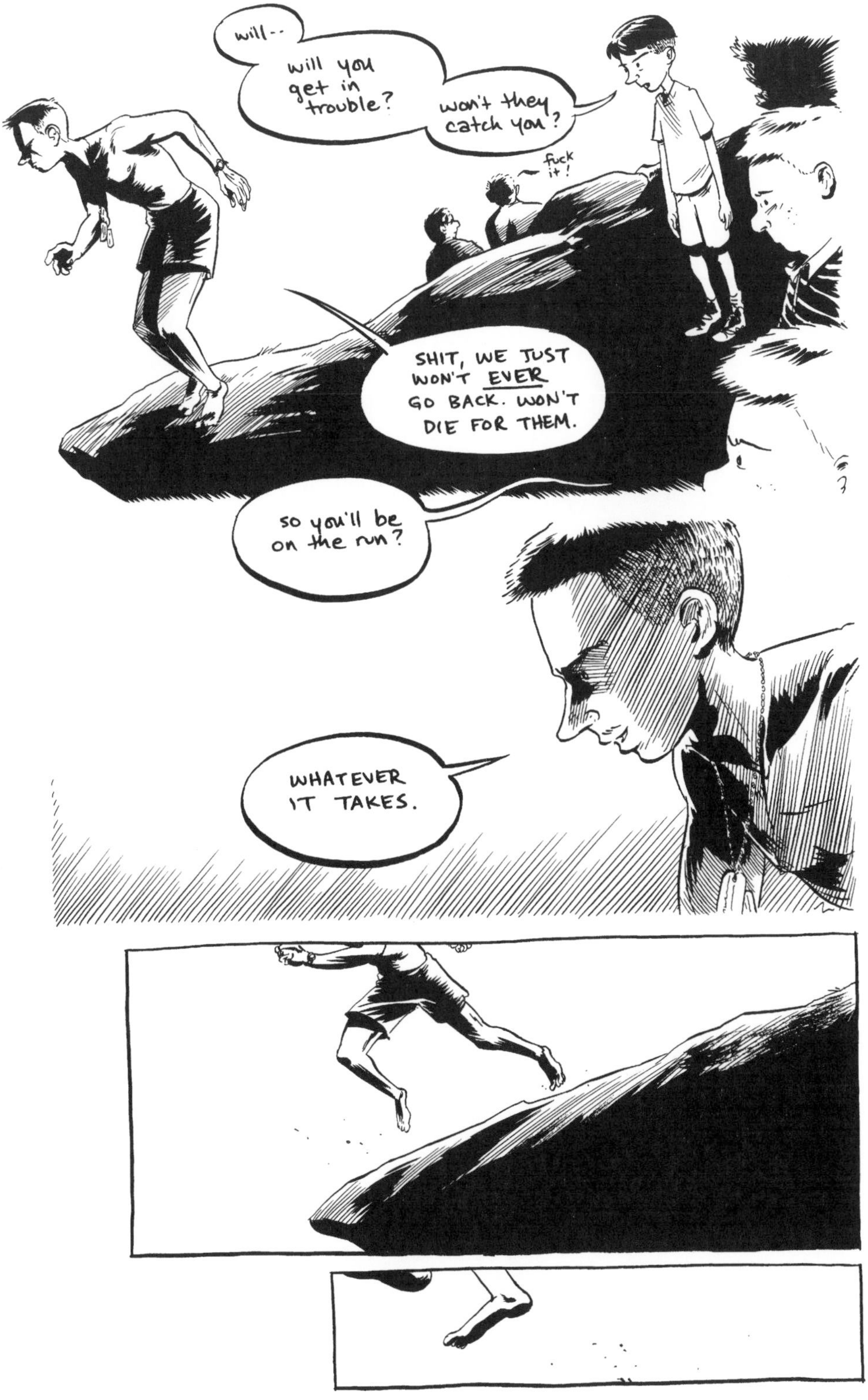
will--
will you get in trouble?
won't they catch you?
fuck it!
SHIT, WE JUST WON'T EVER GO BACK. WON'T DIE FOR THEM.
so you'll be on the run?
WHATEVER IT TAKES.

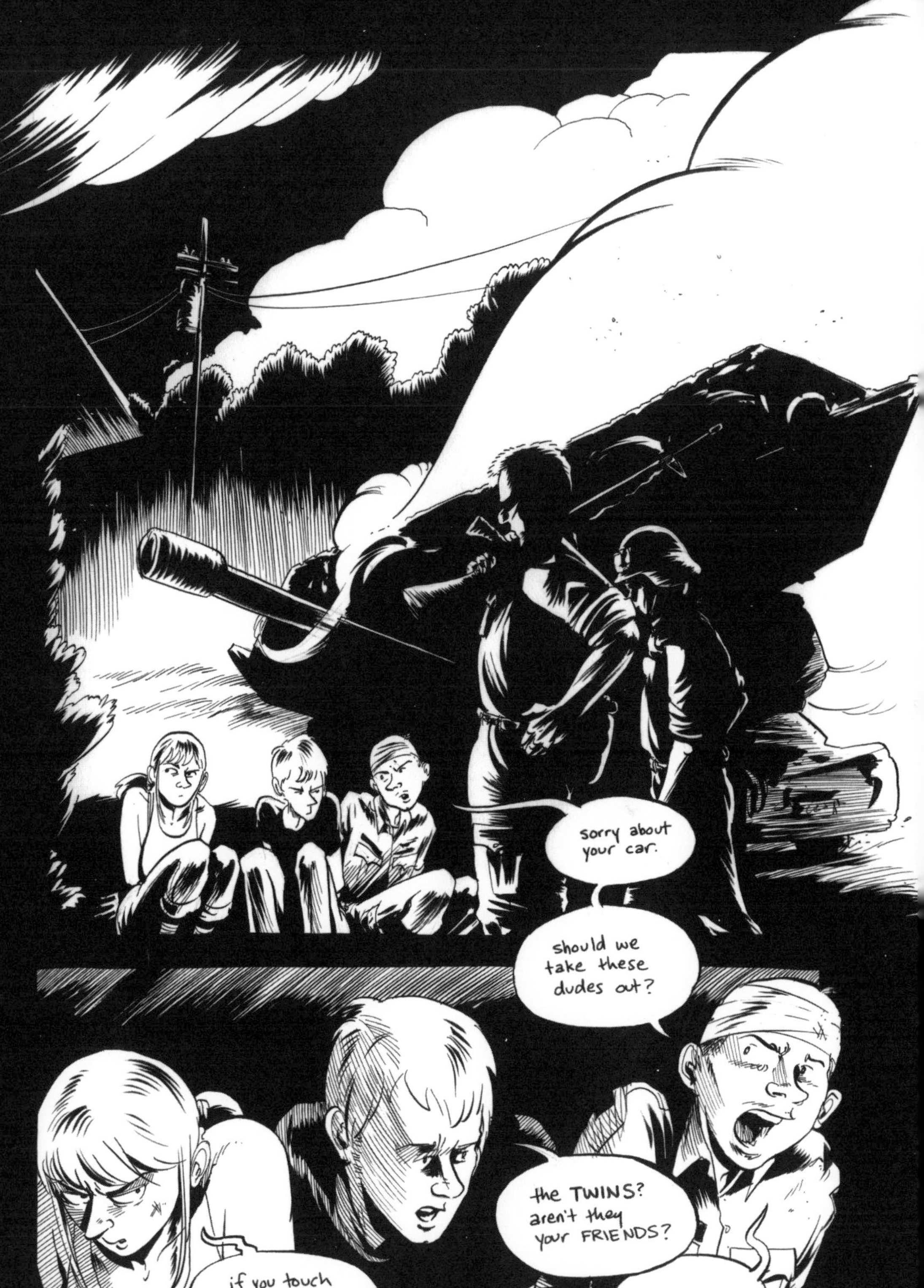
sorry about your car.
should we take these dudes out?
the TWINS? aren't they your FRIENDS?
if you touch my fucking dog i'll kill you.
whatever.

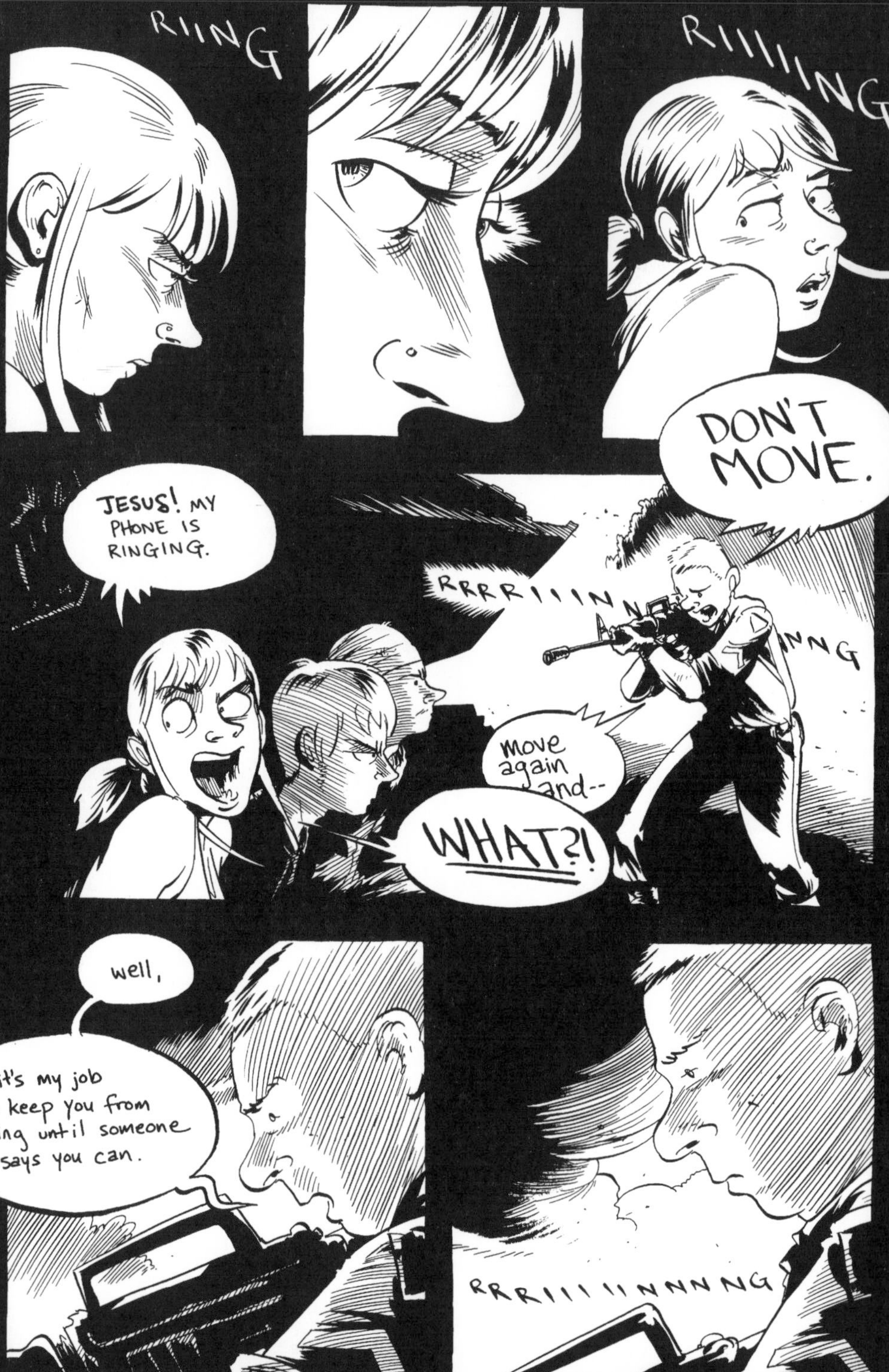

RIING
RIIIIING
JESUS! MY PHONE IS RINGING.
DON'T MOVE.
RRRRIIIINN
NNG
move again and--
WHAT?!
well,
it's my job to keep you from moving until someone says you can.
RRRIIIIINNNNG

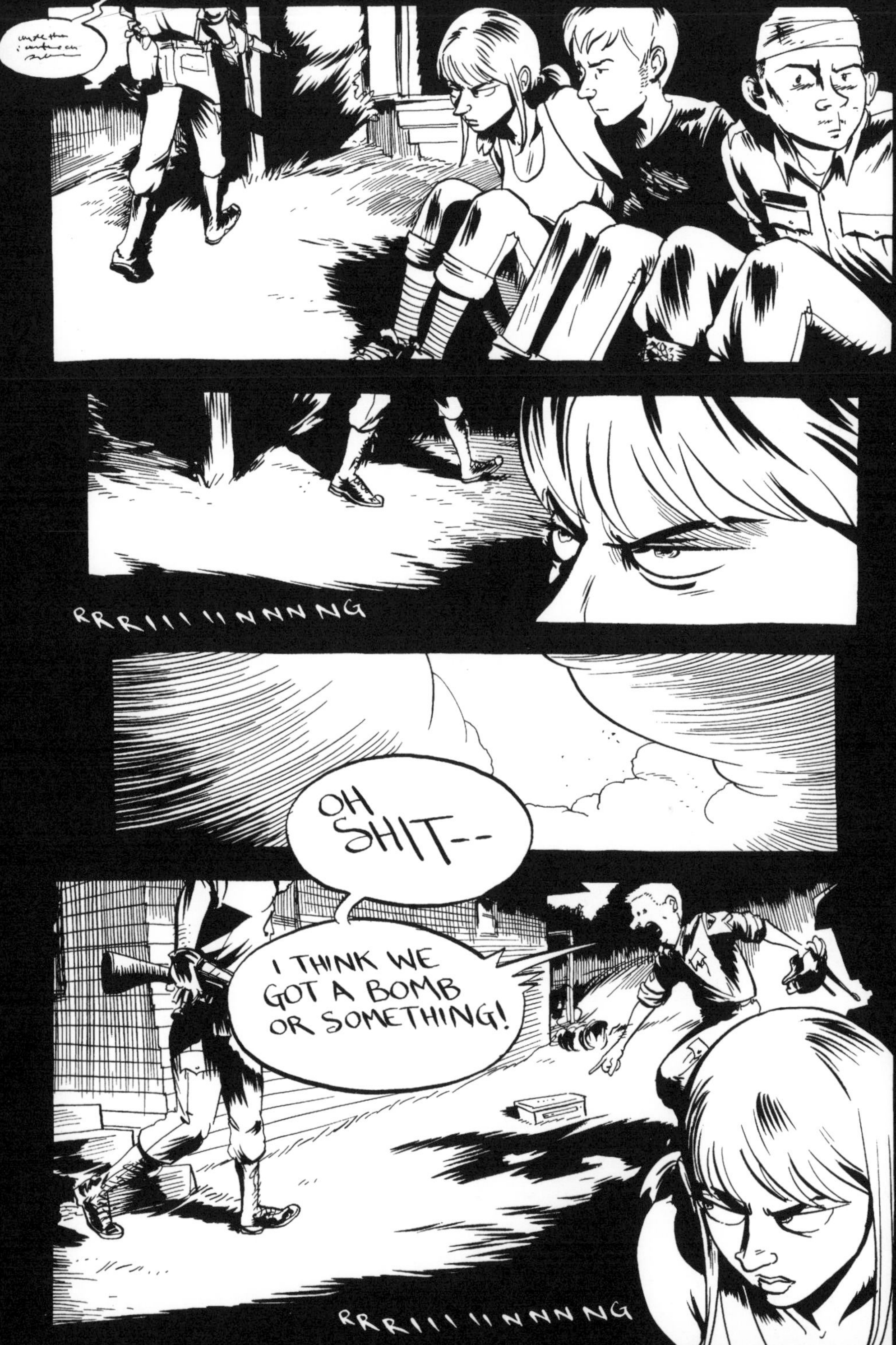
RRRIII IINNNNG
OH SHIT--
I THINK WE GOT A BOMB OR SOMETHING!
RRRIII IINNNNG

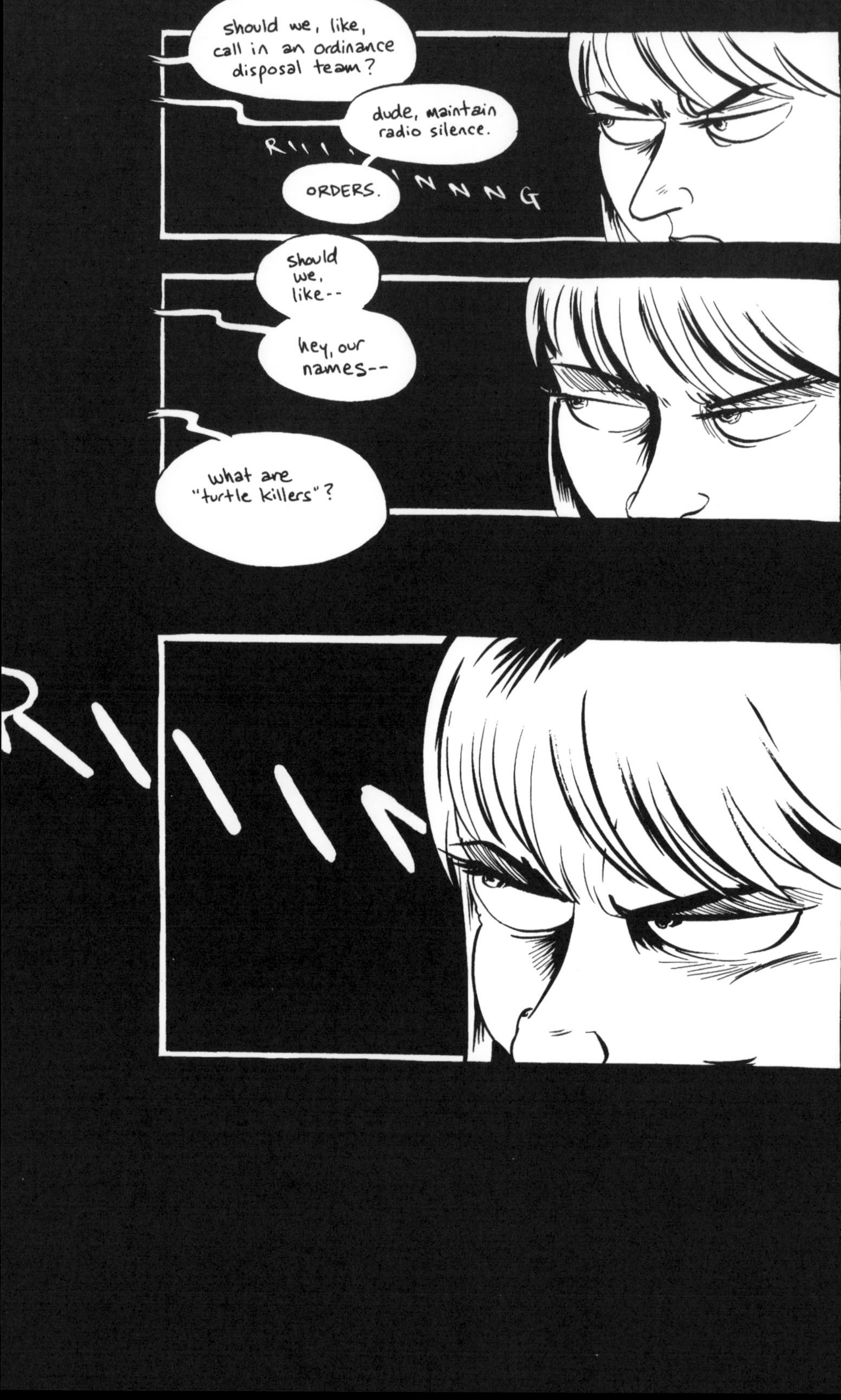
should we, like, call in an ordinance disposal team?
dude, maintain radio silence.
RIII
ORDERS.
NNNG
should we, like--
hey, our names--
what are "turtle killers"?
RIIIN

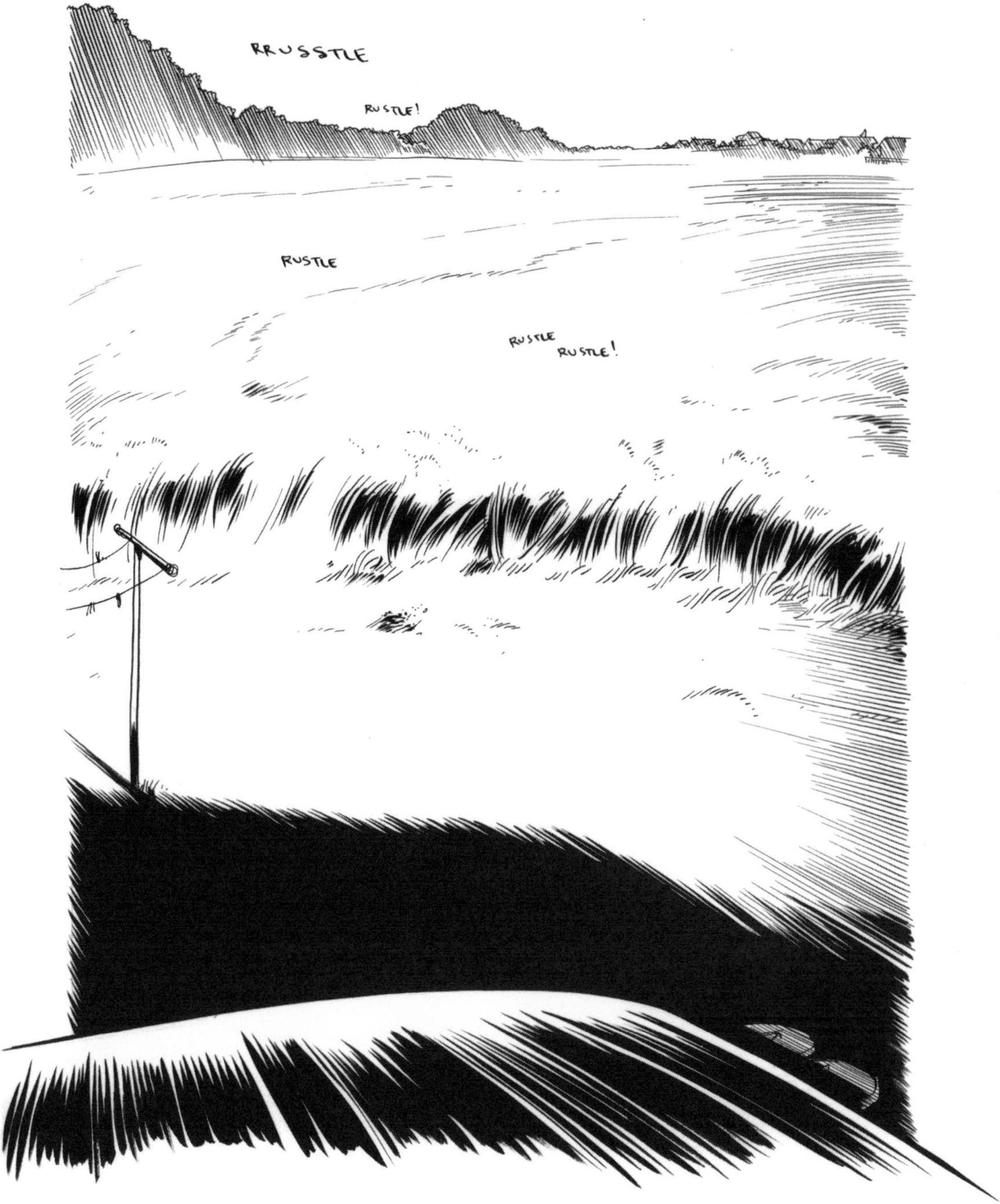
RRUSSTLE
RUSTLE!
RUSTLE
RUSTLE
RUSTLE!

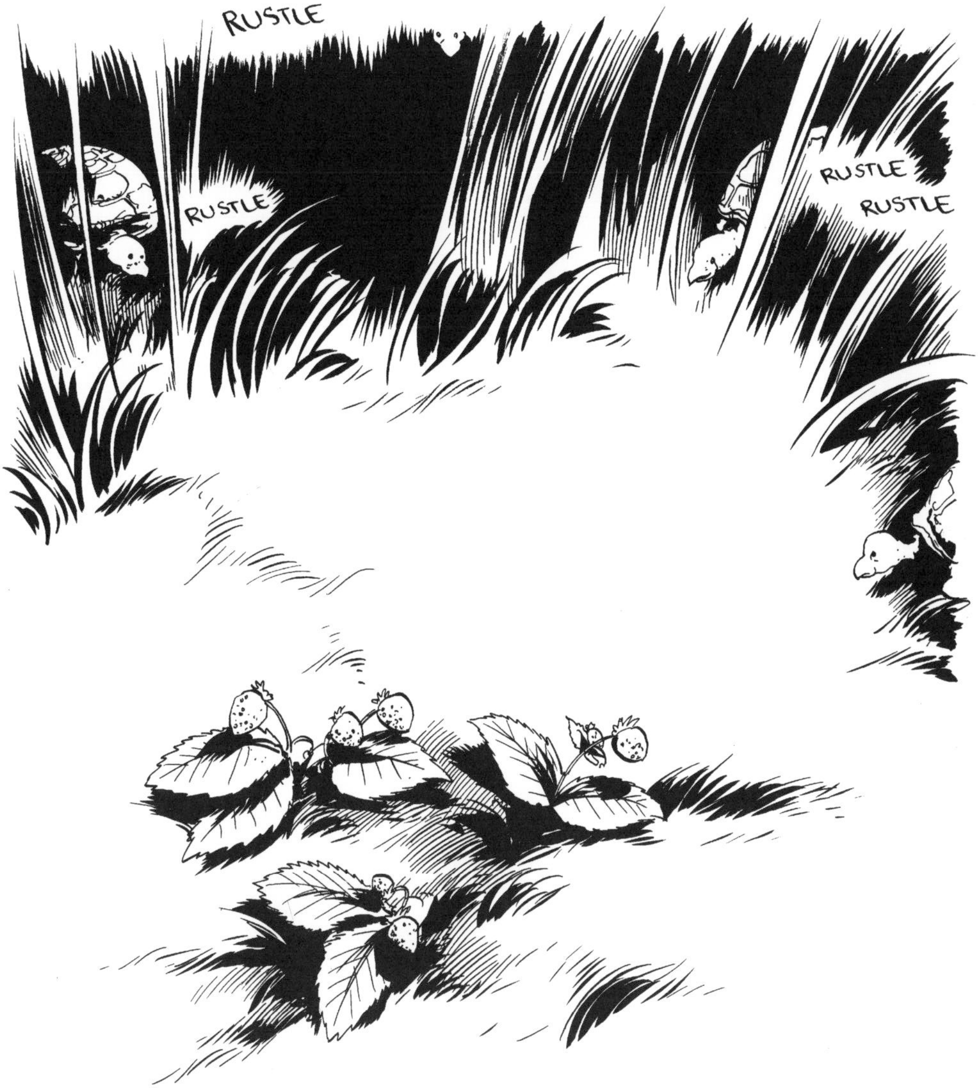
RUSTLE
RUSTLE
RUSTLE
RUSTLE

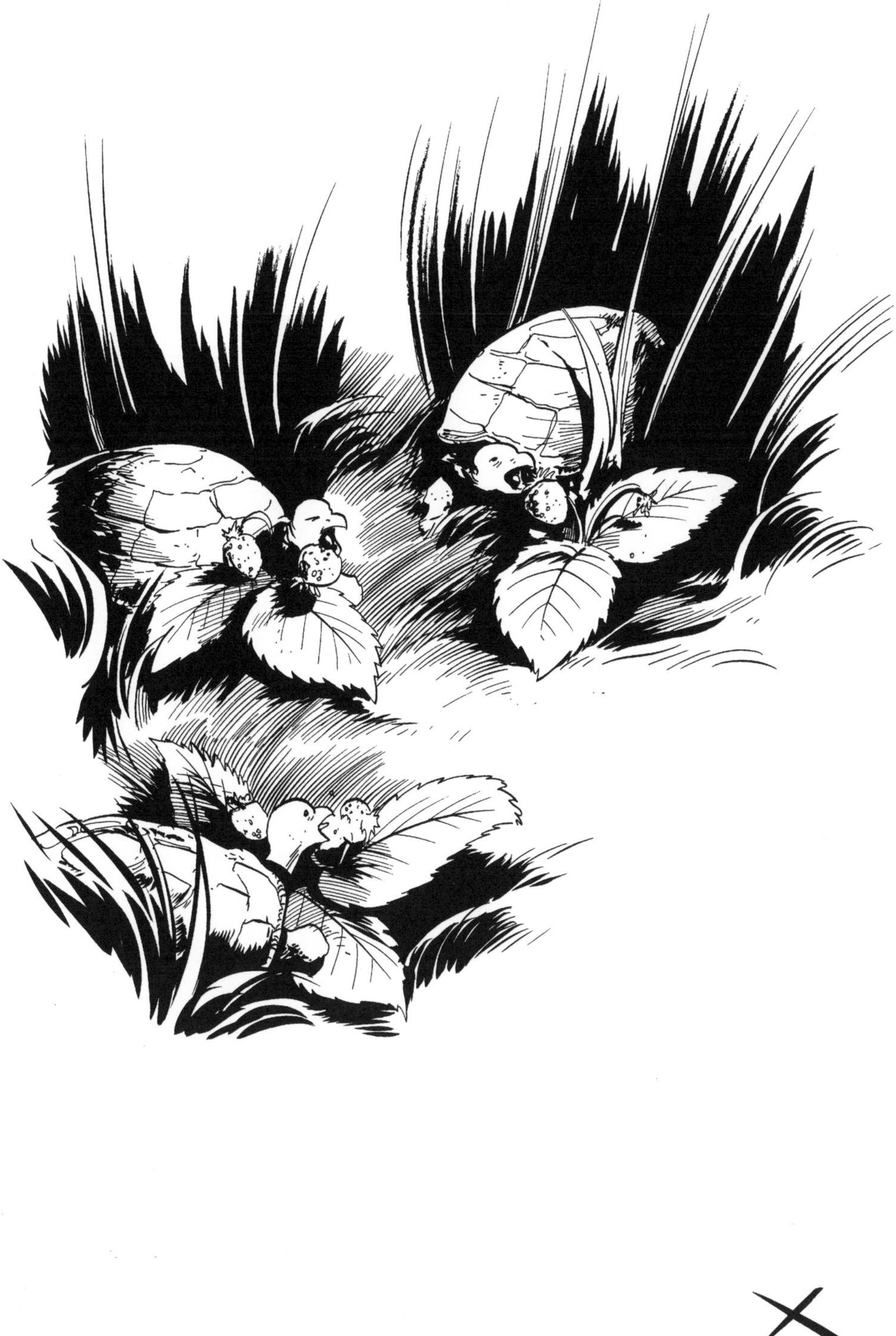
NP.
2/11.

THANK YOU:

CHRIS, BRETT, LEIGH, and ROB at TOP SHELF, RACHEL BORMANN for putting up with me every single day, ERIN TOBEY for constant support, help, and cooperation, the Powell family, TONY ONG, MICHAEL HOERGER, MARALIE ARMSTRONG, NATHAN WILSON, MIKE LIERLY, ELI MONSTER, KIM HIEFTJE, everyone at MICROCOSM PUBLISHING, JEFF LEMIRE, MATT KINDT, JEFFREY BROWN, BRETT WELDELE, and all within the Top Shelf family, DASH SHAW, FRANK SANTORO, AARON COMETBUS, GREG MEANS, GABBY SCHULZ, FAREL DALRYMPLE, NATALJA KENT, NATE BEATY, RYAN SEATON, MIKE TAYLOR, cohorts in UNIVERSE and SOOPHIE NUN SQUAD's ghosts, SIMONE, VINCENZO, FRANCESCA, and all at LIZARD, VINCENT, NADIE, and all at CASTERMAN, MAT and PETER at SHERPA, KIRA and SAMIR who stare at me all day every day, and everyone who's given me a floor to sleep on or a tour of their town.

DEDICATED to JOSH BORMANN
(1981 – 2010)

NATE POWELL was born in Little Rock, Arkansas in 1978, and began self-publishing at age 14. He graduated from School of Visual Arts in 2000.

His work includes SWALLOW ME WHOLE (Eisner Award winner for Best Graphic Novel, LA Times Book Prize finalist, and Ignatz Award winner), EDIBLE SECRETS, CAKEWALK, PLEASE RELEASE, THE SOUNDS OF YOUR NAME, IT DISAPPEARS, TINY GIANTS, the self-published WALKIE TALKIE series, and contributions to the PAPERCUTTER, SYNCOPATED, and MEATHAUS anthologies.

From 1999 to 2009, Nate worked full-time supporting adults with developmental disabilities. He has managed DIY punk record label Harlan Records since 1994, and has performed in the bands Universe, Divorce Chord, Wait, Soophie Nun Squad, and Boomfancy. He lives in Bloomington, Indiana with his wife Rachel Bormann, a bastard kitty and an overly-sensitive dog.

PO Box 3382
Bloomington, IN
47402 USA

seemybrotherdance@yahoo.com
www.seemybrotherdance.org

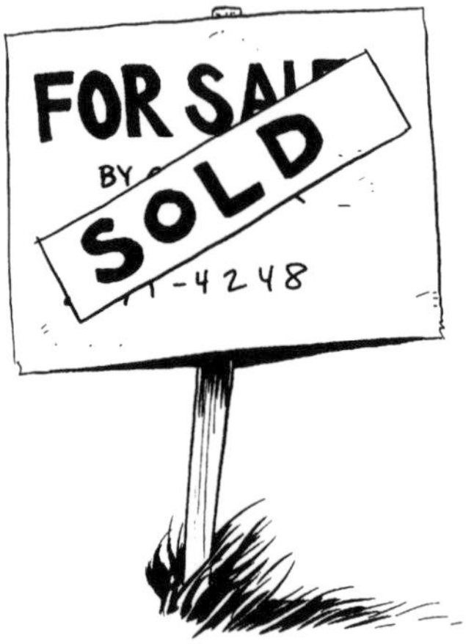
FOR SAL
BY
SOLD
-4248